Reading Process and Practice

THIRD EDITION

Reading Process and Practice

THIRD EDITION

Constance Weaver
Western Michigan University

with a chapter by
Margaret Moustafa
California State University
Los Angeles

HEINEMANN
Portsmouth, NH

Heinemann
A division of Reed Elsevier Inc.
361 Hanover Street
Portsmouth, NH 03801–3912
www.heinemann.com

Offices and agents throughout the world

The author and publisher wish to thank those who have generously given permission to
reprint borrowed material:

Excerpt from "Understanding the Hypothesis, It's the Teacher that Makes the Difference" by Jerome C. Harste, in *Reading Horizons* (1977), College of Education, Western Michigan University, Kalamazoo, Michigan.

Excerpt from *Psychology of Language* by David S. Palermo. Copyright © 1978. Reprinted by permission of Pearson Education Inc. Upper Saddle River, NJ.

Excerpt from *A Camel in the Sea* by Lee Garrett Goetz. Copyright © 1966 by McGraw-Hill Book Company. Reprinted by permission.

Appendix from "Validating the Construct to Theoretical Orientation in Reading Instruction" by Diane DeFord, in *Reading Research Quarterly,* Spring 1985. Reprinted by permission of Diane DeFord and the International Reading Association.

Excerpt from "Looking at Reading Instruction: Sociolinguistic and Ethnographic Approaches" by David Bloome and Judith Green in *Contexts of Reading,* edited by Carolyn N. Hedley and Anthony N. Baratta. Copyright © 1985. Published by Ablex.

Excerpt from "Cultural Schemata and Reading Comprehension" by Ralph E. Reynolds, Marsha A. Taylor, Margaret S. Steffensen, Larry L. Shirey, and Richard C. Anderson in *Reading Research Quarterly,* Vol. 17, No. 3. Reprinted by permission of Ralph E. Reynolds and the International Reading Association.

Excerpt from *Dandelion Wine* by Ray Bradbury. Reprinted by permission of Don Congdon Associates, Inc. Copyright © 1953 by Gourmet Inc.; renewed 1981 by Ray Bradbury.

Excerpt from "The Law and Reading Instruction" by Robert J. Harper and Gary Kilarr in *Language Arts* 54 (November/December 1977). Copyright © 1977 by the National Council of Teachers of English. Reprinted by permission.

Excerpt from "Literacy in the Classroom" by John R. Bormuth in *Help for the Reading Teacher: New Directions in Research,* edited by William D. Page. Copyright © 1975 by the National Council of Teachers of English. Reprinted by permission.

Excerpt from "Poison" in *Someone Like You* by Roald Dahl. Copyright © 1950 by Roald Dahl. Reprinted by permission of Alfred A. Knopf, Inc.

Excerpt from *The Glorious Conspiracy* by Joanne Williamson. Copyright © 1961 by Alfred A. Knopf. Reprinted by permission of Alfred A. Knopf, Inc.

Excerpt from "Jimmy Hayes and Muriel" by O. Henry, in *The Complete Works of O. Henry.* Copyright © 1937 by Garden City Publishing Company Inc. Reprinted by permission of the publisher.

Excerpt from *A Magic Box* and *Opening Doors* from the Macmillan Reading Program by Albert J. Harris and Mae Knight Clark. Copyright © 1965 by Macmillan Publishing Company. Reprinted by permission.

Excerpt from *Morris Has a Cold* by Bernard Wiseman. Copyright © 1978 by Bernard Wiseman. Reprinted by permission of Dodd, Mead & Company, Inc.
Credits continue on p. 430.

Library of Congress Cataloging-in-Publication Data
Weaver, Constance.
 Reading process and practice / Constance Weaver.—3rd ed.
  p. cm.
 Includes bibliographical references and index.
 ISBN 0-325-00377-7 (alk. paper)
 1. Reading. 2. Psycholinguistics. 3. Language awareness in children. I. Title.
 LB1050.22 .W44 2002
 372.4—dc21   2001007546

Editor: Lois Bridges
Production service: Patricia Adams
Production coordination: Abigail M. Heim
Typesetting: TechBooks
Cover design: Lisa Fowler
Manufacturing: Louise Richardson

Printed in the United States of America on acid-free paper
06 05 04 03 02   RRD   1 2 3 4 5

For Lois,
whose support and encouragement have been unfailing

For Peter,
who alternately cheered me up and cracked the whip

And for Rollie,
the wind beneath my wings

Contents

8 Developing a Reader Profile: From Assessment to Instruction   *184*

9 Revaluing Readers, Retrospective Miscue Analysis, and Other Strategies for Helping Readers   *212*

Addressing Students' Needs in a Comprehensive Literacy Program   *231*

Reading Research from Differing Perspectives   *251*

Website (http://www.heinemann.com/weaver)

Preface

It's been eight years since the 1994 publication of the second edition of *Reading Process and Practice*. In those eight short years, much has changed in literacy education. While more and more teachers have learned about the development of literacy and effective ways to foster it, we are increasingly being faced with government and corporate intrusion into our classrooms as we experience more and more politically determined state and national mandates, not to mention federal funding with ideological strings attached—all of which restrict our decision making as professional educators. One of my aims in this third edition has been to provide accurate data, informed critique, and results of oft-ignored research studies that may help you counteract what is promoted or mandated by the State, when informed practice tells us that the mandated teaching is harmful to kids. Obviously the other major aim for *Reading Process and Practice* is, and always has been, to provide information about the reading process, the research behind our understanding of that process, and concrete, teacher-tested ideas for implementing exemplary literacy instruction: to offer you information crucial for supporting and teaching your students in ways that will enable them to become proficient, eager, lifelong readers. Those of us who teach know that the art of teaching remains unchanged, regardless of what the State may require. Effective instruction stems from a sensitive, informed response to students' needs; my aim is to help you achieve that goal.

To that end, I approached the third edition of *Reading Process and Practice* with four additional goals: to make the book shorter; to include more specifics on assessing and helping individual readers; to update material as needed; and to make the text accessible and helpful to both graduate and undergraduate students as well as to new and veteran teachers alike. For example, in support of the three latter goals, the second edition's chapter on analyzing miscues has been replaced with five new chapters: Chapter 6, "Understanding What Miscues Can Tell Us About Readers' Strategies"; Chapter 7, "Analyzing Miscues and Looking for Patterns"; Chapter 8, "Developing a Reader Profile: From Assessment to Instruction"; and two chapters on helping readers with particular needs: Chapter 9, "Revaluing Readers, Retrospective Miscue Analysis, and Other Strategies for Helping Readers" and Chapter 10, "Addressing Students' Needs in a Comprehensive Literacy Program." These new chapters provide, I think, enough information to do miscue analysis successfully, to develop a reader profile, and to draw upon such assessment to determine and carry out instructional support for individual readers within a comprehensive literacy program.

The goal of making the third edition accessible to both undergraduates and graduates, preservice teachers and experienced teachers, has been addressed in three additional ways: (1) the interior design of the book is visually open and appealing, with several recurring features; (2) definitions and concepts are repeated throughout the book, thus providing multiple entry points into key understandings and issues; and (3) a new chapter describing what a comprehensive literacy program might include and how it might be structured is included as well as practical chapters that flesh out specific components of such a program. On the other hand, I have still included the discussions of research for which *Reading Process and Practice* is known.

An exciting new feature of the third edition is a Web page relating to the book: <*http://www.heinemann.com/weaver*>. Initial features of this page include case studies to complement the chapters relating to assessment and its application in teaching students who need additional help. Written mostly by Lisa Schade, the case studies deal with students having different reading patterns and needs, at different instructional levels: first grade, fourth grade, and junior high. The Web page also contains a superb annotated professional bibliography for teachers. Compiled and annotated by first-grade teacher Catherine Compton-Lilly, this bibliography has more than twenty sections on reading, teaching reading and writing to various and varying student populations at all grade levels, and more. In addition, the bibliography contains brief sections on professional journals and professional videos for teachers.

There is, of course, a logic to the way the chapters are ordered. After the introductory chapter, Chapters 2, 3, 4, and 5 explain the reading process. Chapters 6, 7, 8, 9, and 10 deal with assessing readers' strengths and needs, then addressing those needs. Chapter 11 is central to understanding major differences between contrasting views of what counts as reading research—or for that matter, what counts as *reading.* As a pivotal chapter, it also lays the groundwork for Chapter 12, by discussing some of the research supporting a comprehensive approach to literacy, and Chapter 13, by discussing concerns about the "skills emphasis" research on reading. Thus, Chapters 11, 12, and 13 go together, followed by a chapter on teaching comprehension strategies and phonics skills in a comprehensive literacy program. Chapter 15, by Margaret Moustafa, rounds out the book by briefly describing experimental research studies that suggest the superiority of a comprehensive, teacher-designed literacy program in the classroom.

Other clusterings, however, are possible. For instance, Chapter 4 demonstrates what we've learned about the reading process from the miscues of proficient readers, which in turn helps us understand what a reader's pattern of miscues can tell us about that person's reading strategy strengths and needs. Thus, Chapter 4 could be clustered with Chapters 6, 7, and 8, the chapters that deal with miscue analysis and reading assessment. Designing and implementing a comprehensive literacy program could begin with Chapter 12, proceed to Chapter 14, then end with the two chapters that deal with helping individual readers: Chapters 9 and 10. Chapters 11, 13, and 15 are research-intensive, so they could be clustered together as well. Chapter 5 also links with Chapters 11 and 13. Therefore, teacher educators might want to consider some of these alternative orderings, depending upon their purposes and the nature of the course they are teaching. As a teacher educator myself, I have found it extremely important to help my students understand key concepts *before* assigning the chapter in which they are discussed. Often it helps to do activities from, related to, or based on, the upcoming readings.

By including definitions of key terms like *phonics* in more than one chapter, I have tried to make the various chapters reasonably independent of one another. However, the first major section of Chapter 13 describes phonics-related terms and concepts in by far the greatest detail, so no matter in what order the chapters are clustered, that section of Chapter 13 should precede the last half of Chapter 14, on teaching phonics in a comprehensive literacy program.

I am indebted to many people for making this book a reality: to Margaret Moustafa, for contributing the final chapter; to Catherine Compton-Lilly, for the extensive annotated bibliography that is on the Web page Heinemann has created for this book; to Lisa Schade, for writing two of the three case studies in miscue analysis, which are also located on the Web page; to those who sent copies of their doctoral dissertations or articles stemming from them and allowed me to draw generously from their materials, namely Peter Duckett, Alan Flurkey, and Eric Paulson; to Joel Brown and Marge Knox for their assistance; to the staff developers and lab teachers at the Public Education and Business Coalition in Denver, and especially to Anne Ebner for permission to describe her classroom; to Peter Krause, for his assistance with research and many time-consuming details; to Lorraine Krause and Anick Leclerc for allowing me to include a piece their first graders wrote and to describe the collaborative writing process and the scaffolding they provided; to Nichole Martin and Katherine Gauthier for allowing me to draw upon their miscue projects; to Jean Patt for critiquing a section of the manuscript; to certain students and their parents, especially Angel and Pamela Cieremans; Victoria and Tracy Niebor, Jacob Williams and Lisa Schade, and to my many students who, over the years, keep helping me discover what I need to explain more thoroughly. I am deeply grateful, also, to the many classroom teachers from whom I have learned and continue to learn, and to my original intellectual mentors, Frank Smith and Kenneth Goodman. Their research and insights set me upon my intellectual journey with regard to reading.

This third edition of *Reading Process and Practice* has truly been a collaborative venture with my wonderful editor and friend, Lois Bridges, whose support has known no bounds. Lisa Fowler graciously put her artistic talents to work in designing the cover. Other major contributors to the success of this book are Abby Heim, Heinemann's production supervisor, who orchestrated the complex production process with consummate skill; Patty Adams, whose conscientious attention to detail has been a lifesaver; Elizabeth Tripp, who expertly copyedited the manuscript; Karen Ettinger and her ''miracle worker'' at TechBooks; and Karen Clausen at Heinemann, whose assistance with various parts of the manuscript has likewise been absolutely invaluable. Thank you, all!

1 Definitions of Reading: They Make a Difference

> Our findings suggest that both teachers and learners hold particular and identifiable theoretical orientations about reading which in turn significantly affect expectations, goals, behavior, and outcomes at all levels.
>
> —Jerome Harste

THE IMPORTANCE OF A DEFINITION

What is *reading,* anyway? Here are some answers from children (Harste, 1978, p. 92):

"It's filling out workbooks."

"Pronouncing the letters."

"It's when you put sounds together."

"Reading is learning hard words."

"Reading is like think . . . you know, it's understanding the story."

"It's when you find out things."

There is considerable variation in these definitions. One emphasizes a medium of instruction, the workbook; others emphasize words or parts of words; and still others emphasize meaning. Of course, children do not often stop to define reading. Nevertheless, their approach to reading itself is guided by what they think reading is.

Responses to interview questions in Figure 1.1 clarify two children's understanding of reading. Interestingly, it is the first grader who has the better grasp of reading as a meaning-making process, judging by her independence in dealing with problem words and her apparent use of meaning in the process. The third grader conceptualizes reading mainly as a matter of getting the words.

What's the Problem Here?

Occasionally one of my students completes a reading interview that, in part, goes something like this:

Q: What do you do in your head when you're reading?
R: Think what I'm reading about.
Q: When you are reading and come to a word that you don't know, what do you do?
R: Sound it out.
Q: What else could you do if you were reading with nobody around to help you?
R: I wouldn't read.
Q: Why not?
R: I wouldn't know how.

Sometimes even adults who are learning to read respond much the same way, when asked if they have practiced reading between tutoring sessions. What do you think may cause learners to respond this way?

Jenny, Grade 3

I: What do you think reading is?

J: Something that um, helps you learn words.

....

I: What do people do when they read?

J: They just read the words that are in the book.

I: They read the words in the book? Anything else? No? Okay, when you're reading something and you come to a word that you don't know, what do you usually do?

J: Sound it out.

I: Sound it out? Do you ever do anything else? No? Okay. Who is a good reader that you know?

J: Shaun.

I: Who is Shaun?

J: My sister, her friend um, her brother, he keeps on reading and he tries to do jump rope when he's reading a book.

I: What do you think makes Shaun a good reader?

J: He went to speech where um, they um, teach him how to read and stuff real good.

I: Do you think Shaun ever comes to a word or something in a story that he doesn't know?

J: Sometimes.

I: Sometimes? What do you think Shaun would do if he came to a word he didn't know?

J: Sound it out.

I: You think he'd sound it out too.

....

I: If you knew someone who was having trouble reading, what do you think you would do to help them?

J: Ask and see if they would sound it out and maybe that would help.

I: Sound it out? Is there anything else you might do to help them? What if they couldn't sound it out?

J: I would tell them the word.

I: Oh, you'd tell them the word.

Barbara, Grade 1

I: What do you think reading is?

B: When you read, it's um, kind of like you're just looking at a book but you're just saying the words because you think they're easy, but they're really not so easy. And, like, stuff like that.

I: That's a good answer of what you think reading is. When you're reading and you come to a word that you don't know, what do you do?

B: Kind of like I sound it out. It's kind of like you come to a word and you think, "Well, should I sound it out, or should I just ask somebody?" Then you see that all the people you want to ask are busy and you kind of sound it out.

I: Do you ever do anything else when you come to a word you don't know?

B: Um, most of the time I skip it.

I: After you skip a word, do you find it easier?

B: Yeah. Like when you skip a word and then go to the end, you can go back to it and read it.

I: Does this help more than sounding it out?

B: Yeah.

Figure 1.1   *Two children's reading interviews (Weaver, 1990).*

Where do children get such definitions of reading? Mainly from literacy experiences (or the lack of them) in the home and/or from what is emphasized (or not emphasized) in school.

Not surprisingly, there is a significant correlation between teachers' approach to reading instruction and children's understanding of what reading is and what it involves. Furthermore, children are influenced more by how teachers teach reading than by what they say about the purpose of reading, if teachers' beliefs are not supported by their actions. For example, teachers may believe that the purpose of reading is to get meaning, but they may teach as if the purpose of reading is to identify words—especially if they are required to use programs that focus on phonics skills first.

Underlying the skills approach being promoted by powerful forces such as business and government that are mostly outside of education (see Chapter 11) is the implicit notion that reading means identifying words, by learning letter-sound relationships first and decoding words letter-by-letter. This approach emphasizes isolating the separable sounds (phonemes) in words, teaching and learning phonics (letter-sound relationships and patterns for identifying words), and fluency—defined recently as being able to read all the words in a text accurately and rapidly. Or in other words, a skills approach starts with the smallest pieces of language and works "upward," only later giving children meaningful texts to read and expecting them to read for comprehension. In such classrooms, the teaching of writing may also reflect a "back to basics" approach, wherein the teaching focuses on learning and writing letters of the alphabet conventionally, printing neatly, spelling correctly, and using sentence punctuation appropriately before children are allowed to write more than—or as much as—a sentence. What these approaches to learning to read and write obviously have in common is that they start with the smallest parts of language and work upward toward constructing meaning. They consider mastery of bits and pieces of language to be essential before meaning can be addressed.

Underlying a comprehensive literacy approach is the conviction that first and foremost, reading means constructing meaning, and using everything you know in order to do it. Such an approach often involves reading simple rhymes, poems, songs, and stories to and with children before dealing with words and letter-sound patterns within the context of literature and other texts. Both predictable texts (including simple versions of folktales and fairytales) and less predictable but high-quality literature are typically enjoyed, reread, and used for instruction in reading strategies and skills. The teacher and students attend to skill-related knowledge like phonics by drawing examples from the texts being read and relating the skills back to their reading—that is, using phonics knowledge as part of effective reading strategies, not only to identify words but to construct meaning. Children in the primary grades may be encouraged to write as best they can from the very first day of school, even if their writing consists of no more than marks accompanying a picture they have drawn. As their experiences with reading enable the children to make letters, they will be encouraged and helped to write the sounds they hear in words—perhaps the best way of all to teach letter-sound relationships: that is, phonics. Gradually children are taught strategies for spelling and checking and correcting their spellings; the conventional spelling of frequently used words; and the conventional use of punctuation. Typically, teachers in comprehensive literacy classrooms help children master letter formation, spelling patterns, and punctuation when the children use writing as a means of expressing themselves, communicating, and coming to know and understand new concepts and experiences.

Children's concepts of both reading and writing often reflect the kind of instruction they have received (e.g., Rasinski & DeFord, 1988; Freppon, 1991). Thus, if the teacher spends a lot of time teaching correspondences between letters and sounds, at least some children will conclude that reading means pronouncing letters and sounding out words, or "getting the words." If the teacher spends a lot of time reading texts to and with children and discussing the meanings with them, most children will conclude that reading means getting meaning. Whatever the instructional approach, it is likely to affect many children's implicit definitions of reading, and hence, their strategies for dealing with written text. And ironically, those children who are least successful at reading may be the very ones who try hardest to do just what the teacher emphasizes. They concentrate on just these one or two strategies—like "ask somebody" or "sound it out"—rather than on the multiple language cues and strategies that must be integrated in order to read for meaning successfully.

> Ironically, those children who are least successful at reading may be the very ones who try hardest to do just what the teacher emphasizes.

Studies investigating children's definitions of reading have found, too, that poorer and younger readers tend to conceptualize reading as a matter of decoding and getting words, whereas older and more proficient readers generally conceptualize reading as more a matter of understanding the text (e.g., Baker & Brown, 1984; Johns, 1986).

If children infer their definitions from the instructional program and approach, as frequently seems to be the case, the instructional approach is obviously crucial in helping children develop a productive definition of reading and effective reading strategies.

To summarize: children's success at reading reflects their reading strategies; their reading strategies typically reflect their implicit definitions of reading; their definitions often reflect the instructional approach; and the instructional approach reflects a definition of reading, whether implicit or explicit. In fact, the instructional approach may reflect a definition quite different from that consciously espoused by the teacher (Levande, 1989).

It is crucial, then, for teachers to have an in-depth understanding of reading and learning to read, so that they can be knowledgeable decision makers, choosing an approach that reflects their informed understanding. In that case, teachers may be able to design and develop their own comprehensive literacy program (Chapters 12 and 14). Even if teachers are required to use a program that denies their own knowledge base, they can often modify their teaching to better meet the needs of their students. In order to do that, teachers also need to assess individual readers' strategies and to be "kid-watchers" (Y. Goodman, 1978, 1985). One of the primary purposes of this book, then, is to help teachers become knowledgeable enough to foster good reading strategies in children, perhaps despite the approach of the reading materials provided by the schools.

CHARACTERIZING READING AND READING INSTRUCTION

As people become increasingly knowledgeable about the reading process, they typically modify their definitions of reading. But it is helpful to become aware of where you stand at the outset. The remainder of this chapter consists mainly of three activities intended to help you determine your own views of reading and reading instruction.

Activity 1

First, please read the following paragraph from David Palermo's excellent *Psychology of Language* (1978, p. 38):

> At least four theoretical variants of the interpretive semantic theory have appeared in the literature since Chomsky first grappled with the problem of semantics. In the late 1960s, alternatives were offered by Lakoff (1968), McCawley (1968), and Ross (1967). Their arguments centered around the idea that it is not possible to separate the semantic and syntactic components of the grammar. According to these

linguists, there is no single base phrase marker but, rather, sentence generation begins with the semantic component and subsequent interaction between lexical insertion and transformational rules leads eventually to the surface structure and the application of the phonological component. Thus, the focus of linguistic inquiry should give at least equal billing to the semantic component rather than merely relegating semantics to a role of interpreting the syntactic component. The generative semanticists, as these linguists have come to be called, have argued that the underlying structures in standard theory are too concrete. Once the presuppositions and implications of sentences are analyzed in more detail, it becomes necessary to postulate more abstract underlying structures which make the deep structures of sentences deeper and more complex. Ross (1974), for example, shows how a simple causative sentence such as "Dr. Grusel is sharpening the spurs" involves more than seven underlying sentence forms or propositions encompassed within its meaning including, for example, the presuppositions that Dr. Grusel and the spurs exist.

Were you able to read the paragraph, as requested? What difficulties did you have, if any? Do you think you were really reading? It should be interesting to discuss your response with others who have tried to read this same paragraph.

Activity 2

Probably the most effective way of determining how a person goes about the task of reading is to examine his or her reading miscues. In order for you to do this more readily, it should help to have some terms defined. Kenneth Goodman first used the term *miscue* in the 1960s to describe any departure the reader makes from the actual words of the text (e.g., K. Goodman, 1965). For example, if a reader substitutes one word for another, adds or omits a word, or reorganizes a sequence of words, he or she has made a *miscue*. By replacing the negative term *error* with the "neutral" term *miscue,* we can more readily examine the reader's departures from the text without prejudice. We can consider the strategies the reader is using and come to understand not only that departures from the text can reflect good reading strategies, but that they may occur *because* the reader is using good strategies. We are not likely to have such insights until we abandon the notion that departures from the text are errors. On the other hand, the term *miscue* does indicate a missed cue. When we see what language cues the reader is and isn't typically using, we can draw informed inferences as to what strategies the reader is using well and what strategies the reader might need help with, if any.

As a first step toward that understanding, let us consider the three kinds of language cues within a written text:

Syntactic cues—that is, grammatical cues like word order, function words,[1] and word endings. (For a quick overview of grammatical cues within language, see Figure 8.4, p. 198).

Semantic cues—that is, meaning cues from each sentence and from the evolving whole, as one progresses through the entire text.

Graphic cues—that is, cues from letters and letter patterns. These combine with our knowledge of letter-sound patterns (phonics) to enable us to identify words automatically, or sometimes to try to sound them out letter-by-letter (very inefficient) or in letter-sound chunks, like l-ake for *lake,* str-ing for *string,* and so forth. Graphic cues would also include punctuation and other visual aspects of the written words (but not the pictures); however, we can settle for defining graphic cues as cues from letters and letter patterns.

Rarely does a miscue show attention to only one of these language cue systems. The following examples include some of the "purest" ones I have found, but even in most of these cases, the reader has paid attention to more than one kind of language cue:

truck
"The little ~~monkey~~ had it."

Attention to syntactic cues, since the miscue fits grammatically in the sentence. (The reader may also have attended to a picture cue.)

...to see if there was any

afraid
danger. He ~~heard~~ the...

Attention to semantic cues, because the miscue fits with the meaning of what came before. Possibly the reader picked up on some graphic cues, too.

'*s*
"This here Muriel," said Hayes...

The reader said "here's," to make the phrase into a grammatical and meaningful sentence.

tear
Their senses were ~~their~~ instruments.

Attention to graphic cues only.

flusk
Stacey swallowed to ~~flush~~ his anger.

Attention to graphic cues only.

expert
Every day ~~except~~ Friday,...

Attention to graphic cues. The miscue also fits with the grammar of what came before, so the reader may have been using syntactic cues up to and including the miscue.

Given these definitions and examples, compare David's miscues with Tony's, in the following two transcripts of a selection they each read aloud. In each case, do the miscues suggest that the child is using implicit knowledge of *syntactic cues* (grammar) to predict words that are grammatically acceptable in context? Do the miscues suggest that the child is using *semantic cues* (meaning) to predict words that are meaningful in context? Do the miscues suggest that the child is using *graphic cues* and letter-sound knowledge (phonics) to pronounce or sound out words? Which child would you say better integrates the language cues into effective reading strategies? What do you think each child's implicit definition of reading is? Again, discuss this activity with others, if possible.

The following key indicates how to interpret the major markings in the transcripts below:

may
Substitution   They ~~did~~ not have books....

(A word written over another word indicates a substitution. The cross-out shows what was replaced by the substitution.)

Omission   ...they dove into (the) waves.

(A circle around a word or group of words indicates an omission.)

Insertion   *high*
...splashing and spraying the water. ...

(A caret points to whatever is inserted.)

Correction   ...in the shade of a tall palm ~~tree.~~ © *twee*

(The © indicates that the miscue was corrected, and the underlining indicates what portion of the text was repeated as the reader made the correction.)

Repetition   ® "Why don't you do my work some day?"

(The ® indicates a repetition, and the underlining indicates what words were repeated.)

Multiple attempts   How lucky he was to live in a ~~Somali~~ village...   2 *Sammon* 1 *Sam-*

(Multiple attempts at a word are numbered consecutively.)

Partial word   *Mo−* Mohamed loved to go swimming in the sea.

(One or more letters followed by a hyphen indicate that the reader uttered what he or she apparently considered only part of a word, judging by the reader's intonation.)

The reading selection is adapted from *A Camel in the Sea* (Goetz, 1966), pp. 11–14. The adaptation is from *Fiesta*, one of the Houghton Mifflin readers (1971). The line divisions differ in the two transcripts because the story was typed differently for each child.

David's Miscues

Mohamed (mo-hah' med) loved to go swim-

ming in the sea. How lucky he was to live in a

① *Sami*   ② *village* ③ *on the right hand or*
~~Somali~~ (so-mah' lee) ~~village~~ ~~right on the Indian~~

Ocean! The sandy shore rang with the happy

© ④
shouts and cries of the village boys and girls.

They liked to race one another into the surf,

splashing and spraying the water into ⑤ ⓐ white

dancing foam before they dove into ⑥ ⓣⓗⓔ waves.

⑦ *younger* ⑧
Mohamed and his ~~young~~ sister, Āsha (ie' shuh),

spent all the time they could in the cool, clean

⑨ ⑧ ⑩   ⑪ *in the water*
~~Sea,~~ ~~swimming~~ and playing ~~water games~~. They

s ⑫
were good swimmers because their mother had taught them.
^

Every day except Friday, Mohamed went to

school with the other village boys. The class

was outdoors, and the children sat on little

benches in front of the teacher in the shade of

⑬ ⓒ *twee*   *may* ⑭
a tall/palm ~~tree.~~ They ~~did~~ not have books, so

the boys repeated everything the teacher said,

⑮ *again*
over and over until they knew their lessons by
^

heart. The girls of the village did not go to school,

for the people thought that school was not as

important for girls as it was for boys.

Tony's Miscues

① *Mo –*
Mohamed (mo-hah' med) loved to go swimming in the sea.

② *a Sammon / Sam-*   ③
How lucky he was to live in a ~~Somali~~ (so-mah' lee) (village)

④ *ran*
right on the Indian Ocean! The sandy shore ~~rang~~ with the happy

⑤ *souts*   ⑥
~~shouts~~ and cries of the (village) boys and girls. They liked

⑦ *high*
to race one another into the surf, splashing ^ and spraying

⑧ *drase*
the water into a white ~~dancing~~ foam before they dove into the

⑨ *Mola*   ⑩ *yūng*   ⑪ *Asla*
waves. ~~Mohamed~~ and his ~~young~~ sister, ~~Asha~~ (ie' shuh),

⑫
(spent all the time they could in the cool clean) sea,

swimming and playing water games. They were good swimmers

because their mother had taught them.

⑬ *expert*   ⑭ *Molda*
Every day ~~except~~ Friday, ~~Mohamed~~ went to school with the

⑮   ⑯
nother viner
~~other~~ ~~village~~ boys. The class was outdoors, and the children

⑰ *beaches*   ⑱ *frose*   ⑲ *shape*
sat on little ~~benches~~ in ~~front~~ of the teacher in the ~~shade~~

of a tall palm tree. They did not have books, so the boys

⑳ *ramped*
~~repeated~~ everything the teacher said, over and over, until

㉑ *other classrooms hurt*   ㉒ *vengil*
they knew ~~their lessons by heart.~~ The girls of the ~~village~~

did not go to school, for the people thought that school was

㉓ *imprentice*   ㉔ *to*
not as ~~important~~ for girls as ~~it~~ was for boys.

Activity 3

Having tried to read a paragraph for which you may not have had much background, and having compared the miscues of two children, you should be able to select or formulate a definition of reading that accords with your beliefs at the present time. Below are some definitions and characterizations of reading and the reading process, arranged more or less from simple to complex. Quite possibly none of these will be entirely satisfactory. In that case, you might draw upon two or several of them to formulate your own definition or characterization.

> Reading means getting meaning from certain combinations of letters. Teach the child what each letter stands for and he can read. . . . Johnny must learn, once and for all, that words are written by putting down letters from left to right, and that they are read in the same direction. (Flesch, 1955, pp. 10, 31)
>
> Reading is a precise process. It involves exact, detailed, sequential perception and identification of letters, words, spelling patterns and larger language units. (View denounced in K. Goodman, 1967, p. 126)
>
> Printing is a visual means of representing the sounds which are language. Meaning is in these sounds. We want to equip the child to turn the written word into a spoken word (whether he actually utters it or not) so he will hear what it says, that is, get its meaning. . . .
> (Walcutt & McCracken in *Lippincott Basic Reading,* 1975, Teacher's Edition for Book E, p. xiv)
>
> Reading is the active process of reconstructing meaning from language represented by graphic symbols (letters), just as listening is the active process of reconstructing meaning from the sound symbols (phonemes) of oral language.   (Smith, Goodman, & Meredith, 1970, p. 247)
>
> Reading is the process of constructing meaning through dynamic interaction among the reader's existing knowledge, the language of the text, and the context of the situation.
> (Michigan Department of Education's definition of reading)
>
> If the words remain words and sit quietly on the page; if they remain nouns, and verbs and adjectives, then we are truly blind. But if the words seem to disappear and our innermost self begins to laugh and cry, to sing and dance, and finally to fly—if we are transported in all that we are, to a brand new world, then—only then—can we say that we can READ!   (Wayman, 1980, title page)

In choosing a definition or formulating your own, consider this: is there any difference between "getting" meaning and "constructing" meaning? If so, what—and does it matter? If so, why and how?

For Further Exploration

1. Compare the following four sketches of children in first-grade classrooms (King & Watson, 1983, p. 70). Try to decide which of the above definitions of reading might underlie each of the approaches implicitly illustrated. Which of the children do you think will become the better reader(s)? Why? Discuss.

   Jamie sits looking at a list of words: *fat, pat, bat, sat, cat, hat.* . . . Later she sees, "The fat cat sat on the bat. Pat the fat cat."

   Josie is waiting her turn in a group whose members are reading aloud a story in which the words *green, table,* and *wood* appear ten times each. Later she will do skill exercises in her workbook.

   Harold looks at a page with *spɷn, baʋl, riŋ, ʃhout, chəer,* and *tæks*

   on it. Later he will write a story using the symbols he has learned in school.

Hildy sits on the floor and reads along with her friends and teacher a story the class has just written. Later she will write a letter to a friend about the book she has just finished reading.

2. Interview some children about their views of reading and experiences with reading. You can use, or draw from, the interview form in Figure 8.1, or use the questions below. Based on the interview, what do you find especially positive in each child's responses? Do you have any particular concerns about the reader's concept of reading or use of reading strategies?

   a. What do you think reading is? What are people doing in their heads when they're reading something?

   b. When you are reading and come to something you don't know, what do you do? (After receiving a response, ask a follow-up question: "What else do you do?" Depending upon the child's response, you might still ask, "Do you do anything else?" and if the response is yes, then ask, "What?" If the response is no, you might ask, "What else *could* you do?")

   c. Who is a good reader you know?

   d. What makes _____ a good reader?

   e. Do you think _____ ever comes to something he/she doesn't know? (After receiving a response, ask: "Suppose _____ does come to something he/she doesn't know. What do you think _____ would do?")

   f. If you knew someone was having trouble reading, how would you help that person?

   g. What would a/your teacher do to help that person?

   h. How did you learn to read?

   i. What would you like to do better as a reader?

   j. Do you think you are a good reader? Why?

3. If possible, observe several teachers during reading instruction. What kinds of direct instruction do they give? How do they respond to children's miscues? How do the activities in which children are involved differ from one classroom to another? Why? Try to decide what each teacher's implicit definition of reading must be. Later, ask each teacher how he or she would define reading and how reading should be taught. Compare these interview results with what you observed and what you inferred from the observation. In each case, does the teacher's definition of reading seem consistent with his or her teaching practices? Discuss.

   If in carrying out this activity you discover teachers with widely differing instructional approaches and/or definitions of reading, it might be particularly interesting to try a further project with some students from the most diverse teachers. With the teachers' permission, interview some of the poorest and some of the best readers from each class. If possible, tape-record the interviews for later study. You could ask the questions in number 2 above, or draw upon my interview form in Figure 8.1 (pp. 186–187).

4. In an article reviewing thirty years of inquiry into students' perceptions of reading, Johns (1986) mentions, among others, a study of 1,655 students from grades 1 to 8. The students were asked three questions: (1) "What is reading?" (2) "What do you do when you read?" and (3) "If someone didn't know how to read, what would you tell him or her that he or she would need to learn?" Johns points out that students often know more than they reveal in such brief interviews. In any case, many of the students' responses had to be classified as "meaningless"—no response, "I don't know," or a vague, circular, or irrelevant response. In many instances, such responses may have indicated that the student did not understand what the question might mean. In responding to the question "What is reading?" fewer than 20% of the students made any reference to getting meaning through reading (the percentage

was higher with the older students, and lower with the younger ones). Most of the students described reading as decoding (e.g., sounding words out), or as an activity involving a textbook and occurring in a classroom or school environment (Johns & Ellis, 1976, as reported in Johns, 1986, p. 36). What do you think accounts for this low percentage of children who define reading as having to do with getting meaning? Do you think this might be fairly typical today, too? What do you think of the apparently high percentage of children who describe reading only as something occurring in school? Again, do you think this pattern is typical today? Do you think either of these observations should be a matter of concern to teachers, parents, and schools? Why or why not? Discuss.

5. If it isn't possible to observe or interview teachers, perhaps you could get some teachers, or students in teacher education programs, to fill out the questionnaire in number 6 below, after you have done so yourself. Talk about your responses together, if possible.

6. To explore further your own views of reading and reading instruction, respond to the following questionnaire; you might also use it during the interviews suggested above. For each question, circle the answer that best reflects the strength of your agreement or disagreement (SA means "strongly agree"; SD means "strongly disagree"). This questionnaire is the DeFord Theoretical Orientation to Reading Profile (TORP), included and discussed in DeFord (1985.)[2]

		1 2 3 4 5
1.	A child needs to be able to verbalize the rules of phonics in order to assure proficiency in processing new words.	1 2 3 4 5 SA SD
2.	An increase in reading errors is usually related to a decrease in comprehension.	1 2 3 4 5 SA SD
3.	Dividing words into syllables according to rules is a helpful instructional practice for reading new words.	1 2 3 4 5 SA SD
4.	Fluency and expression are necessary components of reading that indicate good comprehension.	1 2 3 4 5 SA SD
5.	Materials for early reading should be written in natural language without concern for short, simple words and sentences.	1 2 3 4 5 SA SD
6.	When children do not know a word, they should be instructed to sound out its parts.	1 2 3 4 5 SA SD
7.	It is a good practice to allow children to edit what is written into their own dialect when learning to read.	1 2 3 4 5 SA SD
8.	The use of a glossary or dictionary is necessary in determining the meaning and pronunciation of new words.	1 2 3 4 5 SA SD
9.	Reversals (e.g., saying "saw" for *was*) are significant problems in the teaching of reading.	1 2 3 4 5 SA SD
10.	It is a good practice to correct a child as soon as an oral reading mistake is made.	1 2 3 4 5 SA SD
11.	It is important for a word to be repeated a number of times after it has been introduced to insure that it will become a part of sight vocabulary.	1 2 3 4 5 SA SD
12.	Paying close attention to punctuation marks is necessary to understanding story content.	1 2 3 4 5 SA SD
13.	It is a sign of an ineffective reader when words and phrases are repeated.	1 2 3 4 5 SA SD

14. Being able to label words according to grammatical function (nouns, etc.) is useful in proficient reading.

   1 2 3 4 5
   SA   SD

15. When coming to a word that's unknown, the reader should be encouraged to guess upon meaning and go on.

   1 2 3 4 5
   SA   SD

16. Young readers need to be introduced to the root form of words (*run, long*) before they are asked to read inflected forms (*running, longest*).

   1 2 3 4 5
   SA   SD

17. It is not necessary for a child to know the letters of the alphabet in order to learn to read.

   1 2 3 4 5
   SA   SD

18. Flash-card drills with sight words is an unnecessary form of practice in reading instruction.

   1 2 3 4 5
   SA   SD

19. Ability to use accent patterns in multisyllable words (pho´-to-graph, pho-to´-gra-phy, and pho-to-gra´-phic) should be developed as part of reading instruction.

   1 2 3 4 5
   SA   SD

20. Controlling text through consistent spelling patterns ("The fat cat ran back. The fat cat sat on a hat") is a means by which children can best learn to read.

   1 2 3 4 5
   SA   SD

21. Formal instruction in reading is necessary to insure the adequate development of all the skills used in reading.

   1 2 3 4 5
   SA   SD

22. Phonic analysis is the most important form of analysis used when meeting new words.

   1 2 3 4 5
   SA   SD

23. Children's initial encounters with print should focus on meaning, not upon exact graphic representation.

   1 2 3 4 5
   SA   SD

24. Word shapes (word configuration) should be taught in reading to aid in word recognition.

   1 2 3 4 5
   SA   SD

25. It is important to teach skills in relation to other skills.

   1 2 3 4 5
   SA   SD

26. If a child says "house" for the written word *home*, the response should be left uncorrected.

   1 2 3 4 5
   SA   SD

27. It is not necessary to introduce new words before they appear in the reading text.

   1 2 3 4 5
   SA   SD

28. Some problems in reading are caused by readers dropping the inflectional endings from words (e.g., *jumps, jumped*).

   1 2 3 4 5
   SA   SD

2 Schemas and Transactions in the Reading Process

Normal reading seems to begin, proceed, and end in meaning, and the source of meaningfulness must be the prior knowledge in the reader's head. Nothing is comprehended if it does not reflect or elaborate on what the reader already knows.

—Frank Smith

Questions for Thought and Discussion

1. How would you define reading, as you begin this chapter?

2. How do we, as readers, determine the meanings of individual words?

3. How do our experiences, beliefs, and knowledge—our "schemas"—affect our understanding of texts and even our perception and understanding of individual words? Consider examples from your own life and the lives of those you know.

4. Why is it that readers necessarily create a personal text that is parallel but not identical to the author's text? And why do we say that reading is a "transaction" between reader and text, occurring within various kinds of contexts?

5. What is a "skills" view of reading? A "sociopsycholinguistic" view of reading? In what major ways do they differ? Which view better reflects your own experiences as a reader and as a child trying to learn to read? Which view better reflects the kind of reading instruction you had as a child? How did that instruction work for you? Which view do you think offers a better basis for reading instruction, and why?

COMPREHENDING AND LEARNING TO READ

You may never have given much thought to *how* words, sentences, and texts mean. In your daily life, you understand much of what you hear and read, while other things you doubtless don't understand. However, you may seldom have reflected upon the how or why of comprehension; you may never have constructed from your own experience a theory about *how* language means. It is important for teachers of reading to have such a theory, however, in order to approach the teaching of reading in a manner that accords with what is known about how meaning is constructed from oral and written language.

Of course everyone agrees that the ultimate purpose of reading is to arrive at meaning, but there are differing views about what is involved in learning to read. Most reading instruction is based, implicitly if not explicitly, on one of the three following views:

View 1. Learning to read means learning to pronounce words.

View 2. Learning to read means learning to identify words and understand their meaning.

View 3. Learning to read means learning to bring meaning to a text in order to get meaning from, or understand, a text.

The first view, that learning to read means learning to pronounce words, is increasingly dictating beginning reading instruction in our schools. This view seems to reflect an assumption that once words are pronounced, meaning will take care of itself. The second view of learning to read assumes that once the meaning of individual words is determined, the meaning of the whole (paragraph, text) will take care of itself. In sharp contrast, the third view assumes that meaning results not necessarily from the precise identification of every word in a sentence, but from the constant interplay between the mind of the reader and the language of the text. This is a *psycholinguistic* view of reading, as will be explained below.

Many people would find the first definition unsatisfactory, incomplete: it is not enough to pronounce the words because that does not guarantee comprehension. If readers cannot also get meaning, they are not really reading. This, indeed, may have been your response to the paragraph on generative semantics (activity 1 in "Characterizing Reading and Reading Instruction" in Chapter 1). You may have been able to pronounce most of the words, yet felt that such word identification did not really constitute reading.

While rejecting as inadequate the view that learning to read means learning to pronounce words, many people unthinkingly adopt the second view: they assume that reading means identifying words and getting their meaning. The implication, of course, is that the meaning of the whole sentence and text will automatically follow from the meaningful identification of words. Since this view also seems to underlie much of our reading instruction in the United States, it is important to examine the assumption that meaning is built up from smaller parts to increasingly larger wholes.

THE MEANING OF WORDS AND SENTENCES: A FIRST LOOK

Since the mid-twentieth century, many psychologists and linguists have turned to the investigation of how people learn their native language and how they produce and comprehend sentences. There arose a hybrid discipline called *psycholinguistics* (from *psyche,* meaning 'mind,' and *linguistics,* meaning 'the study of language'). Since the early 1970s, when a psycholinguistic view of reading was first popularized through the books of Frank Smith (*Understanding Reading,* 1971, *Psycholinguistics and Reading,* 1973) and the miscue research of Kenneth Goodman and his colleagues (K. Goodman & Burke, *Theoretically Based Studies,* 1973), scholars in related disciplines have come to essentially the same conclusions about how language means.

Such scholarly research by sociopsycholinguists, schema theorists, semioticians, literary theorists, and reading educators simply confirms what we ourselves might conclude from thoughtful observation of how we and others comprehend. So—let us work inductively, together building a theory of comprehension.

To begin, please take a moment to write five to ten sentences using the word *run.* Try to create sentences in which *run* has different meanings.

The following are some of my sentences:

1. Can you run the store for an hour?
2. Can you run the word processor?
3. Can you run the 500-yard dash?
4. Can you run in the next election?
5. Can you run next year's marathon?
6. I helped Samuel with his milk run.
7. They'll print 5,000 copies in the first run.

8. Sherry has a run in her hose.

9. There was a run on snow shovels yesterday morning.

10. It was a long run.

Doubtless you have thought of several additional meanings of *run*.

Now the question is, in these and other sentences, how does the reader (or listener) know what *run* means? One of my small dictionaries lists nearly forty meanings for the word *run;* one of my desk dictionaries lists over eighty. Can readers arbitrarily take any one of the meanings of *run* from their mental dictionaries and apply it to the word *run* in these sentences? Clearly the answer is no. More often than not, meaningless sentences would result.

From even this simple example, then, it should be obvious that we do not simply add together the meanings of individual words to get the meaning of a sentence. To determine the meanings of the words, we use contexts of various sorts:

1. *Grammatical context within the sentence.* In the first five sentences above, *run* occurs in a context that signals its use as a verb. The grammatical context partially delimits the meaning of *run.*

2. *Semantic context within the sentence.* In "run the store" we know that *run* means something like 'manage'; in "run the word processor," we know that *run* means something like 'operate'; in "his milk run," we know that *run* means something like 'route'; and so forth. Interestingly, in the sentences where *run* is a verb, the precise meaning is determined by a noun that comes after it, rather than before.

3. *Situational, pragmatic context.* A sentence like "It was a long run" has several possible meanings, depending on the context in which it is uttered or written. In the context of stockings, *run* would refer to a tear (notice that the meaning and pronunciation of *tear* depends on its context, too). In the context of a dog kennel, *run* would mean an enclosure. In the context of fishing, *run* would mean migrating fish. In the context of skiing, *run* would mean a downhill path or route. In the context of theater, "It was a long run" would mean that the play was performed for a long period of time. And so forth. Situational context can be either verbal or nonverbal or both, as you can readily imagine from the preceding examples.

4. *Schematic context.* This refers to knowledge in our heads: a mental *schema* is simply an organized chunk of knowledge or experience. If we did not have mental schemas, we could not make practical use of the other kinds of context mentioned. For example, if we did not have an intuitive sense of grammar, we could not use grammatical context to limit a word's possible meanings to those that are appropriate for the verb function of the word (as in examples 1 through 5) or to limit the word's possible meanings to those that are appropriate for the noun function (as in examples 6 through 10). This process of grammatically delimiting a word's possible meanings is so automatic that we are not often aware of it, but it nevertheless occurs—and is made possible by our grammatical schemas.

Since our schemas develop as we interact with the external world, we may often lack appropriate schemas for understanding what we hear or read. For example, if you take your dog to be boarded at a kennel while you're on vacation, then return home and reassuringly tell your young children, "Gretchen's okay, she's got a long run," this sentence may make no sense to them. They may not be able to make use of the *verbal* situational context unless they have experienced the *nonverbal*—that is, unless they have actually seen the enclosure called a "dog run" at a kennel. Thus the children's schemas may be inadequate for making sense of what you've said.

From the examples and discussion so far, we can make several preliminary observations about how words and sentences mean:

1. Clearly, we do not just add together the meanings of the individual words in a sentence to get the meaning of the whole. We cannot know what a word means until we see it in context. Oddly enough, the supposedly simplest words like *in, on, at,* and *by* typically have at least fifteen to thirty meanings listed in a desk dictionary. In isolation, words have only *potential* meanings, a range of meanings that a dictionary attempts to characterize (e.g., Halliday, 1975). It is only when the word is used in context (of various sorts) that one or more of these meanings is actualized.

2. Without knowledge in our heads, our schemas, we could not make use of the information provided by other kinds of context: grammatical, semantic, situational—and social, too.

3. The observations above strongly suggest that meaning does not arise from part to whole but in some much more complex way. Bizarre as it sounds, we are able to grasp the meanings of individual words only when we see how they interrelate with each other. Thus, meaning arises from whole to part more than from part to whole.

Thus, as a first approximation of how sentences mean, we may say that *the meaning of a sentence arises or develops by means of transactions among words whose meanings are not identifiable except in context, where context includes at least grammar, semantics, and situation. It is the readers' and listeners' schemas—their individual contexts—that enable them to make use of these other kinds of context to comprehend language.* The truth of this observation should become clearer as the chapter progresses, when we focus on schemas and transactions, deep structure and surface structure, and contrasting views of language processing and reading. The use of context in identifying words will be discussed further in Chapters 3 and 4.

SCHEMAS: WHAT ARE THEY?

In recent years, those interested in how the mind operates have postulated the existence of cognitive schemas. As stated earlier, a *schema* is simply an organized chunk of knowledge or experience, often accompanied by feelings (e.g., Anderson, 1994; Anderson, Spiro, & Anderson, 1977; Adams & Collins, 1979; Rumelhart, 1980; Iran-Nejad, 1980; and Iran-Nejad & Ortony, 1984).

To get some idea of what a schema is and how it operates in our daily lives, let us explore for a moment our schemas for restaurants (as suggested by Pearson & Johnson, 1978). What are some of the different kinds of restaurants you can think of—not specific restaurants or even restaurant chains, but categories into which these might be organized? A preliminary list might include truck stops and greasy spoons, fast food restaurants, cafeterias, ethnic restaurants, family restaurants, and fancy/expensive/gourmet restaurants. In addition, I have a concept for what might be called a cocktail restaurant. It's something between a family restaurant and a fancy restaurant: a place where you may go for drinks, a nice but not too expensive meal, and maybe entertainment on Friday or Saturday night—without the kids. Figure 2.1 shows these categories in a hierarchic, branching-tree diagram. You might add the additional categories you have thought of.

Notice that it is difficult to say exactly how big or little a schema is. We may have an ethnic restaurant schema that is part of a general restaurant schema, but the ethnic restaurant schema can be further subdivided into schemas for Greek restaurants, Italian restaurants, Mexican restaurants, Chinese restaurants, Thai restaurants, and so forth. Your own schemas for ethnic restaurants will depend a lot upon where you live and what cities and countries you have visited. Then, too, our original category, "restaurants," is itself part of a larger schema, "places to eat."

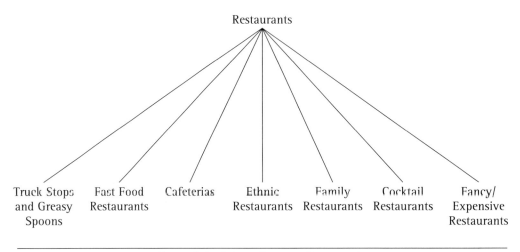

Figure 2.1   *Schema for types of restaurants.*

Other places to eat might be at home, at Grandma's, in the park, in the school cafeteria, or even in bed. Obviously our schemas for these various places to eat will also differ from one another.

Most if not all of these categories are what Arthur Koestler (1969) called *holons:* each is simultaneously a whole, with its own subparts, and yet a part of something else. For example, the category "ethnic restaurants" has its own subcategories yet is itself a subcategory of "restaurants."

How are categories related to schemas? A schema is the organized knowledge we have about a category. Let's compare, for instance, our schema for fast food restaurants with our schema for fancy/expensive restaurants. Some of the obvious differences are given in the list below, but doubtless you can add others.

Schema for Fast Food Restaurants	*Schema for Fancy/Expensive Restaurants*
Limited menu, often consisting of hamburgers plus a few other items	Generally a wide selection of foods, often including European cuisine
Order food across a counter	Order food from waitress or waiter (often the latter)
Pay before receiving your food	Pay after eating
Eat quickly	Eat slowly, with food served in several courses
Use paper napkins and plastic utensils	Use cloth napkins and silverware

Notice that cutting across the *category schemas* for types of restaurants are various *operational schemas* for selecting food, ordering, paying, and eating (see Figure 2.2). From these operational schemas, we can select elements that together will uniquely characterize each type of restaurant.

The distinctions within these operational schemas can be amazingly subtle. For example, take the schema of paying for the food. In a fast food restaurant, you usually pay for the food before receiving it. In a cafeteria, you pay for the food after receiving it, but before taking it to a table to eat. In drugstore counter restaurants (not included in the previous list), you receive the check as soon as you are served, and may be asked to pay for the food then. In family restaurants, you often receive the check as soon as you are served, but you pay as you leave. In cocktail restaurants,

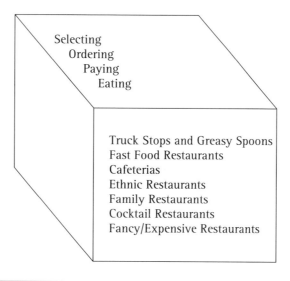

Figure 2.2   *Category and operational schemas.*

you usually do not receive the check until after you have finished eating and have had an after-dinner drink or a cup of coffee—or at least have been invited to do so. Your waitress or waiter may take the check to the cashier for you, or you may pay on the way out. In a fancy restaurant, of course, the waitress or waiter (traditionally a waiter) will present the check on a platter or in a menu-like booklet and take the check to the cashier for you.

A moment's reflection will reveal the importance of schemas in our daily lives. Suppose someone has a well-developed schema for fast food restaurants and for family restaurants, but has never been to a fancy restaurant before. If a child, this person will surely be unprepared to endure the lengthy wait for one course after another, or the interminable adult discussions, or being repeatedly admonished to sit still and keep quiet. Where is the playground outside the restaurant? Where are the video games? Even as an adult, a person may not know what to do with the "extra" silverware and may not realize that the reason the check is served on a tray or platter is so that the diners can put their money on it for the waitress or waiter to take. As for wine tasting—what's that? One of my students related her father's first experience in a fancy restaurant. The waiter opened a bottle of wine and handed her father the cork to sniff. Not knowing what was expected, he looked at the cork and said, "Yup, that's a cork all right." Another student admitted that when first confronted with a finger bowl at a gourmet restaurant, she drank the water. Obviously their schemas for fancy restaurants did not include what to do in situations like these.

Can you think of examples when your own cognitive schemas were obviously not adequate to the situation? Can you remember times when you tried to understand an explanation or a lecture, a textbook or a library book, and found your schemas inadequate? What are some of the implications for teaching?

SCHEMAS IN READING

To explore the importance of schemas in the reading process, read one or the other of the following paragraphs once, without rereading. Then write a brief summary of what you have read.

Cost or Other Basis (on the topic of capital gains and losses)

In general, the cost or other basis is the cost of the property plus purchase commissions, improvements, and minus depreciation, amortization, and depletion. If you inherited the property or got it as a gift, in a tax-free exchange, involuntary conversion, or "wash sale" of stock, you may not be able to use the actual cash cost as the basis. If you do not use cash cost, attach an explanation of your basis.
—Internal Revenue Service, booklet on *1040 Federal Income Tax Forms and Instructions* (1985)

Dissipative Structures (based on Prigogine & Stengers, 1984)

Ilya Prigogine has demonstrated that when an "open system," one which exchanges matter and/or energy with its environment, has reached a state of maximum entropy, its molecules are in a state of equilibrium. Spontaneously, small fluctuations can increase in amplitude, bringing the system into a "far-from-equilibrium" state. Perhaps it is the instability of subatomic "particles" (events) on the microscopic level that causes fluctuations on the so-called macroscopic level of molecules. At any rate, strongly fluctuating molecules in a far-from-equilibrium state are highly unstable. Responding to internal and/or external influences, they may either degenerate into chaos or reorganize at a higher level of complexity.
—Constance Weaver, "Parallels Between New Paradigms in Science and in Reading and Literary Theories" (1985)

Now check your summary with the original. Did you leave out any important ideas? Distort any ideas? Or can't you even tell? Many of us simply do not have schemas adequate for this task. Because we do not already know something about capital gains and losses or about dissipative structures, we cannot understand much of what we are reading, and therefore we find it difficult to summarize the passage or even to evaluate our summary afterwards. We simply have no cognitive schemas for these topics.

Now let's take a slightly different situation. Again, read the following passage and then summarize it in writing without looking back. Check your summary with the original.

The procedure is actually quite simple. First you arrange things into different groups. Of course one pile may be sufficient depending on how much there is to do. If you have to go somewhere else due to lack of facilities that is the next step, otherwise you are pretty well set. It is important not to overdo things. That is, it is better to do too few things at once than too many. In the short run this may not seem important but complications can easily arise. A mistake can be expensive as well. At first the whole procedure will seem complicated. Soon however, it will become just another facet of life. It is difficult to foresee any end to the necessity for this task in the immediate future, but then one never can tell. After the procedure is completed one arranges the materials into different groups again. Then they can be put into their appropriate places. Eventually they will be used once more and the whole cycle will then have to be repeated. However, that is a part of life.
—John D. Bransford and Nancy S. McCarrell, "A Sketch of a Cognitive Approach to Comprehension" (1974)

Many people find that their summaries of the above passage are inadequate—not because they can't understand the passage, but because they can't place the operations described within a context that makes sense to them. They understand the passage as they read, but they recall relatively little.

Now ask someone else to read and summarize this passage, but tell the person beforehand that the passage is about washing clothes. Compare the two summaries. Is the other person's summary more complete? Did this person include anything about washing clothes that was not explicitly stated in the passage? Often people will mention sorting the clothes into light colors and dark, or going to a laundromat if a washing machine isn't available at home. Clearly these ideas can be inferred from the passage, but only if you know or think that the passage is about washing clothes—and if you know something about that process. Only when we have cognitive schemas adequate to what we are reading and only when these schemas are somehow activated will we have much understanding and recall of what we hear or read.

This issue of activating one's schemas is crucial, as the terms *metalinguistic awareness, metacognition,* and *metacomprehension* suggest. Basically these terms refer to being aware that you have such strategies, and being able to use them consciously. For instance, having metalinguistic awareness means you are aware that you have linguistic knowledge (schemas) that you can use in listening and reading, as for example in predicting that a noun will come soon after the word *the.* Being aware that you have such knowledge, you can use it consciously when necessary. Here, in contrast, is an example of a college student who seemed unaware that she had cognitive strategies to monitor her own comprehension; at any rate, she had apparently not learned to use those strategies effectively in reading her textbooks. This student had just flunked her last introductory psychology exam (Santa, 1981, p. 168; italics mine):

> She had the proper "good student facade"; she underlined essential points in her text and had an adequate set of lecture notes. She also claimed to spend a considerable amount of time studying. After having her [the student] reread a short selection from her psychology text, I was somewhat amazed that she could not even answer the simplest question. Thinking she might have a poor memory, I asked her several other questions allowing her to look back in her text for the appropriate answer. Still, she had no success. *What is interesting is that she was very surprised that she had comprehended so little.* She had assumed she had understood without ever testing her assumption and *appeared totally oblivious to strategies which might help her monitor her own comprehension.*

Thus we might say that not only was this student neglecting to activate whatever schemas she might have had relevant to the understanding of psychology, she was even unaware of having strategies or schemas that might enable her to determine whether or not she was comprehending. Obviously readers need to mobilize such self-monitoring strategies as well as schemas relevant to the content of what they are reading.

SCHEMAS AND TRANSACTIONS

This discussion of schemas leads naturally to the concept of *transaction.* To gain experientially an understanding of this concept, read the following poem as many times as you wish. Please do not read farther in the text until you have written down what you think the poem says.

To Pat

On the day you died
my lover caught a fish
a big-mouthed bass
nineteen inches long
four and a half pounds strong
they measured it.

They measured it,
stretching the tape to match
  its length,
piercing its mouth to heft
  its bulk.

They measured, examined,
   praised it.

"Fish, dear fish," he said,
"you are too beautiful to eat.
I will put you back."

But it was too late.
Like you, the fish could not
   be revived.
He died in the kitchen sink.

And now I have eaten
of his sweet flesh,
the communion denied me
by the church of your people.

It is finished.

Typically, people will give different responses to the poem. One student suggested that the author—or at least the "I" of the poem—had been in love with Pat, but that the church had kept them from marrying. Another student, in a similar vein, suggested that the writer couldn't have Pat because he was a priest. Some people have interpreted "On the day you died" metaphorically: on the day you died to me, the day our friendship or romance ended. Others have taken the line literally, as describing the physical death of the person addressed. Some students take the line about communion as referring to sexual communion. Others interpret the line as referring to the taking of the sacraments in church; for some of these students, this interpretation seems to be fostered by the knowledge that certain churches forbid nonmembers to take communion ("the communion denied me / by the church of your people"). Still other students have taken "communion" as signaling both meanings, sexual and religious communion. Some students have seen religious elements in various parts of the poem after reading the last line. Others, not knowing that Christ's last words on the cross were "It is finished," have seen no religious elements at all. Often, of course, students have modified their opinion of what the poem says during the social give-and-take of classroom discussion.

Clearly each reader has brought to bear his or her own schemas in grappling with the poem—including a schema for interpreting poetry, which often goes something like this: "There must be a deep meaning here that I don't immediately get. It probably has to do with sex and/or religion." An interesting commentary on the experience students have had with reading poetry in school, is it not? Notice, too, that although I have asked students to tell just what the poem said, not what they thought it meant, most students have not separated the two. This is common: after a very brief interval, readers typically cannot distinguish between what they've actually read and what is a logical inference from what they have read. You may have observed this with people who summarized the "washing clothes" passage knowing what it's supposed to be about. As readers internalize what they have read, recall and inference and interpretation become inseparable. (Again, you might consider the implications for teaching and learning.)

Each person's experience of the poem above, and of everything else he or she reads, is influenced by the person's own schemas—the person's knowledge and experience and feelings. Recognition of this fact is, however, a sharp departure from an earlier (and, in some quarters, a still popular) concept of comprehension. For a long time after the introduction of Shannon's revolutionary concepts of information theory (Shannon, 1948), it was thought that a message would travel pure and unchanged from sender to receiver, provided the channel—the medium through which the message was transmitted—did not contain "noise"—that is, something that would distort the message. Shannon's basic concept can be represented as follows:

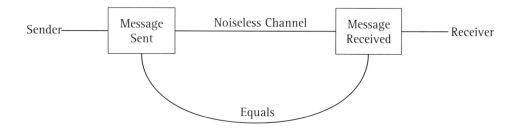

Now we understand, however, that in human communication the message received is *never* identical to the message sent, whether the communication is oral or written. This is true not because there is necessarily any noise in the channel, though there may be. Rather, the message received is inevitably different from the message sent because the receiver—the reader or listener—brings to bear his or her schemas in interpreting the message. The speaker or writer tries to encode a message in language, but because no two people's experiences, thoughts, and feelings are ever identical, the message received is never quite identical to the message sent. This view can be represented as follows:

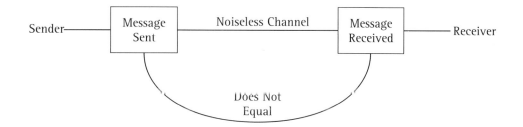

From the listener's or reader's point of view, then, meaning is not in the spoken or written word, the text itself. Rather, meaning arises during a transaction between the words and the listener or reader. The reader constructs what Kenneth Goodman calls a "personal text," which is parallel to, but not equivalent to, the written text.

The person who has stimulated widespread understanding of the concept and term *transaction* is Louise Rosenblatt (e.g., 1938, 1964, 1978), who borrowed and popularized the concept of transaction introduced by Dewey and Bentley (1949). To clarify the concept of transaction, Rosenblatt (1978) defines some key terms:

- *The Reader* is the person seeking to make meaning by transacting with (actively reading) a text, of whatever kind.
- *The Text* is the collection of word symbols and patterns on the page, the physical object you hold in your hand as you read.
- *The Poem* is the literary work created as the reader transacts with the text. ("Poem" refers metaphorically to *any* literary work—not just a poem in the usual sense, but a short story, novel, play.)

The crucial point is that meaning is not in the text itself, whether the text be literary or otherwise. Rather, meaning arises during the transaction between reader and text, while the author can only hope that the reader will bring similar knowledge and experiences (similar schemas) to the reading event. Thus *reading* is a process, a transaction between reader and text in a given situational context, an event during which meaning evolves.

To elaborate: the writer has, let us say, a novel in his or her head (though, of course, much of the novel typically develops as one writes). The writer chooses word symbols and patterns to represent that novel, usually knowing full well that from the text thus created, the reader will create his or her own novel. No two novels, so created, will ever be alike. The novel I created from Anya Seton's *Katherine* (1954) at age fifteen is not the same novel I created upon re-transacting with the text at thirty-five, and certainly the novel you create will never be the same as either of mine. We bring different life experiences, different schemas, to the word symbols and patterns of the text.

PRAGMATICS: SITUATIONAL, SOCIAL, AND CULTURAL FACTORS IN READING

Our schemas depend in part on a variety of social factors: our cultural, ethnic, and socioeconomic background; our age and educational attainment; our interests and values; and so forth. For convenience, we shall consider these as falling within two broad categories: situational and social, including cultural.

Such factors often affect readers' perception of and approach to a reading event, their way of dealing with a particular text, and their understanding of it. For example, a student may read one way when reading silently for pleasure, another way if asked to read aloud without preparation, and still another when reading a multiple-choice test. The reading event is also influenced by other factors, such as the teacher's expectations of a student, expressed verbally and/or nonverbally; whether or not the teacher interrupts the student while reading; and whether the teacher is encouraging or disparaging. A student's reading may also be affected by reading with a buddy or a group, by being a member of a literature discussion group or a book club, or by being labeled as a troublemaker and isolated from classmates to read alone in a corner of the room. And this only begins to touch upon the social and situational factors in the classroom, not to mention the various factors that affect our reading outside of school and throughout our lives.

Such situational, social, and cultural factors may be called the *pragmatics* of reading. They generate schemas that we bring to a text and the reading event. Such schemas are derived from past experience. To be more specific about a previous example: When reading for pleasure, a child may read for meaning, without trying to identify all the words that aren't recognized on sight. When asked to read aloud in school, that same child may read to identify words, because the child has learned that correct word identification is what's expected. In taking multiple-choice "reading comprehension" tests, the child may read merely to locate the phrase in the paragraph(s) that corresponds with the phrase in one of the answers. A personal example comes readily to mind. When my son was in fourth grade, he had vocabulary tests of the matching type: match the word to the definition. One of the words to be tested was *assumption*, defined as "an assuming." I tried to find a more suitable definition in our dictionaries at home, but with little luck; finally, I concluded that the best way to help my son understand the word was with examples from his own life. John's reply, however, was typical of the student who has learned to play the academic game. "Oh, don't worry," he said. "On the test, I'll just match *ass*'s" (the first three letters of *assumption* and *assuming*). Obviously the situational context of the classroom did not demand genuine understanding.

An example of how social and situational factors intersect may help to illuminate both. Seeking to determine why inner-city children typically score lower on reading achievement tests than children from affluent suburbs, various researchers have discovered, not surprisingly, that one difference is that inner-city children less frequently have schemas that would facilitate comprehension of the passages in such tests. The passages are often based on experiences, knowledge, and/or vocabulary that they do not have. More interesting, though, is that many children from nonmainstream cultures (e.g., Black inner-city youth) apparently bring a different mind-set to the testing task itself. Though many children have learned that in responding to questions on a so-called comprehension test you're not supposed to draw upon prior knowledge but only to use information in the passage at hand, many inner-city youth do not operate upon this principle; rather, they answer test questions by using what they know (Nix & Schwarz, 1979).

Bloome and Green (1985) provide an interesting example, with an even more interesting commentary. The passage and question below are taken from a reading workbook, *Reading House Series* (1980, p. 71). The question, of course, is multiple-choice:

> Bill Benson looked only once at his homework assignment. Immediately, he started moaning to his seatmate, Candy Caries, about its length. As he shuffled out of the room after the bell, he couldn't help but remark to his teacher that the room was too stuffy to work in. The teacher only smiled and shook her head at Bill's complaints.
>
>   Faced with the possibility of running an errand for his parents, Bill is likely to say:
> A. "Do I have to go? Why don't you ask Uncle Joe this time?"
> B. "Sure I'll go! Should I walk or take the bus?"
> C. "Okay, Dad. I'll go right after I finish my homework."
> D. "I'm way ahead of you, Pop! I took care of it already."

According to Bloome and Green (1985), one ninth grader explained why he chose option C (a "wrong" answer) instead of A (the "right" answer) by pointing out that Bill Benson had no intention of doing his homework or of going to the store, but that confronting his father—which is the situation in option A—would probably result in punishment. Thus, the student chose C, which superficially indicates compliance, but which may allow Bill to procrastinate indefinitely. Bloome and Green comment (1985, p. 180):

> In answering the question, the student used his own background knowledge as a frame for interpreting the story and the question. However, when high-achieving students from the same grade, school, and background were given the same passage and questions, they gave the answer designated correct by the teacher's guide. In brief, one of the strategies some students may need to learn is to suppress their own background knowledge and assume the interpretive frame of the school.

Bloome and Green thus explain the problem as one of an "interpretive frame," adding that "Differences in interpretive frames may be the result of cultural differences, economic differences, personal experience differences, and so on" (p. 179). Thus, *social context* (the background of the student) may intersect with *situational context* (the testing situation) in such a way as to result in apparent failure to comprehend. Ironically, however, students like the one described above are doing precisely what readers must do in order to read real texts effectively: they are bringing their prior experience and knowledge to the task of making sense of what they read.

To further explore the importance of readers' schemas, read the following letter written by a teenager to his friend (Reynolds, Taylor, Steffensen, Shirey, & Anderson, 1982). Then write down a one- or two-sentence summary of the third paragraph, without looking back at the letter. If possible, compare your responses with others'.

Dear Joe,

I bet you're surprised to be hearing from your old friend Sam. It's been a long time since you moved away so I thought I'd drop you a line to catch you up on what's going on around here. Things haven't changed much. The weather's been really bad but we've only been let out of school a couple days. Everybody in the family is O.K., and my cousin is still asking about you. School has been going O.K. but I did get in some trouble last week.

It started out as a typical Thursday. Typical that is until lunchtime; at that point things started to get interesting. But don't let me get ahead of myself. I'll start at the beginning. Renee, my sister, and I were almost late for school. Renee had trouble getting her chores done and I couldn't leave without her. We barely caught our ride and made it to school just as the tardy bell rang.

Classes went at their usual slow pace through the morning, so at noon I was really ready for lunch. I got in line behind Bubba. As usual the line was moving pretty slow and we were all getting pretty restless. For a little action Bubba turned around and said, "Hey, Sam! What you doin' man? You so ugly that when the doctor delivered you he slapped your face!" Everyone laughed, but they laughed even harder when I shot back, "Oh, yeah? Well, you so ugly the doctor turned around and slapped your momma!" It got even wilder when Bubba said, "Well man, at least my daddy ain't no girl scout!" We really got into it then. After a while more people got involved—4, 5, then 6. It was a riot! People helping out anyone who seemed to be getting the worst of the deal. All of a sudden Mr. Reynolds the gym teacher came over to try to quiet things down. The next thing we knew we were all in the office. The principal made us stay after school for a week; he's so straight! On top of that, he sent word home that he wanted to talk to our folks in his office Monday afternoon. Boy! Did I get it when I got home. That's the third notice I've gotten this semester. As we were leaving the principal's office, I ran into Bubba again. We decided we'd finish where we left off, but this time we would wait until we were off the school grounds.

Well, I have to run now. I've got to take out the trash before Mom gets home. Write soon and let me know what's going on with you.

Later,
Sam

When you summarized the third paragraph, did you say, in one way or another, that the teenagers had gotten into a fight, a physical confrontation? Or did you think that the battle was merely verbal, not physical? If the latter, you're right. What Sam was describing to his friend Joe was an instance of "sounding" or "playing the dozens," a form of ritual insult found especially among Black males. When Black and White eighth-grade students tried to recall the letter and responded to questions about its content, the White students (who were from an agricultural area) tended to describe the events as "horrible," described the two participants as angry, and generally recalled the event as a fight: "Soon there was a riot all the kids were fighting"; "Me and Bubba agreed to finish our fight later, off the school grounds." The Black students, in contrast, more often recognized that the participants were just joking, just having fun. In fact, when told that White students tended to interpret the letter as being about a fight instead of an instance of sounding, one of the Black students looked surprised and said, "What's the matter? Can't they read?" (Reynolds, Taylor, et al., 1982, p. 365).

Reading, then, is not merely a psycholinguistic process, involving a transaction between the mind of the reader and the language of the text. Rather, *reading* is a sociopsycholinguistic process, because the reader-text transaction occurs within situational and social contexts. (See, for example, the longitudinal Bristol study documented in Wells, 1986.) More accurately, there are a variety of social and situational factors, a variety of contexts, that affect the activation of one's schemas and the outcomes of the reader-text transaction. That is, a variety of social and situational factors influence how the person reads and what the reader understands (see, for example, Carey, Harste, & Smith, 1981; Bloome, 1985). Figure 2.3 is an attempt to capture the

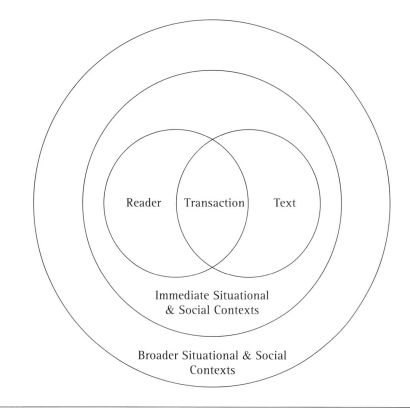

Figure 2.3 *Reading as a sociopsycholinguistic process.*

complexity of these relationships. Indeed, reading is a sociopsycholinguistic process of incredible complexity.

TRANSACTIONS WITHIN THE LANGUAGE OF THE TEXT: GRAMMATICAL SIGNALS

The reader-text transaction that takes place within an immediate situational context and broader personal and social context is by no means the only transaction taking place during the reading process. In particular, there are also numerous transactions, on various levels, within the language of the text itself.

Some of these transactions are signaled by grammatical cues: word endings, function words, and/or word order. Take, for example, word endings. The ending *-ed* indicates past action, as in "She *chaired* the meeting." The ending *-er* indicates one who does something, as in "Cindy is a top-notch *runner*." The ending *-en* denotes an action, as in "Bleach will *whiten* your clothes." And *-ly* indicates the manner in which an action is carried out, as in "She examined it *closely*." What, however, do these same endings indicate in the following sentences?

1. The *exhausted* doctor slept all day.

2. I can't run any *faster*.

3. The tomato is *rotten*.

4. Her cocker spaniel is very *friendly*.

Here, the -ed indicates a condition or state, the -er indicates the manner of an action, the -en indicates a condition or quality, and the -ly indicates a quality or characteristic. Our knowledge of words and the endings they can take, plus our recognition of how the italicized words are functioning in the above sentences, tells us that this time the endings are functioning differently than before. Both the meaning and the part of speech are different, as readers intuitively know.

Thus, although word endings do help to signal the meanings of words and the kinds of semantic and syntactic transactions into which they can enter, nevertheless we often do not know the meaning of an ending until we see it in the word to which it is attached—and, in some cases, not until we see how that word is used in the sentence. For example, in addition to its use as an adjective, *exhausted* can be a verb, as in "The recent demand for computers *exhausted* all our supply." Thus, in isolation, *exhausted* has the potential to be either an adjective or a verb.

Function words are another major grammatical signal, for they glue together the content words—the nouns and pronouns, verbs, adjectives, and adverbs that carry most of the meaning of a sentence. Thus, the major function words or signal words are noun determiners (ND), including the articles *a, an,* and *the*; verb auxiliaries (VA); prepositions (P); and conjunctions (C). Note the examples of function words below.

After it *had* rained *for an* hour, *the* young people gave up *their* idea
  C   VA   P ND   ND   ND

of camping out. Instead they rented *a* room *at a* motel where they
 P   ND   P ND

could swim *in a* pool *and* eat *by the* poolside.
 VA   P ND   C   P ND

Like word endings, such function words serve as useful but not infallible signals of what is coming next in a sentence. The word *this,* for example, usually works as a noun determiner, to signal that a noun is coming up in a sentence, as in "*This* problem is difficult." However, the word *this* can also work as a pronoun taking the place of a noun, as in "I can't understand *this*." Somewhat similarly, the words *will* and *can* commonly work as verb auxiliaries, to signal that a verb is coming up, as in "Terry *will* do it" and "Maryellen *can* come." However, both words sometimes function as nouns, as in "She has an iron *will*" and "He couldn't open the *can*." Thus, although function words help to signal the relations among words, we don't always know whether something is even a function word or not until we see how it fits with the other words in a sentence.

Even when we know something is a function word, we cannot tell its precise meaning in isolation. Take, for example, the preposition *by* in the following sentences. In each case what does it mean, and *how do you know?*

1. That was prescribed *by* Dr. Lucy.

2. Charlie sat down *by* Dr. Lucy.

3. Woodstock went *by* plane.

4. *By* the way, how old do you think Snoopy is?

5. *By* Snoopy's calculations, it ought to work.

The fact that *by* is a preposition tells us little about how it relates to the other words in a sentence. It is actually the other words that give *by* a specific meaning, rather than the other way around. *By* acquires meaning by transacting with the other words in the sentence.

In fact, the meaning of the function words and often the precise function words themselves can be predicted from the content words. Try again to read the sentence about giving up camping, as reproduced below. You will probably find that you can supply most of the missing words, getting at least the gist if not the actual words of the original:

_____ it ___ rained ____ _ hour, ___ young people gave up _____ idea _ camping out. Instead they rented _ room _ _ motel where they _____ swim _ _ pool ___ eat _ ___ poolside.

If indeed you could read the passage with little trouble and supply most if not all of the missing words, what might this suggest about the importance of function words in signaling grammar and thus meaning? Clearly, function words are useful in signaling the relations among words, but they may not be nearly so vital as is commonly supposed. (For a similar activity from which this conclusion may likewise be drawn, see the Kent State passage in Chapter 4, p. 109.)

Word order is more reliable than either word endings or function words in signaling the relationships among words. Compare, for instance, the following pairs of sentences:

1. Snoopy kissed Lucy.
   Lucy kissed Snoopy.

2. Dog bites man.
   Man bites dog.

3. Wendy loves Greg.
   Greg loves Wendy.

4. Cook the roast.
   Roast the cook.

In each case, our knowledge of English word order tells us that the first word indicates the doer of the action, while the third indicates the recipient of the action. The two sentences in each pair contain the same words, but the differing word order signals different relations, different transactions among the words. Note that the sentence "Roast the cook" may sound either cannibalistic or nonsensical to some readers, while other readers may have a schema that allows for an interpretation like the following: "Have a ceremony in which we honor the cook by seeming to dishonor him or her."

So far, then, it should be clear that word endings, function words, and word order all help us determine the meanings of words and the relations among the words in a sentence. But we have also seen that word endings are not infallible clues to word function or meaning. Function words are also limited in their usefulness. What appears to be a function word may not always be working as one; the meanings of some function words (particularly the prepositions) can by no means be determined out of context; and, in any case, many function words are often dispensable in a given context, being themselves predictable from the nouns, verbs, adjectives, and adverbs. These limitations leave us with word order as the best clue to word relationships. However, we shall see in the next section that even word order is often not adequate to signal the basic relations among the words of a sentence.

SURFACE VERSUS DEEP STRUCTURE

The grammatical clues of word endings, function words, and word order are surface structure clues—that is, clues that are visible in written language or audible in speech. As adults who know the language, we perceive many kinds of relationships that are not signaled, or not signaled adequately, by grammatical aspects of surface structure. These cues are part of the *deep structure,* a term coined by Noam Chomsky in the early 1960s to denote those relationships among words that are intuitively clear to a native speaker of the language, but that are not overtly signaled in the flow of language itself (see, for example, N. Chomsky, 1965).

Chomsky emphasized deep, underlying relationships that he considered grammatical. Take, for example, the following pair of sentences:

The operation was performed by a new surgeon.

The operation was performed by a new technique.

The two sentences have the same grammatical surface structure, but they "mean" in different ways. On the surface, "operation" is the subject, "was performed" is the verb phrase, and "by a new surgeon" and "by a new technique" are both prepositional phrases; the surface grammar is essentially the same. However, we know that in the first sentence it is the surgeon who performed the operation. "Surgeon" is the agent or doer of the action and hence the "deep" subject, as we can demonstrate by turning the sentence around and making it active: "A new surgeon performed the operation." We also know that the parallel word in the second sentence, "technique," is *not* the doer of the action or the deep subject: it would not make sense to say "A new technique performed the operation." The deep subject is, in fact, unspecified. For all we know, the operation may have been performed by a barber or a butcher. Or the operation may be of a totally different kind, having nothing to do with surgery.

Structurally ambiguous sentences provide further evidence that surface structure, including word order, is not always adequate to signal deep structure, the underlying relationships among words. Take, for example, the following sentences. What do they mean?

Visiting relatives can be a nuisance.

They asked the police to stop drinking.

The surface grammar of the first sentence gives us no clue to the deep grammar, to *who* is do-ing the visiting. Does the sentence mean that relatives who visit can be a nuisance? Or does it mean that the act of going to visit relatives can be a nuisance? In the second sentence above, the surface grammar similarly gives no clue as to the deep subject of *drinking:* are the po-lice to stop other people from drinking, or are they themselves to cease drinking? The sur-face grammar, including word order, is insufficient to make the meaning or the deep grammar clear.

In context, however, such sentences are usually understood. In fact, we understand the deep grammar precisely because we understand the meaning of the sentences, given a particular situational context. Chomsky's insistence on the importance of the deep structure *grammar* (as opposed to meaning) no longer seems as important as it once did. Historically, however, Chomsky's distinction between surface and deep grammar was of tremendous significance, paving the way for the widespread recognition that meaning does not lie in language itself but rather arises during the transaction between reader and text.

Modernizing Chomsky's definitions of surface and deep structure, then, we can say that *surface structure* is the visible or audible text, the squiggles and vibrations that are interpreted as words and word patterns—including the grammatical signals of word endings, function words, and word order. The *deep structure* is the underlying relationships that are perceived by, or rather constructed by, the reader or listener, on the basis of his or her prior knowledge and experience—schemas, in other words. Surface structure is what you see or hear. Deep structure is what you don't see or hear, but nevertheless understand.

SURFACE STRUCTURE Visible—Supplied by the Text			DEEP STRUCTURE Invisible—Supplied by the Reader		
Vibrations in the air or squiggles on the page	Words on the page	Surface grammar (word endings, function words, word order)	Possible word meanings	Relational meanings among words in sentences	Listener's or reader's schemas

Figure 2.4 *Surface-deep structure continuum. Language processing occurs in both directions, surface to deep and deep to surface, and is even more complex than is reflected here.*

Figure 2.4 summarizes these aspects of language and language processing in a surface-deep structure continuum. As the previous discussion suggests, however, we do not simply go from surface to deep structure in interpreting sentences. For example, if you have ever listened to someone speak a language that you do not know, you may have found that you could not even tell when one word ended and another began; the spoken words may have been little more than noises to you. For someone who has no acquaintance with written language, written words probably look like little more than scribbles or hieroglyphics; such, in fact, is our own experience when first encountering a radically different writing system. What enables us to make sense of language is our storehouse of schemas, including our schemas about the structure of the language in question and, for written language, our schemas about the nature of print in that language. Thus, language processing goes as much or more from deep to surface structure as the other way around.

To solidify our understanding of how sentences mean, let us work through one more set of examples, considering how syntactic and semantic context, situational context, and schemas all play a role. First, quickly define the words *chair, white, run, close,* and *love,* in your head or on paper. Now see if your definitions are appropriate for these contexts:

1. Get Shirley to *chair* the meeting.
2. Separate the *white* from the yolk.
3. Angie can *run* the outfit.
4. That was a *close* call.
5. I *love* you.

In the first sentence, surface grammar is enough to signal the meaning. That is, *chair* coming immediately after *to* must be a verb, and for most of us that verb has only one possible meaning: to take charge of, to preside over. In the second sentence, *the* indicates that *white* is a noun, but we don't know much about that noun *white* until we see it in context with *yolk;* here, we must have recourse to semantic cues within the sentence. In the third sentence, *can* clearly signals that *run* is a verb, but what does that verb mean? And what does the noun *outfit* mean—clothing? A business operation? The two words *run* and *outfit* can be understood only in transaction with each other.

In the fourth sentence, grammatical context indicates that *close* is an adjective rather than a verb and *call* is a noun rather than a verb, but what about the meaning of the phrase "a close call"? We need to know more about the situational context in which the sentence occurs. Is the speaker/writer describing a baseball game, a near-accident, or what?

On the surface, the word *love* in "I love you" appears clear enough: it is a verb, with *I* as subject and *you* as object. The transaction among the words is clear, but what does it mean to the person who hears or reads it? To one who does not know English, the sentence will mean nothing at all, unless the nonverbal context makes it clear. To those who know the language, it will still have different meanings under different circumstances and with different individuals. Under some circumstances, one may interpret the words "I love you" to be merely a verbal enticement to sexual gratification, while under other circumstances one may interpret the same words as an expression of lifelong devotion. It all depends upon the situation and the schemas, the deepest of deep structures that the individual brings to bear.

These examples again illustrate what we have already seen: that comprehension is not a one-way process from surface structure to deep structure. Indeed, as we interpret what we hear or read, we in effect impose deep structure on surface structure. Our prior knowledge and experience determine our understanding of the relations among the words in a sentence—or our inability to understand what a sentence means. Perhaps more surprising, however, is the fact that our entire system of knowledge and belief can affect even our perception of individual words and parts of words. While reading a story to my son, I once made the following miscue:

older
The ~~other~~ seals knew better.

In the context of the story, the other seals were in fact older. However, my students have insisted that this miscue was caused not so much by the preceding context of the story as by my unwarranted assumption that to be older is to be wiser. Probably they are right.

CONTRASTING MODELS OF READING AND LEARNING TO READ

We began this chapter by discussing contrasting views of learning to read, views that seem related to contrasting views of reading itself, and, still more generally, to contrasting views of how language means. Let us consider one more example of how language means before turning to models of reading.

Comprehending Language in Reading

It will help you develop your own model or theory of language comprehension and reading if, once again, you participate wholeheartedly in the activity suggested. Read the following paragraph silently, not worrying about how the words are pronounced. Just see if you can get some sense of what the passage is about, rereading the passage as necessary. Incidentally, the seeming nonsense words are actually antiquated, "lost words" (Sperling, 1977) that have been revived for the occasion:

> The blonke was maily, like all the others. Unlike the other blonkes, however, it had spiss crinet completely covering its fairney cloots and concealing, just below one of them, a small wam.
> This particular blonke was quite drumly—lennow, in fact, and almost samded. When yerden, it did not quetch like the other blonkes, or even blore. The others blored very readily.
> It was probably his bellytimber that had made the one blonke so drumly. The bellytimber was quite kexy, had a strong shawk, and was apparently venenated. There was only one thing to do with the venenated bellytimber: givel it in the flosh. This would be much better than to sparple it in the wong, since the blonkes that were not drumly could icchen in the wong, but not in the flosh.

Were you able to get any sense from the passage at all? Much to my initial surprise, I have found that people typically *do* get some meaning on a first or second reading. Typically they get the impression that the blonke is an animal of some sort, one who is obviously different from the others of his kind. Often, students comment that something seems to be wrong with this particular blonke. Can you see how they might get that impression? See if that impression becomes more obvious as you reread the passage knowing that a *blonke* is a large, powerful horse, and that *drumly* means something like 'sluggish.' As you reread the last paragraph, do you get any idea as to what might be wrong with the blonke, what might have made him so sluggish?

Upon rereading that paragraph, you may have concluded, rightly, that the blonke's *bellytimber* is a good clue to the problem. What do you suppose bellytimber is? And what do you suppose *venenated* means? Often, I have found, readers are able to get the general drift: that bellytimber is food, and that something is wrong with the food—it is spoiled or poisoned. Correct! Now please reread the entire "story" again, knowing the meanings of the key words *blonke, drumly, bellytimber,* and *venenated.* In general terms, what do you suppose is being recommended in the last two sentences, and why? You will surely find that you do *not* need to know the meanings of the "nonsense" words in those two sentences in order to get the general drift of the meaning.[1]

Why? Because, of course, you are using your schemas. You are using your knowledge of real-life situations to conclude that somehow the poisoned food must be put in a place where the other blonkes can't get to it, so they won't get sick too. Frankly, I still find it amazing that we can get so much meaning with so many of the key words unknown, yet this illustrates what children who become voracious readers do all the time. They read materials that are supposedly far beyond their ability to comprehend, but because they use their schemas and all kinds of context cues within what they are reading, they get most of the essential meaning of stories even when they do not already "know" many of the words. I distinctly recall, for example, that when my son John was much younger, I found him reading a book based on the Flintstone characters Pebbles and Bam-Bam, wherein the two children went on some kind of space adventure. A quick glance at the book convinced me that *many* of the words would be beyond John's previous acquaintance: they were words he had never even heard of, much less seen in print. Nevertheless, he enjoyed the book thoroughly.

Unfortunately, we may deny children such satisfying experiences with books if we assume that first and foremost, reading means identifying the words and getting their meaning. It is all too common to assume that word identification precedes comprehension, whereas in fact it is clear that in large part language comprehension works the other way around: because, or if, we are getting the meaning of the whole, we can then grasp the meanings of the individual words. The words have meaning only as they transact with one another, within the context of the emerging whole.

Thus we have two contrasting models of reading and language comprehension: one assumes that language is processed from part to whole, and the other asserts that language processing occurs just as much or more from whole to part. Let us contrast these views in somewhat more detail.

A Skills View of Reading and Learning to Read

A skills view of reading assumes that reading proceeds from the bottom up, starting with letters and letter-sound relationships, then words. Some proponents of this model also seem to assume that meaning takes care of itself, after the words are identified. Meaning is viewed as a property of the text, not as arising from a transaction between the reader and the text. Thus reading is viewed as an outside-in process only.

Some prominent researchers and summarizers of research promote a skills view of reading. For example, Marilyn Adams (1990) writes:

> . . . when reading for comprehension, skilled readers tend to look at each individual word and to process its component letters quite thoroughly. The other aspect of skilled readers' performance that is

underscored by this research [eye movement research] is the remarkable ease and speed with which they achieve such letter-based word recognition . . . . (p. 102)

In a similar vein, Frank Vellutino (1991b) writes:

. . . the research supports the following generalizations: a) The most basic skill in learning to read is word identification; b) an adequate degree of fluency in word identification is a basic prerequisite to successful reading comprehension; c) word identification in skilled readers is a fast-acting, automatic and in effect modular process that depends little on contextual information for its execution . . . . (p. 442)

Keith Stanovich, too, belittles the role of context in identifying words by noting that reading words in context rather than in isolation reduces the duration of eye fixations on words by only a few milliseconds (summarized and referenced in Stanovich, 1991, p. 432; see, for instance, McConkie & Zola, 1981).

Such researchers have typically not considered other kinds of evidence, or evidence from other eye movement and fixation studies, showing that context plays a definite role in identifying words. They have interpreted eye movement and eye fixation research from the 1980s, plus research on the teaching and learning of isolated skills, to mean that reading proceeds from the smallest units to the largest. Thus they assume that context, meaning, and prior knowledge play no essential role in the identification of words. For convenience, we can call this a "skills" view of reading. This view naturally leads to what we described briefly in Chapter 1, a "skills" approach to reading instruction.

Some advocates of a bottom-up skills approach (the most vocal of them not being reading educators) have claimed that phonemic awareness—the ability to hear the separate, or at least "separable," sounds in words—precedes the learning of letter-sound correspondences. This is not true; generally, the research shows that phonemic awareness develops most readily when sounds and letters are taught together (see Chapters 13 and 14). However, the strongest advocates for phonemic awareness first don't necessarily examine the actual research studies. Figure 2.5 captures their version of a skills model of reading. Starting from the bottom up, reading allegedly

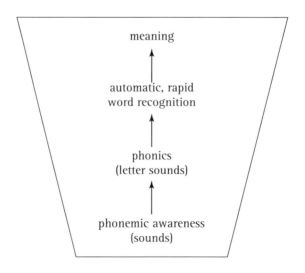

Figure 2.5 *Part-to-whole, "skills" model of reading.*

involves first the development of the ability to hear and to manipulate separate sounds in words (phonemic awareness); then the development of letter-sound knowledge (phonics), followed by the ability to decode texts wherein about 75 to 80% of the words reflect simple phonics patterns; and only later the ability to read texts for meaning.

Such a model is incorporated in a set of principles and steps for teaching reading, as set forth by Bonita Grossen (1997) and abbreviated by Robert W. Sweet, the founder and at that time president of the self-styled National Right to Read Foundation. These seven principles or steps were listed in the NRRF's Web page as follows (1997):

1. Teach phonemic awareness directly in kindergarten.

2. Teach each sound-spelling correspondence explicitly.

3. Teach frequent, highly regular sound-spelling relationships systematically.

4. Teach students directly how to sound out words.

5. Teach students sound-spelling relationships using connected, decodable text.

6. Teach reading comprehension using interesting teacher-read stories.

7. Teach decoding and comprehension skills separately until reading becomes fluent.

You've doubtless noticed that this list never does get to a point where the child is reading texts independently, for meaning! Nor does the list show any recognition of the roles that context and the reader's schemas play in identifying words and determining their contextually appropriate meanings, let alone in constructing meaning from the sentences and paragraphs of a text. It will probably not surprise you, then, to learn that Grossen's claim about these being research-based principles is not solidly anchored in research at all (e.g., Allington & Woodside-Jiron, 1998b, 1999).

True, the research focusing on the development of skills taught and tested in isolation does provide some justification for steps 1 and 3, and step 4 seems logically to follow. But there is no research that justifies the explicit teaching of "each" spelling-sound correspondence; none that shows that beginning readers should be required to read "decodable" texts; none that suggests "reading comprehension" should initially be taught only through listening; and none that indicates decoding and comprehension "skills" should be taught separately until reading becomes fluent. Indeed, the emphasis on teaching reading skills first seems both unnecessary and inappropriate when we consider more fully the nature of the reading process itself (Chapters 3–5 especially) and the greater positive effects overall of a comprehensive, literacy program on children's development of literacy (Chapters 11 and 15).

If you doubted that anyone really believes in the first view of reading that was mentioned at the beginning of this chapter, doubt no more. "Learning to read means learning to pronounce words" seems, in fact, to be exactly the view that some organizations and individuals are promoting in the political and public arena. In 1997, for example, U.S. Representative William Goodling introduced to the House Committee on Education and the Workforce a draft for what came to be called the Reading Excellence Act, H.B. 2614 (1998). Surely it is no coincidence that the bill was introduced shortly after Robert Sweet of the National Right to Read Foundation became an aide to Representative Goodling. Consider the way reading was defined in the first draft presented by Goodling (Reading Excellence Act, draft, 1997):

> The term "reading" means the process of comprehending the meaning of written text by depending on the ability to use phonics skills, that is, knowledge of letters and sounds, to decode printed words quickly and effortlessly, both silently and aloud.

Notice that in this view, phonics leads to word identification, which automatically leads to comprehension. As we shall see in Chapter 11, this bottom-up, skills-first view is also held by G. Reid Lyon, who became the chief advisor on reading to President George W. Bush when he took office in 2001.

A Transactional, Sociopsycholinguistic View of Reading and Learning to Read

We have already begun to see, in this chapter, evidence for a transactional, sociopsycholinguistic view of reading—partly a top-down, whole-to-part view of reading that emphasizes the fact that readers construct meaning from texts rather than absorbing meaning from the page. So before we look at one visual model of such a view, let us first summarize the observations about language and reading comprehension that derive from the activities and discussion in this chapter:

- In isolation, most words do not have a single meaning, but rather a range of possible meanings.
- Words take on specific meanings as they transact with one another in sentence, text, social, and situational contexts.
- Meaning is not in the text, nor will the meaning intended by the writer ever be perceived—or rather, constructed—exactly the same way by a reader.
- Readers make sense of texts by drawing upon their schemas—their entire lifetime of knowledge, experiences, feelings, and beliefs.
- Meaning emerges as readers transact with a text in a specific situational context.
- Thus the process of reading is to a considerable degree whole to part, top to bottom, deep to surface, and inside out (from the reader to the text).

Figure 2.6 presents a "redundancy" model of the reading process, a particular sociopsycholinguistic model that is further supported by research discussed in Chapters 3, 4, and 5. According to this model, each kind of information and processing supports and is supported by each of the others, directly or indirectly. In this chapter we have already seen how context, word perception, and word meanings interact. We have also seen how prior knowledge/experience and social/situational contexts affect the interpretation of words and context, and even the identification of words from the visual text (my reading of "the older seals" rather than "the other seals"). In short, we have already discussed the interactions emphasized by the thicker arrows in Figure 2.6, in one if not both directions. Since the roles of context are crucial in a sociopsycholinguistic model of reading, the three following chapters will discuss in more detail these roles and the interrelationships in which context is involved.

In this chapter we have taken at least small steps toward understanding Kenneth Goodman's concept of reading as a sociopsycholinguistic process involving transactions between the mind of the reader and the written text (e.g., K. Goodman, 1967, 1994). It is a process of comprehending, of constructing meanings from texts. Bartoli and Botel (1988) elaborate on this view as follows:

> Reading comprehension is a process that involves the orchestration of the reader's prior experience and knowledge about the world and about language. It involves such interrelated strategies as predicting, questioning, summarizing, determining meanings of vocabulary in context, monitoring one's own comprehension, and reflecting. The process also involves such affective factors as motivation, ownership, purpose, and self-esteem. It takes place in and is governed by a specific context, and it is dependent on social interaction. It is the integration of all these processes that accounts for comprehension. They are not isolable, measurable subfactors. They are wholistic processes for constructing meaning. (p. 186)

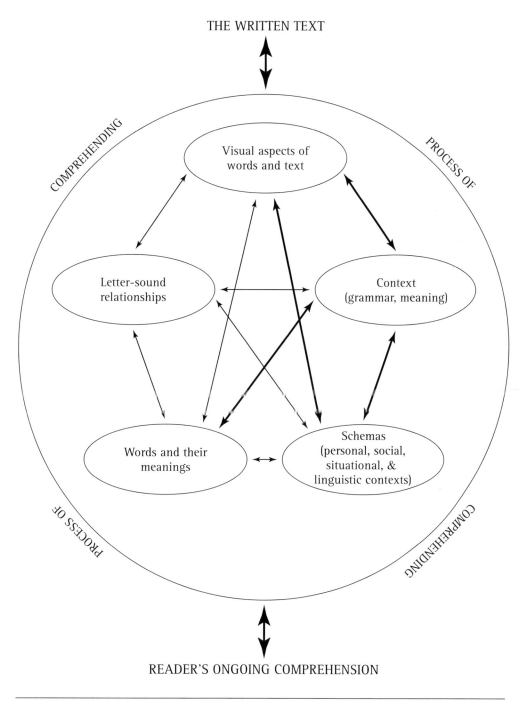

Figure 2.6 *Redundancy model of the reading process.*

Elsewhere, I have tried to express this complexity somewhat poetically, suggesting that the meaning that arises during the reader's transaction with a text may be viewed as an ever-fluctuating dance that occurs more or less simultaneously on and across various levels: letters, words, sentences, schemas; writer, text, and reader; text/reader and context; the reader's present with his or her own past; the present reader with other readers, past and present; and so forth, all connected in a multidimensional holarchy, an interlocking network or web of meaning, a synchronous dance (Weaver, 1985, p. 313).

This is the view of reading that underlies the ways of teaching reading described in this book and the comprehensive literacy program within which they and the students flourish.

FOR FURTHER EXPLORATION

1. To further explore the role of schemas and the various kinds of context in determining the meanings of words, you might try the following activity. Drawing from the following list of ten words, plus any others you might want to add, compose several sentences using at least two of the words in each sentence. Then consider *how* you know what the words mean in each case.

   baste, coat, cook, hose, part, rag, roast, run, store, wash

2. Playing around with idioms is another interesting way to convince yourself that we cannot determine precisely what words mean before we see them in context, and that therefore we do not comprehend sentences simply by adding together the meanings of the individual words. Take, for example, some of these idioms with *run:*

   a. They ran up the flag at sunrise.

   b. They ran up a huge bill at the doctor's.

   c. The bathtub ran over.

   d. Let's run over our notes quickly.

   e. Let's run over to the store.

   f. We've run out of soap.

   g. She might run out on him.

   h. We might run short of food.

   i. I had a run-in with my boss.

   j. He gave her a run for her money.

   Note that in most of these cases, *run* or *ran* is followed by another word that functions along with it, as a single unit: *ran up, ran over, run over, run out, run short, run-in,* and maybe *run for.* No wonder idioms are difficult for children and foreigners to learn!

   If possible, try out these or some other idioms with early elementary children and/or people who have learned English as a second language. Find out whether they can read the words of the sentences and, if so, whether they can explain the idiomatic meaning.

   An interesting and useful source of idioms is *A Dictionary of American Idioms* by Boatner, Gates, and Makkai (2nd ed., 1987). There are some delightful books of idioms that attempt to capture children's humorous misinterpretations of common idioms. Several of these are by Fred Gwynne: *The Sixteen Hand Horse* (1987), *A Chocolate Moose for Dinner* (1988a), *The King Who Rained* (1988b), and *Little Pigeon Toad* (1990). Upper elementary children typically enjoy creating such books of their own.

3. As you may have concluded from this chapter, we need to consider students' schemas—their background of knowledge and experience—when we give them reading assignments and when we interpret their results on tests. Nix and Schwarz (1979) interviewed ten inner-city high school students, asking them to explain answers to test questions. The investigators found that these students brought to bear a different system of assumptions than members of the majority culture. This led them to answers that were often "wrong," but that generally made sense from their perspective. As Reynolds, Taylor, et al. (1982, p. 356) point out,

> The research on cultural schemata has implications for the education of minority children. Standardized tests, basal reading programs, and content area texts lean heavily on the conventional assumption that meaning is inherent in the words and structure of a discourse. When prior knowledge is required, it is assumed to be knowledge common to children from every background. When new information is introduced, it is assumed to be as accessible to one child as to the next. The question that naturally arises is whether children from different subcultures can generally be assumed to bring to bear a common schema.

Discuss this statement in light of your own experience, as a student and/or a teacher. If possible, administer to one or more students a standardized reading test of the multiple-choice variety. Then interview the student to find out how he or she went about answering the questions and why the student chose the responses given. Discuss.

4. Return to the "blonke" passage earlier in the chapter. This time, do the following things:

a. Read the passage aloud. Did you have much difficulty pronouncing the strange words? If so, why? If not, why not? Were you consciously applying phonics rules in pronouncing the words? If not, what enabled you to pronounce them with little difficulty? Consider the implications for the teaching of phonics rules, such as "When two vowels go walking, the first one does the talking."

b. Answer the following typical kinds of comprehension questions about the passage, without checking the meanings of the strange words:

   ■ *Literal:* Where was the small wam?

   ■ *Translation:* What is "drumly"?

   ■ *Inference:* Why weren't the other blonkes drumly?

   ■ *Reorganization:* In what way(s) was the drumly blonke like/unlike the others?

   ■ *Evaluation:* If bellytimber is venenated, is it wise to givel it in the flosh? Why or why not?

Did you have serious difficulty answering the questions? If you had little difficulty, even though you didn't know many of the words, what does this suggest about comprehension and/or about the typical kinds of "comprehension" questions found in workbooks and on standardized tests?

5. The following is similar to the "blonke" passage, except this time you may have much less of an idea what the passage means. To demonstrate that you, as a typical reader, use syntactic cues like word endings, function words, and word order, read this "corandic" passage, and then answer the comprehension questions that follow. How is it that you are able to answer such questions? Again, what does this experience suggest about the kinds of "comprehension" questions often found on standardized tests?

> Corandic is an emurient grof with many fribs; it granks from corite, an olg which cargs like lange. Corite grinkles several other tarances, which garkers excarp by glarcking the corite and starping it in tranker-clarped storbs. The tarances starp a chark which is exparged with worters, branking a slorp.

This slorp is garped through several other corusces, finally frasting a pragety, blickant crankle: coranda. Coranda is a cargurt, grinkling corandic and borigen. The corandic is nacerated from the borigen by means of loracity. Thus garkers finally thrap a glick, bracht, glupous grapant, corandic, which granks in many starps.

a. What is corandic?

b. What does corandic grank from?

c. How do garkers excarp the tarances from the corite?

d. What does the slorp finally frast?

e. What is coranda?

f. How is the corandic nacerated from the borigen?

g. What do the garkers finally thrap?

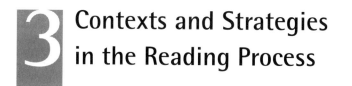

Contexts and Strategies in the Reading Process

The major folklore of reading instruction relates to the "theory" that reading is considered an exact process. In other words, the reader is expected to read everything exactly as printed on the page in order to understand the message of the author. In general the consuming public, legislatures, courts and too many educators hold to this theory. It is like the theory of the world being flat during the time of Columbus.

—Robert Harper and Gary Kilarr

In this chapter and the next, we will consider several kinds of context that affect word perception and identification: the context that letters provide for each other as they combine in familiar word patterns; syntactic and semantic context among words within sentences; and other contexts beyond the sentence and beyond the text. After this brief overview that proceeds from smaller units to larger, we will reverse the order for extended discussion. Chapter 5 then culminates in a model of proficient reading that reflects a synthesis of these insights about word identification and the construction of meaning.

THE VARIETIES OF CONTEXT: AN OVERVIEW

One kind of context in reading is the visual context that letters provide for each other, creating recognizable and familiar patterns. To understand the significance of this kind of context, glance quickly at the column of pseudowords in the left-hand column below, then write down as many as you can remember. Next, do the same with the column of pseudowords on the right (Miller, Bruner, & Postman, 1954, p. 133):

RICANING	YRULPZOC
VERNALIT	OZHGPMTJ
MOISSANT	DLEGQMNW
POKERSON	GFUJXZAQ
FAVORIAL	WXPAUJVB

The pseudowords at the left are much easier to perceive and recall, simply because their letter patterns are much closer approximations to normal English. While we have to read the pseudowords on the right more or less letter-by-letter, we can—and typically do—read the words on the left by perceiving them in syllables: *ri-can-ing* or *ric-a-ning* or *ric-an-ing,* for example. Try reading these two columns of words aloud and see for yourself.

Given our internalized knowledge of letter patterns, it should not be surprising that we can identify a word in about as much time as it takes to identify a single letter. Indeed, we can identify a related group of words in about the same length of time as it takes to identify a single word. Research shows, in fact, that during a normal eye fixation of about one-fourth second, we can identify about four or five unrelated letters, or about ten or twelve letters organized into two or three unrelated words, or about twenty to twenty-five letters organized into a sequence of four or five related words (see, for example, F. Smith, 1973, p. 56, and F. Smith, 1975, p. 58). Hence, during a normal eye fixation, we might be able to identify a sequence like *tgojf* (four or five unrelated letters), a sequence like *can't well this* (ten to twelve letters organized into two or three unrelated words), or a sequence like *this frog can't jump well* (twenty to twenty-five letters organized into a sequence of four or five related words). Our perceptual span increases with the relatedness of the units being identified:

4 or 5 unrelated letters	tgojf
10 to 12 letters, organized into 2 or 3 unrelated words	can't well this
20 to 25 letters, organized into 4 or 5 related words	this frog can't jump well

We can identify more letters when they are organized into words, and more words when they are organized into a related phrase or sentence.

In phrases and sentences, we have basically two kinds of context to aid in word identification: syntactic context and semantic context. *Syntactic context* consists of the signals provided by word endings, function words, and word order (see Chapter 2 and Figure 8.4, p. 198.). *Semantic context* consists of the meaningful relations among the words. In short, *syntax* means grammar, and *semantics* means meaning.

To see how grammar and meaning aid in the identification and recall of words, look for a moment at the following four strings of words. Which string would be easiest to process? Which would be hardest? Why?

1. Furry wildcats fight furious battles.
2. Furry jewelers create distressed stains.
3. Furry fight furious wildcats battles.
4. Furry create distressed jewelers stains.

As you might suspect, the first string is typically easiest to process, because it has both grammar and meaning: that is, it preserves normal word order, and it makes reasonable sense. The fourth string is typically hardest to process, because it has neither grammar nor meaning: the string does not preserve normal word order, and it does not make sense. Processing is easier when we have either normal word order (string 2) or some semblance of meaning (string 3). (For details, see Marks & Miller, 1964, pp. 1–5.)

Various laboratory experiments indicate that both grammar and meaning aid in the identification and recall of words. That is, both syntactic context and semantic context are important.

Another revealing activity is the so-called *cloze test*, sometimes used to assess a reader's comprehension and his or her use of reading strategies. The standard cloze test typically requires supplying every fifth word of a text, as in the following example from Bormuth (1975, p. 70). Try to fill each blank space with whatever you think was omitted from the original text (in some cases a number or a part of a hyphenated word has been omitted). As you fill in the blanks, try to be conscious of how you are using context and what kinds of context you are using:

The Beaver

Indians call beavers the "little men of the woods." But they (1) _____ really so very little. (2) _____ beavers grow to be (3) _____ or four feet long (4) _____ weigh from 30 to (5) _____ pounds. These "little men (6) _____ the woods" are busy (7) _____ of the time. That (8) _____ why we sometimes say, " (9) _____ busy as a beaver."
(10) _____ know how to build (11) _____ that can hold water. (12) _____ use their two front (13) _____ to do some of (14) _____ work. Cutting down a (15) _____ with their four sharp-(16) _____ teeth is easy. A (17) _____ can cut down a (18) _____ 4 inches thick in (19) _____ 15 minutes.

At the outset you probably found that to fill in the blanks you had to use both the grammar and the meaning of the preceding part of the sentence. In the first sentence where a blank occurs, "But they _____ ...," the word *they* suggests that a verb will be coming next; this is grammatical context, or syntax. The word *but* suggests that this second sentence will in some way contradict the first, and that the verb should therefore contain a negative marker; this is meaning context, or semantics. Putting both kinds of information together (and some other information as well), we are likely to supply the word *aren't,* and thus to read the sentence as "But they aren't really so very little." This word seems to fit syntactically and semantically with what comes after the blank as well as with what comes before.[1]

In some cases, following context is even more essential than in the first example. Look, for instance, at the sentence "That _____ why we sometimes say '_____ busy as a beaver.'" The word *that* can function as a noun determiner rather than a noun, as in "That fact explains why we sometimes say, 'as busy as a beaver.'" If we did not look ahead, we might supply the wrong kind of word in the blank following the word *that.* And we need to see "busy as a beaver" to know that the word in the second blank should be *as.* When we have adequate background knowledge, about one word in five—at least—can be supplied by the reader (W. Taylor, 1953). In other words, with only about four-fifths of the words present, the reader can still reconstruct the text, creating closure (hence the term *cloze procedure*). This suggests that there is considerable redundancy of information within most texts.

As we began to see in Chapter 2, "context" is far more inclusive than most people realize. We can and do use our entire personal context of knowledge and experience, our schemas (including our entire social and cultural context, our background) to help us identify (and sometimes misidentify) words. Second, we use aspects of the situational context, verbal and/or nonverbal. (An amusing example of a situationally caused miscue is from the sign in a church parking lot that one boy misread for a long time as "Angel parking" rather than "Angle parking.") For simplicity, I would also include under situational context various aspects of the sociolinguistic context. The classroom setting, for example, is a powerful sociolinguistic context, giving rise to particular kinds of assumptions and expectations on the part of both teachers and students. An example would be the expectation that many of my students bring to reading the poem "To Pat" (Chapter 2) in class; namely that there must be some deep, hidden meaning in the poem, a meaning that they probably aren't seeing clearly. Like the context within the reader, the sociolinguistic context can aid or thwart word identification.

In addition to using these kinds of contexts that are outside or beyond the text, we of course use context within the text to identify words. First, we use context before and after the sentence being read, but within the same reading selection. Second, we use context before and after the word being identified, but within the same sentence. For example, you may have used context to get the meaning of the word *thwart* in the sentence "Like the context within the reader,

Context within the text		Context beyond the text	
Within the sentence (before and after the word being read)	Beyond the sentence (before and after the sentence being read)	Within the situation (verbal and nonverbal, including sociolinguistic context)	Within the reader (entire lifetime of knowledge and experience)

Context within the sentence   Context beyond the sentence and the text

Figure 3.1   *Contexts used in word identification.*

the sociolinguistic context can aid or *thwart* word identification." Figure 3.1 summarizes all these major kinds of contexts, while suggesting two major ways of subdividing them: context within the text versus context beyond the text, and context within the sentence versus context beyond the sentence and the text. Since contexts beyond the sentence tend especially to blend together, the following discussion will reflect this latter division. We will deal with the "larger" kinds of context first.

CONTEXT BEYOND THE SENTENCE AND THE TEXT

Using Context to Determine Meaning and Acquire Vocabulary

As proficient adult readers, we are often conscious of using context to determine the meaning of words we do not know (but see Schatz & Baldwin, 1986).

One of my own interesting experiences was with the word *desiccant*. I could pronounce the word with no difficulty, but without context I would have had no idea what it meant. The word was printed on the outside of a little packet that came inside a bag of potato chips, and the manufacturers obligingly indicated that this packet of desiccant was included to absorb moisture and keep the chips fresh. Thanks to this explanation, I realized that the desiccant was not something to be thrown away as soon as the bag of chips was opened.

Writers are not always so obliging, yet often the preceding or following context gives a clue to the meaning of an unfamiliar word. Consider, for example, the context leading up to the word *fragile* and the word *melancholy,* below:

The teacups were delicate, easily broken. So *fragile* that Ellen hardly dared grasp the handle.

It was a gloomy day, more depressing than any that Margo had ever known. She lay motionless in bed, listless and *melancholy.*

Here, the preceding context indicates the meaning of *fragile* rather clearly, and at least supplies an appropriate connotation for *melancholy.* Note also that a reader would be able to get the essential meaning from these contexts, whether or not the words were pronounced correctly. As a matter of fact, I knew the meaning of *melancholy* for years before I finally learned that my mental pronunciation of the word was incorrect (I incorrectly syllabicated and stressed the word: *me-LAN-cho-ly*).

If the context of preceding sentences is not enough to make the meaning of a word clear, often the context of following sentences will come to the rescue. This is what happened when I first encountered the word *scofflaw*. When I read the headline "Scofflaw off to a Bad Start," I thought *flaw* must be the base word, so I mentally pronounced the word like this: *SKO*-fla.

I could not even syllabicate or pronounce it correctly until I had read most of the article. It was the third paragraph that finally triggered my understanding:

> Cooper had ignored 780 parking tickets between 1973 and 1977. He was identified by a computer in 1977 as the city's worst traffic scofflaw. It took nearly a year for police to find him.[2]

In this case, I used the following context to correct my tentative stab at the word. Once I realized that a "scofflaw" is someone who scoffs at the law, I was able to syllabicate and pronounce the word correctly.

In a similar vein, Yetta Goodman cites as an interesting and instructionally useful example the concept of the word *krait* in Roald Dahl's short story "Poison" (1950). Goodman excerpted the following sentences from the story (Y. Goodman, 1976, p. 101). Stop after each sentence and ask yourself what mental picture you have of the krait.

"A krait! Oh, oh! Where'd it bite you?"

"It's on my stomach. Lying there asleep."

Then out of the corner of my eye I saw this krait sliding over my pajamas. Small, about ten inches.

They hang around people's houses and they go for warm places.

The bite is quite deadly, except sometimes when you catch it at once; and they kill a fair number of people each year in Bengal, mostly in the villages.

I was going to be ready to cut the bitten place and try to suck the venom out.

"Shall we draw the sheet back quick and brush it off before it has time to strike?"

"It is not safe," he continued, "because a snake is cold-blooded and anesthetic does not work so well or so quick with such animals."

The author builds suspense by only gradually providing the information necessary to identify the krait as a snake. Note, too, that how quickly a person understands this fact will depend largely upon how much that person knows about snakes. If one knew nothing about snakes, one might have to read even the last of the sentences above to realize what a krait is. Context within the selection must be supplemented by personal context, the totality of one's knowledge and experience.

Our ability to use everything we know in order to understand unfamiliar words in context enables us to learn new vocabulary through reading. It has been estimated that the "average" fifth grader is likely to encounter between 16,000 and 24,000 unknown words per year in the course of reading (R. C. Anderson & Freebody, 1983) and that the typical child adds more than 3,000 words a year to his or her recognition vocabulary—about 16 words per school day (Miller & Gildea, 1987; Nagy & Anderson, 1984; Nagy & Herman, 1987; Nagy, Anderson, & Herman, 1987). Clearly, not this many words are directly taught. The obvious conclusion is that many of these new words—indeed, most of them—are acquired through the act of reading. Usually it takes several encounters for the new word to "take," and for the meanings inferred to become more accurate (Beck, McKeown, & McCaslin, 1983). Nevertheless, during their school years, children apparently learn most of their vocabulary through the act of reading.

This, of course, is one major reason why we should not withhold challenging texts from students until they can recognize nearly all of the words accurately. Such restraint will actually inhibit their acquisition of new vocabulary. In contrast, extensive reading will enhance vocabulary and thus encourage the reading of more sophisticated texts.

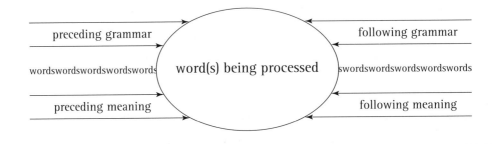

Figure 3.2   *Context before and after the word(s) being processed.*

Using Context to Identify Words

So far we have talked about determining the meaning of words that one might not have understood without context. However, beginning and less proficient readers, in particular, often use context to identify, or to help them identify (that is, to name) words that are in their speaking vocabulary but that they do not immediately recognize in print. We shall soon see that such readers use context within the sentence to identify words that they do not always identify correctly in isolation. However, it is also true that such readers use context from the preceding and following sentences (see Figure 3.2).

Perhaps most remarkable is the fact that readers can use the context of the following sentences to correct the miscues they themselves have made. An example comes readily to mind. As a first grader, my son was having unusual difficulty with a basal story I had asked him to read for a miscue analysis (there are certain disadvantages to being a professor's son). The boy in the story was named Hap. While at a local fair, Hap noticed someone who was jumping high as he walked along. Hap's father explained that the person was able to jump so high because of the pack on his back. Here are the following four sentences of the story, along with my son's miscues on the word *gas*:

"The pack has a kind of ~~gas~~ *gams* in it.

The ~~gas~~ *gangs* is very light.

It helps the boy to jump high."

"What kind of ~~gas~~ *gangs* is it?" asked Hap.

As you might suspect, my son was getting little meaning from this passage. But on the next page of the story, Hap's father explained to him that the gas is called helium. This explanation apparently triggered my son's understanding, because the next time he came to the word *gas* his face lit up and he said, "I got that wrong on the other page. It was *gas* all the time." In this case, the meaning of the word was familiar to the reader, but he did not recognize the word in print until the context of following sentences triggered his own personal context, his prior knowledge of helium and its effects.

Even context within the text is often not enough to facilitate the identification of words. The relative importance of grapho/phonemic cues, context cues, and prior knowledge can often be seen in the miscues of moderately proficient readers. Like most of us, they can use context and grapho/phonemic cues together to "get" words if the words are already within their personal schemas, but otherwise even simultaneous use of these cues may fail them. Consider, for instance, the following examples from Anne, a fifteen-year-old who demonstrated fairly effective use of reading strategies. The passage is from *Bread and Jam for Frances* (Hoban, 1964):

That evening for dinner, Mother cooked

       vail cutelets
breaded ~~veal cutlets,~~ with string beans

and baked potatoes.

             husband
"Ah," said Father. "What is there ~~handsomer~~

on a plate and tastier to eat than breaded

val cutelets
~~veal cutlet~~!"

Anne managed to use all the language cue systems to correct "husband" to *handsomer,* despite the rather unusual and grammatically unpredictable use of the word. Probably she was able to make this correction because she was familiar with the written word *handsome* in other contexts. However, she was not able to get *veal cutlets,* twice more pronouncing it as "vail cutelets." Finally Anne said "cutlets" a page later, but miscued on *breaded:*

             braid
What do cutlets wear before they're ~~breaded~~?

Later questioning revealed that Anne had never heard of veal cutlets. Nor was she familiar with poached eggs, tangerines, or custard, all words on which she miscued. On the other hand, she was usually able to correct grammar-disrupting or meaning-disrupting miscues when the words were within her prior knowledge and experience.

The same thing happens to relatively proficient readers when they don't already know the word. Witness my problems with *melancholy* as a child, and my problems with *desiccant* and *scofflaw* as an adult. If you are still tempted to think that grapho/phonemic cues alone are usually adequate, see Activity 6 at the end of this chapter, or try pronouncing some unfamiliar words in a textbook, and then check their pronunciation in a dictionary. Chances are you'll mispronounce a goodly proportion of them. But even if you get the pronunciation correct (as Anne eventually got the pronunciation of *cutlets*), can we necessarily assume that you have identified the word in any meaningful sense, without prior knowledge or at least adequate contextual information?

Of course, sometimes prior knowledge will lead us astray, as with the third grader who made the following miscue in a story about Henry Ford:

Henry felt that everyone should be able to own a car,

not just the wealthy people. In 1903 he started the Ford

Motor Company. His cars cost much ~~less~~ *more* than other cars

had before.

Then there was the sixth-grade boy who seemed to have read his own role expectations into the following sentences written in the first person:

Sometimes I'm ~~in a~~ *a pilot* ballet costume, dancing on a stage.

Or I'm ~~secretary, writing~~ *psychiatrist waiting* important ~~letters~~ *littles*.

He seems to believe that boys are more likely to become pilots or psychiatrists than to become ballet dancers or secretaries.

One more example of how making good use of one's schemas can actually cause miscues in word identification comes from the fourth-grade son of one of my students. Reading one of the Encyclopedia Brown stories about a fictional ten-year-old "Sherlock Holmes in sneakers," David kept making miscues on the nickname "Encyclopedia," saying things like "Enkeycalapia," "Encaspeelas," and "Incapinkia." His mother was surprised by these miscues, since she thought he was familiar with the word *encyclopedia*. To test her belief, she wrote three sentences for the boy to read, two in which the word *encyclopedia* meant what it typically does, and one in which the word was used as a boy's nickname. She asked her son to read these three sentences:

If you want to find out about Abe Lincoln you can look in the Encyclopedia.

I read in the Encyclopedia all about World War I.

Bob and Danny went to Encyclopedia's house to see if he could play.

This time, David read "Encyclopedia" correctly in all three sentences, but he was convinced he had misread it in the third sentence. In that context, the word simply did not make sense to him. "I got that wrong," he said. "Is it 'Encaplesia'?" Though again the reader has been led astray by his own prior knowledge, David's problem with *Encyclopedia* illustrates the strength of what is usually a productive and in fact crucial reading strategy: using everything you know (or think you know) to try to make sense of what you read.

Miscues will not always be corrected, of course, but far more often than we realize, even young readers are capable of noticing when they have made a miscue. They may not express their realization overtly, though, as my son John did with the miscues on *gas*.

Still, we must realize that children can and will do a lot of self-correcting, internally if not out loud. And we must give them opportunity and encouragement to correct their own miscues if they disrupt meaning—or to simply read on, when their miscues do not disrupt meaning or when their attempts to get the word and/or its meaning do not readily result in meaningful text.

	Preceding Context	*Following Context*
Syntactic Context	Preceding syntactic context indicates the word is a noun or a noun modifier.	Following syntactic context confirms that the word is a noun.

The cruel giant fell into the water and drowned.

	Preceding Context	*Following Context*
Semantic Context	Preceding semantic context suggests the word should indicate something into which one can fall.	Following semantic context shows that the word should indicate something in which one can drown.

Figure 3.3   *Context within the sentence.*

CONTEXT WITHIN THE SENTENCE

You may be most aware of context within the sentence. Yet even this kind of context has various aspects. On the one hand, we use both syntactic context and semantic context, both grammar and meaning. On the other hand, we use both preceding context and following context, both what comes before and what comes after the word being identified. Figure 3.3 provides a visual representation of how these aspects of context operate as we read the words on the page.

As an example, Figure 3.3 suggests how each aspect of context—syntactic and semantic, preceding and following—helps us identify the word *water* in the sentence "The cruel giant fell into the water and drowned." The word *the* indicates that the next word must be a noun or noun modifier, while the word *fell* suggests that the word after *the* should indicate something into which one can fall. The word *drowned* confirms that the word in question must indeed be a noun; further, *drowned* shows that the word should indicate something in which one can drown. The word in question could be *water, lake, pond, river, ocean, well,* or *moat* (to name some likely alternatives). The various kinds of contexts within the sentence have helped us narrow the alternatives to such a point that we need to use only a small amount of visual information from the word itself to identify the word in question as *water.*

In looking at the sentence in Figure 3.3, you may have thought, "That's silly. I already know the word *water*. I don't need to use context in order to identify that word." No doubt that is true. Nevertheless, the identification of words proceeds much faster and more efficiently when we are using the context provided by connected text. The fact is that fluent readers use context so automatically that they are rarely conscious of doing so. We become aware of our reliance on context mainly when we come to a word whose meaning we do not know, or when we make a miscue because of our reliance on preceding context.

To understand better this automatic use of context, read aloud the following sentences, without looking them over beforehand:

1. Can you read rapidly?
2. There was a strong wind blowing.
3. He wound the string up tightly.
4. I looked up and read the sign.
5. Her dress had a tear in it.

6. I saw a tear in her eye.

7. She looked at the minute printing on the label.

8. He made her a bow and arrow.

Each sentence contains a word that has, potentially, more than one pronunciation. In sentences 1–4, the preceding syntactic context is enough to signal the appropriate pronunciation of *read, wind, wound,* and *read.* In sentence 5, we need the preceding semantic context to tell us that *tear* should rhyme with *dare* rather than with *dear.* In sentences 6–8, we need following semantic context to signal the appropriate pronunciation of *tear, minute,* and *bow.* In short, we use preceding context to predict what is coming next, and we use following context to confirm or correct our predictions. This use of following context is facilitated by the fact that our eyes typically register about four words beyond the word we are focusing upon[3]—in fact, the semantic information from these following words may be available to us even before we have consciously identified the words (McKean, 1981; see also Bishop, 1993). If we do not use following context to help identify a word correctly in the first place, we use following context to tell us when we have made a miscue. Thus, if you incorrectly pronounced *bow* to rhyme with *now* in sentence 8, you surely recognized the miscue when you noticed the word *arrow.*

Although such sentences as these are somewhat atypical, they do help us understand the nature of proficient reading. We do not normally rely just on *grapho/phonemics,* our knowledge of letter-sound relations. Rather, we use context to complement and reduce our reliance on grapho/phonemic cues.

In other words, we use nonvisual information to reduce our dependence on visual information.

It should come as no surprise, then, that beginning readers and nonproficient readers can often read words better in context than in isolation. Here are some examples from first and second graders. On the left is the word misread in isolation, with the miscue indicated above the word. On the right is a sentence in which the same child read the word correctly:

has
~~his~~ . . . said his father.

hot
~~not~~ His father said, "You are not old enough for that."

want
~~went~~ The next day Hap and his mother and father went to the fair.

which
~~with~~ "Hap can come with me."

wig
~~wag~~ All morning Peter tried to make the turtle wag its tail.

now
~~know~~ "I know you would," said his mother.

don't
~~didn't~~ But she didn't bring it back to Peter.

our
~~your~~   "Come on, Lassie," said Peter. "Wag your tail."

tall
~~tail~~   He wanted the turtle to wag its tail.

made
~~named~~   Peter named his fish Lassie.

An early study showed that words are easier to recognize in familiar contexts than in relatively unfamiliar contexts. Even the function words tended to cause more recognition problems in the Group B sentences than in the Group A sentences below, for the less proficient beginning readers tested (Reid, 1958, p. 297):

Group A	*Group B*
You must do your best work.	You must not go back on your word.
I can see his face in the darkness.	No man can do more than his best.
We went back to the deep mud.	Darkness was upon the face of the deep.
Can you give me more words to read?	We must not give up when work is hard.

The best readers had no trouble with either set of sentences, but the less proficient readers had difficulty with many of the words in what was, to them, an unfamiliar context. Murphy's study (1986) produced comparable results.

Similarly, others have found that beginning readers may know color names like *brown* and *green*, but not be able to recognize these words when they are used in names like *Mr. Brown* and *Green Street*. Or the word *had* may be recognizable in a sentence where it indicates possession (as in *I had a dog*), but unrecognizable in a sentence where it indicates past perfect (as in *He had left already*). Unfamiliar idioms may cause word identification problems for many speakers of English as a second language, as well as for younger or less proficient readers; an example is the word *mustard* in the expression "He couldn't cut the mustard."

My favorite example of such difficulty comes from my son John. Early in his first-grade year, we visited Chicago's Field Museum of Natural History. As we were looking at the bird exhibits, my husband excitedly called John's attention to a display of Weaver birds. "Look, John. What kind of bird is this?" he asked, pointing to the identifying label. But in such an unfamiliar and unexpected context—indeed, without any sentence context at all—our son could not recognize his own name.

The classic study demonstrating the importance of context was undertaken by Kenneth Goodman. In context, his group of first graders correctly read 62% of the words that they had missed in isolation. His second graders correctly read 75% of the words they had missed in isolation. And his third-grade group correctly read 82% of the words they had missed in isolation (K. Goodman, 1965, p. 640). If these figures seem astonishingly high, it may be partly because the words were presented first in lists, and then in context. Thus, by the time the words were seen in context, prior experience with the words in lists might have made recognition easier. So reasoned P. David Pearson, who reported that when he gave children the same list twice, there was a 20% improvement without any context help. Furthermore, in his attempt at replicating Goodman's study, Pearson found that context produced gains of only 40% among first graders and 50 to 60% among third graders, when the list was presented first (Pearson, 1978). Still, these figures suggest that context helps substantially.

Tom Nicholson has further pointed out that Goodman's study did not differentiate between good and poor readers' use of context. (For present purposes, we can define "good" readers as those who typically make effective and efficient use of language cues and reading strategies and readily comprehend appropriate text; poorer readers are those who are less proficient in one or both respects. In miscue studies that have led to such a definition, "good," "average," and "poor" readers are often preidentified by other means, such as standardized measures.) In any case, Nicholson, in more recent studies, has eliminated the order effect and considered how context affects the reading of poor, average, and good readers, at ages six, seven, and eight. Across the three studies, Nicholson found that younger readers and poorer readers of all ages generally read words more accurately in context. The results for the good older readers were less consistent; indeed, in the most recent study, the eight-year-old good readers did better with the list, when given the context passage first (Nicholson, 1991).

Beginning readers and nonproficient readers can often read words better in context than in isolation.

In general, research on word identification suggests that context improves the identification of words for younger and less proficient readers more than for older and more proficient readers (Stanovich, 1980, 1991; Perfetti, 1985; Share & Stanovich, 1995; Nicholson, 1991). However, in view of the fact that good readers read for meaning, not to identify words, it is not surprising that the older good readers in Nicholson's study (1991) read the words better *in lists!* For one thing, they read the passage first. For another, they may have read the passage for meaning (the experimental procedures encouraged this), but read the list to identify the words. And as the next section helps explain, reading for meaning may have resulted in *more* miscues rather than fewer.

In general, the evidence from nearly three decades of miscue research demonstrates that:

1. Words are easier to identify in context than in isolation, at least for younger and less proficient readers.
2. Words are easier to identify in familiar contexts than in unfamiliar and unpredictable ones, at least for younger and less proficient readers.
3. Contextual information speeds and facilitates reading for proficient as well as nonproficient readers; it also facilitates the understanding of many words that the reader may not be able to pronounce or identify.
4. Proficient readers use contextual information in combination with prior knowledge and grapho/phonemic information.

LANGUAGE CUES AND READING STRATEGIES

When we analyze miscues, we consider how a reader has used language cues and reading strategies. The major *language cues* are syntactic, semantic, and grapho/phonemic. Our intuitive knowledge of syntax, our grammatical schemas, enables us to use word endings, function words, and word order as cues to word identification. These syntactic cues are complemented by semantic cues, the meaning relations among words and sentences in the text we are reading. In addition, we bring to bear various situational cues and our entire store of personal knowledge and experience. We use not only the syntactic and semantic cues available in the text and the situation, but also our entire experience with language and with life. Of course, reading could not exist without the graphic cues, the letters and words on the page, and our intuitive knowledge of letter-sound relations and patterns (unless, of course, we are reading Braille). However, our reading would be both ineffective and inefficient if we relied just on grapho/phonemic cues. As Paul Kolers has written, "Reading is only incidentally visual" (Kolers, 1969). At this point, such an outrageous statement should begin to make sense.

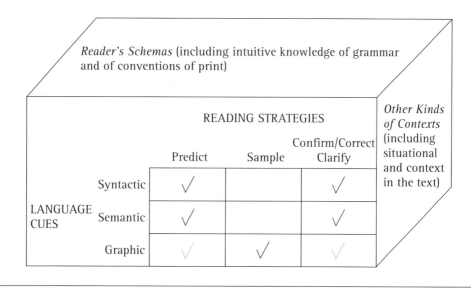

Figure 3.4 *Language cues and reading strategies.*

Figure 3.4 indicates how language cues give rise to reading *strategies*. Whether conscious or unconscious, such strategies are plans for carrying out mental operations—in this case, the operation of reading. Of course during normal reading, all kinds of processing are going on simultaneously. But in order to understand some of this complexity, it may help, temporarily, to think of reading as a matter of identifying words. In order to identify a word, proficient readers first use syntactic and semantic knowledge and cues to *predict* what is coming next. We do not necessarily predict a specific word, but at least we subconsciously narrow down the possibilities, which helps us identify the word or recognize when we have made a miscue that does not fit with what came before. Thus, only a limited number of words might reasonably complete the sentence "The cruel giant fell into the _____."

After mentally restricting the possibilities, we normally look at the word itself—that is, we use graphic cues, which in turn call forth our grapho/phonemic knowledge. But because prediction has narrowed down the number of reasonable alternatives, we need to use only a minimum of visual information to tentatively identify the word. In the sentence about the giant, we would need to process only two or three consonant letters or parts of them in order to decide that the word is *water* rather than one of the other reasonable possibilities. Apparently as proficient readers, we only sample the graphic cues, first identifying the word, and then almost simultaneously perceiving the letters within. Finally, we use following syntactic and semantic cues to confirm our tentative identification of the word, to correct if we have made a miscue that does not fit with the following context, or to clarify in some other way. The word *water* fits not only with the preceding context but with the following context in "The cruel giant fell into the water and drowned." Hence we would confirm our identification of the word in question. Figure 3.4 depicts this relationship between language cues and reading strategies, suggesting in addition the use of other contextual cues and the fact that it is our schemas that enable us to make use of the cues provided by text and situation.

Figure 3.5 attempts to suggest the simultaneity of these strategies: at one and the same time, we are sampling new graphic cues, confirming or correcting what we've just read, and making new predictions about what is to follow. "Each [system and strategy] follows the others but at the same time precedes them, always moving toward constructing a text and making meaning" (Y. Goodman, Watson, & Burke, 1987, p. 33).

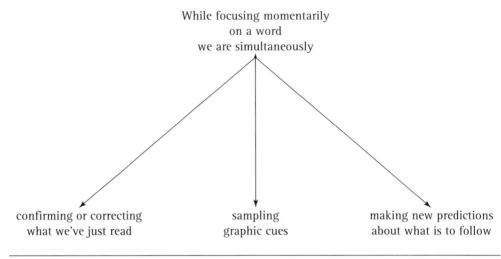

While focusing momentarily
on a word
we are simultaneously

confirming or correcting   sampling   making new predictions
what we've just read   graphic cues   about what is to follow

Figure 3.5   *Simultaneous processes in reading.*

In Chapter 7, the forms for analyzing miscues invite us to consider significant aspects of these relationships between language cues and reading strategies. We ask, "Did the miscue go with the grammar and meaning of what came before?" If the answer is yes for a high percentage of the miscues that are analyzed, we can infer that the reader is making good use of prior context to *predict.* We also ask of each miscue analyzed, "Did the miscue go with the grammar and meaning of what followed?" If the answer is yes for a substantial percentage of the miscues, we can infer that the reader is using following context to help monitor comprehension. Both strategies are important: not only in "getting" words but, more crucially, in constructing meaning from a text.

Context in Reading: Review and Preview

Sometimes *context* has been conceptualized rather narrowly, as the words surrounding a particular word in question, within a sentence or phrase. In the last four decades, though, it has become increasingly evident that context means many things—even the context relevant to reading just an individual word. Context includes the grammar of sentences and the meanings of words; a paragraph; a whole story or other text. Context is also taken to include the reader's expectations and purposes for reading; various aspects of the location and situation in which the person is reading; and even the person's culture and times—in short, the reader's schemas, his or her entire background of knowledge and experience (e.g., Brown, 1997). These various factors operate simultaneously for proficient readers; they usually operate quite unconsciously; and they can affect the identification of single words as well as the reader's understanding of an entire text. The automatic use of context—of multiple contexts—is a crucial part of the reading process, though most people don't realize it.

Various research studies, and differing kinds of research, indicate that context plays a major role in reading. The following observations review points already made and preview points to be made more fully in Chapters 4 and 5.

1. First, proficient readers just naturally attend to context as they read; they do so
   automatically. This is demonstrated by various kinds of research (e.g., as summarized by
   F. Smith, 1994/1971), but particularly the research that has analyzed the patterns of readers'

miscues. In the 1960s, Kenneth Goodman chose the term *miscue* to designate observed reading responses that differed from what was expected—from what was "on the page" (K. Goodman, 1965). Various important inferences about the nature of reading have been drawn from the substantial body of research that has followed (K. Goodman & Burke, 1973; J. Brown, Goodman, & Marek, 1996).

Critical to the initial research studies was a comparison of the ways in which the patterns of proficient readers' miscues differed from the patterns of not-so-proficient readers—the good and poor readers in the study, as previously determined by standardized measures. One of the key conclusions was that good readers are more sensitive to context. For one thing, their miscues, though relatively infrequent, more often fit with what came before in the sentence and text, suggesting that they were unconsciously predicting (and sometimes mispredicting) as they read. Even more noticeable, though, was the fact that proficient readers were much more likely to notice and try to correct miscues that didn't fit with the context that followed the miscued word. Such monitoring and correction demonstrate that the reader was thinking about what was being read. Furthermore, the more proficient readers made more miscues on the little, so-called "sight words" than less proficient readers, because the good readers would predict words and even grammar that fit the context and didn't change the essential meaning. From such observations as these, we can reasonably infer that proficient readers automatically use context—all kinds of context—to predict ("think ahead"), and to try to correct when something doesn't sound right or isn't making sense. In other words, they use context to think about what they are reading. Furthermore, this is true even of first graders and kindergartners who can read simple but new texts independently (predictable or natural texts, not phonically regular, "decodable" texts). The following examples from first graders are typical of the miscues that proficient readers make, both adults and children, particularly when they are reading aloud:

- Get ~~a~~ **the** ball, Mary.

- Who ~~rides~~ **can ride** with Mike?

- I can't play with Jeff and Mary. **But** I can play ball.

- Bill the circus boy ~~led~~ **let** Penny the elephant into the circus ring. [was corrected]

- ~~Everybody~~ **Everyone** forgot to eat popcorn.

- Carlo the clown ~~ran~~ **went** up to Trixie.

To put it another way, automatically drawing upon various contexts is as integral to the reading process as automatically identifying a majority of the words.

This is crucial for emergent and other nonproficient readers to learn and to practice, if they have not done so already: to read for meaning, to think ahead as they do so, and to use various "fix-it" strategies when something does not sound right or is not making sense.

2. Proficient readers use context-based strategies more than less proficient readers, for the most part. Proficient readers use context to "think ahead": to predict words that might be coming next (whether the prediction turns out right or wrong), or at least to anticipate, in general, what might make sense as they read on. Proficient readers also use context to monitor comprehension, and to confirm or try to correct miscues that don't fit with the context. In addition, they use context to get at least an approximate meaning for individual words. For example, readers draw upon such contextual aids as prior knowledge and experience; direct definition or description, such as may be included in appositive constructions; parallel constructions; closely related terms or synonyms; antonyms or other kinds of contrast; meaningful word elements; type style, such as boldface or italics; and other cues, such as the overall mood or tone of a text or paragraph (e.g., Dulin, 1969; Ames, 1966; Artley, 1943; McCullough, 1943). Various studies suggest that less proficient and/or less experienced readers generally make less effective use of context than more proficient readers (K. Goodman, 1965; K. Goodman & Burke, 1973; Dulin's 1969 review of earlier studies; Weber, 1970; Gates, 1979; Hughes, 1977; Hudelson-Lopez, 1977; Wood, 1976).

3. Proficient readers do not *need* to use context to identify many of the words they read. Nevertheless, they *do* use context to direct their eyes where to fixate next as they read, thus reducing the number of fixations and the amount of time needed to identify words (see summary by Paulson & Goodman, 1998; and see Chapter 5). Even though this reduction in time may amount to only a few milliseconds per word (summarized and referenced in Stanovich, 1991, p. 432), this brief reduction in the time required for identifying a word is due to the use of context.

4. Furthermore, there is substantial evidence that proficient readers identify familiar words faster than, and apparently before, they perceive individual letters. Proficient readers draw upon some of the visual information in the letters to identify the word, and then may perceive individual letters as letters (though this "perception" may be an after-the-fact reconstruction by the brain, which "knows" the word and its letter components). We can simulate this process by whiting out parts of the letters in a coherent sentence. If the content and vocabulary are reasonably predictable in the context, a proficient reader can usually read the sentence or phrase. Individual words are often readable, too, when a lot of their visual information has been omitted (see examples in Chapter 5).
   Research shows that:

   ■ whole words can be read as fast or faster than their individual letters (F. Smith, 1994/1971; see F. Smith, 1973, p. 56, and 1975, p. 58; Huey, 1908/1968);

   ■ all but the least experienced readers will read real words, and also strings of letters that reflect the letter patterns in real words, faster than strings of unrelated letters that don't resemble English (McCaughey, Juola, Schadler, & Ward, 1980; Lefton & Spragins, 1974; Miller, Bruner, & Postman, 1954);

   ■ readers can read words under conditions that do not permit the identification of single letters, such as too great a distance or insufficient light (Erdmann & Dodge, 1898, as reported in Huey 1908/1968 and in F. Smith, 1994/1971; see also Rayner & Pollatsek, 1989); and

   ■ we do not typically recode printed words to speech before accessing their meanings (Banks, Oka, & Shugarman, 1981), and indeed, some sense of the meaning of a word can be perceived when a person isn't even aware of having seen the word at all, much less its individual letters (Marcel & Patterson, 1978).

5. Less proficient readers use context too, but somewhat differently. They are more likely to *need* context to identify words that they don't immediately recognize in print. This is true

both of emergent readers who haven't yet had much experience with words and of older, less proficient readers if they haven't acquired an extensive stock of words they recognize on sight. Context provides temporary support, known as "scaffolding," until these readers have encountered new print words often enough to recognize them anywhere they might occur.

6. Nagy, Herman, & Anderson (1985) conclude from their research that "our results strongly suggest that a most effective way to produce large-scale vocabulary growth is through an activity that is all too often interrupted in the process of reading instruction: Reading." Why? Because, of course, various kinds of context facilitate the learning of vocabulary. These researchers point out that one's understanding of a word's meanings arises gradually, as the word is encountered in more and more contexts. Although the probability of learning a word from just one exposure is quite low, given an average amount of reading, a child would learn about 800 to 1,200 words a year reasonably well: "well enough to pass fairly discriminating multiple-choice items" (Nagy, Anderson, & Herman, 1987, p. 262). This is about three to four times the number of words often taught each year as vocabulary words. Interestingly, there was no significant difference between proficient and less proficient readers' learning of words from context, in the particular study reported in depth in Nagy, Anderson, & Herman (1987).

7. Various kinds of evidence suggest that many emergent and less proficient readers develop phonics knowledge most readily by learning whole words and deriving phonics knowledge from them, rather than by learning phonics first (Moustafa, 1997; for related research, see also Ehri, 1994, 1995; Goswami, 1986, 1988). In order to do this, they have to spend a lot of time reading. And as they read to become more proficient readers, they will still need to use context as a temporary support to get words they don't recognize. Part of what needs to happen is a chain reaction: using context will help less proficient readers get the words; repeated exposure to words will make the words identifiable on sight; an increased repertoire of sight words will facilitate knowledge of letter-sound relations, and the ability to use sight words, phonics, and increasingly sophisticated aspects of context will enable children to become more involved, proficient, effective, and competent readers: who can actively learn and achieve through reading.

FOR FURTHER EXPLORATION

1. To determine for yourself whether words are easier to read in context or in isolation, choose a reader to work with, either a beginning reader (late first grade, or second grade) or a poorer reader of any age. Then choose a reading selection that should be appropriate for this reader: not easy, but not terribly difficult either. The selection should be about 250 words long or longer (except for the youngest readers, who may find this too much). It might be wise to photocopy the selection for your later convenience in analysis and discussion. Once you have chosen the reading selection, type from it a list of about 50 words for the person to read (fewer if the reader is a nonproficient beginner). One possibility would be to make a list of all the different function words in the selection. Another possibility is simply to choose every fifth word (avoiding duplications). Have the reader read the list of words and then the entire selection. Instead of trying to take notes on the reader's miscues as he or she reads, just tape-record the session for later study. To facilitate discussion, mark each of the miscues on the word list and each of the miscues the reader made on the reading selection itself. For the most part, the marking symbols introduced in Chapter 1 should be adequate. Consider such questions as the following:

   a. On the whole, did the reader seem to be using context to predict what was coming next? What examples support your conclusion?

b. Did the person read in context any of the words that he or she missed in isolation? If so, what are some examples? How or why might the context have helped?

c. Did the person read in isolation any words that he or she later missed in context? If so, what are some examples? Why do you suppose these words were read correctly in isolation but not in context?

d. On the whole, would you conclude that words are easier to read in isolation, or in context?

2. Even words that are central to a passage can often be determined from context. What word or words would you put in the blanks below? Essentially the same item belongs in each blank. The paragraph is from Ray Bradbury's *Dandelion Wine* (1957, p. 34):

Somehow the people who made _____ knew what boys needed and wanted. They put marshmallows and coiled springs in the soles and they wove the rest out of grasses bleached and fired in the wilderness. Somewhere deep in the soft loam of the _____ the thin hard sinews of the buck deer were hidden. The people that made the _____ must have watched a lot of winds blow the trees and a lot of rivers going down to the lakes. Whatever it was, it was in the _____, and it was summer.[4]

You might try finding or creating similar passages to use with children.

3. We can often get the meaning of a word from context (even though we may never pronounce the word correctly). Try it:

a. First, jot down a definition for the following words: *deng, tolchock, veck,* and *viddy.* Just make up a definition that seems reasonable.

b. Now see if you can tell what the words mean, as used in this sentence from Anthony Burgess' novel *A Clockwork Orange* (1963): "Our pockets were full of *deng,* so there was no real need . . . to *tolchock* some old *veck* in an alley and *viddy* him swim in his blood while we counted the takings . . ." (pp. 1–2). Discuss what cues enable you to determine what the words mean.

c. Try essentially the same procedure again. Write down a definition for these words:

creech	malenky	razrez
droogs	messel	skorry
glazzies	millicents	spatted
goloss	poogly	zoobies

Did you notice yourself using any fairly consistent principle for determining what the words might mean? Discuss.

d. Now read the first chapter of *A Clockwork Orange.* In each case, how do you finally determine what the word means?

4. Many children who tend to deal with each word in a text as if it stood in isolation will make habitual confusions of one sort or another. They may confuse *then* with *than,* the word *the* with *they,* or the word *and* with *can,* and so forth. The solution is not to drill students on these words in isolation, but to help them learn to use context to disentangle the confusion. You can begin with passages in which both grammar and meaning strongly signal the word intended. For example, if a person commonly reads "can" for *and* and vice versa, you might construct a passage beginning as follows:

Jim called to ask his friends Bob *and* Mike, " *Can* you come to the fort today?" Bob answered, " Yes, we *can.* But let's go get some pop *and* cookies to take with us."

You might even initially omit the problem words and ask the reader to supply whichever one is appropriate in context.

As an activity, then, create several passages that might be used to help readers overcome habitual confusions between pairs of words like those listed above. You might first create a passage where only one of the words is appropriate, and create a companion passage for the other word. You might then create a passage that includes blanks where the two words belong. Finally, you might create a passage like the one above, where both words are explicitly included. It would be better yet to find appropriate passages from children's literature and blank out the relevant words, since artificially constructed passages tend not to have the supportive language and meaningful context that make it possible for readers to supply or read the troublesome words. If possible, try these passages with readers who habitually confuse the words. (For various kinds of strategy lessons to use with middle-grade children and older, see Y. Goodman, Watson, & C. Burke, 1996.)

5. As indicated earlier in the chapter, the "basic" cloze procedure, first developed by Wilson Taylor in 1953, involves the reader's supplying every fifth word, on the assumption that about one of every five words in a text can be predicted from context. Various modifications of the cloze procedure may be useful in helping students learn to use all the language cue systems and the strategies of predicting and confirming or correcting—though Kucer's research (1992) suggests that students may not perceive the purpose of the activities, despite repeated explanations!

If you think it worth trying some cloze activities, you might prepare some mini-lessons, using one or more of the following suggestions:

a. Omit the last word of a sentence, if it is highly predictable—or include just the first letter of the last word. This is particularly useful with beginning readers. The procedure works especially well when the last word of a line rhymes with the end of a preceding line.

b. Omit inflectional endings, to help readers recognize their own syntactic knowledge.

c. Omit function words, to help readers realize their ability to predict these words from the content words, word order, and context.

d. Omit key concept-carrying words (as in the passage from Bradbury in activity 2 above), to help readers see how words can be understood from context.

e. Omit every fifth word (or whatever) and have students read just for meaning, not to fill in the words, in order to help them see that comprehension is possible without identifying all the words.

f. For less confident readers, omit only words and sentences that are highly predictable, to assure success.

You might use a variety of materials: songs, poems, and stories; content-area textbooks; newspapers and magazines; and anything else that might be suitable. Whatever the variations and materials used, however, it is important for students to read through the entire cloze activity before filling in any of the missing parts, in order to help them see the value of using following context to identify and/or get the meaning of difficult words. Of course, you should accept any and all responses that reasonably fit in each blank, not just the actual word omitted. It is crucial for students to discuss their answers to a cloze exercise. They need the opportunity to share and compare their responses with those of other students, and the challenge of defending their choices or rejecting them in favor of something better. Perhaps even more crucial is explicitly discussing what the activity suggests about reading normal texts, including the need for using schemas and context in dealing with problem words. Kucer's research suggests that students are not too likely to make these connections for themselves.

6. Try reading the following words quickly:

zeugma	riata
sarsaparilla	plesiosaur
vitiate	demesne
sycophant	extravasate
submandibular	dissepiment
sapogenin	inqenue
samizdat	botryoidal

Now check the correct pronunciations on p. 85. Did correct pronunciations clarify the words' meaning? Did incorrect pronunciations hinder your understanding of any word? What conclusions would you draw from these and other examples?

4 What Miscues Tell Us About Reading and Readers: Reciprocal Insights

Reading miscue research was undertaken for the express purpose of providing knowledge of the reading process and how it is used and acquired.

Our research has made it possible to infer from their miscues the control that readers are exercising over the reading process.

Miscue research has led us away from a word focus to a comprehension focus. As we have looked at reading from a psycholinguistic perspective, we have come to see that the word is not the most significant unit in reading.

—Kenneth Goodman

Questions for Thought and Discussion

1. Consider the above statement that "As we have looked at reading from a psycholinguistic perspective, we have come to see that the word is not the most significant unit in reading." What do you think has led Goodman to this conclusion? Do you agree? Why or why not?

2. When we talk about readers bringing "prior knowledge" or "prior knowledge and experience" to the reading event, what do we mean?

3. What kinds of miscue patterns and reading strategies are typical of proficient readers? What kinds are common among less proficient readers?

4. Do proficient readers identify every word accurately and read smoothly and fluently? What evidence supports your views?

5. Why do we say, from a psycholinguistic perspective, that accurate word identification is not the primary factor differentiating proficient from less proficient readers?

6. What kinds of evidence do we have (see Chapter 3) that we identify words partly through their functions in a sentence, and that we identify words before saying them aloud, rather than afterwards?

7. How does the evidence referred to in question 6 support the view that dialect miscues are evidence that the reader is comprehending, rather than an impediment to comprehension? What about miscues that result from the reader not being a native speaker of the language being read?

As the introductory quotes from Kenneth Goodman indicate, miscue analysis was originally designed to offer insights into the reading process itself. Goodman and his collaborators (K. Goodman & Burke, 1973) examined the miscues of good readers to determine how they used language cues and reading strategies like predicting, sampling text, monitoring comprehension, and confirming/correcting. Similarly, these researchers examined the miscues of average and poorer readers to gain insight into what they didn't do that good readers did. The research process in effect became cyclical: good readers' strategies provided insights into the nature of the reading process, and an understanding of the reading process enables us to understand the strategies of individual readers and assess the effectiveness, or probable effectiveness, of those strategies.

Before proceeding further, we need to define some terms. The concept of a *proficient* reader is key. Kenneth Goodman (1978) talks about proficient readers being "effective" and "efficient":

> Proficient readers are both efficient and effective. They are effective in constructing a meaning that they can assimilate or accommodate and which bears some level of agreement with the original meaning of the author. And readers are efficient in using the least amount of effort to achieve effectiveness. (p. 6)

Drawing upon Goodman's concepts of the effective, efficient, and proficient reader, I have developed the following definitions for use in this text:

- An *effective* reader is one who succeeds in constructing meaning from texts for which he or she has adequate background knowledge and meaning.
- An *efficient* reader is one who doesn't waste time and effort in the quest for meaning.
- A *fairly proficient* reader is one who is both effective and efficient.
- A *moderately proficient* reader is typically effective but not as efficient.
- A *nonproficient* reader is neither effective nor efficient.
- A *good* reader is one who is at least reasonably effective in constructing meaning. Such a reader may or may not also be efficient, at least to some degree. Thus, as I use the term henceforth, a *good* reader would be a proficient or moderately proficient reader.

Later in this chapter (p. 70), I shall characterize readers' degrees of effectiveness, according to their use of reading strategies. After discussing readers' miscues and how they suggest reading strategies and effectiveness, we shall consider the importance of the individual word and the significance of dialect miscues and miscues reflecting the fact that the reader is not a native speaker of the language being read.

> Good readers use syntactic and semantic context automatically and efficiently, to reduce their reliance on graphic cues and grapho/phonemic knowledge.

READING PROFICIENCY AND THE USE OF CONTEXT

Good readers use syntactic and semantic context automatically and efficiently, to reduce their reliance on graphic cues and grapho/phonemic knowledge. Good readers also draw upon their personal schemas, their "prior knowledge and experience." In effect this phrase is shorthand for

- the reader's pragmatic knowledge—prior knowledge of and from situational, social, and cultural contexts;
- the reader's already-existing knowledge, experience, beliefs, values; and
- the reader's intuitive knowledge of how grammar works, how words can relate meaningfully to one another, and how letters relate to sounds.

Figure 4.1 suggests how various kinds of cues and contexts are used in the reading process. While sampling the letters in words for graphic cues, a proficient reader *thinks back* to what has just been read, in order to confirm or correct, and also simultaneously *thinks ahead* to predict (or mentally to limit) the possibilities for what will follow. In thinking back and thinking ahead, the reader uses both syntactic and semantic context within the text and his or her own personal

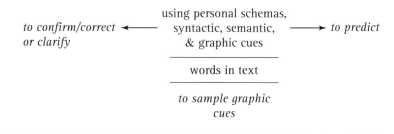

Figure 4.1 *Cues and strategies in the reading process.*

schemas. The major language cues within the text are *graphic* (letters), *syntactic,* and *semantic.* The major reading strategies are *predicting* (thinking ahead), *monitoring comprehension* (thinking back), and *confirming* (thinking back) or *clarifying* (reprocessing meaning and language cues as needed or reading on to construct meaning).

This section will consider related observations about good and less proficient readers: (1) the fact that both good and less proficient readers may make miscues on simple "sight words," but that good readers' miscues are more likely to preserve grammar and sense; (2) the fact that good readers use both preceding and following context effectively, sometimes even reconstructing text in their efforts to construct meaning; and (3) the fact that ineffective use of context is often an indication of lesser proficiency in reading—that is, lesser proficiency in constructing meaning from texts.

Miscues on Basic Sight Words

Though good readers generally make fewer miscues than less proficient readers, they may actually make as many or more miscues involving pronouns and simple function words—the so-called basic sight words. This occurs because they are reading to construct meaning, rather than to identify words. Good readers tend to substitute one pronoun or function word for another, and to omit or insert optional function words. The following are examples (some from K. Goodman & Burke, 1973). To recap the meaning of the symbols: a caret points to an insertion; a circle indicates an omission; one or more words written above the text indicate a substitution; and, later in the chapter, a ⌐⌐ indicates a reversal:

- White men came from ~~the~~ *their* cities.

- ~~That~~ *It* took us about an hour.

- "You ~~may~~ *might* be right."

- She made her own paints from ⟨the⟩ roots.

- ... but after a month we saw ⟨that⟩ nothing was growing.

- Mr. Tully beat me more often and more cruelly than Mr. Coffin had ⟨done⟩

- Billy feasted on *the* roast corn ...

- ... it was enough to wake *up* the dead.

- They told him *that* he had been foolish to plant sesame ...

In each of the foregoing examples the meaning is preserved even though the surface structure is altered, and the sentences are still grammatical. The reader has made miscues precisely because he or she is constructing meaning rather than merely trying to identify words.

The following excerpt from a miscue analysis offers further evidence that good readers often miscue on simple words as they use context to construct meaning from a text. The reader is a sixth grader named Billy; the passage is from Joanne Williamson's *The Glorious Conspiracy* (1961, pp. 17–18):

Life went on as usual. Mr. ~~Tully~~ ①*Tü lly* beat me more often

and more cruelly than Mr. Coffin had ②(done). But I was

used to that now. And there were ways a poor boy could

find of having a bit of fun once in a while—like daring

the other apprentices to steal ③④ /a bit *of* from the shops and

watching to see if they got caught. If they did get

caught, they would be hanged at Gallows Mill, so that was

a real dare. Or one could throw bits of garbage in the way

of gentlemen in wigs and hide around the corner to see

them slip and fall ④(down). There wasn't much time for

such sports, ⑤*though* ~~so~~ we made the most of what time we had.

My granddad had become pretty sick about this time.

He had the lung fever. He had ⑥(had) it a long while, but

now it was beginning to be bad, and Aunt Bet was begin-

ning to look frightened. I began to be scared, too, hearing

him cough so much and seeing him look so pale and ill.

And when I got through work at eight or nine ~~of the~~ ①o'clock

~~clock,~~ I took to hanging about the streets, tired and hun-

gry as I was, hiding out of the way of ⑧(the) watchmen, so

as not to go home till I had to. I knew this made Aunt Bet

even more frightened; and that made me ashamed and

even more anxious not to go ⑨ to home.

One night after I had scrubbed down Mr. Tully's fish

house and come ⑩(out) into the street, I saw a man come out

of a chandler's shop. I knew ⑪(who) he was—Mr. Watson,

a ropemaker and an excellent workman, so everyone said.

I didn't want ~~him to see me~~ ⑫ to see him, for I meant to tell Aunt Bet

that I had been kept late, and go ⑬(looking) for mischief.

So I hid in a doorway and watched ~~for him to go by.~~ ⑭ him go by

Many of Billy's miscues involve the omission, substitution, or insertion of pronouns and function words—the allegedly simple sight words. Billy is reading to construct meaning, more than to identify each and every word.

Interestingly, it is mainly proficient readers who make miscues like these. The percentage of miscues involving pronouns and function words tends to increase as one becomes a more proficient reader (see K. Goodman & Burke, 1973, pp. 165–166, 184).

When less proficient readers make miscues on such basic sight words, the miscues may sometimes reflect the fact that the reader is not succeeding at constructing meaning, perhaps because the reader conceptualizes reading more as a matter of identifying words. One example comes from Tony's miscues (see Chapter 1):

... The girls of the ~~village~~ *vengil*

did not go to school, for the people thought that school was

not as ~~important~~ *imprentice* for girls as ~~it~~ *to* was for boys.

In this sentence at least, Tony apparently was not succeeding in constructing meaning—which is probably why the miscue "to" for *it* was not corrected. This is rather typical of the sight word miscues of a less proficient reader: the miscues may have some letter(s) in common with the word in the text and be of similar length, but they don't necessarily preserve good grammar or good sense. They don't fit with the context—especially the following context. And often, they aren't corrected.

It is important to realize, though, that some students who have been viewed as poor readers may actually be using good reading strategies and may be making the same kinds of miscues with function words and pronouns as more obviously proficient readers do. In general, it is important not to assess a reader's strengths and strategies based on standardized test scores or on how smoothly the person reads aloud. Instead, we need to examine how the reader's miscues fit with the context and considers how well the reader comprehends normal texts in untimed situations. See Chapters 6–8.

Constructing Meaning and Reconstructing Text

The following example further shows how good readers typically construct meaning as they read, and sometimes even reconstruct the grammar of texts in doing so. Once you can read the passage fluently, making the same miscues this sixth grader, Jay, did, it may be revealing to ask someone to try to remember the miscues as you read the passage aloud. The passage is from an O. Henry story, "Jimmy Hayes and Muriel" (Porter, 1936, p. 670):

After a hearty supper Hayes joined the smokers ~~about~~ ① *around*

the fire. His appearance did not settle all the questions in ② *at all*

the minds of his brother rangers. They saw ③ simply a loose,

lank ④ ⓒ youth with tow-colored sunburned hair and a berry-

⑤ *ingenious*
brown, ~~ingenuous~~ face that wore a quizzical, good-

natured smile.

"Fellows," said the new ranger, "I'm goin' to interduce

⑥   ⑦ *much about*   ⑧
you to a lady friend of mine. Ain't (ever) heard (anybody)

⑨   ⑩   ⑪ *a*
(call) her (a) beauty, but you'll all admit she's got ~~some~~ fine

points about her. Come along, Muriel!"

Ⓒ   ⑫
He held open the front of his blue flannel shirt. |Out (of)

⑬   ⑭ *toad*
(it) crawled a horned ~~frog~~. A bright red ribbon was tied

⑮ *the*
jauntily around its spiky neck. It crawled to ~~its~~ owner's

⑯ *it*
knee and sat there motionless.
∧

⑰ *s*
"This here Muriel," said Hayes, with an oratorical wave
∧

⑱ *She's* ⑲
of his hand, "~~has~~ got qualities. She never talks back, she

⑳
always stays (at) home, and she's satisfied with one red

dress for everyday and Sunday, too."

㉑ *d*
"Look at that blame insect!" said one of the rangers
∧

㉒ *toads*
with a grin. "I've seen plenty of them horny ~~frogs~~, but I

㉓ Ⓒ
never knew anybody to have one for a (side) partner. Does

the blame thing know you from anybody else?"

㉔ *her*
"Take ~~it~~ over there and see," said Hayes.

Proficient reading is not miscueless.

Almost all of Jay's miscues fit the context: the preceding syntactic and semantic context, and the following syntactic and semantic context. In fact, when Jay made a miscue that would disrupt the structure of the text, he made others that restored grammatical structure. He drew upon prior knowledge, changing *frog(s)* to "toad(s)," and he even added to the dialect O. Henry was trying to portray by reading *blame* as "blamed." In fact, Jay's rendition of the story was so smooth, despite the numerous miscues, that when I read the passage aloud, reproducing Jay's miscues, usually only two are correctly identified by my listeners—and these are the two that disrupt grammar, though they do not seriously affect the sense.

Together, David's miscues (Chapter 1) along with Billy's and Jay's in this chapter help to illustrate the nature of proficient reading. It is not miscueless. Though many good readers do make fewer miscues than substantially poorer readers, the critical difference is the quality of the miscues. In other words, a good reader could make as many miscues as a less effective reader, but the use of language cues and reading strategies would mostly be different. Typically this difference is reflected in their differing use of context.

Good Versus Less Proficient Readers' Use of Context

Even beginning and less proficient readers typically make some use of context as they read, especially in classrooms where reading is treated as a meaning-making process. An early study by Rose-Marie Weber sought to determine what percentage of a group of first graders' miscues were acceptable with preceding syntax only, and what percentage were acceptable with following syntax as well. The following examples illustrate the two types of miscues:

- Acceptable only with preceding context: Spot ~~can~~ *and* help Dick.

- Acceptable with both preceding and following syntax: Spot can ~~help~~ *hear* Dick.

The miscue "and" for *can* is syntactically acceptable up to that point in the sentence, but not beyond it. However, "hear" for *help* is syntactically acceptable with the following context as well (though of course it does change the meaning).

Weber found that about 90% of these first graders' miscues were acceptable with the preceding syntax. This startlingly high percentage was true for the low-proficiency group as well as for the high-proficiency group. Furthermore, 72% of the high group's miscues and 63% of the low group's miscues were acceptable with the following syntax as well. The major difference between groups was in the correction of miscues that did not fit with the following syntactic context (miscues like "and" for *can* in *Spot can help Dick*). The high group corrected 85% of these, while the low group corrected only 42% (Weber, 1970, pp. 153, 160, 161). Thus, a major difference between proficient and nonproficient readers lies in the correction of miscues that are unacceptable with the following syntactic context.

Weber's study focused just on the use of syntactic context. However, the broad conclusions are equally applicable to the use of semantic context as well. Emergent readers can indeed use both syntactic and semantic context as a means of word identification and meaning construction. Furthermore, many emergent readers tend to do so, especially if they are already well acquainted with books and the joys of being read to. Here, for example, are miscues from John, a child with only two months of reading instruction. The sentences are from *Opening Doors* in the Macmillan Reading Program (1965):

- Get ~~a~~ ball, Mary.   *the*

- Who ~~rides~~ with Mike?   *can ride*

- Mary said, "Play ball, Jeff.

  Mike and I want to play." *ball* ∧

- Mike said, "I can't ride.

  I can't play with ~~Jeff and Mary.~~ *Mary and Jeff*

  I can play ball." *But* ∧

The child's miscues make sense in context, but even more: some of the miscues seem to improve upon the original, making the deep structure—the meaning—even more explicit. Paradoxically, John's miscues allow us to see that he uses context in reading.

In contrast, we have seen with Tony's miscues in Chapter 1 that less proficient readers may make less efficient use of context in identifying words and constructing meaning. They may over-attend to graphic cues and underattend to syntactic and semantic cues. In an extensive study of reading miscues, it was found that the miscues of low proficiency eighth and tenth graders frequently looked and sounded more like the text word than the miscues of high proficiency readers (K. Goodman & Burke, 1973, pp. 51, 53). But often this careful attention to grapho/phonemic cues produced nonwords like Tony's "souts" and "ramped," or words that did not fit the context. Such overreliance on graphic cues and letter-sound knowledge actually hindered word identification, as well as the construction of meaning. Indeed, one sometimes gets the sense that a reader is hardly even trying to make sense of a passage. He or she is reading just to identify the words.

It should be noted, though, that sometimes in the early stages of learning to read, good readers will progress from merely trying to supply a sensible word to trying to get the exact word, using graphic cues and letter-sound knowledge (Biemiller, 1970). For example, a child who earlier might have said "bird" for *canary* may now try to sound out the word, producing a nonword like "cainery." This is growth on the reader's part, reflecting the fact that the reader is now trying to integrate all three major language cue systems. Evidence that the child is trying to use graphic cues and letter-sound knowledge *along with* prior knowledge and context cues comes from the retelling, when the child talks about the bird in the story—or even the canary! Indeed, even less proficient readers will often demonstrate that they understood an important word or concept, though they may never have pronounced the word correctly while reading (see the example of Danny, pp. 78–79). These observations underscore not only the need for having a reader retell and discuss the story read, as part of a reader profile (see Chapter 8), but also the importance of knowing the reader's pattern of growth in interpreting any particular sample of miscues.

Now to summarize. Decades of miscue analysis give rise to the following observations about effective readers and many less effective readers, where "effective" readers are defined as those who succeed at constructing meaning from texts for which they have adequate prior knowledge:

1. *Highly effective* readers' miscues typically go with the previous grammar and meaning. This leads us to infer that they use preceding syntactic and semantic context, along with their schemas, to think ahead and *predict* what might be coming next—that is, to predict particular words or just to be sufficiently aware of what might logically follow so as to notice if the upcoming words don't sound right (grammatically or semantically) with what came before.

2. *Highly effective* readers' miscues usually go with the following grammar and meaning, as well. This leads us to infer that they use the following syntactic and semantic context, along with their schemas, to *monitor their own comprehension* and to *confirm* their prediction—or to *try to correct,* if needed.

3. *Moderately effective* readers' miscues often fit with the preceding syntactic and semantic context, leading us to infer that they use preceding context along with their schemas to think ahead, to predict. However, they tend to be less successful in noticing when grammar or meaning has gone awry—or at least, they are less likely to try to correct aloud when their miscues do not go with what follows the miscue.

4. *Somewhat effective* readers' miscues may fit with the preceding syntactic context, though perhaps as little as 40 to 60% of the time. Thus we can infer that they use preceding syntactic context to predict, at least part of the time. However, their miscues often do not go with previous meaning, suggesting that they don't make equally good use of the preceding semantic context to predict.

5. *Ineffective readers'* miscues don't often go with even the preceding syntactic context. Their miscues suggest they are reading almost as if the words were arranged in a list rather than in sentences. Unfortunately, this tendency seems to be increasing as more and more children are taught to read by phonics alone.

Of course, not all less effective or ineffective readers underrely on context and overrely on phonics—that is, on letter-sound knowledge. Emergent readers, particularly, may read a text primarily by looking at the pictures and making up a story, or relying on memory and their reading of a few words, if the story has been read to them repeatedly. This is a normal developmental phase, but such readers need help if they don't make a transition to attending more completely to the words on the page. Some older readers have not caught on to the fact that there are relationships between letter patterns and sound patterns, or they may find it difficult (perhaps despite extensive phonics training) to convert letter patterns into sound patterns. These readers too may be somewhat ineffective, or quite ineffective, and in need of help. See, however, the discussion in Chapter 13 of highly accomplished professionals who are quite successful readers and writers, though they still have difficulty with word-level skills like decoding.

In general terms, miscue analysis has led to the following important points about the reading process:

1. Constructing meaning from a text is far more important than identifying all the words—even though, obviously, many of the words have to be identified or at least understood conceptually, if the reader is to construct meaning effectively.

2. Effective and efficient reading requires the integration of prior knowledge and experience—our schemas—with all the major kinds of language cues: syntactic, semantic, and graphic. The latter call forth our grapho/phonemic knowledge (schemas) as well.

3. To read effectively, it is crucial to draw upon these sources of information—schemas, syntactic and semantic context, letters—and to orchestrate these kinds of information into successful reading strategies: predicting, sampling, monitoring comprehension, and confirming or correcting.

A key implication for reading instruction is also clear: The goal of reading instruction should not be the accurate identification of every word, but rather the effective and efficient use of reading strategies in order to construct meaning.

Many readers can make effective use of such key reading strategies, even if they make a number of miscues. Making effective use of reading strategies is a reasonable goal for all readers. On the other hand, completely accurate word identification is not a reasonable goal for any reader. The following section will further examine why "getting all the words" is not a reasonable goal for readers or for reading instruction.

> The goal of reading instruction should not be the accurate identification of every word, but rather the effective and efficient use of reading strategies in order to construct meaning.

WHY NOT WORD IDENTIFICATION?

We have already seen one argument for not emphasizing accurate word identification as a goal of reading: this does not reflect what proficient readers actually do. Therefore in emphasizing accurate word identification with those who are obviously less proficient readers, we may actually be impeding their growth toward reading proficiency.

In this section, we will consider three more arguments for the inappropriateness of exact word identification as a goal: (1) the fact that more than one word or group of words can signify a particular entity or concept; (2) the fact that we can often get the essence of a passage with its function words missing, or supply missing function words to fit the context; and (3) the fact that the precise words of a text are quickly forgotten anyway. All of these facts and factors lead to the conclusion that efficient and effective reading is a matter of constructing meaning, not of identifying words.

Words as Symbols

Many people think that words uniquely stand for things and must therefore be identified precisely. However, it is rare for anything—or any action or quality—to be designated by one and only one word. Look, for example, at the italicized words and phrases in the following sentences:

- Here, *Daisy*.
- Don't let *the dog* in.
- Look at *'er* go!
- *She's a handsome animal.*

All of these expressions and more could be used to designate a particular dog. Usually more than one word or expression can be used to designate an entity; more than one word can be used to express an action or a quality; and so forth. As speakers and writers, we choose whichever word best suits our immediate purpose. And as listeners and readers, we may well substitute a contextually equivalent word or expression for that of the original.

One example is Jay's substitution of "toad" for *frog* in the O. Henry story "Jimmy Hayes and Muriel":

- Out of it crawled a horned ~~frog~~. *toad*

- I've seen plenty of them horny ~~frogs~~ . . . *toads*

Though Jay's term was different, it still designated the same entity: Muriel. Like me, Jay had probably heard of horned toads but not of horned frogs. Instead of reflecting a loss of meaning, his substitution showed that he got the essential meaning of the author but translated it into something that made more sense to him.[1]

Especially common is the substitution of an appropriate pronoun for the noun to which it refers, a miscue made by a second grader reading the following passage from Bernard Wiseman's *Morris Has a Cold* (1978):

Boris said,

"Beds do not jump.

Beds do not run.

Beds just stand still."

"Why?" asked Morris.

"Are ~~beds~~ lazy?" *they*

In this context, it was perfectly reasonable to substitute the pronoun "they" for the repeated noun *beds*. Jay made a similar miscue, substituting one pronoun for another:

"Take ~~it~~ over there and see," said Hayes. *her*

In context, "her" made perfectly good sense, because Muriel was female.

Constructing Meaning Without All the Words

It is mainly proficient readers who make substitutions like those in the preceding examples. As mentioned earlier, the percentage of miscues involving pronouns and function words tends to *increase* as one becomes a more proficient reader (see K. Goodman & Burke, 1973, pp. 165–166 and p. 184). Insofar as they serve to signal relations between words, pronouns are like function words. And we can often supply many of the function words ourselves, if we are getting the essential meaning. That is, the content words, word order, and the total context are often adequate to signal many of the relations among the words in a sentence, if we have adequate background knowledge. To test this, consider the following passage. You may want to read it just for meaning first. Then try to fill in the missing function words (the original is from the *New York Times*, May 5, 1970, p. 17):

██ crack ██ ██ rifle volley cut ██ suddenly still air. It appeared ██ go on, ██ ██ solid volley, ██ perhaps ██ full minute ██ ██ little longer.

　　Some ██ ██ students dived ██ ██ ground, crawling ██ ██ grass ██ terror. Others stood shocked ██ half crouched, apparently believing ██ troops were firing ██ ██ ██ air. Some ██ ██ rifle barrels ██ pointing upward.

　　██ ██ top ██ ██ hill ██ ██ corner ██ Taylor Hall, ██ student crumpled over, spun sideways ██ fell ██ ██ ground, shot ██ ██ head.

　　██ ██ firing stopped ██ slim girl, wearing ██ cowboy shirt ██ faded jeans, ██ lying face down ██ ██ road ██ ██ edge ██ ██ parking lot, blood pouring ██ ██ ██ the macadam, ██ 10 feet ██ ██ reporter.

People usually find they can supply reasonable function words—often the precise one that was omitted from the original.[2] Just as words can typically be identified from only part of the visual information normally available, sentences can normally be understood from fewer than the total number of words available. We are able to recreate part of the surface structure from our understanding of the deep structure.

Since meaning is the goal of reading, we hardly need to insist that every word be identified accurately. Instead of demanding an accurate rendition of the surface structure, we might better call for a reasonable interpretation of the deep structure.

Some will argue that there are times when it is vital to read every word accurately, and this is probably true. In savoring a poem, for example, one often dwells on the significance of virtually every word and every mark of punctuation. And surface accuracy may sometimes be important in getting the deep structure of warranties and guarantees, application forms, recipes and other directions, and legal contracts. But even with such materials, surface accuracy is not as important or as helpful as commonly supposed. The proof of this is in our everyday experience. Many of us have had the frustrating experience of being able to read all the words in a set of directions or a contract, yet been unable to determine precisely what was meant. We are often able to get the surface structure, yet unable to get the deep structure—the intended meaning.

An experience of my own seems pertinent. Several years ago I was asked to render an expert linguistic opinion in a court case involving a life insurance claim. The deceased had died piloting his own plane. The linguistic question involved the following exclusion clause in the insurance policy, and in particular the word *passenger*. The insured person was not covered by the policy "while engaged in or taking part in aeronautics and/or aviation of any description or resulting from being in any aircraft except while a passenger in an aircraft previously tried, tested, and approved." The insurance company claimed that the word *passenger* excluded the pilot of a plane, and hence the man was not covered by the policy at the time of his death. The family claimed that the man *was* covered at the time of his death, because the pilot of a plane is also one of its passengers. Both parties agreed on the word and its basic meaning, but not on the meaning most relevant to that context. And it was a crucial $50,000 difference.[3]

Once again the conclusion seems clear: what's most important is not the surface structure, but the deep structure. The proficient reader reads more for meaning than for every surface detail.

Constructing Meaning and Forgetting the Words

You will learn most from the following example if you treat it as an experiment. Read through the following passage just once, at a normal pace, trying to fix it verbatim in your mind. Then write the sentences as you remember them, without looking back at the original. Alternatively, you might read the passage aloud to someone, asking the person to try to remember and write the passage verbatim. It is taken from Graham Greene's *The Power and the Glory* (1940, p. 139):

> The young men and women walked round and round the plaza in the hot electric night: the men one way, the girls another, never speaking to each other. In the northern sky the lightning flapped. It was like a religious ceremony which had lost all meaning, but at which they still wore their best clothes.

You (or your listener) may have found that you could not recall all of the passage after just one reading. This is typical. But in trying to recall as much as possible, you probably preserved the essential meaning, making only or mostly superficial changes in surface structure. Among the more common changes are these:

"around" for *round*   "flashed" for *flapped*
"women" for *girls*   "that" for *which*
"the other" for *another*   "to which" for *at which*

In addition, it is common to find the first sentence divided into two sentences, or even three:

> The young men and women walked round and round the plaza in the hot electric night. The men went one way and the girls another. They never spoke to each other.

Obviously the wording and sentence structure may be changed in several other ways while still preserving the essential meaning. Most of the deep structure is retained, but some of the surface structure is lost. There is perhaps no definitive answer to precisely how fast surface structure is lost, but an experiment by Sachs suggests that we begin to forget the actual words within about half a second of reading them (Sachs, 1967).

Koestler (1969, p. 201) offers a succinct example of how the spoken word resolves itself into increasingly more abstract mental representations for the listener, just as the written word does for the reader:

> You watch a television play. The exact words of each actor are forgotten by the time he speaks his next line, and only their meaning remains; the next morning you can only remember the sequence of scenes which constituted the story; after a month, all you remember is that it was about a gangster on the run or about two men and a woman on a desert island.

In a few months, you may not remember the show at all, though it may have affected your available gangster-movie schema or your love-triangle schema. Words, scenes, even whole texts may be quickly forgotten.

Why, then, be so concerned about getting the exact words of the text, as long as the essential meaning is preserved?

IMPLICATIONS FOR UNDERSTANDING DIALECT MISCUES

It used to be common for teachers to think that miscues reflecting a reader's spoken dialect were wrong and needed to be corrected for understanding to occur; perhaps it still is. However, this assumption should be reconsidered in light of the evidence that understanding usually precedes oral verbalization and in light of the evidence that proficient readers make miscues that reflect their predictions, their prior knowledge, and even their preferred language structures (e.g., Jay's miscues, given earlier).

To understand how common it is to translate a text into our own language patterns precisely because we *are* understanding (getting the deep structure), you might try the following experiment with someone you consider to be a reasonably proficient reader. Without giving any hint of your purpose, have the person read the following passage aloud, while you take careful note of any miscues that are made. The passage is from Zachary Ball's *Bristle Face* (1962, p. 75), discussed in Rigg (1978, p. 287):

> He nodded. "Some good mud cats in there. That bluff you speak of, I denned me a bear in the rocks up there oncet."
> "A bear! When was that? Lately?"
> He chuckled. "Naw , that was way back yonder, when I was a boy, no older'n you. Ain't been no bear around here for sixty year, about. That was the last one ever I heard of hereabouts."

For those whose dialect is different from this rural mountain speech, "sixty years" for *sixty year* is a common miscue. As I checked this quote for accuracy, I first read "I ever" for *ever I*, changing the syntactic pattern to one more common in my speech. Your reader may have made other miscues that preserved the deep structure but changed the surface structure to a more familiar pattern.

A second dialect passage may again help demonstrate the fact that we do not necessarily have to get all the words right in order to get the meaning. If possible, try this passage on yet another reader, someone who does not know your purpose. The passage is from Claude Brown's *Manchild in the Promised Land* (1965, p. 39):

> "Seem like nobody can't make him understand. I talk to him, I yell at him, I whip his ass, but it don't do no good. His daddy preach to him, he yell at him, he beat him so bad sometimes, I gotta run in the kitchen and git that big knife at him to stop him from killin' that boy. You think that might break him outta those devilish ways he got? Child, that scamp'll look Jesus dead in the eye when he standin' on a mountain of Bibles and swear to God in heaven he ain't gon do it no more. The next day, or even the next minute, that little lyin' Negro done gone and did it again—and got a mouthful-a lies when he git caught."

Among the numerous possible dialect miscues here, the more common are "he's got" for *he got,* and "he's standin'" for *he standin'.* Another is "gonna" for *gon,* which should be pronounced with a nasalized vowel and no final consonant. You may also find that your reader adds third person singular verb endings, saying, for example, "seems" for *seem,* "yells" for *yell,* and "beats" for *beat.* With miscues such as these, the reader has gotten the meaning without getting all the words entirely right. Indeed, it is *because* the reader has gotten the meaning that he or she makes such miscues.

In reading the passage from *Manchild,* speakers of a standard English dialect may add some of the surface grammatical features that would be normal for their dialect. In contrast, speakers of other dialects may read a passage written in standard English and omit some of the surface grammatical markers that are not always present in their dialect. What we often fail to realize is that such dialect translation would not be possible unless the reader had understood the deep structure of the author's sentence. Actively transacting with the text, the reader has simply expressed it in his or her own surface structure.

Usually, teachers are most disturbed by miscues that reflect a pertially different grammatical system: "we was" for *we were,* "he don't have none" for *he doesn't have any,* and so forth. But such miscues as these are relatively rare. The more common grammatical miscues involve just pieces of words, the grammatical endings. Kenneth Goodman and his associates have found, for example, that among inner-city Black children, the following are the most common dialect-related miscues that appear to involve grammar. Most of these miscues involve grammatical elements attached to or manifested within a word (adapted from K. Goodman & Buck, 1973, p. 9).[4]

- Absence of past tense marker
  "look" for *looked,* "call" for *called,* "wreck" for *wrecked,* "love" for *loved,* "pound" for *pounded,* "help" for *helped,* "use" for *used,* "run" for *ran,* "have" for *had,* "keep" for *kept,* "do" for *did*
- Absence of plural noun marker
  "thing" for *things,* "work" for *works,* "story" for *stories,* "prize" for *prizes*
- Absence of third person singular verb marker
  "look" for *looks,* "work" for *works,* "hide" for *hides*
- Absence of possessive noun or pronoun marker
  "Freddie" for *Freddie's,* "Mr. Vine" for Mr. *Vine's,* "one" for *one's,* "it" for *its*
- Substitution and omission of forms of *to be*
  "was" for *were,* "is" for *are,* "we" for *we're,* "he be talking" for *he'd been talking*
- Hypercorrections (the use of two grammatical markers of the same type)
  "likeded" for *liked,* "helpded" for *helped,* "stoppded" for *stopped*

In the late 1970s, Kenneth and Yetta Goodman (1978) and their associates completed a massive study of miscues among second, fourth, and sixth graders who spoke a nonmainstream dialect or who spoke English as a second language. The dialect groups were downeast Maine, Mississippi Black, Appalachian, and Hawaiian Pidgin. The second-language groups were Texas Spanish, Hawaiian Samoan, Arabic, and Navajo. The most common kind of grammatical miscue, for both the dialect speakers and the ESL speakers, was again the absence of grammatical inflections on the ends of words. This is a common "interlanguage" feature among people learning English as a second language (Selinker, 1972).

From their impressive study, in which they examined not only the children's miscues but also their comprehension, the Goodmans concluded that there is "no evidence that inability to cope with Book English is a general problem for any group" (1978, p. 3–5). The students' dialect or interlanguage influence was evident in their reading, "but it is not in itself a barrier to comprehension" (p. 3–22).

With oral reading, then, we do not ordinarily need to be concerned about the absence or use of such features as those cited by Goodman and Buck. Such miscues typically reflect not a lack of understanding, but only an alternative surface structure common in the reader's everyday speech. Having understood the deep structure, the reader simply expresses it in an alternative oral form. Such a process is reflected in Figure 4.2. This model indicates that, as mentioned earlier, when we read aloud, our understanding is usually ahead of our voice. Unless we are having unusual difficulty, we get the meaning *before* speaking the words, rather than vice versa.

Given this fact as well as the specific research into dialect miscues and ESL miscues, the Goodmans point out that special reading materials are not needed for *any* of the low-status dialect groups studied, nor is special methodology needed (p. 8–5). What *is* needed, however, is a positive attitude toward reading miscues in general and toward dialect and ESL miscues in particular.

This point can hardly be emphasized enough. In a survey in which 94 Midwestern elementary teachers rated miscues as acceptable or unacceptable, Tovey (1979) found that when miscues

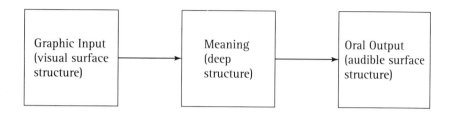

Figure 4.2 *A simplified model of proficient oral reading.*

were syntactically and semantically appropriate in the teacher's dialect, only 16% of the teachers would not accept the miscues. However, when the miscues reflected translation into the reader's dialect, 60% of the teachers would not accept the miscues. An earlier study by Cunningham produced similar results (1977). Teachers, then, must have the knowledge, the experience, and the *attitudes* that will enable them to recognize and accept miscues that merely reflect an alternative spoken dialect. This is essentially one of the conclusions that can be drawn from the famed Ann Arbor decision of 1979, in which a group of black children won their court suit charging that the school had failed to take their home language into account in teaching them to read (see *Ann Arbor Decision,* p. 9 in particular).

In his excellent book on what was then described as Black English Vernacular, Robbins Burling offered some particularly pertinent remarks (1973, pp. 158–159):

> What should a teacher do when her children make such "mistakes"? She may be willing to accept the idea that children should be permitted to read aloud in their own natural pronunciation, but grammatical changes [or apparent grammatical changes] seem far more dramatic. To most teachers they look like out-and-out errors and they seem to warrant correction. Nevertheless, these "errors" give far better evidence of comprehension than would more literal and "accurate" recitation of the words. Word-for-word recitation may amount to no more than parroting. It may be no different from reading a word list in which the words have no relation to one another. Conversion to nonstandard forms, so long as the meaning is preserved, amounts to a kind of translation that would be quite impossible if the child did not understand. If reading with comprehension is our goal, then these "errors" prove that we have been successful.

At least some research indicates that it is the *best* readers who produce the most dialect-based miscues (Hunt, 1974–1975), supporting the observation that good readers tend to express the author's deep structure in a surface structure that is partially their own. They are less concerned with surface detail than with meaning.

REVALUING READERS

Recognizing that reading is more a matter of constructing meaning than of identifying words should encourage us to revalue readers we might previously have considered to be poor readers. In part, this recognition should prompt us to revalue those we might have mistakenly considered less proficient because of their dialect miscues. It should also prompt us to revalue the many readers who are not very good at "getting" all or even most of the words, but whose miscues show good use of reading strategies and who comprehend well.

The example of Danny comes readily to mind. When the following sample of his miscues was generated, Danny was a third grader reading *What's the Matter with Carruthers?* by James

Marshall (1972), from *Windchimes* in the Houghton Mifflin basal reading program. In the story, the bear Carruthers is grumpy when greeted by his friends Emily and Eugene—a pig and a turtle, respectively. Emily and Eugene try to cheer up Carruthers by playing music for him, inviting him over for a lunch of tea and honey cakes, taking him to an amusement park, and finally trying to keep him busy raking leaves. Nothing works.

Here is an excerpt from the text, with Danny's miscues marked. He was several pages into the story:

① E g e n
"Well," ~~Eugene~~ began, after a long pause.

②
"Whenever I'm (in a) grouchy and unpleasant

mood, I always listen to beautiful music. In no
③   ④
I'm feeling   ⑤
time at all ~~I feel~~ much better, (and) I'm sure that

I'm much more pleasant to be around."
⑥   Ⓒ a
"That gives) me an idea," said Emily. "Come

with me."
⑦   Ⓐ
The two friends hurried home, but (in) a (few
⑧ later
minutes ˄ they were back in the park with their
⑨   ⑩ carried
musical instruments. Emily (was) ~~carrying~~ her
E g e n   ⑪ trumpet
tuba. ~~Eugene~~ had his ~~tambourine~~.
⑫   E g e n
(What) a good idea," said ~~Eugene~~. "When we
⑬ Caluthers' ⑭ plumped ⑮ nerv-es
smooth ~~Carruthers'~~ ~~rumpled~~ ~~nerves~~ with our

beautiful music, he'll be his old friendly self
⑯
again. I'm sure that he'll be (so) grateful."

Ⓡ   Caluthers
⌐Turning the bend, they saw ~~Carruthers~~ still

      © ⑰   Ⓒ gl- ⑱
sitting in (the (same) place, still (gazing at the

                  Ⓒ e-
falling leaves. And (ever so quietly they tiptoed

              ⑲
              them
up behind ~~him~~) ⑳

㉑ Prancing a ㉒
   ~~Placing the~~ mouthpiece of her tuba to her lips,

              ㉔ ㉕
       ㉓ the keeth
Emily puffed (up) ~~her cheeks~~ and began to play,

          ㉖   ㉗
              quiet   Eqen
softly at first and (then) ~~quite~~ loudly. ~~Eugene~~

   ㉘ the ㉙
      the trombone
tapped on ~~his~~ ~~tambourine~~.

"Um-Pah Um-Pah Tap Tap. Um-Pah Um-Pah

                  ㉚   Ⓡ
Tap Tap." It sounded ~~something~~ (like (that) ㉛

       Caluthers
But ~~Carruthers~~ was not impressed. Instead
㉜ ㉝
he listened
~~of listening~~ to the music, he put his paws to his

ears and growled, "That is the most awful noise I

      ㉞
have (ever) heard in my life!"

Ⓡ ㉟
⌐And (he) promptly got up and walked away.

If we conceptualized reading as first and foremost a matter of identifying words, we would see Danny as a weak reader who has missed a number of words in a short passage. But if we look at his strategies, we will see a reader who makes effective use of prior knowledge and context to predict, and who sometimes restructures text to keep a stretch of words grammatical, at least with what came before. These strategies, along with the many miscues that fit the context without needing correction (for instance, "trumpet" for *tambourine* and "trombone" for *trumpet*), suggest that Danny is reading to construct meaning, and probably succeeding. This impression is confirmed by the following excerpt from his retelling:

> There was a bear friend of—of—of two [thinks about it] girls, I can say. And one person, that bear, wasn't being friendly. He wasn't being polite. And so they tried to play soft, beautiful music, but that didn't work. They invited him to honeycake and took him to an amusement park, but that didn't work. And finally they found out that it was time for him to hibernate.

Interestingly, Danny knew that Carruthers' friends had taken him to an amusement park, even though Danny didn't say the word *amusement* correctly when he encountered it in the text. Also, the story didn't use the word *hibernate* at all; Danny appropriately inferred it from the plot. He may not have known that "Eugene" is a boy's name, and thus assumed that both of Carruthers' friends were girls.

For whatever reason, correct word identification does not come easily to Danny. A traditional solution might be to give him flash cards to get him to memorize more sight words, or to give him more phonics instruction, on the assumption that he should be sounding out unfamiliar words. However, close examination of his reading strategies suggests that he is rather effective in coordinating prior knowledge and context with letter cues to predict, sample, monitor comprehension, and sometimes to correct. It is possible that he does a lot of correcting silently, for he seems well able to get the essential meaning of the text. Emphasizing sight words or sounding out words could easily divert Danny from his goal of constructing meaning.

In time, and if he does a lot of reading, his word recognition will surely improve. Meanwhile, if I were his teacher or tutor, I would demonstrate and discuss his effective reading strategies with him. Since his previous teachers noticed only his frequent miscues and his lack of fluency, my highest priority would be to help him revalue himself as a reader: to recognize and celebrate his effective strategies and his strengths as a reader. Chapter 9 includes examples of how this can be done.

REVIEW AND BEYOND

Chapters 3 and 4 have dealt with a variety of interrelated topics: various kinds of context available to a reader, language cues and reading strategies, reading proficiency and the use of context, why it is inappropriate and unproductive to conceptualize reading as involving accurate identification of all the words, implications for understanding and accepting dialect miscues, and revaluing readers.

Among the more important conclusions and implications are the following:

1. Readers do not have to rely on graphic cues and letter-sound knowledge alone, as an increasing number of reading programs would have them do when starting to learn to read. When reading predictable and other natural-sounding texts, readers have available both syntactic and semantic context within the text as well as their own schemas.

2. Context can help all readers identify or at least understand words they don't immediately recognize, but context is especially helpful for younger and less proficient readers. For them, words are clearly easier to identify in context than in isolation.

3. Language cues—syntactic, semantic, and graphic—give rise to reading strategies, especially predicting, sampling, monitoring comprehension, and confirming or correcting (or trying to correct).

4. Proficient readers, those who are both effective and efficient in constructing reading, focus primarily upon the construction of meaning from text, not upon identification of all the words.

5. Less proficient readers are often those who overrely on graphic cues and phonics, usually because they think they have to say all the words correctly. Ironically, overusing phonics while underusing context and schemas makes even word identification more difficult.

6. On the other hand, some readers may need help in learning to use graphic cues and phonics knowledge more effectively, *along with* context and schemas. That is, they may need help in orchestrating all the language cues and sources of information into effective reading strategies.

7. Many words and sentences, sometimes even whole paragraphs, are not critical to the meaning of the evolving whole of a text. Most texts contain a significant degree of redundancy, especially at the word level.

8. Accurate word identification is appropriate only for *rehearsed* reading performances, if at all. When reading aloud to an audience, readers may try to read all the words, especially if the listeners have a copy of the text. On the other hand, some of us find that we make the most miscues when reading to an audience, because we are trying to maintain eye contact as well. In such cases, I often notice myself making miscues and restructuring text, if necessary, to maintain not only the meaning but acceptable grammar too.

9. Dialect-related miscues and miscues related to the learning of English as a nonnative language indicate that the reader has processed the text for meaning, then converted it into his or her own surface structure. Such miscues are best viewed as evidence of effective reading.

10. We need to revalue readers who are effective at getting meaning, even if they are slow or halting and sometimes struggle with words. We need to revalue them, and to help them revalue themselves and their effective reading strategies, as well as to become more efficient at constructing meaning, if needed.

Later chapters will address many of these points and related topics in greater depth.

FOR FURTHER EXPLORATION

1. Consider the miscues made by Anne, a first grader reading Jene Barr's *Little Circus Dog* (1949). Which of Anne's miscues fit with the preceding context? Which fit with the following context as well? Based on her miscues, would you say that Anne is a good reader? Why or why not?

Now the band began to play. Then the lions roared.

Peter the pony ran ~~around~~ the ring. Bill the circus boy
①about

Ⓒ let ②
~~led~~ Penny the elephant into the circus ring. ~~Everybody~~ Everyone ③

forgot to eat popcorn. They forgot to drink soda pop.

They forgot to wave balloons. ~~The~~ circus man made a bow.
④ A

Trixie ran into the middle of the ring. She sat and

⑤ went
waited. Carlo the clown ~~ran~~ up to Trixie. Trixie jumped

⑥ on   ⑦ the
up and sat ~~in~~ his hand. Carlo put Trixie on ~~a~~ box. Trixie

stood on her hind legs. Then she jumped onto Carlo's head.

Trixie looked very funny sitting on Carlo's head. Every-

⑧ one
~~body~~ laughed.

2. Look again at David's and Tony's miscues in Chapter 1. What language cues and reading strategies does each child seem to have been using? Ask yourself the same question about the miscues recorded below. The examples in (a) are from a kindergartner. Examples (b) through (f) are from second graders; and the others are from older readers (sixth, eighth, and tenth graders) (K. Goodman & Burke, 1973, pp. 210–211, 230–231, 250, 258, 310).

not getting anything
a. I'm ~~getting nothing~~ for Christmas. [a line from a song]

mean inside
"No, no," said Boris. "I ~~don't mean outside~~."

② didn't do
Boris growled, "That's because you ~~did~~ it the wrong way."

[The reader started to say, "You didn't do it right."]

to get down
b. Here is something ~~you can do~~.

I have not help the little kitten will we want little kitten to play?
c. ~~I am not too little to help with little things, am I?~~

truck
d. "The little ~~monkey~~ had it."

him
e. . . . a voice calling, somewhere above.
              ∧

up
f. . . . it was enough to wake the dead.
                          ∧

know   fun was   sky
g. Bill ⓨ ~~knew~~ that ~~fawns~~ ~~were~~ always very ~~shy~~.

h. I ~~leaned~~ *liked* over ~~the crib, pointing~~ *a crab potted* a finger . . .

i. Billy was so ~~pleased~~ *proud* by the hunter's words.

j. . . . to see if there was any danger. He ~~heard~~ *afraid* the . . .

k. . . . stop driving until we (can) see Los Angeles.

l. . . . I went (over) to his bed.

m. . . . when the children begin assuming *the* control of the country.
   ∧

n. . . . the door ~~of~~ *to* Harry's ~~room~~ *bedroom* . . .

o. . . . a pair of pyjamas (with) blue, brown ~~and~~ *and* white stripes. *with*
   ∧

3. If you know of any teachers with widely differing instructional approaches and/or definitions of reading, it might be interesting to compare their reactions to Anne's miscues (p. 81–82) or Jay's (pp. 66–67) or Billy's (pp. 64–65), or all of them. Do the teachers think most of these miscues are serious, a matter for concern? If not, why not? If so, what kind of instructional help would the teachers recommend? Compare the responses from the different teachers.

4. To compare proficient reading with nonproficient reading, try our blacked-out *New York Times* passage (p. 73) with both good and poor readers of about junior high age or beyond. First, be certain that each person can identify all of the content words in the selection; if necessary, read these words for the person one or more times. Then ask the person to write in the missing function words (you may want to use a photocopy of the passage for this purpose). Are the good and poor readers equally able to supply reasonable possibilities for the missing words? If not, what does this suggest about their differing approaches to the task of reading?

5. Examine the dialect-related miscues that a college student made in reading the passage below. All of the miscues are numbered in this passage from the dialect reader *Friends*, by Joan Baratz and William Stewart (1970, pp. 24–30). What do you think caused the reader to make each of these miscues? Discuss.

One morning Ollie and Leroy was getting ready to

go to school. Leroy, he put on one of Ollie socks

'cause he lost his. Ollie say, "Boy, give me my *back* ①
   ∧

② *he*
sock" but Leroy wouldn't give it to him. Leroy
                    ∧

                        ③ *knew*
say "It's my sock." But Ollie ~~know~~ it wasn't

                                ④   *'s*
'cause it wasn't even the same color as Leroy
                                        ∧

other sock. Ollie kept on begging and begging

Leroy for the sock. But Leroy still wouldn't

                                    ⑤ *into*
give it to him. Ollie hit Leroy. And they got ~~to~~

⑥ *a fight*   ⑦ *ed*
~~fighting~~. Leroy hit Ollie in the nose and it start
                                            ∧

to bleeding. Then, Ollie got real mad and hit Leroy

on the arm as hard as he could. Leroy hollered real

loud. Big Momma must have heard them fighting 'cause

⑧ *come*
she ~~come~~ running in the room and she stop the fight.

                    ⑨ *ed*
She say "All right, who start this mess?" Ollie say
                                ∧

Leroy start it and Leroy say Ollie start it.

Big Momma say, "I done told you about fighting

before. Since don't nobody know who start this

mess I'm just going to whip both of you."

Incidentally, I have typed this just the way it was typed by the student who carried out the experiment with her college friend. Along with four other errors in copying, my student made two dialect miscues in reading and typing the passage![5]

6. Sometimes people think that children need instruction in phonics in order to be able to spell better. To test this assumption before going on to Chapter 5, dictate the following words to a group of adults, perhaps your class. Repeat the words if asked, but don't use them in a sentence. Afterwards, compare the different ways these words have been spelled. What do you think our chances are of spelling words conventionally if we use basic letter-sound knowledge alone?

a. Real words: sun, brake, rowed, mete

b. Nonsense words: keak, glite, wraim, /nē' der lē/[6]

c. Real words that few people know:

coriaceous /kor' ē ā shəs/

deraign /di rān'/

escharotic /es' kə ra(h)t' ik/

gaudeamus /gau' dā a(h) mo͞os/

isochronal /ī sa(h)k' rə nəl/

mesophyte /mes' o fīt/

piceous /pis' ē əs/

I often give this spelling test at the end of class. Then I ask that students look up the words in group C in a large desk dictionary before the next class. Subsequent discussion on the difficulty of locating these words proves most illuminating.

7. Put the following words (enlarged) on a transparency and show them to an audience, one row of words at a time, on an overhead projector. Ask your audience to read the words aloud quickly, without struggling over them. As they read the words, listen for how they have tackled the words, and of course listen for miscues that you can discuss afterwards.

zeugma /zo͞og' mə/   riata /rē a(h)' tə/

sarsaparilla /sas pə ri' lə/   plesiosaur /plē' sē ə sor/

vitiate /vi' shē āt/   demesne /di mān', di mēn/

sycophant /si' kə fənt/   extravasate /ik strav' ə sāt/

submandibular /səb man dib' yə lər/ dissepiment /di sep' ə mənt/

sapogenin /sa pə jen' ən/   ingenue /an' zhə no͞o/

samizdat /saam ēz daat/   botryoidal /ba(h)t' rē oid' əl, ba(h)-trē oi dəl/

After your audience has read the words, you might ask such questions as these:

■ Who tried to read the words letter-by-letter? (Usually nobody does this, so you could then ask, "Why not?")

■ Who tried to read the words mostly by chunking them into syllables? (This is a common strategy.)

■ Who tried to read the words by sampling the letters more or less all at once? (You may have noticed this while your audience was reading the words. This is the strategy that leads to the most miscues.)

■ What words do you know the meaning of, or think you know the meaning of?

■ Did pronouncing the words give you insights into their meanings? (Follow up if/as appropriate.)

- How do you handle unknown words when you encounter them in normal reading?
- What do you think are the implications of this experiment and discussion for how we should help students deal with unfamiliar print words? (This is indeed meant as an open-ended question, for many people will suggest that it depends on the age and/or proficiency of the reader.)

8. Begin an in-depth investigation of the federal agenda to promote the teaching of phonics first. This agenda has been spurred by various legislative acts and actions that have initiated, supported and greatly enlarged the role of the National Institute of Health and Human Development in deciding what counts as reading research and what research will be funded. This agenda has been carried out largely by G. Reid Lyon, head of Child Development and Behavior and the reading research agenda within the NICHD. In that capacity, he has shaped legislation and policy by gaining the ear of President George W. Bush, who has, according to the media, made Reid Lyon his "reading czar."

    On January 8, 2002, the U.S. government passed, and President Bush signed into law, a redesigned and reauthorized Elementary and Secondary Education Act (ESEA), popularly known as "No Child Left Behind" since it reflects so much of George W. Bush's presidential campaign agenda, particularly with respect to reading (Law: P.L. 107 (H.R. 1). Section B deals specifically with the teaching of reading; it starts at *http://www.ed.gov/legislation/ESEA02/pg4.html*. A primary—and no doubt intended—effect of this legislation will be to line the coffers of the largest publishers of reading programs, tests, test preparation materials, teacher training programs, and ancillary materials. Another intended effect: to make politicians look good. (Teachers can later be blamed for not carrying out the federal agenda or the reading program properly; it is never the intent of politicians or large corporations to take responsibility for promoting methods and materials that don't work well.)

    Though claiming to be based upon "scientific research" showing how to teach reading, the Reading First and related initiatives are based more upon the belief systems of those with sufficient powerful connections, political influence, and government-allocated funding to enable them to be heard by legislators and other politicians. As you investigate various items and articles dealing with this federal reading initiative, combine new information with your previous understanding of teaching and learning to consider the validity of these statements:

    > What legislators have legally approved is not a scientific basis for reading instruction but simply a belief that narrowly conceived, experimental laboratory science provides the best—indeed, the only—model for measuring complex human phenomena, in this case reading and learning to read. They have passed legislation supporting a belief about the nature of human learning that is contradicted by myriads of evidence. They have reified—if not deified—a view of teaching and learning that is not merely inadequate but demonstrably false.

    There are many sources to draw upon as you investigate. For example, Chapter 11 here includes numerous references critiquing the National Reading Panel report summary (2000, c), which is taken as support for the federal reading agenda. Among these important references are various articles in the *Phi Delta Kappan* and books by Garan (2002), Allington (2002), and Coles (2003). (See p. 385 for references, and see Chapters 11 and 13 for my own critiques.) Historical background is provided by several articles included in K. Goodman (1998). Two other references crucial for tracing the influences and understanding the agenda of the "Reading First" initiative are Metcalf's "Reading Between the Lines" (2002) and Altwerger and Strauss' "The Business Behind Testing" (2002).

9. As Chapters 3 through 5 indicate, proficient readers draw upon context in order to make more efficient use of graphic cues and letter-sound knowledge—phonics—as they read. Educators who understand readers who use phonics knowledge together with context often teach phonics in the context of reading and writing whole texts. In addition to benefiting readers more directly, teaching phonics in context avoids the typical problem that skills

taught in isolation do not readily transfer into use. Teaching phonics in context is not only effective, but efficient.

Teaching phonics first may have temporary benefits when phonics and word reading skills are essentially the only outcomes measured (see Chapters 11 and 13), but the limitations and drawbacks outweigh the benefits. As you read the rest of this book, and perhaps carry out investigations yourself, you can use the following comparison to help organize the information encountered. Then critique the comparison and make any modifications that seem more accurate to you.

Phonics First	Phonics Within Whole Language
Part-to-whole	Parts in context of whole
Isolated skills first	Skills in context; skills as part of reading strategies
Phonemic awareness taught as prerequisite	Phonemic awareness developed in context, as part of phonics and by spelling sounds within words
Starts with more abstract, harder tasks and texts	Starts with easier tasks and texts that reflect developmental patterns
Uses "decodable" texts that are harder to read	Uses easier-to-read texts: patterned, rhymed, and other natural and familiar texts that provide usable context for decoding words
Phonics is taught from commercial programs	Phonics is taught mostly from the texts that children are reading and writing
Phonemic awareness and phonics are typically taught in a predetermined sequence to the entire class, reflecting a "one size fits all" assumption	Though some phonics may be taught to the whole class, teachers use small groups and individual conferences to tailor instruction to children's particular needs
"Success" equals mostly the scores on tests of word skills and word reading, through grade 1	"Success" equals the ability to use grapho/phonemic (phonics) knowledge to carry out effective strategies for constructing meaning
Research procedures and questions are narrowly defined, tightly controlled by legislation and funding, then labeled "scientific"	Research includes teacher research, other observational research, and experimental research
Research typically focuses on the effects of teaching one particular skill, such as phonics, without regard for effects on the development of other skills, the process of reading as a whole, or attitudes and motivation	Research typically focuses on multiple, interacting causes and effects; much (not all) of the experimental research compares different overall approaches to literacy in different classrooms

5 Word Perception in the Reading Process

Vision and perception are two different phenomena. Vision involves the eyes and the optical nerves. Perception is what the brain does with the visual input. Nor is the brain a prisoner of the eye. The brain directs the eye—deciding on where it should fix and the direction it should move.

—Kenneth Goodman

Questions for Thought and Discussion

1. What role do the eyes play in reading? What are the roles of the brain?

2. What is the difference between "sight" (as defined here) and "visual perception"?

3. What parts of words are especially useful in identifying words?

4. What does it mean to say that we read new print words by analogy with parts of known print words? Is this easier or more difficult than decoding new words one letter-sound at a time? What do you think about the need for teaching individual letter-sound correspondences for the purpose of decoding words?

5. What does it mean to say that we "process" or "perceive" many or most of the words in a text, or even most of the letters in the words? How are most people misled by such statements?

6. What do eye fixation studies show about the roles of context in facilitating the processing of words and texts?

7. Why aren't proficient readers necessarily fluent readers? Why aren't fluent readers necessarily proficient readers?

8. How does the concept of proficient reading as "flow" differ from the concept of proficient reading as fluent?

9. How and why does a "redundancy" model of the reading process help us understand that slow and halting readers may nevertheless be able to construct substantial meaning from conceptually suitable texts?

10. What do you think are the most important concepts about the reading process that you have been reading about in this text?

Let me introduce this chapter by asking you to read a short story written by Kenneth Goodman. Please read the passage straight through, without looking back or rereading the passage. Then cover up the passage and jot down what you remember reading. Here is the passage:

"The Boat in the Basement"

A woman was building a boat in her bastement. When she had finished the the boot, she discovered that it was too big to go though the door. So he had to take the boat a part to get it out. She should of planned ahead.

If you are doing this in a group setting, talk about what you have jotted down. Did any of you write down the passage word-for-word? (Not likely. Why?) How did you decide what to write? And did you notice any errors in the passage as you read? It's common to notice that the fourth line ends with *he*, so you may have mentally corrected to "she," or you may have asked yourself something like "Who's *he*, anyway? Her husband? Son? Boyfriend?" For me, at least, the placement of *he* at the end of the line accentuates the discrepancy between what we anticipate, "she," and the actual word. Without looking back at the story, think a minute: Did you notice any other errors? What were they? There are *seven* errors in the paragraph. How many did you notice when you first read the story? Now reread it and see if you can locate all seven errors!

Many readers may notice two to four errors on a first reading, but in a research study (Gollasch, 1980), most people couldn't find all six of the original errors, even when given unlimited time to search for them. (I have added a seventh error myself.) The original passage can be found in K. Goodman (1996, p. 38), and the errors are listed here in an endnote.[1]

The major point, however, is not to find all the errors, but to consider why most people don't notice all of them, perhaps hardly any of them, on a first reading. What do you think? The primary reason seems to be this: we are reading for meaning, not to hunt for errors. We may even perceive the misspelled words as spelled correctly. Did you notice, on a first reading, that the word starting with *b* was actually *boot*, not *boat*? Or did you simply anticipate that the word would be *boat,* and consequently read it that way? Did you notice that *basement* was spelled *bastement* in the second line? (That's the error I added.) Or that the fifth word in line 3 was actually *though*, not *through?* Most people do not notice all of these errors. Nor do most of us notice that the beginning of the second sentence reads as follows: (When she had finished the the boat . . .). Did you notice the repetition of the word *the* this time?

While there has been some research suggesting that readers notice errors as they read, the nature of the altered texts has typically made the errors more obvious. What our little experiment and Gollasch's (1980) research suggests, however, is that we do not identify all the letters in a word before identifying a word, even if the word occurs in isolation. Indeed, we do not necessarily identify all the letters, period. What's even more surprising is that proficient readers, when they *do* perceive all the letters, may be determining the letters after they have identified the word.[2]

At first thought, such a statement may seem outrageous, but consider, for instance, the experimental results described in Chapter 3, in which readers could identify five four-letter words organized into a sentence in about the same time as they could recognize four or five letters from a string that that did not follow normal English spelling patterns (Cattell, 1947; reported in Huey, 1908/1968, pp. xvii, 69–73, and F. Smith, 1971, p. 91). Sure, the research subjects could identify the letters in those four words, but they must not have identified the letters separately before identifying the words. Research studies like these help us understand what Kenneth Goodman means when he writes, "Vision and perception are two different phenomena." The eyes provide data from the external world, while the brain—more accurately, the mind—organizes, selects from, and perceives that data.

THE EYES AND THE BRAIN

The distinction between what the eyes do and what the brain does during reading is extremely important. I doubt, though, that "vision" is the best word to describe the role of the eyes, since that term is often associated with the creation of mental images—with what the brain does. Perhaps we might say that "sight" is what the eyes engage in. The eyes receive data from the external world; they mediate between the external world and the brain. But the eyes don't record entire images; rather, images are "perceptions" created by the brain. As psycholinguist Frank Smith has explained, "What goes into the open eyes is a diffuse and continual bombardment of electromagnetic radiation, minute waves of light energy that vary only in frequency, amplitude, and spatial and temporal patterning. The rays of light that impinge on the eye do not in themselves carry the color and form and texture and movement that we see." Rather, these are constructions of the brain (F. Smith, 1988, p. 68). So too in reading: the eyes receive waves of light energy that are transmitted to the brain as a series of neural impulses. Initially, the written symbols may be perceived as sets of bars, slits, edges, curves, angles and breaks (Gough, 1972, p. 332; see also F. Smith 1979, Chapters 8 and 9).

How do the eyes actually pick up these waves of light energy that are transformed into words? In 1879, the Frenchman Émile Javal discovered that the eyes move along a line of print with a series of jerky movements he called *saccades,* meaning 'jerks' (Huey, 1908/1968). There is no useful vision during the eye movements themselves (Dodge, 1900; Wolverton & Zola, 1983), as you can demonstrate by looking into a mirror with your head held still while moving your eyes from left to right between two imaginary points. As you will discover, you cannot see your eyes in motion. Neither can you read with your eyes in motion (I. Anderson & Dearborn, 1952, p. 101). The saccades, or eye movements, take up only a small fraction of total reading time—about 10% of the time in rapid reading and about 5% of the time in slow reading (I. Anderson & Dearborn, 1952, p. 107). The rest of the time is taken up by eye fixations, or pauses. It is during these fixations that the eyes receive the stimuli that the brain has directed them to attend to, the stimuli that are transformed into visual images in the brain. This process of selecting, organizing, and interpreting data picked up by the eyes is what is commonly called visual perception. We use our prior knowledge and experience to guide even the most elementary aspects of visual perception.

Thus when someone claims that skilled readers "perceive" most of the words in a text, such a statement (to the extent it is true) does not mean that the words were identified prior to interpreting the phrase in which they occur. Even if we "perceive" most of the letters in most of the words—if or when we've chosen to read more or less line-by-line (a topic to which we shall return)—this does not mean that the letters are perceived separately before the word is perceived. When we read for comprehension, it seems clear, in fact, that we do *not* first identify the smallest units of language, letters, and then work upwards.

A Few Terms Defined

1. *Sight:* What the eyes do, which is pick up data from the external world. The eyes mediate between the external world and the brain. The eyes themselves do not form the data into the images we perceive.

2. *Vision:* Sometimes used synonymously with *sight,* but can also refer to mental pictures. Therefore, we need to determine the meaning of *vision* from its context. Clearly in the opening quote from Goodman, *vision* meant essentially the same as *sight.*

3. *Visual perception:* The brain's perception of the data gleaned through the eyes. Though we commonly think of perception as what the eyes do, that's not accurate. Perception is not a passive act of receiving information through the eyes, but an active process of selecting what data to attend to, then organizing and interpreting that data as visual images. We may think of visual perception as a transaction between the brain and the external world. *In the case of reading, visual perception is a transaction or "dance" among the reader's brain and the external world of texts, print, and the people, situations, and other factors that affect the reading event. But it is the reader's brain that leads in this metaphorical dance.*

could
short
a! ·ut
voice
tr··st
s:·nrf
drunk
_.·ost
which
:tand

Figure 5.1 *Mutilated words.*

PARTS OF WORDS AT WORK

Various kinds of laboratory experiments make it abundantly clear that we do not need all the visual information normally available to us in order to identify familiar words. For example, you can probably read all or most of the words in Figure 5.1 fairly easily, though some are significantly mutilated by the omission of visual information. Furthermore, you may find that you have read each word more or less as a whole, without consciously identifying all the letters.[3]

Proficient readers automatically draw upon the most salient and useful visual cues. (The relevant meanings of salient are 'projecting beyond a line, surface, or level'; 'prominent'; 'standing out conspicuously.') Such visual cues enable us to identify familiar words at a glance. The following three activities are designed to help you determine which parts of words are especially useful and which are less useful in cueing the recognition of words. These informal "experiments" are highly unscientific. There has been no strict control over vocabulary or sentence length and structure, and, most important, the words are presented in context rather than in isolation. But these experiments are more fun and easier to carry out than more scientific kinds of experiments on isolated words, and in most cases the conclusions are likely to be the same.[4]

Activity 1

You can use a stopwatch, or a watch or clock with a second hand, to time yourself or someone else reading the following two sets of sentences, which constitute the beginning of a little story:

Vowels Absent

-nc-   -p-n   -   t-m-   th-r-   w-s   -   h-nds-m-   y- -ng   w-lf   n-m-d   L-b-.
L-b-   l-v-d   w-th   h-s   m-th-r   -nd   f-th-r   -t   th-   -dg-   -f   -   d- -p,
d-rk   w- -ds.   -v-r-   d- -   L-b-   w-nt   t-   h-nt   -t   th-   n-rth   -dg-   -f
th-   w- -ds,   n- -r   th-   l-ttl-   v-ll-g-   -f   C-l- -s.

Consonants Absent

-o-e-i-e-   a- -   -o-o   -ou- -   -i- -   -a-   a   -i-e-e-   o- -   -a- -e-   o-   -i-
-i-e,   -o- -i- -   i-   - -e   -ie- - -   -ea-   - -e   -oo- -   o-   -i- -i- -   -e- -ie-   i-
- - e   - -i- - e-.   A-   o- -e-   -i-e-,   -o-o   -i- - -   -e   -u- -y   e-ou- -   -o   -i- -
a   - -u- -,   -ui-y   - -i- -   - -a-   -a-   -i-o-eye-   i- -   -a-e- - -   a- -   - - -aye-
-oo   -a-   - -o-   -o-e.

After this experiment, it should be obvious that consonants are more important than vowels in cueing word recognition. This can be explained, at least in part, by two simple facts. First, there are considerably more consonants than vowels in English, and hence the consonants are more distinctive, more able to narrow down the number of possible alternatives that any given word could be. Second, consonants occur more frequently than vowels; that is, in most cases there are more consonants per word. Given these factors, it is hardly surprising to find that consonants are more useful in cueing word recognition. Indeed, written Arabic omits the vowels altogether, except in beginners' books (Gibson & Levin, 1975, p. 524).

Activity 2

This activity is related to the first. Again, time yourself or someone else reading the following two sets of sentences, a continuation of the story:

Bottoms Absent

One day as Lobo was skirting the edge of the forest he came upon a little girl in a red hood. Her cheeks were so rosy and her arms so nuday that Lobo knew she would be delicious. "Oh," she replied, "I'm taking this basket of goodies to my grandmother on the other side of the woods. Grandma isn't feeling very well."

Tops Absent

Lobo thought for a moment. He could hardly wait to devour this scrumptious child, but then again he was hungry enough to eat the grandmother too. "Which house does your grandmother live in?" asked the wolf. "In the house by the three big oak trees," said Red Riding Hood (for that is what she was called). "She lives there all by herself."

Which paragraph took longer to read? Which part seems to be more important in cueing word recognition: the tops of words, or the bottoms? Most people conclude that the tops are more important, and this is indeed what research suggests. If you have not already figured out why, then look at the following list of the letters in our alphabet. How many ascend above the top line? How many descend below the bottom line?

a b c d e f g h i j k l m n o p q r s t u v w x y z

As you can readily see, about twice as many letters ascend above the top line, making them visually more prominent. Note, too, that more than half of the consonants either ascend above the top line or descend below the bottom line, while none of the vowels do (with the exception of *y*, which is only sometimes a vowel). Hence, not only are consonants more numerous and more frequently occurring than vowels, but many are also more prominent visually.

Activity 3

Again, time yourself or someone else reading the following passages, in order to determine the relative importance of the beginnings, middles, and ends of words:

Middles Absent

"W-at   a   mar- - -ous   oppo- - -nity!"   th- - -ht   L-bo.   He   t-ld   t-e   c- -ld to   s-op   a-d   p-ck   fl- - -rs   f-r   h-r   gran- - -ther   on   t-e   w-y   th- - -gh t-e   w- -ds,   t-en   t-ok   o-f   on   a   s- -rt   c-t   t-at   o-ly   t-e   wo- -es k-ow   a- -ut.   S-on   he   ar- - -ed   at   t-e   grand- - -her's   co- - -ge.   "I-'s me,   Gr- - -ma,"   L-bo   s-id   in   a   t-ny   v- -ce,   as   he   kn- - -ed   on t-e   d-or.   He   pu- -ed   t-e   d- -r   o-en   a-d   w-nt   in.

Ends Absent

Lob-   wen-   strai- - -   to   th-   grandmoth- -'-   be-   an-   gobb- - -   he-   up.
He   donn- -   he-   ca-   an-   gow-   an-   clim- - -   int-   be-,   feel- - -   non-
to-   wel-   hims- - -.   By   th-   tim-   Litt- -   Re-   Ridi- -   Hoo-   ha-   arri- - -,
howe- - -,   he   ha-   overc- - -   hi-   atta- -   of   indigest- - -   and   wa-   rea- -
fo-   dess- - -.   He   answe- - -   Red'-   kno- -   in   an   ol-,   crack- -   voi- -:
"Com-   in,   dea-.   Jus-   com-   on   in."

Beginnings Absent

-obo   -as   so   - - -enous   -hat   he   - -dn't   -ait   -or   - -ttle   -ed   - -ding
-ood   to   -sk   -er   "- - -ndma"   -ow   -he   -as   or   -o   - -ing   -er   -he
- -sket   of   - - -dies.   He   - -rew   -ack   -he   - -vers,   - -mped   -ut   of   -ed,
-nd   -an   -ver   to   -he   - -ild.   -he   - - -eamed   -nd   -an,   -ut   it   -as
-oo   -ate.   -obo   - - -bled   -er   up.   - - -erwards   he   -at   by   -he   - - -eside
- - -king   - - -ndma's   -ipe,   - - -aming   of   - -icy   - -ttle   - -rls.

Once again, which set of sentences took longest to read? Which took the shortest? From this experiment, you have probably concluded that the beginnings of words are more important in word identification than the middles or the ends. This is also what the research suggests. Various kinds of research also clearly indicate that the ends are more important than the middles. (If your results suggested otherwise, it was probably due to the flaws in the design of this particular experiment.)

Again, we may ask why these results occur. First, it seems that the beginnings and ends of words are important just because they are visually prominent, being either preceded or followed by white space. Second, the beginnings of words are particularly important because we read the words of a text more or less from left to right. In addition, the beginnings of words are less predictable than the ends, and therefore more necessary. The ends of words are more predictable than the beginnings because they often consist of grammatical endings, many of which are predictable from context. Thus, endings are less important cues to word recognition than beginnings, because endings are more predictable. On the other hand, endings are more important than middles, partly because they often do carry grammatical information. (For a discussion of many of the experiments that give rise to such observations, see I. Anderson & Dearborn, 1952, Chapter 5.)

Children pay increasing attention to the beginnings and ends of words as they become more proficient at reading. In one study, for example, the spaces between words were filled in with a symbol created by superimposing an x on a c (see✗Spot✗run). Groups of children in the first and second grade read such a "filled" version of a story, as well as an "unfilled," or normal, version of a story. The filled version took significantly longer to read, but the difference was most noticeable for the better readers. The less proficient, slower readers were affected relatively little by the filled-in text (Hochberg, 1970, pp. 87–88). Since the poorer and slower readers were not much affected by the lack of spaces between words, it seems that these readers had not yet learned to pay particular attention to the beginnings and ends of words (see R. Brown, 1970, pp. 169–170). And this, in fact, might be one reason why these children *were* less proficient readers.

Parts of Words in Review

Clearly, we can recognize familiar words from only part of the visual information available to us. Which parts of words are particularly important in cueing word recognition? We have found that:

1. Consonants are more important than vowels.

2. Beginnings of words are more important than middles and ends, and ends are more important than middles.

3. Some people may be relatively nonproficient readers at least in part because they have not learned to attend particularly to the parts of words that provide the most useful information.

How We Perceive Words

As the foregoing discussion suggests, the brain does not just passively interpret the data relayed through the eyes. In fact, the brain is in large measure independent of the eye. In normal vision, the picture that the eye registers is upside down, but the brain rights it. And as Frank Smith observes,

> In a number of perceptual experiments, many men and animals have been fitted with special spectacles which completely distort the information received by the eye, switching top to bottom, or left to right, or distorting form or color. But within a very short while the brain "adapts" and the perceived world reverts to its normal appearance. No further distortion is perceived until the trick spectacles are removed, whereupon the "normal" pattern of stimulation produces a topsy-turvy percept which persists until the brain readapts. (F. Smith, 1971, p. 89; for more details, see Kohler, 1962).

The brain performs equally marvelous feats in normal reading.

We have seen that some visual cues are more important than others in cueing word recognition—namely, consonants and the beginnings of words (which are often consonantal). But are these the cues *actually* used the most in perceiving words? The answer seems to be yes and no.

Before further investigating how consonants and vowels contribute to word perception, let's deal with the widespread assumption that words are processed in serial fashion, letter-by-letter, from left to right.

Activity 1

First, try the following exercise on formulating phonics rules. In each of the words below, one letter is printed in italic boldface type. Determine how each italic boldface letter should be pronounced, and what part of the word signals the pronunciation of the italic boldface letter. In other words, try to formulate a rule for producing the correct pronunciation of the italic boldface letters. You will need at least one rule for each of the three sets.

Set A

hat	hate
hatter	hater
pet	Pete
petted	Peter
bit	bite
bitter	biting
mop	mope
mopping	moping
cut	cute
cutter	cuter

Set B

*w*rap	*w*ar
*w*ren	*w*et
*w*ring	*w*in
*w*rong	*w*on

Set C

*c*ar	*c*ent
*c*are	*c*ereal
*c*oat	*c*ite
*c*ough	*c*ity
*c*ube	*c*yclone
*c*ut	*c*yst

For the first column of words in Set A, you may have formulated a rule something like this: a vowel is short when it is followed by just a single consonant, or when it is followed by a double consonant plus an ending of some sort. For the second column of words in Set A, you may have formulated a rule something like the following: a vowel is long when it is followed by a silent *e*, or when it is followed by a single consonant plus an ending of some sort. Complicated, yes? The words in Set B should have been easier to deal with. You may have formulated a rather simple rule such as this: when a word begins with a *w* followed by an *r*, the *w* is not pronounced; otherwise, it is pronounced as a /w/. For the words in Set C, you might have formulated a rule something like this: when *c* is followed by *a*, *o*, or *u*, it is pronounced /k/; when *c* is followed by *e*, *i*, or *y*, it is pronounced /s/.

Doubtless these are not the only rules possible, nor are they necessarily the best rules. But note that in each case *the pronunciation of the italic boldface letter is determined not by what precedes, but by what follows*. We could not possibly pronounce the listed words correctly if we processed and pronounced them merely letter-by-letter, from left to right. Furthermore, most of these words are not exotic words that we encounter only once or twice in a lifetime; most are relatively common words that we encounter fairly often. As Venezky put it in *The Structure of English Orthography*, "A person who attempts to scan left to right, letter by letter, pronouncing as he goes, could not correctly read most English words" (1970b, p. 129).

Activity 2

Activity 1 leaves open the possibility that we might process each letter separately, even if not left to right. To test this possibility, try replicating the following experiment, from Edmund Huey's *The Psychology and Pedagogy of Reading* (1908/1968, p. 100). For this experiment, you will need either a stopwatch or a watch or clock with a second hand. Figure 5.2 contains a column of letters, a column of four-letter words, and a column of eight-letter words. Time yourself or someone else reading the column of letters as rapidly as possible, either simply identifying each letter mentally or pronouncing it aloud. Repeat the same procedure for the column of four-letter words and the column of eight-letter words.

Even though you may have stumbled over some unfamiliar words, you probably found that it did not take nearly four times as long to read the column of four-letter words as it took to read the column of single letters; nor, surely, did it take eight times as long to read the column of eight-letter words. Huey's four experimental subjects read the columns aloud, averaging 15.7 seconds for the isolated letters, 17.3 seconds for the four-letter words, and 19.6 seconds for the

y	pool	analysis
w	rugs	habitual
u	mark	occupied
s	send	inherent
q	list	probable
o	more	summoned
m	pick	devotion
k	stab	remarked
i	neck	overcome
g	your	resolute
e	dice	elements
c	font	conclude
a	earl	numbered
z	whit	struggle
x	ants	division
v	role	research
t	sink	original
r	rust	involved
p	ware	obstacle
n	fuss	relative
l	tick	physical
j	rasp	pastness
h	mold	lacteals
f	hive	sameness
d	four	distract

Figure 5.2   *Huey's list of letters and words.*

eight-letter words (Huey, 1908/1968, p. 101). When I first tried the experiment, I read the columns silently. It took me 7 seconds for the single letters, 7 seconds for the four-letter words, and almost 8 seconds for the eight-letter words.

Clearly, fluent readers do not process words letter-by-letter. Just as we do not comprehend sentences merely by combining the meanings of individual words, so we do not perceive words merely by combining the perceptions of individual letters.

Given the examples in the preceding discussion, it should not be surprising that words can be identified under conditions that make it impossible to identify individual letters. More than a century ago, Erdmann and Dodge (1898) determined: (1) that words can be recognized when lying too far from the eyes' fixation point to permit recognition of individual letters; (2) that words can be recognized when they are constructed of letters so small that the letters cannot be singly identified; and (3) that words can be recognized from distances at which the letters, exposed singly, cannot be recognized (see Huey, 1908/1968, pp. 73–74). It has also been found that words can be identified under lighting conditions that do not permit the identification of single letters.

In one experiment, even first graders could identify familiar three-letter words at lower light intensities than they needed for identifying single letters (see F. Smith, 1971, p. 141).

To get an idea of what these experiments are like, suppose that two letters are flashed upon a screen in front of you and that you are told these letters form an English word. Suppose too that you cannot identify either of the letters with certainty, but you can see enough features to determine that the first letter must be *a* or *e,* and the second letter must be *f* or *t.* Since this limits the possible combinations to *af, at, ef,* and *et,* you can readily identify the word as *at.* Because only one of the possible combinations forms a word in standard written English, you can identify the word without being able to identify either letter by itself (see F. Smith, 1979/1996, p. 125).

A similar thing happens when you play the travel game of locating first one letter of the alphabet and then the next on road signs as you travel down the highway. If you have ever played this game with a young child just learning to read, you may have realized that your tremendous advantage is the fact that you identify the *words* first, and then recognize the letter you are looking for. The child who knows letters of the alphabet but few words must, of course, look for the individual letters. Your ability to recognize whole words aids your perception of individual letters.

In a similar vein, some rather startling experiments indicate that a person can get some sense of a word's meaning without consciously being able to identify it. McKean (1985) mentions, for example, the work of Anthony Marcel at Cambridge, England. Using a tachistoscope to flash words on a screen for an extremely brief period of time, Marcel noted that his volunteer readers were able to get some sense of the meaning of the word, even though they hadn't seen the word long enough to identify it. For example, if the word on the screen was *queen,* people would guess it as "king," or if the target word was *yellow* they would guess it as "blue." Odd as it sounds, the people in the experiment retained a subconscious impression of a word's meaning—not only without knowing its identity, but even when the visual exposure was so brief that they weren't sure they had seen any word at all. (See Marcel & Patterson, 1978). Recent studies of brain-damaged individuals confirm that a person can recognize some key features of a word's meaning while being totally unable to recall other key features that they "know" (Bishop, 1993).

At this point, we can see in more detail what it means to say that we bring meaning to the written page in order to get meaning from it. We bring not only our knowledge of the world and our intuitive knowledge of grammar, but even an internalized knowledge of letter and sound patterns. Consider, for a moment, the following list of words. Which ones look like English words? Which ones do not?

glung	rpet	cratn	drepm
tsont	dremp	terp	stont
pret	lgung	crant	tepr

Without ever having been told, we know what is possible in English, and what is not. For example, we know that *glung* and *dremp* are possible, while *lgung* and *drepm* are not (see Gibson, Shurcliff, & Yonas, 1970, p. 59; Gibson, 1972, p. 13). Just as we do not consciously think of how sentences are structured as we speak, so we do not consciously think of how words are structured as we listen or read. Nevertheless, even before learning to read, we have acquired an internalized knowledge of sound patterns, and we quickly begin to acquire a similar internalized knowledge of letter patterns. Thus, our internalized knowledge of letter patterns enables us to identify words from only a fraction of the visual information available.

We use a minimal amount of visual information and a maximal amount of nonvisual information. The brain does not passively interpret data gathered by the eyes. On the contrary, the brain tells the eyes what data to gather, which parts of words to attend to. As stated earlier, visual perception is in fact more a function of the brain than of the eye.

An anecdote may help to solidify this point. Bateman reports the following (1974, p. 662):

At a meeting several years ago, an opthalmologist presented a paper on the eye and reading. After the introduction he came to the podium and stood silently for a moment. Slowly and deliberately he delivered his paper—"Ladies and gentlemen, there are no important relationships between the eye and reading. Thank you." And he returned to his seat.

An exaggeration, certainly, but one containing much truth.

Syllables: A Perceptually Salient Unit

In reading the eight-letter words from Huey's lists, perhaps you had some sense of dealing with the words in syllables. And in fact, some of the research on word perception suggests that this is how proficient readers accomplish the visual part of word processing: by drawing upon part of the visual information within chunks of letters that more or less correspond to syllables (Mewhort & Campbell, 1981, cited in Adams, 1990). Perhaps this relationship between the visual and spoken chunks we call syllables partially accounts for the fact that proficient readers typically "hear" what they read in their mind's ear (Perfetti, Bell, & Delaney, 1988; Tanenhaus, Flanigan, & Seidenberg, 1980), even though—as we saw in Chapter 4—mentally hearing or actually saying a word does not occur before the understanding of its meaning (Spoehr, 1981).

Research demonstrates that it is much easier for young children to identify spoken syllables than to abstract either words or sounds (phonemes) from the stream of speech (see Adams, 1990, pp. 296–300). This is not surprising, for a syllable is the smallest unit that can be spoken in isolation. Even when we say the names of letters, we necessarily say them as syllables. For example, we cannot pronounce letters like *b* without adding a vowel sound to them ("buh").

A syllable may be said to consist of two major parts, the *onset* and the *rime*. The *rime* consists of a vowel, which is the obligatory part of a syllable, plus any consonants that might follow it. Thus, the following words consist of one syllable, and that syllable has just the rime: *a, I, am, and, earn, up.* Many syllables, of course, have an onset as well. The *onset* consists of any consonants that precede the vowel: *ma, pi, Sam, hand, learn,* and *cup.* For a more detailed discussion of onsets and rimes, see Chapter 13, which also refers to studies showing that children demonstrate awareness of onsets and rimes before they can demonstrate awareness of phonemes—the "separate" sounds—within words (see, for example, the excellent summary of research in Chapters 1–4 of Goswami & Bryant, 1990).

But, back to syllables: does the fact that the only obligatory part of a syllable is a vowel *sound* (as in *a, eye, I*) mean that the vowels are the most important parts of words, after all? No, not for most words. From one perspective, vowels are the least useful parts of written words, because they carry much less visual information. Adams (1990) cites an interesting study in which Miller and Friedman (1957) found that when all the vowels were removed from printed texts, adults could reconstruct the texts almost perfectly:

```
Ths   dmnstrts   tht   txt   s   stll   mr   r   lss   lgble
whn   th   vwls   hv   bn   rmvd.
```

On the other hand, when a similar proportion of randomly selected letters had been removed, readers reconstructed the text with only 20% accuracy (that was the median, not the mean):

```
Tis   dosts   that   ex   bome   elatey   ilgi   when   a   pabl
ropoon   f   rndoml   lec   etters   a   ben   eov.[5]
```

The random omission of letters may be more confusing than the systematic omission of certain kinds of letters. However, we have already seen for ourselves the difficulty of reconstructing text with all the consonants systematically omitted, which shows that consonants are more important.

On the one hand, then, the vowels are visually not very distinctive or prominent, and therefore the *specific* visual information they carry is not very helpful in identifying words. They become even less necessary when prior knowledge and context can be used along with consonants, as in normal reading. And yet, vowels seem to attract consonants to them (particularly the preceding consonants), and thus they help us group letters into visual patterns that correspond roughly to syllables. The vowel letters seem to pull consonants to them to create visually salient patterns—that is visually prominent patterns—that we can readily recognize. Perhaps, as Marilyn Adams suggests, the most useful function of vowels is simply to *be there* (Adams, 1990, pp. 118–121, 219).

A quick caveat is in order, though. When we read, it surely is not important that we chunk words into syllables as defined by the dictionary or by linguists; the important thing is to cluster letters into visually identifiable chunks, whatever those may be. Thus, it's not really important whether we see *medical* as *me-di-cal* or *med-i-cal, elephant* as *el-e-phant* or *ele-phant, crumple* as *crum-ple* or *crump-le.* The point is that the chunks are ones we recognize at a glance.

MORE ON READING BY ANALOGY

The following informal experiment should help demonstrate how we chunk letters into syllables and other recognizable patterns. Read the following paragraph aloud, as smoothly as possible:

> Corandic is an emurient grof with many fribs; it granks from corite, an olg which cargs like lange. Corite grinkles several other tarances, which garkers excarp by glarcking the corite and starping it in tranker-clarped storbs. The tarances starp a chark, which is exparged with worters, branking a slorp. This slorp is garped through several other coruscs, finally frasting a pragety, blickant crankle: coranda. Coranda is a cargurt, grinkling corandic and borigen. The corandic is nacerated from the borigen by means of loracity. Thus garkers finally thrap a glick, bracht, glupous grapant, corandic, which granks in many starps.

You were no doubt able to pronounce most of the words in the paragraph. But did you *consciously* apply any phonics rules (rules for relating letters to sounds)? If so, which ones? If not, how did you know or decide how to pronounce the words? Once having recovered from the shock of seeing so many nonwords, most people are able to read the paragraph rather well, and without consciously applying many (if any) phonics rules. They have simply internalized enough knowledge of spelling-sound correspondences to be able to pronounce most of the words with little trouble. In fact, I have found that most adult readers who once had phonics instruction cannot verbalize many (if any) of the rules, whereas most adult readers who have never had phonics instruction can apply phonics rules anyway.

In effect, what we are doing is reading words and their syllables *by analogy* with familiar words and word parts, as we did in Chapter 3 with the pseudowords *ricaning, vernalit, moissant, pokerson,* and *favorial.* We scarcely even become conscious of reading new print words by analogy, except perhaps where there is more than one model for us to draw upon. Shall we pronounce *lange* like the *lang-* part of *language,* or shall we draw upon some word like *range* or *orange* for the rime part of the syllable? Subconsciously we recognize that there is more than one possible model, and we tend to hesitate, even in a mostly fluent rendition of the passage. Such conflicting analogies may also cause problems with a few of the words in the "blonke" passage in Chapter 2.

The fact that we can read most of these nonsense words fluently without resorting to phonics rules strongly suggests what research demonstrates: that proficient readers seem to process unfamiliar words by analogy with familiar letter patterns, and to do so in syllables and/or smaller units like onsets and rimes (Glushko, 1979; Lenel & Cantor, 1981; Bradley & Bryant, 1983, 1985; Perfetti, 1985; Stanovich, 1984; Gunning, 1988, 1995; Treiman & Chafetz, 1987; Goswami, 1986, 1988; Kirtley, Bryant, MacLean, & Bradley, 1989; Wise, Olson, & Treiman, 1990; Haskell et al., 1992). This observation lends further support to what we have already seen: that we draw upon internalized patterns of letter and letter-sound relations to minimize the use of visual information as we read.

Some Key Terms

Syllable: The largest sound unit within a word. By definition, a syllable contains a vowel sound as its nucleus. It may or may not have consonant sounds. Examples: *I, a, eye* are all one-syllable words that have no consonant sounds. In contrast, the one-syllable words *use, cake, church, string, them, drip,* and *park* all have one or more consonant sounds in addition to the vowel.

Rime: The vowel of a syllable, plus any consonants that may optionally follow the vowel. Examples from the one-syllable words above: *I, a,* and *eye* have a vowel sound but no following consonant sounds. The rimes in the other one-syllable words are represented by the following letters: *-ake,* in *cake; -urch,* in *church; -ing,* in *string; -em,* in *them; -ip,* in *drip; -ark,* in *park*. Notice, however, that in most of these instances, there are more letters than there are sounds in the rime.

Onset: Any consonant sound or sounds that may, optionally, occur before the vowel in a syllable.

Decoding: The ability to sound out words. Sometimes *decoding* is used to mean the identification of words by whatever means—that is, not limited to sounding out.

Phonics: Letter-sound relationships, and the related skills used in analyzing words into phonemes or larger units and blending them to form recognizable words. Some researchers define phonics as *teaching* letter-sound relationships, or teaching relationships between the spelling and sound systems in a language.

Phonics knowledge: A knowledge of letter-sound relationships, whether explicit (conscious) or implicit (functional knowledge that is not conscious).

Children, too, read new print words (words new to them in print) by analogy with the parts of words they already can identify in print. Gunning (1995) describes several studies wherein children and adults used pronounceable word parts to decode words. Furthermore, several studies demonstrate that children can use onset and rime chunks to pronounce new print words before they are able to identify single sounds, known as phonemes (Moustafa, 1990, 1995; Goswami, 1986, 1988; Wagner, Torgeson, & Rashotte, 1994; Peterson & Haines, 1992; Tunmer & Nesdale, 1985; Wylie & Durrell, 1970; see discussion in Moustafa, 1997, Chapter 5). Moustafa's (1990) research, discussed more fully in Chapter 13, is particularly of interest. Working with seventy-five children in their last six weeks of first grade, she assessed children's knowledge of common words having an onset or rime that was included in the uncommon words (real or "pseudowords") that she asked them to read. ("Pseudowords" are also called *nonsense words* or *novel words*.) Moustafa also assessed the children's ability to identify the separate sounds (phonemes) associated with the letters in these uncommon words. She writes:

> While the children's knowledge of the common words accounted for 95 percent of the unusual words they were able to pronounce, the children's knowledge of letter-phoneme correspondences accounted for only 64 percent of the unusual words they were able to pronounce. That is, 36 percent of the time the children were able to correctly identify an unusual word, they could not correctly identify the sounds of all the letters and digraphs that constituted the word. For example, many children who correctly pronounced *rue* also correctly pronounced both *red* and *blue* but told me that *r* was /r/, and *ue* was /u/ and /e/. (1997, p. 47)

In other words, it appears that children use their knowledge of letter patterns that correspond with onset-rime chunks more than their knowledge of single letter-sound relationships to read unfamiliar print words. Moustafa's (1990) study provides further evidence that children read new print words by analogy with parts of known words, and that they do so before they can accurately segment words into phonemes. These parts or "chunks" of words are typically syllables, onsets and rimes, or other pronounceable chunks (Gunning, 1985).

THE ROLE OF PHONICS RULES IN THE READING PROCESS

Clearly phonics patterns—that is, letter-sound patterns—are crucial if we are reading a text in normal print, rather than Braille. But what role do phonics "rules" play in the reading process? One is tempted to simply say "little or none" and leave it at that.

Your own experience reading the "blonke" and "corandic" passages surely led you to realize that adults don't often consciously apply phonics "rules" as they read. Neither do children: they, too, read new print words by analogy with known words or word parts, as just discussed. So demonstrating common onset and rime patterns seems much more useful than teaching phonics rules and then expecting children to apply them consciously and deliberately. Indeed, one of my son's primary-grade teachers taught phonics rules but then advised the children, "Just sound it out the best you can."

Another problem with teaching phonics rules is that the often-taught rules frequently don't apply to a high percentage of words. Take, for example, the oft-taught rule that "When two vowels go walking, the first one does the talking." Examples are *nail, bead, ceiling, pie, boat, suit.* But what about words like *said, head, neighbor, chief, cupboard,* and *build?* The "rule" holds about 45% of the time. Or take the silent *e* rule: "When a word ends in a vowel + consonant + *e,* the *e* is usually silent and the other vowel is long." Examples are *cake, late, scene, chime, bone, June.* But what about exceptions like *have, bare, come, move?* This rule holds about 63% of the time (Clymer, 1963). Of course the patterns themselves are no more consistent than the rules; see—and enjoy!—the poem in Figure 5.3. However, the unreliability of the rules calls into question the desirability of teaching them. We simply have to learn which way the different words are pronounced, and that can be facilitated by examining words with the same letter-sound pattern in sets together. As for the rules that *are* quite reliable (Clymer, 1963), there's no need to teach them; we can demonstrate the patterns without the rules, if that seems necessary for some children.

Clearly, however, these patterns are not simple. If our language were strictly phonetic as well as alphabetic, each distinctive sound would be represented by one consistent symbol, and vice versa: only one symbol would represent one distinctive sound. But one-to-one correspondence does not hold even at the subword level. Take, for instance, the following exceptions to the one-to-one principle:

There are several consonant digraphs, wherein two letters represent a single sound: *ch, sh, th* (which has two different sounds), *wh, gh, ph, ck, ng*

There are some consonants that have different pronunciations, depending upon what vowel follows:

- *c* is pronounced /k/ before *a, o, u,* but /s/ before *e, i, y*
- *g* is usually pronounced /g/ before *a, o, u,* but /j/ before *e, i, y* (some notable exceptions are *get, give, girl*)

There are some consonants that combine with vowels to produce different consonant sounds. For example:

- *t* joins with the *i* to become "sh" in *-tion* (*action, motion, nation,* etc.)
- *c* joins with the following *i* to become part of "sh" in *-cial* (*crucial, special,* etc.), in *-cian* (*musician, physician,* etc.), and in *-cious* (*atrocious, conscious,* etc.)
- *s* joins with the following *i* to become "zh" in *-sion* (*confusion, fusion,* etc.)

And so forth.

"Phonics Fun"

Let's see now: Where, oh where, to start?
Some say the head and some the heart.

Heart, as a maverick, rhymes with *hart.*
Head rhymes with *bed,* but not with *bead*—
And *lead* with either *dead* OR *deed.*
How spelling doth mislead: indeed!

We see the rule of silent *e*
In *plate* and *scene* and *bite* and *cove,*
But *come* rhymes not with *home* and *tome,*
Nor *move* with *love* and *shove,* or *stove,*
While *dove,* a word more versatile,
Can rhyme with either *love* OR *rove.*

A's not the same in *bat* and *bank,*
no matter what the books may say.
And *fat*'s not *fat* at all in *father,*
Nor *moth* in *mother, broth* in *brother*
Indeed, what rhymes with *father? Bother!*

A *cough* is not a *cough* in *hiccough*
Nor *-ough* the same in *tough* and *though.*
Though rhymes, in fact, with *slow* and *grow,*
And also rhymes with *no* and *know.*
Know rhymes with *hoe,* but not with *chow;*
But *bow* can rhyme with *no* OR *now.*

And then there's *route,* which rhymes with *snoot*—
But also rhymes with *snout* and *shout!*

A hundred rules or so will do
To account for *sue,* and *shoe, shoo*
For *flew* and *flue* and others *too.*
Dear me, 'tis enough to make me blue.
                              —Connie Weaver

Figure 5.3   *Phonics poem (Weaver, Gillmeister-Krause, & Vento-Zogby, 1996, p. T5.1).*

This list comes nowhere close to illustrating all the possible pronunciations of the consonants—and the possibilities are far more numerous for vowels.

In short, the conditions governing spelling-sound correspondences are often far more complex than is generally recognized (Venezky, 1967, 1970a, 1970b). Mapping the spelling-sound relationships in a good majority (80 to 90%) of English words—that is, ignoring true exceptions—has demonstrated that hundreds of correspondences are involved (Hanna et al., 1966, as cited in Adams, 1990, p. 242). Nor is this complexity confined to words that are used primarily by adults rather than children. In one of the more extensive studies, Berdiansky and her associates tried to establish a set of rules to account for the spelling-sound correspondences in more than six thousand one-syllable and two-syllable words among those in the comprehension vocabularies of six- to nine-year-olds. The researchers discovered that their 6,092 words involved 211 separate spelling-sound correspondences—that is, 211 correspondences between a letter and a sound, or between two letters functioning together (like *qu* or the digraphs above) and a sound. Of these 211 correspondences, 166 occurred in at least ten words out of the set of 6,092 different words, while 45 of the correspondences occurred in fewer than ten words (Berdiansky, Cronnell, & Koehler, 1969, p. 11; see F. Smith, 1979/1996, pp. 139–140). Thus, while it may be said that about 80 to 90% of English words are regular, in that they follow a recognizable pattern, hundreds of patterns are involved (Hannah et al., 1966).

Research such as this should certainly convince us of the ridiculousness of Rudolph Flesch's simple prescription: "Reading means getting meaning from certain combinations of letters. Teach the child what each letter stands for and he can read" (Flesch, 1955, p. 10). In fact, as my friend Bonnie Regelman has pointed out to me, Johnny could not even read the print on the cover of Flesch's *Why Johnny Can't Read* (1955) by using phonics rules alone! Nor could Johnny read the vast majority of the 150 most common words in schoolbook English (Adams, 1990, p. 273).

So much for the oft-asserted opinion that we should teach phonics so that children will learn to spell correctly.

Furthermore, sound-to-spelling patterns are not consistent or predictable with much precision, either. For example, applying the rules of Berdiansky and her associates in reverse, Cronnell found that they generated correct sound-to-spelling translations for fewer than half the words in his corpus (Cronnell, 1970, as cited in Adams, 1990). Furthermore, using the 300 rules developed by Hanna and her colleagues (Hanna et al., 1966), fewer than 50% of the 17,000 words in their corpus would be spelled correctly. No wonder that, as Adams notes, "in a spelling bee between fourth graders and a computer that had been programmed with these rules, the fourth graders handily won out" (Simon & Simon, 1973, cited in Desberg, Elliott, & Marsh, 1980; Adams, 1990, p. 390). So much for the oft-asserted opinion that we should teach phonics so that children will learn to spell correctly. When we invite children to spell the sounds they hear in words, this is only a stepping-stone to conventional spelling.

Neither phonics terms nor rules for pronouncing parts of words are particularly useful when reading.

Most children cannot remember abstract phonics terms and rules, yet they can apply such rules unconsciously in their reading. Marilyn Adams has expressed it this way: "For neither the expert nor the novice can rote knowledge of an abstract rule, in and of itself, make any difference" (1990, p. 271). Tovey explored the utility of phonics-related terms in a study of children from grades 2 to 6, with five children from each grade. Though their teachers indicated that the children had learned terms like *consonant, consonant blend, consonant digraph, vowel, long vowel, short vowel, vowel digraph,* and *diphthong,* the children's responses suggested otherwise. The only term acceptably defined by over half of the children was *silent letter.* More than half of the terms were acceptably defined by only 20% or fewer children.

The time spent on learning phonics terms would be better spent reading, which, among other benefits, would give children the opportunity to read more and more words by analogy with the parts of words they already know, to come to recognize many of these words automatically after several exposures, and to internalize more and more of the frequently occurring letter-sound patterns in our language.

Interestingly, Tovey notes that second graders produced only two acceptable responses to questions about terms, and that sixth graders seemed relatively less able to deal with phonics terms than children in grades 3 through 5—probably, I would assume, because upper elementary students have not traditionally received phonics instruction. However, all the children did much better on a phonics test that required them to pronounce nonsense words and to deal with the kinds of elements listed above (plus others) in reading actual text. On this test, all the scores were 55% or above, with the percentage rising steadily from 55% at grade 2 to 79% at grade 6 (fourth graders broke the gradually rising pattern temporarily with 83%). The children were able to make use of phonics knowledge that they were not conscious of, that they could not verbalize. Tovey (1980) concludes: "Instruction which requires children to deal constantly with the abstract or technical language related to phonics does not warrant the time and effort often expended. This time might better be spent reading" (p. 437), which, among other benefits, would give children the opportunity to read more and more words by analogy with the parts of words they already know, to come to recognize many of these words automatically after several exposures, and to internalize more and more of the frequently occurring letter-sound patterns in our language.

In short, neither phonics terms nor rules for pronouncing parts of words are particularly useful when reading. We shall see in Chapter 14, however, some ways of helping children internalize letter-sound relationships and patterns.

WORD PARTS AND WORD PERCEPTION IN REVIEW

Drawing mostly upon the foregoing activities and the research from which they derived, we can articulate several generalizations about word recognition in fluent reading:

- We do not simply process a word from left to right.
- We do not separately identify each of the letters in a word prior to identifying the word itself.
- We apparently process words in letter chunks, typically syllables and/or onsets and rimes, selectively using only part of the visual information available to us. The consonants are most visually distinctive and thus provide the most information, but the vowels help by drawing the consonants into syllables.
- Words can be identified when their constituent letters cannot be, or have not been, separately identified. Indeed, the perception of words seems to precede the perception of individual letters in proficient reading.
- If proficient readers typically "see" the individual letters in a word (Rayner & Pollatsek, 1989), this is not because they need or use all the letters or all the visual information to identify words. The brain constructs the letters from the bars, slits, lines, curves, and such perceived by the eye. Thus, in this sense, *see* is being used to describe a mental act.
- Both adults and children decode unfamiliar words by analogy with familiar words and word parts, particularly syllables and the units within them, onsets and rimes.

Notice that for the purposes of this discussion, we are considering the perception of words in isolation, or as if the words occurred in isolation. We have already seen, both in Chapters 3 and 4 and in some of our activities here, that proficient readers automatically draw upon prior knowledge and context as they read normal text, making word perception even more of a top-down process and further reducing the need for visual information during normal reading.

We shall see in the next section of this chapter that the notion of word perception as partly a top-down process is not universally accepted, though it is strongly supported by decades of miscue research and more than a century's research on word and letter perception and processing.

Eye Movement and Eye Fixation Studies and the Perception of Words

In the last decade or so, it has been popular to claim that readers fixate on or at least process every word, or nearly every word, as they read. Some researchers who have cited research on eye fixations in support of this claim have also said that readers process each letter. Such statements of these researchers, and the propulsion of their claims into the public and political arena, have seemed to provide justification for a proliferation of programs for teaching letter-sound correspondences to children before they learn to read. As we shall see, however, such statements are sometimes inaccurate, and at best misleading to those who are not experts in the field of eye movement research.

Popular Claims by Oft-Cited Researchers

Paulson (2000, pp. 99–100, 115–116) and Duckett (2001, pp. 156–158) offer quotes from frequently cited researchers in which they make claims about eye fixations and/or word and letter processing, typically citing studies of eye movements/fixations. Quoting some of these statements myself, I shall then turn to contradictory statements and other evidence about skilled reading from eye fixation researchers themselves, and finally return to examine the following statements quoted from oft-cited researchers.

Linnea Ehri (1998) has written:

> Studies reveal that the eyes fixate on practically every word in a text, sometimes more than once (McConkie & Zola, 1981; Rayner & Pollatsek, 1989). Few words are skipped [not fixated], usually only high frequency words such as *the*. Even words that can be predicted with 100% accuracy are not skipped. This indicates that the eyes are picking up and processing each word when reading. (p. 10)

Marilyn Jager Adams (1999) has said:

> When reading for meaning it turns out that good readers do read word by word, left to right, and line by line. (Adams, in a report to the Arizona State Reading Success Task Force, September 9, 1999; as cited in Duckett, 2001, p. 156)

Also, Adams (1990) has written:

> Even if skilled readers look at every word, they might not process every word in equal detail. Do skilled readers sample the visual features of predictable text less thoroughly?
> No. Regardless of semantic, syntactic, or orthographic predictability, the eye seems to process individual letters. (Adams, 1990, p. 101; she cites McConkie & Zola, 1981)

In addition, Adams (1990) has written:

> . . . when reading for comprehension, skilled readers tend to look at each individual word and to process its component letters quite thoroughly. The other aspect of skilled readers' performance that is underscored by this [eye fixation] research is the remarkable ease and speed with which they achieve such letter-based word recognition, requiring only a few one-hundredths of a second to recognize each additional letter. (p. 102; Adams references Just & Carpenter, 1987)

I. Liberman and A. Liberman (1992) have written:

> The elegant studies of eye movements during reading by Rayner and his associates have shown conclusively that good readers read every word (Rayner & Pollatsek, 1989). It's only the poor readers who sample the print, picking out words here and there, and then guessing the rest. (p. 352)

Keith Stanovich (1992) has written:

> Furthermore, the study of the processing of visual information within a fixation has indicated that the visual array is rather completely processed during each fixation. It appears that visual features are not minimally sampled in order to confirm "hypotheses," but instead are rather exhaustively processed, even when the word is highly predictable. (p. 7)

Frank R. Vellutino (1991b) has written:

> With regard to the predictive role accorded context by whole-language advocates, the contrary evidence is also definitive. For example, it is known from eye movement [studies] (Just and Carpenter, 1987; Rayner and Pollatsek, 1989) that, barring very high frequency words such as *and*, *the*, and *of*, skilled readers process virtually all of the words encountered in connected text and typically all of the letters in these words. (p. 438)

Unfortunately, most people are likely to draw some very inaccurate conclusions from such statements, especially when they are taken together. Most people are likely to assume that good readers identify individual letters before identifying words, that they identify words without using context, and that they identify all the words in a text accurately and rapidly. Research on letter and word perception and identification (for example, that cited in Chapter 3 and previously in this chapter) and miscue research (for example, K. Goodman & Burke, 1973; and studies annotated in Brown, Goodman, & Marek, 1996) together demonstrate the falsity of such assumptions. But these assumptions are also contradicted by studies of eye fixations and eye movements themselves.

Eye Fixation Research

Eye fixation researchers themselves make some rather different observations and generalizations from the research:

> Rayner (1997) writes: "... at least 20% to 30% of the words in text are skipped altogether [that is, not fixated upon]" (p. 319).

> Just and Carpenter (1987) write: "... about 68% of the words [in their study] are fixated" (p. 37).

> Hogaboam (1983) writes: "In fact, in the present study about 40% of the words were skipped [not fixated on]" (p. 160).

These studies, and indeed all the eye movement and fixation studies I have ever read about, show quite clearly that skilled readers do not *focus* on every word. It seems clear, then, that claims like Ehri's (1998), about skilled readers fixating on "practically every word," are simply inaccurate. Even the first-grade readers in Duckett's (2001) study did not fixate on all the words: their individual rates of non-fixation varied from 9 to 34% of the words in the text (p. 235).

Studies showing that short words can be read as rapidly or almost as rapidly as individual letters also suggest that statements like "the eye seems to process individual letters" (Adams, 1990, p. 101) are also inaccurate (Huey, 1908/1968). The *brain* may indeed be able to identify the letters *after* the word has been identified, but there is ample evidence that identifying the individual letters does not come first (see also the beginning of Chapter 3). The fact that letter perception is a function of the brain rather than the eye explains why, during an eye fixation of about one-fourth second, we can identify about four or five unrelated letters, or about ten or twelve letters organized into two or three related words, or about twenty to twenty-five letters organized into a sequence of four or five unrelated words (F. Smith, 1973, p. 56; 1975, p. 58). Once we have identified the words we can then determine the letters, but that's a function of the brain, not the eyes themselves. Generally speaking, eye fixation research does not demonstrate that letters are identified before words in normal reading. Indeed, it suggests just the opposite.

Various eye fixation studies also have found that context plays a role in determining the location and/or duration of eye fixations, and consequently in the perception and identification of words. During an eye fixation, the eye actually has access to three viewing regions. The central region, the one we think of as being in clear focus, is the *foveal* region; six to eight letters are typically in focus during reading, with average size print. The region around the foveal region is the *parafoveal* region, which extends the visual field to about fifteen to twenty letters, though letters in the parafoveal region are not as clearly seen. Beyond the parafoveal region is *peripheral vision* (Rayner & Sereno, 1994). The parafoveal region, in particular, may provide contextual information that readers draw upon in directing their eyes where to focus next.

Furthermore, studies of eye movements and fixations show just the opposite of what is claimed in some of the quotes in the preceding section. Instead of showing that syntactic and semantic context play no role in the identification of words, they show that context *does* play a role (see summary by Paulson & Goodman, 1998):

- O'Regan's (1979) study shows that sentence structure exerts some influence on eye movements and fixations—on the decisions the brain makes about what words to move to next and to fixate upon. Syntactic cues apparently enable readers to skip (not fixate upon) words that have been confirmed from the parafoveal region.

- In a study involving college students, content words were fixated upon more frequently than function words. Just and Carpenter found that readers fixated upon content words 83% of the time and function words 38% of the time (Carpenter & Just, 1983; Just & Carpenter, 1980). In his study with first graders, Duckett (2001) found that on average for all readers, 82% of non-fixated words were function words. These substantial differences suggest that the readers were using syntactic information as well as visual information from the parafoveal region to make decisions about where to fixate next.

- Underwood, Clewes, and Everatt (1990) conclude, from their research, essentially the same thing about semantic information: that readers must use semantic information from the parafoveal region to guide the eyes to their next fixation. Or as Paulson and Goodman (1998) express it, "This conclusion indicates that readers are able to sample semantic information from the parafoveal field, which enables them to use as textual cues the most informative part of a word—a good example of one of the numerous ways readers make efficient use of text" (section on "Eye movements and perception," tenth paragraph).

- A study by Rayner and Well (1996) found that words that were relatively predictable (highly or moderately constrained by context) required less fixation time than words that were less predictable (having low textual constraint). Furthermore, readers were more likely to fixate on the words that were less predictable (having either low or medium contextual constraint) than on words that were highly predictable (highly constrained by context). This suggests that predictability does play a role in the processing of words and texts.

- Balota, Pollatsek, and Rayner (1985) explored the influence of context and parafoveal information, concluding that "a strong context helps readers fill in information that is not totally available in their parafovea" (p. 374).

- Fisher and Shebilske (1985) concluded that their results "support the generality of the hypothesis that expectations based on contextual constraints can interact with parafoveal information to determine the guidance of fixations" (p. 154).

Together these research studies on eye movements and fixations, which mostly used different techniques from one another, point to the general conclusion that syntactic and semantic context play a significant role in the visual perception and identification of words.

Together these research studies on eye movements and fixations, which mostly used different techniques from one another, point to the general conclusion that syntactic and semantic context play a significant role in the visual perception and identification of words.

Various studies of eye movements and fixations *do* suggest that information from the parafoveal region is processed during reading, even though words in that part of the visual field may not be fixated upon. From that perspective, it may be true that skilled readers "read" most words and can even identify most of the letters in these words, but these identifications of words and letters are mental decisions about what the eyes have processed. Also, the fact that readers can identify whole words in about the same amount of time as individual letters (e.g., Huey, 1908/1968) suggests that the identification of the letters in a word comes *after* the identification of the word!

Dispelling Some Myths About Eye Fixations

Paulson (1999) identified some myths about eye fixations that are important to dispel. Some of these myths are refuted by studies discussed previously, and all of these myths are refuted by Paulson's 2000 and in-press studies and by Duckett's (2001) study. To avoid misinterpretation, I will preface each of these myths with a disclaimer based upon such research:

■ *It is not true*—indeed, it is far from being true—that readers fixate upon every word when they read. See the preceding discussion.

■ *It is not true* that readers' eyes move serially from word to word, left to right, line to line. For example, Rayner (1981) states that 15 to 20% of eye movements in reading are regressive.

■ *It is not true* that readers' fixations are all about the same duration.

■ *It is not true* that readers' oral reading miscues are caused by faulty eye movements like not fixating on the word in question, or not fixating on the word long enough.

With respect to the last two myths, the results of Paulson's (2000, & in press) and Duckett's (2001) studies are particularly interesting. Paulson (in press) found that when the college students in his study made substitutions, 75% of the words receiving substitutions were directly fixated before the miscue was produced, a percentage that is higher than the fixation percentage for all the words in the text—readers were more likely to fixate a substituted word than they were a word that was orally produced verbatim to the text. These were not short fixations; in fact, the durations of fixations on substituted words tended to be almost 25% longer than the overall average fixation duration. In Duckett's study with first graders, 94% of the time, all of these readers "fixated miscue words well beyond their personal average fixation duration prior to miscue production" (p. 237).

What are we to make, then, of statements like "Regardless of semantic, syntactic, or orthographic predictability, the eye seems to process individual letters" (Adams, 1999, p. 101)? Or what are we to make of Adams' reference to "the remarkable ease and speed with which they [skilled readers] achieve such letter-based word recognition, requiring only a few one-hundredths of a second to recognize each individual letter" (p. 102)? *If* Adams means to imply that in normal reading, individual letters are perceived before words or the frequently occurring letter chunks within words, then there is plenty of research evidence to indicate that she is in error. Definitely incorrect is Adams' (1999) statement that "When reading for meaning it turns out that good readers do read word by word, left to right, and line by line." Or at least this statement is wrong as it would likely be interpreted by most people.

With regard to good readers, research on eye movements and fixations confirms what we have seen from miscue research:

- Good readers do not read word-by-word if this means fixating on every word or reading every word as it is printed on the page.

- Good readers do not read word-by-word as if the words were in a list rather than in context; rather, they use context not only to perceive and identify words but to do so with slightly greater speed and fewer eye fixations.

- Good readers do not read strictly left to right, either, when reading for meaning; they often regress to correct, to repeat for confirmation, or just to reconsider the words and the meaning mentally. They may look ahead, too, to help them in identifying words or clarifying meaning.

Furthermore—an observation from everyday life—good readers do not read word-for-word or even line-by-line when they choose to read more rapidly than that, as many good readers do, especially when reading for their own pleasure and their own purposes—even when their purpose is to gain information.

Which parts of the quotes from Liberman and Liberman (1992), Stanovich (1992), and Vellutino (1991b) are most likely to be derivable from studies of eye movements and fixations, and which do not seem to be reasonable inferences, given that body of research and other research previously discussed in this text? Statements about the reader "processing" most words could be valid, if by "processing" the authors mean *perceiving* rather than fixating upon. Why? Because the brain can perceive words in parafoveal vision. Thus we can indeed perceive and identify most of the words, if we choose, and thereby identify most of the letters. Other statements, however, are not justified by the eye movement/fixation research or any other body of research.

It is demonstrably false that "it's only the poor readers who sample the print" (Liberman & Liberman, 1992, p. 352). Stanovich's related statement is interesting, for he says, "It appears that visual features are not minimally sampled to confirm 'hypotheses'" (1992, p. 7). This statement seems clearly disproven by research on word versus letter identification (see the beginning of Chapter 3). However, Stanovich continues in the same sentence to indicate that visual features "are rather exhaustively processed, even when the word is highly predictable," a statement that is true if "processed" means that various features within words—not necessarily letters—are picked up by the eyes *before* the words or chunks of letters are perceived and before words (much less the individual letters) are identified by the brain. Vellutino might be somewhat close to accurate when he states that skilled readers "process virtually all of the words encountered in connected text [barring very high frequency words] and typically all of the letters in these words" (1991b, p. 438). This is assuming, of course, that these skilled readers choose to read that way—an interesting assumption, since proficient readers, those who are effective and efficient at constructing meaning, do *not* necessarily read that way. But again we must emphasize that *processing* letters does not mean consciously identifying the individual letters, either before or after perceiving the word in which they occur.

Even if all these claims about readers and reading were entirely true, which miscue research shows they are not, they would not disprove—as Vellutino seems to have thought—the counterclaim that context plays a predictive role in reading. Ironically, Vellutino cites some of the same eye fixation researchers whose work *does* suggest that context plays such a role. For example, Balota, Pollatsek, and Rayner (1985) concluded that "the data imply that when the word is skipped, only the beginning two or three letters of the parafoveal word were actually identified.

Thus, on these occasions, a strong context helps readers to fill in information that is not totally available in their parafovea" (p. 374).

To conclude this section, let me simply say that eye movement and fixation research does not justify a part-to-whole model of reading. On the contrary, the body of such research supports a psycholinguistic, constructivist model of reading in which context plays a significant role in the mind's decisions about where to fixate the eyes as well as its perceptions of words and their meanings, and even the letters within words.

PROFICIENT READING: "FLOW" RATHER THAN "FLUENCY"

A 1997 study by Flurkey (1997, 1998) describes how reading rate varies within a text as readers use reading strategies in constructing meaning. His study challenges the popular notion that fluency is crucial for effective reading.

But let's consider first the claims about the importance of reading fluently. Traditionally, reading smoothly has been part of the concept of fluency, along with the idea that fluent readers read with expression. In the last decade or so, however, fluency has more and more been defined as identifying words automatically and rapidly. Stanovich (1991), for example, has written that "Cognitive psychologists who study reading conceive of reading fluency as the ability to recognize words rapidly and accurately" (p. 19; see also Adams, 1990). Fluency as automatic and rapid word identification has been claimed to be important by "skills" researchers, as I refer to them in Chapter 11. Such researchers typically try to isolate one factor that contributes to proficient reading—word identification, for example—and then use timed, standardized tests to determine the importance of that factor, or the effects of teaching that factor intensively. Such an assessment procedure naturally privileges those who can read rapidly, whether they do so by reading words fast or by skimming. Therefore, students who read more slowly and struggle to identify words will usually score lower on such timed tests—unless they play the multiple-guess game and win. How well or how much they are able to understand from their reading is not accurately measured by a timed assessment of any kind, much less a standardized test.

With a background in miscue analysis and the comment from Prisca Martens that readers read at different rates within different parts of the same text (e.g., Martens, Goodman, & Goodman, 1993), Flurkey (1997) decided to investigate how time intervals correlate with reading miscues and strategies, using readers of various ages. Discovering that reading rate varied among and within sentences where no miscues were produced, Flurkey also found that, in general, the amount of time that readers spent reading sentences in a connected text varied with the quality of the miscues that they produced. Take, for example, sentences in which high-quality substitutions were produced—substitutions that resulted in no loss of meaning. The reading rates for those sentences were generally higher than the rates for sentences with regressions and low-quality miscues. In fact, some sentences with high-quality miscues were read at higher rates than sentences with no miscues in them. These findings disprove the frequent suggestion that the production of miscues necessarily results in lower reading rates and a lack of "automaticity."

On the other hand, when the readers in Flurkey's study were attempting to solve syntactic and/or semantic problems that they encountered in reading a text, they did spend more time at the point of miscueing, even when they substituted a word for the word in the text. This disproves (as does Duckett's 2001 study) the frequent suggestion that readers make miscues because they don't examine the visual display adequately. Flurkey's study showed that the more the reader seemed to be focusing on constructing a meaningful text, as assessed by the nature and number of the miscue attempts in one location, the longer the time interval spent at that point in the text.

Flurkey (1997) found a greater variability of reading rate in a proficient seventh-grade reader, Kelly, than in an effective but not so efficient fourth-grade reader, Betsy. Figure 5.4 shows the difference in their words per minute across the successive sentences of entire texts, and

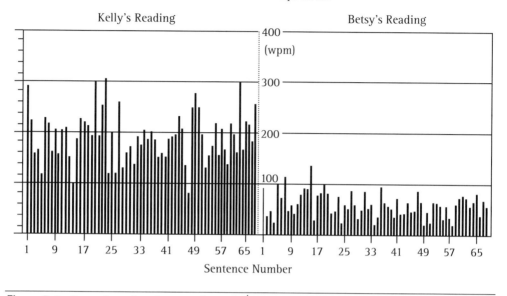

Comparison of Rates for Efficient and Effective Readings
for Successive Sentences Across Entire Text
Text: *The Man Who Kept House*

Figure 5.4 *Comparison of reading rates for proficient reader Kelly and effective reader Betsy (Flurkey, 1997, p. 224).*

Figure 5.5 shows the variability in rate correlated with "reading strategy use" for one of the sentences in Betsy's reading. Flurkey also examines reading rate in comparison with pauses and regressions, again showing how reading strategies correlate with reading rate.

We see from Flurkey's study that reading rate varies across a text, that pauses and regressions typically correlate with the use of strategies for constructing meaning, and that therefore, oral fluency performance is not an appropriate measure of underlying reading competence. In place of the concept of "fluency," Flurkey suggests that we might better investigate the "flow" of reading, including the ebb and flow of reading rate. He describes "flow" as "a reader's dynamic response to a text, of speeding up and slowing down, acceleration and deceleration across a text" (1997, p. 155). Important to his investigation are also the preceding decades of miscue research. "Each of a reader's unexpected responses (miscues) to a text tells us something of interest: the concern for meaning evident in the 'double backing' of simple regressions, self-corrections, or multiple attempts at producing a meaningful structure; the economy produced by omissions; the enrichment provided by meaningful insertions" (Flurkey, 1997, p. 154).

As more researchers use Flurkey's investigational techniques, we may even find that smooth, rapid, expressive reading is more likely to occur when a reader is *not* attending much to meaning, but rather trying to perform for an audience. Meanwhile, Flurkey's study contributes to the evidence against a skills view of reading, as does the eye fixation research of Paulson (1999), Duckett (2001), and others. This research adds to the picture developed from Chapter 2 onward and strongly supports the view that reading is a transactive, constructive, psycholinguistic process.

TOWARDS A MORE COMPLETE MODEL OF THE READING PROCESS

In Chapter 2, we developed a simple sociopsycholinguistic model of the reading process, emphasizing the fact that reading proceeds at least as much from whole to part as from part to

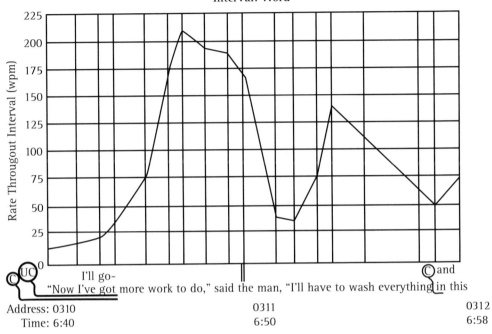

Figure 5.5   *Word interval rate and strategy use for one of Betsy's sentences (Flurkey, 1997, p. 211).*

whole, with readers' prior knowledge and experiences (schemas) and various pragmatic (social and situational) factors playing a role not only in the comprehension of texts but even in the identification of words. Chapter 3 deepened that discussion by focusing on various kinds of contexts in the reading process. Chapter 4 further elaborated on those insights by considering research that sheds light on the reading process through consideration of readers' miscues (e.g., K. Goodman, 1973; Brown, Goodman, & Marek, 1996). In this chapter, we have further expanded our perspective by examining research on word perception, focusing especially on the perception of words when reading connected text, and drawing especially from a range of studies on eye movements and fixations. Taken together, such research demonstrates that:

- The meanings of individual words contribute to the meaning of the evolving whole, yet the evolving whole also determines the appropriate meanings of individual words.
- Context reduces the amount of visual information that readers need in order to identify words and their constituent letters.
- The eye mediates between the external world and the brain; thus "sight," a sensory process, contributes to the brain's insights, in reading as well as otherwise (in sighted persons, of course).
- Visual processing, though, is a function of the brain. The brain tells the eyes where to look and what to look for; orchestrates the lines, curves, slits, and such that the eye gleans from written texts; and interprets the data as meanings, words, and letters. This, in turn, informs the next brain-eye-brain cycle.

- In proficient (effective and efficient) reading, context and the use of prior knowledge play a significant role.
- Unless they are skimming, proficient readers automatically "process" most of the words in a text visually, even though they may not fixate on nearly all of the words, and even though they may not read all of the words orally or to themselves exactly as the words were printed on the page.
- Proficient readers automatically use prior knowledge and context to construct meaning as they read, as well as to reduce their reliance on visual information. (The term *skilled readers,* used by researchers from the bottom-up tradition of reading research, does not mean the same as the term *proficient readers.* Readers labeled as "skilled" are apparently those who can read aloud smoothly and at a good pace, and/or readers who can score well on tests of isolated skills, including comprehension skills. "Skills researchers" (see Chapter 11) use measures of reading achievement to assess reading ability, with *reading achievement* being a code word for scores on standardized tests. Researchers who view reading as a transactional process use a variety of measures to assess readers' comprehending and understanding of texts, and they realize that any reader will demonstrate differing degrees of proficiency in reading different texts, or even different parts of the same text. See Chapter 11 for a more in-depth treatment of the differing research perspectives.)
- Proficient readers usually go directly from print to meaning, even if they afterwards "hear" the words in their mind's ear. Only occasionally do they recode written words into spoken words in order to get meaning. When they seem to have "seen" all the letters, they have actually constructed letters from incomplete data from the eyes, usually determining the words before determining the letters. Using prior knowledge of letters and letter patterns, the brain constructs a complete visual image from the partial data supplied by the eye, and may even use context and prior knowledge to construct an inaccurate complete image.
- Proficient readers do not need to use context to identify most of the words they read, but they use context and prior knowledge anyway. Their reading is thus more efficient and more reflective of effective reading strategies. They are "strategic" readers, not mere word-callers. (And their effective use of strategies may even cause reading miscues as they seek to construct meaning from texts.)
- Effective readers, both adults and children, tend to read new words by analogy with the parts of words they already can read. These parts or "chunks" may be syllables, onsets and rimes, or some other pronounceable chunks.
- Many not very efficient readers are nevertheless rather effective at constructing meaning, even though they have difficulty with word identification and especially using phonics skills to decode, and even though they identify considerably fewer than all the words. Their focus on meaning minimizes the effects of their problems with specific words and the fact that they are not fluent readers. (Standardized tests, of course, require reading either fluently or selectively, not slowly and haltingly as many of these readers do.)
- Thus, reading fluency is not necessary for constructing meaning from texts.
- Many less proficient readers do not succeed very well at constructing meaning from texts, even though—or because—they try hard to identify all the words. Their focus on identifying words diverts them from the goal of constructing meaning.
- Some less proficient readers may not be very effective (much less efficient) at constructing meaning or at getting the words, even though—or because—they try hard to sound out words they don't immediately recognize. They make inadequate use of other reading strategies and cues, such as prior knowledge and context.

■ Some less proficient readers may not succeed very well at getting the words of a text; even though—or because—they try to identify words on sight. They make inadequate use of other reading strategies and language cues, such as context and letter-sound patterns.

This list of points reflects research discussed in the preceding chapters and attempts to put into perspective the research on reading "skills" and thus on "skilled readers." Much of that research is summarized in detail by Adams (1990), succinctly by Stanovich (1991), and more recently in the National Reading Panel report (2000b). Even most of the complex models of reading still tend to assume that prior knowledge and context play no or a very little role in the automatic word identification of proficient readers. Taking into account a broader range of research, especially research that involves recording and analyzing miscues, shows quite a different picture. Such research is, of course, foundational in Kenneth Goodman's transactional, sociopsycholinguistic view of reading, but it is also important in the other models of reading and literacy processes found in the fourth edition of *Theoretical Models and Processes of Reading* (Ruddell, Ruddell, & Singer, 1994). There seems to be ample evidence from other experimental studies as well as from miscue research that proficient readers do use prior knowledge and context to construct meaning and also to reduce their reliance on visual information in identifying words.

Figure 5.6 is an attempt to capture the previously listed insights into the nature of the reading process, as discussed in this and the preceding chapters. I call this a redundancy model of reading because each kind of information and information processing facilitates the others; each is connected, directly or indirectly, to all the others, and they function together more or less simultaneously. For simplicity, I have chosen to include in Figure 5.6 just the kinds of information processed, and not to name the kinds of processing. *Schemas* encompass personal knowledge, experiences, and beliefs, including cultural and social background and experiences, plus the situational and social context. The use of schemas and context within a text to predict upcoming text facilitates the processing of words and the smaller units within them, and of course the triggering of relevant word meanings. The recognition of words leads to potential word meaning, while our schemas enable us to select contextually appropriate meanings. Recognition of words also leads to recognition of letter patterns and letters, even though letter recognition may be more subconscious than conscious among proficient readers; after all, they are concentrating on meaning, not on letter identification. The recognition of words also facilitates the development of schemas and the further use of both schemas and context in identifying subsequent words. Nevertheless, there is also reciprocal action, especially for emergent readers and for proficient readers encountering unfamiliar print words: that is, the processing of letters can trigger not only phonological and grapho/phonemic knowledge to pronounce unfamiliar print words, but—especially with the simultaneous use of context and schemas—the processing of letters can also trigger perception of the words, plus recollection or understanding of the appropriate meanings of words. And so forth. In other words, the processing systems each work in concert with and support of one another, which is why we say that readers need to "orchestrate" the various language cueing systems and sources of information to construct meaning from a text. This need becomes most obvious, perhaps, when visual processing (a mental act) does not lead to immediate word recognition. Then, if a word is in the person's listening vocabulary, the reader can get the word by processing the word grapho/phonemically, all the while automatically using context, schemas, and relevant knowledge of word meanings to help identify the word.

In a redundancy model of reading, one processor, one kind of processing, might be capable of a given task, such as identifying a word. But in the reading of normal texts, readers can use other routes to meaning—though unfortunately, this is not so possible when reading "decodable texts" like "Nan can fan Dan" (discussed in Chapter 11). Proficient readers typically use all routes to meaning, but alternative routes are particularly crucial for readers having difficulty with word recognition. The redundancy within the reading process as well as within texts can help us

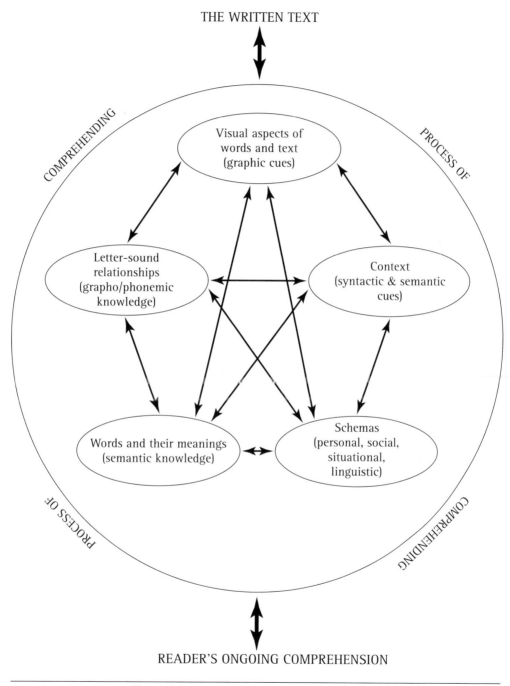

Figure 5.6   *Redundancy model of the reading process.*

understand how less proficient readers may construct meaning without necessarily identifying most of the words, and without being equally effective in using all kinds of language cues and strategies. "Less proficient" does not necessarily mean ineffective.

FOR FURTHER EXPLORATION

1. Most people think of phonics in connection with the teaching of letter-sound correspondences, relationships, and patterns. I use the term mostly this way, too, but sometimes refer to functional "phonics knowledge" or "phonics know-how" as something acquired and used by the reader, irrespective of whether, or how, letter-sound connections have been taught. Such phonics knowledge may well be unconscious rather than conscious. Indeed, it is such unconscious phonics knowledge that proficient readers use in processing letter patterns into their corresponding sound patterns.

   With that observation as background, consider the case of Jan, a fourth grader who was a good student and who considered herself a good reader, as did her teacher and her parents (Watson, 1996). Given a worksheet on the three main sounds of *ea*, Jan completed less than half of the seventy-two items, and missed nearly half of the thirty-one items she attempted. Examine this worksheet to try to determine why Jan might have had problems with it. Discuss this with others, if possible.

Jan's worksheet

The vowel digraph ea has three sounds: long e, short e, and long a. If a word is unfamiliar, try each of the three sounds. You should then recognize the word. Show the sound of ea on the line after each word. Show the sound of a short e with an unmarked e.

−14 (−41)   KEY: EACH ē   HEAD e   GREAT ā

1. TREATMENT ē	25. CREAKING ē	49. TREACHEROUS
2. STEADIER a ✓	26. JEALOUSY ✓	50. HEADQUARTERS
3. STEALTHY ✓	27. APPEAL e_ ✓	51. CLEANLINESS
4. TEAK ā ✓	28. DECREASE ē	52. MEANT
5. GREATEST ā	29. BEEFSTEAK e	53. UNDERNEATH
6. WREATH ē	30. PEASANT e	54. BREAKTHROUGH
7. DEALT e	31. PEACEABLE ✓	55. REPEAL
8. CONGEAL ē	32. REVEAL	56. STREAKED
9. SHEATH ✓	33. WEAPON	57. WEATHERED
10. CREASED ā ✓	34. CLEANSING	58. MEANTIME
11. MEASLES ē	35. BEAGLE	59. EAGERNESS
12. BEACON ā_ ✓	36. SNEAKERS	60. EAVES
13. BREAKNECK ā−	37. FEATHERY	61. THREATENED
14. HEATHEN e ·✓	38. FEAT	62. LEASED
15. HEAVENLY e	39. FLEA	63. LEASH
16. EASEL ē	40. MEANWHILE	64. BREAKWATER
17. SWEAT ē	41. CEASE	65. DEAFEN
18. UNHEALTHY e	42. HEAVILY	66. EASTERN
19. SEASONING ē	43. PEALED	67. RETREATING
20. CHESAPEAKE ✓	44. WEASEL	68. BLEACHERS
21. STREAMLINED ē	45. DREAD	69. DEATHLESS
22. TREACHERY ē ✓	46. EATABLE	70. HEADACHE
23. DEFEATED ē_	47. INCREASING	71. LEAKY
24. PHEASANTS ē ✓	48. DEALER	72. SNEAKY

Finish your Work! (−41)

Frustrated by her failure, Jan cried herself to sleep the night that the worksheet was returned. Equally frustrated and concerned, her parents consulted reading expert Dorothy Watson, who prepared for Jan a passage containing several words exemplifying four different *ea* sounds. Watson called this a "determining lesson" because it was designed to help the teacher determine whether or not Jan had particular problems with *ea* words within connected text. Here is the passage, with the *ea* in bold in those words, just for our convenience in locating them. Also, Jan's miscues are marked.

(R) When hunting season comes Uncle Bill is almost as eager

to head for the woods as Babe and Bingo are. Babe and Bingo

are beautiful beagles, but Uncle Bill calls them eager beavers

when it comes to pheasant hunting.

(C) re- When Uncle Bill releases those dogs from their steady

leash, you should see them streak across the meadow at (R) break-

neck speed. They can really work up a sweat!

Aunt Joan dreads hunting season. Babe and Bingo's

2 deefing / deef steady stream of barking is ~~deafening~~ and gives her headaches (a)

(C) b- She can't bear to think of one feather on a bird being harmed.

Uncle Bill gives the pheasants to a neighbor. Babe and Bingo

howl.

In context, Jan was able to read three of the words, or variants thereof, that she had not been able to get in isolation: *sweat, pheasants,* and *steadier.* In context, she had trouble with few of the *ea* words.

Does it seem to you that reading independently requires the ability to "do phonics" in isolation? Why or why not?

2. To test for yourself the assertion that grammatical endings are often predictable when a word occurs in context, try to provide the endings missing from the following sentences (the same sentences from which the consonants were earlier omitted). As before, the dash indicates an omitted letter:

Sometime- all Lobo could find was a wizen-- old farm-- and his wife, work--- in the field- near the wood- or pick--- berri-- in the thicket. At other time-, Lobo might be luck- enough to find a plump, juic- child that had disobey-- its parent- and stray-- too far from home.

Did you find it easy to provide the grammatical endings? What do you think of the notion that we should teach grammatical endings to children in order to help them identify words?

3. If you are not familiar with the symbols of the Initial Teaching Alphabet, try the following experiment (or try it with someone else who is not familiar with the ITA). First, try to decide what sounds are probably represented by the following symbols:

$$\text{æ} \quad \text{ʊ} \quad \text{ω} \quad \text{ie} \quad \text{th} \quad \text{ʒ} \quad \text{ʃh} \quad \text{dʒ} \quad \text{ŋ}$$

Now, simply read the paragraph below. This is an alternative conclusion to our story about the wolf and Red Riding Hood:

þe littl girl taested deliʃhous but loeboe hardly had tiem tω enjoi þe flaevor befoer somwun nakt at þe doer. þe wωlf skrambld bak intω bed and sed, "Cum on in. just oepen þe doer." in stroed a big wωdsman. hee recogniesd þe wωlf at wuns, and loeboe berly had tiem tω jump out ov bed and thrw a windoe befoer þe wωdsman's aks fel. tω this dae, loeboe has never gon bak tω þe south edʒ ov þe wωds. hee staes nir hoem, settliŋ for wizend oeld farmers and þer wievs.

What words caused particular difficulty, and why? On the whole, were you able to read the preceding paragraph fairly easily, even if you did not know what sound each of the symbols represents? If so, how were you able to read the passage without knowing all the letter-sound relationships?

4. To continue exploring the idea that the use of context can reduce our need for visual information during normal reading, have someone try to supply the words that are missing from the following, our story about the wolf and Red Riding Hood. The first letter of each missing word is provided as a clue, along with dashes to represent the missing letters:

Once upon a t--- there was a handsome y---- wolf named Lobo. Lobo l---- with his mother and f----- at the edge of a d---, dark woods. Every day L--- went to hunt at t-- north edge of the w----, near the little village o- Calais. Sometimes all Lobo c---- find was a wizened o-- farmer and his wife, w------ in the fields near t-- woods or picking berries i- the thicket. At other t----, Lobo might be lucky e----- to find a plump, j---- child that had disobeyed i-- parents and strayed too f-- from home.

One day a- Lobo was skirting the e--- of the forest, he c--- upon a little girl i- a red hood. Her c----- were so rosy and h-- arms so pudgy that L--- knew she would be d-------. "Where are you going, l----- girl?" he asked. "Oh," s-- replied, "I'm taking this b----- of goodies to my g---------- on the other side o- the woods. Grandma isn't f------ very well."

Lobo thought f-- a moment. He could h----- wait to devour this s---------- child, but then again h- was hungry enough to e-- the grandmother too. "Which h---- does your grandmother live i-?" asked the wolf. "In t-- house by the three b-- oak trees," said Red R----- Hood (for that is w--- she was called). "She l---- there all by herself."

"W- - - a marvelous opportunity!" thought L- - -. He told the child to stop and pick flowers f- - her grandmother on the w- - through the woods, then t- - - off on a short c- - that only the wolves k- - - about. Soon he arrived a- the grandmother's cottage. "It's m-, Grandma," Lobo said in a t- - - voice, as he knocked o- the door. He pulled t- - door open and went i-.

Lobo went straight to t- - grandmother's bed and gobbled h- - up. He donned her c- - and gown and climbed i- - - bed, feeling none too w- - - himself. By the time L- - - - - Red Riding Hood had a- - - - - -, however, he had overcome h- - attack of indigestion and w- - ready for dessert. He a- - - - - - - Red's knock in an o- - -, cracked voice: "Come in, d- - -. Just come on in."

L- - - was so ravenous that h- didn't wait for Little R- - Riding Hood to ask h- - "grandma" how she was o- to bring her the b- - - - - of goodies. He threw b- - - the covers, jumped out o- bed, and ran over t- the child. She screamed a- - ran, but it was t- - late. Lobo gobbled her u-. Afterwards he sat b- the fireside smoking grandma's p- - -, dreaming of juicy little g- - - -.

Which kinds of missing words were easier to supply: content words or function words? Was it possible to get the essential meaning even without being able to supply all the words?

5. If you know of a reader who is considered to be in need of phonics instruction, try developing a "determining lesson" similar to the one Dorothy Watson prepared for Jan (activity 1 in this section). Or simply have the reader read connected text and do a miscue analysis to determine if he or she is making adequate use of graphic cues and letter-sound knowledge in the context of meaningful reading. If the majority of the reader's miscues fit with the preceding context and also fit with the following context or are corrected, then adequate use is probably being made of letter cues and letter-sound knowledge.

6. If interested, you might examine Janet Norris' expansion of my redundancy model of reading (Norris, 1998). Labeling her expanded model as a "Constellation of perceptual and conceptual processes functioning interactively during reading," Norris writes: "Within the elaborated redundancy model, all of the processing units form a constellation, with each unit connected directly and/or indirectly to all of the others. Anything that happens at one point within the constellation has consequences at all other points (Rumelhart & McClelland, 1986; Seidenberg & McClelland, 1989; Weaver, 1994a [the second edition of this book]" (p. 517).

6 Understanding What Miscues Can Tell Us About Readers' Strategies

> Miscue analysis reveals the reader's strengths and weaknesses and provides a continuous window on the reading process.
>
> —Kenneth Goodman

Questions for Thought and Discussion

1. What is a reading miscue?
2. How can miscues lead to inferences about reading strategies? (See also Chapter 3, where language cues are related to reading strategies.)
3. What is a "proficient" reader? An "effective" reader? An "efficient" reader?
4. What are key major characteristics of "good" readers, those who are reasonably effective and possibly efficient as well?
5. How can miscues be marked on a copy of the selection?
6. How can we infer from a reader's miscues whether or not the reader tends to predict, or "think ahead" when reading?
7. Why is there no reason to be concerned about miscues that simply reflect the reader's immature speech or dialect, or the fact that the reader is a nonnative speaker of English and in the process of learning it? (See also Chapter 4.)
8. What kinds of miscue patterns and reading strategies suggest that a reader is monitoring his or her comprehension?
9. What is the nature of miscues that suggest nonefficient reading?
10. What is the nature of miscues that suggest noneffective reading?
11. What are some of the possible relationships, both effective and ineffective, between a reader's use of graphic cues and his or her use of syntactic and semantic cues?
12. What is characteristic of miscue analysis in the Goodman tradition?
13. What are some crucial ways that miscue analysis differs from running records?

In the 1960s, Kenneth Goodman chose the term *miscue* to refer to the unexpected responses of readers, both children and adults, as they read a text orally. In addition, the term *miscue* indicates that the reader has missed one or more language cues: graphic (word, letter pattern, and letter cues), syntactic (grammar cues), and/or semantic (meaning cues). (See Chapter 2 and Figure 8.4, p. 198 for clarification of grammatical cues in English.)

Of course readers make unexpected responses when reading silently, too: that is, they make responses in their head that differ from the words on the page. But it is only through oral reading that an observer can notice the miscues. Analysis of miscue patterns will reveal whether a reader's miscues are or are not typically productive, reflecting good reading strategies. Based on the patterns that are and aren't typical of the best readers—readers who are both effective and efficient—people often come to refer to some miscues as "good" miscues. However, the term *miscue* itself is neutral as to whether it is productive or nonproductive.

My aim in helping teachers understand and do miscue analysis is first to help them gain insight into the reading process. As Y. Goodman, Watson, and Burke express it (1987), "Once professionals concerned with reading have developed miscue analysis techniques they will never again listen to readers in the way they did in the past" (p. 4). This, then, is my first and primary aim: to help you gain appreciation for reading as a unique transaction between reader and text, to help you learn to perceive the productive reading strategies that often cause readers to make miscues, and to help you understand that there may or may not be a close correlation between miscues and comprehension. In order to gain such insights, it is important to begin by analyzing miscues in some detail; later, when you have learned to listen to readers in a new way, you can use simpler procedures for analyzing the reading strengths and needs of students with whom you work (see Chapter 7).

What We Can Learn by Analyzing Miscues

As we shall see, the actual miscues cannot "tell" us exactly what the reader was thinking or trying to do when he or she made them. Miscue analysis requires us to draw *inferences* about what the miscues and miscue patterns tell us. We can make our analysis more objective if, immediately after the reading or retelling, we invite the reader to listen to the tape recording of the reading with us and to speculate as to why he or she made certain miscues. Teachers should not worry about the fact that they have to draw inferences in miscue analysis, though. In so-called objective, machine-scored tests, everything but the machine scoring itself is subjective—the testmaker's thinking and the student's thinking, which do not necessarily match. Miscue analysis requires an understanding of the reading process and the ability to apply that knowledge and understanding to make inferences, to look for and see patterns, and to draw tentative conclusions to guide instruction. Miscue analysis is the product of a caring and informed teacher who tries hard to understand the reading of the students in his or her charge.

Getting Acquainted with Miscue Analysis

Brown, J., Goodman, K. S., & Mareck, A. M. (1996). *Studies in Miscue Analysis: An Annotated Bibliography.* Newark, DE: International Reading Association.

Goodman, Y. M., Watson, D. J., & Burke, C. L. (1987). *Reading Miscue Inventory: Alternative Procedures.* Katonah, NY: Richard C. Owen.

Wilde, S. (2000). *Miscue Analysis Made Easy: Building on Student Strengths.* Portsmouth, NH: Heinemann.

A brief review of key concepts is in order. With the first set of miscue studies, Goodman and his collaborators found the following to be key characteristics of good readers (as previously identified by "reading levels") (K. Goodman & Burke, 1973, p. 13):

- They read to construct meaning from texts, not just to identify words.
- They predict, or "think ahead," as they read.
- They monitor comprehension; that is, they are continually noticing whether what they've read makes sense or not. They also notice if something they've said doesn't sound grammatical.
- They typically try to solve the problem when something doesn't make sense or sound grammatical.

Such readers are *effective*: they succeed in constructing meaning from texts for which they have adequate background knowledge and language. Readers are *efficient*, too, if they can understand what they read without struggling again and again to sound out words that don't seem crucial to the meaning or to correct miscues that are completely appropriate in context; in short, readers are efficient if they don't waste time and effort in their quest for meaning. As Kenneth Goodman expressed it, readers are *proficient* if they are both effective and efficient. Often, I may use the more common but less precise description "good readers" to refer to readers who are at least reasonably effective in constructing meaning, and possibly efficient as well.

As we shall see, we can learn many things from analyzing a reader's miscues. This chapter's discussion focuses on miscues that reflect good predictions, miscues that reflect the reader's normal language patterns, and miscues that indicate the reader is monitoring comprehension. All of these are "good" kinds of miscues, the kinds of miscues made by readers identified as good by standard measures as well (K. Goodman & Burke, 1973). In addition, we will look at some miscues that reflect inadequate reading strategies.

This discussion is intended not only to help you understand miscues and what they can show us but to begin preparing you to analyze miscues yourself. First, however, you need to become familiar with the miscue markings used in this book.

MISCUE MARKINGS

For the most part, I use the symbols originally developed by Kenneth Goodman to mark miscues for analysis or discussion. A slant line indicates a line division in the text that the reader read.

Substitution

- "Blow your nose ~~into~~ the Kleenex."   [*with* written above *into*]

- On ~~sunny days~~, . . .   [*Sunday* written above *sunny days*]

Note that it is useful to draw a thin line through the word or words that the reader did *not* say. The substitution is simply written over the text.

One punctuation mark can also be substituted for another, as in the following example, where the reader made a period-like pause after "hand," to restructure the grammar after his previous miscue:

- "This here Muriel," said Hayes, with an oratorical wave   [a comma-like mark inserted after *here*]

of his hand, "~~has~~ got qualities."   [*. She's* written above *has*]

Fairly often, what traditionally would have been considered a substitution is more likely a prediction, an instance of "thinking ahead." When this seems to have been the case, the miscue should be indicated as an insertion, illustrated below.

Insertion

- "You should just suck cough drops."   [*on* inserted with caret before *cough*]

- The teacher told first grade how to do / the test.   [*the* inserted with caret before *grade*]

- "You bumped into me. Now you apologize."
  2 when the—
  1 when you —

- Once upon a time there lived a family of dragons.
  was

In the first two examples, the reader probably was looking ahead sufficiently to insert a word that would make the sentence sound more grammatical. In the last two examples, the reader seems to have made a prediction that amounts to an insertion. In the last sentence one might traditionally have considered "was" as a substitution for *there*, but I think the more likely explanation is that the reader predicted "was" before even noticing the word *there*. That is, the reader predicted the familiar structure "Once upon a time there was . . . ." For this reason, I would code "was" as an insertion.

Sometimes a reader makes a period-like stop where there was no punctuation mark in the text. This is indicated as an insertion:

- That first day, Mohamed felt quite grown-up and superior ⊙

  when he saw his mother and Asha carrying a heavy basket to the

  beach.

Omission

- "I will make you some (hot) tea."

- It sounded something⌐like that⊙
  that —

In the second example, the reader reversed *something like,* repeated it as if uncertain of what he had said, then said "that" as if he expected something to follow: "It sounded like something that—" We use the dash to indicate that the reader's intonation suggested the sentence was not yet complete and mark the period at the end as an omission, by circling it.

Partial

- Jenny's mother (sighed).
  2 sig—
  1 si—

- With these (reservations) out of the way . . .
  re—

Sometimes intonation suggests that the reader realizes he or she is uttering only part of a word. On the worksheet, use a hyphen to indicate what seems to be said as a partial word, judging by the intonation. If the reader does not "correct" the partial by saying the whole word accurately, there are two possibilities: (1) it will be sounded out or said inaccurately, in which case it is coded according to what is said; (2) it will be left as a partial, in which case we normally code it as an omission if it does not provide enough information for us to consider how it fits in context. Thus you might want to circle the partial to remind you to code it as an omission, as in the second example. In that example, the period must also be marked as an omission.

Reversal

- "No, no," Boris said.

    The reader said, "'No, no,' said Boris."

Correction

- I first saw Claribel when I ~~was~~ *saw* working in my office.

The underlining attached to the © indicates what part of the text was repeated as the reader made the correction.

Unsuccessful Attempt at Correction

- His mother . . . scrubbed and ~~pounded~~ *a putty / pondy* the clothes. . . .

Successive attempts at a word or phrase are numbered 1, 2, 3, and so forth. If a miscue is never corrected, the last unsuccessful attempt at correction is the miscue that's coded. In this case, that's the miscue numbered 2.

Abandoning a Correct Response

- He left home to make his ~~fortune~~ *future*.

    The reader first said "his fortune," then abandoned this response and said "his future."

Repetition

- "Why don't you do my work some day?"

When the reader repeats a word or phrase not for the purpose of correcting but apparently for the purpose of reflecting or of getting a running start on what comes next, this can be marked as above, with underlining to indicate what part was repeated. In analyzing miscues, such repetition is considered a strategy for dealing with text, not a problem.

Pause

- The ~~Mayor~~ *mother* said, "I will ask Mr. Pine . . ."

When the reader pauses significantly, this can be indicated with a P whose tail is inserted where the pause occurred. In this instance, the reader may have paused while processing what was coming next.

Sounding Out

- *br-oo-t*
  "I have ~~brought~~ you / some things to wear," he said.

- Harry was a white dog with black spots

  who liked everything,
  3 excapect
  2 exc-
  1 ex-
  ~~except~~ . . . getting a bath.

- *kert-anly*
  . . . a trick he ~~certainly~~ had never done before.

Whether the reader sounds out a word mostly letter-by-letter or in chunks, it is important to indicate how the word was sounded out, to give insight into the reader's strategies for reading. Sounding out may, of course, produce the word that was on the page, another word, or a nonword. This will affect how it is later coded.

Mumble

- *con* ~~~
  "Because of the boa ~~constrictor~~."

- *s-* ~~~
  "Yeah, and the chickens started ~~squawking~~ and flying around."

When the reader seems to be mumbling a word or part of a word, it can be marked as above.

MISCUES THAT REFLECT GOOD STRATEGIES

Miscues may reflect a reader's lack of knowledge of a word or a concept, but they may also reflect other, positive strategies that the reader is using. They may reflect good predictions, good use of the reader's conceptual and/or language background, and/or good strategies for constructing meaning, monitoring comprehension, and "fixing" the reader's reading when meaning or grammar goes awry.

Miscues That Reflect Good Prediction

Most readers, especially those who are very effective at constructing meaning, will predict or "think ahead" as they read. This may cause them to make miscues, perhaps many miscues, that fit with the text that came before:

- Emily was carrying her

  trumpet
  tuba. Eugene had his ~~tambourine~~.

- Eugene

  trombone
  tapped on his ~~tambourine~~.

The context before the first of the examples above mentions musical instruments. The reader, a second grader, read *tuba* correctly, but made two different miscues on *tambourine*. The first time he said "trumpet" and the second time "trombone," which are musical instruments he was more likely to have heard of. The next examples show an even closer fit with the letter cues and the meaning:

- *Grandpa*
  Grandma and ~~Grandpop~~ and all / the aunts and cousins. . . .

- *around*
  Hayes joined the smokers ~~about~~ / the fire. . . .

- *glanced*
  I stopped and ~~gazed~~ over my shoulder. . . .

In the three instances above, the readers have sampled the visual cues and used preceding context (grammar and meaning) plus prior knowledge to make miscues that better reflect the words they would use in such a structure. That's true in the following two sentences as well. In the first case, the reader, a first grader, has changed the grammar to a more natural language pattern, "can ride." In the last instance, the reader, a sixth grader, has changed the word *frog* to "toad"—not, of course, because he can't read the word *frog,* but because he's never heard of horned frogs, only of horned toads (or "horny toads," as I've heard them called). Here are the two examples:

- *can ride*
  Who ~~rides~~ with Mike?

- *toad*
  Out of it / crawled a horned ~~frog~~.

Here are some other interesting examples that I shall let stand without comment:

- ⊙ *went*
  He sneaked in and ~~what~~ did he see?

- ⊙ *very*
  Droofus awoke the next morning feeling very lonely / and ~~ever~~ so hungry.

- "Help! Help! A mouse!"

  ⊙ *Where*   *I crashed*
  ~~There~~ was a scream. Then ~~a crash~~.

- *@ library*
  A ~~lady~~ from the principal's office

came to the first grade.

plate   pie
She had a big ~~pile~~ of ~~papers~~ with

little boxes all over them.

the ⊘   read
- Their teacher told (first grade how to ~~do~~

the test. She said, "Read the questions

places
carefully. Then take your ~~pencil~~ and

s
fill in the box next to the right answer."

Miscues Involving Pronouns and Function Words

Good predictions often involve *function words*, the little glue words that hold major content words together in sentences. Other good predictions may be *pronouns*, the general words that often "stand for" more specific nouns (words like *he, she, we, they; this, these, those*). The percentage of miscues involving pronouns and function words tends to *increase* as one becomes a more proficient reader (K. Goodman & Burke, 1973, pp. 165–166 and p. 184). Some of the miscues in the preceding main section illustrate this pattern, as do some of the following examples. All of these miscues were made by the same reader:

- *me*
  "Are you kidding?" said Buster, "Of course!" [pronoun inserted]

- *your party*
  "When is ~~it~~?" [pronoun replaced by specific noun]

- "This Saturday afternoon? (But) that's when I'm / having my party!" [function word omitted]

- *at*
  Wednesday ~~before~~ school, the boys had a meeting. [one function word replaced by another]

- *ought to*
  "I think we ~~should~~ stick together," said Buster. [a function word replaced by a function word phrase]

- *the*
  "Who needs girls?" [function word inserted]

- *in*
  "Everyone find a place to hide," said Arthur. [function word inserted]

- *should*
  "Muffy ~~will~~ be here any minute!" [one function word replaced by another]

This reader's miscues look a lot like the high-quality miscues made by Jay in Chapter 4, do they not? The reader who made the miscues above, in reading *Arthur's Birthday,* by Marc Brown (1998), was a six-year-old.

Miscues That Reflect Readers' Language Patterns

Readers—especially those who are reading to construct meaning may make miscues that reflect their own concepts, their own background knowledge and experience and therefore their expectations. Again, an effective and important strategy can actually cause miscues. We have already seen above, under the heading "Miscues That Reflect Good Prediction," some miscues that reflect the reader's conceptual background or a language pattern that is more natural for the reader. Here, we shall see examples of miscues that reflect the reader's own natural speech in different ways: miscues that reflect simply immature pronunciation or grammar, ones that reflect an ethnic or social dialect, and ones that reflect the fact that the reader is learning English after having learned another language as his or her native language.

It is crucial to realize that miscues reflecting immature speech, dialect, and the normal speech of those who did not learn the language natively do not interfere with the reading process. Instead, they actually *demonstrate* how proficient readers process text. Such miscues indicate that the reader has processed the text for meaning, then "translated" it into his or her normal speech.

Immature Speech Pattern

- How lucky he was to live in a

  willage
  Somali (so-mah' lee) ~~village~~ . . .

- *twee*
  . . . in the shade of / a tall palm ~~tree~~.

These two examples—a "w" for an initial *v* and "tw" for initial *tr*—are well-documented patterns in the research on child language acquisition. The reader who made these miscues was a third grader. He corrected both of the miscues, suggesting that these were childish pronunciations he was trying to overcome.

Here is another kind of example:

- *drived*
  They put them in Miss / Tizzy's red wagon and ~~delivered~~ them all over town . . .

Here, the young reader has not only used a different word, but regularized its past tense, saying "drived" rather than "drove." This kind of immature language feature, regularizing a past tense, is more common among young readers than the sound features just illustrated. Such regularization can also be part of a reader's dialect, but not in the case of the reader who said "drived" instead of "delivered."

Ethnic, Social, or Regional Dialect

The following dialect miscues were made by a young woman who uses informal African American English in her daily speech:

- One Saturday, Mom ~~asked~~ *aksed* me to fold clothes . . .

- If it rains, Dad / ~~carries~~ *carry* her . . .

- Dad ~~washes~~ *wash* clothes and cleans the garage.

- I, Patty Jean / Piper, ~~call~~ *calls* her Princess Pooh.

- Mom / ~~says~~ *sāys* there's no / money to send / ~~me~~ *you* to camp.

The pronunciation "aksed" for *asked* is common in African American English. So are the other features (see Chapter 4 regarding dialect miscues). The last miscue above is particularly interesting because the typical AAE pattern would be "Mom say." Here, the reader has changed the vowel of *says*, pronouncing it like *say*. However, the reader has also maintained the -s ending of *says* (which is pronounced as a /z/ sound).

The following miscues are typical of African American English as well, but they are also common among speakers of many ethnic backgrounds if they do not use, or when they are not using, the dialect forms considered "standard," "mainstream," or characteristic of "the Green dialect" (the language of money—that is, the language of power and influence):

- I hide so well that my friend

~~won't ever~~ *wouldn't never* find me.

- We always have fun when

it's just my (friend) and me . . .

These and other dialect forms were common in the speech I heard at home from my grandmother. Others were single words: *amongst* rather than *among*, and *towards* rather than *toward*. These single-word dialect forms were originally regional rather than social, but *amongst*, especially, would sound uneducated to native residents of the state where I live now. *Amongst* and *towards* would be dialect miscues if they occurred in reading most texts (unless the writer was actually representing the dialect with these spellings).

Sometimes a writer tries to represent characters' dialects in a novel or story. In this case, a reader may miscue by supplying the "standard" form:

- "Yeah, she *'s* the one," answered Mr. Simms.

Or the reader may add a dialect marker that is consistent with the dialect being represented, but not included in the text:

- "Look at that blame insect!"

[handwritten "d" inserted above "blame" with caret]

ESL-Related and EFL-Related Miscues

People who are learning or have learned English as a second language are often called ESL speakers: speakers of English as a Second Language. People who have studied English in school as a foreign language are referred to as EFL speakers: speakers of English as a Foreign Language. In this text, I shall use the term *ESL speakers* to refer to both.

When people do not speak English as their native language, their speech in English may typically reflect the sound system of the native language. Interestingly, the grammatical differences between their English and that of native speakers do not seem to reflect the native language, but simply the fact that they have not yet mastered some of the grammatical signals and patterns of English. Indeed, native speakers of very differently structured languages make mostly the same grammatical miscues in English, reflecting a common "interlanguage" (Selinker, 1972).

Omission of a grammatical ending is quite common. Also, the way we use, or don't use, the articles "a," "an," and "the" is extraordinarily difficult for nonnative speakers of English to learn. Finally, the prepositions of our language, words like "in" and "on," are problematic because not all languages have prepositions, and even if they do, the meanings of our prepositions often do not match one-to-one with a seemingly similar *pre*position (or *post*position) in another language. The use of a non-expected verb form may also occur, especially if the English verb is "irregular" in the way it forms its past tense.

The following examples of ESL-related miscues are from a Hispanic student (Miramontes, 1990):

- Ramon ~~crept~~ *creeped* to the door and slowly opened it.

- "I'm ⓐ scary ghost!"

- "I'd know your cowboy boots anywhere," Steve said.
- . . . to make spooky noises.

The following miscues are from a college student who spoke Korean as his native language. Most of his ESL-related miscues involve omission of the past tense marker, as in the first two examples:

- And, in speaking these words / there ~~came~~ *come* out of out her mouth two roses, . . .

- "Alas, sir! my mother has turned me out of doors."

The following omission suggests the student's difficulty with our article system in English:

- As for her sister, the gift of the fairy remained with her . . .

In English, "the gift of fairy" is not quite right grammatically when referring to a specific fairy.

It is crucial to realize that miscues reflecting immature speech, dialect, and the normal speech of those who did not learn the language natively do not interfere with the reading process. Instead, they actually *demonstrate* how proficient readers process text. Such miscues indicate that the reader has processed the text for meaning, then "translated" it into his or her normal speech. (See the discussion in Chapter 4, pp. 74–77).

Miscues That Result from Monitoring Comprehension

Of course we have already been examining miscues that result from monitoring comprehension: predictions, and miscues that reflect readers' concepts or language patterns. None of these would occur if the reader weren't reading for meaning and monitoring for comprehension. But there are additional categories as well, especially those discussed below.

Restructurings

Restructurings of the text often suggest that the reader is not only monitoring comprehension, but monitoring for grammatical acceptability as well. Thus, when a reader makes a miscue that doesn't fit with the grammar that follows, he or she may restructure the following text so that it is both meaningful and grammatical.

Here are two rather simple restructurings of text:

- Jenny sat in the circle all

  that
  ~~through~~ (the) night, . . .

- Every day except Friday, Mohamed

  went to the school with

  another
  ~~the other~~ village boy~~s~~.

In the first example, the reader said "that" for *through,* then restructured by omitting *the,* to produce the grammatical phrase "that night." In the second example, the reader probably predicted "another" as he moved from one line to the next. Having done that, he made *boys* singular, producing "another village boy." These restructurings suggest that the readers were monitoring for comprehension—and for grammar, too.

The following miscues were made by Jay (Chapter 4):

- "Ain't (ever) heard (anybody)
  much about
  ‸

  (call) her (a) beauty, . . ."

- Out ⓞf

ⓘt crawled a horned frog.

- "This here ⸍s Muriel," said Hayes, with an oratorical wave

  . She's
  of his hand, "~~has~~ got qualities."

In each case, Jay made one miscue that caused him to make others, in order to produce a sentence that was both meaningful and grammatical.

Regressions to Correct

Corrections indicate, of course, that a reader is monitoring comprehension. Sometimes corrections require or encourage the reader to regress. In the examples below, the underline attached to the Ⓒ indicates the stretch of text that was redone, during the correction.

- I started past ⓒthe ~~her~~ again, . . .

The reader read "I started past the again," then regressed to correct, saying "her again" as she corrected.

- I swung back around, ⓒ and kicking ~~at~~ the sidewalk, . . .

The reader reread "kicking" as she corrected her miscue.

- ⓒ ⓒ not He was a mean-look-

  ⓒwith a   4 bar
              3 barned
  ing man, red ~~in the~~ face   2 burned
  and ~~bearded~~.   1 burned

First the reader regressed to correct her insertion of "not." She corrected "with a," then she read to the end of the sentence and apparently noticed that what she had said didn't sound quite right. So she started again at the beginning of the sentence and read the entire sentence correctly.

I would not bother mentioning regressions to correct as evidence of monitoring comprehension if it weren't for the fact that some informal reading inventories have penalized readers for regressing. Surely a scheme for assessing a reader should not penalize the reader for regressing to correct.

Repetitions and Pauses

Often, a reader repeats a word or a stretch of words to confirm that what he or she has said is right:

- I braced myself

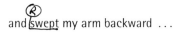
and Ⓡswept my arm backward . . .

The word *swept* is not very logical after "I braced myself," so it's hardly a surprise that the reader reread/repeated the word to confirm its correctness.

- "I ain't nasty,"

I said, properly holding my ⟨temper⟩ in check.

The reader may have repeated "temper" to confirm that it was correct. Perhaps she predicted that the "I" of the story would be holding something concrete, an object, and needed to reread/repeat "temper" to confirm that she had read the word accurately. The long-tailed P indicates that the reader also paused after "temper," perhaps to confirm and perhaps to process the words ahead.

Readers pause for many reasons, such as to confirm what they've read, to look and think ahead, to ponder words and concepts that puzzle them, and to reconsider a miscue that doesn't fit with what follows and perhaps to correct mentally, if not orally. The following example may fit the last of these situations:

- All Alexander wanted was a few crumbs and yet

  every time ~~they~~ saw him/they would scream for help
  (*he* written above *they*)

  or chase him with a broom.

I would hypothesize that the reader read up to the word *him*, realized that "he saw him" was not going to make sense in context, and may have mentally corrected "he" to the text word *they* before going on.

MISCUES THAT SUGGEST INEFFICIENT READING

Of course, miscues suggesting nonproficient reading do not alone tell the whole story. We need to weigh the frequency of such miscues against the frequency of miscues that do use good reading strategies. As always, it depends upon the patterns of miscues and their relative frequency. Miscue patterns may suggest, for example, that a reader is effective but not very efficient, or that a reader is neither effective nor efficient.

Overcorrection of Miscues

Overcorrection of miscues may reflect effective but inefficient reading—at least if overcorrections occur frequently. As the Goodmans have defined *overcorrections*, these miscues involve only minor grammatical differences, such as the change of a word involving a contraction to the non-contracted form, or the opposite.

- "I ~~do not~~ want you to help us any more ..."
  (©*don't* written above *do not*)

- He ~~did not~~ purr anymore.
  (©*didn't* written above *did not*)

In each instance, the reader created a contraction that reflected her informal speech patterns. And in each case the reader apparently felt compelled to "correct" this perfectly normal variant.

Contractions can occur with various other combinations, such as the following:

Uncontracted words	Contraction
does not	doesn't
I am	I'm
she is	she's
we/they are	we're; they're
would have	would've
they have	they've
he had	he'd known
there is	there's

Other corrections, though not technically "overcorrections" as defined by the Goodmans, may likewise be totally unnecessary:

- We like to play with my ~~racing~~ ⓖrace cars.

I remember that my son and I called them "race" cars, too; there is no need to correct this miscue to say the exact word that was on the page.

If overcorrections and other totally unnecessary corrections occur infrequently, there is no reason for concern. But sometimes such miscues are accompanied by other evidence of inefficiency, such as numerous struggles to "get" various words, when reading onward would probably be the wiser choice. Here is one example that seems to have stemmed from difficulty with the word *whipped*, in this particular context:

```
6 ............ my hands
5 I waved my hands
4 I waved
3 I whispered
2 I whispered
1 whis-
```

- As soon as we were outside, I ~~whipped~~ my hand

  from his.

This reader (Erica, at the end of this chapter) told me, indeed, that she absolutely had to try, and try again, to "get" every word. Perhaps this was the result of her six years of tutoring in phonics.

Readers who overcorrect and those who correct when it's totally unnecessary may be inefficient readers, if such miscues occur often. Even more inefficient is the reader who struggles repeatedly to "get" a word that isn't logical in the context or, more often, a word that isn't in the reader's listening vocabulary anyway—in other words, a word that the reader doesn't know, in any sense. It's better to try to get a sense of the word's meaning from context, if possible, and then read on.

Such inefficient reading strategies as unnecessary correction and repeated struggling with words are often accompanied by miscues suggesting that the reader reads more or less word-by-word, without attending to whether the miscue fits in context. Indeed, readers who seem to read word-by-word are neither efficient nor effective.

MISCUES THAT SUGGEST INEFFECTIVE READING

This category is not as simple or straightforward as it might seem, for such miscues are not necessarily an indication that the reader doesn't read for meaning. As always, we must consider whether there is a frequent pattern of such miscues. Equally important, we must consider other situations and other kinds of evidence.

For example, not correcting miscues on difficult words, words likely to be difficult for that particular reader, may simply be an indication that the text is too difficult—or at least some of the words in it are. With some readers, not attempting to correct miscues on difficult words may simply reflect a healthy strategy of "getting on" with the reading. That is, the reader may determine that he or she doesn't know the word and probably still wouldn't know it if the word were sounded out correctly (which is often difficult or impossible to do anyway, if you don't know the word). Especially if the miscued word doesn't seem crucial to the meaning, the reader may simply have made an instantaneous decision to just read on.

Readers may also tend to correct silently, in the head, rather than out loud. Sometimes we have no evidence of this whatsoever. In other cases, the reader's silent correction may be cued by a pause, or even a repetition suggesting that the reader is trying to confirm or disconfirm. Such pauses and repetitions would suggest that the reader does monitor comprehension and does at least try to correct if it seems important to the meaning.

On the other hand, miscues that severely disturb meaning but aren't corrected may indeed reflect lack of correcting as a productive, frequently used strategy. This is especially true if the miscues also do not at least go with the grammar of the sentence, particularly with the grammar of what comes before. Here are some examples of miscues that severely disturb meaning, taken from the miscue analysis of readers who also didn't get much meaning from what they read.

- "Well, ~~what finally stopped~~ it?"
  the family tripped

  "Well, we ~~heard~~ the ~~farmer's wife screaming~~."
  had   farn   wif   scring

  "Why was ~~she screaming~~?"
  the scrunked

In this passage, *some* of the reader's miscues at least go with what came before. They are a reasonable prediction. That's not so often true, though, of the miscues from another reader, in the following passages:

- That ~~tool~~ was the body ~~itself~~.
  tol   interest

  Their senses were their instruments. They ~~listened~~ to the
  leachened

  heart and felt the ~~heat~~ of fever. They smelled the odor of
  heart

  ~~decaying~~ flesh or watched a ~~wound~~ heal.
  doctor's   word

- *Those* a cim/es *already larger*
  ~~These accomplishments awaited~~ a ~~later~~

stage of (childhood)

Though some of these miscues preserve grammatical structure, most do not preserve meaning, nor do they suggest a meaning appropriate to the context. Indeed, the reader does not seem to have been reading for meaning. There's little evidence that she thought the text should sound meaningful when she read it.

We must be very cautious, however, about drawing the conclusion that meaning-destroying miscues really do affect the reader's essential comprehension of a sentence or a text. As we shall explain in Chapter 8, we need also to have the reader retell and discuss what was read in order to draw the most accurate conclusions from miscues that appear to disrupt meaning. Some of the reasons are illustrated in the next section.

THE USE OF GRAPHIC CUES IN RELATION TO OTHER CUES

There are various possibilities for how a reader's use of graphic cues (words, letter patterns, letters) may relate to his or her use of syntactic and semantic cues, as well as to prior knowledge and experience.

Effective Use of Graphic Cues Along with Other Cues

The effective use of graphic, syntactic, and semantic cues together is a mark of a good reader. Here are some examples:

- *trampled*
  They ~~tramped~~ through the snow.

- *raced   the*
  Toad ~~rushed~~ past trees and rocks.

- "I AM ALL ALONE!"

  shouted
  ~~screamed~~ Toad.

All four of these miscues were from the same reader. The following example is from Erica (see the end of this chapter), who was typically successful at constructing meaning from text:

wearily
Stacey laughed ~~wryly~~.

This miscue not only shows attention to all three kinds of language cues but fits Stacey's character and the situation perfectly. Then there is the following miscue, also from Erica:

a-a-ah- ā - ā - āpō- apŏ'/a- gĭz- ā pō/ah'gĭz

- "Well, ~~apologize~~," she ordered.

"What?"

₂ when the-
₁ when you-

"You bumped into me. Now you apologize."

As Erica's miscues on this passage suggest, she was typically able to "get" words when she could use context along with graphic cues. When the word *apologize* first occurred, apparently Erica did not anticipate that the word might be *apologize*. But two lines later, "You bumped into me" cued her to read the last word in the line as "apologize."

Fairly often, readers will make good use of graphic cues, with two major parts or "chunks" of the word resembling the text, and in addition, preserve the grammatical ending of the text word. Usually this happens because the reader does not know the word in print. Therefore, coming close to the word in pronunciation doesn't cue the reader to the word itself. For example:

witch- safed
The cruel witch ~~vouchsafed~~ me not one word of answer.

Of course this miscue was probably cued partly by the preceding word, *witch,* though the pronunciation of the vowel is not the same. Probably the thirteen-year-old who made the miscue was not familiar with the word *vouchsafed,* neither as a word in print nor as a word in his listening vocabulary. Chapter 7 includes similar examples, in the discussion of coding miscues as to how they fit with preceding and following context. As we saw in Chapters 3 and 4 (p. 60 and p. 00) it is difficult for even adults to "correctly" sound out a multisyllabic word especially, if the word is not among the words they know orally.

Underuse of Graphic Cues

Many young, emergent readers—often preschoolers and kindergartners—learn to retell favorite stories from the pictures and a few remembered words. A little later, they may recognize some key words but still mostly tell stories from pictures instead of reading, or trying to read, the words. Or they may start reading a sentence but end up creating most of it. During the first-grade year if not earlier, such rendering of text will usually give way to reading more and more, perhaps most, of the words. If this does not appear to be happening, the reader may benefit from additional help, perhaps from the classroom teacher, a Reading Recovery teacher, or some other tutor. Or the reader may merely need more predictable texts to read and reread, until more and more words can be read easily.

Overuse of Graphic Cues and Underuse of Other Cues

In the following examples, the miscues do not fit with grammar or meaning, either before or after the miscue. In the first two sentences, the miscues are real words. In the next two sentences, the miscues are nonwords.

fatter
- Have you seen a photo of your mother or your ~~father~~ at / your age?

ever went come
- Nothing stopped him—not ~~even wet cement~~.

-    ... the people thought that school was / not as ~~important~~ *imprentice* for girls as it was for boys.

-    I was in ~~real trouble~~. *ruh duhroo*

In these times when intensive phonics *first* has been promoted by state legislatures and now is being promoted by federal legislation and agencies (see Chapter 4, p. 86), it is not surprising that many readers today show this pattern of miscues that is common among ineffective readers: that is, overuse of graphic cues and underuse of syntactic and semantic cues as well as prior knowledge and context.

When readers have not said or sounded out a word "correctly," it has traditionally been assumed that the reader does not have adequate phonics skills. Rarely, however, is the problem best construed as a lack of phonics. Why? Using context to help construct meaning enables readers to make more effective use of graphic cues and phonics knowledge and actually reduces the number of miscues, particularly for readers who are not yet proficient. Furthermore, looking on beyond the miscue, often just a word or two, will frequently help readers correct some of their miscues—silently if not orally. In short, using graphic cues alone is rarely if ever the best solution to an apparent problem with reading a word. The best solution is to use all three kinds of language cues—semantic, syntactic, and graphic—along with prior knowledge and experience. Independent readers have learned to orchestrate these cues successfully.

Related but Different Approaches to Miscue Analysis

The work of Kenneth Goodman and many others reflects the original procedures for miscue analysis—procedures that are quite detailed, because they were developed for research purposes (K. Goodman & Burke, 1973). The major simplification of these procedures for classroom teachers is *Reading Miscue Inventory: Alternative Procedures* (Y. Goodman, Watson, & Burke, 1987), which includes an extensive discussion of the reading process and of the authors' most complex RMI form, along with other forms. For simplicity, I shall henceforth refer to their form(s) as the Goodman form(s), the most detailed of which is reproduced here as Figure 6.1.

As you can see, the form asks the analyst to consider whether miscues are syntactically acceptable, whether they are semantically acceptable, and whether there is a meaning change. There are also columns devoted to meaning construction, grammatical relationships, graphic similarity, and sound similarity. Most of these items deal with the reader's use of language cues: syntactic, semantic, and graphic. Sandra Wilde's procedure in *Miscue Analysis Made Easy* (2000) is based on procedure 3 from the Y. Goodman, Watson, et al. (1987) book.

Over the years, I have developed a series of slightly different forms that look at the semantic and syntactic acceptability of the miscues indirectly, as we examine whether a miscue goes with the meaning and grammar of what comes before and what comes after.

Of course, we must keep in mind that it is the miscue *patterns* we are looking for. In order to code columns 2 and 3 on my miscue form in Figure 6.2, we have to decide whether each coded miscue goes with the grammar (syntax) and meaning (semantics) of what came before in the sentence. If a majority of the miscues go with the grammar and meaning of what came before, we can infer that the reader tends to predict or "think ahead" while reading. If a substantial percentage of the miscues also go with the grammar and meaning of what follows (column 3), we can infer that the reader's eyes may typically be ahead of the voice in reading aloud. In addition, by comparing the results of column 3 with the information in the correction column (column 5), we can also gain insight into whether the reader uses following context to cue at least an attempt at correction. Similarly, we can compare column 4 with column 5 to see whether

MISCUE ANALYSIS PROCEDURE I CODING FORM ©1987 Richard C. Owen Publishers,. Inc.

LINE No./MISCUE No.	READER / TEXT		1 SYNTACTIC ACCEPTABILITY	2 SEMANTIC ACCEPTABILITY	3 MEANING CHANGE	4 CORRECTION	See 2,3,4 MEANING CONSTRUCTION			See 1,2,4 GRAMMATICAL RELATIONSHIPS				5 GRAPHIC SIMILARITY			6 SOUND SIMILARITY		
							No Loss	Partial Loss	Loss	Strength	Partial Strength	Overcorrection	Weakness	H	S	N	H	S	N
	READER	TEXT																	

READER _____ DATE _____
TEACHER _____ AGE/GRADE _____ SCHOOL _____
SELECTION _____

a. TOTAL MISCUES _____
b. TOTAL WORDS _____
a ÷ b × 100 = MPHW _____

COLUMN TOTAL
PATTERN TOTAL
PERCENTAGE

(Goodman, Watson, Burke)

Figure 6.1 *Goodman, Watson, & Burke's miscue analysis procedure I coding form (1987).*

a loss of meaning at the sentence level seems to cue the reader to try to correct. Thus by its very nature, the form also suggests insights into whether the reader might need help with monitoring comprehension and perhaps trying to correct.

The use of any of these strategies—predicting, looking ahead, trying to correct when appropriate—gives evidence that the reader is monitoring comprehension while reading. Use of these strategies together suggests that the person is a "strategic reader," to use the popular term.

Neither the Goodman miscue form nor mine offers any opportunity to code the use of picture cues or the use of prior knowledge and experience (schemas) or any other pragmatic cues. Teachers using our forms must simply record and use that knowledge as appropriate.

Miscue Analysis in the Goodman Tradition

A word of warning is in order. The term *miscue* is being used frequently these days to refer to departures from the text, even when they are really being viewed as errors, period. Likewise, the phrase *miscue analysis* is sometimes used to refer to procedures that emphatically are not in the tradition of Kenneth Goodman and those whose procedures for analysis basically follow his underlying principles. If alleged miscue analysis procedures reflect the original intent of miscue analysis, they will:

1. By their very nature, reflect the conviction that constructing meaning is more important than reproducing surface detail.

READER'S NAME						
Grade Age						
Coder's name						
Date						
Text that was read						

Code columns 2 through 4 as if the miscue weren't corrected, even if it was.

In coding columns 2 & 3 don't ask whether the miscue made *the same* grammar and nearly the same sense. Just ask if it makes *good* grammar and a sensible stretch of words with what came before (column 2) and after (column 3).

1 Did the miscue reflect the speaker's ordinary speech patterns?

I = immature speech
D = dialect
E = ESL or EFL learner

If a miscue is coded I, D, or E, all the rest of the columns are coded Y, except for column 6, which is coded as usual

2 Did the miscue go with the grammar and meaning of what came before?

Y = yes, the miscue fit with both the preceding grammar and preceding meaning
G = the miscue fit with the preceding grammar only
M = the miscue fit with the preceding meaning only
N = the miscue fit with neither

3 Did the miscue go with the grammar and meaning of what followed?

Y = yes, with both
G = with grammar only
M = with meaning only
N = no, with neither

4 Did the miscue leave the *essential* meaning of the sentence intact?

Y = yes, this particular miscue, by itself, left the *essential* meaning of the sentence still intact

N = no, this miscue did not leave *essential* meaning of the sentence intact

5 Was the miscue corrected?

Y = yes, corrected
UC = unsuccessful attempt at correction
N = no, not corrected, and this miscue is not an attempt at correction
O = overcorrection; a miscue involving a contraction was corrected unnecessarily

6 Was the miscue graphically similar?

Y = high similarity
P = some (partial) similarity
N = no similarity

Apply to substitution miscues only.

7 Was the sentence, as the reader finally left it, semantically acceptable within the whole original selection that was read?

Bracket the miscues that came from each sentence, and then code the sentences:

Y = yes, acceptable; there wasn't any essential change in the meaning of the selection
P = partial; there was inconsistency, loss, or change of a *minor* idea, incident, character, fact, sequence, or concept in the selection
N = not acceptable; there was inconsistency, loss, or change of a *major* idea, incident, character, fact, sequence, or concept in the selection

	TEXT SAYS	READER SAYS	I	D	E	Y	G	M	N	Y	G	M	N	Y	N	Y	UC	N	O	Y	P	N	Y	P	N
1																										
2																										
3																										
4																										
5																										
6																										
7																										
8																										
9																										
10																										
11																										
12																										
13																										
14																										
15																										
16																										
17																										
18																										
19																										
20																										
21																										
22																										
23																										
24																										
25																										

Figure 6.2 *Weaver's miscue analysis coding form # 1 (from Constance, Weaver, Reading Process and Practice, 3rd ed., Heinemann 2002; © 2002 by Constance Weaver; may be reproduced for use).*

2. Consider miscues only in context, distinguishing between those that are appropriate in context and those that are not. In fact, the procedure might note as overcorrections those miscues that are corrected even though they fit the context and reflect no essential loss of meaning; in such cases, the correction is unnecessary.

3. Provide insight into the reader's strategies, particularly into how well the reader uses context to predict what is coming next, to monitor comprehension, and to correct those miscues that do not make sense in context. Thus, the procedure offers a starting point for acknowledging the reader's already-effective strategies and strengthening other strategies.

4. Be more concerned with reading strategies than with reading speed, fluency, or accuracy. Many readers are rather proficient at getting meaning, even though they read neither quickly, fluently, nor with near accuracy. To label them as deficient and give them skills work rather than real reading is to deprive them of the experience that will most contribute to better reading: the experience of reading and perhaps rereading interesting, coherent, and connected texts. Furthermore, skills work in isolation is much less valuable than direct help in using reading strategies and skills as one reads, or reflecting on one's miscues together with the teacher while listening to and discussing a tape recording of what one has read. (See the section on Retrospective Miscue Analysis in Chapter 9.)

5. Focus attention on readers' strengths as well as their possible weaknesses. For example, omitting basic sight words may be a strength, when the meaning is kept intact; not sounding out a difficult word may be a strength, when the word seems unimportant to the sentence; and repetitions and pauses may be evidence of effective strategies, as the reader tries to deal with upcoming words.

6. Be conducted as part of a more comprehensive analysis that considers, in addition, not only the reader's ability to reflect upon and discuss the selection read, but the reader's understanding of the reading process, conscious awareness of reading strategies, and other factors that offer insight into the person's reading and the reader's habits and interests as a reader. (See Chapter 8.)

Philosophically, my miscue coding practices and forms, and the components of the reader profile as described in Chapter 8, lie within the Goodman tradition.

Crucial Differences Between Miscue Analysis and Running Records

The growing popularity of Marie Clay's Reading Recovery program for first graders (Clay, 1985) has brought with it the "running record," wherein the teacher records miscues while the student is in the process of reading. The major advantage is obvious: there is no need for tape-recording and later playback. In fact, the teacher does not even need a typescript or photocopy of the reading selection for marking the miscues; only a sheet of paper is needed. Every word read correctly is indicated with a check mark or simply a slanted line. Thus, the teacher's running record consists of checks (or slanted lines) interspersed with the reader's miscues. A running record of Anne's rendition of "Little Circus Dog" (see p. 81) for example, might look like Figure 6.3.

Even a quick glance at this example should begin to suggest the concern that many educators have with the running record: it implicitly encourages us to consider miscues without regard to how they relate to the context. Although Clay explains that miscues should be analyzed for how they fit the context, her procedure discourages this. Clay also emphasizes accuracy. She categorizes texts as easy, instructional/learning, or hard based on the number of miscues. And she considers it important that students in the Reading Recovery program read a selection with 95% accuracy (including self-corrections) before they attempt more difficult texts (Clay, 1985, pp. 17–22; 1991). Her point is to use texts that are easy enough to support the reader in developing

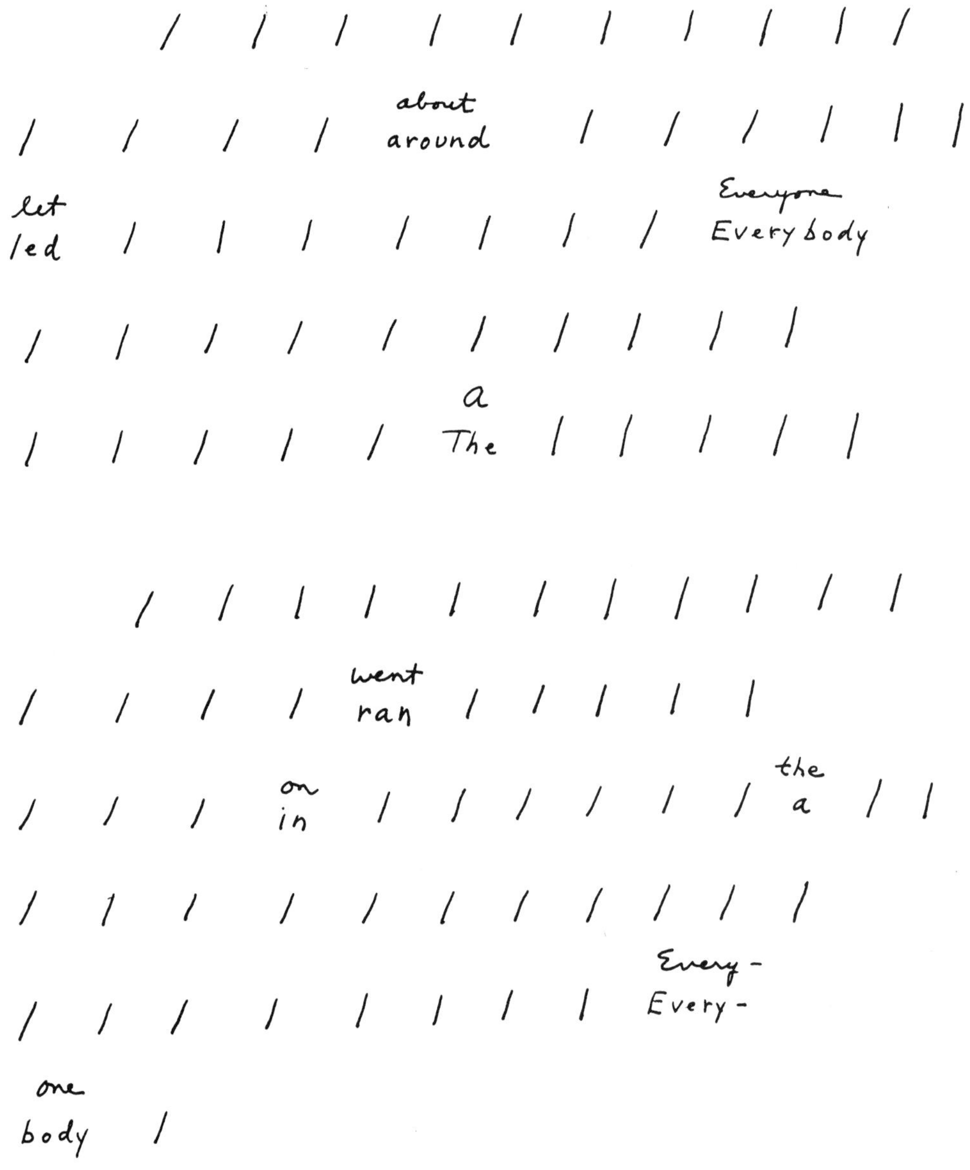

/ / / / / / / / / /

/ / / /   about
          around   / / / / / /

let
led   / / / / / /   Everyone
                    Everybody

/ / / / / / / / / /

/ / / / /   a
            The   / / / / /

/ / / / / / / / / /

/ / / /   went
          ran   / / / / /

/ / /   on
        in   / / / / / /   the
                           a   / /

/ / / / / / / / / /

/ / / / / / / /   Every-
                  Every-

one
body   /

Figure 6.3   *Running record of Anne's miscues.*

reading strategies, but researchers experienced in miscue analysis have not found this degree of textual support to be necessary.

Despite Clay's own sophisticated understanding of miscues and what they reveal about reading strategies, and despite the fact that both teachers and students in the Reading Recovery program are encouraged to develop such an understanding, the analytical procedure and certain instructional practices seem to encourage more emphasis on accurate word identification than on reading strategies. They imply that the quantity of miscues is more important than the quality. Also, the child is not necessarily required to read more than a hundred to two hundred words of the selections chosen to establish reading level (Clay, 1985, p. 17), so the reader has insufficient opportunity to get mentally into the text and demonstrate his or her reading strategies and ability at their best. Thus, there are some important conceptual and philosophical differences between the miscue analysis procedures developed by Kenneth Goodman and his associates (K. Goodman, 1965; K. Goodman & Burke, 1973; Y. Goodman, Watson, & Burke, 1987) and the running record procedures that Marie Clay developed for the Reading Recovery program (Clay, 1979, 1985, 1993a). Perhaps the greatest difference is in how proponents of miscue analysis view the miscues they analyze, as opposed to how Clay views and deals with "errors." We may summarize as follows some of the critical differences, including some previously mentioned:

1. Clay's procedure was developed for recording the miscues of first graders reading texts they could read close to word-perfectly. She suggests that for analyzing the reader's errors, the text should be one that the child is likely to read with between five and ten errors per hundred words—within what she and Johnston call the "learning range" (Johnston & Clay, in Johnston, 1997, p. 213). Thus there is no need to tape-record the miscues, because the teacher can rather easily keep up with the coding. Goodman's miscue analysis procedure was developed for use with readers of any age, and regardless of how many miscues the reader might make. Thus it is necessary to tape-record the reading and analyze the miscues later.

2. Clay counts all uncorrected substitutions, omissions, and insertions as "errors." Goodman considers all departures from the text as miscues, including those that have been corrected. That way, the reader's self-corrections become part of what is analyzed, leading to insights about good reading strategies that can all too easily be lost when self-corrections are excluded from further analysis.

3. Clay counts virtually all uncorrected substitutions, omissions, and insertions—literally. She is concerned with the quantity of a reader's miscues (including the percentage of errors, the percentage of words read accurately, and the percentage of self-corrections), because she wants to base instruction for an emergent reader on texts that the reader can read with 90% accuracy. That way, she believes, the text will support the reader in constructing meaning and in self-correcting when an error is made. Clay also appears to believe that children should be getting precise messages from books, at least when they are emergent readers dealing with relatively simple texts (Clay, 1993a). In contrast, the standard miscue procedure does not involve counting miscues, because the reader's use of strategies is considered far more important than the quantity of miscues. Indeed, miscue researchers have learned to distrust measures of quantity because they can mislead observers into drawing inaccurate inferences about the reader's understanding of the text. Miscue research has demonstrated that many readers can effectively construct meaning from text even when they have made numerous miscues (e.g., K. Goodman & Burke, 1973; K. Goodman & Y. Goodman, 1978; and much of the research cited in Brown, Goodman, & Marek, 1996).

4. With the exception of self-corrected miscues as mentioned above, what Clay calls "errors" are similar to the miscues that Goodman and others choose for analysis. However, the errors in Clay's system are always viewed as failures in some respect; these errors are counted, and the Reading Recovery teacher helps children develop strategies for getting the exact word. In contrast, the miscues in Goodman's procedure will be considered good miscues if they preserve the essential meaning, or at least partially good miscues if they reflect the use of important reading strategies, like using prior knowledge and context to predict what's coming next. From the perspective of miscue analysis and the supporting body of miscue research, it is inappropriate—even counterproductive—to have the reader try again to get the exact word if the reader's miscue preserves the essential meaning. This is why some miscue forms have had a category of "overcorrection" or "unnecessary correction."

5. When reading for a running record in the Reading Recovery program, the child may be given the word when he or she stops for a few seconds and seems unwilling to go on. It is considered important to facilitate fluent reading and to encourage the reader by providing such backup support. When having the reader read for a miscue analysis, on the other hand, it is considered important not to help the reader, usually, since the intent is to analyze how the reader deals independently with words that aren't immediately recognized on sight. The teacher can simply remind the child to do whatever he or she would do if no one else were around. If absolutely necessary, the teacher can say "Just go ahead; read on."

In Johnston and Clay's chapters on running records (Johnston, 1997), the authors discuss various factors that are important to consider, such as the fact that the percentage of miscues may bear little relationship to how frustrated a reader might or might not be in reading a text and the fact that it's difficult and rather arbitrary to decide what to consider as an "error," I certainly agree. Nevertheless, it is clear that a running record is not merely a less time-consuming way of doing miscue analysis. Differences in underlying principles are involved.

Of course it is possible for a teacher who understands miscue analysis to glean the same information from running records, if the teacher compares the running record with the original text (e.g., Johnston & Clay, in Johnston, 1997, 221–223). Similarly, one could create columns for analysis in the margins of a running record that are the same as the columns one would use for miscue analysis in the Goodman tradition, procedure 3 (Y. Goodman, Watson, & Marek, 1987). Or one could create, on a running record, some or all of the columns from one of my miscue forms (see especially Chapter 7) and simply analyze the "errors" as I suggest for miscue analysis, by considering how the miscues fit in the context. This will work if the reader is limited to reading a text on which he or she will make few enough miscues that the teacher can keep up with doing the running record. Personally I would not want teachers to select only such texts, but the advantage, of course, is that the teacher does not have to tape-record the reading nor make a photocopy of the selection in order to analyze the miscues. Analysis can be done simply by taking the miscues noted on the running record sheet and putting them back into the original context mentally to analyze and code them.

Obviously, then, I prefer miscue analysis myself, and if teachers are going to do running records, I think they need the understanding gleaned through miscue analysis. That understanding will greatly enhance what they can learn about a reader's strategies, enabling teachers to determine instructional needs from the combination of recording via running record procedures and analyzing via miscue analysis procedures.

Useful References on Running Records

Johnston, P. H. (2000). *Running Records: A Self-Tutoring Guide.* York, ME: Stenhouse. 64 pp. + 40-minute audiotape.

Johnston, P. H. (1997). *Knowing Literacy: Constructive Literacy Assessment.* York, ME: Stenhouse. Includes two chapters, coauthored with Marie Clay, on recording and interpreting running records. Since this comprehensive book includes the audiotape for learning to do running records, plus much more about literacy assessment, it is by far the better bargain.

FOR FURTHER EXPLORATION

1. Review the symbols for marking miscues (pp. 122–125). Then, read the following passage with Betsey's miscues marked (the line divisions maintain those in the text that Betsey was given to read). Try to read the passage as Betsey read it, with the miscues. Then consider her reading strategies. Does she frequently use preceding context to predict what might come next? Does she frequently use following context to monitor comprehension and correct, or

try to correct, miscues that don't fit with what follows? Do her miscues and her use of reading strategies change in nature or effectiveness, from the beginning of her reading to the end?

① Mahoad ②s   ③ -minging
~~Mohamed~~ loved to go swimming, in the sea. How lucky he was

④ island   ⑤
to live in a Somali village right on the ~~Indian~~ Ocean! The sand(y)

shore rang with the happy⌐shouts and cries of the village boys

⑥ 2 surfy ⑦
  1 surfing SP-
and girls.⌐They liked to race one another into the ~~surf,~~ ⌐splash-

⑧ form   ⑨ the
ing⌐and spraying the water into a white dancing ~~foam~~ before ~~they~~

           Mohema   ⑩ a Ala
                            1 Almea
dove into the waves. ~~Mohamed~~ and his young sister, ~~Asha,~~ spent all

the time they could in the cool, clean sea swimming and playing

water games. They were good swimmers because their mother had

taught them.

⑪ especially   ⑫
Every day ~~except~~ Friday, Mohamed went to(the)school with

⑬ another   ⑭
~~the other~~ village boy(s). The class was outdoors, and the children

⑮ a   ⑯   ⑰ and 2 shell ⑱
                                  1 sand
sat on little bench(es) in front of the teacher ~~in~~ the ~~shade~~ of

⑲ the
~~a~~ ⌐tall palm tree. They did not have books, so the⌐boys repeated

⑳ .   ㉑ were ㉒ learned
everything the teacher said, over and over, until they ~~knew~~ ~~their~~

㉓ it   ㉔
~~lessons~~ by heart. The girl(s)of the village did not go to school,

㉕ taught   ㉖ s were ㉗
for the people⌐~~thought~~ that school ~~was~~ not as important for girls as it

was for boys.

On ~~sunny days~~ [Sunday] (28), as soon as school was over, ~~Mohamed~~ [Madoona] went with

his mother and ~~Asha~~ [Ashes (C) wa-] ~~(to wash~~ (29) ['s] the family clothes. His mother stood

in the water and scrubbed ~~and~~ [the] (30) ~~pounded~~ [a putty / pondy] (31) the clothes until they were

clean. Then she ~~handed~~ [had (32)] them to ~~Mohamed~~ [2 Madoona / 1 Madoo] and ~~Asha~~ [Ash], who took them

and ~~arranged~~ [agreed (33)] them on the beach to dry.

~~Mohamed~~ [Madoona] had helped his mother and (Asha) (34) wash (35) [ed] the clothes ever

since he could remember. He was very much surprised, therefore,

one day not long before his tenth birthday, when his mother told

him not to come with her and (Asha) (36).

"I ~~do not~~ [(C) don't (37)] want you to help us any more, ~~Mohamed~~ [2 Madoona / 1 Madoosa]," his mother

said. "It is time that ~~Asha~~ [Ashes] had more work to do around the

house. Beside~~s~~ (38), in two more years you will be ~~thought~~ [taught (39)] of as a

man by our ~~tribe~~ [troubles (40)], and it is not fit~~ting~~ [ing (41)] that people see you

always doing women's work. From now on, you [will (42)] help your father in

the ~~shop~~ [skip (43)] ~~and~~ [we (44)] (Asha will) (45) help me at home."

That first day, ~~Mohamed~~ [Madoona] felt quite grown-up and ~~superior~~ [surprised (46)]

when he saw his mother and ~~Asha~~ [Azza] carrying a heavy basket to the

beach. But this feeling did not last long. He had no one to

(47) had Azza
play with! He ~~and Asha~~ had played together for so long that the

other children were used to his not playing with them.

2 Madoona
1 Madoosa   (48)
~~Mohamed~~ stood and watched the other boys play "kick (the)

(49) the   (50)
ball" and "hunt for robber" and "water tag" When no one
          ^

(51) the
called him for ~~a~~ game, he turned and walked down the beach,

(52) (53) a   (54) tried   (55) thoughtful
kick(ing) up ~~the~~ sand with one foot, and ~~trying~~ to look as ~~though~~

(56) did   (57) ed
he really ~~didn't~~ care or want to play.
                              ^

(58) Hamasam
Finally, he decided to take his problem to his father, ~~Hassan.~~

(59) 's
"Mother doesn't want me to help wash the family clothes any more,
                                            ^

Madoosa   Asha
Father," ~~Mohamed~~ told his father. "~~Asha~~ has her work and her

friends, but now I have no one to play with."

(60) Probably   Madooha
"~~Perhaps~~ your mother is right, ~~Mohamed,~~" his father said,

(61) © help
and he put down the piece of board that he ~~held~~ in his hand.

ship
"It is time that you should learn to help me in the ~~shop.~~"

(62) © when
Hassan was a builder of fishing boats that ~~went~~ out to sea

every morning and returned to the shore every evening. His

ship
small ~~shop~~ was right on the beach.

"When you come home from school each day, ~~Mohamed~~ *Madooha*," said

his father, "I will show you the beginning of your ~~trade~~ ⑥③ *trouble*. You

will be a builder of boats like me."

"But father, when will I have time for games?" ~~Mohamed~~ *Madooha* asked.

"You help me a little, and I shall see that you have plenty

of time to yourself," ~~Hassan~~ *Hansa* promised. He laughed ~~softly~~ ⑥④ *slowly*. "I do

remember that boys need to have time to think and play.

You shall have it, my son."

⑥⑤ *desert*
That summer was the ~~driest~~ one that anyone—even the oldest

people in ~~Mohamed's~~ *Madooha's* village—could recall. It did not rain at all.

Each day the people would look up at the sky to see if they

could see any rain clouds. But each day the sun shone brightly.

2 *hiding* ⑥⑦
1 *hidden*
There was not even one cloud ⑥⑥ (to) ~~hide~~ the sun⑥⑧(s) face for a while.

Soon all the leaves of the trees started to turn brown. The

⑥⑨ *dropped* ⑦⓪
flowers ~~drooped~~ low(er) and lower on their stems. Finally they

became dry as paper. When the wind blew the dry leaves, they

⑦①
made a noise like a snake͜s slipping through the sand.

Day after day the sun beat down, and there was no shade from

(73) *leaves*   (73) *Jane*   (74) *Julie*

the ~~leafless~~ trees. ~~June~~ and ~~July~~ came and went without rain.

August was nearly over and still no rain.

2. Consider Erica's miscues and reading strategies, below, in the same way you did Betsey's. Background: Erica was a bright fifth grader who enjoyed discussing literature and offered insightful comments into the characters' feelings and motivations. However, both her writing and her reading were rather slow and painful–much less fluent than one would have predicted from her intelligence and liveliness. Each week she attended reading classes with two different special reading teachers. Therefore, her classroom teacher and I decided to see what we could learn from analyzing Erica's miscues. The class was reading and discussing *Roll of Thunder, Hear My Cry,* by Mildred Taylor (1976); I was reading the book and discussing it with the least proficient readers, including Erica. Below is a passage she read while her teacher, Ruth Perino, listened and tape-recorded the session. The story concerns a black girl, Cassie, and her family in the rural South in the 1930s. At this point in the story, Cassie has just been ignored by a storekeeper as soon as white customers entered the store, then scolded and told to leave the store when she protested this treatment. Shortly after she and her older brother Stacey part outside the store, she has another painful awakening: she accidentally bumps into a white classmate, Lillian Jean, on the sidewalk, and is humiliated by being forced to apologize and then to walk in the street.

(1)   6 .... *my hands*
     5 *I waved my hands*
     4 *I whispered my hands*
     3 *I whispered*
     2 *I whispered*
     1 *whis-*

As soon as we were outside, I ~~whipped~~ my hand

(R2) R_2 = *repeated twice*

from his. "What's the matter with you? You know he

was wrong!"

(C) *gruffily*
          3 *gruf-*
(2) 2 *flusk*   (3) *he* 2 *gruf-* (4)
   1 *flu-*   1 *gruf-*

Stacey swallowed to ~~flush~~ his anger, then said ~~gruf-~~
                                   ^

~~fly,~~ "I know it and you know it, but he don't know it,

(5) *you* (R2)
and that's where the trouble is. Now come on 'fore you
                       ^

(6) *got*
~~get~~ us into a real mess. I'm going up to Mr. Jamison's to

(R2)
see what's keeping Big Ma."

Ⓡ Ⓡ²   ⑦ stopped
⌐"What 'bout T. J.?" I called as he s̶t̶e̶p̶p̶e̶d̶ into the

street.
              ⑧ wearily   Ⓒ,Ⓡ   ⑨
Stacey laughed w̶r̶y̶l̶y̶. "Don't worry 'b̶o̶u̶t̶ T. J. He
                                  Ⓡ
      ⑩ Ⓒwhat   ⑪ Ⓒ ²sʊl-
knows exactly h̶o̶w̶ to act." He crossed the street ¹siʃen-
                                              s̶u̶l̶l̶e̶n̶l̶y̶
   ⑫
then⌐his hands jammed in his pockets.
              ⑬ he
I watched him go, but ᵪdid not follow. Instead, I
  r   ⑭   ρ
ambled along/the sidewalk trying to understand why
 ^
                                        Ⓡ
Mr. Barnett had acted the way he had.⌐More than once
     ⑮ glanced   ⑯ ²mircantēl   [teacher then
I stopped and g̶a̶z̶e̶d̶ over my shoulder at the m̶e̶r̶c̶a̶n̶- ,mir   gave her the word]
         ³a good mind to go back Ⓡand find out what had
    ⑰   ²a   into the back to find out Ⓡwhat had
          ¹to go mind into
tile. I had a̶ ̶g̶o̶o̶d̶ ̶m̶i̶n̶d̶ ̶t̶o̶ ̶g̶o̶ ̶b̶a̶c̶k̶ ̶i̶n̶ ̶a̶n̶d̶ ̶f̶i̶n̶d̶ ̶o̶u̶t̶

w̶h̶a̶t̶ ̶h̶a̶d̶ made Mr. Barnett so mad. I actually turned

once and headed toward the store, then remembering

what Mr. Barnett had said about my returning, I
              ⑱
         Ⓒ and
swung back around,⌐kicking at the sidewalk, my head
AC ²bōw-   ^
⑲⌐ ¹bl-   AC = abandoning a correct form
   b̶o̶w̶e̶d̶.   [teacher then said "You got it - 'bowed.'"]
            ⑳ ²Linna
                ,Lin-
It was then that I bumped into L̶i̶l̶l̶i̶a̶n̶ Jean
�21 ²Sil
     ,Som
Simms.

"Why don't you look where you're going?" she

(22) said ~~asked~~ huffily. Jeremy ~~and~~ her two younger brothers were

with her. "Hey, Cassie," said Jeremy.

"Hey, Jeremy," I said solemnly, keeping my eyes

on ~~Lillian~~ Jean.

(25) a-a-ah-ā-ā- āpō-apō'la gīz- ăpō/ah' gĭz
"Well, ~~apologize~~," she ordered.

"What?"

(26) when the- / when you-
"You bumped into me. Now you apologize."

(27) don't
I ~~did not~~ feel like messing with ~~Lillian~~ Jean. I had

other things on my mind. "Okay," I said, starting past,

(28) 2 willa Jean / 1 willa
"I'm sorry."

Lillian Jean sidestepped in front of me. "That ain't

(29)
enough. Get down in the road."

(30) You're
I looked up at her. "~~You~~ crazy?"

(31) Don't ca-
"~~You~~ can't watch where you going, get in the road. (32) to

(33)
Maybe that way you won't be bumping into ~~decent~~ (34) discount

(35) ha-
white folks with your little nasty ~~self~~."

This second insult of the day was almost more than

(36) Mrs.
I could bear. Only the thought of ~~Big~~ Ma up in Mr.

(37) James'   Linny   (38) s
Jamison's office saved Lillian Jean's lip. "I ain't nasty,"

(39) C 2 proudly (40)   R
        1 proudl-
I said, properly holding my temper in check, "and if

you're so afraid of getting bumped, walk down there

yourself."

              G the (41)
I started past her again, and again she got in my way.

C let's (42) 2 Linnean
              , Lilly
"Ah, let her pass, Lillian Jean," said Jeremy. "She

ain't done nothin' to you."

   "She done something to me just standing in front
(43) C What's   (44) C 2 apen-
                                   1 at -
of me." With that, she reached for my arm and at-

tempted to push me off the sidewalk. I braced myself

R   (45) s
and swept my arm backward, out of Lillian Jean's

(46)   (47) me
wrists
reach. But someone caught it from behind, painfully

        (48) a C shovel back (50)
                  (49)
twisting it, and shoved me off the sidewalk into the

road. I landed bottom first on the ground.

   Simson   (51) Then   gla- (52) [Erica paused before
Mr. Simms glared down at me. "When my gal Lil-   saying "gla-." Finally
                                                 her teacher gave her
2 Linnean   the word.]
1 Lin-   (53) ll
lian Jean says for you to get yo'self off the sidewalk,

you get, you hear?"
(54) C 2 me there was   C 2 Mivin (55)
        1 was   , Mar-
Behind him were his sons R. W. and Melvin. People

   C be-   (56)   Simsons (57)
from the store began to ring the Simmses. "Ain't that

(58) 3 was caught in / 2 was caught / 1 that caught — caught in

the same little nigger ~~was cuttin~~ (up) back there at Jim's (60) (61) ^Lee's?" ~~someone~~ asked.   (62) L- everyone

"Yeah, she's the one," answered Mr. ~~Simms~~ Solomon (R) (63) ("You

hear me talkin' to you, gal? You 'pologize to Miz ~~Lil~~ Lig- [Teacher corrected her.]

lian Jean this minute."

(64) (I) ~~stared~~ starred (65) up at Mr. Simms, (66) and (67) (frightened). Jeremy ap- ^friendly

peared frightened, too. "I—(68) apologize already."

Jeremy seemed relieved that I had spoken. "She

(69) d- (70) r-r- (71) f- f-
d-did, Pa. R-right now, 'fore y'all come, she did—"

Mr. ~~Simms~~ Simm or turned an angry ~~gaze~~ (72) upon his son and

(73) 2 flattered / , flattened (R) (74)
Jeremy ~~faltered~~, (looked) at me, and hung his head.

(R3)
Then Mr. Simms jumped into the street. I moved

(75) keep (R) (76) not
away from him, trying to ~~get~~ up. He (was) a mean-look-

(C) with a (77) (78) (79) 1 burned 2 burned 3 barned 4 bar
ing man, red ~~in the~~ face and ~~bearded~~. I was afraid he [when she reached the end of the sentence, she started again at the beginning and read the entire sentence accurately.]

was going to hit me before I could get to my feet,

(80) ed
but he didn't. I scrambled up and ran blindly for the

(81) (C) found (C) at-
wagon. Someone grabbed me and I ~~fought~~ wildly, at-

(82) a
tem-
tempting to pull loose. "Stop, Cassie!" Big Ma said.

(83) (84) (85)
this min- You're
"Stop, ~~it's me~~. ~~We're~~ going home now."

㊏86㊏   ㊏87㊏she
"Not 'fore she 'pologize/s/to my gal, y'all ain't," said

㊏88㊏
Mr. (Simms)

Big Ma gazed down at me, fear in her eyes, then
㊏89㊏ 3 grōwling
       2 crowling
       1 growling
back at the ~~growing~~ crowd. "She jus' a child—"

㊏90㊏ Annie
"Tell her, ~~Aunty~~."

                                        ㊏91㊏cracked
Big Ma looked at me again, her voice ~~cracking~~ as

she spoke. "Go on, child . . . apologize."

Ⓡ
⌐"But, Big Ma—"

               ㊏92㊏look ㊏93㊏said
Her voice hardened. "~~Do~~-like I ~~say~~."

I swallowed hard.

"Go on!"

Ⓡ Ⓡ
⌐⌐"I'm sorry," I mumbled.

       ㊏94㊏ Ⓒ Lin   Ⓒ de-   Soloms
"I'm sorry, Miz ~~Lillian~~ Jean," (demanded Mr. ~~Simms~~.
       ㊏95㊏ 2 baked
            1 bi-   [Teacher then supplied
"Big Ma!" I ~~balked~~.   the word.]

"Say it, child."

A painful tear slid down my cheek and my lips

trembled. "I'm sorry . . . M-Miz . . . Lillian Jean."

When the words had been spoken, I turned and

fled crying into the back of the wagon. No day in all
       ㊏96㊏ Ⓒcurled
my life had ever been as ~~cruel~~ as this one.

7 Analyzing Miscues and Looking for Patterns

Once professionals concerned with reading have developed miscue analysis techniques they will never again listen to readers in the way they did in the past.
—Yetta Goodman, Dorothy Watson, and Carolyn Burke

Questions for Thought and Discussion

1. Given that miscue analysis is an art rather than an exact science, what are some situations and issues that make miscue analysis quirky?
2. How can we code miscues in the margins of a copy of the selection read?
3. What additional information can we learn from a more detailed miscue analysis form?
4. What miscue analysis patterns are common with proficient readers?
5. What miscue patterns may we find with nonproficient readers—that is, those who often do not make much meaning from texts?

Analyzing miscues is not an exact science, but an art.

Analyzing miscues is not an exact science, but an art. There are certain set procedures to follow (some of which I have modified from the Goodman original), but we will always find that reality never quite fits our predetermined schemes for analysis. Or to put it another way, teachers who understand reading strategies, the use of language cues in reading, and miscue analysis will always find that some readers and some miscues fit predetermined forms and miscue analysis schemes awkwardly, at best. Informed teacher judgment must always take precedence over a rigid scheme, and the data on a form will rarely tell us all we need to know about what is being analyzed. Nevertheless, a scheme such as a miscue analysis coding form can lead teachers to insights they otherwise wouldn't have had, particularly if their prior experience has led them to view all unexpected responses to text as merely "errors" to be avoided.

It should be emphasized that analyzing every miscue in a stretch of text does *not* mean that we consider the identification of every word to be crucial. Indeed, the most proficient readers are those who are not only effective in constructing meaning, but efficient in that they do not waste time struggling with words that seem relatively unimportant in their quest for meaning. Even though we may analyze miscues for whether or not they were corrected, the point is not necessarily that they "should" have been corrected. On the other hand, if a reader seldom tries to correct miscues that disrupt meaning, this tells us something about the reader's approach to reading and *perhaps* suggests that he or she is not reading to make meaning of text. In that case, helping the reader notice when miscues are not meaningful may be one important way to encourage the reader to read for meaning. Nevertheless, meaning is the goal, not precise identification of all the words.

It should be emphasized that analyzing every miscue in a stretch of text does *not* mean that we consider the identification of every word to be crucial. Indeed, the most proficient readers are those who are not only effective in constructing meaning, but efficient in that they do not waste time struggling with words that seem relatively unimportant in their quest for meaning.

The next three sections of this chapter deal with (1) miscues and the use of context; (2) analyzing and coding miscues on the selection copy (a photocopy or typescript of the selection read); and (3) analyzing, coding, and interpreting the data from Tony's miscues, as an example.

The rest of the chapter focuses on helping you do miscue analysis yourself. First, the chapter offers recommendations on marking and numbering miscues for coding, which is information you will need whether you analyze and code miscues in the margins of a copy of the selection, or use some coding form. This discussion is followed by more on how to code miscues, with particular reference to my detailed analysis form; an example using the detailed form for coding a student's miscues; and finally a brief section on alternative miscue analysis procedures and forms.

MISCUES AND THE USE OF CONTEXT

When a reader makes a miscue, it may or may not go with the grammar and/or the meaning of what came before, as Figure 7.1 may help you visualize.

Proficient readers use context to think ahead or "predict" as they read. Typically their eyes are ahead of their voice (or thinking) when they read, so their miscues often fit with the following context as well. And if not, they will often use the context following their miscues to look and think back, correcting their miscue if possible—silently if not orally. Thus, if many or most of the reader's miscues fit with what came before, we can infer that the reader tends to predict, or "think ahead." Likewise, a miscue may or may not go with the grammar and/or meaning of what comes afterwards. If many or most of the reader's miscues fit with what follows, we can infer that the reader's eyes are likely to be ahead of the voice while reading. (The difference between where the eyes are and what the reader is saying aloud is called the *eye-voice span*). If the miscues do not fit with what follows *and* if the reader does not try to correct, this may mean:

- The reader is not reading for meaning.
- The reader is correcting silently.
- The reader is making sense of the text without the miscued word(s).
- The reader assumes that he or she can't "get" the word anyway.
- Or perhaps some combination of the above.

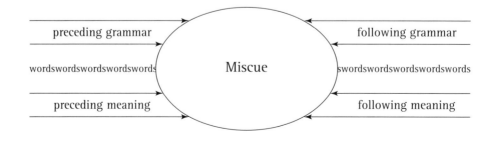

Figure 7.1 *Context before and after a miscue.*

When we code a miscue as to whether it goes with the preceding context, we read the preceding part of the sentence as the reader left it: with preceding miscues left uncorrected, if they weren't corrected by the reader. When we code a miscue as to whether it goes with the following context, we do not take into consideration miscues that have not yet been made, unless it seems virtually certain that the reader was looking ahead.

You may need to review the miscue markings in Chapter 6 before continuing with this chapter (pp. 122–125).

Below are some examples of how certain miscues would be analyzed for the use of preceding context (PC) and following context (FC). For the most part, these examples are given according to what we commonly see as the proficiency of a reader progressively decreases, from highly competent to less competent. I have numbered the miscue examples below, so that you can easily refer to them in discussion. In addition, so that you can see the codings visually, I have included the codings regarding preceding and following context on part of a miscue form (Figure 7.2). *These examples are not from just one reader or text.* The sentence numbers below correspond with the miscue numbers on the coding form. Here, then, are examples that illustrate different patterns.

The following miscues fit with the preceding grammar and meaning and with the following grammar and meaning, so they would be coded as Y for both:

1. "Are you kidding?" said Buster, "Of course!"
   me (inserted after "kidding")

2. George carefully drew (in) a carrot / so the test people would know.

3. "Take *her* over there and see," said Hayes.

4. There were ~~baseball~~ *basketball* caps and / straw hats with bright, red bands.

In sentence 4, the miscue "basketball" makes a grammatical and meaningful stretch of words with what comes before in the sentence and with what follows, even though the meaning is not precisely the same.

5. After that Droofus gave up ~~eating~~ *his* grasshoppers and beetles. . . .

In sentence 5, the grammar of the miscue was actually different, but the miscue fits grammatically as well as meaningfully with what comes before *and* with what follows. The meaning was clear from the preceding sentences in the text.

The following miscues fit with the preceding grammar and meaning and with the following grammar *or* meaning, but not both. These would be coded as Y for preceding context, and as either G or M for following context, whichever is appropriate.

6. It was (a) perfect day for flying. . . .

7. There was not even one cloud to hide the sun(s) face for a while.

READER'S NAME

Various readers

Coder's name

c s w

Date *6/6/01*

Text that was read

Various texts

In coding these columns don't ask whether the miscue made the same grammar and nearly the same sense. Just ask if it made *good* grammar and a *sensible* stretch of wor s with what came before (column 2) and after (column 3).

	Did the miscue go with the grammar and meaning of what came before?	Did the miscue go with the grammar and meaning of what followed?
	Y = yes, the miscue fit with both the preceding grammar and preceding meaning	Y = yes, with both
		G = with grammar only
	G = the miscue fit with the preceding grammar only	M = with meaning only
		N = no, with neither
	M = the miscue fit with the preceding meaning only	
	N = the miscue fit with neither	

	TEXT SAYS	READER SAYS	Y	G	M	N	Y	G	M	N
1	—	me	✓				✓			
2	in	—	✓				✓			
3	it	her	✓				✓			
4	baseball	basketball	✓				✓			
5	eating	his	✓				✓			
6	a	—	✓						✓	
7	sun's	sun	✓						✓	
8	loaded	looked	✓					✓		
9	shook	took	✓					✓		
10	heard	had	✓							✓
11	except	expert	✓							✓
12	arranged	agreed	✓							✓
13	taller	talling		✓						✓
14	seat	sit			✓		—			
15	racing	raising		✓				✓		
16	rustled	resteled		✓				✓		
17	fields	felds		✓				✓		
18	cautiously	contisly		✓				✓		
19	now	how			✓				✓	
20	gracious	gra-use			✓				✓	
21	howl	hine			✓		—			
22	cement	come			✓		—			
23	camp	comp			✓		—			

Figure 7.2 *Sample miscue codings.*

looked
8. He ~~loaded~~ up his dump truck with oatmeal cookies, . . .

took
9. The doctor / came and went. He ~~shook~~ his head and looked / very serious.

In sentence 6, the omission of the word *a* makes the sentence ungrammatical. I consider omissions completely acceptable with preceding context. However, this omission is acceptable with only the meaning of the following context. In sentence 7, "sun" is completely acceptable with what precedes but goes only with the meaning of what follows. Thus, both 6 and 7 would be coded Y for preceding context and M for following context. In sentences 8 and 9, the miscue likewise fits with the preceding grammar and meaning, but with the following grammar only (the miscues are verbs, and the same kind of verb as the text word). Thus the miscues in sentences 8 and 9 would be coded Y for preceding context but G for following context.

The next miscues fit with the preceding grammar and meaning (Y) but not with the following grammar *or* meaning (N):

had
10. She ~~heard~~ / the children singing, and she loved it.

11. They were good swimmers / because their mother had taught them.

expert
Every day ~~except~~ Friday, . . .

12. Then she handed them to Mohammed and Asha, who took them

agreed
and ~~arranged~~ them on the beach to dry.

In sentence 10, "had" is a good prediction, but it doesn't go with what follows—at least not within the context of the original story. In sentence 11, the same is true with the miscue "expert," which can be considered a reasonable prediction not only syntactically but semantically, given preceding sentences in the story. The miscue in sentence 12 likewise fits with preceding grammar and meaning but not the following, even though the miscue "agreed" is the same general part of speech—a verb—as the word in the text. However, the text word *arranged* takes an object and "agreed" does not, so the miscue is not acceptable with even the grammar of what follows.

Here are miscues that fit with the preceding grammar or meaning, but not with both:

talling
13. Sally was ~~taller~~ than Tom.

14. One day Miss Tizzy took off her purple hat with

sit
the white flower and laid it on the window ~~seat~~.

The following miscues do not fit with even the preceding grammar or meaning:

15. "Queen Angelica will ~~now~~ *how* show you the second / good manner."

16. "Your ~~gracious~~ *gra-use* queen says 'Thank you.'"

17. That night Clifford was ~~so~~ *s-* *lane* lonely / he ~~began~~ *i been* ~~to~~ *to* ~~howl~~ *abe* *hine* *go*. [Only "hine" has been coded in Figure 7.2.]

18. Nothing stopped him—not ~~even~~ *ever* ~~wet~~ *went* ~~cement~~ *come*. [Only "come" has been coded in Figure 7.2.]

19. Then ~~he~~ *she* took (us) all ~~back~~ *black* to ~~camp~~ *comp*. [Only "comp" has been coded in figure 7.2.]

I have marked all the miscues in sentences 17 through 19, because they help us realize that most of the miscues in these sentences do not fit with even the grammar or meaning of what preceded them in the sentences, as the preceding text had been read aloud by the reader.

Here are miscues that fit with grammar only:

20. But / all she saw were the cars and / trucks ~~racing~~ *raising* along the busy / road.

In sentence 20, I do not think the miscue "raising" is sensible with what came before or what came after. However, it is a verb form ending in -*ing,* just like the original. Therefore I consider it to fit with the preceding grammar and following grammar, though not with meaning.

21. Night birds called and / the trees ~~rustled~~ *rēsteled*.

22. Where the town had stood / there were ~~fields~~ *felds* of / grass.

23. When she ~~cautiously~~ *contisly* opened / the flap of her tent, . . .

In sentences 21 through 23, the miscues are nonwords. We code nonwords as acceptable if they preserve the grammatical ending of the original word. "Rēsteled" preserves the past tense ending of the text word *rustled*; "felds" preserves the noun plural ending of the text word *fields*; and "contisly" preserves the adverb ending on *cautiously*.

It is important to realize that nonwords may have different significance for different readers. Some readers tend to sound out unfamiliar print words without trying to make meaning from texts; these are typically not very proficient readers, such as Tony, in this chapter. Other readers may get the essential meaning—or even the exact word—mentally, but still try to sound out the word, as Danny did with the word *amusement* in *amusement park* (Chapter 4). And still other readers may, at least when reading aloud, say something that resembles the text word graphically, but that isn't a word they automatically know on sight (and maybe not at all) and that doesn't seem to be crucial to the meaning of what they are reading. Often, the latter are proficient readers: that is, readers who not only make meaning from texts but who do so efficiently, without wasting time. (See the examples in Chapter 6, where the use of graphic cues along with other cues is discussed.)

MARKING AND CODING MISCUES ON THE SELECTION COPY

To simplify miscue analysis for everyday use, we can mark and code miscues on a copy of the selection that the person read (let us call this the *selection copy*). If needed, you can again return to Chapter 6 to review how miscues are marked. After marking them on the selection copy, we can simply use a ruler to create columns in the margins for coding the miscues, as done with Tony's miscues in Figure 7.3, a little later in the text.

Coding the Miscues

There are four major questions I would ask about miscues, and thus four columns on the copy of the selection (Figure 7.3), labeled as follows:

■ Question on use of *preceding context*, coded in the column I have labeled PC:
"Did the miscue go with the grammar and meaning of what came before?"

Responses to this question are coded as follows:

Y = Yes, the miscue fit with both the preceding grammar and the preceding meaning.

G = The miscue fit with the preceding grammar only.

M = The miscue fit with the preceding meaning only.

N = No, the miscue fit with neither.

The pattern of responses to this question gives us insight into whether the reader was typically predicting, or "thinking ahead" while reading.

■ Question on the use of *following context,* coded in the column I have labeled FC:
"Did the miscue go with the grammar and meaning of what followed?"

Responses to this question are coded as follows:

Y = Yes, the miscue fit with both the grammar and the meaning of what followed.

G = The miscue fit with the following grammar only.

M = The miscue fit with the following meaning only.

N = No, the miscue fit with neither.

The pattern of responses to this question gives us insight into whether the reader was typically looking ahead to following context while reading aloud. If so, many of the miscues are likely to fit with the following context; if not, quite a few of the miscues will probably not fit with the following context.

■ Question on *correction,* coded in column C:
"Was the miscue corrected?"

Responses to this question can be coded as follows:

Y = Yes, the miscue was corrected.

UC = The reader attempted to correct the first miscue made, but was unsuccessful.

N = No, the miscue was not corrected.

Miscue | Sentence

| | PC | FC | C | SS | |

① Mo –
Mohamed (mo-hah' med) loved to go swimming in the sea.

② 2 Sammon / 1 Sam-   ③
How lucky he was to live in a ~~Somali~~ (so-mah' lee) (village)

④ ran
right on the Indian Ocean! The sandy shore ~~rang~~ with the happy

⑤ souts   ⑥
~~shouts~~ and cries of the (village) boys and girls. They liked

⑦ high
to race one another into the surf, splashing and spraying

⑧ drase
the water into a white ~~dancing~~ foam before they dove into the

⑨ Mola   ⑩ yūng   ⑪ Asla
waves. Mohamed and his ~~young~~ sister, ~~Asha~~ (ie' shuh),

⑫ (long omission ordinarily not coded)   long omission
(spent all the time they could in the cool clean) sea, not coded

swimming and playing water games. They were good swimmers

because their mother had taught them.

⑬ expert   ⑭ Molda
Every day ~~except~~ Friday, Mohamed went to school with the

⑮   ⑯
nother viner
~~other~~ ~~village~~ boys. The class was outdoors, and the children

⑰ beaches   ⑱ frose   ⑲ shape
sat on little ~~benches~~ in ~~front~~ of the teacher in the ~~shade~~

of a tall palm tree. They did not have books, so the boys

⑳ ramped
~~repeated~~ everything the teacher said, over and over, until

㉑ other classrooms hurt   ㉒ vengil
they knew ~~their lessons by heart~~. The girls of the ~~village~~

did not go to school, for the people thought that school was

㉓ imprentice   ㉔ to
not as ~~important~~ for girls as ~~it~~ was for boys.

Miscue	PC	FC	C	SS	Sentence
1	—	Y	N	Y	1
2	Y	Y	UC	Y	2
3	Y	Y	N		
4	Y	G	N		3
5	G	G	N	Y	
6	Y	Y	N		
7	Y	Y	N	Y	4
8	N	N	N		
9	Y	Y	N		5
10	N	N	N	Y	
11	Y	Y	N		
12					
				Y	6
13	Y	N	N		
14	Y	Y	N	Y	7
15	N	N	N		
16	N	N	N		
17	Y	Y	N		8
18	N	N	N	Y	
19	Y	Y	N		
20	G	G	N	P	9
21	G	—	N		
22	N	N	N		
				P	10
23	N	N	N		
24	Y	N	N		

PC   12 Y = 54%   3 G = 14%   7 N = 13%

FC   10 Y = 45%   3 G = 14%   9 N = 41%

C   1 UC = 4%   22 N = 96%

SS   8 Y = 80%   2 P = 20%

12Y	10Y	1UC	8Y
3G	3G	22N	2P
7N	9N		
22	22	23	10

Figure 7.3   *Tony's miscues.*

By comparing the G only, M only, or N codings for following context with the codings for correction, we can see whether the following context may have cued the reader to try to correct.

■ Question on the *semantic acceptability* of the *sentence* with the whole *selection,* coded in the column I have labeled SS for "sentence within the selection":
"Was the sentence, as the reader finally left it, semantically acceptable within the whole original selection (text) that was read?"

Responses to this question are coded on the selection copy as follows:

Y = Yes, acceptable; there wasn't any essential change in the meaning of the selection.

P = Partial; there was inconsistency, loss, or change of a minor idea, incident, character, fact, sequence, or concept in the selection.

N = No, not acceptable; there was inconsistency, loss, or change of a major idea, incident, character, fact, sequence, or concept in the selection.

I do have a concern with the "partial" option, though. I am concerned that some teachers may be inclined to mark virtually every miscue as P for "partial," if they haven't marked it N. That is, they may view almost every miscue as a loss of essential meaning, to a greater or lesser degree. That would be unfortunate, and a complete misunderstanding of a major concept associated with miscue analysis. Teachers need to realize that many miscues have essentially no effect on the meaning of the sentence as a whole, much less on the entire selection.

> Teachers need to realize that many miscues have essentially no effect on the meaning of the sentence as a whole, much less on the entire selection.

It can be very informative to analyze and code *all* the sentences on the selection copy in this manner, to get a more complete sense of what the reader might have comprehended while reading.

ANALYZING, CODING, AND INTERPRETING THE DATA FROM TONY'S MISCUES

Miscue analysis and codings require us to draw inferences about the individual miscues. Further interpretation stems from examining the miscue patterns and the semantic acceptability of what has been read.

Analyzing and Coding Tony's Miscues

My discussion of Tony's miscues, and Jay's later in this chapter, will surely demonstrate just how much of an art is involved in making decisions about miscues in order to code them. Miscues are a window to the reading process, but only an indirect window, and coding miscues requires us to draw inferences—that is, to *think* about the miscues. With that warning, then, I shall turn to a discussion of Tony's miscues.

Before coding, it is helpful to read through the selection with the miscues marked, making the same miscues that the reader did, to get a sense of the reader's miscues and strategies. The selection copy with Tony's miscues marked is included here as Figure 7.3. The numbers to the left of the columns indicate the miscue number. The numbers to the right of the columns indicate the sentence number.

The following comments should help clarify some of my codings on the selection copy. The numbers that follow refer to the miscue numbers:

1: Ordinarily a "partial" like "Mo-" for *Mohammed* would be coded as an omission. In this case, however, I assumed that Tony could still tell that the word was the name of a person, so I chose to code it accordingly. In the PC column, I drew a line to indicate that there was no prior context within that sentence, but I gave the miscue a Y in the FC column, because I assumed Tony knew that *Mohamed* was the name of a person. I have had teachers argue that not reading *Mohamed* correctly causes a loss of meaning, since the name would suggest a Middle Eastern setting, and that is important to the story. But if Tony knew that "Mohamed" is a common Middle Eastern name, I expect he would have read the name correctly. Basically, I doubt that reading *Mohamed* correctly would have clued Tony as to the setting.

2: We always code the last miscue made on a word or stretch of words, which in this case was "sammon." As with the previously discussed miscue, I chose to assume that Tony realized this was a noun, in this case the name of a place or a thing that one could live in. The miscue is coded UC in the correction column, for an unsuccessful attempt at correction.

3: Coding miscue #3 was a challenge, since we don't know for sure whether Tony assumed "sammon" was something you could live in. However, I decided to make that assumption. That is, I decided to assume that Tony was making a grammatical and mostly meaningful sentence when he read "How lucky he was to live in a sammon right on the Indian Ocean." Therefore, I coded the omission of *village* as acceptable with both the preceding and the following context, and as preserving the essential meaning of the sentence. Of course, someone else might have made a different assumption about "sammon" and thus about the omission of *village*. I chose to consider and code these miscues the way I did partly to illustrate the complexity of thought involved as we make decisions about how to code miscues.

4: Interestingly, miscue #4 seems to make a meaningful stretch of words with what came before. One way we can tell is, paradoxically, to see if we can imagine the sentence continuing grammatically and meaningfully. I can imagine "The sandy shore ran" continuing with something like "along the beach for miles." Thus I interpreted the miscue as going with the preceding context and coded it as Y in the PC column. In the FC column, I coded the miscue as G, because it goes with the grammar that follows, but not with the following meaning.

5: When a nonword substitution preserves the grammatical ending of the text word, we code it as going with the preceding and following grammar, but not with meaning; that is, we code it G in the PC column and the FC column. This is true of "souts" for *shouts* and for miscue #19 as well, "ramped" for *repeated*. Why consider as grammatically acceptable the nonwords that appear to retain the grammatical endings of the text words they replace? Goodman and Goodman report that "Our data on readers' word-for-word substitutions, whether nonwords or real words, show that, on average, 80 percent of the observed responses retain the morphemic markings of the text" (1997; p. 112 in Weaver, 1998). The "morphemic markings" are mostly grammatical endings on words.

6: We code the same omission again because the grammatical context is different.

8 and 10: When a nonword like "drase" or "yūng" replaces a text word that has no grammatical ending, it is simply coded N in columns 2 and 3.

12: The miscue "expert" for *except* is coded as going with what came before, because "Every day expert…" is acceptable up to and including the miscue. However, the miscue does not go with the grammar or meaning of what follows.

15: Notice that after omitting *village* twice, Tony starts giving it a try. This can be a positive sign, though as mentioned in Chapter 6, it can often be a waste of time to make repeated, different attempts at the particular ("proper") names of people and places, such as *Mohamed* and *Somali*.

20: Here, Tony seems to have given up trying to read the exact words of the text, simply saying "other classrooms hurt" instead of *their lessons by heart.* Sad to say, perhaps he was drawing upon his own classroom experience, plus lack of experience in memorizing information.

20–22, 23–24: Each of the two sentences seems to have lost a minor concept about how the boys were taught. The same seemed to hold true for the sentences containing miscues 19 and 20, and again for 21 through 23.

Such process-oriented data needs to be complemented by a retelling and discussion, described in the next chapter.

Interpretation of Tony's Miscue Patterns

In brief, Tony's miscue patterns look like one major pattern found among nonproficient readers. In the preceding context column, only 50% of Tony's miscues fit completely with the preceding context, and this is a rather low percentage for that column, suggesting that Tony doesn't try to think ahead as he reads but mostly deals with words one at a time. It's true that another 18% of his miscues fit with the preceding grammar, but these miscues are mainly nonwords, again suggesting that Tony uses mostly graphic cues, along with some grammatical cues. The statistics from the following context column are similar, but slightly less positive than those from before. The fact that Tony doesn't even try to correct more than one of his miscues (the C column) is also telling, given the low percentage that fit in context (the PC and FC columns).

The data from the last column, the semantic acceptability of the sentence within the selection, is not strongly encouraging, either, though I did code 70% of Tony's sentences in this part of the selection as being semantically acceptable. (I do not have the data for coding the rest of the sentences in the selection.)

Considering this information all together, I have come to the following conclusions about Tony's reading—conclusions that are the same as his teacher's, after she did the analysis:

- Tony tends not to read for meaning, judging by his weak retelling of the story.
- Tony's miscues suggest that he tends to read words without a great deal of regard to their sounding right or making sense in the story (though his miscues do fit better with the grammar than with the meaning).

Tony needs help, then, in learning to read for meaning, and in learning to use grammar and meaning *along with* graphic cues, to make it easier to "get" words as well as to construct meaning from texts.

Another Way of Coding Tony's Miscues

In Chapter 10, we shall begin to discuss literacy experiences and instruction that can help readers like Tony, as well as readers showing different miscue patterns. Chapters 12 and 14 will continue that discussion. Here, however, I want to continue by showing how Tony's miscues might be coded according to procedure 3 in Y. Goodman, Watson, & Burke (1987). Here are the questions that are asked of each *sentence* (1987, pp. 116–117). I have added a few comments in square brackets:

- Question 1: *Syntactic acceptability:*
  Is the sentence syntactically acceptable in the reader's dialect and within the context of the entire selection?

  Y—The sentence, as finally produced by the reader, is syntactically acceptable.

  N—The sentence, as finally produced by the reader, is not syntactically acceptable (partial acceptability is not considered in this procedure).

■ Question 2: *Semantic acceptability:*
Is the sentence semantically acceptable in the reader's dialect and within the context of the entire selection? (Question 2 cannot be coded Y if Question 1 has been coded N.) [In my own procedures, we code semantic acceptability even if the miscue is not syntactically acceptable.]

Y—The sentence, as finally produced by the reader, is semantically acceptable.

N—The sentence, as finally produced by the reader, is not semantically acceptable (partial acceptability is not considered in this procedure).

■ Question 3: *Meaning change:*
Does the sentence, as finally produced by the reader, change the meaning of the selection? (Question 3 is coded only if Questions 1 and 2 are coded Y.) [In my own procedure, we nonetheless ask "Was the sentence, as the reader finally left it, semantically acceptable within the whole original selection that was read?"]

N—There is no change in the meaning of the selection.

P—There is inconsistency, loss, or change of a *minor* idea, incident, character, fact, sequence, or concept in the selection.

Y—There is inconsistency, loss, or change of a *major* idea, incident, character, fact, sequence, or concept in the selection.

[Notice that a positive response—no change in the meaning of the selection—is coded N, while a negative response is coded Y.]

■ Question 4: *Graphic similarity:*
How much does the miscue look like the text item?

H—A high degree of graphic similarity exists between the miscue and the text.

S—Some degree of graphic similarity exists between the miscue and the text.

N—No degree of graphic similarity exists between the miscue and the text.

To code for graphic similarity, the H, S, or N is placed directly above each word-level substitution on the selection copy.

Figure 7.4 shows these questions applied to Tony's sentences (and question 4 to the substitution miscues). Only the question about meaning change is comparable to one of my questions, question 7 on my miscue form. However, the Y and N answers are reversed because the question is worded just the opposite on the two forms.

Why, you may ask, have I included this different way of coding miscues on the selection copy? Because some teachers may prefer not to code individual miscues (except perhaps for graphic similarity), but rather to code whole sentences instead. In that case, teachers might especially like Sandra Wilde's (2000) book on miscue analysis made easy, which uses the Goodman procedure 3 form. Clearly, coding whole sentences is much less time-consuming than coding individual miscues, because it requires hardly any analysis. Furthermore, coding sentences on the selection sheet can provide comparative data over time, if you absolutely must keep quantifiable data (and if you use "leveled" or "graded" passages so that the comparisons might have some chance of being meaningful). Personally, though, I find this procedure inadequate because it doesn't tell me much about reading strategies, which I want to know in order to plan for instruction (see Chapter 9). Therefore, I prefer my coding procedures or Procedure 1 in Y. Goodman, Watson, & Burke (1987).

① Mo S̲
Mohamed (mo-hah' med) loved to go swimming in the sea.
② a Sammon / Sam- S̲   ③
How lucky he was to live in a ~~Somali~~ (so-mah' lee) (village)
④ ran H̲
right on the Indian Ocean! The sandy shore ~~rang~~ with the happy
⑤ souts H̲   ⑥
~~shouts~~ and cries of the (village) boys and girls. They liked
⑦ high
to race one another into the surf, splashing and spraying
⑧ drase S̲
the water into a white ~~dancing~~ foam before they dove into the
⑨ Mola S̲   ⑩ yŭng H̲   ⑪ Asla H̲
waves. Mohamed and his ~~young~~ sister, ~~Asha~~ (ie' shuh),

⑫
(spent all the time they could in the cool clean) sea,

swimming and playing water games. They were good swimmers

because their mother had taught them.
⑬ expert H̲   ⑭ Molda S̲
Every day ~~except~~ Friday, Mohamed went to school with the
⑮ H̲ ⑯ S̲ nother viner
~~other village~~ boys. The class was outdoors, and the children
⑰ beaches H̲ ⑱ frose S̲   ⑲ shape H̲
sat on little ~~benches~~ in ~~front~~ of the teacher in the ~~shade~~

of a tall palm tree. They did not have books, so the boys
⑳ ramped H̲
~~repeated~~ everything the teacher said, over and over, until

㉑ other classrooms hurt N N S̲   ㉒ vengil S̲
they knew ~~their lessons by heart.~~ The girls of the ~~village~~

did not go to school, for the people thought that school was
㉓ imprentice H̲   ㉔ to N̲
not as ~~important~~ for girls as ~~it~~ was for boys.

syntactic acceptability	semantic acceptability	meaning change	Sentence
Y	Y	N	1
Y	N	–	2
Y	N	–	3
Y	N	–	4
N	–	–	5
Y	Y	N	6
N	–	–	7
Y?	Y?	N?	8
Y	N	–	9
N	–	–	10
7Y 3N	3Y 4N	3N	

Figure 7.4 *Tony's miscues, coded according to Y. Goodman, Watson, & Burke (1987).*

Informal Reading Inventories

From a psycholinguistic perspective, informal reading inventories published for teacher use are usually inadequate or inappropriate. One reason is that they typically suggest "reading levels" based on the percentage of miscues, often with no regard to the quality of the miscues and certainly with no consideration for what is appropriate for an individual student. Another major concern is that the passages are usually too short for the reader to have an opportunity to learn from the text and thereby to begin making better-quality miscues. Also critical is the typical nature of the "comprehension" questions: on short passages, the testmaker may be forced to include mostly questions that focus on detail and recall of fact, rather than the more challenging kinds of questions that stimulate sophisticated inferencing or critical reflection.

Having raised these concerns, there is one informal reading inventory that appears to be a notch above several others on the market:

Leslie, L., & Caldwell, J. (2001). *Qualitative Reading Inventory—3*. New York: Longman.

Using the "total acceptability" criterion for independent, instructional, and frustration levels is much better than using the "total accuracy" alternative that the authors also mention. However, I still think the percentage suggested for "total acceptability" is substantially higher than appropriate for each of the levels (pp. 56–57). Therefore, I advise not taking the "level" designations seriously.

MARKING MISCUES FOR CODING

Before we can analyze and code miscues, we need to mark them on a copy of the selection. This may be a photocopy (enlarged, if necessary, to give more space between the lines), or a copy we have typed ourselves. If we type a copy, we need to leave three spaces between lines and end each line exactly where it was ended in the original text, so we can see if the line endings might have encouraged some of the miscues. Again, we call the copy of the selection on which we mark the miscues simply the selection copy, for convenience.

How to Mark Miscues on the Selection Copy

When the reader has said a nonword, or "nonsense" word, we use as much of the spelling of the original as possible in representing the reader's pronunciation. Suppose, for example, that the text word is *psychology,* and the reader has said /SI - ko - lo - gi/. Write this as PSYkology, not as SIkology. If the text word is *wrapped* and the reader has said it with a long *a*, write the miscue as "wrāpped" or "wraped," not as "rāpt" or "raped." In other words, don't make changes in spelling unless they reflect actual changes in sound.

Numbering the miscues requires understanding and judgment. It is not just a mechanical act.

Once we have marked the miscues on a copy of the reading selection, we must number the miscues to be analyzed. In the early miscue research, Kenneth Goodman and his colleagues found that coding 25 miscues was usually sufficient to demonstrate miscue patterns that suggest certain reading strategies, or the lack thereof. However, if the reader has made more than 25 miscues, it is usually a good idea to discard the miscues on approximately the first 200 words of text (if, of course, this leaves at least 25 miscues). After that, we can code the next 25 numbered miscues consecutively, without omitting any numbered miscues. This procedure will usually provide a representative sample of the reader's strategies. However, we might choose 25 miscues from the middle of the selection to code, if they seem more representative. Or perhaps we might compare one stretch of miscues from the beginning of the text with two more stretches of text: one from the middle and a final one from the end of the text read. Rarely is it necessary to code more than 50 miscues to establish a reader's patterns.

Notice that I have said we code 25 consecutive *numbered* miscues. Numbering the miscues involves understanding and judgment. It is not just a mechanical act. Here are some basic guidelines for numbering the miscues.

1. It can be useful for later discussion to number the miscues starting from the very first one, even if the first 25 are not included on the miscue coding form.

2. If the reader omits most or all of a line of text (or more), we need not number the miscue for later analysis, though we should make note of such omissions, if they occur at all frequently. Alternatively we may code the omission as a single, complex miscue (see item 6 below), but that is not commonly done.

3. In the original miscue analysis procedures, it was not considered necessary to number and analyze miscues that merely reflect the sound system of a reader's dialect or the reader's native language, or the fact that English has some sounds not part of the reader's native language. For example, if a reader normally said "hep" for *help* or "picher" for *picture*, such a miscue was not coded. Neither were miscues like "dis" for *this* or "herro" for *hello*, when they reflected a different dialect or language pattern. But for our own learning purposes, we may choose to number and code these sound features, if we are using a detailed form like the one in Figure 6.2 (repeated in this chapter as Figure 7.5). Miscues that reflect the reader's own grammatical or semantic system have always been coded and analyzed, but considered completely acceptable in columns 2, 3, and 4: dialect miscues such as "We was" for *We were*, for example, or "quarter of nine" for *quarter till nine*. The same is true for miscues that occur because a nonnative speaker of English has not completely mastered the grammatical system of English, such as "He want it" for *He wanted it* or "He was amazed to found it" for *He was amazed to find it*. (See the next section on coding miscues.)

4. Do not consider a partial attempt at a word as a miscue to be numbered and analyzed, if the partial is then completed (that is, "corrected"). For example, if the text says *psychology* and the reader says "psy-" and then "psychology," we mark the partial word miscue on the worksheet but don't number it for coding. (Such miscues may indicate a useful word attack strategy.) On the other hand, if a partial word is not corrected, we also mark and then code it as an omission, since a partial word ordinarily provides too little information to make coding decisions about how it fits with context. Mumbles are additionally marked and coded as omissions.

5. If a reader more than once makes exactly the same substitution for a content word (that is, a noun, verb, adjective, or adverb), then we number and analyze only the first occurrence. On the other hand, each *new* substitution for a content word, and each substitution for a function word (new or not) should ordinarily be coded. Nevertheless, there are exceptions. For example: in reading *A Camel in the Sea*, Betsey made so many miscues on the proper (specific) names that listing each new pronunciation would mean that a large percentage of the 25 coded miscues would involve proper names. Since this would give a very distorted picture of Betsey's miscues and reading strategies, I chose not to number the various substitutions for names (see pp. 145–149 at the end of Chapter 6). Such repeated attempts should be noted elsewhere on the selection copy, however, or on a separate sheet.

6. If one particular miscue seems to have caused one or more others, it may be best to consider them together as a single complex miscue. Here is one possible example, from

Jay's miscues:

Ain't (ever) heard (anybody)   *much about*

(call) her @ beauty.

Instead of three omissions and one insertion, we might consider this to be one longer substitution miscue: "much about her beauty," instead of *anybody call her a beauty.* On the other hand, it can be reasonably argued that coding these as one complex miscue obscures rather than highlights the fact that additional miscues may result from readers accommodating following text to previous miscues, as Jay surely did. For the latter reason, I have chosen to number and code the miscues separately in this stretch of text.

The following section deals with coding miscues once they have been marked on the selection copy and numbered appropriately.

General Principles and Procedures for Coding Miscues

Questions always arise when teachers new to miscue analysis, or new to my miscue form, try to code miscues and look for patterns. This section anticipates some of those questions with clarifications and information that may prove helpful.

Here are some general directions, this time keyed to my detailed coding form (Figure 7.5).

- If the miscue is an insertion, simply draw a line in the column headed "Text says" and write the miscue in the column "Reader says." See example 1 in Figure 7.2.
- Conversely, if the miscue is an omission, write the text word(s) in the column "Text says" and draw a line in the column "Reader says." See example 2 in Figure 7.2.
- If the reader tries unsuccessfully to correct a miscue, it's the last attempt at correction that is written in the "Reader says" column. However, it can be useful to write the first attempt as well if there is more than one, so that we can immediately tell that the reader has made an unsuccessful attempt at correction.

The following questions correlate with the questions on the miscue analysis form in Figure 7.5.

Question 1: Did the miscue reflect the speaker's ordinary speech patterns?

If the miscue reflects a well-documented pattern of immature speech, put a check mark (or I) in column 1, under the I. If it reflects a well-documented feature of an ethnic, social, or regional dialect other than the dialect of your region, mark the miscue under D for dialect. Similarly, if the miscue reflects the learning of English as a nonnative language, mark it under E for ESL (English as a Second Language) or EFL (English as a Foreign Language). Common dialect and ESL miscues are given in Chapter 4, pp. 74–77. See also the discussion of such miscues in Chapter 6, pp. 129–131. Usually dialect miscues that reflect simply a sound pattern of the dialect are not coded, but you might choose to record these if they aren't frequent within the stretch of miscues you are coding.

READER'S NAME

Grade   **Age**

Coder's name

Date

Text (selection) that was read

Code columns 2 through 4 as ___ the miscue weren't corrected, even if it was.

In coding columns 2 & 3 don't ask whether the miscue made *the same grammar* and nearly the same sense. Just ask if it makes good grammar and a *sensible* stretch of words with what came before (column 2) and after (column 3).

		1 Did the miscue reflect the speaker's ordinary speech patterns? I = immature speech; D = dialect; E = ESL or EFL learner. If a miscue is coded I, D, or E, all the rest of the columns are coded Y, except for column 6, which is coded as usual			**2** Did the miscue go with the grammar and meaning of what came before? Y = yes, the miscue fit with both the preceding grammar and preceding meaning; G = the miscue fit with the preceding grammar only; M = the miscue fit with the preceding meaning only; N = the miscue fit with neither				**3** Did the miscue go with the grammar and meaning of what follows? Y = yes, with both; G = with grammar only; M = with meaning only; N = with neither				**4** Did the miscue leave the *essential* meaning of the sentence intact? Y = yes, this particular miscue, by itself, left the *essential* meaning of the *sentence* still intact. N = no, this miscue did not leave essential meaning of the sentence intact		**5** Was the miscue corrected? Y = yes, corrected; UC = unsuccessful attempt at correction; N = no, not corrected, and this miscue is not an attempt at correction; O = overcorrection; a miscue involving a contraction was corrected unnecessarily				**6** Was the miscue graphically similar? Y = high similarity; P = some (partial) similarity; N = no similarity. Apply to substitution miscues only.			**7** Was the sentence, as the reader finally left it, semantically acceptable within the whole original selection that was read? Bracket the miscues that came from each sentence, and then code the sentences: Y = yes, acceptable; there wasn't any essential change in the meaning of the selection. P = partial; there was inconsistency, loss, or change of a *minor* idea, incident, character, fact, sequence, or concept in the selection. N = not acceptable; there was inconsistency, loss, or change of a *major* idea, incident, character, fact, sequence, or concept in the selection		
TEXT SAYS	**READER SAYS**	I	D	E	Y	G	M	N	Y	G	M	N	Y	N	Y	UC	N	O	Y	P	N	Y	P	N
1																								
2																								
3																								
4																								
5																								
6																								
7																								
8																								
9																								
10																								
11																								
12																								
13																								
14																								
15																								
16																								
17																								
18																								
19																								
20																								
21																								
22																								
23																								
24																								
25																								

Figure 7.5 *Miscue analysis coding form #1 (from Constance Weaver, Reading Process and Practice, 3rd ed., Heinemann, 2002; © 2002 by Constance Weaver; may be reproduced for use).*

At your discretion, you might choose to check an informal miscue like "cause" for *because* as D in column 1. However, such a miscue reflects simply the normal speech of everyone, not a dialect feature. This is important for teachers to realize.

When a miscue is coded I, D, or E in column 1, then columns 2 through 4 are all coded Y. That is, the miscue is coded as completely okay in these columns if it simply reflects such normal speech patterns.

If there is no reason to code a reader's miscues as I, D, or E in column 1, then leave the column blank.

Question 2: Did the miscue go with the grammar and meaning of what came before?

Question 3: Did the miscue go with the grammar and meaning of what followed?

Figure 7.1 was included to help you visualize the fact that a miscue can be analyzed with reference to preceding grammar and meaning and following grammar and meaning. The following discussion is slightly repetitive of the previous discussion, but the material probably bears repeating.

When a reader makes a miscue, it may or may not go with the grammar and/or the meaning of what came before. If many or most of the reader's miscues fit with what came before, we can infer that the reader tended to predict, or "think ahead," when reading the selection. Likewise, a miscue may or may not go with the grammar and/or meaning of what came afterwards. If many or most of the reader's miscues fit with what followed, we can infer that the reader's eyes were likely to be ahead of the voice while reading (see "eye-voice span" in Chapter 3). If the miscues did not fit with what followed and the reader did not try to correct, perhaps (1) the reader was not reading for meaning; (2) the reader was correcting silently; (3) the reader was making sense of the text without the miscued word(s); (4) the reader assumed that he or she couldn't "get" the word anyway; or (5) some combination of the above.

> When we code a miscue in column 2 as to whether it went with the preceding context, we read the preceding part of the sentence as the reader left it: with preceding miscues left uncorrected, if they weren't corrected by the reader. When we code a miscue in column 3 as to whether it went with the following context, we do not ordinarily take into consideration miscues that have not yet been made.

I chose to discuss together the questions in columns 2 and 3 of the miscue form, because they raise the same kinds of issues for coding:

- In column 2, the miscue is coded Y if it fit with both the grammar and the meaning of what preceded. Likewise, in column 3, the miscue is coded Y if it fit with both the grammar and meaning of what followed.

- In column 2, the miscue is coded G if it fit with the grammar of what came before, but not the meaning of what came before. Likewise, in column 3, the miscue is coded G if it fit the grammar of what followed, but not the meaning of what followed.

- In column 2, the miscue is coded M if it went with the meaning of what came before, but not with the grammar of what came before. Likewise, in column 3, the miscue is coded M if it went with the meaning of what followed, but not the grammar of what followed.

- In column 2, the miscue is coded N if it fit with neither the grammar nor the meaning of what came before. Likewise, in column 3, the miscue is coded N if it fit with neither the grammar nor the meaning of what followed.

- When we code a miscue in column 2 as to whether it went with the preceding context, we read the preceding part of the sentence as the reader left it: with preceding miscues left uncorrected, if they weren't corrected by the reader.

■ When we code a miscue in column 3 as to whether it went with the following context, we do not take into consideration miscues that have not yet been made, unless we are fairly certain that the reader tends to look ahead while reading aloud.

Notice that columns 2 and 3 ask us to consider not whether the miscue makes *the same* grammar and *the same* sense with what comes before and after, but only if it makes a grammatical and/or meaningful stretch of words with what came before (column 2) and what came after (column 3). One example I particularly remember from the early miscue work was the text sentence *He looked up and saw a canary.* Some children read this as "He looked up and saw a carrot." Seeing a carrot is certainly not the same as seeing a canary, but this miscue was coded as completely acceptable with what came before (and with the period afterwards), since it is possible—at least potentially sensible—to look up and see a carrot hung in the air. As a balance to such codings, column 4 on my miscue form gives us the opportunity to indicate if the essential meaning of the sentence was changed by the miscue, as it clearly was in this instance.

Question 4: Did the miscue leave the *essential* meaning of the sentence intact?

The word *essential* is key here. How do we know whether a miscue affected the essential meaning of a sentence? It is easier to suggest when the miscue probably did *not* affect the essential meaning—at least when we examine substitutions. A miscue is not likely to have affected the essential meaning when (1) it involved an unimportant describing word, like "huge" in *great big, huge bear;* (2) the essence of the word miscued was suggested by another word or words in the sentence; or (3) the miscue occurred in a relatively unimportant part of the sentence. Here are examples of miscues that don't seem to have affected the essential meaning of the sentence:

- The sandy shore rang with the happy

  souts
  ~~shouts~~ and cries of the village boys and girls.

In the above example, the accurately read word *cries* suffices to clarify the meaning, since it, too, is modified by the word *happy:* "the happy... cries of the boys and girls."

- On ~~sunny days~~ *Sunday*, as soon as school was over, Mohamed went with

  his mother and Asha to wash the family $'s$ clothes.

In the context of the story, it is relatively unimportant whether the reader reads the beginning phrase as "On sunny days" or as "On Sunday." It's true that the meanings are not identical, but the meaning difference is not important to main idea of the sentence in context.

Sometimes a miscue is not coded for meaning in columns 2 and 3 the same way it is coded in column 4. Take, for example, the miscue in this sentence:

- "Your ~~gracious~~ *gra-use* queen says 'Thank you.'"

In this case the miscue is a nonword, so it is coded as not going with the meaning of what came before or after. However, the word *gracious* is relatively unimportant in that sentence, so I would code the miscue Y in column 4, to indicate that the miscue left the essential meaning of the text intact. The opposite, or near opposite, pattern can also occur. One reader, for instance, read *Hiram was usually the caboose* as "Hiram was using a chalkboard." The miscue "using a chalkboard" makes a sensible stretch of words with what comes before in the sentence, so I would code it as Y in column 2. It receives just a straight line in column 3, because there is no following context within the sentence. In column 4, however, the miscue would be coded N, because the miscue certainly does change the essential meaning of the sentence.

Question 5: Was the miscue corrected?

The miscue is coded Y if it was corrected and N if it wasn't. However, column 5 includes two other special circumstances. If a reader tried unsuccessfully to correct a miscue, the (last) attempted correction is written on the coding sheet and coded UC in column 5, for unsuccessful attempt at correction. Second, if a miscue involving a contraction was corrected unnecessarily, it is marked Y in column 5, but also O in column 5, for overcorrection. An example would be if the text said *do not,* the reader miscued with the contraction "don't," then corrected it unnecessarily to "do not." (See Chapter 6, pp. 133–134, for other examples.) At your discretion, you may also indicate other unnecessarily corrected miscues the same way in this column. However, I would advise reserving this coding for miscues that are almost a perfect match, in terms of grammar and meaning preservation.

My miscue form does not offer any special way to code a miscue if the reader read the text correctly, then abandoned the correction for a miscue. That miscue simply is coded as N in column 5. (See Chapter 6, p. 124, for how such a miscue is written on the selection copy.)

Question 6: Was the miscue graphically similar?

For substitution miscues, we can ask whether the miscue had high, partial, or no similarity to the word in the text. In general, we can code a miscue as highly similar if at least two "parts" of the miscue are graphically similar—the beginning and end of the word, for example, or the beginning and middle, or the middle and end. Some examples are "rēsteled" for *rustled,* "felds" for *fields,* and "contisly" for *cautiously* (sentences 21 through 23 previously discussed). Examples of real-word miscues with high graphic similarity are "looked" for *loaded* and "took" for *shook* (sentences 8 and 9 as discussed). When the miscue resembles the text word somewhat, with a similar beginning, middle, or end, we can code the miscue as P, which is commonly used for "partial." No graphic similarity is coded N.

It's important to keep in mind that graphic similarity is not necessarily a desirable characteristic. On the one hand, readers may try to say or sound out words without regard to meaning, as with the previous examples of "rēsteled," "felds," and "contisly." If the reader had been reading for meaning, I suspect that he would have read correctly at least the word *fields* and possibly the word *cautiously.* But instead, he settled for meaningless near misses to the words.

On the other hand, making miscues like these may represent a phase in a good reader's developing strategies. A good reader who previously read *I saw a canary* as "I saw a bird" may later read the same sentence as "I saw a cainery," as the reader now attempts to identify the specific kind of bird, or just to say the exact words on the page. Also, we see many miscues that bear little or no graphic similarity to the text word, but that fit the sentence syntactically and semantically, with no meaning change—as in these examples, mostly from Chapter 6:

- "Chocolate!" ~~said~~ ^{shouted} Arthur.

- "When is ~~it?~~" ^{your party}

- Wednesday ~~before~~ ^{at} school, the boys had a meeting.

- *should*
  "Muffy ~~will~~ be here any ~~minute~~!" *second*

- Out (of)/(it) crawled a horned frog.

These are examples from highly proficient readers, who read for meaning rather than precise identification of all the words.

Teachers need to realize that many miscues have essentially no effect on the meaning of the sentence as a whole, much less on the meaning of the entire selection.

Question 7: Was the sentence, as the reader finally left it, semantically acceptable within the whole original selection that was read?

For the wording of the alternative choices, I have rephrased those in procedure 3 of Y. Goodman, Watson, and Burke (1987, p. 117), so that a Y for "yes" is positive and an N for "no" is negative, in terms of the sentence being semantically acceptable. The options on my form are as follows:

Y = Yes, acceptable; there wasn't any essential change in the meaning of the selection.

P = Partial; there was inconsistency, loss, or change of a *minor* idea, incident, character, fact, sequence, or concept in the selection.

N = Not acceptable; there was inconsistency, loss, or change of a *major* idea, incident, character, fact, sequence, or concept in the selection.

Let me say it one more time: it is important for teachers to realize that many miscues do not really affect a reader's comprehension of the entire selection read, even though teachers are accustomed to making that assumption. If this is your tendency, I encourage you think again!

ALTERNATIVE MISCUE ANALYSIS PROCEDURES AND FORMS

This section includes some alternative forms for analyzing miscues and recording data and/or examples.

The procedure for analyzing miscues that was discussed in some detail involves marking the miscues on a copy of the selection read, then coding a consecutive sample of miscues on a coding form. The detailed miscue form in Figure 7.5 is what I think of as a basic "learning about miscues" form, with important explanations for coding included on the form. But once you understand how to use this form, it is handy to have a form with fewer explanations and more space in the rows. Figure 7.6 was developed to meet this need.

If you code miscues in the margins of a copy of the selection read, you do not need a coding form at all. Then, if you need to do a separate data sheet for record-keeping, miscue data from the margins could be entered in the boxes of the miscue analysis record form in Figure 7.7. You could add a "correction" box, too, but I did not do so because I'm concerned that correction might become an end in itself, without regard for whether the miscue needed to be corrected.

In addition to or instead of using such a miscue record form, teachers may find it helpful for instructional purposes to record not just numbers but examples that illustrate conclusions from the data. Miscue form #3, in Figure 7.8, can be used for that purpose. The use of this latter form will be illustrated in Chapter 8.

READER'S NAME		1 Did the miscue reflect the speaker's ordinary speech patterns?			2 Did the miscue go with the grammar and meaning of what came before?				3 Did the miscue go with the grammar and meaning of what followed?				4 Did this miscue, by itself, still leave the essential meaning of the sentence intact?		5 Was the miscue corrected?				5 Was the miscue graphically similar?			7 Was the sentence, as the reader finally left it, semantically acceptable within the whole original selection that was read?		
Grade	Age																						
Coder's name																							
Date																							
Text (selection) that was read																							
TEXT SAYS	READER SAYS	I	D	E	Y	G	M	N	Y	G	M	N	Y	N	Y	UC	N	O	Y	P	N	Y	P	N
1																								
2																								
3																								
4																								
5																								
6																								
7																								
8																								
9																								
10																								
11																								
12																								
13																								
14																								
15																								
16																								
17																								
18																								
19																								
20																								
21																								
22																								
23																								
24																								
25																								
TOTALS																								
PERCENTS																								

Figure 7.6 *Miscue analysis coding form #2 (from Constance Weaver, Reading Process and Practice, 3rd ed., Heinemann, 2002; © 2002 by Constance Weaver; may be reproduced for use).*

Reader   Rater

Date

Text (selection) read

MISCUE	Preceding context		Following context	
	number	*percent*	*number*	*percent*
Y = yes, acceptable				
P = partially acceptable				
N = no, not acceptable				
Total		100%		100%

MISCUES (substitutions)	Graphic (visual) similarity	
	number	*percent*
High graphic similarity		
Some graphic similarity		
No graphic similarity		
Total		100%

MISCUES	Meaning acceptability within sentence as the reader left it (columns 4 & 5)	
	number	*percent*
Y = yes, acceptable		
P = partially or unclear		
N = no, not acceptable		
Total		100%

SENTENCE	Meaning acceptability within text as the reader left it (column 7)	
	number	*percent*
Y = yes, acceptable		
P = partially acceptable		
N = no, not acceptable		
Total		100%

Figure 7.7 *Miscue analysis record form (from Constance Weaver,* Reading Process and Practice, *3rd ed., Heinemann, 2002; © 2002 by Constance Weaver; may be reproduced for use).*

READER _____ GRADE/AGE _____ DATE _____

RATER _____

TEXT READ _____

How well did the reader use prior knowledge and context to predict effectively? Circle or underline one option, then provide examples.

       Almost never / seldom / about half the time / frequently / almost always

How well did the reader use following context to correct, or try to correct, miscues that didn't fit with the following context and/or miscues that didn't leave the essential meaning of the sentence intact? Circle or underline one option, then provide examples.

       Almost never / seldom / about half the time / frequently / almost always

How appropriately did the reader use graphic cues along with preceding and following context, plus prior knowledge? Circle or underline one option, then provide examples.

       Almost never / seldom / about half the time / frequently / almost always

---

Figure 7.8 *Miscue analysis form #3 (adapted from Constance Weaver,* Reading Process and Practice, *3rd ed., Heinemann, 2002; ©2002 by Constance Weaver; may be reproduced for use).*

Analyzing miscues in context gives us glimpses into the reader's process of comprehending, and the strategies he or she uses to process text. However, it is crucial to balance a miscue analysis with more direct measures of the reader's comprehension—that is, the understanding demonstrated during a retelling and discussion of the selection read.

The next chapter describes additional procedures that are a "must" for developing a more complete profile of a reader. At a minimum, these include a reading interview and a retelling and discussion of the text that was read for miscue analysis. Thus the next chapter includes more forms, too: a reading interview form; a form for recording information from the retelling and discussion; a form for summarizing crucial data in some detail and making an instructional plan; and a very brief analysis/retelling/summary/planning form adapted from Y. Goodman, Watson, and Burke (1987), procedure 4. With all these examples, surely you can find or create a form or forms that work for you in the classroom.

ANALYZING JAY'S MISCUES

Before analyzing Jay's miscues on my detailed form (Figure 7.5), let us first examine his miscues on the passage from "Jimmy Hayes and Muriel" (Chapter 4). To get a feel for Jay's reading process, it should help to read through the passage, making the same miscues Jay did as you read:

After a hearty supper Hayes joined the smokers ~~about~~ ① *around*

the fire. His appearance did not settle all the questions in ② *at all*

the minds of his brother rangers. They saw|simply a loose, ③

lank ~~youth~~ with tow-colored sunburned hair and a berry- ④ ⑤ *young*

brown, ~~ingenuous~~ face that wore a quizzical, good- ⑤ *ingenious*

natured smile.

"Fellows," said the new ranger, "I'm goin' to interduce

you to a lady friend of mine. Ain't (ever) heard (anybody) ⑥ ⑦ *much about* ⑧

(call) her (a) beauty, but you'll all admit she's got ~~some~~ fine ⑨ ⑩ ⑪ *a*

points about her. Come along, Muriel!"

He held open the front of his blue flannel shirt. ⓒ ⑫ Out of

⑬ It crawled a horned ⑭ toad ~~frog~~. A bright red ribbon was tied

jauntily around its spiky neck. It crawled to ⑮ the ~~its~~ owner's

knee and sat there motionless. ⑯ it

"This here ⑰ 's Muriel," said Hayes, with an oratorical wave

of his hand, "⑱ She's ⑲ ~~has~~ got qualities. She never talks back, she

always stays ⑳ at home, and she's satisfied with one red

dress for everyday and Sunday, too."

"Look at that blame ㉑ d insect!" said one of the rangers

with a grin. "I've seen plenty of them horny ㉒ toads ~~frogs~~, but I

never knew anybody to have one for a ㉓ ⓒ side partner. Does

the blame thing know you from anybody else?"

"Take ㉔ her ~~it~~ over there and see," said Hayes.

Figure 7.9 shows how I have coded Jay's miscues. Jay speaks the mainstream dialect for his region and does not have any immature features in his speech, so I have not coded any miscues in column 1. I shall comment on some of the codings for certain miscues, keying my comments to the miscue number on the selection copy and the form.

1: Miscue #1, "around" for *about*, is probably more natural for Jay. However, I would not code it as a dialect form. Regarding column 6: When coding graphic similarity, I look for whether one, two, or no parts of the miscue resemble the text word when written. By parts, I mean the beginning, middle, and end of the word.

2: With miscue #2, the line in the "Text says" column indicates that there was nothing in the text where the reader said "at all." In other words, the miscue was an insertion. Miscue #2 is not coded in column 6, because only substitution miscues are coded for graphic similarity.

READER'S NAME Jay

Grade _____   **Age** _____

Coder's name CSW

Date 6/14/01

Text (selection) that was read "Jimmy Hayes and Muriel"

Code columns 2 through 4 as if the miscue weren't corrected, even if it was.

In coding columns 2 and 3... don't ask whether the miscue made the same grammar and nearly the same sense. Just ask if it made good grammar and a sensible stretch of words what came before (column 2) and after (column 3)

Column 1 — Did the miscue reflect the speaker's ordinary speech patterns?
I = immature speech
D = dialect
E = ESL or EFL learner
If a miscue is coded I, D, or E, all the rest of the columns are coded Y, except for column 6, which is coded as usual

Column 2 — Did the miscue go with the grammar and meaning of what came before?
Y = yes, the miscue fit with both the preceding grammar and preceding meaning
G = the miscue fit with the preceding grammar only
M = the miscue fit with the preceding meaning only
N = the miscue fit with neither

Column 3 — Did the miscue go with the grammar and meaning of what follows?
Y = yes, with both
G = with grammar only
M = with meaning only
N = with neither

Column 4 — Did the miscue by itself, still leave the essential meaning of the sentence intact?
Y = yes, this particular miscue, by itself, left the essential meaning of the sentence still intact
N = no, this miscue did not leave essential meaning of the sentence intact

Column 5 — Was the miscue corrected?
Y = yes, corrected
UC = unsuccessful attempt at correction
N = no, not corrected, and this miscue is not an attempt at correction
O = overcorrection; a miscue involving a contraction was corrected unnecessarily

Column 6 — Was the miscue graphically similar?
Y = high similarity
P = some (partial) similarity
N = no similarity
Apply to substitution miscues only.

Column 7 — Was the sentence, as the reader finally left it, semantically acceptable within the whole original selection that was read?
Bracket the miscues that came from each sentence, and then code the sentences:
Y = yes, acceptable; there wasn't any essential change in the meaning of the selection
P = partial; there was inconsistency, loss, or change of a *minor* idea, incident, character, fact, sequence, or concept in the selection
N = not acceptable; there was inconsistency, loss, or change of a *major* idea, incident, character, fact, sequence, or concept in the selection

#	TEXT SAYS	READER SAYS
1	about	around
2		at all
3	saw simply	simply saw
4	youth	young
5	ingenuous	ingenious
6		ever
7		much about
8	anybody	—
9	call	—
10	some	a
11	of	—
12	it	—
13	frog	toad
14	its	the
15		it
16	here	here's
17	here	⊙
18	has	she's
19	at	—
20	blame	blamed
21	side	toads
22	it	her
23		
24		
25		
	TOTALS	
	PERCENTS	

Figure 7.9 Jay's miscues.

4: Miscue #4 went with the following meaning but not with the following grammar (column 3); this is no doubt why Jay corrected the miscue (column 5).

5: Jay probably did not know the word *ingenuous,* which, in context, means that Jimmy Hayes is pretending to be simple and innocent when he really isn't. I coded this miscue N in the column dealing with preservation of the sentence meaning, because the miscue "ingenious" lost this insight into Jimmy Hayes' character. Nevertheless, I coded the entire sentence as semantically acceptable within the context of the story (Y in column 7).

7 and 8: I've coded miscue #7 as an insertion of "much about," followed by an omission of the text word *anybody* (#8), though frankly I'm not absolutely certain whether "much about" should be coded as a substitution for *anybody* instead. It is decisions like this that mark the human teacher from the robotic scantron that scores standardized, "fill in the bubble" tests. We teachers will be wrong sometimes, but at least we are *trying* to figure out where the reader was coming from. A scantron can't do that.

8, 9, and 10: Because of miscues #7 and #8 the sentence would not have been grammatical if Jay had read the rest of the words as written. So, Jay made two more omissions, miscues #9 and #10, keeping this part of the sentence grammatical as well as meaningful. First came the insertion of *much about* and the omission of *anybody,* as I chose to code them (miscues #7 and #8), followed by the omission of *call* and *a* (miscues #9 and #10). The text said *Ain't ever heard anybody call her a beauty,* while Jay read "Ain't heard much about her beauty."

12 and 13: By omitting not only *of* but also *it,* Jay maintained a grammatical and meaningful stretch of words: "Out crawled... " However, Jay read as far as "crawled," then backtracked and corrected omission miscues #12 and #13. The line attached to the ©️ indicates how far Jay read before correcting—that is, through the word *crawled.*

14: Miscue #14, "toad" for *frog,* simply indicates Jay's strong drive for meaning (not an inability to read *f-r-o-g*). Like me, he had probably heard of horned toads ("horny toads," we call them) but not of horned frogs.

17, 18, and 19: Once again, Jay made one miscue that led him to make two others, in order to maintain grammatical flow and sense. Having made a complete sentence from the first stretch of words, Jay had to "substitute" period-like intonation and add a new grammatical subject, producing " 'This here's Muriel,' said Hayes, with an oratorical wave of his hand. 'She's got qualities.'" You'll notice that although miscue #18 seems to be the "substitution" of one mark of punctuation for another, I didn't code it for graphic similarity in column 6.

The rest of the codings seem fairly straightforward.

Interpretation of Jay's Miscue Patterns

I totaled the number of miscues in each subcolumn, writing the totals as a fraction of the total miscues coded in each column. With Jay, I had only 24 miscues to code in columns 2 through 6. These miscues occurred in 12 sentences (column 7). I computed the percentages in each subcolumn, dividing the upper number of the fraction by the lower number. You will notice in column 2 that 100% of Jay's miscues fit with the preceding context, showing his strategy of thinking ahead, or predicting. I have found that proficient readers usually have 80-some or 90-some % Y in that column. In column 3, 75% of Jay's miscues went with the following context as well—again a strong percentage, suggesting a proficient reader.

Often a proficient reader will correct miscues that don't go with the following context, but that wasn't usually the case with Jay (compare column 3 with column 5). Instead, he almost always restructured text to keep the sentence grammatical and meaningful, as explained above. Column

4 indicates that Jay preserved the essential meaning of the sentence with all miscues but one, that being the miscue "ingenious" for *ingenuous*. Jay corrected relatively few of his miscues, but correction was seldom called for, since most of the miscues either fit with the context or involved restructuring the text. Fully half of the substitution miscues were not graphically similar, but low graphic similarity is also common among more proficient readers, who go for meaning rather than for letters and their sounds—a key example being "toad" for the text word *frog*. His miscues involving function words almost always preserved both grammar and meaning, too, but bore no graphic similarity to the word they may replace.

All of the sentences involved in this stretch of text are semantically acceptable with the whole text. Indeed, all but one of the miscues seems to preserve the meaning admirably. Of course it is possible to read a text aloud as well as Jay did and get virtually no meaning from it. This often happens to me when I am reading aloud, because I'm concentrating on performance rather than meaning. That's often true for our students, too. Clearly, then, we need to assess a reader's comprehension of the text, his or her understanding of it, separately from the coding of miscues. In this instance, I no longer have the specific data at hand, but I do know that Jay's comprehension was excellent, as was his use of reading strategies.

Whatever way we go about analyzing miscues, whether in the margins or on a form, we can gain valuable insights into a reader's use of key reading strategies and draw tentative inferences as to how much of that particular text the reader might have been comprehending. The next chapter will enable you to complement such data with a reading interview and a retelling/discussion session. Taken all together, these assessment measures provide valuable data for planning instruction.

FOR FURTHER EXPLORATION

1. For practice, fill out my miscue form #3 (Figure 7.8) for Tony.
2. Review the miscue markings on pp. 122–125. To gain practice in analyzing and evaluating miscues, you might begin by analyzing David's (pp. 7–8) or Anne's (p. 81–82) or Billy's (pp. 64–65); you can create columns in the margins as I did for coding Tony's miscues. When you feel comfortable analyzing one of these easier samples, then try analyzing Danny's miscues (pp. 78–79). By then, you may feel comfortable in using miscue analysis coding form #2 (Figure 7.6).
3. Analyze, code, and interpret Betsey's miscue patterns, as marked on the selection copy near the end of Chapter 6 (pp. 144–149). Use either coding form #1 (Figure 7.5) or coding form #2 (Figure 7.6). But this time, analyze miscues #1 through #27 as a separate group, #28 through #57 as another separate group, and #58 through #74 as a separate group. Compare the miscue patterns from the separate groups. What pattern differences and other differences do you notice? What might we infer from such differences? Betsey was reading from *A Camel in the Sea* (Goetz, 1966). The repeated miscues on the proper names *Mohamed* and *Asha* have not been numbered for coding, nor have the long omissions. Again, the line divisions reflect the way the material was presented to the reader. To give a more balanced picture of the reader's strategies when you code them, this time I have numbered only the first substitution for each of the proper names, even though the subsequent substitutions are not always the same.
4. Analyze Erica's miscues, pp. 149–154, using a form or forms of your choice.
5. Fill out a miscue record form (Figure 7.7) for a reader whose miscues you have analyzed on one of the coding forms.

8 Developing a Reader Profile: From Assessment to Instruction

A miscue analysis always includes a retelling by the reader, since we need to know what she understands from her reading as well as what her miscues are like. Since teachers often underestimate how much a reader can get out of a text even despite many miscues, a retelling helps ensure that we base our assessment of the reader on a full range of evidence.

—Sandra Wilde

Questions for Thought and Discussion

1. What do you think are the most important matters to ask about in a reading interview? Why?

2. What are some reasons why we can't assume that an unaided retelling accurately reflects a reader's comprehension or understanding of a particular text, much less his or her reading "ability"?

3. What else might we need to do to assess someone's reading fairly?

4. What are some important things to keep in mind when doing a reading interview? When guiding a retelling and discussion session?

5. What are some important things to remember when analyzing and interpreting data from a reading interview? From a miscue analysis? From a retelling/discussion session after the oral reading?

6. What points and pointers are important to keep in mind as a teacher, regardless of whether you ever do a (or another) reader profile, as described in this chapter?

As Sandra Wilde points out in the opening quote, a reader's miscues, even numerous miscues, do not necessarily prevent a reader from getting quite a bit of meaning from a text. Nor can we assume that nearly perfect oral reading means the reader *did* comprehend what was read. The reader's comprehension depends upon many factors: the conceptual difficulty of the text for that reader, whether or not the reader is actually reading for meaning while reading aloud, the nature of the reader's miscues and strategies, how the reader feels about making miscues, how the reader feels about reading aloud for assessment, and more. Teachers need to understand such factors, which can be investigated by having the reader retell the selection and discuss not only it, but the reading experience: how he or she felt about the reading, where the reading was difficult and what caused the problem, and other factors deemed relevant by the teacher or the student.

Before having someone read aloud for miscue analysis, it is often helpful to do a reading interview if you do not know the person well, or if you want to inquire about certain things in particular. We can learn what the reader thinks is the purpose of reading and the process of reading; what strategies the reader is aware of, and/or aware of using; what the reader likes to read, and/or to read about; how the reader feels about reading at school and reading at home, or reading different kinds of fiction and nonfiction; how the reader feels about himself or herself as a reader; what the reader thinks might make him or her an even better reader; and so forth.

This chapter includes discussion of the reading interview and the retelling/discussion session; a list of questions in Figure 8.1 that can be used for a reading interview with primary-grade children; a form that can be used to record information from and about the retelling and discussion session; and two additional, alternative forms that can be used to record data from the interview, oral reading and miscue analysis, and retelling/discussion session, along with space to write a plan for instruction. The chapter also includes minimal information drawn from a case study, along with an instructional plan, in order to illustrate how the data from a reader profile can be used to inform instruction. Other case studies may be found on the Web page associated with this book: *<http://www.heinemann.com/weaver>*.

As a classroom teacher, you may find, of course, that you need to simplify some of the procedures, to better meet your needs. For now, however, I will offer a few suggestions for doing a reading interview and a retelling/discussion session.

Whether you are an inservice or preservice teacher, doing just one reader profile in detail should help you begin to develop a deeper understanding of the reading process, reading strategies, and the possible relationships between how the reading sounds and what the reader understands from the reading. It should also help you begin to see some of the strengths and needs of an individual student. A current version of directions I provide for my students can be obtained from the Web page relating to this book. I strongly recommend that you collect data for the reader profile analysis in two (or more) separate sessions, not just one. Practicing teachers will probably need to schedule the sessions before or after school or during lunchtime, because when you are just learning to gather data for such a reader profile, you will need more time than when you know both the student and the procedures better. Not to worry: later, you will find your own ways to assess more rapidly. Most teachers who have done even just one miscue analysis find that they listen to readers with much greater ability to assess reading strategies and needs, so they can do briefer and even anecdotal records as they listen to and confer with individual students. Teacher Ruth Davenport has even developed what she calls "over the shoulder" procedures for listening to students and recording miscue data while walking among students and stopping to listen to them read.

Davenport, R. (2002). *Miscues Not Mistakes: Miscue Analysis in the Classroom.* Portsmouth, NH: Heinemann.

THE READING INTERVIEW AND THE FIRST SESSION

Figure 8.1 (following pages) presents questions that can be asked in a reading interview, including questions that are most appropriate for young readers. These questions draw heavily from the Burke Reading Interview.

The Reading Interview

The reading interview traditionally used in miscue analysis is that developed by Carolyn Burke and reprinted in Y. Goodman, Watson, and Burke (1987) (pp. 219–220). Here are Burke's ten questions, designed for readers of any age:

1. When you are reading and come to something you don't know, what do you do?

2. Do you do anything else?

3. Who is a good reader you know?

4. What makes _____[name of person] a good reader?

5. Do you think _____[name of person] ever comes to something she/he doesn't know?

READER _____ Grade _____ Age _____

Interviewer _____ Date _____

NOTE: These questions are for you to draw upon during the interview. Tape-record the interview. Later, you will transcribe it for analysis and evaluation, not only of the reader but of yourself as an interviewer. Try not to ask "leading questions" that offer the responses you hope to hear, or questions that can be answered with a simple "yes" or "no." Be sure to follow up the reader's responses with other useful questions whenever appropriate.

1.   What do you do for fun? What else are you interested in?
[There are two major purposes to these questions: (1) to "break the ice" with the reader; (2) to help you choose books for oral reading and retelling. Explore briefly.]
2.   How do you feel about reading? [This is designed as an open-ended question. You may want to ask follow-up questions.]
3.   What do you read? What do you like to read?
[Explore to get a sense of the reader's range of reading. Reading material might include not only books, magazines, and newspapers, but everyday, practical things like the TV guide, signs and labels, Nintendo, things found on the Web. As for what the reader likes to read, you might inquire about topics, series, specific books, specific authors—but don't go on and on with such questions.]
4.   Do your parents like to read? What do you see your parents reading for themselves?
[To get insight into what is modeled in the home.]
5.   What do you think your parents do when they come to a word they don't know?
[To gain insight into how the reader thinks proficient readers read. Explore as needed.]
6.   Do/did your parents read to you?
[Explore to find out more about what (or if) the parents read to the child, and how often.]
7.   How did you learn to read? What do/did your parents do to help you learn to read? What did your teachers do to help you learn to read? [Explore as needed.]
8.   What does your teacher this year do to help you learn to read (or to help you learn to read better)? What other reading activities do you do (if any)? [Explore. This question is not necessary, of course, if it has already been covered by discussion of the preceding question.]
9.   Who usually chooses what you read in school? What about at home? Do you like to choose what you read? Why/why not? [Explore as needed.]
10. Why do people read? Why do you read? [Explore to see if your interviewee realizes that people read for many purposes. Does the reader him/herself read for similar purposes, and/or for purposes like getting the words, learning new words, and other task-related reasons?]
11. What do people do when they read? What do you do inside your head when you read?
[Another way to clarify might be to ask, "How do you deal with the text?" while pointing to the written text in a book. The purpose is to see what readers understand about the reading process itself—what they think it is, and how they go about it. Rephrase the questions as needed.]
12. Be sure to ask all three questions:
a. When you are reading and come to a word you don't know, what do you do? Does this help?
b.   What else do you do, when you come to a word you don't know?

Figure 8.1   *Reading interview questions for early to intermediate grades.*

c.   What else do you think you could do, if you were reading by yourself, with no one to help you? [Explore. Below are some kinds of responses you might receive.]

Word-based strategies:	Meaning-based strategies:	Assistance-based strategies:
(Try to) sound it out	Think what it means	Ask someone
Say the letters	Go back and reread	Use a dictionary
Spell it out	Look at the context	
Look at word parts	Read on and come back to it later	

13. Do you know anyone in your class besides the teacher who you think is a good reader? Who? What do you think this person [use name] does when he/she comes to a word he/she doesn't know?

14. Do you like to read in order to find out about things you're interested in? What do you read about? [Explore as needed. Omit this item if the answers are already clear from previous questions.]

15. How do you feel about reading your assignments (and/or doing your reading assignments) in school, or for homework? [Explore or omit if the reader has already clarified.]

16. How do you feel about yourself as a reader, in general? [Explore as needed.]

17. What do you do well as a reader?

18. What would you like to do better as a reader, if anything? [Explore.]

Figure 8.1   (*Continued*).

"Yes" When _____ [name of person] does come to something she/he doesn't know, what do you think he/she does?

"No" Suppose _____[name of person] comes to something she/he doesn't know. What do you think she/he would do?

6. If you knew someone was having trouble reading how would you help that person?

7. What would a/your teacher do to help that person?

8. How did you learn to read?

9. What would you like to do better as a reader?

10. Do you think you are a good reader? Why?

Burke's questions 1 through 5 are designed to elicit the reader's awareness of strategies for dealing with "something she/he doesn't know." Questions 6 and 7 are likely to reflect how the person was taught to read, either at school or at home, while question 8 directly asks, "How did you learn to read?" Questions 9 and 10 ask the reader to reflect on himself or herself as a reader.

After using the Burke interview questions for years, I have developed—and redeveloped—some of my own, in addition to the kinds of questions that Burke includes. The form in Figure 8.1 is designed to be used with a child in the early to intermediate grades whose interests and reading background you do not know. You will quickly realize that some questions need to be omitted, added, or changed for other readers. For example, an interview with secondary or even middle school students might include questions like "How do you feel about reading literature?" and "When you read literature in or for school, is that the same as reading for pleasure?" These and related questions can be important, for they may sometimes reveal that the teaching of literature in traditional ways actually turns students off to reading.

The interview flows best if you engage in a conversation with the questions as triggers, instead of grilling the reader in simple question-and-answer format.

Preparing for and Conducting the First Session

During the first session, you will conduct the reading interview, tape-recording it for later analysis. It is also wise to have the person read a page or two from three books of differing levels of difficulty, to get some idea of what you might have the person read orally during the second session. In considering what texts you might take as possibilities for the reader to read from later, keep in mind that in order to do a miscue analysis of the oral reading, the reader will need to have made at least twenty-five miscues. Other directions for choosing a selection are included in "Preparing for and Conducting the Second Session," later in this chapter.

I am writing my suggestions as directions and advice for preservice teachers, on the assumption that inservice teachers will be able to modify the procedures as appropriate.

What to Have with You for the First Session

1. A tape recorder with healthy batteries, and a 60-minute blank tape that you won't need for anything else. Try the tape recorder well in advance of the first session, to be sure it tape-records well. For your first experiment(s) in miscue analysis, it is important to tape-record everything.

2. An interview form such as Figure 8.1 or a list of the questions you plan to ask. Study this form ahead of time, so you will be better prepared to use it insightfully and to ask appropriate follow-up questions. Paradoxically, perhaps, thinking in advance about where the reader's responses might lead should make it easier for you to conduct the interview more like a conversation.

3. Three books you think a child at this age or grade level might be able to read, while making at least 25 miscues. These will be used just to get ideas for the oral reading later.

4. A permission form, if needed. Preservice teachers are almost always required to obtain a parent's permission to develop a reading profile for a child, or at least the teacher's permission. Teachers may want a parent's written permission, too.

What to Do at the First Session

1. Gather whatever information you can about how the child is perceived as a reader, how well the child succeeds in school, the child's age and grade, if the child has been "labeled," and so forth.

2. Let the reader talk into the tape recorder and play it back, to help the reader relax and to be sure the tape recorder is working and is picking up the reader's voice.

3. Ask the interview questions prepared in advance. But don't be tied to only or exactly these questions. Here are more suggestions:

   - With the questions about what the reader does for fun and what the reader likes to read, feel free to share your own interests. This helps turn the interview into a conversation.

   - Listen to the reader's responses and ask good follow-up questions, as appropriate. Don't just go on to the next question on your list!

   - Try not to ask "leading questions" that offer the responses you hope to hear, particularly questions that can be answered with a simple "yes" or "no."

- In general, if you should ask a yes/no question, follow up with a question that probes for more information or clarification.
- Don't ask two or three questions at once. Instead, give the reader plenty of wait time to respond. Then rephrase questions as necessary.
- If you find yourself repeating the reader's responses, be sure to do so in a positive tone of voice, not a tone that suggests you question what the reader has said. You might even explain that you are repeating in order to be sure the tape recorder is picking up the information. It would be better, of course, not to keep repeating what the reader has said, but I've found that a lot of us do this in order to gather our thoughts as to where to go next with our questioning.
- In general, don't give the reader the impression that you are surprised or disappointed by a response. Watch especially your tone of voice and nonverbal reactions.

4. If time permits, have the reader read from one or more of the selections that you have at hand. This can help you get some idea of the difficulty of the selection that you'll want to use for the oral reading during session 2. Finding out what the reader does for fun and what he or she likes to read can also help you choose. Perhaps you can also ask the advice of a parent—or the teacher, if you are doing the analysis in someone else's classroom.

5. If relevant, obtain the permission of the parent, the teacher, or other adult responsible for the student, if the student is under eighteen. Even if the reader is an adult, obtain a written note of permission.

Recording the Data from the Interview

In my classes for preservice or inservice teachers, those just learning to do reading interviews type out the reading interview and the retelling/discussion session in a "he said, she said" transcript, like a play. They are also expected to add, in square brackets, comments on things they should or shouldn't have done, or should have done differently. This is the most important reason for writing out the entire discussion as a transcript. Even experienced teachers can learn much more about their interviewing strengths and weaknesses by doing a transcript of the session. Here is an example that includes both a clarifying comment in square brackets (always useful) and self-critiquing comments, both positive and negative:

Katie: So, when you are reading and come to a word you don't know, what do you do?
Angel: Ask for help.
Katie: What if you are at home and there is nobody to ask for help?
Angel: Ask Michael. [He is her brother.]
Katie: What if Michael is not here?
Angel: Sound it out or look at the picture.
Katie: What else do you do when you come to a word you don't know? [I'm glad I kept pursuing the issue.]
Angel: Skip it.
Katie: Skip it . . . go on and come back to it. [Oops, I was putting words into her mouth. Maybe she doesn't go back at all, but just skips the word!]
Angel: [nods her head "yes"]

It is helpful to do a thorough interview for each student in the class during the first two months of the school year, but of course you will have to find a much briefer way to record important data. To assist with this, I have a form, Figure 8.2, that clusters questions together

READER _____ Grade _____ Age _____	
Interviewer _____ Date _____	

Reader's interest in reading, and particular reading interests
(possibly question 1; questions 2 and 3; parts of 9 and 11; questions 14 and 15)

Home background for reading (especially questions 4, 5, 6, and part of 7)

Reader's perception of how he or she learned to read, including how the reader has been
taught and is being taught to read in school (questions 6, 7, 8; possibly question 15)

Reader's ideas about reading, such as why people read and what reading is
(questions 10, 11, and 12)

Reader's awareness of strategies for reading, and awareness of own reading strategies
(question 12; also 5 and 13)

How the reader feels about himself or herself as a reader
(especially questions 2, 16, 17, and 18, but possibly question 1 and other earlier questions
also, and question 15)

Figure 8.2   *Topics addressed by the reading interview questions.*

into topics from the interview form in Figure 8.1. You could use this form to record the most important information, and simply keep the tape recording in the child's literacy portfolio in case you need it for any purpose. Or you might want to write even briefer comments on one of the summary forms later in this chapter (Figures 8.7 and 8.8).

Here are the topics culled from the questions:

1. The reader's interest in reading, and particular reading interests: See possibly question 1; questions 2 and 3; parts of 9 and 10; plus questions 14 and 15.

2. Home background for reading: See especially questions 4, 5, 6, and part of 7.

3. How the reader learned to read, and how the reader has been taught and is being taught to read in school: See questions 6, 7, and 8.

4. The reader's ideas about reading, such as why people read and what reading is: See questions 10, 11, and 12. With question 12, note that readers who think reading is just getting the words are less likely to use meaning-based strategies.

5. The reader's strategies for reading: The reader's awareness of possible reading strategies is assessed by 12, but also by 5 and 13. The reader's own strategies for reading are assessed by question 12, especially the third item, "What else do you think you could do, if you were reading by yourself, with no one to help you?"

6. How the reader feels about him/herself, as a reader: See especially questions 2, 16, 17, and 18, but earlier questions may give insight, too, and possibly question 15.

PREPARING FOR AND CONDUCTING THE SECOND SESSION

During the second session, the oral reading is followed by a retelling and discussion of the selection and the reading situation.

Preparing for the Reading

Choose an appropriate text (story, article, or other informational selection) and familiarize yourself with your choice(s). It may be best to choose three selections, based on the reader's interests and whatever you know or can find out regarding the difficulty of the material the person typically reads. In choosing a selection, keep in mind these guidelines:

1. Choose something the reader hasn't read before. The selection must be entirely new to the reader, but the content should be something that he or she can understand and relate to. Pattern books are not a good choice, because the text isn't varied enough. The language of the text should be as natural as possible (not like "Look, Spot, look," or "Nan can fan the man"). The selection must be difficult enough to cause the reader to make miscues, too. You will need to code 25 miscues, but repeated miscues on "content words" (nouns, verbs, adjectives, adverbs) don't count! Repeated attempts at the names of persons and places aren't usually numbered and coded, either. And when possible, we don't code the miscues marked for the first 200 words of the text, since the nature of the miscues often changes (improves) noticeably beyond about that point, as the reader settles into the text and uses the evolving meaning to prevent or solve difficulties (Menosky, 1971). Thus for a miscue analysis, it is usually helpful if the reader makes more than 25 miscues. The text(s) should be selected accordingly, keeping in mind that the reading should not be too difficult for the reader, either.

2. Choose something that has a sense of completeness (for example, a picture book; one or more stories in something like the Frog and Toad books; a chapter that has its own plot, in a chapter book; an article; a section in an informational book).

A sense of completeness is important for the retelling. Therefore, for example, the first chapter of a book won't do if it consists mostly of introducing the setting and maybe some characters. Such a chapter offers too much detail and too little organization to facilitate recall (as, for example, a sequence of events and a plot provide organization, or as the structure of a textbook section or an informational article provides organization).

3. Choose something that has 500 words or more. Two or three shorter stories can be selected for children for whom something like the Frog and Toad books are appropriate, but often the child's miscue patterns are quite clear from just one story, if the child has made at least 25 miscues on that story.

Preparing for the Retelling and Extended Discussion

It is wise to prepare to conduct a retelling and discussion relating to more than one selection, in case the one you try first is too easy or so difficult that the reader becomes *extremely* frustrated, begins to cry, and/or just gives up. On the other hand, teachers need to realize that a slow and halting reading that frustrates us as adult listeners may not necessarily frustrate the reader excessively. Thus we should not be quick to turn to an easier selection.

Many readers give very little information during the first unaided retelling, especially if they have never been asked to retell a story before. Therefore, it is crucial that you prepare to ask good follow-up questions about the selection to be read. It may be helpful to prepare notes on the selection first, then prepare possible follow-up questions. However, don't plan to ask questions about picky details, such as relatively unimportant information about the characters, or characters who don't play a substantial role in a story, or irrelevant information about the setting. Instead, prepare to ask inferential questions and questions that encourage the reader to relate to, think about, and reflect on the story, if a story has been selected.

There are other reasons, too, to be judicious in what you think the reader "should" recall. Remember that a reader's recall can be affected by many factors:

- Whether the selection was too difficult or too unfamiliar conceptually for the reader
- Whether or not the reader has had experience retelling a story or other selection
- Whether the reader was actually trying to comprehend while reading aloud, or only to get the words and perform for a listener
- Whether the reader was trying to recall information, as well as to comprehend while reading
- Whether the reader was interested in the story or other selection
- Whether the reader was interested in the topic and became interested in the selection
- The reader's prior knowledge—beliefs, thoughts, emotions, feelings, and information relevant to the settings, experiences, and concepts found in the reading selection
- Whether the reader is a detail person, or a general picture person (learning style, corresponding roughly to what we once called "left brained" or "right brained")
- How the reader feels about himself or herself as a reader, his or her ability to succeed at the task, the interviewer (positive, negative, uncertain), and the situation (location, noise, being kept from doing something fun in order to do the task, sick, hungry, etc.)

Preparing to Ask Questions About a Story

Considering that so many factors can adversely affect the reader's understanding and recall, you can probably see why it is important to plan ahead of time an outline of things you might ask about, if the reader doesn't volunteer the information or initially demonstrate much understanding. Of course we won't always choose a story as the reading selection, but for a story, you might consider asking about such elements as the following:

Characters: Which characters might the reader reasonably be expected to recall? What might the reader be likely to remember about the main character? This could include such aspects as physical appearance (if important to the plot), attitudes and feelings, behavior, relationships with other characters, problems or conflicts, character development, and so forth. But don't overdo it with what you expect the reader to remember about characters.

Events: What events might the reader reasonably be expected to recall? What should the reader remember about the sequence of events?

Plot: What might the reader reasonably be expected to tell about the central conflict or problem of the story?

Theme: If there seems to be a theme, an underlying idea, what might be some alternative ways of expressing it? Often, it is not appropriate to expect children to perceive or express a theme the way we might as adults. And many times it seems to be quite a stretch to imply that a particular story has a theme at all.

Setting: If the setting is important to the story, what might the reader reasonably be expected to describe and discuss about the setting?

The form for recoding data from the retelling session, Figure 8.3, can help you in planning ahead what you might ask. Here are some guidelines for asking such questions:

1. Try to avoid asking questions that can be asked with a simple "yes" or "no." Instead, ask questions that begin with so-called WH words like *who, what, when, why,* and *how:* "Who else was in the story?" "What happened after that?" "Why do you think [mention a certain character] did that?"

2. Instead of giving the reader information, try to build upon information already supplied by the reader, using such WH word questions. You can begin by restating information the reader has already given you: "You mentioned that so-and-so was in the story. Who else do you remember?" "You mentioned that *X* happened. What happened after that?" If you happen to ask yes/no questions inadvertently, you can always ask a WH word question as a follow-up.

3. Ask probing questions that will elicit the reader's responses to the story and that will stimulate further thinking about the story, its relationship to other stories and/or the reader's life, other possible endings or how the reader predicts the story might continue or end in the next chapter(s), and so forth. Here are some questions you might ask to elicit the reader's responses to the story:

   ■ How did you feel when . . . ?

   ■ Why do you think so-and-so did such-and-such? Would you have done that? Why (or why not)?

   ■ Have you ever been in a similar situation? What did you do?

   ■ Did you like the way the story ended? Why (or why not)? If not: how would you have ended it?

   ■ Does this story remind you of anything else you've ever read? Why (or how)?

   ■ Overall, did you like this story? Why (or why not)?

4. If desired, and if it looks as if you will still have time for questions relating to items 5 and 6 below, you can ask one or more questions designed to stimulate further thinking about the story and related issues: specifically, to stimulate what Piaget called "formal operational

Reader		Grade	Age
Date			
Text (selection) read			

Score(s), if desired	
Information from text	**Inferences, predictions, and connections beyond the text**
Important characters and character development	
Events and plot	
Inferences about theme, larger meaning	
Other connections, predictions, comments	
Misconceptions	
Teacher comments	

Figure 8.3 *Retelling and discussion notes (adapted from Y. Goodman, Watson, & Burke, 1987; Wilde, 2000; and Board, 1976).*

thought." Questions of this nature are appropriate for many elementary children as well as for older students. For example:

- Invite the reader to think about abstract ideas and concepts, and to apply such concepts to the reading. ("What is a true friend? Do you think so-and-so was being a true friend when he or she . . . ? Why/why not?")

  - Invite readers to reason hypothetically. ("If so-and-so had done such-and-such, what do you think might have happened?")

  - Invite the reader to systematically consider multiple causes/explanations/factors and weigh their relative importance. ("You mentioned three reasons why you think so-and-so did such-and-such. Which reason seems most important to you? Why?")

5. If the reader miscued on a key word, ask about the meaning of that word, using the reader's own pronunciation: "What is a 'typeical' baby, anyway?" (The text word was *typical,* and it was important to the story that the baby was ordinary, not unusual.) Here is another example: "You said this word (point in the text to *canary*) was 'cainery.' What is a 'cainery,' anyhow?" (This may tell you if the reader realizes that a "cainery" is a bird.)

6. Also, find out where the reader thought the reading went well, where it didn't go well, and why. ("Where did the reading go especially well for you?" "Was there anywhere you had particular trouble with the reading? Show me where." You can then explore the problem and, if it's a single word, help the reader develop an effective strategy for dealing with the word.)

Obviously certain kinds of questions will have to be developed in response to what the reader has said about the story, but some advance planning can certainly be done.

Conducting the Oral Reading and Retelling/Discussion

You may need more time for the oral reading and the retelling/discussion than you needed in order to do the reading interview and to sample the reader's oral reading.

What to Have with You for the Second Session

1. A tape recorder with healthy batteries, and at least one sixty-minute (or a ninety-minute) blank tape that you won't need for anything else. Again, everything needs to be tape-recorded.

2. The selection(s) you have chosen to try with the reader.

3. Possible follow-up questions about the selection(s) and about how the reading went (see the preceding section here).

4. Your own copy of the selection(s), if that's possible, so you can more easily follow along as the reader reads.

What to Do at the Second Session

1. Again let the reader talk into the tape recorder and play it back, to be sure the tape recorder is working and is picking up the reader's voice as well as yours.

2. Start the tape recorder and record everything.

3. Perhaps explain to the reader that you are trying to learn how people/children read, and that therefore you actually need for the reader to make "errors" (miscues). Explain to the reader that he or she has been specially chosen to help you learn about reading itself.

4. Tell the reader that after the reading, you will ask him or her to tell you all about the selection. Emphasize that the reader should read for meaning and try to understand and remember what is being read.

5. Then, perhaps review the strategies the reader mentioned, in the previous session, for dealing with problem words. Tell the reader that you won't be able to help him or her, because you are trying to find out what readers do when they have difficulty with a word when they are reading all by themselves. (This gives us insight into their reading strategies.) Remind the reader that he or she can use the strategies previously mentioned, plus any others that would help.

6. Assuming you have available three selections with differing degrees of difficulty, try the middle level of difficulty first. If the reader makes almost no miscues in the first twenty sentences or so, switch to the more challenging selection. If the reader keeps making several miscues per line, even after reading twenty or so lines, you might switch to the easier selection. You can modify these suggestions as necessary for the particular reader, considering such factors as the reader's conceptual background, his or her self-confidence as a reader, the length of the lines in the text (e.g., an "I Can Read" book for beginners has fewer words per line, compared with a young adult novel).

7. Have the person read the entire selection orally. Don't help him or her with problem words. If the reader looks to you for help during the reading, remind the reader to do whatever he or she would do if nobody were there. (Of course, "stop reading" is not ordinarily an option during a miscue analysis!)

8. Ask the reader to tell you everything he or she remembers about the selection. Sometimes it helps to say something like, "Pretend you're telling your best friend all about the story." Don't forget that this unaided retelling should be done before you ask specific questions.

9. After the reader has given you an unaided retelling, ask questions that probe to see if more was remembered and/or understood. Then ask relevant questions designed to uncover deeper understanding and personal connections, plus questions designed to elicit the reader's reflection upon the reading experience and/or upon his or her reading strategies. You should have planned such questions and questioning as discussed in the previous section, "Preparing for the Retelling and Extended Discussion." On the other hand, don't follow your list of questions as if it were a script, but instead respond conversationally to the reader's responses.

10. If the retelling and discussion have been somewhat unsatisfactory, have the person read the selection again silently, then retell and discuss again. Or, you might have the person read and retell/discuss a different selection that seems more suitable. Unfortunately, it may be necessary to set up another time to get together with the reader.

Reminders and Warnings

1. Choose a selection that the person hasn't read before, and one that has a sense of completeness about it (a plot, for example). It is good to have three selections of differing degrees of difficulty available, and to be prepared to ask follow-up questions on all of them. Try the selection from the middle level of difficulty first. If the reader is making hardly any miscues after twenty sentences or so, switch to the more challenging selection. If the reader is making several miscues per line, even after twenty or so lines, consider switching to the easier selection. Encourage a frustrated reader to keep reading, perhaps by reminding the reader of reading strategies he or she has previously mentioned. If desperate, you can even suggest that the reader skip a problem word, even if the reader hasn't mentioned this as a strategy he or she uses. If the reader then omits a lot of words, probably the selection is too difficult.

2. Remember to ask the reader to tell you all about the selection first, then ask follow-up questions.

3. Don't assume that a brief unaided retelling means the reader got very little from the selection. Many readers will say very little at first, but remember and understand quite a bit when you ask questions and engage the reader in discussing the selection.

4. If the retelling and discussion are weak, do one of the following: (1) have the reader reread the selection silently and then engage in another unaided retelling and discussion; or (2) have the reader read another selection silently and follow up with a retelling and discussion session.

5. In drawing upon the retelling session(s) to assess the reader's comprehension, be sure *not* to overgeneralize your conclusions about the reader's *ability* to comprehend text. The reader's recall will depend upon a lot of factors, previously discussed. If the reader doesn't have strong recall, consider these other factors. Be especially alert for the possibility that the reader may not have had sufficient background knowledge for the concepts and/or experiences included in the text. Lack of prior knowledge will cause miscues as well as diminish recall.

Recording the Retelling Data

When doing your first reader profile project, it can be extremely valuable to type out the reading and discussion session, too, in "he said, she said" transcription format. This helps you recall information accurately and again is useful in critiquing your own questioning and discussion strategies. But for regular classroom use, you will certainly not have time to do this: you will need a simpler form. I suggest the one in Figure 8.3 as a possibility, because it can be used first in preparing for the retelling/discussion session, and then afterwards, for record-keeping.

Recording the Miscues on the Selection Copy

In order to mark the reader's miscues, you will need to have a copy of the selection that you can write on. I recommend making a photocopy of it. If necessary, you may be able to enlarge the page while copying, in order to give you more space between the lines. If you type the selection yourself, leave three spaces between the lines, end each line where it ends in the copy that the reader will read aloud, and mark page divisions with a line.

Before recording the miscues on the selection copy, it is important to do the following:

- Review the miscue markings in Chapter 6, pp. 122–125
- Review how to mark and number the miscues, Chapter 7, pp. 168–170

Coding the Miscues and Analyzing Patterns

My students are normally asked to use my more detailed miscue form to code miscues, but even if you are doing the coding on the selection copy, it is important to review the general principles for coding miscues, in Chapter 7, pp. 170–175.

In addition, Figure 8.4 on grammatical cues in the reading process may help you review these cues and consider whether the miscues you're coding do or don't fit with the preceding and following grammar. See columns 1 and 2 on the detailed form in Figure 8.5. In general, if a miscue "sounds right" with what came before, it probably fits with the preceding grammar. If the miscue "sounds right" with what comes after, it probably fits with the grammar that follows.

When my students analyze the miscue patterns in order to start thinking about recommendations for instruction, they actually write a comprehensive paper, because it allows them to explain the patterns and the insights about the miscues and the readers' strategies more thoroughly than a form would, and it gives them the opportunity to discuss other insights that are not captured or encouraged by the detailed miscue form itself. For classroom use, however, it can be helpful to use Figure 7.8 (p. 178), which I have used later in this chapter for recording data about

Grammatical signals in English

There are three major grammatical signals in English. In descending significance, these are:
1. Word order
2. Function words (also called *signal words, glue words*)
3. Word endings that signal number or possession on nouns,
    tense and aspect on verbs; other word endings that signal noun, verb, adjective, adverb

Word order

In Old English, it didn't make much difference how the words were ordered in a sentence, because there were endings to tell things like which word was the subject (usually the doer of the action), which word was the direct object (the receiver of the action), which word was the verb (the action), and so forth. But in recent centuries, word order has replaced these endings.

Thus *The man chased the dog* is not the same as *The dog chased the man.*
    Carly kisses the parakeet is not the same as *The parakeet kisses Carly.*

Function words

Function words are also important signals in English. There are several kinds of function words, such as articles (*a, an, the*) and other "determiners," particularly *this, these, that, those, his, her, its, their,* and *our,* when they modify a noun that follows. Other kinds of function words are prepositions, auxiliary (helper) verbs, and conjunctions. See Chapter 2 for other examples.

This chocolate lab is *a* friendly puppy, *but her* barking makes her *a* nuisance, too.
Sally *will* meet Harry *by the* pond *in an* hour.
The man *was* chased *by the* dog.
I'*ll* go to the musical *if* you *will* buy *the* tickets.

Word endings

There are two kinds of word endings in English that signal grammatical function.

1. One kind of word ending is called *inflectional.* There are noun plural and possessive endings, plus verb endings for present tense and past tense, present participle and past participle.

Carmen *borrows* the *boys' bicycles* every spring. She *borrowed Charlie's* bike last week.
Charlie is *riding* a motorcycle now. He hasn't *ridden* his bike all year.

2. Other grammatical endings, called *derivational suffixes,* signal a word's part of speech (noun, verb, adjective, adverb). (Sometimes one ending can signal more than one part of speech, so context is needed to clarify which one.)

Compare, for instance: *construct,* which is often a verb (He'll *construct* the house); *construction,* which is a noun (Let's get started with the *construction*; and *constructive,* which is an adjective (Give only *constructive* criticism).

The *-ion* ending, variously spelled, is one of many that signal a noun (*construction, invitation, incision*).

The *-ive* ending signals an adjective (*innovative, legislative, lucrative, demonstrative,* etc.).

Figure 8.4 *Grammatical signals in English.*

READER'S NAME					
Grade	Age				
Coder's name					
Date					
Text (selection) that was read					

Column headings:

1. Did the miscue reflect the speaker's ordinary speech patterns? (I D E)
2. Did the miscue go with the grammar and meaning of what came before? (Y G M N)
3. Did the miscue go with the grammar and meaning of what followed? (Y G M N)
4. Did this miscue, by itself, still leave the essential meaning of the sentence intact? (Y N)
5. Was the miscue corrected? (Y UC N O)
6. Was the miscue graphically similar? (Y P N)
7. Was the sentence, as the reader finally left it, semantically acceptable within the whole original selection that was read? (Y P N)

	TEXT SAYS	READER SAYS
S1	you	they
S2	boa	boing
S3	constrictor	"trick/tricker
S4	boa	bagging
S5	constrictor	a tricking teacher / stricken teacher
S6	yeah	yah
S7	doing	ido-/a digging
S8	the	a
S9	brought	broat
S10	took	look
S11	it	
S12	squawking	sgui-
S13	around	away
S14	happened	i holding
S15	excited	extra
S16	an	a
S17	landed	laided
S18	.	?
S19	broke	brock
S20	yucky	yuck
S21	thought	throwed
S22	Tommy	Tommy's
S23	threw	threw
S24	so she	
S25	him	on

Annotation in Column 7: "Uncoded miscues on 'boa constrictor' made this sentence a line."

Note: Contrary to usual procedures, I coded not just one instance of "boa" + "constrictor," but two. I stopped coding them at that point though the semantic acceptability of sentence 4 was also affected by miscues on "boa constrictor."

Figure 8.5 Angel's miscues.

Angel's miscues (Figure 8.6). This form can also be useful to my students for making note of examples they plan to discuss in their papers, since I ask them to address, in their papers, the three major questions on the form and give examples of their conclusions, plus counterexamples if significant:

1. How well does the reader use prior knowledge and context to predict effectively?

2. How well or how appropriately does the reader use following context to correct, or try to correct, miscues that don't fit with the following context and/or miscues that don't preserve the essential meaning of the sentence?

3. How appropriately does the reader use graphic cues *along with* preceding and following context, plus prior knowledge?

Before analyzing the miscue patterns and drawing tentative conclusions about reading strategies from them, it can be extremely helpful to review the sections of Chapters 6 and 7 that haven't already been mentioned for review. These sections can help you consider miscue and strategy patterns you might look for, plus other insights you might gain by examining, analyzing and coding, then reanalyzing the miscues and looking for patterns that suggest insights into reading strategies. And patterns are indeed the issue here, not an isolated miscue or two.

DEVELOPING A READER PROFILE: TANGLING WITH THE MESSINESS OF REALITY

Angel was a seven-year-old second grader when one of my students, a preservice teacher, did a reader profile project with her. I've chosen to draw from this project in illustrating the beginnings of a reading profile, simply because the miscue patterns are interesting and the situation gives us the opportunity to think about certain issues that teachers need to be aware of. As always, it seems, the data is less complete than I would wish, and even I found it challenging to make coding decisions about some of the miscues. These matters, of course, are but two kinds of "messiness" that the classroom teacher has to deal with daily.

For brevity, I will share just some highlights from the reader profile information gathered by Katie, my student. I have included her reflections after she typed the interview, to illustrate not only the "messiness of reality" but the difficulty of developing an accurate reader profile. Katie has engaged in the kind of reflection we all need to do before assuming that the data we have gathered is an accurate reflection of the reader.

The Reading Interview

Below is an excerpt from the reading interview, with an example of how the interviewer critiqued her own interviewing in her write-up. A stands for Angel and K stands for Katie, the interviewer.

K: Angel, what do people do when they read? What do you think is inside their head when they read?

A: Words.

K: The words are going through their head?

A: [nods her head]

[Oh, oh: I abandoned the quest to find out what processes she thinks readers go through as they read. Maybe I could have asked something like, "What are readers thinking when they read?" Would that have been a "leading question"?]

K: Angel, when you are reading and come to a word you don't know, what do you do?

READER _Angel_   AGE/GRADE _7/2_   DATE _7/15/01_

RATER _CSW_

TEXT READ _The Day Jimmy's Boa Ate the Wash_

How well did the reader use prior knowledge and context to predict effectively? Circle or underline one option, then provide examples.

Almost never / seldom / <u>about half the time</u> / frequently / almost always

52% fit completely with the preceding context; 12% fit with preceding grammar only; 36% didn't fit at all.

Examples of ones that didn't fit

          2.holding
          1.holding

#48 "What ~~happened~~?"

#59 She got mad because she thought Tommy threw it,
       so she threw / one at ~~him~~. *(on)*

               look
#44 "You mean he ~~took~~ it into the hen house?"

                 fam   wif   sering
#75, 76, 77 "Well, we heard the ~~farmer's wife screaming~~."

How well did the reader use following context to correct, or try to correct, miscues that didn't fit with the following context and/or miscues that didn't leave the essential meaning of the sentence intact? Circle or underline one option, then provide examples.

<u>Almost never</u> / seldom / about half the time / frequently / almost always

She corrected only one miscue, which happened to fit with the preceding, ~~following~~ context:

                  look Ⓒ
    "You mean he ~~took~~ ⓘⓣ into the hen house?"

Out of 25 coded miscues, she corrected only 1 and attempted to correct 4 others — 2 of which were miscues on <u>constrictor</u>.

How appropriately did the reader use graphic cues along with preceding and following context, plus prior knowledge? Circle or underline one option, then provide examples. *It depended.*

Almost never / seldom / <u>about half the time</u> / frequently / almost always

Sometimes her miscues showed the use of all three language cueing systems:
                           extra   *a*
#49, 50, 51 "Well, one hen got ~~excited~~ and laid ~~an~~ egg,
        laided
        and it ~~landed~~ on Jenny's head."
Sometimes her miscues showed the use of grammar and graphic cues as she constructed a sentence that didn't fit semantically with the surrounding context:
                   the family tripped
#71, 72, 73 "Well, ~~what finally stopped~~ it?"
Several miscues, especially toward the end, showed overuse of graphic cues and underuse of grammar and/or meaning:
                 brock
#53 "No, the egg. And it ~~broke~~ — yucky...."
                     Also #93, 97, 98 ...

Figure 8.6 *Angel's miscue patterns.*

A: Ask for help.

K: What if you are at home and there is nobody to ask for help?

A: Ask Michael [her brother].

K: What if Michael is not here?

A: Sound it out or look at the picture.

K: Okay, what else do you do when you come to a word you don't know?

A: Skip it. [I think I was doing a good job of getting her to tell me *all* the strategies she could think of.]

K: Skip it . . . go on and come back to it.

A: [nods her head]

K: That's a good idea.

[Oh, dear, I put words in her mouth. Maybe she doesn't go back; maybe she just skips it. But I said what I hoped she would do, and once again she nodded her head "yes."]

K: What else could you do if there was no one else to help you?

A: Just make up a story for it.

K: You ever make up stories for the pictures when you are reading or when you don't want to read the text?

A: [shakes her head "no"]

K: Angel, you said you try and sound out the words, right?

A: [nods her head]

K: You say the letters and then say it out loud and put them together and then try and say it all at once. Like, sound it out and then say it faster and faster until you get the word. [I have previously observed Angel reading.]

A: At school. [I should have explored more into what she meant by "at school."]

K: At school, and sometimes you ask somebody what the word is. [If I was going to summarize her strategies, why didn't I also mention skipping the word?]

K: Do you ever think about what the word actually means? Like, when you are reading the sentence and you think about what the sentence might mean, then try to get the word from that?

K: Yeah. [But again, I told her what I wanted to hear!]

As we can see from this transcript, Angel's first strategy in dealing with problem words apparently is to ask somebody, not to try to deal with the words independently. This is further confirmed by other responses from the reading interview. She uses two other strategies that she's aware of: sound it out, or skip the word. These, of course, are strategies she can use independently.

Another exchange from the interview suggests that Angel might be overattending to words and underattending to meaning:

K: Angel, why do people read?

A: So they know what they want to do when they grow up.

K: Pretty good idea. Why do you read?

A: So when I want to read a book I know what the word is.

Angel also admits, though, that she likes to read to find out about things that interest her, and that she likes to read funny stories. Therefore, she might not be as word-bound as one might have suspected from the response "So when I want to read a book I know what the word is."

Given Angel's later reading and retelling, it seems that these discussed aspects of the interview are most relevant.

The Retelling and Discussion

Katie asked Angel to read and retell *The Day Jimmy's Boa Ate the Wash,* by Trinka Hakes Noble. As with many readers—probably most who have never done a retelling before—Angel's initial, unaided retelling was quite brief:

> They went to a farm. And, uhm, they were throwing eggs at each other. And a pig came home with them on the bus.

Instead of including another stretch of dialogue between Katie and Angel, I shall simply mention a few points:

- Angel knew that children had gone to a farm for a field trip with their teacher.
- She knew they had thrown eggs and corn.
- She thought they had gotten on the bus to go home (a logical inference, though they probably had to go back to the school first).
- She knew that Jimmy left the "bonga bonga" (boa constrictor) at the farm, and that, in place of it he took home the pig that was on the bus.
- She knew initially that Jimmy brought a "bonga bonga" to the farm, but rather than ask her what the "bonga bonga" was, Katie *told* her it was a snake, a boa constrictor. Instead, Katie should have asked, "What's a 'bonga bonga'?" Since she didn't, we don't really know whether Angel understood during her reading that Jimmy had brought a snake to the farm, though she probably did, because of the pictures. However, Angel probably didn't know how this kind of snake attacks its predators and prey: by wrapping itself around them and squeezing them to death, hence the name "constrictor." Of course, in a teaching situation, we would explain about boa constrictors before inviting the child to read the book. But in this assessment situation, we want to see how the reader will navigate the text without help.

Katie's questions dealt mostly with events. She didn't begin her questioning by trying to find out what Angel remembered about Jimmy's bringing the boa constrictor to school, though, or whether Angel realized that every person and animal would be frightened by the boa, or whether Angel understood that the boa could cause havoc on the farm. Rather, Katie began asking about events with the question "What were they throwing?" Katie never really attempted to find out whether Angel understood the plot: the fact that Jimmy's bringing his pet boa initiated a hilarious sequence of events. Nor did she determine whether Angel appreciated the humor of the story.

Miscues, Miscue Patterns, and Reading Strategies

Analyzing and coding Angel's miscues was an interesting challenge (see Figure 8.5). Here is the part of the selection I chose to analyze—not the very beginning, but the part where we first learn about the boa constrictor.

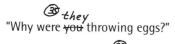

(38) bagging (39) a tricking teacher
              1 tricker
"THE ~~BOA CONSTRICTOR~~!"

(40) Yah   bow
"~~Yeah~~, Jimmy's pet ~~boa~~ (constrictor)."   [After two examples of the
                                                   miscues on boa constrictor, I
                                                   didn't number any more for coding.]
                    bow conteacher 1 do
"What was Jimmy's pet ~~boa~~ ~~constrictor~~ (41) a digging (42) ~~doing~~ on ~~the~~ farm?"

(43) br-oō-t
"Oh, he ~~brought~~ it to meet all the farm animals,

but the chickens didn't like it."

(44) look (E (45)
"You mean he ~~took~~ (it) into the hen house?"

Yah   (46) squi-   (47) away
"~~Yeah~~, and the chickens started ~~squawking~~ and flying ~~around~~."

(48) a holding
     1 helding
"Go on, go on. What ~~happened~~?"

(49) extra   (50) a   (51) laided
"Well, one hen got ~~excited~~ and laid ~~an~~ egg, and it ~~landed~~ on Jenny's head."

"The hen?"
(52) ? (53) brock   (54)
"No, the egg. And it ~~broke~~-------yuck(y)-------all over her hair."

"What did she do?"
(55) throwed   (56) 's throw (57) (58)
"She got mad because she ~~thought~~ Tommy ~~threw it~~, (so she) threw

(59) on
one at ~~him~~."

It's tempting to explain the reasoning behind some of my codings, but I've chosen instead to invite you to try coding them yourself and compare our codings (see the "For Further Exploration" section at the end of this chapter). Here, I will simply respond to the questions in Figure 8.6, a miscue recording form from Chapter 7 that you can use for briefly describing miscue patterns, as a prelude to drawing tentative conclusions about a reader's use of reading strategies.

■ How well did the reader use prior knowledge and context to predict effectively?

Only 52% of Angel's coded miscues fit completely with the preceding context, and only 12% more fit with the preceding grammar only. This leaves a disturbingly high 36% that do not fit with the preceding context. Here are some examples:

2 holding
1 helding
#48 "What ~~happened~~?"

throwed   's throw
#59 "She got mad because she ~~thought~~ Tommy ~~threw~~ it, ⟨so she⟩ threw

on
one at ~~him~~."

look
#44 "You mean he ~~took~~ it into the hen house?"

fam   wif scring
#75, 76, 77 "Well, we heard the ~~farmer's wife screaming~~."

In miscue #48, Angel made two attempts at the text word *happened,* but neither of the miscues fit with the grammar or the meaning of what came before. Miscue #59 is similar. Miscue #44, "look," shows the use of a verb for a verb, but it doesn't fit the preceding grammar because the text word *took* is a past tense verb, while the miscue "look" is not. The miscue "look" doesn't really fit with the preceding meaning in the story, either. As she read the story, Angel made several miscues like #75, #76, and #77. These are nonwords that have no meaning and that don't preserve the grammatical ending of the text word, either. (The "-ing" of "scring" isn't a *grammatical* ending because "scr" by itself isn't the base of a verb.)

■ How well or how appropriately did the reader use following context to correct, or try to correct, miscues that don't fit with the following context or preserve the essential meaning of the sentence?

Angel succeeded in correcting only one miscue, the omission of *it* (#45). Here is the sentence with Angel's miscues marked:

look ⓒ
#44 45: "You mean he ~~took~~⟨it⟩into the hen house?"

However, the miscue fit with the following context, so that can't have been the reason for correction. In any case, I suspect that the essential meaning of the sentence was lost, so I coded the miscue accordingly.

Angel's attempts at correcting her initial miscues on *boa constrictor* were nowhere near successful, but at least she tried. The only miscue she might have tried to correct because of a poor fit with context was actually a miscue that didn't fit with the *preceding* context:

2 holding
1 helding
#48 "What ~~happened?~~"

Angel read this first as "What helding?" then as "What holding?"

Angel did not try to correct the other 20 miscues coded. Given that she surely could not have corrected the miscues on *boa* and/or *constrictor,* that still means that there was no attempt to correct several miscues that either failed to fit with the following context, failed to preserve the essential meaning of the sentence, or both.

■ How appropriately did the reader use graphic cues along with preceding and following context, plus prior knowledge?

This question can only partly be answered by looking at the codings for question 6, "Was the miscue graphically similar?" We see that 45% of Angel's miscues were coded as having high graphic similarity, which means that at least two of the three "parts" of the word were graphically similar: the beginning, middle, or end. Another 41% showed low (partial) graphic similarity, usually the same beginning letters when the miscue was written (though sometimes only the very first letter was the same). We can't really tell the significance of this information, though, until we simultaneously consider how these miscues fit with the context. This is easiest to do by simply looking at the copy of the selection with the miscues marked.

There, we see that some miscues that have high or some graphic similarity do fit with the context, and do make reasonably good sense in context:

#47   "Yeah, and the chickens started squawking and flying ~~around~~." *away*

#49, 50, 51   "Well, one hen got ~~excited~~ and laid ~~an~~ egg, and it ~~landed~~ on Jenny's head." *extra* *a* *laided*

The miscue "extra" for *excited* doesn't fit the context as well as the others, but at least it doesn't seem to detract from the meaning.

Unfortunately, we also see among Angel's miscues many that show high graphic similarity but that don't fit well with the preceding and/or following context:

#53   "No, the egg. And it ~~broke~~-------yucky-------all over her hair." *brock*

#93   "Boy, that sure ~~sounds~~ like an exciting trip." *sends*

#97, 98   "Yeah, I suppose, if you're the ~~kind~~ of ~~kid~~ who likes *klinged* *¹king* *²kid* *³kidding*

class trips to the farm."

The miscue "brock" shows high attention to the letters of the text word, but none to the preceding context. Angel seems not to have even tried to come up with a word that would be meaningful. The miscues in the last two example sentences are from later in the book. The miscue "sands" has high graphic similarity with *sounds*, but it is not even grammatical with what comes before. The same is true of "klinged" for *kind* and "kidding" for *kid*.

Interestingly, as Angel read well into the selection, she also made more miscues that produced a grammatical and meaningful sentence, especially up to and through the miscue, but these miscues didn't preserve the essential meaning of the story. For example:

#71, 72, 73   "Well, ~~what finally stopped~~ it?" *the family tripped*

"Well, the family tripped it?" is a sensible sentence, but it doesn't fit the context of the story.

In the following example, the miscues "had" and "the story" fit with the preceding context, but not with the following context:

#83, 84, 85, 86   "We never ~~found~~ *had* out, because Mrs. Stanley made us get on the

bus, and ~~we sort~~ *the story* of left in a hurry ~~without~~ ©*went* the boa constrictor."

The miscue "went" didn't even fit with the preceding context, but Angel did correct it.

What might we tentatively conclude from all of this? Angel showed some ability to draw upon all three kinds of cues effectively, as in some of the preceding examples. It looks as if Angel was initially inclined to make too much use of graphic cues and too little use of context. Then she began making more and more miscues that fit the grammar and meaning of what preceded—miscues that typically didn't bear much or any graphic similarity to the text words. However, these miscues often did not fit with the following context, and she generally didn't try to correct them or indicate, by tone of voice, pauses, or repetitions, that she knew the miscues were unsuitable.

Based on the evidence we have, I think she needs the following kinds of help:

- Help in learning to use preceding context to think ahead
- Help sounding words out in letter-sound chunks, refusing to settle for nonsense, and using context to come up with a word that fits
- Help in looking at least a word or two ahead when she's having trouble with a particular word
- Help in learning to ask, "Does that sound right?" and "Does that make sense?" when she's made a miscue
- Help in figuring out how to decide when to keep trying to get a word (for example, by rereading and/or looking or reading ahead, and in either case reprocessing the graphic display of the word), when to just try to figure out what would fit in terms of meaning, and when to just go on

The first four kinds of instructional help can enable Angel to become more effective in constructing meaning from a text, while the latter set of suggestions can help her become more efficient. Both, of course, will help her become increasingly independent, so that her first thought when encountering an unfamiliar word won't be "Ask somebody."

An Instructional Plan

Deciding what kind of help the reader needs is obviously the first step towards making an instructional plan. Assuming I had already developed a comprehensive literacy program in my classroom, I would, if I were Angel's teacher, continuing providing her with many opportunities to be read to, to discuss readings (not be quizzed on them, even orally), to write in response to what she's reading, to read books of her own choice, to read collaboratively with peers, and to read with me. I would also provide books on tape that had been recorded at a pace that Angel could follow. I would see that she had help (mine or another adult's) in making her own books, reading and rereading them, and reading them to others. In short, I would provide as many as possible of the experiences described in Chapter 10, including some that would be provided only to students who need to use all the language cues together to construct meaning more effectively, or who need to become more efficient in their reading. One more experience I would particularly provide is echo reading, where the student reads along orally with a more proficient reader, or as an "echo" when necessary.

The major kind of individual help I'd provide, though, would be through Retrospective Miscue Analysis procedures, used with a small group having similar needs and with Sarah individually, in a conference. Retrospective Miscue Analysis is discussed in Chapter 9.

ADDITIONAL FORMS FOR RECORDING DATA

When you are confident that you can determine many readers' miscue patterns and strategies by just listening, you might find useful a form like the one in Figure 8.7. The summary form in Figure 8.8 is still briefer, as it requires tabulating and calculating only the percentage of sentences that fit semantically in the context of the story.

READER _____ AGE/GRADE _____ DATE _____

RATER _____

TEXT READ _____

Does the sentence, as the reader left it, make sense within the context of the whole text?
  (Do a running tally on the Yes and No lines, total them, then compute the comprehending score and the number of miscues per No sentence.)

Yes _____ TOTAL _____

No _____ TOTAL _____

Comprehending score = number of Yes sentences, divided by the total number of sentences
RATIO _____ PERCENT _____
Miscues per No sentence = number of miscues in the No sentences, divided by total number of No sentences (can be computed if the miscues have been recorded):
RATIO _____ PERCENT _____

NOTES FROM READING INTERVIEW

NOTES ON MISCUE PATTERNS AND READING STRATEGIES

Figure 8.7 *Reader profile summary form, long (adapted from Y. Goodman, Watson, & Burke, 1987); from Constance Weaver,* Reading Process & Practice, *3rd ed., Heinemann, 2002; © 2002 by Constance Weaver; may be reproduced for use.*

NOTES FROM RETELLING AND DISCUSSION SESSION

SUMMARY OF STRENGTHS AND NEEDS AND/OR OTHER COMMENTS

INSTRUCTIONAL PLAN

Figure 8.7 (*Continued*).

READER _____ AGE/GRADE _____ DATE _____

RATER _____

TEXT READ_____

Does the sentence, as the reader left it, make sense within the context of the whole text?
(Do a running tally on the Yes and No lines, total them, then compute the comprehending score and the number of misues per No sentences.)

Yes_____ TOTAL _____

No _____ TOTAL _____

Comprehending score = number of Yes sentences, divided by the total number of sentences
RATIO_____ PERCENT _____
Miscues per No sentence = number of miscues in the No sentences, divided by total number of No sentences
RATIO_____ PERCENT _____

OVERALL SUMMARY OF STRENGTHS AND NEEDS

INSTRUCTIONAL PLAN

Figure 8.8 *Reader profile summary form, short (adapted from Y. Goodman, Watson, & Burke, 1987; from Constance Weaver,* Reading Process & Practice, *3rd ed., Heinemann, 2002; © 2002 by Constance Weaver; may be reproduced for use).*

Other Aspects of a Reading Portfolio and Profile

Ideally, a reader profile would be based on a broader array of data than just a reading interview, a miscue analysis, and a retelling/discussion session. Ideally, too, the reader profile would be only part of a more complete literacy profile or a still more comprehensive learning profile. See Chapter 12 for more aspects of reading that may become part of a reading/literacy profile, which, in turn, guides teaching and documents learning.

For Further Exploration

1. For more practice in analyzing and coding miscues and determining a reader's possible strategies, you can photocopy miscue coding form #2 from Chapter 7 (Figure 7.6) and code Angel's miscues in this chapter yourself. Then compare with my codings to see the differences. See if you can understand the reasons for my codings, but don't necessarily consider your different codings "wrong"; actually, I found it quite a challenge to make some of the decisions, too. Sure, in some cases your different codings might have resulted from confusion about how to code miscues, but if you have already analyzed some, such as those of the readers in the last chapter, then some or most of the differences may simply reflect legitimate differences in our thinking patterns. Talk with others about these differences, if you have the opportunity to do so.

2. Consider what kind(s) of instructional help, if any, you would provide individually or in a small group for Betsey and/or Erica, whose miscue samples are provided at the end of Chapter 6. If desired, you can look ahead at Chapters 9 and 10 for more ideas.

3. Read the case studies included on the Web page associated with this book: <*http:www.heinemann.com/weaver*>. See if you agree wih the conclusions Lisa Schade and I drew in writing up these case studies. Are there other elements you would add to our instructional plans?

9 Revaluing Readers, Retrospective Miscue Analysis, and Other Strategies for Helping Readers

We have . . . assumed that children in the lower [reading achievement] groups cannot engage in real reading and writing, and so offered them steady diet of isolated skills activities . . . . The differential instruction typically provided lower-achieving children too often works to perpetuate continued use of ineffective reading strategies and continued low achievement . . . . It is important that the regular classroom provide the kinds of literacy experiences that all children need, but that some especially need to receive *in school.*

—Richard Allington

Questions for Thought and Discussion

1. Why do you think reading instruction has traditionally focused on the mastery of isolated skills for children who have been placed in lower reading groups? What do you think the effects have been, and why?

2. How would you yourself define *reading fluency?* How important do you think it is to read fluently? To read efficiently? What are your reasons?

3. Why do some readers need to reconsider what reading effectively actually requires and to revalue themselves as readers?

4. What are some of the many ways that Retrospective Miscue Analysis can be used to help readers?

5. Why would it be valuable to have readers who don't read for meaning hear the teacher demonstrate think-alouds, and then do think-alouds themselves?

The opening quotes from Richard Allington offer us some idea of what does *not* help children who have had few literacy experiences (or at least few prior experiences with books); who score low on standardized measures of reading achievement; and who often just try to read—or to sound out—the words of a text, with little concern for meaning. Allington details some of the ways in which we have shortchanged such children, in comparison with their more fortunate peers (1998, pp. 556–557):

Various studies (e.g., Stanovich, 1986) indicate that children placed in higher-achievement groups (misnamed higher "ability" groups) have more actual opportunities to read, especially to read silently; their instruction is more often focused on comprehension after reading than on the pronunciation of words during reading; they are encouraged to use cross-checking strategies to identify and verify unknown words instead of just being told to "sound it out" or being given the word; they are asked more thoughtful questions about what they read, rather than mostly literal recall questions, and so forth. In contrast, children in the lower groups are kept busy with more round-robin oral reading peppered with interruptions focused on sounding and matching, more isolated skills and drills, fewer comprehension-stimulating activities, and more dependency-creating instruction; because of this they also do less reading and writing (Allington, 1983).

Allington (1998) mentions other, research-confirmed differences, too, between the instruction provided to children placed in lower reading groups—often as early as kindergarten—and those placed in higher groups. Always the differences serve to further disadvantage children in the lower groups. Is it any wonder that once labeled as "lower ability" or "lower achievement," few children become as competent at reading and writing as their differently labeled peers? Though administrators, teachers, and parents mean well, often we have actually held such children back as readers, through our instructional methods.

This chapter and the next are designed to help you focus on the *real* needs of children who have, or seem to have, difficulty with reading—needs identified through miscue analysis and retelling, in particular, rather than through scores on standardized tests. While considering some particular ways of helping such readers, we must constantly keep in mind that such instructional help will achieve its full potential only if *all* readers in the classroom are immersed in a rich array of literacy activities.

We shall return to that topic in the next chapter and, in much greater detail, in Chapter 12.

Why Do You Suppose ... ?

In 1998 and 2000, fourth graders taking the National Assessment of Educational Progress test in reading were asked how often their teachers help them break words into parts. Those who responded "never or hardly ever" had the highest overall NAEP reading scores, compared with those who responded "once or twice a week" (the next highest scores) or "every day" (the lowest scores).

In response to the question or to how often their teachers help them understand new words, those who responded "once or twice a week" or "once or twice a month" had higher overall reading scores than the other two categories (see National Assessment of Reading Progress, 2001).

PHONICS, WORDS, AND READING

Currently, the reading profession is plagued with false claims that children have to learn to read simple, "decodable" texts with regular letter-sound patterns accurately and fluently before they should be given texts to read for comprehension or enjoyment. The same is prescribed for older students who struggle over words and do not read fluently. These false claims stem from a skills-first model of reading and learning to read, which is promoted in the public arena by researchers, special interests, and politicians who look at only a very narrow and select base of research studies, refer to these studies as "scientific research," and even encourage or pass legislation based upon these claims. I will discuss some of the research in Chapters 11 and 13, and Margaret Moustafa will do so in Chapter 15. Meanwhile, let me point out that this skills-first teaching is exactly the kind of instruction that Allington and others have found to hold back children who have been assigned to lower reading groups.

We can help readers give appropriate attention to letter-sound patterns as they use effective strategies not only to decode words but to construct meaning while reading and writing texts, as indicated near the end of this chapter and especially in the next. Listening to books on tape can help readers internalize not only words but letter-sound patterns, as indicated in the next chapter. Chapters 13 and 14 also describe what is often called "analogy phonics," another way that readers can be helped to internalize letter-sound patterns.

However, this chapter on supporting and helping readers does not focus on teaching phonics in isolation, for several reasons:

- Developmentally, most children (and adults) learn whole words and/or whole, simple texts first, before they develop knowledge of letter-sound patterns.

- Reading more and more words enables most readers to pick up on chunks of letters and letter-sound patterns, and they then use this knowledge in reading other words that are not yet familiar in print.

- Unfamiliar print words are harder to recognize by those who are not very strong readers if they use graphic cues and letter-sound knowledge alone, without reference to context. *Later*, they will recognize more and more words on sight and become more automatic in their word recognition.

- Reading texts and words (with support, of course) before focusing on letter-sound patterns enables readers to focus on meaning, which needs to be the starting point of reading as well as its goal. It is highly motivating to be able to read meaningful texts, and reading for meaning first will keep most readers from starting to overemphasize mere word identification, as if the words stood in isolation. (See particularly the discussion of "shared reading" in this chapter and especially in Chapter 12.)

Some of the research behind these assertions has been discussed in Chapters 3 and 4 particularly, while other research evidence will be discussed in Chapters 11 and 15.

EFFICIENT READING AND FLUENCY

We have noted, in Chapter 6, a distinction between "effective" readers and "efficient" readers. Effective readers are those who succeed in constructing meaning from texts that are appropriate in concepts and language. Efficient readers are those who, in addition, construct meaning without wasting time unnecessarily. Proficient readers are those who are both effective and efficient.

As more and more demands are placed upon students to learn from texts independently, it becomes increasingly important to become efficient and not merely effective as a reader. Skimming can help substantially with efficiency, but first we need to learn to determine what is most important in what we are reading—sometimes what's most important to us, but at other times what teachers or testmakers are likely to deem most important. Indeed, with regard to questions on standardized tests (not to mention questions at the end of selections in basal reading programs), many students have learned that it is most efficient to read the questions first, then skim the text for the information required. For "literal" questions, the answer comes directly from the text and can usually just be matched with the appropriate answer among the multiple choices. Thus skimming can be a valuable test-taking strategy, reflecting one way to read efficiently.

What does test taking have to do with fluency? Well, another way to get through standardized tests rapidly is to identify most of the words automatically and thereby read the text "fluently" and quickly. If students haven't been taught other ways of reading efficiently, it is hardly surprising that they would be hampered on standardized tests by not reading rapidly. Even scores on "comprehension" would be affected by slow, inefficient reading. Is it any wonder that the current rage for automaticity and reading fluency comes from those who usually use timed, standardized tests as their only measure of "reading achievement"? It's a larger leap, though, when they and others begin actually equating automaticity and fluency with reading comprehension, and when they begin claiming that automaticity and fluency must precede reading for meaning. Miscue analysis and teachers' classroom experience show the fallacy of thinking that fluency is necessary for comprehension or, on the other hand, that fluency is a surefire indicator of comprehension.

Cautions About Current Claims Regarding Fluency

Some researchers claim that fluent reading with automatic word identification ("automaticity") is crucial for concentrating on meaning (e.g., Adams, 1990). However, such claims are typically based upon laboratory research involving word-for-word recall as a measure of what can be chunked into short-term memory at once (as, for instance, in the studies discussed at the beginning of Chapter 5). Such claims are *not* derived from research on the important information readers *actually* remember and understand from reading real texts. Miscue analysis studies (e.g., Flurkey, 1997, and earlier chapters) confirm what observant, inquiring classroom teachers have long noticed:

- Fluent reading doesn't guarantee comprehension.
- Comprehension doesn't require fluent reading.
- Thoughtful reading is often—perhaps usually—not fluent.
- Fluent reading may actually mask a *lack* of attention to meaning.

Of course it is also true that those who read slowly and struggle over words may not be attending to meaning, but that is another matter. It has more to do with their concept of reading than with their lack of fluency. Therefore, we need to be sure that when we ask or invite students to reread texts until they can read them fluently, we are not sending the wrong message about what reading is. *Fluency must not replace a focus on meaning as the goal of reading.*

Nevertheless, most readers want to be able to read words and texts with relative ease and efficiency, even if not word-perfectly, and to read texts with "flow," as proficient readers do. I think "fluency" is a desirable long-term goal if redefined this way. Notice, however, that I said long-term goal, not fluency first, nor fluency as a condition for constructing meaning from texts. We can help readers develop fluency in this sense as they read and reread familiar and enjoyable texts, during shared reading and perhaps guided reading, during the sustained reading that they do without a teacher's help, and when reading along in a book while listening to a tape recording of it—especially a tape recording that has been specially tailored to the reader's rate of reading. In fact, many of the literacy experiences that are part of a comprehensive literacy program promote not only the enjoyment of meaningful texts but the development of fluency. Many reading and writing activities can also be structured so as to promote the development and use of letter-sound knowledge.

We need to be sure, however, that when we ask or invite students to reread texts until they can read them fluently, we are not sending the wrong message about what reading is. Fluency must not replace a focus on meaning as the goal of reading.

REVALUING READERS

It was tempting to refer to "struggling readers" in the title of this chapter, since that is a current buzzword (or phrase). I chose not to use that term, however, for several reasons. First, the phrase *struggling reader* seems to have an air of permanence about it, as if we were saying "once a struggling reader, always a struggling reader." That is simply not true. Second, the so-called struggling reader may be struggling more with other people's perceptions of him or her as a reader than with reading itself. Third, and similarly, the reader may be struggling to meet other people's expectations and/or to score well on their assessment measures, even though the reader may actually be competent at constructing meaning from age-appropriate texts. For example, teachers, administrators, and parents may expect a child to read word-perfectly and fluently, even though proficient readers often don't do either (see Chapters 4, 5, and 6). Or adults may want a child to score well on standardized, timed tests, even though the reader comprehends perfectly well when reading more slowly. Fourth, and often as a result of these kinds of expectations and demands, the reader may mostly need help in revaluing himself or herself as a reader, and otherwise, help via basically the same kinds of literacy experiences that are offered to children perceived as good readers. In fact, what is most important for all readers is a comprehensive literacy program within which individual readers' needs can be met. See in the next chapter the brief definitions of major components of such a literacy program, and see the detailed information in Chapter 12.

When teachers consider or label students as "struggling," "lower ability," or—worse yet— "poor" readers because they cannot read age-appropriate texts fluently, such labeling and possible tracking commonly damages the reader's self-esteem and has further negative effects on the reader, often causing the reader to try even harder to get the words right, at the expense of meaning. When a school psychologist labels students as "dyslexic" or "learning disabled" because of their scores on tests of isolated skills, the negative effects only deepen—for students as human beings, and for them as readers. The negative effects are particularly devastating when the classroom teacher interprets such test results as indicating that the children need work on isolated skills rather than more opportunities to read—and to write—connected, interesting texts and more help with strategies while they are reading and writing such texts.

In such situations, students need for their teachers to better understand the reading process, the nature of proficient reading, and what promotes effective strategies. But the students also need help themselves in understanding the nature of proficient reading, effective reading strategies and good miscues, and the fact that they need not be word-perfect readers in order to be good readers. They need to understand that the purpose of reading is to construct meaning and gain understanding from what they read. They need to be encouraged to approach reading this way, to be guided in using strategies for getting meaning, to appreciate their own good miscues, and to recognize that they are better readers than they thought. They need to revalue themselves as readers, and to do so they first need to reconsider and reconceptualize reading itself.

ERICA: FROM ANALYSIS TO ASSISTANCE

The following information about Erica and her reading was included at the end of Chapter 6, in the section "For Further Exploration." For convenience, that information is reproduced here, followed by a discussion of why and how I did Retrospective Miscue Analysis with Erica, in order to encourage her to revalue herself as a reader.

When I first met her, Erica was a bright fifth grader who enjoyed discussing literature and offered insightful comments into the characters' feelings and motivations. However, both her writing and her reading were rather slow and painful—much less fluent than one would have predicted from her intelligence and liveliness. Each week she attended reading classes with two different special reading teachers.

Erica's classroom teacher and I decided to see what we could learn from analyzing her miscues. The class was then reading and discussing *Roll of Thunder, Hear My Cry,* by Mildred Taylor (1976), and I was reading and discussing the book with the least proficient readers, including Erica. Below is a passage she read while her teacher, Ruth Perino, listened and tape-recorded the session. The story concerns a black girl, Cassie, and her family in the rural South in the 1930s. At this point in the story, Cassie has just been ignored by a storekeeper as soon as white customers entered the store, then scolded and told to leave the store when she protested this treatment. Shortly after she and her older brother Stacey part outside the store, she has another painful awakening: she accidentally bumps into a white classmate, Lillian Jean, on the sidewalk, and is humiliated by being forced to apologize and then to walk in the street. Erica's miscues are marked for the first part of this passage:

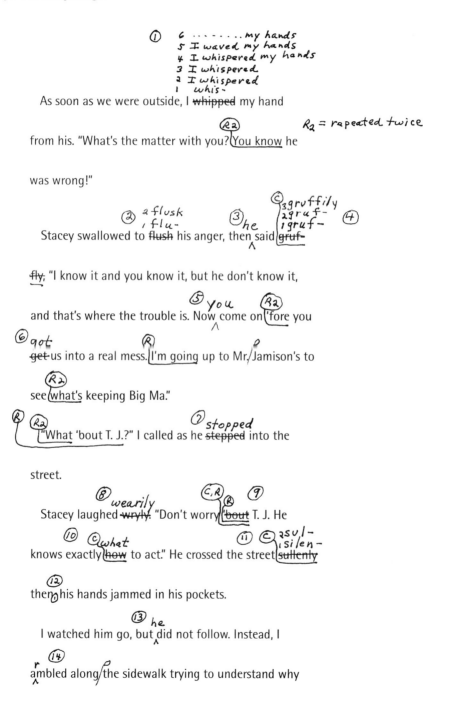

Mr. Barnett had acted the way he had. ⟨R⟩|More than once

⑮ glanced   ⑯ ₂mircantēl   [teacher then
I stopped and ~~gazed~~ over my shoulder at the ~~mercan-~~   ,mir   gave her the word]

          ⑰ ₃ a good mind to go back ④and find out what had
                ₂   into the back to find out ⑧what had
tile. I had ~~a good mind to go back in and find out~~   ₁ to go mind into

~~what had~~ made Mr. Barnett so mad. I actually turned

once and headed toward the store, then remembering

what Mr. Barnett had said about my returning, I

                    ⑱
          ⓒ   and
swung back around,|kicking|at the sidewalk, my head

⒜Ⓒ₂bōw-   AC = abandoning a correct form
⑲ ₁bl-   [teacher then said "You got it – 'bowed.'"]
   ~~bowed.~~

                ⑳ ₂Linna
It was then that I bumped into ~~Lillian~~ Jean   ,Lin-

㉑ ₃Sil
   ,Som
   Simms.

"Why don't you look where you're going?" she

               ⓒ ₂an- ㉓
㉒ said   ₁a-
   ~~asked~~ huffily. Jeremy|and| her two younger brothers were

with her. "Hey, Cassie," said Jeremy.

               ⓒ   ㉔
"Hey, Jeremy," I said solemnly,|keeping|my eyes
   ₂Lin
   ,Lill-
on ~~Lillian~~ Jean.

㉕ a-a-ah-ā-ā- āpō- apō'la- gīz- āpōlah' gīz
   "Well, ~~apologize~~," she ordered.

"What?"

          ㉖ when the-
               when you-
"You bumped into me. Now you apologize."
               ^

(27) (C) *don't*
I did not feel like (R) messing with ~~Lillian~~ *Willa* Jean. I had

(C) *o-*
other things on my mind. "Okay," I said, starting past,

(28) *2 Willa Jean*
1 Willa
"I'm sorry."ʌ

Lillian Jean sidestepped in front of me. "That ain't

(29)
enough. Get down (in) the road."

(30) *You're*
I looked/up at her. ρ "~~You~~ crazy?"

(C) *Don't ca-* (31)   (32) (C) *to*
"~~You can't~~ watch where you going, get (in) the road.

(33) (C) *'s*   (34) (C) *discount*
Maybe (that) way you won't be bumping into ~~decent~~ ʌ

(35) (C) *ha-*
white folks with your little nasty ~~self~~."

This second insult of the day was almost more than

(36) (C) *Mrs.*
I could bear. Only the thought of ~~Big~~ Ma up in Mr.

(37) *James'*   *Linny* (38) *s*
~~Jamison's~~ office saved ~~Lillian~~ Jean's lip. "I ain't nasty,"ʌ

(39) (C) *2 proudly* (40)
1 proudl-   (R) ρ
I said, ~~properly~~ holding my/temper/in check, "and if

you're so afraid of getting bumped, walk down there

yourself."

Analyzing Erica's Miscues

In analyzing Erica's miscues, I asked the three questions on the form in Figure 7.8 and concluded that Erica's miscues rated an "almost always" response in each instance. Below are the questions, with examples that clarify my strong affirmative.

■ How well did the reader use prior knowledge and context to predict effectively?

I would say "almost always," as illustrated by the following examples:

wearily
Stacey laughed ~~wryly~~.

glanced
I stopped and ~~gazed~~ over my shoulder. . .

2 *when the -*
1 *when you -*
"You bumped into me. Now you apologize."

2 *proudly*
1 *proudl-*
"I ain't nasty," I said, ~~properly~~ holding my temper in check.

Each example shows Erica making an appropriate prediction from context. Her understanding of Stacey's character and state of mind is evident in the miscue "wearily" for *wryly.* The miscue "proudly" for *properly* was a perfect description of Cassie.

- How well or how appropriately did the reader use following context to correct, or try to correct, miscues that didn't fit with the following context and/or that didn't leave the essential meaning of the sentence intact? Again, I would say "almost always." Here are some examples:

© *Don't ca-*   © *to*
"~~You~~ can't watch where you going, get ~~in~~ the road.

's   © *discount*
Maybe that way you won't be bumping into ~~decent.~~

white folks with your little nasty self."

In each instance, Erica corrected the miscue when it did not sound like language or make sense with what followed in the sentence.

- How appropriately did the reader use graphic cues along with preceding and following context, plus prior knowledge?

2 *flusk*   *gruffily*
1 *flu-*   *gruf-*
Stacey swallowed to ~~flush~~ his anger, then said ~~gruf-~~
                                   gruf-

~~fly,~~ . . .

2 *sull-*
1 *silen-*
He crossed the street ~~sullenly~~. . .

a-a-ah-ā-ā- āpō- a pō'la - gĭz - āpō lah 'gĭz
"Well, ~~apologize,~~" she ordered.

"What?"

when the -
when you -
"You bumped into me. Now you apologize."

These examples show Erica making good use of graphic cues and letter-sound knowledge along with prior knowledge and context. When the actual word is not something that makes sense to her in context (*flush,* in the first example, and *apologize,* the first time it occurs), she is unable to get the word using graphic cues and letter-sound knowledge alone. But when context supports her sounding-out strategy, she is able to get the word. Indeed, she doesn't need to sound out *apologize* the second time she encounters it: the word makes sense to her in this context. Thus Erica is quite effective in using graphic cues and letter-sound knowledge along with semantic and syntactic cues.

I also asked the miscue-related question in Figure 8.7, slightly paraphrased here:

■ Did the sentences, as the reader left them, make sense within the context of the whole text? (Or, did the sentences preserve meanings essential to the story?)

Yes, as almost all of the foregoing sentences would suggest. Indeed, though Erica did not regress and overtly correct her first prolonged attempt at sounding out *apologize,* it is obvious from her reading as well as later discussion that she realized what the word had been.

In short, Erica made highly effective use of reading strategies. She was able to orchestrate all the language cues into strategies for constructing meaning from the text.

Helping Erica Revalue Herself as a Reader

Erica had been labeled as "dyslexic" in the first grade, primarily because she had difficulty with isolated skills, such as identifying words out of context, and word attack skills, such as phonics. Then began her years of resource room tutoring by a teacher with training in the Orton-Gillingham approach, which emphasizes a multimodal approach to phonics. The final report from her third-grade resource room teacher was focused entirely on isolated skills, such as the identification of single consonants, short vowels, syllable patterns, syllable divisions, spelling rules and generalizations, and a few other areas.

In Ruth Perino's fifth-grade class, Erica was involved, like the other children, in many interesting reading, writing, and oral language experiences. She loved reading literature; demonstrated generally excellent understanding of what she read; used effective reading strategies like predicting, monitoring comprehension, and correcting; and dealt effectively with problem words by using semantic and syntactic cues along with letter-sound knowledge and prior knowledge of what had come before in the book she read from. Therefore, her teacher and I concluded that what Erica needed most was a lot more experience in reading itself, not skills or strategy work.

Nevertheless, I did use the tape recording of Erica's reading to help her gain self-confidence as a reader. Earlier, her literature discussion group had made with me a list of strategies for dealing with problem words. I asked Erica to review these briefly, then told her we would replay the tape and I'd like her to stop the tape whenever she heard herself making a good miscue or using a good strategy. Of course she was then to explain why it was a good miscue and what good reading strategies she was using. I regret not tape-recording this session, as Erica was absolutely thrilled to hear herself making good miscues and to be able to explain why they were good. This one session seemed to significantly boost her self-confidence as a reader—that is, to enable her to revalue herself as a reader.

RETROSPECTIVE MISCUE ANALYSIS

My instructional procedure with Erica is a variation of what is known as Retrospective Miscue Analysis, or RMA. Notice that the basic "reading miscue analysis" procedure is done for assessment. Retrospective Miscue Analysis is a teaching/learning procedure, though it too requires or involves assessment of the reader's miscue patterns and strategies. Actually, Retrospective Miscue Analysis is a collection of teaching/learning procedures that can be done after the reading; hence "retrospective" (from Latin *retro,* meaning 'back,' and '*specere,*' meaning 'to look').

The "Classic" on Retrospective Miscue Analysis

Goodman, Y. M., & Marek, A. M. (1996). *Retrospective Miscue Analysis: Revaluing Readers and Reading.* Katonah, NY: Richard C. Owen.

Originally developed in the 1970s by a Canadian secondary school reading specialist, Chris Worsnop, Retrospective Miscue Analysis has been popularized by Yetta Goodman and Ann Marek (1996). In Retrospective Miscue Analysis, we are able to "look back" at miscues the reader has made, because the reading has been tape-recorded. Tape recording not only allows for later reflection and teaching but encourages us as teachers not to interrupt the reader while reading, but rather to allow the reader to deal with problems and miscues independently. This is important if we want our students to become independent readers who don't wait for others to "give" them words. Furthermore, in the long run it is much better to have given the reader a strategy to use than to have given the reader just a word, or several words. Retrospective Miscue Analysis enables us to do just that: help readers develop effective and efficient strategies for reading.

Teachers Choosing the Miscues for Discussion

Often, the teacher selects miscues for discussion, and the reader and the teacher later consider the miscues together, either by looking at the miscues marked on a copy of the selection, by listening to the tape, or both. That is, together they consider in retrospect the reader's miscues and the reading strategies these miscues reflect—or don't reflect. A particularly powerful variation of RMA is having students in a small group discuss their own and one another's miscues; this possibility will be briefly discussed a little later in the chapter. In both one-on-one and group settings, readers can speculate as to why they made different miscues, reconsider the nature of the reading process, revalue themselves as readers, and focus on developing and/or reinforcing strategies for effective and efficient reading.

Below are some reader characteristics, with suggestions for the kinds of miscues a teacher might choose for discussion in each case. The suggestions are a combination of Ann Marek's (1989, 1992) and mine.

Why do we suggest contrasting miscues that *do* exemplify a desirable strategy with those that *don't?* Simply to demonstrate to the reader that he or she is capable of using the strategy and just needs to use it more consistently.

Reader Characteristics and Needs	*Kinds of Miscues That Could Be Examined*
Thinks reading means getting all the words; needs to understand that reading is not an exact process.	Select miscues that fit the context appropriately, and discuss. Might also consider the completely acceptable miscues of someone else who is clearly a good reader—perhaps the teacher, or perhaps classmates.
Lacks self-confidence, often because he or she doesn't read all the words correctly and thinks that good readers identify each word accurately.	Same as above.

Doesn't seem to understand that reading is supposed to make sense, which can be evidenced by a lot of miscues that don't fit with the preceding context.

Select miscues that do go with the preceding context, and discuss with the reader how he or she may have "thought ahead." Then consider miscues that don't go with the preceding context. When listening to miscues that don't fit with what came before, teachers can ask, "Does that make sense?" and/or "Does that sound like language?" You can then invite the reader to predict something that would fit with what came before. When the reader has become successful at this thinking ahead and is clearly trying to make meaning from texts, select instances where prediction plus the initial letters of the word are likely to enable the reader to predict the exact word; look at the rest of the word and confirm. But keep reinforcing the emphasis on meaning first.

Further evidence that a reader doesn't read for meaning may be several nonword miscues that suggest underuse of syntactic and semantic cues and overuse of graphic cues and letter-sound knowledge. Such miscues may often result if the reader tries to sound out words but, as indicated, doesn't pay attention to whether the words sound right together grammatically or make meaningful sentences together.

Keep in mind that even the most proficient readers may often make such miscues if the concepts and/or vocabulary of the selection are beyond their experience. If, however, the reader is making nonword miscues on words that you think should be common words in the reader's vocabulary, the strategies suggested in relation to prediction should help. You can also select miscues wherein all three kinds of language cues—syntactic, semantic, and graphic—were used effectively, and contrast these with miscues that reflect a sounding-out strategy, with insufficient regard for meaning.

Seldom corrects or tries to correct miscues that don't fit with the following context. May not even demonstrate recognition, by pausing or repeating, that the miscue doesn't sound right as the reader goes on.

Before even dealing with correction, you might help the reader learn to look a couple of words ahead while reading, especially when dealing with a problem word. Focus on correction only if the reader already seems to read for meaning and only if the reader already makes good predictions, as evidenced by miscues that fit with the preceding context.

If the reader meets these criteria, select appropriately corrected miscues and discuss, to demonstrate effective use of correction

	strategies *if/when* correction *is needed and seems possible* (that is, if the word is likely to be in the reader's listening vocabulary). Perhaps you will find that the reader often corrects such miscues silently. If not, and as a next step, select miscues you think the reader could easily correct and discuss them with the reader. Invite the reader to try again and/or to use this strategy "next time."
Reader is beginning to grasp that reading should make sense and beginning to make more good (meaning-preserving) miscues, but still has some tendency to sound out simple unfamiliar (or even familiar!) print words more or less letter-by-letter.	Select miscues where the reader has successfully sounded out words that were familiar orally, and sounded them out in chunks rather than letter-by-letter. (Such chunks might be the separable parts of syllables—see the discussion of onsets and rimes in Chapter 13—or syllables themselves.) Reinforce this chunking-out strategy as useful, as long as the reader is reading for meaning. Review, reminding/helping the reader to use context to think about possible words and meanings before chunking, and to aim for a real word that makes meaning in the sentence. Using following context to confirm or reconsider the "chunked-out" word is also important. However, be sure the reader does not keep trying to chunk out a word again and again and again. If chunking out doesn't work after a couple of tries, even though the reader is also attending to meaning, it is usually better just to read on.
A relatively proficient reader makes nonword miscues on longer words that are probably within the reader's listening vocabulary. This often happens because the reader figures he or she will never get the "long word" anyhow, or the reader figures that the word isn't all that important anyway. In such instances, even a relatively proficient reader may just say something that reflects some of the letters in the word, then read on.	If the reader is losing significant meaning frequently with this "say something and go on" strategy, it may be helpful to encourage the reader to use context to determine the probable/possible meaning of the word before going on. Or it may be useful to help the reader chunk out words while focusing all the while on coming up with a real word that would be meaningful in the context. But if the reader doesn't often lose significant meaning by dealing with longer words in this way, it may be wise just to accept and reinforce the "say something and go on strategy," which is a strategy that proficient readers use to keep reading efficiently as well as effectively.

Readers Selecting Their Own Miscues for Discussion

Though teachers often take the lead in selecting miscues and strategies for discussion, the reader can take more ownership over the selecting of miscues and strategies for discussion—especially once the reader understands the reading process and has begun to understand effective reading strategies. After the reading has been tape-recorded, for example, you can invite the reader to listen for certain kinds of miscues to discuss with the teacher, if warranted by the reader's pattern of miscues. For instance:

1. While following along in the text, the reader can be invited to listen for miscues that fit the context appropriately and therefore don't need to be corrected. This procedure is for the reader who thinks reading means completely accurate word identification. Such readers may try to correct even miscues that are perfectly acceptable in context. They may also lack self-confidence as readers.

2. The reader can listen for miscues that reflect good predicting, but that don't go with following context. This reinforces the predicting and also demonstrates the need for correction, when that situation occurs. This is for the reader who makes good predictions but shows little concern for miscues that don't fit with the following context, even if these miscues should be easy to correct in context. (We need to talk with the reader, though, to find out if he or she already tends to correct such miscues silently or to get the gist of the stretch of words even without mental correction.)

3. The reader can listen for miscues that don't sound like language. (This is for the reader who underuses syntactic as well as semantic cues and may overuse graphic cues and letter-sound knowledge.)

Of course, similar instructional strategies can be used on the spot, with immediate playback of a paragraph just tape-recorded. And the discussion can be more open-ended. For example, the teacher can simply ask the reader to stop the tape at trouble spots as they listen to the tape together. The reader can explain why this spot was a problem and how he or she tried to deal with it; then together they can discuss any other strategies that might have been effective. Such instructional strategies as these can be discussed and developed as the teacher—or the reader—sees the need.

In "Reader-Selected Miscues," Watson and Hoge (1996) offer excellent ideas for launching Retrospective Miscue Analysis with a whole class:

> One way to implement the RSM strategy is to allow at least thirty minutes for personal silent reading. Students are told that they will be exploring how reading works by examining places in the text that cause them problems. Before the reading period begins, students take several blank bookmarks (approximately two inches by eight inches). They read as they normally would except that when they have difficulty they place a marker in their books at the trouble spot and continue reading. Ten minutes before the close of reading time, students [who had trouble in at least one place] examine their trouble spots and select three miscues that confused or distracted them and affected their overall understanding or enjoyment of the work. Each student writes a sentence containing a selected miscue on the marker [bookmark], underlines it, writes his or her name on the marker, and returns all bookmarks to the teacher. (p. 157)

As a teacher, what are some ways you might follow up with the bookmarks? What are some variations on this procedure that you might try?

Retrospective Miscue Analysis with Pairs or Groups

Chris Worsnop, the teacher who first began using what is now known as Retrospective Miscue Analysis, worked first with individual readers, next with pairs of seventh graders, and then with groups of ninth graders. In all instances he was working with students from "remedial" or special reading classes.

Chris and the student(s) listened together to the tape recording of a student's reading, whoever first heard the miscue stopped the tape recorder, and each of them marked the miscue on their own copy of the selection. After each miscue had been marked, they went through a hierarchy of questions:

1. Does what the reader said mean the same as what is in the book? (semantic similarity)

2. Does what the reader said still sound like language? (syntactic similarity)

3. Does what the reader said look like what is in the book? (graphic similarity)

4. Does what the reader said sound like what is in the book? (phonic similarity)

The beauty of treating these questions as a hierarchy was that the students and the teacher stopped the first time that a question was answered "yes." This procedure in effect placed the highest emphasis on meaning and the lowest on whether the miscue looked and/or sounded like the word in the text (Worsnop, 1996, pp. 152–153).

Worsnop makes several important observations about the success of RMA with these readers who needed extra help:

■ Often the students answered "no" to the first two questions about semantic and syntactic acceptability, but "yes" to the questions about graphic and phonic similarity. "In these cases the students readily admitted that they could sound out the word after an attempt or two, but that they still did not understand it" (p. 153).

■ Worsnop and a classroom teacher who also worked with some of the students repeatedly praised their good miscues, strategies, and insights. Most of the students became more cheerful and confident. "They began to verbalize their belief that they might be able to 'make it' in reading after all" (p. 154).

■ By the end of the school year, all of the students that Worsnop and the classroom teacher worked with were handling "progressively more difficult material while either maintaining or improving their miscue profiles when compared to those with which they had started" (p. 154).

■ Their subsequent work with classes of students (in Worsnop's case, eight ninth-grade students in a special reading class) lent further support to Worsnop's earlier conclusions: that the significant difference occurred first in *"the improvement of the students' images about themselves as readers,"* and that *"reading improvement and self-confidence are interdependent"* (p. 155).

Other teachers have reported group miscue analysis to be highly successful with middle school readers as well.

THE "THINK-ALOUD" STRATEGY

A think-aloud procedure can be used with students who have difficulty comprehending texts and typically do not realize that the purpose of reading is to understand. Thinking aloud about what one is reading can be modeled by teachers, then used by students to help them focus on meaning, develop effective reading strategies, and reflect on their reading. Of course teachers can also use student think-alouds to assess students' ongoing reading strategies and to plan for instruction. The following suggestions for launching the think-aloud process are drawn from Opitz and Rasinski (1998, p. 14), who based them on Davey (1983):

1. Select a passage to read aloud. Choose something that will interest the students and that also will pose some difficulties, such as words that are ambiguous or likely to be unknown to the students.

2. Begin reading the passage aloud as the students follow along. Ideally the students should not only listen to you, but be able to follow along with a written copy of the passage. When you come to a trouble spot, stop and think it through aloud while students listen.

3. When you have completed the reading in this manner, invite students to add their own thoughts about these trouble spots or offers they themselves encountered.

4. Pair students and have them practice the procedure with each other. Students can take turns reading and responding to each other.

After the students have learned to do think-alouds in pairs, how might you use think-alouds for assessment and instructional planning? How might you get students to make such thinking procedures part of their silent reading as well? An excellent resource is Jeffrey Wilhelm's *Improving Comprehension with Think-Aloud Strategies* (2001).

HELPING READERS DEVELOP NEEDED CONCEPTS, VOCABULARY, AND STRATEGIES

Teachers are usually aware that students need help with concepts and vocabulary when new topics or units are introduced in science or social studies. However, we often do not think about students' probable lack of background knowledge for reading simple storybooks. Take, for example, one of the books in the Clifford the Big Red Dog series, namely *Clifford Takes a Trip* (Bridwell, 1966). In several instances, nine-year-old Jaime's miscues in reading this book probably stemmed from her not being familiar with the experiences, concepts, and vocabulary in the story. Take, for example, an incident near the end of the book, where Clifford crosses a toll bridge. Extending across most of two pages is the picture of the bridge, a suspension bridge with cables that extend downward in arcs from high suspension points above the bridge. (Obviously such a bridge is even difficult to describe, and if you have never seen such a bridge, you may not be able to construct a mental picture from my description.) The left-hand page shows Clifford stopped by a man in uniform in front of a toll booth that has the sign "TOLL BRIDGE—25¢," and another man in the toll booth holding out his hand for money. The sentence began on the preceding page, and this page begins with the words *he came to a toll bridge.* Jaime read this as "he came to a tall beginning." This makes a lot of sense if you don't know what a toll bridge is, have never seen a large suspension bridge, and are looking at the picture and the initial consonants in the words for help. The bridge did indeed have a "tall beginning" in the picture. See Chapter 14 for examples of other "simple" books that pose conceptual challenges to many children.

It is important for teachers to realize that what appears to be a problem identifying or even sounding out words may stem from something much deeper: a lack of experience, concepts, and the language used to express them in the text. Being reminded of the potential for such problems, classroom teachers can often become more sensitive to them and thereby prevent some potential reading difficulties before they have the opportunity to occur. Teachers may also need to help certain students learn to use their prior knowledge—including what they have just acquired in the classroom—as part of their strategies for making sense of text. Clearly, however, some individual children will need more help than the classroom teacher can provide.

Extra Help Through Shared Reading and Constructive Reading Strategies

An increasing number of teachers are engaging primary-grade children in shared reading experiences based upon the scaffolding techniques involved in Don Holdaway's "Shared Book Experience" (1979, 1982). The experience can be shared between an adult and a child or with a group of children or even a whole class, as long as the copy of the text (book, chart, transparency) is large enough for all the children to see and read. Indeed, emergent readers of any age can be aided in learning about various aspects of language, especially written language, through shared reading experiences.

Derived from Holdaway, the following are key procedures in the shared reading experience:

- Rereading favorite selections together
- The teacher running a finger under the words
- Later focusing on reading strategies and various aspects of the text, through discussion
- Independent rereading of the texts shared (ideally with small copies of the text and perhaps with an audio recording that accompanies the text)

Following are some of the aspects of language that can be addressed as the teacher extends the shared reading experience with one or more students:

Orthographic (Letter) and Orthographic/Phonological (Letter-Sound) Aspects of Written Language and Reading

- Understanding conventions of print, such as the fact that we read pages from to top to bottom and left to right in English
- Understanding the concepts of *word* and *letter*
- Developing a stock of words recognized on sight
- Recognizing letters and letter clusters
- Developing letter-sound knowledge—particularly an ability to read common onsets and rimes (defined in Chapter 13)
- Understanding conventions of punctuation and how these relate to intonation patterns

Syntactic and Semantic Aspects of Language

- Using grammatical markers to signal reference and relationships (e.g., pronouns, prepositions, coordinating and subordinating conjunctions)
- Reviewing, activating, and using schemas to process text; adding to one's repertoire of schemas
- Understanding story structure
- Drawing inferences
- Analyzing, synthesizing, evaluating; thinking critically
- Distinguishing between fact and fantasy or opinion
- Exploring the meanings of metaphorical and figurative language
- Responding personally and emotionally to texts; relating texts to personal lives

Strategies for Processing Language and the Metacognitive Awareness of Such Strategies

- Predicting a logical sequence of events or actions ("What do you think might happen in this story? Why?" "What do you think might happen next? Why?")

- Predicting what would fit next grammatically and semantically ("What would make sense here? Why?")
- Monitoring comprehension and appropriate word identification ("Does that sound like language?" "Does that make sense?")
- Using the visual aspects of words and letter-sound knowledge to check initial identification of words ("Does that word look/sound like . . . ?")
- Reprocessing text to clarify meaning and particular words

These and the other reading and cognitive strategies that children labeled as learning disabled or dyslexic need to learn about language and reading can be taught during the context of a shared reading experience. So can other aspects of spoken and written language. For example, the teacher can help children like Jaime with the pronunciation of words, explore ways of conversing effectively through the conversations between characters in texts, and work on using explicit, decontextualized language.

In a videotape (not commercially available) on improving oral and written language abilities in mild-to-moderately handicapped children, Janet Norris and Paul Hoffman (no date) demonstrate how the speech-language teacher can use the basics of the shared book experience with children who have difficulties with language and/or reading. Basically they provide more conceptual and linguistic scaffolding with such children than the regular classroom teacher might do, and they proceed at a slower pace. Such modifications have been demonstrated to be more effective than a typical alphabet-based curriculum for at-risk students (Hoffman & Norris, 1994).

In the aforementioned tape, Norris explains their focus on "communicative reading strategies" (see Norris 1988, 1991). For beginning or very weak readers, they use written language with simple predictable texts to simultaneously address the oral as well as the written language needs of children like Jaime, who was assessed as needing help with language development. Written language provides a context for learning to comprehend and use both oral and written language. Instead of being divided into skills, each of which is taught in a separate activity, the language remains integrated and communicative. The interactions between the teacher (interventionist) and the student(s) are conducted as something of a dialogue. Such interactions are not really reading and not really a discussion, but a combination of both.

For example, the teacher activates student background knowledge and supplies additional background knowledge as needed, sometimes almost sentence-by-sentence or word-by-word; guides children in using various kinds of cues to predict events and words; defines and uses unfamiliar words or phrases in additional contexts; expands upon the language of the student(s); models how to understand characters and interpret events; explains abstractions; demonstrates the meanings of grammatical elements and words by clarifying how they work in the written context; leads the student(s) to explain the sequence of events; guides them in using and developing metacognitive awareness of reading strategies; and so forth. Instead of correcting a miscue overtly, the teacher can use the actual text word(s) in a paraphrase sentence of her own, thus clarifying what the text said in a conversational way. Most often, Norris and Hoffman work with only one or two readers at a time.

This, then, is the kind of instructional focus that speech-language clinicians who understand the reading process have found to work best with children like Jaime. They attend to skills—such as Jaime's difficulty with recognizing words or using letter-sound knowledge—within the context of reading and discussing stories. In one of the case studies on the Web page related to this text (*http://www.heinemann.com/weaver*), we shall see detailed examples of how "communicative reading strategies" could be used with Jaime.

Meanwhile, the following chapter will further explore ways of addressing students' needs with and within a comprehensive literacy program.

For other ideas on teaching reading strategies, see Chapter 14.

FOR FURTHER EXPLORATION

1. Reid Lyon and Louisa Moats, leading promoters of skills-based research on reading, made the following claim in a 1997 article: "It is generally accepted among reading scientists that the primary pheno-typic manifestation of developmental reading disability (RD) is inaccurate and dysfluent decoding of single words out of context" (p. 578). They cite several researchers and their studies, which typically focus on teaching some aspect of the sound system and/or letter-sound relationships and decoding, then they further claim that "In fact, one of the most reliable indicators of reading disability is poor performance on novel-word-reading and pseudo-word-reading tasks" (reading new words and nonsense words).

   But who has made the decision to define reading disability in this way? It appears that it may have been Reid Lyon himself (1995), head of a division within the National Institute of Child Health and Human Development. Subsequently, the National Institutes of Health (of which the NICHD is a part) defined dyslexia thus:

   > Dyslexia is one of several distinct learning disabilities. It is a specific language-based disorder of constitutional origin characterized by difficulties in single word decoding, usually reflecting insufficient phonological processing abilities. . . .

   By no means would everyone define dyslexia this way, with respect to reading. (Indeed, not everyone would agree to a concept of dyslexia at all.) Therefore, it becomes important to ask ourselves who benefits from dyslexia being defined in this way? Who is, or may be, hurt by such a definition? (Also, who has decided which researchers are reading "scientists" and which aren't—and what are the potential consequences of such a division?)

2. Examine some high-quality picture books intended to be read to young children, or books like the Clifford series that are also intended to be read by primary-grade children themselves. For each book, consider the kinds of prior experiences, concepts, and vocabulary that the book requires in order for the reader's comprehension to be rich and meaningful.

3. Drawing upon what you have learned from this chapter, consider the kinds of instructional help you would want to provide for Tony, whose miscues were analyzed in Chapter 7. Tony was not able to retell or discuss much from what he had read.

10 Addressing Students' Needs in a Comprehensive Literacy Program

> Several conclusions and faulty assumptions have blinded educators to the effects of their educational policies and practices. Probably the most pernicious of these is the belief that we must "slow it down and make it simple" for children of poverty and others labeled "at risk," learning disabled, and so forth. This assumption puts children at risk even more than their family's socioeconomic status or their being labeled as deficient in some way. Instead of a slow-it-down curriculum, these children need an accelerated and rich literacy program if they are to catch up with their peers. . . . It is important that the regular classroom provide the kinds of literacy experiences that all children need, but some especially need to receive *in school*.
>
> —Richard Allington

Questions for Thought and Discussion

1. Which aspects of a comprehensive literacy program seem to offer the most opportunities for addressing readers' individual needs?

2. How can a comprehensive literacy program be structured so that the needs of all readers can be addressed?

3. How and why would reading books of their own choice in school help students become better readers?

4. What are some important ways and reasons that composing their own reading materials can support and help many readers in need, including even secondary students and adults?

5. What are some problems with "round-robin" reading, and what are some oral reading experiences that offer particular benefits to less proficient readers?

6. What are some literacy experiences and instruction that can help readers who demonstrate different reading characteristics?

Clearly Allington's point in the quote introducing this chapter applies to readers with particular needs, whether or not they have been labeled as "at risk," "struggling," "dyslexic," or "learning disabled."

If you haven't previously developed a classroom literacy program that includes a variety of literacy experiences and events as well as various instructional opportunities, you may be wondering how you could find time to work with students individually to do Retrospective Miscue Analysis or to address students' individual needs in other ways. In truth, if you are required to teach a reading or phonics program for a substantial part of your school day and truly dare not deviate from it, the only opportunities might be while teaching the reading of texts in other content areas, such as social studies and science. Or you might be able to work with individuals and small groups before or after school (e.g., Allington, 2001).

Shared reading	Sustained reading	Sustained writing	Choices
	Read alone Read with partner Listen to book on tape and follow in the book	Write alone Write with partner Read to get ideas for writing	Read/write alone Read/write with partner Listen to book on tape and follow in the book Read/write with adult
	Guided reading	Shared writing	Have a conference* Do a special project
	Individual conferences	Individual conferences	Write in response to book**
	Literature groups		Choral reading or readers theater

Read-aloud time can be held after lunch or recess.
*The student initiates the conference.
**This might include writing in a journal or literature log, a letter in response to the main character, a story that imitates the pattern or structure of a book, and so forth.

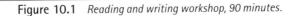

Figure 10.1   *Reading and writing workshop, 90 minutes.*

If your concern is a time and classroom management issue over which you have control, there are various ways you can "make time" for working not only with the whole class but with small groups and individuals, too. Chapter 12 ends with some possible formats for reading workshops, or reading and writing workshops, of different time lengths. The figure for a possible ninety-minute reading/writing workshop is reproduced here as Figure 10.1, just to provide a handy example of some possibilities. As this figure suggests, while most students in the class are engaging in sustained reading, you could do "guided reading" with a small group of children, hold a few individual conferences, or even conduct a literature discussion group. You could confer individually with students during literacy "choice" time, too.

MAJOR COMPONENTS OF A COMPREHENSIVE LITERACY PROGRAM

Since not all readers of this book will be familiar with concepts like "guided reading" or "literacy discussion groups," I will briefly describe here some major components that are common in teacher-developed classroom literacy programs. These components are discussed in much more detail in Chapter 12. However, brief descriptions here should help illuminate some of the recommendations yet to come in this chapter for working with students who need reading support and help. Perhaps most important, though, is this reminder that students who need support and help with reading will flourish best in a classroom that offers them such a rich array of literacy experiences and learning opportunities as those mentioned here.

Chapter 14 will deal with teaching reading strategies and phonics within the context of such literacy experiences.

READ-ALOUD By reading aloud, teachers demonstrate how to read with expression and how to portray characters' voices. They can read texts that are beyond the students' ability to read independently, thus introducing more complex situations, sentence structure, concepts, and vocabulary. It is important to involve the children in thinking and talking about the book, too, and even in predicting what might happen next. The major predictor of success in reading and in academic study is children's experience in being read to. Reading aloud has important benefits, no matter what the students' age.

SHARED READING Initially, shared reading techniques were developed by Don Holdaway (1979) and classroom teachers in New Zealand, for use with primary-grade children. The idea was to capture the most helpful features of parents reading books to, and discussing them with, their children, interactively, typically just before bedtime. In the classroom, the activity begins by reading to the children a new selection that is displayed for all to see and large enough for all to read (Big Books or charts or transparencies containing songs, poems, stories, or information, such as a morning message). As the teacher rereads the text and points to each word, the children are encouraged to chime in whenever they can.

During repeated readings across several days, the children are more and more able to "read" the common text, together and individually. And they usually have individual copies of the text from which to practice reading as well. Concepts about print, reading strategies, words, phonics, and decoding can all be taught and explored as the text is reread and reexamined over several days.

GUIDED READING This term seems to be used in several ways, but especially to refer to temporary reading groups that are determined on the basis of students' individual needs at the time, not on alleged reading ability. Thus, for the entire small group, the teacher may focus on reading for meaning and not just words; using phonics along with other cues to read for meaning; understanding the use of quotation marks to indicate who's speaking—in short, literally any aspect of reading the students need to work on. The teacher may invite the students to sit around him or her and then listen to the students read aloud all at the same time, intervening with individual readers as needed to teach a strategy or skill, including letter-sound patterns and decoding.

SUSTAINED READING The more common terms are *independent reading* and *sustained silent reading*, but some readers may need to listen to a book on tape and follow along, to read with a buddy, or to read along with an adult. In any case, a great deal of research, such as that summarized in *The Power of Reading* (1993) by Stephen Krashen, demonstrates that to develop and refine not only word and phonics knowledge but reading for meaning, it is crucial to read, read, read! Even kindergartners can at least "read" the pictures of a book and tell the story to themselves and others. This helps develop the expectation that "I can read this!" even though they may not yet be attending much to the print. Such interactions with a book are important daily experiences for emergent readers, as well as for children who are already independent readers.

The Importance of "Free Voluntary Reading"

In his important book *The Power of Reading* (1993), Stephen Krashen discussed the importance of "free voluntary reading," or reading texts for pleasure. Krashen reviewed 41 comparisons of sustained silent reading in school with traditional instructional programs and reported that in 38 cases, those in sustained silent reading did as well or better than comparison groups on tests of reading comprehension. Programs that lasted for a year or longer showed the most positive results. Sustained reading in school is all the more crucial for children from low-income families, who typically have little access to appropriate and interesting reading material in the home or in community libraries (see Krashen, "Recreational Reading," in press).

INDIVIDUAL READING CONFERENCES It's crucial for teachers to structure their literacy program so as to have time to confer with students individually about their reading. Various things can be done and discussed during individual reading conferences, but here are some of the most important: (1) interview the student about himself or herself as a reader; (2) invite the student to tell about what he or she is currently reading; (3) have the student read aloud a section of the book he or she is currently reading, and listen for the reading strategies being used or not used well (tape-recording the reading can be useful); (4) read and discuss the student's reading journal or "literature log" entries in response to the reading that has recently been done; (5) teach strategies that will help with problem words, monitoring comprehension, reading to draw inferences and develop understanding; (6) assess the student's progress as a reader, in various ways. Of course, Retrospective Miscue Analysis done during individual conferences can be crucial for many readers. For example, some readers may need help learning to decode words by using letter-sound knowledge along with context. Others may need help learning to think ahead or to monitor comprehension, while some may need guidance in learning to read for meaning rather than just to identify words.

LITERATURE GROUPS In literature discussion groups, also called *literature circles,* the students all read a book and then discuss it, typically with the teacher but alternatively just with peers. Beyond the early grades, this requires having text sets with several copies, usually of several books. Typically the book is self-chosen by the group, or the group is assembled according to the choice of book. One way of preparing for literature discussion circles is to have the group read the entire book first, over several days or a week (with the teacher, in the lower grades). After the students have read the book, the teacher will set up time for literature discussions with the group. The teacher is an organizer and fellow discussant, not an inquisitor or a dispenser of what the text "really" means. Literature discussion groups can be valuable for each and every student in the class.

INQUIRY, OR READING TO LEARN It's crucial for teachers to guide students in developing skills for dealing with informational texts and not merely assume that because the students can read, they can read informational texts effectively and efficiently, or remember and use what they have read. Reading to inquire and learn also involves writing.

WRITE-ALOUD By writing aloud, the teacher can demonstrate various aspects of how one writes. The piece of writing is the teacher's own, not something being composed by the class together (see "Shared Writing," below). Using chart paper, the overhead projector, or the chalkboard, the teacher writes aloud, talking about certain writing decisions as they are made. The teacher may solicit the students' ideas and help whenever appropriate. Writing aloud can be another opportunity to teach letter-sound patterns, and/or to assess children's knowledge of such patterns.

SHARED WRITING The teacher helps the students compose something—a morning message, a note home to parents, a letter to the principal, a chart of "what we know" and "what we want to know" about a topic, a patterned story, a poem, or whatever. That is, the teacher helps the students brainstorm, shape their ideas, revise, and edit, as appropriate. Here, too, letter-sound knowledge can be taught and assessed, if needed.

GUIDED WRITING In addition to sometimes being another name used to describe shared writing, guided writing is a term for teacher-planned groups that are based on the teacher's observation of common needs among certain writers. Usually the members of the group are working on their own individual pieces, though collaborating on a piece is also possible. The teacher typically offers a mini-lesson at the beginning of the guided writing session, then guides individual writers as needed in applying the skill. Obviously letter-sound knowledge can be taught during this literacy activity.

SUSTAINED WRITING Often this is called *independent writing,* but as with reading, sustained writing might involve not just individual writing, but writing in pairs and trios. Similarly, we might call it *choice writing,* except that sometimes the teacher may determine or narrow the range of topics, specify the audience and/or the genre, and so forth. In other words, sustained writing will often be free-choice writing, but not always.

INDIVIDUAL WRITING CONFERENCES Individual conferences are an important part of writing in a comprehensive literacy program. For example, the teacher may hold an instant mini-conference during sustained writing time, stopping to ask, "Do you need help writing the sounds in that word?","How's it going?", "Is there a part you really want to share with me?", or "Is there anything you need help with?" The teacher may be able to respond adequately during this brief, spontaneous conference, or the instant conference may lead to the teacher's scheduling a longer conference with the student. Other mini-conferences and mini-lessons occur during guided writing, as explained above.

JOURNALS Students can be asked or invited to keep journals for a variety of reasons: to record and respond to books read or discussed; to describe personal experiences and express feelings; to jot down ideas for writing; to record observations in science; to try to solve math problems; and more. Journals are an important part of writing to learn.

INQUIRY, OR WRITING TO LEARN Writing to learn occurs most obviously in the content areas and in conjunction with inquiry through reading. Journal entries can be very important, but students also need help learning to take notes in efficient ways, so that the notes will be useful later. Note taking can take many forms, ranging from a phrase or sentence on a note card to outlines and related formats for brainstorming and planning, including webs, charts, time lines, and other visually clarifying forms.

OTHER LITERACY EXPERIENCES FOR READERS IN NEED

Developmentally, whole-word reading comes before dealing with letter-sound relationships, as children learn to read signs, labels, and other words in their environment.

The preceding section has briefly characterized elements widely accepted as crucial in an effective literacy program. But for readers who need additional support and help, other kinds of literacy experiences may also be vital. These include, but are not limited to, choral reading, readers theater, echo reading, and buddy reading; audiotapes of books, especially audiotapes paced to closely match individual readers' rate of reading; "language experience" or individualized guided writing and reading; plus other experiences that involve students in reading more interactively through discussion, through writing, and through the arts. Several of these will be discussed in this section.

Developmentally, whole-word reading comes before dealing with letter-sound relationships, as children learn to read signs, labels, and other words in their environment (Ehri, 1994; Vellutino & Scanlon, 1987; Ehri & Wilce, 1980; Gough & Hillinger, 1980; Perfetti, 1985; K. Goodman & Y. Goodman, 1979; F. Smith, 1988). As we shall see in Chapter 13, letter-sound knowledge and use develops naturally for many children, as they learn more and more words and also as they write the sounds they hear in words. However, some effective ways of teaching phonics will be described in Chapter 14.

Language Experience and Guided Writing

What is "language experience"? At one time considered an "approach" to reading and literacy, language experience is now primarily considered an activity within a total approach. The teacher draws upon children's language and experiences by writing down what they want to write using the children's own words (Van Allen, 1976). This is—or was—done either with a group of children or for an individual child. The text thus written is relatively easy for the child to read and reread, because the ideas and language are the child's own. Reading their own dictated texts can be a real breakthrough for students who have virtually no command of the reading process.

Today, "language experience" has virtually been replaced in the classroom by two other kinds of writing experience. Often, children are now encouraged to do the writing themselves, spelling the words the best they can, though the teacher may later supply conventional spelling—

especially if the child creates and publishes a classroom book from what he or she originally wrote. The other activity that has typically replaced "language experience" is guided writing, wherein the teacher helps the student(s) shape the writing and doesn't merely act as a scribe taking dictation.

To emphasize the importance of supporting readers by helping them write their own reading material, I want to share two anecdotal accounts before discussing guided writing in more detail.

SERGIO AND RUDY: DOING LANGUAGE EXPERIENCE TOGETHER The following example of the power of language experience writing and reading is excerpted and adapted from the section written by Suki Stone for the second edition of my *Reading Process and Practice* (1994a, pp. 531–533):

> When preservice teacher and instructional aide Sergio Cordova first met Rudy, he found that fifth-grade Rudy had been labeled learning disabled. Doubtless Rudy's reading difficulties were caused, at least in part, by his educational history. His parents moved between Texas and California every year doing migrant work, and his family spoke only Spanish, while Rudy needed to speak English at school. Results from his achievement tests in fourth grade showed him to be still functioning at a preprimer level: that is, his language arts/reading level was at a readiness stage, as measured on standardized tests. Before working with Sergio, he had never learned (or retained knowledge of) the alphabet. Although he had received special education services since fourth grade, Rudy was still having difficulty reading. As an eleven-year-old nonreader, Rudy was easily frustrated and unsuccessful while learning to read using traditional basal materials and methods. He had also developed low self-esteem as a result of his academic difficulties.
>
> Knowing that passionate involvement generates a love for learning (Freire, 1970), Sergio became acquainted with Rudy's greatest interests, his passions. One of many things Sergio learned about Rudy was his willingness to help with cutting, pasting, and building projects in the classroom. Rudy also talked about his love for animals. Then Sergio approached him with a group of magazines containing pictures of things Rudy had talked about, telling Rudy to cut out anything that interested him. Rudy chose animal pictures and wanted to write animal stories.
>
> Sergio wrote the first couple of stories Rudy dictated. The first story was about a shark, and Rudy read it about 90% correctly. He reread the story three or four times, practicing until he could read it perfectly. After reading the shark story to the other resource room aide, he received much praise and encouragement from both that aide and Sergio. Then he read the shark story to a substitute teacher who had developed rapport with Rudy while teaching in his class.
>
> After the initial story, Rudy wrote a different story every three days, putting them into a photograph album. He began to build self-confidence as the teachers and aides complimented his ability to read. He was so proud of his book of stories that he brought a picture of himself as a three-year-old and put it in the beginning of the photograph album. Then he wrote an autobiographical piece for the front of the book, naming it his story book.
>
> As he became more self-confident, Rudy began to be comfortable with oral reading. While Rudy read his second story aloud to Sergio, students in the classroom stopped their work and listened attentively. Rudy began looking forward to reading the stories he created and shared with Sergio. At the end of six stories, Rudy remarked that he had to write only ninety-four more stories to complete his book!
>
> During the time Sergio worked with him, Rudy was continuing in the class basal. In the fourth grade he hadn't gone past the third story in the basal, but through writing and reading his own stories he soon accumulated enough sight words and vocabulary to read fifteen of the stories in the basal reader. His progress and interest in reading helped him develop in other academic areas as well. By capitalizing upon one of Rudy's passions, animals, and by helping him write his own reading material about animals, Sergio enabled Rudy to make a breakthrough to reading, writing, and learning.

SECONDARY STUDENTS LEARNING THROUGH LANGUAGE EXPERIENCE Some students have learned to think of reading as a matter of identifying words rather than constructing meaning. Or at least they approach a text in that manner, thereby short-circuiting the reading process, since constructing meaning from texts actually helps us get words as well as meaning. When students read more to identify words than to construct meaning, this is usually the result of classroom instruction, and often from teachers and/or parents continually saying "sound it out" when the reader encounters a difficult word. In such instances, the reader often has just two main strategies for dealing with problem words: "ask somebody" or "sound it out."

Older readers who exhibit such a pattern benefit from the same kinds of assistance as young emergent readers, though of course they do not want to read what they perceive as "baby" texts. This is one reason why language experience or guided writing is so important for these readers. Not only do they compose what they want to write, but they accept what they themselves have composed as suitable reading material; indeed, they are proud of it.

The importance of using reader-composed texts was discovered in an exemplary three-year program in which British secondary school English teachers worked intensively, one-on-one, with secondary-level readers in difficulty. Margaret Meek explains (1983, p. 214):

> When we began, our pupils had one reading strategy. They held it in common because they had all been taught it when they first had reading lessons in school. They were efficient sounders and blenders and decipherers of initial consonants; so efficient, indeed, that words they could have recognized "at sight" were subjected to the same decoding as those they had never seen or heard before.

What these secondary students could not do effectively was use their letter-sound knowledge and sampling skills appropriately in a coherent approach to constructing meaning from a text.

The teachers working with these students tried focusing on their apparent needs (based in part on an analysis of their miscues). What proved most effective, however, was adopting a language experience approach. The teachers became scribes for each student, writing to the student's dictation, inviting the student to reread the evolving text to see if he or she had said what was wanted, then writing and discussing some more, and finally providing opportunities for the student to read the finished text to an appreciative audience. That approach did more than anything else to affect the students' view of themselves as readers and to increase their competence.

> What worked the best was a language experience approach. That did more than anything else to affect the students' view of themselves as readers and to increase their competence.

LEARNING LETTER–SOUND RELATIONSHIPS THROUGH WRITING Assisting students in actually writing down parts of stories they themselves are composing can also help older students gain greater mastery of letter-sound correspondences.

Just as one might help beginning writers write letters for the sounds they hear, so we can help an older writer/reader in this way. The older writer/reader need not write out the entire text being composed, for that might become a laborious process that would inhibit composition and the sense of satisfaction that would otherwise come from having created a longer and more adult piece of writing. However, guided assistance in hearing and writing the sounds in words greatly facilitates acquisition of the basic letter-sound knowledge that one needs to acquire in becoming an independent reader and writer. With older students as with young children, though, one must remember that a reasonable phonetic spelling is the aim for a first or rough draft—not "correct" spelling. Emphasis on perfect spelling would defeat the purpose for having the writer sound out and write words for himself or herself.

See also the section on shared writing in Chapter 12 and the discussion of teaching phonics through writing in Chapter 14.

GUIDED WRITING To give a sense of how guided writing might occur, I have developed a sequence with a particular child in mind: a fourth grader, Jaime, whose word recognition and reading strategies were both fairly weak. This is the same Jaime whose need for help with concepts and vocabulary was discussed in the preceding chapter. An adult and Jaime working together might do the following:

- Decide upon a topic and a form, perhaps the form of a patterned story Jaime had been reading or an original story about a favorite book character such as Clifford the big red dog (Jaime's favorite)
- Brainstorm for events, perhaps with the adult writing down key words and phrases in a semantic web, branching tree diagram, or time line (thus the adult would also provide some conventional spellings that Jaime could draw upon)
- Orally rehearse some of the sentences Jaime might use to communicate her ideas in writing, so that grammar and word selection are planned in advance of writing
- Get a first draft written, with Jaime using invented spelling and her knowledge of letter-sound relationships when she does not know the conventional spelling of a word (perhaps she could write on a computer)
- Discuss the evolving text as she writes, with the adult encouraging her to reread and see if she has written what she wants to write (especially if using a computer, which makes rereading and revision easier)
- Reconsider what she has written, including things like the sequence of events, cause-effect relationships, and connections between words and ideas
- Do a second draft if needed, ideally with Jaime or the adult typing the text on computer (if the adult did the typing, he or she would use conventional spellings at this point)
- Divide Jaime's written text into chunks that she would illustrate, each on a separate page
- Edit her writing for spelling and punctuation, if she did the typing
- Assemble the book
- Encourage Jaime to read and reread the book (when together, the adult would help her focus on reading strategies as needed)

This sounds like a lengthy process, and clearly it might take several tutorial sessions. However, the results in motivation and learning are well worth the time and effort, especially if such collaborative processes are continued for a while. When we "scaffold" students' learning by helping them do what they cannot yet do alone (Bruner, in Ninio & Bruner, 1978), we are modeling the processes involved and enabling the learners to become a little more competent each time to carry out the processes themselves. With guided writing, we are also helping students create suitable texts for them to read. Last, but perhaps most important, we are fostering engaged and passionate learning.

> When we "scaffold" students' learning by helping them do what they cannot yet do alone, we are modeling the processes involved and enabling the learners to become a little more competent each time to carry out the processes themselves.

Books on Tape

The value of having children read along with a tape recording of a book was illustrated by a research study reported in an early article titled "After Decoding: What?" by Carol Chomsky

(1976). She worked with five eight-year-olds, whom she described at the outset of the tutoring program as follows (p. 288):

> These children were not nonreaders. They had received a great deal of phonics training and had acquired many phonetic skills. They met regularly with the remedial reading teacher with whom they had worked intensively since first grade. After much effort, they could "decode," albeit slowly and painfully. What was so frustrating was their inability to put any of this training to use, their failure to progress to even the beginnings of fluent reading. . . . In spite of their hard-won "decoding skills," they couldn't so much as read a page of simple material to me. The attempt to do so was almost painful, a word-by-word struggle, long silences, eyes eventually drifting around the room in an attempt to escape the humiliation and frustration of the all too familiar, hated situation.

Chomsky obtained for the children two dozen picture books, also recorded on tape, from which the children were to make their own selections. The children were asked to listen to the tape of their chosen book and to read along in the book again and again, until they had become familiar enough with the book to read it fluently. In effect, they would be first memorizing the book and then learning to read it: attending to the whole and then to parts as necessary. Chomsky explained her rationale (1976, p. 289):

> When it comes to memorizing a book, these eight-year-olds are in a very different position from the pre-reader. They have already had two years of drill in word analysis, long and short vowels, word endings, blending, and so on. They can sound out words and have a fair sight vocabulary. They are beyond needing introduction to the alphabetic nature of the English writing system. What they need is to shift their focus from the individual word to connected discourse and to integrate their fragmented knowledge. It is the larger picture that they need help with, in learning to attend to the semantics and syntax of a written passage, and in developing reliance on using contextual clues from the sentence or even longer passages as they read.

Using pages that the children could already "read" fluently in semi-rote fashion, Chomsky and her graduate assistant supplemented the reading with gamelike activities involving mostly word recognition and analysis. In addition, the children did substantial writing connected with their reading.

Progress at first was slow: it took four of the five children about a month to learn to read their first book fluently. After that slow beginning the pace increased, and subsequent books took less and less time, so that when the children were on their fourth or fifth book, they were able to finish it in a week. Soon there seemed less and less need for the analytical work; after a while, the tutoring sessions became opportunities for simply reading the books and discussing the story, doing some writing, or discussing some stories the children had written. Those children who progressed the most improved in both reading and writing.

It appears that with repeated readings of familiar texts, readers not only add more words they can recognize on sight but internalize letter-sound "chunks" that they then can use in dealing with print words they haven't specifically learned to identify on sight.

In general, the children improved dramatically, not only in fluency but also in their attitude toward reading. They began reading TV commercials, cereal boxes, and magazines at home. They began picking up books to read instead of avoiding reading at all costs. In short, they began to feel and act like readers.

Repeated rereading of familiar, self-chosen texts seems to be extremely valuable if not absolutely critical in helping not only younger but older readers develop proficiency, as the previous examples of the success of language experience techniques also suggest. It seems clear that with repeated readings of familiar texts, readers not only add more words they can recognize on sight but internalize letter-sound "chunks" that they can then use in dealing with print words they haven't specifically learned to identify on sight. This process of reading new print words by analogy with "old" words is well supported by research (see Chapters 13 and 15). It also helps explain why, by their fourth or fifth book, the children in Chomsky's study no longer required a month to read their book fluently but could finish a new book in a week.

Where to Buy Tape Recordings of Books?

There are various sources of books on tape for children, including publishers of books and programs for children; Scholastic is particularly notable for audio recordings of children's literature <*http://www.scholastic com*> Another prolific source of audiobooks is Recorded Books, which includes some children's books on tape <*http://recordedbooks.com*>. Your local bookstore may have tape-plus-book combinations, too.

BOOKS SPECIALLY RECORDED Numerous publishers of reading programs for children sell audiotapes of some of their children's books, so that children can listen to a book on tape while following along with the book. Other companies that produce hundreds of recorded books for adults also produce some for children; the Recorded Books company is perhaps the most prolific. Even making your own tapes can be a wonderful support for readers who read in a monotone, who are in the process of learning English, or who cannot keep up with the class if you are using a class novel for discussion and extension activities. (I did this for two chapters of *Roll of Thunder, Hear My Cry* [Taylor, 1976] for Erica's little group of slower readers, and they loved it.) Purchasing or making a tape recording of a book, or even just some chapters when needed, enables teachers to engage all students in the class with a book that challenges them intellectually and touches their emotions. We don't have to give the slower readers something babyish to read instead of the more interesting book that most of the class is reading.

On the other hand, emergent readers (of any age) may find that most commercial tape recordings proceed at too fast a pace for them to read along with the text and thus strengthen their own reading. Indeed, that may be a major reason why the eight-year-olds in Carol Chomsky's research study typically took a month to read their first recorded book fluently.

For learning to read, it may be far better to have books specially recorded just a tiny bit faster than the person can currently read. When the reader has mastered the reading at that pace, it is helpful to provide at least one or two more tape recordings, each recorded at a still slightly faster pace. The same material can be recorded at a faster pace, and/or some text farther in the book can be recorded at the faster pace. Pace itself, however, is only part of the issue. It is important to record the sentences of the book in increasingly larger phrases, so as to model how proficient readers chunk words into phrases as they read. For example, suppose the book to be recorded begins with the sentence "Once upon a time, a little old man and a little old woman lived in a cottage by the sea." The first recording for a reader who recognizes almost no words in print might be chunked thus: "Once / upon / a time, / a little / old man / and a little / old woman / lived / in a cottage / by the sea." The next recording might be chunked like this: "Once / upon a time / a little old man / and a little old woman / lived in a cottage / by the sea." Eventually, of course, the reader should be able to read along with a normally recorded audiotape of the book.

Marie Carbo, founder of the National Reading Styles Institute and the "Carbo Recorded-Book Method™" (e.g., Carbo, 1978), has produced commercially available recordings at slower and then increasingly accelerated paces for more than 150 books representing a variety of reading demands and interests *<http://www.readingstyles.com>*. However, you may want simply to do such recordings yourself, or to ask a parent volunteer who reads aloud especially well to make some recordings—being sure, of course, that the parent understands what is needed.

Support from Another Reader

Of course support from another reader may take many forms, such as reading with a partner or "buddy," with an older student, or with an adult. One possibility is for the pair to read aloud together, at not too fast a pace, so that the reader in need can speak up like an "echo" when he or she can't readily read some of the words. Of course the other reader must be someone who reads aloud fluently, so often it will be an adult or an older reader.

Another version of "paired" or "buddy" reading occurs when the proficient and less proficient reader sit next to each other, perhaps even reading a different book. The more proficient reader reads silently, while the less proficient reader reads silently or perhaps aloud and asks for help from time to time. Of course such paired reading works well only if the more proficient reader is willing to give such assistance. I have seen this form of support function especially well in Debbie Manning's multiage class, where she has obviously taught readers effective reading strategies, but also taught the more proficient readers to help their less proficient buddies use strategies to get a problem word themselves, instead of just telling their buddies the word.

Something else reading buddies can do is each read a page (or slightly shorter or longer section) themselves, then stop and discuss the page with each other. Buddies might draw pictures about what they have just read and discuss them. In addition or alternatively, buddies might engage in a "written conversation" about what they have read. These procedures can work well even with one buddy who speaks English as his or her native language and another buddy who speaks a different language as his or her first.

A Wonderful Resource on Reading Aloud

Opitz, M. F., & Rasinski, T. V. (1998). *Good-Bye Round Robin: 25 Effective Oral Reading Strategies*. Portsmouth, NH: Heinemann.

The authors explain why to avoid "round-robin" reading, wherein the teacher has children take turns reading aloud while the rest of the class or reading group supposedly listens. The authors offer twelve reasons plus twenty-five strategies for effective oral reading practices that do not put individual readers on the spot to read unrehearsed text or make other readers waste their time listening, or pretending to listen. They also offer suggested texts for using the different oral reading strategies with children.

Unrehearsed Reading: The Pitfalls of "Round–Robin" Reading

In *Good-Bye Round Robin*, Opitz and Rasinski (1998) offer several reasons not to have students take turns reading unrehearsed texts aloud. Here is my own list of favorite reasons, which naturally overlaps with theirs:

- Children who can't read well aloud wait in fear to be called upon, and they typically feel humiliated after they have read.
- If the teacher uses a clear rotation pattern for calling on readers, most students look ahead and practice silently the part they think they'll have to read aloud. Thus they aren't focusing either on the reader or on the emerging meaning of the selection.
- Children who can read well are especially bored by round-robin reading.

- Many students find it difficult to concentrate on meaning even when they try to listen to a classmate read aloud. Unless the reader is exceptionally good at reading for expression, their attention wanders.

- Most students can read silently faster than they can read aloud. Thus the round-robin procedure wastes readers' time—time they could be using to read and understand the selection, or to read something of their own choice.

- Alternatively, some readers will read ahead and ignore the oral reading. Good readers especially may employ this survival strategy—and then perhaps be caught not knowing where to begin when called upon to read aloud!

- Such oral reading gives students the impression that reading is equated with identifying all the words; that is, with reading word-perfectly. Thus, round-robin reading can also encourage ineffective reading strategies.

Note, too, that when we read aloud in normal life situations, the audience often doesn't have a copy of what we are reading (Opitz & Rasinsky, 1998, p. 7), and even if they do, we often make miscues that are scarcely noticed at all, because our oral rendition preserves meaning and grammatical acceptability. Personally, I often make several departures from the text as I read aloud, because I am concentrating on making eye contact with listeners and thinking ahead as much as reading ahead.

Choral Reading and Readers Theater

While unrehearsed oral reading has many drawbacks, rehearsed oral reading can have various benefits. Some of the effective reading strategies discussed in *Good-Bye Round Robin* (Opitz & Rasinsky, 1998) have already been discussed in this chapter, but I want to mention two others in particular: choral reading and readers theater.

To put it simply, choral reading involves readers taking different parts as a selection is read aloud. The parts are rehearsed, and less proficient readers can volunteer for—or be assigned to—parts that have more than one person reading at a time. For both of these reasons, less proficient readers usually feel comfortable with choral reading. Poems, songs, or stories with refrains are especially good for choral reading, as are poems with different voices. My personal favorite is Paul Fleischman's *Joyful Noise: Poems for Two Voices* (1988; suitable for the intermediate/middle grades), but of course there are many possibilities for both younger and older elementary students and beyond.

Readers theater is a more formal kind of oral reading, usually with just one reader reading each part. Plays are commonly used for such oral reading, but there are no costumes, props, or actions other than the facial expressions and gestures the readers may make as they sit or stand to read aloud. Poems with a distinctive voice also make good texts for readers theater; I think, for example, of the humorous poems of Shel Silverstein. After sufficient rehearsal, readers theater can be performed for other classes in the school or for parents night. So can choral reading, of course.

CHOOSING APPROPRIATE TEXTS

Of course teacher instruction and assessment should be based on the reading and discussion of selections that are appropriate for the reader, in terms of concepts and the reader's prior knowledge, and in terms of language. But what is appropriate for any given reader cannot be determined by any handy formula or miscue count, though there are plenty of these available, especially as part of the "informal reading inventories" that are commercially available for teachers to use.

In Peter Johnston's *Knowing Literacy* (1997, p. 213), he and Marie Clay comment on the appropriateness issue as follows:

> First, all errors are not created equal. Some suggest difficulty with the text whereas others do not.... Some children seem to have a higher tolerance for different kinds of word level errors than do others. Some children's reading processes seem to fall apart when they reach an error rate of about one in twenty (5 percent). Other children seem to feel comfortable, showing healthy reading processes, even in material they read with an error rate of one in eight (12.5 percent). There also appear to be developmental differences in manageable error rate.

Notice that Johnston and Clay talk about "errors," not miscues (Clay, 1993a). I appreciate the fact that Johnston and Clay have noticed that the mere percentage of miscues does not tell whether a selection is or isn't too difficult for a reader. In response and in addition, I have five observations to make:

- Readers who are disturbed if they make one miscue in twenty words (5%) may need help understanding the nature of the reading process and revaluing themselves as readers.
- Many readers aren't disturbed at making more miscues than one in eight words (12.5%), provided they are enjoying the text, know they aren't being harshly judged for their miscues, and are allowed to read without being interrupted with corrections.
- It's important for even less proficient readers to read texts of some length and substance, because texts themselves help teach the reader (Meek, 1988).
- All readers should read at least some texts that are relatively easy for them, but readers should also have the opportunity to read books that are somewhat more challenging, if they are interested in the topic and the text.
- Readers tend to choose more challenging texts for themselves than teachers choose for them. This may happen when they choose books primarily because of interest rather than familiarity with most of the words on a sample page or two. Also, readers may choose more challenging texts if they know that they can probably succeed in constructing enough meaning from the text to satisfy themselves—and if they know that when reading to and for themselves, silently, their miscues won't matter so much.

Thanks to My Teachers!

I often think how lucky I was to have, in the elementary grades, mostly teachers who let us read silently instead of making us take turns reading aloud, "round robin." I am sure that if I were in elementary school today, many of my teachers, armed with leveled books, readability formulas, and popular advice on how to choose a book that's not too difficult, would discourage or downright prevent me from reading those engrossing books I remember reading from grade 3 onward. Fortunately, when I was in school, nobody told me to put a book back because it was too difficult; nobody listened over my shoulder to make sure I wasn't making "too many" miscues. As a result, I could follow my interests, and in the process learn new vocabulary, too (if not always the conventional pronunciation).

MATCHING INSTRUCTION TO READERS' VARIED NEEDS

Choosing appropriate texts for assessment is important, and we may want to let the reader's own choice of reading material be a guide, at least to some extent, in what we choose to have a reader read and discuss afterward. A reader profile, including at least a reading interview, miscue analysis, and retelling and discussion, can be very helpful for determining someone's reading strengths and needs.

Of course there is no magic formula for translating the perceived characteristics, strengths, and needs of a reader into instructional strategies. What may be valuable, though, are some suggestions based on many teachers' experience (revised somewhat from Weaver with Stone, 1998). Following is a list of reader characteristics and possible teaching strategies, including, as appropriate, Retrospective Miscue Analysis and the other teaching possibilities discussed in this and the previous chapter. By "reader characteristics," I don't mean to imply anything inherent in the reader. For me, however, this phrase works as a convenient cover term for things like observed behaviors, expressed concepts and beliefs about reading and reading strategies, and needs assessed by the teacher.

The following set of reader characteristics, possible evidence, and possible teaching strategies is based, then, on the assumption that the reader has been assessed on his or her reading and discussion of a text that is appropriate for that particular individual.

READER CHARACTERISTIC Reader doesn't seem to know that reading should make sense.

Possible Evidence

- Reader sounds out a lot of words and settles for words that don't fit the context, or for nonwords.
- Miscues don't fit with even the preceding grammar and meaning at least 60% of the time.
- Miscues often do not fit with the following grammar or meaning, but the reader seldom or never tries to correct.
- Reader cannot tell much about the selection, even if the selection is appropriate for the reader's prior knowledge and concepts, the reader has read or reread the selection silently, and good questions have been asked to draw out the reader's recall and understanding.
- *In addition* to one or more kinds of evidence just mentioned, the reader may sound like he or she is reading word-by-word, reading in a monotone, and/or not honoring punctuation marks with appropriate intonation.

Possible Teaching Strategies

- During a shared reading experience (group or one-on-one), preview the book about to be read. From the title and the cover, invite the reader to predict what the book might be about. Go through the book together, looking at the pictures and predicting.
- Read books to the class, and discuss.
- Involve all members of the class in literature discussion groups, including this reader.
- Do language experience with the individual reader; that is, write down what the reader wants to say about a topic or event, and have the reader read it back—again and again, until the reader is fluent. Perhaps the writing can be done, or redone, on a computer, with space on the pages for the reader/writer to illustrate. REMINDER: In various settings and situations, a language experience approach to reading has proved more effective than anything else with older readers who have little ability to read—even with secondary students and adults. In this chapter, see the earlier section on language experience.
- Do guided writing, which is similar to language experience except that the teacher helps shape the writing. Individual guided writing may produce even better results than language experience techniques, because the resulting text may be more coherent and thus more predictable for the reader. Again, see the section earlier in this chapter.
- Provide tape recordings of books for the reader to listen to, along with copies of the books. If possible, start with specially made tape recordings wherein the person on tape has recorded

the book in phrases, just slightly faster than the learner can read. Help the reader notice how the voice on the tape emphasizes meanings. Encourage the reader to reread the book while listening to the tape until the reader can read the book independently and fluently, with appropriate expression. (This may literally take weeks, but the next book will usually go faster, because the reader recognizes more words and has absorbed more letter-sound patterns.)

■ Have the reader read with a buddy and stop after every page to discuss.

■ Use Retrospective Miscue Analysis (see Chapter 9). Tape-record the reader reading, and play back part of it. Stop the tape recorder when the reader has made a miscue that doesn't make sense. Ask, "Does that make sense?" Invite the reader to reread, offering help with reading strategies as appropriate.

■ Provide time daily for this reader and all members of the class to engage in sustained reading.

READER CHARACTERISTIC Reader doesn't yet recognize many words or have much knowledge of letter-sound patterns.

Possible Evidence

■ Reader tells the story from the pictures more than reads the words on the page, even though most peers are reading the words.

■ Reader skips or misreads a huge proportion of the words in a simple text.

■ Reader cannot pronounce even the first letter of very many words, if asked.

In short, the reader is clearly an emergent reader, whatever his or her age.

Possible Teaching Strategies

■ Provide for the reader the same kinds of instruction you would for a first grader, but use age-appropriate texts. This might be language experience texts that the reader has dictated to a scribe, or texts that the reader has been helped to compose during guided writing. It might be simple pattern books, if the reader doesn't find them too babyish. Often, though, we can appeal to older students and adults on the grounds that they can read such books to their own children, after they've become fluent with them. Suitable texts might alternatively be simple messages or even letters that the learner wants to write (e.g., Freire, 1970), especially if the learner is an adult.

■ Be sure the reader is focusing on constructing meaning from texts, not just trying to identify or sound out words. See, for instance, the suggestions in the preceding section for readers who don't seem to know that reading should make sense.

■ Do shared reading experiences with the reader or a group of readers with similar needs, being sure to point to words so the reader(s) can begin to make connections between spoken words and written words. Have readers take turns pointing to the words as they read. This can be done not only with younger readers who might be reading from a Big Book or a chart, but with older readers whose shared reading might be projected onto a screen or a wall.

■ Use the shared reading experience as an opportunity to focus on selected and particularly relevant aspects of letter-sound patterns, such as the onsets of one-syllable words that begin the same, and/or identical rimes in some one-syllable words. In a syllable, the initial consonant sound(s)—if there are any—constitute the "onset," such as the /s/ in *sip*, the /sh/ in *ship*, and the /str/ in *strip*. The rime part of a syllable is the vowel plus any consonant sound(s) that might follow: the /ip/ in the words above, for example. See Chapter 13 for more details and examples.

- Do guided writing with the group of readers, being sure to focus on key letters and how they sound. Identify a sound and then invite emergent readers and writers to write the sound they hear. They can do this one at a time on large chart paper where the group composition is being written, or they can do this on individual chalkboards that they can readily hold up for the teacher to check.

- Do this kind of guided writing with individual learners of all ages. Focusing on writing the sounds they hear will enhance their phonics knowledge. If desired, you can use Elkonian boxes for writing/spelling (as used in Reading Recovery, e.g., Clay, 1993a, p. 33), having the individual write key sounds and supplying the other letters yourself.

- Involve all members of the class in literature discussion groups, including this reader.

- Provide time daily for this reader and all members of the class to engage in sustained reading.

READER CHARACTERISTIC Reader doesn't seem to use prior knowledge and context to predict what's coming next. Reader may not know that this is an important reading strategy that makes even word identification easier.

Possible Evidence

- Miscues often don't fit the preceding grammar or meaning.

Possible Teaching Strategies

- See suggestions for a reader who doesn't seem to know that reading is supposed to make sense and try those suggestions that seem appropriate—including the recommendations for conducting literature discussion groups and for providing sustained reading time daily.

- Use Retrospective Miscue Analysis to help the reader learn to "think ahead" and use prior knowledge and context to deal with problem words.

- Do and discuss relevant strategy mini-lessons, such as those in Debra Goodman's *Reading Detective Club* (1999; see Chapter 14) or particularly relevant lessons from Yetta Goodman, Watson, & Burke's *Reading Strategies:* Focus on Comprehension (1996). Another example: In a passage where one key word is repeated, you might construct a strategy lesson by copying the passage and blocking out the word with a marker, then having the student(s) try to determine what the word is, using context and prior knowledge. (See relevant activities at the end of Chapter 3.)

READER CHARACTERISTIC Reader doesn't seem to monitor comprehension.

Possible Evidence

- Miscues often do not fit with the following grammar or meaning, even though they may fit with the preceding grammar or meaning.

- Reader cannot tell what the selection is about—perhaps not even after reading silently a selection that is appropriate to his or her interests and background knowledge.

Possible Teaching Strategies

- See suggestions for the reader who doesn't seem to know that reading should make sense and the suggestions for the reader who doesn't seem to use prior knowledge and context to predict, and try those suggestions that seem appropriate—including literature discussion groups and daily sustained reading.

- Take turns reading with this reader. Stop after each page (and/or after key paragraphs) to retell and discuss what was read.

- For a story, create together (teacher-student, or peer-peer) a semantic web of key information, such as characters, plot, and so on.

- For informational selections, develop and use together some strategies for monitoring comprehension, such as:

  - Discussing trouble spots

  - Stopping after each paragraph or so and restating what it was about

  - Rereading or looking up key terms that are troublesome

  - Preparing a visual organizer of some sort: semantic web, time line, graph, outline, chart, map, or whatever is appropriate to the selection

READER CHARACTERISTIC Reader lacks self-confidence and/or reader thinks that reading means saying all the words correctly.

Possible Evidence

- Reader struggles again and again to get each word not recognized on sight.

- Reader says that he or she can't read.

- Reader says that he or she doesn't like to read. (May indicate nonproficient reading and/or lack of confidence in reading.)

Possible Teaching Strategies

- Do shared reading experiences with young emergent readers: the more proficient readers will support the less proficient. With older readers who are relatively nonproficient, an age-appropriate text can be written on a chart or projected onto a screen or a wall for shared reading.

- Use Retrospective Miscue Analysis to point out good miscues and good reading strategies, if possible. It's important to wean the reader from the idea that good reading is word-perfect reading and that good readers know all the words.

- Use reading strategy mini-lessons, as suggested for readers who don't seem to use prior context and knowledge to predict. It is important to demonstrate to the reader that he or she can get the essence of a passage without reading all the words. The "Kent State" passage in Chapter 4, p. 73 is one illustration of such a passage. Other variations on the cloze procedure may be suitable; again, see some of the activities at the end of Chapter 3.

- Help the reader develop a wider range of strategies for dealing with problem words independently, instead of always asking someone or giving up. This can be done through Retrospective Miscue Analysis.

- Invite the reader to listen to a book on tape and follow along, practicing reading the book until he or she can read it fluently.

- Provide for echo reading, wherein a more proficient reader reads a text and the less proficient, less self-confident reader reads along, sometimes a fraction of a second behind, echoing the more proficient reader.

- Provide for buddy reading, wherein a peer can help when needed, but help with developing strategies or by discussing the reading, not just by telling the unconfident reader what some words are.

- Provide for choral reading, wherein the unconfident reader can practice reading certain parts of a selection with other readers until they can all read it fluently. Perform for a real audience.
- Involve all members of the class in literature discussion groups, including this reader.
- Provide time daily for this reader and all members of the class to engage in sustained reading.

READER CHARACTERISTIC Reader doesn't seem to be able to sound out words in pronounceable chunks, though he or she does read for meaning.

Possible Evidence

- Reader deals with problem words by saying a word that includes some of the letters, but doesn't fit the context.
- Reader makes nonword miscues that include some of the letters but don't reflect an attempt to sound out the word in pronounceable chunks—even though the word is probably one in his or her listening vocabulary.

Some of the following strategies are appropriate for young emergent readers, especially if modified appropriately. However, I did have more proficient readers in mind with these suggestions.

Possible Teaching Strategies

- First, consider the possibility that the reader is dealing with problem words this way because doing so enables him or her to be more efficient as a reader. If the miscues aren't frequently causing the reader to lose important meaning, it may be best not to worry about such miscues.
- Second, consider the possibility that the miscued words often aren't ones in the reader's listening vocabulary anyway. It can be virtually impossible for even adult proficient readers to sound out such words in chunks (to "chunk out" such words), and it may be useless or unnecessary anyway, in terms of meaning. Instead of focusing on the "chunking out" of such words, it may be better to encourage the reader to try to get the essence of the meaning from them by using context, then read on. We saw from the example of Danny in Chapter 4 that readers may even grasp the exact word (in his case, "amusement," in *amusement park*) even though they never pronounce it conventionally. This, too, should be kept in mind.
- Next, be sure that the reader is reading to make sense of text, to predict, and to monitor comprehension, before working on "chunking out" words. Be sure these strategies are firmly established.
- Then, when the reader comes to a troublesome word, have the reader predict what might make sense. If the reader's predictions include the actual word, focus on the printed word to help the reader realize this; often, attention to just the initial letters will be sufficient to confirm the prediction. If the reader has not included the actual word among his or her predictions but the word is fairly predictable using prior knowledge, context, and the initial letters, try encouraging the reader to use all of this information to make a prediction. Guide as necessary.
- If needed, help the reader sound out the word in pronounceable chunks and try to determine whether the word makes sense in the context. It's not important to apply rules for determining syllables, but only to sound out words in chunks. You may need to help the reader try alternative ways of chunking, too—not only to get the particular word in question but to realize that if at first one doesn't succeed, chunking the word differently may help. Again, help the reader use context to confirm or correct the chunked-out word. Remember that if the word is not in the reader's listening vocabulary, the reader may find it difficult or

impossible to sound out the word correctly, or to decide whether the word fits the context. This is typical of proficient as well as less effective readers.

- Involve all members of the class in literature discussion groups, including this reader.
- Provide time daily for this reader and all members of the class to engage in sustained reading.

READER CHARACTERISTIC Reader doesn't read fluently or efficiently.

Possible Evidence

- Reader already reads to construct meaning and has good reading strategies, but the reader reads in a monotone, reads through punctuation marks as if they weren't there, and otherwise reads aloud without appropriate intonation for an audience.

Possible Teaching Strategies

- Provide tape recordings of books for the reader to listen to, along with copies of the books. Help the reader notice how the voice on the tape emphasizes meanings. Encourage the reader to reread the book while listening to the tape until the reader can read the book independently and fluently, with appropriate expression. (This may literally take weeks, but the next book will usually go faster, because the reader recognizes more words and has absorbed more letter-sound knowledge.)
- Engage the reader, and perhaps other readers—even the whole class—in activities where they have the opportunity to practice their oral reading before reading aloud as performance. Choral reading and readers theater are two possibilities.
- Teach strategies for reading efficiently. These include strategies for dealing with words that can't be easily pronounced or "chunked out," plus strategies for skimming text to look for what's most important.
- Provide time daily for this reader and all members of the class to engage in sustained reading, and encourage readers to read efficiently.
- Involve all members of the class in literature discussion groups, including this reader. Include brief discussion of the strategies readers used, or could have used, to read the book efficiently.

A Must-Read Book!

Allington, R. L. (2001). *What Really Matters Most for Struggling Readers: Designing Research-Based Programs.* New York: Addison Wesley Longman.

I highly recommend this book to classroom teachers as well as language arts curriculum specialists and administrators. (Although I don't agree with Allington on the absolute necessity for fluency, I find his practical teaching suggestions regarding fluency the best and most comprehensive I've seen—and the book overall is excellent.)

In Conclusion

Many readers of this chapter will surely have realized that the strategies suggested for readers who need extra help are essentially those that effectively enable most young children to learn to read without special help. This is no accident. More isolated skills work is not the answer for readers in so-called lower-ability groups, or even for readers labeled as "learning disabled" or "dyslexic." Yes, we need to provide extra support and help for certain readers, but the needed reading strategies and skills can most easily be taught, learned, and applied in the context of authentic, meaningful, and enjoyable texts.

For Further Exploration

1. Drawing upon what you have learned from this chapter, now consider what *additional* kinds of literacy experiences and instructional help you would want to provide for Tony, remembering that he was not able to retell much from what he had read. (Tony's miscues were analyzed in Chapter 7.)

2. If you have developed a reader profile for some other reader who clearly needs support and help, make a list of literacy and literary experiences and instructional techniques you would want to use with that reader.

3. Discuss with others how you could fit such experiences and instruction into a comprehensive literacy program and what kinds of support you might seek from parents or other instructional aides, if that's possible.

11 Reading Research from Differing Perspectives

Charles Sanders Peirce described four ways that people "fixate belief." One is by trying things out and seeing what happens, then believing in the results. "The three other ways are believing what one wants to believe; believing what one has always believed; and believing what an authority says is true.... [But] 'truth' and 'proof' are more complicated for professional researchers."

—Diane Stephens

Questions for Thought and Discussion

1. How do we, or could we, determine "what works" in teaching reading?

2. What are some of the differences between the assumptions, practices, and research methods of skills researchers compared with comprehensive literacy researchers? What are some common differences between the applicability of their conclusions?

3. Should reading instruction be based solely on "scientific research" results? Why or why not?

4. Should reading educators be permitted to freely choose the research base that will inform their own reading instruction? Why or why not?

5. To what degree, if any, should reading instruction methods be mandated and monitored? By whom, and with what justification?

When claims are made that "research," "the research," or even "scientific research" shows this or that, we need to be wary—and to be wary about making such claims ourselves. With research studies on reading and on teaching and learning to read, we need to ask ourselves questions such as "What theoretical assumptions underlie this study?" "What other, perhaps equally or more plausible, theoretical assumptions were ignored?" We need to ask things like "How was reading success measured?" or "What counted as success?" and "How adequately did the measure(s) of success reflect the reading of authentic texts?" And we need especially to consider also what *wasn't* measured in determining "success." When some aspect of reading instruction is said to "work," we need to ask "Works to accomplish what?" Equally—or more—important, we need to ask, "What *isn't* being accomplished?" As an International Reading Association pamphlet points out,

> Our measures of what "works" are not defined consistently. What do we mean when we say a method works? In some cases a method works if children are able to read lists of words in isolation. In others "works" means that children can answer questions on a multiple-choice test. If there is anything we have learned from methods studies, it is that children learn what we teach them (Pearson & Fielding, 1991). If we teach them how to pronounce pseudo-words, they learn how to pronounce pseudowords and sometimes lists of regular words. If we teach children to summarize, they learn how to give better summaries. Therefore, many methods have a right to claim they "work," but that does not necessarily mean that any of these methods are better than all or most other methods or that any one of them is the "right" method. For all these reasons beginning reading instruction has been controversial. (International Reading Association, 1999)

To expand upon what Diane Stephens says in the opening quote, truth, proof, and even "what works" are complex issues for professional researchers, and one researcher's "truth" may seem meaningless, inaccurate, or totally inadequate to another.

This chapter focuses on reading research from two differing perspectives, with each group of researchers considering the other group's research questions, research, and results as invalid and meaningless, or inadequate and incomplete. For convenience, we shall refer to one group as "skills" researchers and the other group as "comprehensive literacy" researchers, though individual researchers may, of course, cross these division lines. Both groups engage in developing theoretical models of reading. Both lie firmly within the empirical research tradition, which draws evidence from experiment or observation. However, there are some major differences in the two research paradigms, both in general and with respect to research on reading and learning/teaching to read:

Skills Research	Comprehensive Literacy Research
Reflects mechanistic paradigm Reductionistic: reduces whole to parts, which are studied in isolation	Reflects holistic paradigm Holistic: parts are intertwined in an indivisible whole that must be studied as such; parts are studied as they relate to other parts and to the whole
Theoretical models focus on parts of reading, such as models of development in learning to read isolated words	Theoretical models focus on reading as a whole, such as models of development from being a nonreader to being an independent reader
Relies on experimental research; when the research involves comparisons of classroom approaches, it tends to focus on one variable	Relies on observational research particularly; when the research is experimental, it may involve comparisons of entire classroom environments and their approaches to literacy development
Experimental research tries to isolate the variable being analyzed, whenever possible	Observational research, and experimental research when done, is much more broadly conceived, with many variables
Measures reading achievement, where the word *achievement* is a code word for scores on standardized tests, especially subtests of skills like letter-sound knowledge	Describes or compares a variety of factors observed, including some that may not have been anticipated at the outset of the research; rich descriptions are usually part of experimental research as well as observational research
Relates to and promotes a skills approach to teaching reading, where skills are arranged in a hierarchy from smaller to larger, and taught and assessed sequentially and in isolation	Relates to and promotes a comprehensive, interrelational approach to teaching, with various aspects that work synergistically to promote children's literacy development in reading and writing together, along with oral language

Elsewhere, I have tried to describe both kinds of research studies not only fairly but dispassionately (Weaver, 1998a). However, my discussion of skills research will not be dispassionate here. Why? Since I drafted the aforementioned article, false claims about conclusions from the skills research, via a paper by Bonita Grossen (1997), have been widely disseminated across the nation and have been used as a basis for phonics legislation in some states (see critique by

Allington and Woodside-Jiron, 1998b). More than twenty states have passed legislation based on claims about the skills research on teaching phonics and/or phonemic awareness (Paterson, 1998, 2000), including the poorly designed study by Foorman et al. (1997, 1998; see critiques by D. Taylor, 1998; Coles, 2000; and see later in this chapter). Particularly in the wake of the National Reading Panel's summary of its report (2000c), the skills research has been heralded as "scientific" research that tells the country everything it needs to know about how to teach reading. And on January 8, 2002, the U.S. Congress passed, and President George W. Bush signed into law the "No Child Left Behind" Act (P. L. 107), which promotes skills research by claiming that it is "scientific" and implying that no other research on reading or teaching/learning to read should be considered in formulating educational policy.

RESEARCH FROM A SKILLS PERSPECTIVE

Phonics and Phonemic Awareness: Brief Definitions

What is phonics, anyway, and what is phonemic awareness? *Phonics* can be defined as relationships between letters and sounds, whether simple letter-sound correspondences or letter-sound patterns involving more than one letter and more than one sound, like the *str-* pattern and the *-ing* pattern in *string*, and the sounds they represent.

Basically, *phonemic awareness* means awareness of the separable sounds in words, such as the three sounds (phonemes) in *pet:* /p-e-t/. In *car,* there are also three phonemes—that is, three separable sounds though most of us normally hear only two sounds, the /k/ sound and /ar/ together as a unit. The word *string* has five separable sounds, not six: /s-t-r-i-ŋ/. In current research, the term *phonemic awareness* is often used to mean not just awareness of the separable sounds in a word but the ability to manipulate the sounds. An example is being able to hear the word *pet* spoken by an experimenter, mentally remove the first sound, and say "-et" in response.

Chapter 13 explains and illustrates these definitions in considerably more detail.

G. Reid Lyon, director of the Child Development and Behavior Branch within the National Institute of Child Health and Human Development (NICHD), once testified before a Congressional committee that "We have learned that no single method, approach, or philosophy for teaching reading is equally effective for all children (Lyon, July 1997). Now, though, as George W. Bush's chief advisor on reading, he promotes a one-size-fits-all approach to teaching reading. This, he claims, is justified by the only research he considers "scientific": skills research, especially the skills research he has funded through the NICHD and a summary of skills research analyzed by a National Reading Panel. This panel produced a document titled *Report of the National Reading Panel: Teaching Children to Read—An Evidence-Based Assessment of the Scientific Research Literature on Reading and Its Implications for Reading Instruction* (National Reading Panel, 2000b). The summary of the panel's analyses—not the Report itself, but the document called a summary—is the primary basis for President George W. Bush's reading initiatives, embodied in the January, 2002 law.

Reid Lyon is now the chief promoter of the summary of that report (NRP 2000c) and its alleged findings, which include statements that imply far broader benefits from systematic phonics instruction than the detailed data warrant (see NRP 2000b for the data, and see Chapter 13 here for discrepancies between the data and the "summary" and "findings"). According to the law passed in January, 2002, the NICHD will be involved in disseminating "information on scientifically based reading research pertaining to children, youth, and adults" and in supporting "the continued identification and dissemination of information on reading programs" that reflect this skills research. For these and related dissemination activities, a grant of $5,000,000 has been set aside by Public Law 107 of 2002. That's five million dollars to promote a skills view of reading, reading instruction, and commercial programs that reflect skills research. Five million dollars for

Reid Lyon and others to promote a "summary" of reading research that draws upon only a tiny fraction of that research, and research from only a skills perspective. Five million dollars to promote not only actual—though limited—findings, but also "findings" that weren't actually found.

Furthermore, Lyon promotes his own unsupportable beliefs by claiming that they reflect the findings of the NRP report, when in fact they aren't even supported by the overgeneralized claims in the NRP summary, much less supported by the data itself. Here are some of Lyon's key beliefs about reading education—beliefs that he has promoted with members of Congress and the administration, by referring to the National Reading Panel report (at least the summary, 2000c) and the NICHD research and calling their conclusions "scientific." Lyon makes the following claims about phonemic awareness and phonics: "A major prerequisite for learning to read an alphabetic language like English is to understand that the words we use in our speech are actually composed of individual sounds. . . . The individual sounds are called phonemes, which beginning readers learn before proceeding to text. . . . So phoneme awareness is a prerequisite [to phonics], and it allows one to develop phonics skills" (Clowes, 1999). Lyon further implies that learning phonics is also prerequisite to learning to read, or at least to trying to comprehend text.

The NRP panel on phonics found that the most effective way of teaching phonemic awareness was in conjunction with phonics, not prior to it (NRP, 2000b, p. 2-6, p. 2-33; see also the summary, NRP 2000c, p. 8). And the NRP panel did not even investigate whether phonics should or shouldn't be taught prior to other aspects of reading. Rather, the panelists emphasized that phonics is only a means to an end, that children must also be taught to *apply* phonics knowledge in their reading and writing, that phonics should not be taught as if "one size fits all," and—most important—that phonics instruction is only one component of a total reading program for primary grade children (NRP, 2000c, p. 10-11). Indeed, the detailed report on phonics includes the following statements (NRP, 2000b, p. 2-128):

- It is important to emphasize that systematic phonics instruction should be integrated with other reading instruction to create a balanced reading program.
- Phonics instruction is never a total reading program.
- Phonics should not become the dominant component in a reading program, neither in the amount of time devoted to it nor in the significance attached.
- By emphasizing all of the processes that contribute to growth in reading, teachers will have the best chance of making every child a reader.

In short, there is absolutely no justification in the National Reading Panel report for teaching phonemic awareness or phonics first, before helping children read texts collaboratively or before focusing on meaning. That is, there is absolutely no justification even when reading-related skills are assessed in isolation from the whole process of reading. (There is no research justification for using "decodable" texts, either.) Furthermore, skills research cannot readily address the factor of motivation, which educators know full well to be important if not crucial in learning.

Nevertheless, the "No Child Left Behind" act of January, 2002 (P. L. 107) not only embodies a skills view of reading but elevates it to the status of public policy, with emphasis on teaching phonemic awareness starting in pre-school and teaching phonics intensively and systematically in the primary grades.

A Real Threat?

"We're entering a period in education where Congress is asking me whether we have enough background data . . . to determine malpractice in teaching. Malpractice is defined by a departure from known fact in the treatment of human beings when, in fact, the data exists to do it in a more effective way" (Reid Lyon, "What Does Quality Reading Instruction Look Like?" 2001b).

Because a small body of skills research has been politically anointed as "scientific" and all other research studies—that is, thousands upon thousands of research studies relating to reading—have been deliberately ignored and/or dismissed as irrelevant or "unscientific," it seems obvious that teachers, administrators, and parents need to understand some of the weaknesses in the skills research, as well as its limited scope. So, of course, do government officials, businesses who want to promote educational policy, and the public at large.

Major research summaries and critiques will be discussed in the order they were published, beginning with a summary that was supposed to end the controversies surrounding reading education: the report titled *Preventing Reading Difficulties in Young Children*.

An Attempt to Achieve Consensus: Preventing Reading Difficulties in Young Children

In the later 1990s, the first academic report that was supposed to end all controversies about reading instruction was titled *Preventing Reading Difficulties in Young Children* (Snow, Burns, & Griffin, 1998). The report was undertaken by a committee of the National Research Council, which is a branch of the National Academy of Sciences that was organized in 1916 "to associate the broad community of science and technology with the Academy's purposes of furthering knowledge and advising the federal government" (p. iv).

On "Scientific" Research and the "Scientific Method"

(From *Preventing Reading Difficulties in Young Children* (Snow, Burns, & Griffin, 1998):

A particular experimental result is never equally relevant to all competing theoretical explanations. A given experiment may be a strong test of one or two alternative theories but a weak test of others. (p. 35)

The notion of a comparison between a treatment group and an untreated control is often a myth when dealing with social treatments. (p. 37)

Science seeks testable theories—not unquestioned edicts. . . . It is the willingness to give up or alter a theory in the face of evidence that is one of the most central defining features of the scientific method. (p. 35)

This research report focused on children allegedly at risk for learning to read, but the committee came to realize that "Our recommendations extend to all children" (p. 2). All children, perhaps especially those considered at risk of reading failure, need a rich literacy environment and instruction geared to their particular needs. The committee by no means limited itself to experimental research studies, but considered observational/descriptive studies as well. Rather than narrowing their purview to experimental studies, they chose to examine empirical research more broadly, which includes both observational and experimental research. Nevertheless, the panel members acknowledged "the difficulty of integrating them [the differing perspectives] into a coherent picture" (p. 33).

The vast majority of the panelists represented a skills approach to research, so it is not surprising that in the final report, conclusions and recommendations are often ordered or organized in such a way as to imply that skills instruction is what children beginning to read need first and foremost (notice, for example, the way items and topics are ordered and organized on p. 6 and pp. 7–8, and the fact that the "mechanics of reading" are discussed first in the reading recommendations on pp. 321–325). That is, skills are often privileged by being described before comprehension. It is also not surprising, then, that those reading researchers and educators who draw upon different research models than the majority of the committee do not consider the *Preventing Reading Difficulties* report a satisfactory synthesis of research on preventing reading difficulties in young children. Indeed, numerous educators doubt that such a synthesis is even possible.

Before the National Reading Panel Report: Critiques of the Skills Research

Because of the unwarranted claims that are made with reference to the NICHD-sponsored research and to skills research that is similar in design and purpose, such claims and the underlying research must be subjected to rigorous scrutiny. Gerald Coles does precisely this in his book *Misreading Reading: The Bad Science That Hurts Children* (2000). To be fair, however, Coles points out (e.g., p. 21), as I do in Chapter 13, that the individual researchers have not always made the claims that are attributed to their research studies, especially when such studies are grouped together as a body of research. Such claims are more typically made by non-researchers, authors of commercially produced reading programs, or persons in administrative positions who have an agenda to justify or support. Apparently such individuals don't always feel it necessary that their claims be based on conclusions *legitimately* drawn from the research they cite (one example is Grossen, 1997).

Coles (2000) goes into considerable detail about key research studies often cited in support of widespread claims about the skills research, particularly the claim that intensive instruction in phonemic awareness and phonics will prevent reading difficulties. Following are some particularly important points from Coles' examination of certain oft-cited research studies and conclusions drawn from them. Except for the last point below, all of the following points were made by Coles. Many of these points have been illustrated or elaborated upon earlier or later in this chapter:

1. *In general, the claims popularly made about the research go beyond what the research even deals with.* For example, claims are made about the best ways to start teaching children to read, namely phonemic awareness and phonics first. However, the research on which these claims are allegedly based is much too limited in scope and usually much too brief in duration to warrant such claims, as some of the following points will illustrate.

2. *Some of the research is simply "bad science."* It falls short of meeting the criteria for good scientific research with an experimental design. One example of such "bad science" is the study by Foorman, Francis, et al. (1997, 1998) that has been widely embraced as allegedly showing the superiority of the direct instruction, scripted Open Court program over what was claimed to be a whole language program. (For critiques, see Taylor, 1998, pp. 327–330 especially; and Coles, 2000.)

3. *Even with the research that isn't bad science, the researchers' conclusions—or the conclusions of some who have promoted it—often go beyond what the data warrant.* For another example, a research study undertaken by Juel and Roper/Schneider (1985) has sometimes been cited in support of the use of "decodable" texts. However, the use of decodable texts wasn't the only variable addressed in the study, so claims about using decodable texts in particular can't validly be drawn from it. Furthermore, claims about the superiority of a multifaceted phonics-emphasis program can't be drawn from Juel and Roper/Schneider's statistical data either, because the researchers found no significant differences in the end-of-year achievement measures between the experimental, phonics-emphasis group and the control group.

4. *Those who have interpreted the results of various studies—sometimes but not always the researchers themselves—have often interpreted mere correlation as causation, without adequate evidence of causation. Correlation* means simply that two (or more) things are related; that is they co-relate, to greater or lesser degree. When things co-occur, or even when they occur one after another in time, it is not necessarily true that one causes the other. In fact, there may be additional or different causes, and/or each of the factors may have a causal effect on the other(s), as we see in Chapter 13 in the discussion of research on phonemic awareness. When other factors have not been taken into account in the research

study, claims about causation can be risky at best, invalid at worst. (See Coles 2000 for specific examples from the research under discussion.)

5. *The oft-cited research studies do not take into account factors beyond the specific reading "treatments" being examined—factors that might substantially influence the results of their studies.* For example, what if some beginning readers in a study do, and others do not, have ready access—in school, at home, and/or in the community—to high-quality picture books that interest them and/or to simple books they can read themselves, such as the "I can read" books found in bookstores? It is clear that access to suitable reading materials has a positive effect upon literacy development, even when the poverty factor has been eliminated from the results (McQuillan, 1998). Therefore, how might such differences in the availability of good reading material have skewed the results of the oft-cited research studies? Or what about the factor of being read to in the home, which makes a clear difference in children's ability to read? (Trelease, 1995). Factors such as these are not usually taken into account in skills-emphasis experimental research.

6. *The research fails to demonstrate that teaching such skills as phonemic awareness and phonics in isolation has a lasting effect, even just on tests of these skills.* Typically, the effect does not last beyond the primary grades, if that long.

7. *Much of the research fails to demonstrate that training in phonemic awareness and related skills produces better scores on reading comprehension—especially beyond first grade* (Coles, 2000). In the studies that do show first graders scoring higher on tests of comprehension if they have been taught phonics systematically, the "passages" for comprehension are typically not more than a sentence long, so the alleged comprehension measure is little more than another measure of word identification skills. Furthermore, when the studies do show higher test scores on "comprehension" for students being taught phonemic awareness, phonics, and related skills intensively and in isolation, the differences are usually slight, and they do not usually last beyond first grade.

8. *The better a research study succeeds in isolating a single variable that can be accurately assessed by so-called objective measures, the less that study reflects the actual complexities of reading and learning to read.* Troia, in his critical review of the experimental methodology in phonological awareness intervention research, put it this way: "The highest ranked studies of phonological awareness training that met a majority of the evaluative criteria were the least representative of typical classroom instruction." Furthermore, "those studies that met a higher proportion of the internal validity standards concurrently met a lower proportion of the external validity criteria" (1999, p. 50, and other references he cites there). In practical terms, assessing a student's reading only through separate measures of skills and subskills like phonemic awareness, phonics, word identification, and even "comprehension skills" (like identifying the supposed main idea) gives a picture of the student as a reader that is necessarily incomplete and all too often quite inaccurate.

Why the Big Concern?

Coles himself puts into perspective his critique of the phonics-related, skills-based research: "None of the concerns about the distortions in understanding how children learn to read, the failure to consider the multiple influences on reading achievement, or the misrepresentation of the actual findings of studies would matter as much were they not part of a nationwide attack on other literacy approaches and research" (2000, p. 103).

The National Reading Panel Report

The document that has been the major weapon in an attack on other approaches to literacy development and research is the previously mentioned National Reading Panel report, particularly the summary of that report (NRP, 2000c).

> By dividing the research studies into different kinds of reading skills, the NRP research summarizers have in effect supported a skills-based model of reading and a skills-based approach to teaching reading.

In 1997, Congress commissioned a National Reading Panel to "assess the status of research-based knowledge [about learning and teaching to read], including the effectiveness of various approaches to teaching children to read" (NRP, 2000c, p. 1). The National Institute of Child Health and Human Development, a government agency, was charged with carrying out this agenda with Reid Lyon, director of the Child Development and Behavior Branch of the NICHD, in charge of its agenda on reading research. The NICHD convened the panel, charging it with seven questions to address. The first of these questions was "What is known about the basic processes by which children learn to read?" (NRP, 2000a, p. 1; 2000b, p. 1-5, where 1 is the section number and 5 is the page number within the section). Though this question about the processes of learning to read is surely a logical foundation for other questions, the panel did not analyze research that investigated the question. Rather, it turned immediately to questions of methodology and narrowed the research questions.

The panel's search of various databases revealed that approximately one hundred thousand research studies on reading have been published since 1966 alone. However, the panelists decided to consider only experimental research with a control group as well as an experimental group, and further limited their review to studies that included data which would enable the panel to combine studies in a statistical meta-analysis. These and other criteria drastically limited the research to be considered, and indeed, the panelists admitted that "unfortunately, only a small fraction of the total reading research literature met the Panel's standards for use in the topic analyses" (NRP, 2000c, p. 27). In the case of the studies on phonics, for example, the panelists finally included only 38 studies.

> "Their strategy has been to increase their comfort by reducing the questions one is permitted to ask, and the ways one is permitted to answer them" (James Cunningham, "The National Reading Panel Report," 2001, p. 328).

Understanding the concept of "scientific" research that the panel chose to adopt is crucial for understanding the agenda of the panel. In an insightful article on the NRP report, James Cunningham (2001) describes and discusses the NRP's philosophy of science, placing it in historical context. Noting that "The Panel members' repeated and unapologetic appropriation of the term *scientific* to describe the results of their work" (p. 327), Cunningham points out that for more than thirty years, such a claim would "have appeared naïve to anyone familiar with the philosophy of science" (p. 327). Why? Because "no one has yet devised a set of criteria that reliably distinguishes scientific from nonscientific practices" (p. 327). By adopting the contrary stance of the logical positivists (e.g., Comte, 1830/1988) rather than the stance of scientific realists (Marsonet, 1995; Weinberg, 1992), the panelists and consequently their work "reveals a desire for certainty and a willingness to engage in reductionism in order to achieve it. . . . Their strategy has been to increase their comfort by reducing the questions one is permitted to ask, and reducing the ways one is permitted to answer them" (Cunningham, 2001, p. 328).

It is no wonder that Cunningham calls the NRP report "a manifesto for a particular philosophy of science as much as a summary of particular research findings" (p. 326). He also points out that the NRP panel was not consistent in its application of the panelists' avowed criteria.

Several other researchers have critiqued the NRP report, on various grounds. For example, members of the phonics subgroup drew the conclusion that phonics is good for normal, heterogenous classes of kindergartners and first graders. However, this ignores the possibility that some children may not need such instruction and that others may need different instruction, or different instruction *prior to* instruction in phonics (e.g., Garan, 2001a; Cunningham, 2001).

Warning! The NRP Summary's Discussion of Phonics May Be Harmful to Your Child's Educational Health

Who knows how deliberate it was, but the separately published summary of the NRP report (NRP, 2000c) makes a sweeping statement that explicitly contradicts conclusions in the detailed report. The statement: "The meta-analysis revealed that systematic phonics instruction produces significant benefits for students in kindergarten through 6th grade and for children having difficulty learning to read" (NRP, 2000c, p. 9). The reality: "Phonics instruction appears to contribute only weakly, if at all, in helping poor readers apply these [word reading] skills to read text and to spell words. There were insufficient data to draw any conclusions about the effects of phonics instruction with normally developing readers above 1st grade" (2000b, p. 2-108).

Two other misleading statements from the summary will also be addressed in Chapter 13. Together, these three statements amount to a big lie about the effects of phonics instruction. If the actual data rather than these overgeneralizations (to use a kinder phrase) were being used as the basis for policy recommendations, perhaps the consequences wouldn't be quite so disastrous for education. However, it's the summary that is being treated as the final word on how to teach reading—and mostly the sections on phonemic awareness and phonics at that.

Ultimately, the panel refined its selection criteria to cull out a relatively small body of the experimental research on seven topics: phonemic awareness, phonics, fluency, comprehension strategies, vocabulary development, computer technology and reading instruction, teacher preparation to teach reading in general, and teacher preparation to teach comprehension strategies.

By dividing the research studies into different kinds of reading skills, the NRP research summarizers have in effect supported a skills-based model of reading and a skills-based approach to teaching reading. In fact, in some of the subgroup reports, such as the ones on phonemic awareness (awareness of the separable sounds in a word) and phonics, "reading" usually meant scores on tests of skills. At the beginning of the National Reading Panel report, the panelists admitted that "reading was defined to include behaviors such as the following: reading real words in isolation or in context, reading pseudowords that can be pronounced but have no meaning, reading text aloud or silently, and comprehending text that is read silently or orally" (NRP, 2000c, p. 5).

According to the phonics subgroup, "The majority (76%) of the effect sizes involved reading or spelling single words, whereas [only] 24% involved text reading" (p. 2-123). Nearly a third of the 24% involved oral reading that was assessed for accuracy, so only 16% of the total number of comparisons dealt with "comprehension." Furthermore, for the kindergarten and first-grade students, this usually amounted to reading no more than a sentence as a measure of "comprehension" (NRP, 2000b, p. 2-107). Being so defined, "improvement in reading," "reading growth," or "a difference in reading scores" would not reflect normal reading. In fact, typically, the normal reading of a substantial passage and the ability to explain and discuss it was used in almost none of the studies included.

As Yatvin points out in her "Minority View" (NRP, 2000a), the experimental methodology and these topics reflected the research interests of a majority of its members, but by no means reflected everything the panel was expected to do. "The research on language development, pre-reading literary knowledge, understanding of the conventions of print, and all the other experiences that prepare young children to learn to read" should have been examined, but these research topics were not considered (NRP, 2000a, p. 2).

In truth, the researchers could not have investigated more than a fraction of the relevant research in the year and a half they spent on the task. However, the time limit surely was not the only factor in leading the researchers to so severely limit the questions they asked. Indeed, the agenda of the majority of the subgroup is reflected in the way they worded their major goal: "The purpose of this report is to examine the research evidence concerning systematic phonics instruction. The research literature was searched to identify experiments that compared the reading performance of children who had received systematic phonics instruction to the performance of children given nonsystematic phonics or no phonics instruction" (NRP, 2000b, p. 2-81).

Misinformation Proposed as Legislation

It is surely not coincidental that the very same day (April 13, 2000) the NRP report was formally released, a so-called Reading Deficit Elimination Act was introduced into both the House (H. R. 4307) and the Senate (S. 2452) of the U.S. Congress. This bill claimed that the NRP report supported instructional practices that it didn't even examine. Nevertheless the bill would have required sequenced reading instruction based on seven allegedly scientific principles of reading—principles that reflect not the NRP report, but Bonita Grossen's unsubstantiated recommendations (1997), most of which are not supported by the research she claims supports them, namely the research sponsored and funded by the National Institute of Child Health and Human Development. Neither is the sequencing she recommended supported by research. (See the critique by Allington & Woodside-Jiron, 1988a, 1999.)

Though this bill did not pass, and indeed never went beyond the relevant committees in the House and Senate, it demonstrates the kind of misinformation that has been distributed in high places as to what "research says" about teaching reading.

Other Critiques of the NRP Report and Its Methodology

The months and years after the release of the NRP report have seen a growing number of critiques of it, especially the section on phonics and the section where silent reading is discussed primarily in terms of its lack of significant effect on oral reading fluency.

Critiques of the National Reading Panel Report

This is not necessarily a complete list of publications critiquing the NRP report; that list continues to grow.

Allington, R. L. (2002). *Inadequate Evidence*. Portsmouth, NH: Heinemann.

Coles, G. (2001). "Teaching Reading: Using the 'Scientific' Hickory Stick." *Phi Delta Kappan,* 83(3): 205–213.

Coles, G. (Forthcoming, 2003). *Reading Unmentionables: Damaging Reading Education While Seeming to Fix It.* Portsmouth, NH: Heinemann.

Cunningham, J. W. (2001). "The National Reading Panel Report." *Reading Research Quarterly,* 36: 326–335.

Garan, E. M. (2001a). "Beyond the Smoke and Mirrors: A Critique of the National Reading Panel Report on Phonics." *Phi Delta Kappan,* 82(7): 550–506.

Garan, E. M. (2001b). "More Smoking Guns: A Response to Linnea Ehri and Steven Stahl." *Phi Delta Kappan,* 83(1): 21–27.

Garan, E. M. (2001c). "What Does the Report of the National Reading Panel *Really* Tell Us About Teaching Phonics?" *Language Arts,* 77(5): 59–68.

Garan, E. M. (2002). *Resisting Reading Mandates: How to Triumph with the Truth.* Portsmouth, NH: Heinemann.

Krashen, S. D. (2001b). "More Smoke and Mirrors: A Critique of the National Reading Panel Report on 'Fluency.'" *Phi Delta Kappan,* 83(2): 118–121. (See also Krashen 2000d.)

Yatvin, J. (2000). Report of the National Reading Panel: Minority View. *http://www.nichd.nih.gov/publications/nrp/minorityView.pdf.* Also included in NRP, 2000b.

Yatvin, J. (2001). "Hasty and Unconsidered." *Phi Delta Kappan,* 82(10): 801.

Yatvin, J. (2002). "Babes in the Woods: The Wanderings of the National Reading Panel." *Phi Delta Kappan,* 83(5): 364–69.

THE FOORMAN RESEARCH STUDY AND OPEN COURT The study in the National Reading Panel Report that has received the closest scrutiny is the study by Foorman, Francis, et al. (1997, 1998).

The NRP subgroup report on phonics instruction states that "In evaluating the evidence [from the research studies included in the report], the Panel attempted to rule out weak designs as the explanation for any positive effects that were produced by systematic phonics instruction" (p. 2–83). However, the panelists certainly did not succeed with the study directed by Barbara Foorman at the University of Texas-Houston Medical Center (Foorman, Francis, et al. 1997, 1998).

This study is of particular concern because it was initially hailed by opponents of whole language teaching as proving that phonics was superior to whole language. The study was reported in the media more than a year before other researchers had the opportunity to examine and critique the research data and methodology. Meanwhile, though, the media had already assured the public that this NICHD-funded study had demonstrated phonics to be superior to whole language in teaching children to read. Not so, of course, though the damage was already done by the time that other researchers could examine the study itself.

The Foorman, Francis, et al. (1997, 1998) study pitted primary-grade children receiving direct instruction via the Open Court (1995) reading program against children in classrooms that were labeled "embedded phonics" classrooms and against children in "whole language" classrooms wherein phonics is supposed to have been taught in the context of reading and writing (but may seldom have been taught at all, as far as readers of the research report can tell). These were called classrooms in which phonics was taught "implicitly." The first major examination of the Foorman, Francis, et al. research study was undertaken by Denny Taylor and reported in her *Beginning to Read and the Spin Doctors of Science* (1998). Here is some of the data (mostly from Taylor 1998, pp. 327–330) demonstrating why the results of this study cannot be considered valid:

1. First, the samples were biased in favor of the direct instruction/Open Court children. For example:

   ▪ Only 55% of the direct instruction/Open Court (DI/OC group) was drawn from the lower-scoring group that received tutorial help as part of the study; but

   ▪ approximately 84% of the whole language treatment group and the control group was drawn from the lower-scoring tutorial group.

2. The DI/OC groups received significant financial and personnel support from SRA/McGraw-Hill, while the other groups received no extra support for the methods they were to use.

3. Approximately 45% of the children in the DI/OC group received two Open Court lessons per day instead of just one, for the first six months of the study. No other group was given extra treatment.

4. The children in the so-called whole language control group, who received no extra funds nor extra materials and whose teachers received no extra support, actually had higher scores on the Formal Reading Inventory (dealing with text reading) than the children in the DI/OC program (Taylor, 3/26/98, listserv message; used with permission).

5. There was no statistically significant difference in the scores on Foorman's word reading test between the DI/OC first graders after one full year of the Open Court basal reading program and those children entering Foorman's study at the beginning of grade 2, who as first graders had had only the district's preexisting "whole language" curriculum (Taylor, 1998, pp. 327–328).

6. The same is true for the scores on Foorman's phonological processing test.

7. Both the first-grade and second-grade children in the DI/OC group scored higher on the word reading test at the beginning of the school year. This was especially true for the second graders. Thus it is highly "unscientific" to emphasize the end-of-year scores only, as if the children had all started at the same place. But that's exactly what the researchers did in the initial reports of their study, as presented to the media, to then-Governor George W. Bush's Business Council in Texas, and to the Education Committee of the California State Assembly (Taylor, 1998).

Overall, as Taylor puts it in her summary, the "exciting news" and the "impressive gains" that the researchers at first claimed for their study "had evaporated by the time that Foorman and her colleagues wrote the final version of the paper published in the *Journal of Educational Psychology*" (Taylor, 1998, p. 336).

Another crucial point is made by Gerald Coles (2000): namely, that the relatively high overall average score for the direct instruction classes was due to the inordinately high scores of a group of children in just one classroom. Similarly, the relatively low overall score for the "implicit code" whole language classes was due to the inordinately low scores in just one classroom. Thus, these two classrooms skewed the overall average group scores. In the other classrooms in the study, the children in the two treatment groups had fairly comparable scores. Coles discusses the Foorman, Francis, et al. study in considerable detail in *Misreading Reading* (2000).

As for the practical results of Open Court in scores on state-mandated tests, they have not been particularly positive. For example, Moustafa and Land (2002) compared the 1999 SAT 9 reading scores of English-proficient children in schools using Open Court against comparable schools using any of four non-scripted programs in one very large urban school district. When they compared the average second-grade SAT 9 reading scores in schools with like percentages of economically disadvantaged children, they found no significant difference between schools using Open Court and schools using one of the non-scripted programs. Furthermore, when they compared the reading scores of all the elementary grades that are publicly reported (second through fifth grade) in schools with like percentages of economically disadvantaged children, they found that schools that had used Open Court 10 or more years were significantly more likely to have lower SAT 9 reading scores than schools using one of the non-scripted programs.

Nevertheless, more and more schools are jumping on the Open Court bandwagon.

Insufficiency of the NRP Report on Phonics

The National Reading Panel report on phonics, by itself, does not even consider the best ways to teach children to read. It addresses little more than how phonics and word reading skills can be taught and demonstrated the fastest. Certainly such a limited research review is not worthy of the attention it has received in the media, and even less worthy to guide federal, state, or local policy on the teaching of reading in our schools.

RESEARCH FROM A COMPREHENSIVE LITERACY PERSPECTIVE

In *Building a Knowledge Base in Reading*, Jane Braunger and Jan Lewis (1997) examined research from differing research traditions in order to determine the nature and extent of consensus. They write: "In this paper, we attempt to fashion such a consensus by detailing what is known about how children learn to read and the environments that support the process. We have identified 13 core understandings about reading that knowledgeable teachers have, understandings informed by various research traditions and demonstrated by the classroom environments such teachers design" (p. 4). Here, without further explanation, are those thirteen core understandings:

1. Reading is a construction of meaning from written text. It is an active, cognitive, and affective process.

2. Background knowledge and prior experiences are critical to the reading process.

3. Social interaction is essential in learning to read.

4. Reading and writing develop together.

5. Reading involves complex thinking.

6. Environments rich in literacy experiences, resources, and models facilitate reading development.

7. Engagement in the reading task is key in successfully learning to read.

8. Children's understandings of print are not the same as adults' understandings.

9. Children develop phonemic awareness and knowledge of phonics through a variety of literacy opportunities, models, and demonstrations.

10. Children learn successful reading strategies in the context of real reading.

11. Children learn best when teachers employ a variety of strategies to model and demonstrate reading knowledge, strategies, and skills.

12. Children need the opportunity to read, read, read.

13. Monitoring the development of reading processes is vital to student success.

What Researchers with Differing Perspectives Agree On

Braunger, J., & Lewis, J. P. (1997). *Building a Knowledge Base in Reading*. Portland, OR: Northwest Regional Educational Laboratory; Urbana, IL: National Council of Teachers of English; Newark, DE: International Reading Association.

Flippo, R. F. (1999). *What Do the Experts Say? Helping Children Learn to Read*. Portsmouth, NH: Heinemann. Of particular interest is not only the list of teaching practices that foster learning to read, but the list of practices that leading reading educators agree are *not* helpful in promoting reading development. All too many of these practices continue in many classrooms today.

Of course one reason there is considerable agreement about such core understandings is the general way in which they are phrased. For example, the statement about developing phonemic awareness and phonics knowledge "through a variety of literacy opportunities, demonstrations, and models" could be narrowly interpreted as a small range of direct teaching lessons or broadly interpreted as a wide range of reading and writing experiences as well as teacher demonstration, modeling, and direct or indirect teaching. Nevertheless, as worded, the core understandings would be accepted by many educators. What this list should make especially clear, however, is that there is a huge body of research relating to reading and learning to read that is being ignored when only skills research is summarized. This includes, but is not limited to, (1) research on reading acquisition and emergent literacy, the reading process, and learning itself; (2) observational/descriptive research documenting the success of contemporary literacy programs with individual children and classes; and (3) experimental research of various kinds, including comparisons of classrooms that reflect different approaches to literacy and literacy instruction.

The following sections offer examples of the latter two kinds of research.

Research on "Decodable" Texts

Stephen Kucer (1985) conducted an interesting experiment in reading two different passages, which are reproduced here. As a thought experiment, read these passages yourself and decide which passage is more difficult to read and remember, and why:

Passage 1: A Pin for Dan

A man had a tin pin.
It's a pin for a cap.
Can Dad win it for Dan?
Dad wins the pin.
The pin is in a bag.
On the bag is a tag. [a picture of a tag has "For Dan" written on it]
The pin fits on Dan's cap.
Dad pins it on the cap.
The pin is Dan's pin.

Passage 2: The Great Big Enormous Turnip

Once upon a time an old man planted a little turnip. The old man said, " Grow, grow, little turnip. Grow sweet. Grow, grow, little turnip. Grow strong." And the turnip grew up sweet and strong and big and enormous. Then one day the old man went to pull it up. He pulled—and pulled again. But he could not pull it up. He called the old woman. The old woman pulled the old man. The old man pulled the turnip. And they pulled—and pulled again. But they could not pull it up. So the old woman called her granddaughter. The granddaughter pulled the old woman. The old woman pulled the old man. The old man pulled the turnip. And they pulled—and pulled again. But they could not pull it up. The granddaughter called the black dog. The black dog pulled the granddaughter. The granddaughter pulled the old woman. The old woman pulled the old man. The old man pulled the turnip. And they pulled—and pulled again. But they still could not pull it up. The black dog called the cat. The cat pulled the dog. The dog pulled the granddaughter. The granddaughter pulled the old woman. The old woman pulled the old man. The old man pulled the turnip. And they pulled—and pulled again. But they still could not pull it up. The cat called the mouse. The mouse pulled the cat. The cat pulled the dog. The dog pulled the granddaughter. The granddaughter pulled the old woman. The old woman pulled the old man. The old man pulled the turnip. They pulled—and pulled again. And up came the turnip at last!

Which passage was harder for you to read? Was it also harder for you to remember? Why? A child in Kucer's study read the first passage as follows (1985, p. 234):

With the miscues marked	As read with the miscues and corrections
© *from* A Pin ~~for~~ Dan	A Pin from—a Pin for Dan
A man had a tin pin.	A man had a tin pin.
© ® *of* *cup* It's a pin ~~for a~~ ~~cap.~~	It a—it's a pin of a—pin of a cup.
© *Dan* © *wind* Can ~~Dad~~ ~~win~~ it for Dan?	Can Dan wind—win it for Dan—Dad win it
	for Dan?

Dad (wins) the pin.   Dad the pin.

(C)
(The pin is (in) a bag.   The pin is a—The pin is in a bag.

(C) In   (C) t-
(On the bag is a (tag.   In the bag—on the bag is a t-tag.

        first   cup
The pin ~~fits~~ on Dan's ~~cap~~.   The pin first on Dan's cup.

(C) D- pinned   cup
(Dad ~~pins~~ it on the ~~cap~~.   D-Dad pinned it on the cup.

The pin is Dan's pin.   The pin is Dan's pin.

In Kucer's study, "The Great Big Enormous Turnip" was also read by a child at the same grade level as the first. It is relatively easy to read the text with the miscues and to get a sense of the nature of the miscues (1985, p. 235):

Out open on   (C) t-
~~Once~~ ~~upon~~ ~~a~~ time an old man planted a little turnip. The old man

                    (R) li'- (C) t-   set
said, "Grow, grow, little turnip. Grow ~~sweet~~. Grow, grow, little

            (C) st-   (C) gro- Strong st-
turnip. Grow strong." And the turnip grew up ~~sweet~~ and strong and

                                              (R)
big and (enormous). Then one day the old man went to pull it up. He

                agen
pulled—and pulled ~~again~~. But he could not pull it up. He called

                    (C) o-
the old woman. The old woman pulled the old man. The old man

pulled the turnip. And they pulled—and pulled again. But they

could not pull it up. So the old woman called her granddaughter.

The granddaughter pulled the old woman. The old woman pulled the

old man. The old man pulled the turnip. And they pulled—and

pulled again. But they could not pull it up. The granddaughter

called the black dog. The black dog pulled the granddaughter. The

granddaughter pulled the old woman. The old woman pulled the old

man. The old man pulled the turnip. And they pulled—and

pulled again. But they still could not pull it up. The black dog called the

cat. The cat ~~pulled~~ *pulls on* the dog. The dog ~~pulled~~ *pulls on* the granddaughter.

The granddaughter ~~pulled~~ *pulls on* the old woman. The old woman ~~pulled~~ *pulls on* the

old man. The *old* man ~~pulled~~ *pulls on* the turnip. And they pulled—and

pulled again. But they still could not pull it up. The cat called

the mouse. The mouse pulled *on* *And* the cat. The cat pulled *on* the dog. The

dog pulled *on* the granddaughter. The granddaughter pulled *on* the old

woman. The old woman pulled *on* the *old* man. The *old* man pulled the

turnip. *A-* They pulled—and pulled again. And up came the turnip at

last!

It is obvious from a quick glance at the two miscue-marked passages that the child reading "A Pin for Dan" miscued on a considerably higher percentage of words than the child reading "The Great Big Enormous Turnip." What do you notice about the nature and quality of the miscues? Which child do you think was the better reader? Why? Now consider the unaided retellings:

Retelling of "A Pin for Dan"

" Well, his Dad was going to buy, Dan's Dad was going to buy, is going to buy a pin and his Dad bought him a pin and pinned it on his cap." (Kucer, 1985, p. 239)

Retelling of "The Great Big Enormous Turnip"

Apparently the reader must have predicted that the first sentence of this story was going to read something like "Out on an open prairie," because her retelling began "On an open prairie there was a man and he started digging and he dug on the turnip and he pulled on the turnip and he couldn't and he called the old woman." From this point on, the reader told every single detail in sequence, concluding with "The cat ran out and got a mouse and then granddaughter, the granddaughter pulled on the old woman, the old woman pulled on the old man, the old man pulled on the turnip and then, a little after they pulled it popped out and they all fell down." The reader drew upon the pictures for the last details (Kucer, 1985, p. 239).

Which child remembered the most about the passage read? Which child do you think is the better reader—the same one as before, or not? Why?

The passages are from two different basal reading programs. "A Pin for Dan" came from Reader 2 in the Merrill Linguistic Readers (Fries, Fries, et al., 1966), while "The Great Big Enormous Turnip" (Tolstoy, 1971) was from the Scott Foresman Reading Systems. Kucer tells us that the two passages had an average "readability" level of 2.0, according to the Spache criteria (1978). However, he explains that the predictability of the two passages is considerably different, with "A Pin for Dan" being much less predictable than the cumulative story about the great, big, enormous turnip. What do you think makes "A Pin for Dan" especially unpredictable, and therefore perhaps more difficult to read and remember?

Does it surprise you to be told that both passages were read by the same reader, within the same time frame? The child was a third grader who had difficulties with reading. Many people seem to think that "decodable" texts like "A Pin for Dan" are easier to read than other texts, but they aren't (Simons & Amon, 1989; Kucer, 1985; Rhodes, 1979).

If you agree that "A Pin for Dan" is not only less memorable but also less readable, especially for emergent readers or readers having difficulty, then the following may concern you, too: In some states, in order to be considered for the state-approved textbook list in reading, commercial reading programs must have beginning reading materials in which 75 to 80% of the words are "decodable," in that they represent phonics patterns previously taught.

So far as other investigators have been able to determine (Allington & Woodside-Jiron, 1998a), there is no research basis for such a requirement—just people's beliefs. As previously mentioned, the 1985 study by Juel and Roper/Schneider is sometimes cited as demonstrating the superiority of decodable texts to other beginning reading materials, but the study did not isolate this variable, so the claim about decodable texts is "unscientific."

Meanwhile, we do know several important things:

- "Decodable texts" are more difficult to read than uncontrived texts.

- Predictability is much more important than the score from a readability formula in determining how "readable" a text is—how readable it is in general, not to mention how readable it is for a particular person.

- Readability formulas are typically derived from word counts of various kinds, such as the number of words per sentence. Of course the formulas may be more complex than this, but even so, word-related criteria alone are extremely inadequate in determining the readability—and consequently the "level"—of a text. Genuine readability depends upon things like the following:

  - The operative definition of *reading* that the reader adheres to

  - The reader's familiarity with the concepts, vocabulary, and/or experiences that the writer has tried to embody in the words

  - The reader's interest—or lack of it—in the topic and/or the selection

  - The difficulty of the sentence structures for the particular reader

  - The explicitness—or lack of explicitness—of the relationships between ideas and sentences, and consequently the degree to which a reader must draw inferences

  - The reader's familiarity or lack of familiarity with the organizing devices used in the text

■ Differences between the language and grammar used in the text and the reader's own speech patterns—especially if the reader did not learn English as the native language

■ Cultural differences in how information is organized and presented, especially in writing meant to persuade

Examples of one point—the *lack* of explicitness of a connection between ideas—can often be found in materials written for young children. In an attempt to write to the readability formulas, textbook writers often do not connect ideas. For example, they might write, "They plant and harvest crops only two months out of the year. Most of the year it is cold." According to a readability formula, writing these ideas as two sentences would make the text more readable than making the connection explicit within one sentence: "They plant and harvest crops only two months out of the year *because* most of the year it is cold." Despite the readability formula, though, the connected version is easier to understand for a child who has inadequate background or who tends not to draw inferences while reading.

In any case, predictability of various kinds—as partially captured in the preceding list of factors—is much more important for genuine readability than are the levels derived from a readability formula. See, for example,

Davison, A., & Green, G. (Eds.). *Linguistic Complexity and Text Comprehension: Readability Issues Reconsidered*. Maweh, NJ: Erlbaum, 1988.

Classroom Research on the Effects and Effectiveness of Comprehensive Literacy Programs

There are several summaries of research involving comprehensive literacy programs: summaries that focus entirely on, or include, comparative experimental research. These summaries include Kohn, 1999, Appendix A; Daniels, Zemelman, & Bizar, 1999; Weaver, 1998a; Smith & Elley, 1995; Krashen, 1993; Stephens, 1991; Shapiro, 1990; Heald-Taylor, 1989; and Tunnell & Jacobs, 1989.

A primary criterion for inclusion in my own most recent descriptions of such experimental studies (Weaver, 1998a) was the requirement that the studies include both standardized test measures and a variety of other measures. All the located studies involved children in preschool, kindergarten, grade 1, or grade 2. Three studies involved two grade levels and one involved three grade levels; one study and another cluster of studies were longitudinal studies involving children deemed to be at risk of educational failure. These various studies are described in detail on the Heinemann Web page associated with this book: <*http://www.heinemann.com/weaver*>.

Some of the best-quality studies have been conducted by Penny Freppon at the University of Cincinnati and/or by Karin Dahl, now at Ohio State University. Therefore, I shall include only studies involving these researchers in the more limited coverage here. These studies are listed in chronological order.

P. A. FREPPON, 1988, 1991 Freppon's 1988 investigation of children's concepts of the purpose and nature of reading in different instructional settings was also reported in Freppon, 1991: "Children's Concepts of the Nature and Purpose of Reading in Different Instructional Settings," *Journal of Reading Behavior,* 23(2): pp. 139–163. This study was included in the National Reading Panel analysis and listed as comparing sequential phonics with whole language. There were no statistically significant differences in the posttests on the one measure specifically charted: oral reading (NRP, 2000b, p. 2-157). Measures favoring whole language classrooms weren't included.

Freppon compared the literacy development of students in two "skills-based" first-grade classrooms with those in two "literature-based" classrooms. She contrasts what the skills-based teachers typically did with what the literature-based teachers did:

> The skill-based teachers: (a) established ability grouping and round-robin oral reading with an emphasis on reading correctly; (b) emphasized drill and practice on discrete skills such as short vowels, blends, and vocabulary words; (c) used a reading basal series exclusively for instruction; (d) required daily completion of skill-oriented (word and phonics) worksheets and workbooks; and (e) followed a traditional, systematic and sequenced curriculum in teaching phonics and vocabulary.
>
> The literature-based teachers: (a) used book demonstrations and modeled reading strategies such as making connections between their own lives and the events in the text when reading to and with children; (b) promoted children's approximations to conventional reading and did not emphasize *word perfect* reading; (c) structured cooperative reading events such as choral and partner reading; (d) emphasized reading for meaning (requiring children to think about what was going on in the story, discussing sense making, directly commenting on making connections with prior knowledge during reading interactions); and (e) taught children to use specific reading strategies including meaning, predicting, skipping words, rereading *(and getting ready to say the word),* guessing, and using graphophonic information. (1991, pp. 143–144)

The following are some of Freppon's conclusions, with contributing evidence:

1. Students in the literature-based group seemed to have a better sense of what sounds like language. Evidence? Of the literature-based group, 97% rejected words in scrambled sentence order as not being language-like, while only 42% of the skills-based group rejected such sentences.

2. Students in the literature-based group seemed to have a stronger sense that reading involves constructing meaning, not merely getting the words right. Evidence? Of the students in the literature-based group, 92% said that understanding the story or both understanding and getting the words right are important in reading, while only 50% of the skills-based group mentioned meaning or emphasized both as important.

3. Students in the literature-based group reported using more strategies in reading, and were more often observed to do so; also, they more often discussed using meaning to self-monitor.

4. Though children in both groups said they were good readers, those in the literature-based group said they were good readers because they read a lot of books, while children in the skills group said they were good readers because they knew a lot of words.

5. Students in the literature-based group were more successful in using grapho/phonemic cues in conjunction with prior knowledge and other language cues in order to construct meaning. Though the skills group attempted to sound out words more than twice as often, the literature group was more successful in doing so: a 53% success rate compared with a 32% success rate for the skills group. Also, the literature group more often showed a balanced use of language cueing systems in their substitutions of one word for another.

In short, students in the literature-based group seemed to be making greater progress toward becoming literate.

K. L. DAHL AND P. A. FREPPON, 1992 Part of the data described here is reported in other articles: Freppon, 1991; Dahl & Freppon, 1991; Dahl, Purcell-Gates, & McIntyre, 1989.

Two studies were involved in the Dahl and Freppon 1992 comparison: an investigation of children's sense making in skills-based classrooms (Dahl, Purcell-Gates, & McIntyre, 1989) and a similar study in comprehensive literacy classrooms (Dahl & Freppon, 1991). Both studies were ethnographic, spanning a two-year period from kindergarten through first grade, and both studies documented children's evolving hypotheses about reading and writing. The school populations

"were representative of the racial and cultural mix typical of the urban low-income populations in the midwest—African American and White Appalachian" (Dahl & Freppon, 1992). The
learners at each site were randomly selected from among those who qualified for the federally
funded lunch program. Seven learners remained through the two-year skills-based study; twelve
completed the comprehensive literacy study. The "focal learners" were racially balanced in each
study (four African American and three Appalachian White in the skills-based study; six of each
ethnic background in the comprehensive literacy study).

At the beginning of kindergarten and at the end of first grade, all learners in both studies
completed six kinds of tasks assessing various aspects of written language knowledge: (1) an
"Intentionality" task designed to determine to what extent the children understood that written
language is a symbol system conveying meaning; (2) Marie Clay's (1979) Concepts About Print
test; (3) three tasks designed to determine children's knowledge of the alphabetic principle and
their knowledge of letter-sound relations; (4) two tasks designed to determine children's understanding of how written narratives are structured; (5) a task requiring children to pretend to read
a wordless storybook to a doll, in order to determine the children's "Written Narrative Register"
(Purcell-Gates, 1988); and, (6) a writing task designed to elicit children's concepts of writing. The
researchers describe most of these tasks in detail.

Upon entering kindergarten, the children in both studies had a very limited understanding
of written language. The children in the comprehensive literacy kindergartens scored slightly
lower on every pretest measure except one. Two years later, children in the skills-based classrooms showed statistically significant gains on all measures except one (the Written Narrative
Register); those in the comprehensive literacy classrooms showed statistically significant gains
on all six measures. With five of the six assessment measures (all except Story Structure), the
comprehensive literacy children had lower pretest scores than the skills-based children. However, the comprehensive literacy children scored higher on all six of the posttest measures (Dahl
& Freppon, 1992, p. 24). Two of these six differences were statistically significant: the tests of
written register and concepts of writing.

Interestingly, the skills-based group was knowledgeable about "intentionality" (writing as
conveying meaning), though this was not explicitly emphasized during instruction. Similarly,
the comprehensive literacy group had comparable (in fact, slightly higher) scores on the tests
of alphabetic principle and letter-sound relations, though these are taught less directly and less
extensively in comprehensive literacy classrooms. Furthermore, a much greater proportion of the
comprehensive literacy learners consistently applied their knowledge of letter-sound relations
effectively by the end of first grade (Dahl & Freppon, 1992, p. 36).

The more interesting and significant differences between children in the two kinds of classrooms were qualitative, not quantitative. For example:

1. In the comprehensive literacy classrooms, children's ongoing talk as they participated in
   reading and writing demonstrated that they perceived themselves as readers and writers,
   even if they were relatively less proficient readers and writers than their classmates.
   Regardless of their proficiency or degree of success, all the comprehensive literacy children
   tended to persist in reading and writing activities. In the skills-based classrooms, these
   patterns were restricted to just the most proficient readers and writers.

2. Children in the comprehensive literacy classrooms participated actively in the reading and
   discussion of literature, related new books to previously read texts, and developed a critical
   stance toward trade books. The curriculum in the skills-based classrooms did not encourage
   these behaviors in students.

3. In skills-based classrooms, passivity appeared to be the most frequent coping strategy for
   learners having difficulty. In comprehensive literacy classrooms, those having difficulty
   tended to draw upon other learners for support: by saving the phrases and sentences that

others could read, by copying what they wrote, and so forth. The less proficient literacy learners in comprehensive literacy classrooms still attempted to remain engaged in literacy activities with their peers.

4. In reading, comprehensive literacy students at each level of proficiency demonstrated a greater variety of reading strategies and more active engagement in reading.

5. By the end of first grade, a considerably larger proportion of the comprehensive literacy children were writing sentences and stories.

In summary, the children in the comprehensive literacy classrooms demonstrated slightly greater gains on quantitative measures of literacy skills, including knowledge of the alphabetic principle and of letter-sound relations. The greatest differences, however, occurred in the range and depth of attitudes and behaviors characteristic of literate individuals. The authors conclude that "a number of instructional elements and practices were productive for low-SES inner-city children. These included extensive experience with children's literature, writing opportunities with self-selected topics, social contexts where learners could work together, and one-on-one teacher conferences" (Dahl & Freppon, 1992, p. 71). Only the last of these was found in the skills-based classrooms.

P. A. FREPPON, 1993 This study built upon the previously described study of Dahl and Freppon (1992). The same children participated in this follow-up study, now as second graders. One question the investigator wanted to address is the frequently asked question "Do children with experience in a comprehensive literacy curriculum, particularly in the early grades, have the skills necessary for success in a traditional, skills-based curriculum?" Another research question was the extent to which students maintained the literacy abilities, behaviors, and attitudes they had developed through kindergarten and first grade.

One group of eight children from the original comprehensive literacy group in Dahl and Freppon (1992) made a transition to a skills-based second grade (the Transition Group), while the other group of nine continued in a comprehensive literacy classroom in second grade (the Continuing Group). All participating children were given pretests and posttests. Eight focal children, four in each group, were closely followed. Data gathering included written artifacts, reading samples, field notes, and audiotapes and videotapes.

At the end of second grade, there was little difference between groups on the standardized tests, and little difference in their gain from pretest to posttest. Findings from the reading and writing interviews revealed several areas of decline in the Transition Group while the Continuing Group generally remained stable or gained in some areas. For example: the Transition Group, now in a skills-based second grade, showed 37% less identification of items to be read beyond school, while the Continuing Group, still in a comprehensive literacy classroom, showed 33% more identification of items to read beyond school. The Transition Group showed a 30% decrease in responses reflecting megacognitive or strategic knowledge, while the Continuing Group showed a 30% increase. The Transition Group showed a 32% increase in statements that writing was difficult, a 38% increase in preference for writing with others, and stability in citing the story and surface features as important in writing. The Continuing Group showed no increase in statements that writing was difficult, stability in preference for writing with others, and a 30% or greater increase in citing the story and surface features as important in writing (pp. 24–25).

The focal children in the Transition Group concentrated primarily on "getting through" assignments. Persistence in self-selected reading and writing declined in the Transition Group, for all but the most academically proficient child within that focal group. In contrast, the focal children in the Continuing Group maintained talk and action demonstrating a sense of themselves as readers and writers and persisted in self-selected reading and writing during second grade, regardless of their academic proficiency.

The investigator concluded that the children in the Transition Group had the literacy skills necessary for success in the skills-based second-grade classroom, but that some of the children showed a loss of motivation for literacy experiences that was not experienced by the students who continued in a comprehensive literacy classroom (p. 85).

Acquiring Literacy in a Second Language Through Book-Based Programs

Another important body of comparative research is that dealing with the effects of book-based programs in comparison with more traditional programs in promoting the acquisition of literacy in a second language.

Elley (1991) reviews nine studies of the acquisition of English as a second language, most of which were undertaken in the South Pacific and Southeast Asia, including his own earlier study (Elley & Mangubhai, 1983). Typically these studies compared the results of programs based on structured, systematic instruction with "book flood" programs, which exposed children to large numbers of high-interest storybooks. In other words, the studies compared the effects of a direct instruction approach with an indirect approach that might be characterized as "comprehensive literacy" or "natural" language learning. These studies all involved elementary school students.

What I've considered the direct instruction approach typically involved principles articulated by structural linguists (e.g., Bloomfield, 1942) and audiolingual methodology: practice on a carefully sequenced set of grammatical structures, through imitation, repetition, and reinforcement. The book flood studies reflected typical contemporary literacy principles, and usually involved either sustained silent reading of an extensive number of picture books; the Shared Book Experience (Holdaway, 1979), including reading, discussion, and related activities; or a combination of these, which in one instance also included a modified language experience approach.

From these combined studies, the following patterns emerged:

1. Students in the book flood programs did better on almost all standardized measures of reading, including not only comprehension skills but also word identification and phonics skills.

2. Usually favoring the book flood students were differences in measures of oral and written language and vocabulary (e.g., listening comprehension, written story completion), and sometimes differences in other aspects of school achievement as well (see also Elley, 1989).

3. More surprisingly, students in the book flood programs often did better on tests of the grammatical structures explicitly taught in the audiolingual program. Elley notes that this interpretation "was supported by an incidental study in which knowledge and use of English in natural settings was found to be largely unaffected by deliberate instruction in them" (1991, p. 389).

4. Students in Shared Book Experience programs typically showed greater gains on various tests than students in silent reading programs. (Perhaps this result suggests the value of oral reading and discussion, probably including the discussion of letter-sound relationships within the Shared Book Experience.)

5. Students in the book flood programs typically had a more positive attitude toward books and reading. (One wonders if these programs also affected children's attitudes toward English as a second language.)

Elley summarizes, in part, as follows: "That pupils showed equally large gains in the discrete-point tests of grammatical structures and vocabulary as they did in the more integrative measures of reading, listening, and writing is particularly damaging for those who argue that structures and vocabulary should be deliberately taught" (1991, p. 402). If more of the comparisons had included tests of decoding skills, perhaps the same conclusion could be drawn for the direct teaching of phonics.

In short, Elley's comparison of these several studies offers powerful evidence for the assertion of comprehensive literacy advocates that language and literacy are acquired gradually, through opportunities to use the language and to engage in literacy events in meaningful contexts. Elley shows how the earlier book-based programs and studies have been extended to other countries in *Raising Literacy Levels in Third World Countries: A Method That Works* (1998).

Observational Research from the Center on English Learning and Achievement

Researchers under the auspices of the Center on English Learning and Achievement (CELA, 1998) undertook to determine major characteristics of the most effective first-grade literacy teachers in California, New Jersey, New York, Texas, and Wisconsin. They defined *effective* as follows:

> In the most effective classrooms, student engagement in academically relevant activities was consistently high. At the end of the year, most of the students of the most effective first-grade teachers were independently reading books at or above the first-grade level; they were writing multiple sentences that observed the conventions of capitalization and punctuation, and spelling high frequency words correctly, with other spellings accurately reflecting the sequence of sounds in the words; they also demonstrated the ability to look up unfamiliar words on a word wall or in a dictionary. In contrast, the students of the more typical teachers wrote less, showed limited knowledge of spelling and punctuation conventions, and independently read fewer and less challenging books. (CELA, 1998, p. 1)

Pressley, M., Allington, R. L., et al. (2001). *Learning to Read: Lessons from Exemplary First-Grade Classrooms.* New York: Guilford. This book documents and describes the exemplary practices of the first-grade teachers in the CELA (1998) study.

There are nine characteristics in particular that the researchers found to be typical of the most effective classrooms (CELA, 1998, pp. 1, 4):

- High Academic Engagement and Competence:
  Most students (90%) were engaged in things academic most (90%) of the time—even when the teacher left the room. Little misbehavior was observed, and student talk was on task. In some cases, students were so lost in their work that they continued right into recess. Students were reading end-of-grade-1 books at the end of the year and writing multiple sentences, in which they used important conventions such as capitalization and end marks.

- Excellent Classroom Management:
  Teachers in the most effective classrooms managed student behavior, student learning, and instructional aides and specialists effectively and efficiently, using a variety of methods. These classrooms had clear rules and expectations that students were familiar with. Teacher planning was evident in the instruction, which was designed so that students spent more time on academically challenging and engaging tasks than on nondemanding tasks. Instructional specialists and aides were consistently engaged with students in instruction, providing curricular coherence and continuity for students needing their services.

- A Positive, Reinforcing, Cooperative Environment:
  These classrooms were positive places. The rare discipline problems were handled positively and constructively—devoid of harsh, demeaning criticism and with little disruption to the class. Students received a lot of positive reinforcement for their accomplishments, both privately and publicly, and students were encouraged to cooperate with one another and to work cooperatively.

- Explicit Teaching of Skills, in Context:
  Word-level, comprehension, vocabulary, spelling, and writing skills were typically taught in the context of actual reading and writing tasks. Teachers balanced the cues they taught to help with word recognition (i.e., phonics, word parts, looking at the whole word, picture cues, other semantic context cues, syntactic clues). Not only did students have frequent opportunities to practice the decoding and word recognition strategies they learned, teachers were opportunistic about teaching and reteaching—e.g., reviewing these strategies when students encountered difficulties. When explicit teaching and opportunistic teaching were combined, there often were as many as 10–20 skills covered during every hour of literacy instruction.

- An Emphasis on Literature:
  The teachers read outstanding literature to their classes and conducted author studies, during which both students and teacher read and discussed a number of books by the same author. Students in these classrooms selected the books they wanted to read from easily accessible classroom collections.

- Much Reading and Writing:
  These teachers set aside large blocks of time for language arts (at least 45 minutes), providing long, uninterrupted periods for reading and writing. Everyone (both students and teacher) read—to themselves, to a buddy, to a group, to an adult volunteer, to the class as a whole, together—everyday. And everyone wrote everyday—in journals, in response to literature, in groups, alone.

- A Match Between Accelerating Demands and Student Competence, with Teacher Scaffolding:
  The teachers set high but realistic expectations and consistently encouraged students to try more challenging (but not overwhelming) tasks. They monitored students' use of skills and provided prompts on an as-needed basis (scaffolding) during both reading and writing. By the end of the year there were high demands on the students for correct use of punctuation conventions and accurate spelling of high frequency words.

- Encouragement of Self-Regulation:
  The effective teachers taught students to self-regulate; for example, they encouraged students to choose appropriate skills and cues when they faced a task rather than the teacher dictating a particular skill or strategy. Students were taught to check their writing for correct use of conventions and given guidance for determining if a book was too hard for them (more than five unknown words). They were also taught to monitor the use of their time and their own organization and work habits. Moreover, the teachers expected students to work to their capacity; they did not accept work from them that was below par.

- Strong Connections Across the Curriculum:
  These teachers made explicit connections across the curriculum—providing opportunities across the learning day to use the skills students were learning. Reading and writing were integrated, and then, in turn, related to other subjects like science and social studies. Vocabulary learning related to reading, and thematic units drove much of what was learned by students. In other words, in the most effective classrooms, instruction was largely seamless, integrated, and overlapping.

The CELA article indicates that the research team consistently found at least 80% of these characteristics in the most effective classrooms, but they caution that singling out any one factor as a key to improving literacy instruction would be unwarranted. "The most effective teachers daily assemble a mosaic of classroom management and instructional strategies, arranging and rearranging the pieces according to the needs of their students at any given time. The quality and characteristics of these pieces matter, but so, too, does the dynamic way that the teachers use each one in concert with the others" (p. 1).

In a spring 2001 newsletter, CELA researchers show, in effect, that similar ways of teaching are what characterize the teaching of highly effective fourth-grade teachers.

Related CELA* Reports

Allington, R., & Johnston, P. (2001). What Do We Know About Effective Fourth-Grade Teachers and Their Classrooms? Report #13010. 25 pages.

Pressley, M., & Allington, R. (1998), The Nature of Effective First-Grade Literacy Instruction. Report #11007. 32 pages.

*Center on English Learning and Achievement (CELA): <*http://cela.albany.edu*>; email: *cela@albany.edu;* (518) 442-5026.

A crucial point to be made about the comprehensive literacy studies is that they gain in practical, "construct" validity as much—or more—than they lose in the kind of validity associated with replicability. To have substantial construct validity, assessment measures must closely resemble the target behavior they are claimed to measure—in this case, the ability to read and understand authentic texts in everyday life. Most of the assessment measures in comprehensive literacy classrooms stem from and relate to the various reading and writing experiences in the classroom (and thus they are also valuable for setting learning and teaching goals). Such assessment measures are designed to be more accurate reflections of children's overall growth in literacy and in the attitudes and habits of literate persons. Isn't that what reading and writing education is supposed to be all about? And isn't this what we should expect from the assessment measures in research studies that give rise to claims about "what works"?

FOR FURTHER EXPLORATION

1. When the Reading Excellence Act of 1998 was first proposed to the House Committee on Education and the Workforce, the definition/explanation of reading was as follows: "The term 'reading' means the process of comprehending the meaning of written text by (1) using the knowledge of relationships between letters and sounds to accurately and fluently identify printed words, both silently and aloud; and (2) establishing the ability to quickly and accurately apply decoding skills to automatically recognize words." Is this an adequate explanation of what children need to learn to comprehend texts, or of how readers comprehend texts? Discuss.

2. Locate Rona Flippo's 1998 article "Points of Agreement: A Display of Professional Unity in Our Field," The Reading Teacher, 52(1): pp. 30–40. (Or locate her book: Flippo, 1999.) Consider and discuss particularly the "contexts and practices that 'would make learning to read difficult.'" Did you experience some of these practices when you were a child? How did you feel about them? Also consider and discuss why you think prominent researchers in the field of reading agreed that these practices are not good.

3. Revisit the "Questions for Thought and Discussion" at the beginning of this chapter. Have you changed your mind on some and solidified your opinion on others? Discuss if possible.

12 Designing a Comprehensive Literacy Program

> Reading and writing workshop organizes reading and writing experiences in meaningful ways. The workshop may vary depending on the teacher and the grade level, but it always involves large blocks of time, the majority of which is used for reading and writing experiences.... Instruction is an important part of reading and writing workshop and takes a variety of forms.
>
> —Cora Lee Five and Kathryn Egawa

Questions for Thought and Discussion

1. Why is reading aloud to young children so important? How can we help the child interact with the book as we read to him or her?

2. What steps are involved in the shared reading experience? Why is it so valuable in helping children learn to read?

3. Why is it important for children to write, even when they are just beginning to read?

4. How can teachers model good reading and writing strategies for children?

5. Why is it important for emergent readers and writers to read and write every day, even though they are just in the process of developing the strategies and skills of independent readers and writers?

6. How can we assess reading and writing in ways that will reflect children's gradual development of literacy, and provide the teacher with specific information to guide future instruction?

Reading will not flourish in a classroom where there are few books and infrequent opportunities for sustained reading of self-chosen books. Reading will not flourish without writing. Nor will reading flourish in a classroom where "teaching reading" amounts to teaching separate skills and strategies, with little opportunity to read. In the previous chapter, we saw too that teaching to read succeeds best when it involves not only explicit teaching of reading skills in the context of their use, but an emphasis on literature, large blocks of time for language arts, and much more. Effective organization for learning is especially crucial.

Those who wonder how they can spare forty-five minutes to two hours for literacy workshops need to understand the following:

■ Skills are taught in demonstrations, mini-lessons, and as students are writing whole pieces. This eliminates the time otherwise needed for isolated practice, such as doing worksheets. Isolated practice requires time helping students transfer the skills to their actual reading and writing, not to mention the time spent assessing in isolation the skills that are typically taught and practiced that way. Thus, a workshop approach to reading and writing saves time in three different ways, thereby allowing more time for genuine reading and writing.

- Discussion of literature and of students' writing offers plenty of opportunities to develop the language skills of listening and speaking, thus also saving time. Even more important, teaching oral language skills in these contexts makes them practical, makes them "real."

- Literature study is a part of reading workshop, so no additional time is needed for that.

- History, other aspects of social studies, and science may be taught through literature and nonfiction (e.g., biographies and autobiographies), so sometimes instructional time and/or the sustained reading time in reading workshop can accomplish both aims. Some literary works can involve or lead to the teaching of math.

- Longer literacy workshops, especially, may include time for various kinds of responses to literature, such as choral reading, readers theater, and drama. Responses may also involve the other arts, such as drawing, painting, music, dance, and sculpture. The literacy workshop becomes intertwined with various areas and aspects of the curriculum, and vice versa.

- Within a longer literacy workshop, inquiry—involving reading and writing to learn—would usually be devoted to themes and topics in other areas of study, so again, the literacy program can accomplish much more than just developing literacy. Even with emergent readers, learning to read also involves reading to learn.

Providing a variety of learning opportunities, in whole-class, small-group, and individual sessions, as suggested in Figure 12.1, is probably the most important thing we can do to ensure good reading instruction that will be effective, in time, for almost all students. Some emergent or struggling readers and writers may still need additional tutorial help, but a comprehensive classroom literacy program is absolutely crucial as the major form of organization and instruction (Kitagawa, 2000; Routman, 1999). And certainly we cannot settle merely for whole-class instruction and expect it to work for all, or even most, children.

Whole-class instruction
read-aloud
also, (re)read familiar texts as a class
& focus on
concepts of print • strategies
words • letter-sound chunks (phonics)
punctuation • etcetera

Guided reading instruction
in small groups, *according to*
current need

Individual instruction,
according to ongoing/unique need

Extra tutorial help
if needed

Figure 12.1 *Providing comprehensive and effective reading instruction.*

Reading	Writing
Read-aloud	Write-aloud
Shared reading	Shared writing
Guided reading	Guided writing
Sustained reading	Sustained writing
Individual reading conferences	Individual writing conferences
Literature groups	Journals
Inquiry, or reading to learn	Inquiry, or writing to learn
Opportunities for response	Opportunities for response

Figure 12.2   *Major components of a comprehensive literacy program: Reading and writing.*

Figure 12.2 shows some major components of reading and writing workshops. Mini-lessons on strategies and skills are interwoven throughout.

Guiding Principles and Practices

What is "literacy," anyway? We hear a lot of talk these days about technological literacy, and media literacy, but what is print literacy, the literacy that has to do with reading and writing? Is it anything more than the mere ability to read and write minimally? That question deserves a resounding "yes." Print literacy includes the ability to read and write well enough to read signs, labels, TV guides, directions, and other practical kinds of texts. It includes the ability to read well enough to handle the demands of a job, which these days often requires quite sophisticated reading and thinking skills in order to use computer software programs and to read and write business letters, reports, and the like (Burke, 2001). But for many who use the term, *print literacy* includes still more: the ability and desire to read for pleasure and to learn new things. We read fiction and nonfiction to find out what we want to know, to learn about ourselves and others, to explore other lands and cultures, to consider our human diversity and find our common humanity. We write to better understand ourselves and our own thoughts; to communicate with, inform, and persuade others; and to create. We read and write not only because we have to, but because we *want* to, because it fulfills our needs and purposes and enriches our lives. A comprehensive literacy program offers students an opportunity to develop these richer aspects of literacy, not merely to learn to read and write.

How Does Literacy Begin?!

Some children begin their road to literacy by reading signs, labels, and other texts that are encountered in daily life. But viewed from a broader, more holistic perspective, literacy is an activity that first and foremost provides the reader with a sense of wonder and connectedness between what is written and their own experience. Through their imagination, readers are transported into the world created by the author and the characters of the book.   —Peter Krause, *School superintendent emeritus*

Furthermore, a comprehensive literacy program is not just a "balanced literacy program," which typically turns out to be skills like phonics taught in isolation, "balanced" by the isolated teaching of comprehension skills, with perhaps some opportunities to read and write whole texts. Rather, a comprehensive literacy program is more integrative, with skills and strategies taught and used in context, and with emphasis upon the guided and sustained reading and writing of whole, meaningful texts, an emphasis that is sorely needed to help children become both functionally and joyfully literate.

"Must-Read" Articles—and a Tip!

Chomsky-Higgins, P. 1998. "Teaching Strategies and Skills During Readers' Workshop: Setting the Stage for Successful Readers and Writers." In *Practicing What We Know: Informed Reading Instruction*, ed. C. Weaver, 140–153. Urbana, IL: National Council of Teachers of English.

Five, C. L., & Egawa, K. (Eds.). 1998. "Reading and Writing Workshop." *School Talk*, 3(4). This eight-page issue includes articles by Joanne Hindley and Kathy Short as well as Five and Egawa.

Catherine Compton-Lilly's extensive annotated bibliography of professional books, *http://www.heinemann .com/weaver,* includes books and a few articles that are especially helpful with various aspects of a reading workshop. See the sections Teaching Reading and Writing in Elementary School and the section Teaching Reading in the Middle School and High School.

In "Reading and Writing Workshop: What Is It, and What Does It Look Like?" Cora Lee Five and Kathryn Egawa (1998b) succinctly describe key components of reading and writing workshops, which are central to a comprehensive literacy program. Some of their descriptions will be quoted in detail. First, however, are six points about organizing in general, followed by brief comments on assessment.

TIME "Workshop time is scheduled on a frequent, regular basis (e.g., 45 minutes, three to five times a week). Scheduling substantial blocks of time for reading and writing experiences signifies their value. We know students need these big blocks of time in order to become engaged in reading and writing, to try out new strategies, and to grow as readers and writers. Some teachers schedule separate times for reading and for writing; others combine them" (Five & Egawa 1998, 2).

PREDICTABLE STRUCTURE AND ROUTINES "It is essential that students understand the structure and daily routines of reading and writing workshop. As teachers, we introduce the workshop procedures through mini-lessons so that students understand what to do and what is expected of them each day. These predictable routines and expectations enable students to begin work without confusion and to develop greater independence as they take responsibility for their learning" (Five & Egawa 1998, 2).

OWNERSHIP AND CHOICE "Within a workshop environment, students are respected as decision makers from the earliest ages, whether their decisions be choosing their own books and topics for writing, sharing their ideas with peers, or helping shape curriculum units. Sometimes, however, we as teachers guide their choices in order to broaden their experiences as readers and writers" (Five & Egawa 1998, 2).

A COMMUNITY OF LEARNERS Creating a community of learners begins with the teacher, and the teacher must demonstrate that he or she is also a learner in the classroom. As Five and Egawa explain, "In valuing who our students are, as well as their ideas, we work to establish a sense of community that encourages different points of view and respectful interaction, including students' responses to each other, as well as our responses to students. We demonstrate a respect for their backgrounds and their special ways of learning, and trust that even when responses might not seem to make sense, they may indeed be meaningful. It's this kind of environment that allows us to identify and to build upon students' interests and strengths" (1998, 2). Five and Egawa suggest that such an environment offers "response opportunities." I call such an environment, and the individuals within it, a community of learners (see Maniates, Doerr, & Golden, 2001).

SCAFFOLDING AND COLLABORATION The term *scaffolding* was first introduced into education by psychologist Jerome Bruner (Ninio & Bruner 1978; Bruner 1983a, 1983b, 1986). Scaffolding means that the teacher, another adult, or classmates provide temporary support for the learner(s). Scaffolding is a lot like the training wheels on a bike, or water wings in the pool. In each case, the device or person(s) helps learners do what they can't yet do independently. Often, scaffolding takes the form of collaborative effort and accomplishment. Success through working together starts the learner or learners on their way to being able to do the activity or project independently.

RECORD-KEEPING AND ASSESSMENT One general way to keep track of what students are doing in reading and writing workshops is Nancie Atwell's (1998) "status of the class" technique. Basically, the teacher calls each student's name and records that student's plans for the workshop that day. In addition, each aspect of a reading and writing workshop, or of an even more comprehensive literacy program, invites its own kind of record-keeping: by the students themselves, and/or by the teacher.

READING AND WRITING WORKSHOPS: THE HEART OF A COMPREHENSIVE LITERACY PROGRAM

A comprehensive literacy program typically includes reading and writing workshops—separate, and/or interwoven together (e.g., Serafini, 2001; Fletcher & Portalupi, 2001). Such a program involves plenty of time to read and write; instruction in whole-class, small-group, and individual settings; opportunities to learn and share orally, through discussion, and through choral reading, readers theater, drama, storytelling, and other oral and visual arts. Work is done not only individually but in collaboration with teachers and peers, as they provide scaffolding for one another that promotes learning and greater individual competence. To assure the success of all children, classroom instruction needs to be supplemented by additional tutorial help for those who still need more than the teacher can provide during whole-class and group work, plus brief individual conferences.

Reading Workshops

The sections below describe important components of a reading workshop. Keep in mind, though, that some components are defined differently in different sources. See the articles and books previously alluded to (p. 279), which offer detailed discussions and guidance for a reading workshop and/or for some aspect of it.

What About Reading Aloud?

"The single most important activity for building the knowledge required for eventual success in reading is reading aloud to children. This is especially so during the preschool years. The benefits are greatest when the child is an active participant . . ." (Anderson, Hiebert, Scott, & Wilkinson, 1985, p. 23, citing C. Chomsky, 1972; Durkin, 1966; and Heath, 1982).

READ-ALOUD Reading aloud offers a demonstration of what oral reading should sound like. Usually it is the teacher who reads aloud, but of course it may be another adult who reads fluently, or even a student who provides a good model of oral reading. Read-aloud should occur daily in classrooms, because it has been shown to be the most important factor in children's literacy development. Being read to in school is crucial for children who aren't read to in the home, especially primary-grade children. Teachers and the school simply must take responsibility for seeing that such children are read to every day. But reading aloud is important not just for these students, but for all students. Among the many benefits of reading aloud, it "fosters knowledge and love of story, introduces new genres (nonfiction, poetry, biography), contributes to literature appreciation, and helps build classroom community" (Five & Egawa, 1998, 2). The teacher can also model some of his or her reading strategies. For example: "Oops, that doesn't sound right, does it? I'd better go back and reread."

Typically for a read-aloud, there is only one copy of the book, the copy used by the person reading aloud. The book may be a picture book, chapter book, book of poetry, nonfiction—whatever will hold the interest of the listeners.

Research shows that when parents read to their children, it's important to not just read the book from start to finish, while the child sits passively (Heath, 1982). Rather, the parent—or the classroom teacher—needs to get the children interacting with the book. Together they can discuss and predict from the pictures, for example, and/or from what has come before. Such prediction is crucial in helping readers learn to think about what they read, and to think ahead as well. Teachers can share some of their personal responses to the text, while eliciting reactions from the children. Sometimes, children may be invited to confer in pairs, reacting to the parts that they are "dying to talk about" and making connections with their own lives. It is important to allow children the time to discuss the events and especially the characters, to "walk in the shoes" of the characters and feel close to them. By modeling and allowing such talk, the teacher "serves as a role model and mentor, instilling the habits and values of a literate life" (Weaver, Gillmeister-Krause, & Vento-Zogby, 1996, 75).

During one school year, I had read 399 books to the children in my K–6, one-room school, by the end of the last day of school. I asked the children if they wanted to go for 400. Of course they said "Yes."
—Lorraine Gillmeister-Krause, *Soulanges School, Quebec*

In the "Professional Books for Teachers" annotated bibliography on *http://www.heinemann.com/weaver* is a section titled "Choosing Books for Children." Many other kinds of bibliographies, organized by topic, should be available at your local or university library. Jim Trelease's classic read-aloud book is the first choice for many parents and teachers:

Trelease, J. 1995. *The Read-Aloud Handbook*. New York: Penguin.
See his Web page too: < *www.trelease-on-reading.com*>.

SHARED READING Initially, shared reading techniques were developed by Don Holdaway and classroom teachers in New Zealand, for use with primary-grade children (Holdaway, 1979). Their idea was to capture the best of what parents do when reading and discussing books with their children, often just before bedtime (Fisher & Fisher-Medvic, 2000). This may include not just reading and discussing the pictures, plot, and characters, but attending to key words and other aspects of the print itself.

In the classroom, the shared reading activity, or set of activities, is initiated by the teacher reading a new selection to the children. Shared reading differs from read-aloud because all participants, not just the teacher, have access to the same text, whether on chart paper, in a Big Book, on an overhead, or with personal copies (Five & Egawa 1998, 2). First may come a *book orientation* wherein the teacher and students discuss the cover, the title, and—when relevant—the story as revealed through the pictures. These basic procedures can be expanded in various ways, with older as well as younger children, and with chapter books as well as picture books (Wilson, 2000). Book orientations are especially helpful for encouraging emergent and struggling readers to think ahead before and as they read: to engage in the strategy often called "predicting" and the process known as critical thinking.

During shared reading with emergent readers, the book orientation is followed by the teacher reading the selection to the children for the first time, as in read-aloud. After the teacher and children discuss the book, the teacher rereads it, pointing to the words so that the children can begin to match the spoken words with written words. The children are encouraged to chime in whenever they can. During repeated readings across several days, the teacher, or a child, continues to point to the words, and the children become more and more able to read the print itself, not just the pictures. When a new text for shared reading is introduced, the old one becomes the first of the texts to be reread during a shared reading session, followed by the new one that is being introduced for the first time.

It is important to provide opportunities for the children to reread the texts previously read during shared reading. During sustained reading time (see below), they can reread the text independently or in pairs, or reread the text from small, individual-sized copies, perhaps listening to a recording of the text to help them read. If necessary, the teacher sometimes makes small copies for the children.

Many if not most teachers extend shared reading time in a variety of ways, in order to directly help children develop the strategies and skills they need to become more proficient and efficient readers. Here is a list of several things that can be taught and learned through a shared reading experience with primary-grade children (Weaver, Gillmeister-Krause, & Vento-Zogby 1996, T4.8a and b):

- Book handling and conventions of print
- The nature of book language, insofar as it differs from oral language
- Sight vocabulary
- Letter-sound relationships
- Word-level skills
- Strategies for processing written texts, and conscious (metacognitive) awareness of such strategies
- Conventions of punctuation; intonation patterns
- Grammar and text structure in reading
- Understanding meanings; critical thinking
- Characteristics of various genres, including fiction, nonfiction, and poetry

See Figure 12.3 for elaboration upon such aspects of teaching and learning. Several of these aspects of print and reading may need to be taught through a shared book experience with older, less proficient readers as well (see Chapter 10). In this case, the text will often be one projected from a transparency, or students may have individual copies of a regular-sized book. The procedures, too, may be modified for older but struggling readers.

There are various important benefits to shared reading, in addition to guiding students' development as readers (slightly adapted from Weaver, Gillmeister-Krause, & Vento-Zogby 1996, T4.9):

- Children enjoy reading together.
- The rhyme, rhythm, and repetition of many texts used for shared reading in the primary grades will make prediction of words easier, and repeated predictions enable readers to identify these words out of context, too.
- Even the more proficient readers can read more difficult text than they could read independently, because the teacher reads along with the group until most children can read the text confidently.

Shared Book Experience: What Can Be Learned

1. **Book handling and conventions of print**
   - Holding a book right side up; where to begin reading; how to turn the pages
   - Understanding conventions of print, such as the fact that we read pages from top to bottom and left to right in English
   - Understanding the concepts of word and letter

2. **Nature of book language**
   - Understanding conventions that don't occur in speech ("he said," "he exclaimed")
   - Understanding the different vocabulary found more often in print than speech
   - Understanding dialect patterns that may differ from the children's own

3. **Sight vocabulary**
   - Developing a stock of interesting words that can be recognized on sight
   - Developing a stock of functional words that can be recognized on sight
   - Developing the ability to recognize more and more words in predictable contexts

4. **Letter-sound relationships**
   - Recognizing letters and letter clusters
   - Developing letter-sound knowledge—particularly an ability to read common onsets and rimes
   - Developing ability to *use* letter-sound knowledge along with prior knowledge and context to make reasonable predictions

5. **Word attack skills**
   - Developing the ability to use prior knowledge and context to predict words
   - Developing the ability to use letter-sound knowledge along with prior knowledge and context to predict words
   - Developing the ability to confirm predictions by examining the text word in chunks of letters
   - Developing the ability to get the meanings of words by looking at meaningful parts

6. **Strategies for processing written texts, and metacognitive awareness of such strategies**
   - Predicting a logical sequence of events or actions ("What do you think might happen in this story?" "What do you think might happen next?")
   - Predicting what would fit next grammatically and semantically ("What would make sense here?")
   - Making connections, drawing inferences, asking questions, determining importance, creating visual (mental) images, monitoring meaning and comprehension, and others

Figure 12.3 *Shared book experience (slightly adapted from Weaver, Gillmeister-Krause, & Vento-Zogby, 1996, T4.8a).*

- The teacher and more advanced readers support the less proficient as they all read together. That is, the more proficient readers provide scaffolding for the less proficient.

- Less proficient readers join in the reading as they can, even if they are echoing other readers. The less proficient readers' miscues are not so noticeable, and these children are not singled out for their lack of proficiency. Therefore, they take more risks as readers and read more confidently.

■ Every child experiences success, even the less proficient.

■ Children aren't just getting ready to read. They are actually reading.

GUIDED READING "Guided reading is focused reading instruction with a whole book, organized by the teacher in response to his or her assessment of the needs of particular learners at particular times" (Five & Egawa 1998, 3). While guided reading may involve the whole class or just one or two children, many people conceptualize guided reading as instruction with a small group. Such instruction focuses on particular needs and continues as long as the need remains. Thus, guided reading is carried out in flexible groupings that change with readers' changing needs. They are not permanent groups.

Guided reading instruction, then, involves preplanned mini-lessons. But of course the teacher also takes advantage of the teachable moment to teach whatever is needed, when the need arises (Opitz & Ford, 2001).

NOTE: As explained here, shared reading and guided reading are not so different as the labels might imply. Guided reading may occur as an expansion of the shared reading experience, and indeed, it is considered an integral part of shared reading by many teachers. Because of this, and because shared reading includes the use of whole texts, we may also say that the shared reading experience can, and usually does, include guided reading.

What About Sustained Reading?

In 1997–98, the 21 students in Lorraine Gillmeister-Krause's one-room, K–6 school read 2,128 books, an average of about 100 books per student. The next year, her 23 students read 2,611 books, an average of almost 114 books per student. Lorraine explains the importance of sustained reading in school: "If I want children to read outside of school, I must provide time in school. I must make reading valued, not just something kids do when they are finished with other work."

Lorraine reads predictable books to her K–2 students, and to third graders as necessary. She also reads them picture books that are too challenging for them to read independently. In addition, these primary-grade children are required to take two books from the classroom library twice a week, one book to have read to them and one to read themselves (try to, pretend to, read the best they can) during sustained reading time.

After morning routine, Lorraine's grade 4–6 students go to the classroom library area to read, for an hour, on the average. Here are some of these students' comments about sustained reading: "Really good. I get a lot of reading done" (Ally, grade 4). "Like the quiet / chance to read in school. In my old school, we did not read" (Little Man, grade 5). "Good to go read in the library. You trust us" (Karen, grade 6). "It's a privilege" (Alex, grade 4).

SUSTAINED READING There's really no commonly accepted term for what I have in mind here, so I've chosen to call it "sustained reading." Most of the time, students will be reading books they have freely chosen to read, so this might be called *choice reading,* but sometimes the teacher may have students engage in sustained reading of a book that fits a particular theme or topic the class is studying, and there may not be many, if any, choices. At other times, children may be reading a book they have chosen for literature study or for inquiry—that is, a book to read in order to learn about something, to find answers to their own questions (see below). We could call sustained reading time *independent reading,* as many do, but sometimes children may be reading in pairs, with the children helping each other, or the more proficient reader helping the less proficient one. Then there's *sustained silent reading* time (SSR), also known as

SQUIRT (*sustained quiet reading time*) or DEAR (*drop everything and read*). A problem with the SSR and SQUIRT labels is that some children need to read aloud in order to comprehend better, so the reading may not be silent. Indeed, it is possible to have a group of children who read aloud sitting close together, away from those who prefer to read silently, but each reading their own different book aloud! As for DEAR, it should not occur at random times during the school day, which is how some schools are implementing it. Rather, DEAR should occur during a preplanned time when students are not in the middle of doing something else.

Five and Egawa make some important points about sustained reading under their heading of "independent reading": "It is the teacher's role to help students develop strategies for selecting appropriate books—books that involve their interests and support their ability as readers. The classroom schedule ensures time to read daily. Students keep records of books read and teachers confer often with readers. Independent reading is also encouraged at home" (1998, 3).

The time allocated for sustained reading may be relatively brief at the beginning of a school year—say ten or fifteen minutes, perhaps, in the lower grades. Even kindergartners can at least "read" the pictures of a book and tell the story to themselves and others. This helps develop the belief that "I can read," which is important in motivating emergent readers to develop the strategies and skills needed for independent reading. With older readers, the sustained reading time may become quite long, possibly as long as forty-five minutes or more, especially when the sustained reading is done as part of inquiry or preparation for literature study (see below). *Sustained reading is absolutely crucial for helping students become proficient and efficient readers.* See, for example, Stephen Krashen's book *The Power of Reading* (1993) as well as research discussed in the preceding chapter.[1]

Fact

On the average, those fourth graders who spent the most time reading books of their own choice in school scored higher than others in the 1998 National Assessment of Educational Progress (NAEP). Those who read their chosen books almost every day scored higher than those who read books of their own choice only once or twice a week (a score of 224 compared with 217). Those who read books of their own choice in school less often than weekly scored substantially lower than either of the other groups (a score of 208). The pattern of difference was the same in 1992 and 1994 as well (P. L. Donahue, K. E. Voelkl, J. R. Campbell & J. Mazzeo, 1999).

Another Fact

The research of Steve Krashen, Jeff McQuillan, and others demonstrates a strong correlation between reading proficiency and access to books—in classroom libraries, school libraries, and public libraries. Of course, it's also important that these books interest children, which means, among other things, that libraries should include not only classic works of children's and/or adolescent literature, but numerous contemporary works as well (see Jeff McQuillan, *The Literacy Crisis: False Claims, Real Solutions*, 1998).

MINI-LESSONS Mini-lessons are planned, focused lessons or demonstrations, which can be taught during any aspect of reading workshop. Five and Egawa (1998) indicate that they often teach preplanned mini-lessons at the beginning of the reading workshop. "We demonstrate the procedure for reading workshop, teach an aspect of the reading process (see the September 1997 issue of *School Talk*), and discuss elements of literature (characterization, plot exploration, sequence of events, etc.). We discuss selecting and abandoning books, introduce new genres, demonstrate point-of-view or how to reread a text to support one's opinions. These are only a few of the lessons that are taught" (pp. 2–3).

Five and Egawa are talking about preplanned mini-lessons, but obviously instant mini-lessons can be taught spontaneously, at the moment of need.

NOTE: Clearly, mini-lessons and demonstrations can occur during shared reading and guided reading, as well as during any aspect of the reading workshop yet to be discussed, especially individual conferences. Implicit mini-lessons occur also during read-aloud time, whenever the teacher demonstrates a reading strategy or invites children to speculate on what might happen next, using the text and/or pictures.

TEACHING READING STRATEGIES AND SKILLS, INCLUDING PHONICS AND DECODING Throughout various aspects of reading workshop, the teacher helps children use effective strategies such as thinking ahead and monitoring comprehension, which make use of various skills, including—but not limited to—phonological and phonemic awareness, phonics, and decoding. The teacher also promotes the development of fluency, especially by providing for and encouraging repeated rereadings of familiar texts the children enjoy (see Chapter 10). These are such important topics, though, that they will be handled separately, in Chapter 14. Meanwhile, suffice it to say that strategies and skills are often taught through mini-lessons, during various aspects of reading workshop, and within whole-class, small-group, and individual settings.

INDIVIDUAL CONFERENCES ON READING It's important for teachers to structure their literacy program so as to have time to confer with students individually about their reading. Various things can be done and discussed during individual conferences, but here are some of the most important:

- Invite the student to tell about what he or she is currently reading. This might involve the reader in summarizing the story, up to this point; telling the best parts and/or what's happening now, at this point in the reading; discussing connections the reader is making between this book and others, or with his or her own life; showing where the reading was easy for the reader and/or where the reading was difficult; and describing what kinds of problems the reader feels he or she is having with the text.

- Have the student read aloud a section of the book he or she is currently reading. The teacher can just listen; intervene to help with strategies; do a running record of the student's reading (see Chapter 6); tape-record the reading for later miscue analysis and perhaps Retrospective Miscue Analysis; and more. In Retrospective Miscue Analysis, the reader is recorded while reading aloud, after which the teacher and student discuss the reader's strategies and may work on needed strategies, using the text previously read. See Chapter 9 for more details and variations.

- Read and discuss the student's reading journal or "literature log" for the reading that has recently been done. (Teachers generally use one term or the other, but a reading journal and a literature log aren't necessarily different with regard to what they include.)

- Teach strategies that will help with problem words, monitoring comprehension, reading to draw inferences and develop understanding rather than just to read words, and so forth, as needed. Such teaching might include the use of Retrospective Miscue Analysis (see Chapter 9).

- Interview the student about himself or herself as a reader. Teacher and student can focus on what topics, books, authors, and illustrators the reader likes; what strategies the reader is aware of using; how the reader feels about himself or herself as a reader, and why; what the reader thinks his or her reading problems are, if any; and, in short, anything that needs to be dealt with. See Chapter 8 for some reader interview questions.

- Assess the student's progress as a reader. The teacher can record data generated by the other kinds of activities mentioned as potentially part of a reading conference, then use this data for assessment—either on the spot, or in later reflection. The teacher draws upon this assessment to plan appropriate teaching and learning experiences for the reader.

Obviously teachers don't have time to do all of these things in a single conference with a student. In fact, a conference may occur in just one to three minutes as the teacher offers individual assistance during guided reading or moves around to help during sustained reading time. However, it is also important to schedule longer conferences with students, conferences that are about ten minutes long or more. Students should be invited to request a conference as needed, and of course the teacher will request a conference with the student to address an observed need. It is important also to schedule regular conferences about once a week with *all* students, not just those who are obviously in need.

LITERATURE GROUPS Literature discussion or study groups are sometimes called *literature circles,* perhaps to emphasize the fact that they involve conversations about a book, not direct teaching except at the point of need. The teacher participates as a discussant, not as a dispenser of information (except as needed in the course of the conversation), nor as an inquisitor, which teachers have traditionally been by asking students questions about literal recall and other matters. Both students and the teacher may ask questions, but these should be genuine questions, ones to which there is no clear answer, or ones which otherwise invite personal response. For example: "I really wonder what's going to happen to *X* in the next chapter. What do you think?" Often such questions are preceded by a statement expressing the speaker's own curiosity or uncertainty: "I thought *X* was smart in doing *Y*, but I wonder whether you had the same reaction. *Was* she smart, or do you think she should have done something else?"

It is very important to set the stage for literature discussion groups in the early weeks of the school year. Literature discussions will proceed best if students have already developed the habit of sustained reading, and if teachers have already helped the students develop effective skills for small-group discussions (K. Smith, 1995). Developing such skills is part of developing a caring classroom community in general (R. Peterson, 1992). For small literature groups to be effective, it is also important to have held whole-class literature discussions during which the teacher models and demonstrates how to discuss literature, and guides students in discussing a work of literature productively.

Once the students are able to conduct literature study groups themselves, perhaps prompted in part by questions from the teacher and/or from a group leader for the day, the groups can proceed without teacher direction. However, many teachers prefer to participate in these discussions, partly to continue modeling and clarifying what a literature group should be, partly to see that the students respond to each other appropriately, and partly because they have a lot of information and understanding to share, in the ebb and flow of conversation, that may help readers with less background knowledge. In this way, teachers take advantage of the teachable moment. Later, the teacher may want to focus discussion sessions on key literary elements (character, symbol, foreshadowing, etc.), but only after the group has held at least one session during which the members mainly share their personal responses to the book. It is crucial that the teacher participate as discussant, not as inquisitor—even when discussing how key literary elements operate in the story (e.g., R. Peterson & Eeds, 1990). It's also crucial that the teacher treat the students with the same respect, and in the same conversational tone, as he or she would address adult friends. This encourages students to treat each other respectfully, too.

Logistically, teachers need to have available, in the classroom, several copies of each book intended for literature study. Often these are simply "good books," ones that are rich enough to invite sustained discussion. Sometimes, though, books are chosen to reflect a curricular theme, such as the American Revolution or the Civil War, protecting the environment or understanding the effects of recent technology. Books by the same author or illustrator are yet another possibility. The teacher gives a book talk on each option, being sure to read a short part of the text aloud, and inviting readers to discuss whether the book sounds "too easy," "too difficult," or "just right" for them. Often, children will want to read a book that is too difficult, perhaps just because it sounds interesting, or perhaps because some of their friends are choosing it. In that case, the less capable readers in the group can be supported by reading with a more capable partner; by a tape recording of the text; by discussion during sustained reading that precedes literature study discussions; and/or by the teacher.

There are various ways of organizing groups for literature study, but usually the teacher tries to give students their first or second choice, even if they need additional support, as just mentioned. One way to do this is to have each student write down his or her first three choices. The teacher can then take these requests home to determine the groups. The students who don't get their first choice can be assured that they will have their first choice next time.

One way to prepare for literature discussion groups is to have the group read the entire book first, during sustained reading. That way, the students can help each other read and begin discussing the book, listen to the book on tape as they follow along, and use whatever other supports might be needed. During this time they may be asked to keep a journal or literature log on the book. A *journal* usually includes just personal responses (perhaps drawings as well as writing), while a *literature log* may include a record of the student's ongoing reading, personal responses, and perhaps other items specified by the teacher. For example, some teachers might want students to keep a running list of pages where they had particular problems; a list of words that were particularly problematic, along with the page number and location where the word was encountered; and/or perhaps a list of pages where there is something they would like to discuss later, in literature study groups—of course with some indication also of what it is they want to discuss. The teacher may even prepare pages with headings of this sort, to facilitate the students' record-keeping.

Figure 12.4 offers a visual representation of how sustained reading time may be used to prepare for literature study groups. It also suggests that the teacher, especially a teacher who is just beginning literature study groups, can organize the activity so that he or she is dealing with only one literature study group in a given week.

A group's first literature study session will be devoted primarily to personal responses, as a prelude to literary study—and this sharing of responses frequently engages students in clarifying meanings, often by reference to the specific page(s) that have led to different understandings, and sometimes by the teacher supplying background information that the students lack. This is the beginning of collaborative meaning making. Frequently, students and the teacher find themselves making connections during this first session: connections with their lives, and connections to other books, authors, even illustrators. Usually the teacher and students together determine the topic for the next day, one day at a time, as they begin deeper exploration of the text and its literary elements, such as plot, character and character development, and vivid or figurative language—whatever emerges as most appropriate to the book they are discussing. There is no need to cover everything! Indeed, this would likely have the effect of ruining the book for the students.

Though the focus of literature discussion groups is naturally upon the book as literature, these groups offer a good opportunity to clarify understanding, to share problems encountered with the text, and even to discuss strategies for dealing with problem words.

"Must-Read" Articles—and a Short Book

Egawa, K. 1990. "Harnessing the Power of Language: First Graders' Literature Engagement with *Owl Moon*." *Language Arts* 67; 582–588. Reprinted in C. Weaver, ed., *Practicing What We Know: Informed Reading Instruction*, 329–339. Urbana, IL: National Council of Teachers of English, 1998.

Peterson, R., & Eeds, M. 1990. *Grand Conversations: Literature Groups in Action.* Richmond Hill, Ontario, Canada: Scholastic-Tab.

Smith, K. 1995. "Bringing Children and Literature Together in the Elementary Classroom." *Primary Voices K–6*, 3 (2): 22–32. Reprinted in C. Weaver, ed., *Practicing What We Know: Informed Reading Instruction,* 340–351. Urbana, IL: National Council of Teachers of English, 1998.

INQUIRY, OR READING TO LEARN Read-aloud, shared reading, guided reading, and sustained reading are all opportunities to pursue an individual, group, or class inquiry. Readers may read just to learn whatever there is to learn about a topic, given the resources available to them. Often, though, after doing some initial background reading, learners formulate questions they would like to find answered through their reading. Various materials may be used as resources: books, newspaper articles, magazines, encyclopedias, the Internet, CD-Roms, maps, videos, interviews, and more. The teacher or students may gather these materials together as a "text set." During a class or group inquiry, different students may be responsible for reading, taking notes on, and sharing certain materials in the text set. Such reading may lead to other kinds of writing and/or projects, but it can also be undertaken just for the pleasure of learning (Rogovin, 2001).

OPPORTUNITIES FOR RESPONSE Response to reading may take many forms. Students may respond through discussion with a classmate or the teacher; by writing journal or literature log entries; by writing letters to classmates or the teacher; through group or whole-class discussion; through

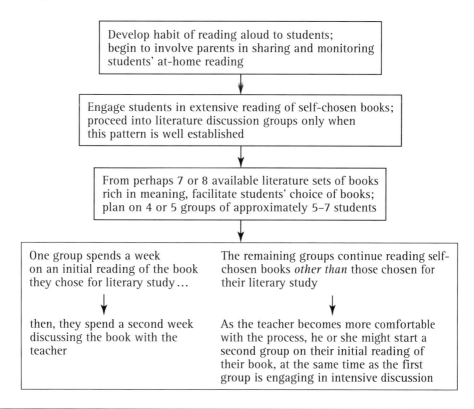

Figure 12.4 *Implementing literature discussion groups (based on R. Peterson & Eeds, 1990).*

choral reading, readers theatre, drama, storytelling, or some other form of the language arts; or through drawing or other art, music, or drama. The possibilities for students sharing what they have read are virtually endless. However, I firmly believe that children should not be made to do some kind of journal entry, report, or project for everything they read. After reading a book, I usually prefer just to read another, and I think students should have the same option. We teachers don't want to give students the idea that they read books just to "do something with them."

That said, here are brief descriptions of choral reading and readers theater, two oral language activities that reinforce reading. For *choral reading,* different parts of a reading selection are assigned to different groups or individuals, who practice their parts; then, the selection is rehearsed and read in its entirety, as a performance. This gives reluctant and struggling readers the opportunity to become fluent with their parts before performing for someone else. *Readers theater* likewise offers the opportunity for readers to practice before performing orally. In readers theater, the script is written like a play, but the children read their parts with expression (and possibly gestures) instead of memorizing their lines and acting them out. The readers sit on a stool and rest their text on a musician's stand, if possible, though in the classroom other arrangements may have to suffice. Both choral reading and readers theater offer students an authentic reason for reading aloud, unlike the daily "round-robin" reading that has characterized so many of our classrooms. The authentic occasion and the opportunity to practice can help reluctant oral readers become enthusiastic readers, since they aren't put on the spot to read unrehearsed text.

Other opportunities for response might be considered *special projects.* For brevity, I shall use that term in charts and sample schedules within this chapter.

Assessment

Ongoing assessment is an integral part of the reading workshop. Here are some important questions we might want to ask about each student's reading progress. These questions are adapted from Weaver, Gillmeister-Krause, & Vento-Zogby 1996, T8.6.

- To what extent does the reader show an *interest* in books?
- To what extent does the reader read for *meaning* and make meaning from suitable texts?
- To what extent does the reader use effective *strategies,* such as predicting (thinking ahead), monitoring comprehension, and various ways to "fix it" when meaning and/or grammar has gone awry?
- To what extent does the reader use meaning and context to deal with problem words, along with letter cues and letter-sound knowledge and meaningful word parts? We may call this employing *word-level skills* in context.
- To what extent does the reader participate in *conversations* about books?
- To what extent does the reader make *connections* among books, authors, and illustrators, and/or between books and real life?
- To what extent does the reader *choose* reading, over other possible activities? (reading as *choice*)
- To what extent does the reader demonstrate interest in an expanded range of *genres*?
- To what extent can the reader describe and assess his or her own *strengths* and *problems or needs* as a reader?
- To what extent can the reader set *goals* for himself or herself as a reader, and work to attain them?

To record the data for responding to such evaluative questions, teachers can create record sheets having a continuum or grid, with markings like "usually," "often," "seldom," and "not yet." While "never" may seem to be the obvious choice for the lowest category, I suggest "not yet" because it's like viewing the glass as potentially full, rather than empty.

A Note on Fluency

You may have noticed that *fluency* is not included in the list of questions above, even though fluency is much talked about these days. There is a reason for this omission—namely, that fluency is often being made a gatekeeper. That is, children are prevented from reading interesting texts, including many patterned texts that are ideal for emergent readers, until they can read many simple words fluently, in nearly meaningless texts. This occurs because some people believe—and publishers have been glad to accommodate this belief—that children must recognize and decode real words and nonsense words fluently before being introduced to more interesting texts. Research clearly demonstrates that this is not true (see Chapters 11 and 13), that in fact children can learn to read short patterned and natural texts, and from rereading these texts, children develop word knowledge and "decoding" skills (e.g., Moustafa, 1997). Other research demonstrates just as clearly that fluency is not necessary for comprehension (Flurkey, 1997; Y. Goodman & Marek, 1996). Furthermore, Flurkey's study suggests that even proficient readers may not read aloud fluently, when reading to comprehend. So, although fluency is indeed a desirable goal when performing for an audience by reading aloud, fluency has been omitted from this list because of the misconception that fluency must be developed *first* and that it is *necessary* for comprehension. Nevertheless, Chapter 10 includes a few suggestions for promoting fluency (see p. 249), and there is an entire chapter on that topic in Allington (2001).

GATHERING AND RECORDING DATA You may be asking yourself, "How and when will I get the data to be able to make such decisions? And how will I record the data?"

Teachers use various means for recording data, especially forms they have devised or borrowed, lists they ask students to make (e.g., an ongoing list of books read), and perhaps notebooks or notebook sections. The trickiest part is recording anecdotal observations made "on the run"—during read-aloud, shared reading experience time, guided reading, and so forth. Here's an overall solution I use, borrowed mostly from other teachers. I keep a loose-leaf notebook for each class, with a divider and section for each student. Anything can be included in that section. With my college students, I begin each section with a summary sheet that has a place for commenting on every project we do, generalizing about the student's work on quizzes and in-class participation, noting attendance, and so forth. There is plenty of room for copying the final comments I've written on each major piece of work. To make daily observations or make notes on papers or projects when I don't want to bother yet with the notebook, I prepare sheets of mailing labels, with each student's name on a label. Since I usually use a sheet with thirty labels, I can ordinarily include all the class on one sheet of labels. To use this for in-class anecdotal notes, I simply put a sheet of labels on a clipboard. I do the same for on-airplane responses to papers, too!

Now for the kinds of data you might want to record. To simplify, I'll make suggestions under the previous headings for aspects of a reading workshop (see also Figure 12.5). But of course this list does not include all the possibilities.

READ-ALOUD During read-aloud and the accompanying discussions, teachers might assess

- Readers' ability to construct meaning (through listening and discussion)
- Readers' interest in books (including particular topics or particular genres, such as picture books, humor, poetry, mystery, historical fiction, autobiography, or biography)
- Readers' willingness and ability to participate in conversations about books
- Readers' inclination to make connections with the book read

	Interest	Meaning	Strategies	Word-level skills, used in context	Conversations	Connections	Choice	Genres	Strengths; problems and needs*	Student goal setting
Read-aloud	✓	by listening ✓			✓	✓		✓	✓	
Shared reading	✓	✓	✓	✓	✓	✓		✓	✓	
Guided reading	✓	✓	✓	✓	✓	✓		✓	✓	
Sustained reading	✓	✓	✓	✓	✓	✓		✓	✓	
Individual reading	✓	✓	✓	✓	✓	✓	✓	✓	✓	✓
Literature reading	✓	✓	✓		✓	✓	✓	✓	✓	
Inquiry reading	✓	✓	✓	✓				✓	✓	

*This applies to either teacher assessment or student assessment of strengths, problems, and/or needs.

Figure 12.5   Topics derived from questions about a reader's progress, correlated with aspects of reading workshop that offer assessment opportunities.

- Readers' demonstration of interest in an expanding range of genres
- Selected aspects of readers' strengths, problems, and needs as readers

SHARED READING Teachers can assess all of the factors that can be noted and assessed during read-aloud, plus the development and use of various strategies and skills, such as

- Predicting story from pictures and text
- Identifying high-interest and common words
- Using prior context, pattern, pictures, rhyme (as relevant) to predict an upcoming word
- Using letter-sound knowledge along with other cues to identify words (also, teachers can make a note of readers who overuse letter-sound knowledge without also using meaning and other cues)
- Using meaning and grammar to cue correction (or attempted correction) of miscues that don't fit with what comes after them

GUIDED READING Any or all of the above.

SUSTAINED READING Any of the above that might be noted as the teacher stops to listen to or talk with a student during sustained reading. In addition, sustained reading gives the teacher a good opportunity to discover what children *choose* to read.

INDIVIDUAL CONFERENCES Depending on what occurs in the specific conference, an individual conference may offer the opportunity to observe, discuss, and record any of the factors listed under shared reading. However, the individual conference is especially useful for gathering data as follows:

- Having the reader read and retell/discuss a selection, with the teacher either doing a running record or tape-recording the reading for later analysis of the miscue patterns and retelling/discussion. These procedures will provide opportunities to observe and assess strategies, word-level skills, reading for meaning, recall, and understanding (through inference, synthesis, analysis, and critical thinking).
- Interviewing/talking with the reader—that is, discussing with the reader such things as
  - The kinds of books the reader likes (topic, format, genre, favorite authors)
  - To what extent the reader reads for meaning and makes meaning from suitable texts
  - To what extent the reader participates in conversations about books
  - To what extent the reader can describe his or her own strengths and problems or needs as a reader
  - To what extent the reader can set goals for himself or herself as a reader, and work to attain them
- Examining and discussing the reader's reading journal or literature log, plus the reader's own record sheets, in order to investigate
  - the kinds of books the reader likes (topic, format, genre, favorite authors); check the reader's ongoing list of books read and attempted
  - to what extent the reader reads for meaning and makes meaning from suitable texts
  - to what extent the reader makes connections among books, authors, and illustrators, and/or between books and real life
  - to what extent the reader enjoys discussing or "having conversations" about books (in this case, through writing)

- how much the reader reads (check record of books read, journal entries)
- how the reader deals with problem words (check journal, if notes on word/vocabulary problems have been required or requested)

LITERATURE GROUPS Of course, these are especially valuable for determining such things as

- To what extent the reader reads for meaning and makes meaning from suitable texts
- To what extent the reader makes connections among books, authors, and illustrators, and/or between books and real life
- To what extent the reader enjoys discussing or "having conversations" about books

In addition, the teacher has the opportunity to observe and record *how* the reader makes meaning; how well the reader understands the plot, characters, and character development in the book being discussed; how well the reader understands figurative language and other literary devices; and more. (See Figure 12.5.)

INQUIRY, OR READING TO LEARN While students are engaged in inquiry and reading to learn, the teacher can observe and record how and how effectively the students scan and skim texts to find the information wanted. It's especially important for teachers to guide students in developing such skills and other skills for dealing with informational texts. Assessment logically follows, in order to determine the need for further teaching. See Figure 12.5 for some other categories of questions for which assessment data can be gathered during inquiry reading.

Writing Workshops

The following components of writing workshop will be discussed: write-aloud, shared (interactive) writing and interactive pen; guided writing; sustained writing; mini-lessons, individual conferences; journals, inquiry, or writing to learn; opportunities for response.

WRITE-ALOUD Just as by reading aloud, the teacher demonstrates good oral reading and effective reading strategies, so by writing aloud, the teacher can demonstrate various aspects of how he or she writes. The piece of writing is the teacher's own, not something being composed by the class together (compare with shared writing, below). Using chart paper, the overhead projector, or the chalkboard, the teacher writes aloud, talking his or her way through certain writing decisions. Teachers may demonstrate writing a first draft, and even solicit ideas from the students to compose their first draft, perhaps by creating a brainstorming list or web of ideas with the students' help. After the first draft is written, further attention can be given to word choice; format and organization; the adding, omitting, or rearranging of detail; and so forth. That is, the teacher demonstrates how to revise. The teacher may also demonstrate how he or she edits for spelling, punctuation, and grammar. Of course students may be invited to help with this, too, as appropriate. Obviously the specific processes demonstrated by the teacher will depend upon the students' readiness to deal with these processes in their own writing.

One of the first things teachers of primary students might do to foster skills is simply emphasize the initial consonant sounds of key words as they write, in order to demonstrate sound-letter correspondences. Alternatively, teachers may invite the children to help with the spelling, by helping sound out part or all of a word, or offering the spelling of a common word that they can spell. Soliciting the students' help, whether with brainstorming, drafting, revising, or editing, is quite common in write-aloud, even though the writing is the teacher's own, and not a class or group composition. Helping the teacher write engages students' interest and helps them learn.

SHARED WRITING In shared writing, sometimes called *guided writing,* the teacher and students compose together. "Compose" in this case can include brainstorming, drafting, revising, and editing—whatever is appropriate for that class or group of students. Shared writing can be done with one student and one co-writer, too—the teacher, another adult, an older student, or a classmate.

Whole-class shared writing often takes the form of a morning message, a note home to parents, a request of the principal or staff, an article for the class newspaper, a chart of "what we know" and "what we want to know" about a topic, a list of information gleaned from a text, or something else that invites whole-class ownership. However, sometimes the class and the teacher may compose a song, poem, or short story together. In the primary grades, class composition of a predictable story is especially popular. Many Big Books have predictable patterns that children love to imitate. The children may, for example, choose to imitate the pattern of a familiar story, song, or poem. The story in Figure 12.6 was composed in June by Anick Leclerc and Lorraine Gillmeister-Krause's class of first graders, 98% of whom did not speak English when they entered the first grade at the end of August that school year. Their story was based on the well-known story of the gingerbread man.

"Sebastian the Unicorn": The Story Behind the Story

As an extended class project, first-grade teachers Anick Leclerc and Lorraine Gillmeister-Krause decided to work from the classic "gingerbread man" story to guide their children in writing their own story, which turned out to be "Sebastian the Unicorn." First they read three versions of *The Gingerbread Man* to the children, to help them learn the story structure and the repetitive pattern. The next step in the project was to make and bake gingerbread man cookies. They also made templates for the sides and roof of a gingerbread house, drawing upon the measurements from a house Anick had made from construction paper. The teachers postponed having the children write their own patterned story based on *The Gingerbread Man* until near the end of the school year, since 98% of the children had started the school year not speaking English. (Their native language is French.) The children brainstormed for animals that might become characters in the story: a unicorn, a wolf, a cheetah, an elephant, a hippopotamus, a bull, an eagle, a koala bear, a black dog, and a white-tailed deer. Then they voted to choose the main character by writing their individual choice on a piece of paper and putting their paper on a graph under the appropriate heading. Of course there just *had* to be a tie vote, so the children voted again on another piece of chart paper, to break the tie between the unicorn and the white-tailed deer. The unicorn won and was named "Sebastian"—pronounced "Sebaschan," the children said, to rhyme with "man." (Besides, this is close to the name's pronunciation in the children's native French: "Sebas-ti-an.")

Sometimes shared writing is called *interactive writing.* The term *interactive pen* generally refers to something more specific, namely to when the teacher guides a student in writing letters for the sounds he or she hears in a word, then takes the pen or other writing instrument and fills in silent letters. See Chapters 13 and 14 on writing as a means of teaching and learning phonics.

GUIDED WRITING In addition to being another name for shared writing, guided writing is a term for teacher-planned groups (theoretically, of any size) that are based on the teacher's observation of common needs among certain writers. Members of the group are working on their own individual pieces, usually, though a joint piece is also possible. The teacher typically offers a mini-lesson at the beginning of the guided writing session, then guides individual students as needed in applying the concept or skill. Such mini-lessons may take various forms, depending upon the need: spelling "as best you can" in a first draft; trying out three spellings to see which one looks most likely; spelling certain common words or using a common spelling pattern (such as the *-ed*) for past tense; using a particular mark of punctuation; organizing and reorganizing;

Sebastian the Unicorn

Once upon a time there was a unicorn. His name was Sebastian. He was inside a house. He was eating flowers that were growing on the floor. He went outside and ran. He met a wolf in the forest. The wolf was sleeping. Then a cheetah came and Sebastian ran away. Sebastian called,

Run run.
As fast as you can.
You can't catch me.
I'm the unicorn Sebastian.

Sebastian went to the jungle A dinosaur was in the jungle and he was going to eat the unicorn. Sebastian called,

Run run.
As fast as you can.
You can't catch me.
I'm the unicorn Sebastian.

Sebastian didn't get eaten by the dinosaur.

Sebastian was going home and he saw a bull playing in the park. He was playing with other bulls and they said that Sebastian could not play with them. Then they catched him. Sebastian called,

Run run.
As fast as you can.
You can't catch me.
I'm the unicorn Sebastian.

He ran by a pond in the park and saw a hippopotamus splashing himself. The hippopotamus said, "Come a little closer," but Sebastian did not. The hippopotamus splashed him and Sebastian called,

Run run.
As fast as you can.
You can't catch me.
I'm the unicorn Sebastian.

Sebastian saw an elephant going for a walk. He invited him home and said, "Come eat flowers with me." They ate lots of flowers and then they went out of the house. They met an eagle but the eagle was nice so Sebastian made a new friend and he made lots of other friends like the koala bear and the black dog and the white-tailed deer and he lived happily ever after.

—First graders, Gault Institute
June 20, 2001

Figure 12.6 *Story by Anick Leclerc and Lorraine Gillmeister-Krause's first graders.*

adding, omitting, or rearranging detail; writing an opening lead to a piece; rewriting a piece in a different genre, or to add voice to it; editing for certain things; and more.

SUSTAINED WRITING Often this is called *independent writing,* but as with reading, sustained writing might involve not just individual writing, but writing in pairs and trios. Similarly, we might call it *choice writing,* except that sometimes the teacher may determine or narrow the range of topics, specify the audience and/or the genre, and so forth. In other words, sustained writing will often be free-choice writing, but not always. Sustained writing occurs during guided writing, too, after a mini-lesson and while the students are then working on their own pieces of writing. Whether during a guided writing session or not, the teacher can always intervene to hold a mini-conference and/or offer a mini-lesson (see below).

MINI-LESSONS Mini-lessons are discussed in the previous section on guided writing. However, spontaneous mini-lessons may also occur during write-aloud, shared writing, inquiry reading and writing, and—of course—individual conferences (Hoyt, 2000).

INDIVIDUAL CONFERENCES Individual conferences are an important part of the writing workshop. For example, the teacher may hold an instant mini-conference during sustained writing time, stopping to ask "How's it going?" or "Is there a part you really want to share with me?" or "Is there anything you need help with?" The teacher may be able to respond adequately during this brief, spontaneous conference, or the instant conference may lead to the teacher's scheduling a longer conference with the student. Other mini-conferences and mini-lessons occur during guided writing, as explained above. It is important to teach writing strategies and skills during guided writing and individual conferences, even when the writer doesn't seem especially needy; we can simply teach something more advanced that the writer(s) could benefit from. As with reading, teaching skills in context makes them more meaningful and more likely to be used.

Frequent writing conferences should be scheduled with all students, so that the teacher can support, record, and celebrate their progress. Of course it's important for students to be able to request a writing conference, too.

JOURNALS Journals can be used for many purposes in a classroom—and indeed, some teachers have students keep several journals, for different purposes. For instance, a journal might be used for recording responses to books read; to write about personal experiences and jot down ideas for more polished pieces of writing; to work and reflect on math problems; to take notes for an inquiry project (see below); and, for science experiments, to make hypotheses, record ongoing data and results, and reflect on the hypotheses in light of the results.

INQUIRY, OR WRITING TO LEARN Writing to learn occurs when students write in reading journals or "literature logs," since writing is a way of coming to know, to understand. However, writing to learn occurs most obviously in the content areas and in conjunction with inquiry through reading. Again, journal entries may be useful. But students also need help learning to take notes in efficient ways, so that the notes will be useful later. Note taking can take many forms, such as outlines and related formats, webs, charts, time lines, index cards, and more.

OPPORTUNITIES FOR RESPONSE Writing itself is, of course, an important response to reading. But students—and teachers—need human response, too, as writers. Often, teachers provide for what is called *author's chair.* The student author sits in a special chair, if possible, and reads his or her piece of writing to a group, or to the whole class, and the listeners respond. There are several variants on this procedure. Someone may read a piece that's in progress and ask for help. In this case, the writer/reader may ask questions of the audience, and the audience may be invited to ask questions of the writer/reader. (Often, suggestions couched as questions are less threatening and therefore more helpful.) Sometimes the writer might ask a classmate to read the piece aloud, so that the writer too can hear how it sounds and learn from that experience. If the writer is reading a final draft to be celebrated, obviously the teacher will make sure the listeners offer only positive responses (Harwayne, 2001).

ASSESSMENT Since this book deals mostly with reading, and since there are many fine books on writing that include assessment of writing, that topic will not be dealt with here. See, however, Catherine Compton-Lilly's annotated bibliography section "Teaching Reading and Writing in the Elementary School," on the web page accompanying this book ⟨*http://www.heinemann .com/weaver*⟩. There are many other fine books on teaching writing, as well.

How Might We Organize a Classroom Literacy Program?

This section includes charts with suggestions—that is, possibilities—for a sixty-minute reading workshop, a seventy-five- to ninety-minute reading workshop, and then two combination reading and writing workshops. Even the two-hour reading and writing workshop does not include all of the components suggested above, especially for writing. The plans included here are possibilities only; individual teachers will surely want to modify any they might choose as a starting point.

Comments on the Sample Schedules

These sample schedules (Figures 12.7 through 12.10) can be conceptualized as time lines, with the component on the left occurring first, and others following as the chart moves toward the right.

In most of the samples, it is assumed that read-aloud will be held at some other time in the day, rather than as a part of reading workshop. Teachers often choose to read aloud to children after lunch, or after recess, as it typically helps the children settle down and then refocus on academics.

Sustained reading can include the reading options under "choices," too: read alone, read with a partner, or listen to a book on tape and follow along in the book. Also, during sustained reading, the students may read the book they are soon to discuss in literature groups.

Of course it is desirable for all members of the class to engage in sustained reading during sustained reading time, but logistically this is not always possible. Thus, during sustained reading

Shared reading	Sustained reading	Choices
	Read alone	Read alone
	Read with a partner	Read with a partner
	Listen to book on tape and follow in the book	Listen to book on tape and follow in the book
		Write response in journal about what's being read
	Guided reading 2 or 3 days a week	
		Literature groups
	Individual conferences 2 or 3 days a week	

Note: Read-aloud time can be held after lunch or recess.

Figure 12.7 *Reading workshop, 60 minutes.*

Read-aloud	Shared reading	Sustained reading	Choices
		Read alone	Read alone
		Read with partner	Read with partner
		Listen to book on tape	Listen to book on tape
		and follow in the book	and follow in the book
			Read with an adult
		Guided reading	Have a conference*
		2 or 3 days a week	
			Do a special project
		Individual conferences	Write in response to
		2 or 3 days a week	book**
			Choral reading or
			readers theater

Read-aloud time can also be held after lunch or recess.
*The student initiates the conference.
**This might include writing in a journal or literature log, a letter in response to the main character, a story that imitates the pattern or structure of a book, and so forth.

Figure 12.8   *Reading workshop, 75–90 minutes.*

time, the teacher may work with one or more small guided reading groups, or hold individual conferences with a few students. Some teachers hold individual conferences three times a week at the beginning of the year and guided reading only twice, because they need the individual conference time to get to know the students and their strengths and needs as readers. Later in the year, teachers may switch to holding guided reading three days a week and individual

Shared reading	Sustained reading	Sustained writing	Choices
	Read alone	Write alone	Read/write alone
	Read with partner	Write with partner(s)	Read/write with partner
	Listen to book on tape	Read to get ideas for	Listen to book on tape
	and follow in the book	writing	and follow in the book
			Read/write with adult
	Guided reading	Shared writing	Have a conference*
			Do a special project
	Individual conferences	Individual conferences	Write in response to
			book**
	Literature groups		Choral reading or
			readers theater

Read-aloud time can be held after lunch or recess.
*The student initiates the conference.
**This might include writing in a journal or literature log, a letter in response to the main character, a story that imitates the pattern or structure of a book, and so forth.

Figure 12.9   *Reading and writing workshop, 90 minutes.*

Shared reading	Sustained reading	Sustained writing	Choices	Inquiry reading, writing, discussion
	Read alone Read with partner Listen to book on tape and follow in the book	Write alone Write with partner(s) Read to get ideas for writing	Read/write alone Read/write with partner Listen to book on tape and follow in the book Read/write with adult	Can involve various genres
	Guided reading	Shared writing	Have a conference* Do a special project	
	Individual conferences	Individual conferences	Write in response to book**	
	Literature groups		Choral reading or readers theater	

Read-aloud time can be held after lunch or recess.
*The student initiates the conference.
**This might include writing in a journal or literature log, a letter in response to the main character, a story that imitates the pattern or structure of a book, and so forth.

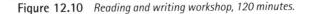

Figure 12.10 *Reading and writing workshop, 120 minutes.*

conferences only two days a week (e.g., Chomsky-Higgins, 1998). Of course the components of guided reading, individual conferences, and literature discussion groups could be scheduled somewhat differently, under the time periods for sustained reading and choices.

In these sample time lines, column headings and other boldfaced items are key components of reading and writing workshop. As previously explained, teacher assessment can occur during any of these components, but especially during shared reading, guided reading, individual conferences, and literature groups, as well as during the similar components in writing workshop.

Writing in response to a book might include an entry in a journal or literature log, a letter in response, a story that imitates the pattern or structure of the book, and so forth. "Do a special project" is my shorthand for the many opportunities for response that the text or the teacher, may offer, or the students may think of.

The preceding and current pages include four possible time frames for reading workshop or a comprehensive literacy program of one to two hours (Figures 12.7 through 12.10). These are followed by a fifth, Figure 12.11 (pp. 301–302) showing how literacy experiences, activities, and teaching can occur throughout an entire school day. This "Literacy Workshop Across the Day" is from Five and Egawa (1998, p. 8).

Of course there are many ways to structure a comprehensive literature program. What's most important, though, is for schools and teachers to provide ample reading opportunities and instruction, in order to enable students to become not only functionally literate in sophisticated contexts and complex ways, but joyfully literate for their own purposes and needs. Children may not have a legal right to instruction that enables them to become broadly and fully literate. However, they have an educational right to schools and teachers that will offer them a comprehensive literacy program that makes such literacy possible.

LEARNING LANGUAGE				
ENGAGEMENT	PURPOSE	POSSIBLE STRATEGIES	ORGANIZING DEVICES	MATERIALS
Read-aloud	To create classroom community To build a shared repertoire of stories, poems, chants, and songs To build a sense of story, as well as of other genres	predicting/think-aloud	list of books read/ anthology of favorite poems	Best-loved and classic stories, poems, songs; award-winning texts, recognized authors
Shared reading interactive writing	To demonstrate literacy processes; to engage all students' participation at current level of ability	partner-reading/ readers theater		Big books, chart writing or poems, texts on overhead; personal copies of text
Independent reading and writing	To read texts independently To select, browse, and read texts of interest To capture ideas; to contribute to thinking		reading log/ writers' notebooks	texts of interest Books at "just right" level
LEARNING ABOUT LANGUAGE				
Strategy instruction Demonstrations Focused lessons Mini-lessons	To focus on the processes, elements, and strategies of reading, writing, spelling, punctuation, and workshop organization: "what to do when I'm stuck" strategies using reference texts/ phonemic awareness/ locating materials/genre characteristics/browsing/ literary elements/ workshop routines/ spelling patterns	Interactive writing/ newsboard/ author's chair/ conferences/ have-a-go spelling	"strategies I can use" sheets	Students' own writing: family stories, inquiry reports, poetry, articles; writing of peers, others' writing; predictable books, literature, poetry, everyday texts (media, newspaper, magazines, etc.)
LEARNING THROUGH LANGUAGE				
Literature study	To read and write stories as a way of helping making sense of life; texts that help readers understand more about themselves and interrogate their world To discuss texts with small groups of interested others To study the author's craft To inform, comment, critique, document	sketch-to-stretch, say something, drama, music, movement, art responses	reading journals "how our group is doing"	Multiple copies of books; stories of significance, often that contribute to broader class theme; text sets; sets of books by one author
Inquiry	To document what one knows; to discover additional information on topics of interest. Paired with literature study, contributing knowledge to a themed inquiry To gather information for projects To publish or present what was learned	browsing/note taking	graffiti boards/ webs/time lines/ inquiry journals	Text sets: a collection of related texts (books [varied ganres], CDs, maps, tapes, artifacts), which contribute multiple perspectives to learners' research

Figure 12.11   *Literacy workshop across the day.*

LEARNING TO CRITIQUE THROUGH LANGUAGE				
Social action projects	To use language to question what seems normal and natural To redesign and create alternate social worlds, through interrogation of the internet, media, advertisements, and other everyday texts.	questioning/ interrogating/ critical talk about books	Audit trail	Books that support critical conversation Everyday texts

M.A.K. Halliday (1980) found that in any meaningful language event, children have the opportunity to learn language, learn about language, and learn through language. They learn language through the "doing" of language—talking, listening, reading, and writing. They learn about language as they explore how language functions and the conventions that support communication. They learn through language as they focus on what it is they are learning. To this we've added learning to critique through language (Egawa & Harste, 2001). All four aspects are essential in every classroom. We don't start with one and progress to the next. Rather, it is the four operating together within a meaningful context that provides the most balanced and supportive learning environment for literacy learners.

Figure 12.11 (*Continued*).

READING	SKILLS/STRATEGIES	WRITING
Read-aloud	CONCEPTS OF PRINT • READING STRATEGIES	Write-aloud
Shared reading	SIGHT WORDS	Shared writing
Guided reading	PHONEMIC AWARENESS • PHONICS • DECODING • WORD ANALYSIS	Guided writing
Sustained reading	FLUENCY	Sustained writing
Individual reading conference	WRITING STRATEGIES	Individual writing conferences
Literature discussions	WRITING FLUENCY	Journals
Reading to learn (inquiry)	SPELLING	Writing to learn (inquiry)
Opportunities for response	WRITING CONVENTIONS	Opportunities for response

Figure 12.12   *Skills and strategies for reading and writing.*

FOR FURTHER EXPLORATION

1. Consider what else you might want to include in a comprehensive literacy program, in addition to what's discussed here. Discuss with others, if possible.

2. Consider how you might use reading and writing as part of inquiry in social studies, science, and math. Discuss with others, if possible.

3. First, consider what reading strategies may need to be taught, at least to some students. Then, on Figure 12.12, draw arrows from the skills and strategies listed in the middle column to the various components of reading and writing workshop wherein these skills or strategies can be fostered. After reading Chapter 14, expand upon this chart as needed. Discuss with others, if possible.

4. Locate additional resources on various components of reading workshop through the ERIC database system (Educational Resources Information Center), or via the Internet. The ERIC system can be accessed easily with this address: <*http://www.askEric.org/Eric*>. This address leads to several ERIC options, including the database.

5. Modify one or more of the sample workshop schedules in this chapter to suit you better, or create an entirely new one.

6. If you're already well informed about the teaching of writing, make a list of questions that you might want to ask about students' growth as writers. Then, if desired, make a grid for writing assessment that resembles the grid for reading assessment (Fig. 12.5, p. 292). The list for reading assessment, pp. 290–291, may give you some ideas.

7. Reconsider the questions at the beginning of this chapter, bringing to bear what you have learned and thought about since beginning the chapter.

13 Research on Learning and Teaching Phonics

> My overall conclusion from reviewing the randomized field studies is that systematic phonics falls into that vast category of weak instructional treatments with which education is perennially plagued.
> —Richard L. Turner

Questions for Thought and Discussion

1. In 1989, Turner reviewed the best of the classroom research studies on teaching phonics directly, in comparison with teaching phonics indirectly or not at all. Why do you think that phonics again became the focus of attention toward the end of the twentieth century and into the twenty-first?

2. Why do you think that teaching phonics not only directly but intensively and systematically has such appeal to many people, particularly those not well versed in a broad spectrum of research on reading, learning to read, and learning in general?

3. Why is the best instruction in "phonemic awareness" actually part of phonics instruction?

4. How does the teaching of phonics, which includes phonemic awareness, impact the learning of phonemic awareness and phonics skills? The ability to read pseudowords? To read real words?

5. How, in comparison, does the teaching of phonics affect reading comprehension "achievement" in first grade? Beyond first grade? What factors do you think account for the drop in effectiveness?

6. Overall, what does the detailed information in the National Reading Panel report suggest about the effects of teaching phonics, and phonemic awareness as a part of phonics?

7. Do you think that the effects on reading skills and temporarily on reading comprehension justify teaching phonics (including phonemic awareness) to preschoolers and/or kindergartners and first graders? If no, why not? If yes, how much time do you think should be spent on teaching phonics to students—and to which students?

8. What are some considerations, cautions, and reminders to keep in mind as teachers plan instruction in phonics, including phonemic awareness?

The opening quote comes from Richard Turner, an assessment expert who attempted to resolve a far-reaching debate between Jeanne Chall and Marie Carbo. Chall believed that research showed the superiority of teaching phonics systematically in the primary grades (1967/1983), but Marie Carbo (1988) demonstrated that much of the research Chall included as the basis for her conclusion had serious design flaws. Turner attempted to resolve the debate by eliminating from consideration all but the best-designed classroom research studies. His conclusion is worth quoting more fully:

> Systematic phonics appears to have a slight and early advantage over a basal-reader/whole-word approach [not the same as whole language] as a method of beginning reading instruction.... However, this difference does not last long and has no clear meaning for the acquisition of literacy in the sense of enhancing vocabulary and improving comprehension. (Turner, 1989, p. 283)

As we shall see, the research of the 1990s leads to much the same conclusion, when the research itself is examined and reported clearly and honestly. That is, phonics taught intensively and systematically to kindergartners and first graders has a moderate effect on tests of word analysis skills, but only a low-to-moderate effect on reading "comprehension scores," which are essentially measures of word identification themselves. Most important, none of these effects appears to last long.

> Phonics taught intensively and systematically to kindergartners and first graders has a moderate effect on tests of word analysis skills, but only a low-to-moderate effect on reading "comprehension scores," which are essentially measures of word identification themselves. Most important, none of these effects appears to last long.

In this chapter we discuss, more fully than in preceding chapters, some key terms like *phonics* and *phonemic awareness*. Next comes research on how children read and learn to read words that aren't immediately recognized on sight (for the moment, setting aside the helpful effects of context). A discussion of research on phonemic awareness follows, with emphasis on the relationships between phonemic awareness and learning to read. This is followed by attention to phonics research, which has already been discussed to some extent in Chapter 11. Since claims in the separately published summary of the National Reading Panel report on phonics (National Reading Panel, 2000a) differ substantially from the evidence actually presented in the detailed analysis (2000b), these discrepancies will be discussed in some detail as well. I will then summarize evidence and major conclusions, mostly from the NRP report. These are followed by considerations, cautions, and reminders with regard to teaching phonemic awareness and phonics more generally.

Clarifying Some Concepts and Terms

In the last few years of the twentieth century, we were hearing more and more about *phonological awareness, onsets* and *rimes,* and *phonemic awareness*—terms that need to be defined and illustrated before we can go very far in discussing either research or practice in helping children develop and use letter-sound knowledge in reading. Then we shall briefly define and discuss *phonics* and the phrase *phonics knowledge* as used henceforth in this book.

Phonological Awareness

Though the term *phonological awareness* is less often found in the professional journals written for classroom teachers, an understanding of the concept provides a basis for defining terms for increasingly smaller units, terms that are basic to today's discussions of phonemic awareness and phonics.

Put simply, *phonological awareness* means awareness of the sound units in a language. There are three kinds of sound units within words in English: (1) syllables; (2) onsets and rimes; and (3) phonemes. These units occur in a hierarchy:

The *syllable* is the largest sound unit within a word.

Onsets and *rimes* are the two parts of a syllable.

Phonemes are the basic parts of onsets and rimes.

Each of these will be discussed in turn, using the same words as examples. See also a list of definitions on pp. 308–309.

SYLLABLES In English, the largest sound unit within words is the syllable. We learned, probably in elementary school, that every syllable has one vowel sound, and that every separate vowel sound is the nucleus of a syllable (or the entire syllable). Many common words in English consist of just one syllable, so we will draw upon such words as examples of the syllable:

I	cake	drip
a	church	string
use	them	park

Each of these words consists of one and only one syllable.

ONSETS AND RIMES Again speaking in terms of sounds, not letters, every syllable has a rime, and many of our syllables have an onset as well. The syllables (one-syllable words) listed below are divided into onsets and rimes. See if you can figure out a good way to describe the rime in a syllable, and then a good way to describe the onset that may occur before it. I will use either words to describe, or slant lines to enclose, my attempts to represent sounds in everyday terms, with an occasional linguistic symbol that should become clear from your own pronunciation of the word.

Word		Onset	Rime
I		none	"long i" sound
a		none	"long a" or a schwa sound /ə/
use		/y/	"long u" + /z/
cake		/k/	"long a" + /k/
church	(a "ch" sound, not /c/ + /h/)	/tʃ/	"r-colored" vowel + /tʃ/
them	("th" sound with the vocal chords vibrating)	/ə/	"short e" + /m/
drip		/dr/	"short i" + /p/
string		/str/	"short i" plus "ng" sound, represented /ŋ/
park		/p/	"r-colored" vowel + /k/

It is probably obvious that the rime part of a syllable consists of the vowel, plus any consonants that may, optionally, come after it. In the examples, the words *I* and *a* have just the obligatory vowel. The onset part of a syllable consists of any consonants that may occur before the rime of the syllable. In the examples, the words *I* and *a* do not have an onset. Multisyllabic words will have one rime for every syllable, and the rime may be preceded by one or more consonants, constituting an onset to the syllable.

Again, it is important to notice that rime and onset have reference to sound units, not to letters. Thus the onset in one of the examples, *use*, does not have a separate consonant letter, though it begins with /y/, a consonant sound. The onset in two of the examples is spelled with one consonant letter (in *cake* and *park*); the onset in two others is spelled with two consonant letters that stand for one sound (in *church* and *them*); and other onsets are spelled with two or three consonant letters representing two or three consonant sounds (in *drip* and *string*).

PHONEMES AND PHONEMIC AWARENESS *Phonemes* are what we have *learned* to hear as separate sounds in the language. Thus *phonemic awareness*, simply defined, is the ability to hear separate phonemes in words, when the words are isolated from meaningful contexts.

This concept, however, is much more complex than one might think, and the task of separating words into phonemes is much more difficult to accomplish than many people might suppose.

For young primary-grade children, and even for adults, it can be difficult simply to separate out sounds from a word, without regard for special problems. In addition, there are indeed special problems with the task. For example, young children hear sounds differently than we adults have learned to perceive them. At some point, emergent readers and writers may hear /tr/ at the beginning of words as /tʃ/, the "ch" sound. This is actually a closer representation of what we say than the two separate phonemes /t/ + /r/. Thus emergent writers acquainted with "CH" as a way to write the /tʃ/ sound sometimes write "CHRAN" for *train*, "CHRE" for *tree*, "CHRAY" for *tray*, and "CHRIBLS" for *troubles*. Likewise, emergent readers and writers may hear /d + r/ as /dʒ/, a "j" sound. Thus they sometimes write "JR" for *dress*, "JRIV" for *drive*, and "JRGN" for *dragon*.

Another problem with hearing separate phonemes is that they aren't always separate! That is, a word isn't always naturally separable into the sounds that literate adults think have been put together to make the word. This situation is especially common when a single vowel letter (not signaling a long vowel) is followed by an *r* or an *l*. For example, do you yourself truly hear the vowel as separate from the /r/ or /l/ in *her* or *candle*? What about *church* and *park*?

It can be illuminating to have literate adults try to say the separate sounds of the words listed below, one sound at a time, without giving these adults time to think:

Word	Phonemes	
cake	k-a-k	
church	ch-u-r-ch	(the *ch* represents a single sound in each instance)
them	th-e-m	(the *th* represents a single sound)
drip	d-r-i-p	
string	s-t-r-i-η	
park	p-a-r-k	

Under such circumstances, even elementary teachers do not always divide all the words into "separate" sounds accurately, as young children are expected to do in phonemic awareness tasks.

Many educators point out that if children can distinguish between words in normal speech that are identical except for closely related phonemes, they certainly have "phonemic awareness," at least at an unconscious, functional level.

However, with the current but erroneous insistence that children must have phonemic awareness before they can learn to read, the ability to hear "separate" sounds has been assessed with isolated words. For example, the researcher—or teacher—may present a child with a single-syllable word that has an onset of one sound, and see if the child can separate the onset from the rime. For example, "I say *cake* and you say *-ake*. I say *sip* and you say *-ip*. Ready? I say *map* and you say—" And the child is expected to say *-ap*. This is one of the easiest phonemic awareness tasks. Other, more difficult measures of "phonemic awareness" are sometimes used in research studies, though normal listening, reading, and writing do not require such skills.

Making tests of "phonemic awareness" a gatekeeper for kindergarten or first grade is not only inappropriate but unjustifiable, especially since children do not need to be aware of separate phonemes before they begin learning to read.

But as we've noted, another fairly simple kind of task, dividing the word into "separate sounds," can cause literate—and even highly educated—adults to make errors. Phonemic segmentation is not a natural task, nor one normally needed for *reading*, beyond the ability to separate an onset from a rime. This fact is important to understand because in some schools, readiness for first grade—or kindergarten!—is being assessed in part by measures of phonemic awareness. Obviously this is an extreme instance of fitting children to the curriculum instead of the more appropriate alternative, fitting the curriculum to the children. Furthermore, the practice of holding back children who do not attain a preset score on a phonemic awareness test encourages schools to label children as failures before they get beyond or even *to* first grade.

Phonological awareness – Awareness of the sound units in a language.

Syllable – The largest sound unit within a word. By definition, a syllable contains a vowel sound as its nucleus. It may or may not have consonant sounds. Examples: *I, a, eye* are all one-syllable words that have no consonant sounds. In contrast, the one-syllable words *use, cake, church, them, drip, string,* and *park* all have one or more consonant sounds in addition to the vowel.

Rime – The vowel of a syllable, plus any consonants that may optionally follow the vowel. Examples from the one-syllable words above: *I, a,* and *eye* have a vowel sound but no following consonant sounds. The rimes in the other one-syllable words are represented by the following letters: *-ake,* in *cake; -urch,* in *church; -em,* in *them; -ing,* in *string; -ip,* in *drip; -ark,* in *park.* Notice, however, that in most of these instances, there are more letters than there are sounds in the rime.

Onset – Any consonant sound or sounds that may, optionally, occur before the vowel in a syllable.

Phoneme – The smallest meaning-signaling unit of sound in a language. Phonemes are what we have learned to hear as the smallest separate, or separable, sounds in a language; the smallest unit of sound that is capable of signaling a difference in meaning, as the /p/ sound in *pit* and the /b/ sound in *bit* differentiate the two words.

Phonemic awareness – Awareness that there are such separable sounds in words; the ability to hear separate phonemes in words. As currently used by skills researchers, *phonemic awareness* usually includes the ability to segment a word into phonemes and to manipulate phonemes in different ways.

Decoding – The ability to sound out words. Sometimes *decoding* is used to mean the identification of words by whatever means—that is, not limited to sounding out.

Phonics – Letter-sound relationships, and the related skills used in analyzing words into phonemes or larger units and blending them to form recognizable words. Some researchers define phonics as *teaching* letter-sound relationships, or teaching relationships between the spelling and sound systems in a language.

Phonics knowledge – A knowledge of letter-sound relationships, whether explicit (conscious) or implicit (functional knowledge that is not conscious).

Additional terms as used in the National Reading Panel Report (2000c, p. 8; and/or 2000b, pp. 2-81):

Analogy phonics – Teaching students to use the parts of known words (such as onsets and rimes) to read unfamiliar print words.

Synthetic phonics – Teaching students explicitly to convert letters into sounds (phonemes) and then blend the sounds to form recognizable words.

Analytic phonics – Teaching students to analyze letter-sound relations in previously learned words, in order to avoid pronouncing sounds in isolation (which cannot be done accurately, especially with sounds like /b/ and /p/).

Figure 13.1 *Commonly used terms relating to sounds, letter-sound relationships, and the teaching of them.*

<u>Embedded phonics</u> – Teaching students phonics skills by embedding phonics instruction in text reading, "a more implicit approach that relies to some extent on incidental learning" (NRP, 2000c, p. 8).

<u>Phonics in context</u> – Teaching students during the reading of texts to use letter-sound relationships along with context and prior knowledge to identify words.

<u>Phonics through spelling</u> – Teaching students to segment words into phonemes and to select letters for those phonemes (i.e., teaching students to spell words phonemically).

Figure 13.1   *(Continued).*

We saw at the beginning of Chapter 9 the kinds of limiting instruction that are often given to children who are placed into lower groups, often called lower "ability" groups, and the same kind of mind-numbing instruction is typically given to children who are held back because of their scores on tests of some skill(s) assessed in isolation from—and instead of—their ability to talk about an appropriate text they have read. Making tests of "phonemic awareness" a gatekeeper for kindergarten or first grade is not only inappropriate but unjustifiable, especially since children do not need to be aware of separate phonemes before they begin learning to read.

Phonics, "Phonics Knowledge," and Decoding

The term *phonics* is used variously by different people, even among researchers and educators. In recent years there has been so much emphasis on teaching phonics that the term *phonics* itself has come to mean, for many people, "teaching letter-sound relationships" (Adams, 1990,  defines it essentially this way). So, how to define *phonics* for the purposes of the discussion in this and following chapters? I still prefer to define it simply as "letter-sound relationships." Then we can talk about teaching phonics or not teaching phonics. We can also talk about teaching phonics intensively and systematically in isolation, compared with teaching phonics mostly as children are reading, enjoying literature, and writing. In addition, we can understand "intensive, systematic phonics" as one—but only one—way of teaching phonics explicitly.

We can also use the phrase *phonics knowledge* to refer to one's knowledge of letter-sound relationships, and further refine that phrase in context and with modifiers. For example, "explicit phonics knowledge" can refer to letter-sound knowledge that readers can verbalize; that is, letter-sound knowledge that they are metacognitively aware of. "Implicit phonics knowledge" then refers to letter-sound knowledge that readers have and can use, even though they may not be able to verbalize it.

Decoding is another concept and term used in relationship to phonics. For some educators, decoding includes any way of identifying words: using letter-sound knowledge, dividing words into meaningful parts, using context and prior knowledge. Usually I use the other common term for this range of processes, namely *identifying words*. Then the term *decoding* can be limited to its other common meaning, pronouncing words by using letter-sound knowledge alone. Usually, *decoding* in this sense refers to sounding out words, whereas recognizing words on sight is simply described as recognizing words automatically, or *word recognition*. Automatic recognition of most words has acquired another term, *automaticity* (see Chapters 5 and 9). Automaticity and rapid decoding are the two basic goals of those who insist we must teach phonemic awareness and phonics first—mostly politicians and those who seek to influence them, not reading researchers.

For handy reference, Figure 13.1 includes a list of these and other phonics-related terms as used specifically in this book—and, with the exception of the term *phonics knowledge,* as used widely in the profession.

Letter–Sound Knowledge in Learning to Read Words

We have already seen, in Chapter 2 (pp. 32–33) and Chapter 5 (pp. 98–99), the fact that adults can read many nonsense words rather easily, at least if they are one-syllable or two-syllable words. We have also discussed the fact that we are probably reading such words *by analogy* with familiar words and word parts, especially syllables and the next smaller units of which they are composed, namely onsets and rimes. Also noted in Chapter 5 is some of the research evidence for this observation, and for the observation that children, too, seem to read unfamiliar print words by analogy with the parts of known words. Such research lends additional support to the other evidence for a key claim of those who have studied reading as a psycholinguistic process: namely, our claim that we draw upon internalized *patterns* of letter-sound relationships as we read, thereby reducing the amount of visual information needed from individual letters.

The question here is: How are these observations relevant to the process of learning to read words that are not yet identifiable on sight? For that, we shall look at additional research.

Reading Words by Analogy

Several research studies suggest that children can demonstrate awareness of syllables in words before they are aware of, or can demonstrate their awareness of, separate phonemes within words. There are also several studies suggesting that children can demonstrate awareness of onsets and rimes before they can demonstrate awareness of phonemes within words (e.g., see the excellent summary of research in Chapters 1–4 of Goswami & Bryant, 1990). Indeed, when defining the terms *phoneme* and *phonemic awareness,* we have already mentioned that children have difficulty analyzing spoken words into phonemes (e.g., Liberman, Shankweiler, et al., 1974; Ehri & Wilce, 1980; Mann, 1986; Treiman & Baron, 1981; Tunmer & Nesdale, 1985; also Peterson & Haines, 1992). It is also notoriously difficult for emergent readers to blend single phonemes into words. On the other hand, young children seem to find it natural to analyze words into onsets and rimes even before they learn to read. In the 1980s, Rebecca Treiman investigated whether children, as well as adults, can analyze spoken words into onsets and rimes. By playing word games with eight-year-olds, she found that the children were able to split the syllables into onsets and rimes (Treiman, 1983, 1985). Usha Goswami, working with children of kindergarten age, first-grade age, and second-grade age, found that younger children, too, can perceive onsets and rimes within syllables and read new print words by analogy with the parts of words they already recognize in print (e.g., Goswami, 1986, 1988, 1993).

A "Must-Read"!

Moustafa, M. (1997). *Beyond Traditional Phonics: Research Discoveries and Reading Instruction.* Portsmouth, NH: Heinemann.

In this book, Moustafa describes research studies more simply yet elegantly than anyone else I know. Her book is a readable and concise treatment of the reading process and research on phonics. Regie Routman writes, "Finally—a terrific book about phonics and reading that is reasonable, research based, and full of workable suggestions" (from the back cover).

Particularly important for teachers is the fact that children find it relatively natural and easy to read new words by analogy with the parts of words they already know in print, an observation introduced in Chapter 5. To further understand this point, we can examine in more detail the study done by Margaret Moustafa (1990, 1995; see also Moustafa 1997 and 1998). Moustafa wanted to know which would be more helpful when emergent readers tried to read unfamiliar print words: their knowledge of individual letter-sound correspondences, or their prior ability to recognize one-syllable words with the same onset or the same rime. She asked the children to read certain nonsense words (nonwords) or words they surely would not know in print, but only after she had determined the extent and nature of their letter-sound knowledge and their ability to read real one-syllable words that had the same onset or rime as the unusual and unfamiliar print "words." For example:

If the child could read *green* with the onset *gr-* and *black* with the rime *-ack,* could the child also read the nonsense word *grack,* which was composed of these two parts? If the child could read *train* with the onset *tr-* and *snake* with the rime *-ake,* could the child also read the nonsense word *trake?* If the child could read *hat* with the onset *h-* and *new* with the rime *-ew,* could the child also read the uncommon word *hew?* And, on the other hand, could the child correctly identify the phonemes when looking at the written word? Which kind of knowledge—word knowledge or letter-sound knowledge—correlated most strongly with (was related most strongly to) the child's ability to read the unusual words?

Moustafa found that the children's knowledge of letter-sound correspondences could account for 64% of the unusual words they were able to pronounce. Or putting it the other way, "36% of the time the children were able to correctly identify an unusual word, they could not correctly identify the sounds of all the letters and digraphs that constituted the word" (1997, p. 47). However, the children's previous knowledge of words in print accounted for 95% of the unusual words that they were able to pronounce correctly. Thus Moustafa's study supports the observation that like adults, children draw upon chunks of known words to read unknown print words. That is, they read new print words by drawing upon the parts of words they already know in print. In general, the more print words the children recognized from the set of real words Moustafa asked them to read, the better able they were to read the unfamiliar print words by making analogies with parts of the familiar print words—whether or not they could identify all the separate phonemes.

There is other evidence, too, that emergent readers find it easier to sound out words in onset-rime chunks than to break the words into separate phonemes and then blend these phonemes to make a word (e.g., Wagner, Torgeson, & Rashotte, 1994; Schatschneider, Francis, Foorman, Fletcher, & Mehta, 1999). In earlier chapters we referred to the ability to process words in chunks (syllables; onsets; rimes) as "chunking out" a word, to distinguish it from the letter-by-letter, sound-by-sound approach that most people think of as "sounding out." The example of Amy, a six-year-old first grader, amply illustrates this difficulty and the resultant nonsense that may be produced. For example, when she attempted the sentence "He loaded up his dump truck with oatmeal cookies, and sent it rolling across the table" she slowly attempted to sound out the letters of most words. The sentence came out sounding something like this: "He d- de- dem truck with uh- oet- m- e- l cookies and s- sh- e— n–t it r- r- ro- a–k— r sh the table." By the time she worked through the sentence, the meaning had been lost. (See the fuller discussion of Amy as a reader on Heinemann's Web page relating to this book: <*www.heinemann.com/weaver*>.)

Developmental Patterns in Review

The findings of Schatschneider, Francis, Foorman, Fletcher, & Mehta (1999) suggest the following developmental order, based on a continuum of easy to difficult tasks: (1) comparison of first sounds: identifying the names of pictures beginning with the same sound; (2) blending onset-rime units into real words; (3) blending phonemes into real words; (4) deleting a phoneme and saying the word that remains; (5) segmenting words into phonemes; (6) blending phonemes into nonwords.

Following is a list of some conclusions drawn from various research studies and summaries, most of them previously discussed:

1. Children find it relatively easy to hear the syllables within words.

2. Children find it easier to divide spoken syllables into the "natural" chunks known as onsets and rimes than to divide spoken words into phonemes.

3. Children who do not yet read find it especially difficult to divide spoken words into phonemes.

4. Children find it difficult to blend phonemes into words, particularly if they are not expecting the result to make a real word that they recognize.

5. Children find it easier to blend onset-rime chunks than to blend phonemes.

6. Children who are learning to read find it easier to deal with unfamiliar print words in letter chunks that correspond to sound chunks, rather than to divide words into separate phonemes and then blend them. That is, "chunking out" an unfamiliar print word is easier and more likely to be successful than what we usually think of as "sounding out."

7. Like adults, children read new print words by analogy with parts of words they already know in print.

Typically, these various studies focus on the processing of isolated words, whether spoken or in print. As we have already seen in earlier chapters, such processing is made easier when the words occur in a meaningful context and the reader is using meaning to help get the individual words in a text as well as to construct meaning from the text.

Observational research suggests a similar developmental pattern for learning to read and write words. These patterns may occur before a child starts school and/or in primary classrooms where children have ample opportunities to read and write, with support and feedback from an adult. Figure 13.2 shows developmental trends in learning to read and write words in meaningful contexts. This model is a slight modification of a figure from Dombey, Moustafa, et al. (1998), who in turn drew upon Frith (1985).

Learning Some Words First

"The data suggest that availability and ready access to the names and meanings of printed words as integrated units facilitates more rapid progress during the initial stages of learning [to read] than does analysis of grapheme-phoneme invariance, quite likely because associative bonds are formed more readily with familiar than with unfamiliar material. It is also likely that mastery of the alphabetic principle depends, in part, on familiarity with an adequate corpus of whole words." (Vellutino & Scanlon, 1987 p. 359)

As the following explanations suggest, *logographic* reading and writing involves treating words like indivisible wholes, or logos; *analogic* reading involves reading new print words by analogy with the parts of words already known in print; *analytic* writing and reading involves analyzing words into sounds (phonemes); and *orthographic* reading and writing uses knowledge of spelling patterns and the spelling system of the language (orthographic patterns and system). In *symbolic* writing, writers may use various kinds of marks to stand for things themselves, without the mediation of words. The terms in capital letters indicate the "pacemakers" that stimulate growth in the same or other mode, reading or writing. That is:

1. *Logographic reading* (reading whole words in the environment or in a written context) typically occurs before *logographic writing* (writing a word, or something that represents a

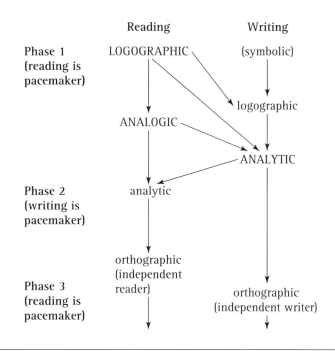

Figure 13.2 *Developmental trends in reading words in context and writing words (slight modification of a figure from Dombey, Moustafa, et al., 1998, p. 23).*

word). In logographic reading, children are developing a "mental lexicon" of words they can recognize and recall.

2. *Analogic reading* (reading new print words by analogy with chunks of familiar words) typically occurs before *analytic writing* (analyzing sounds in a word and writing letters to represent some of the sounds). This fits with the previous observation that blending onsets and rimes to read words by analogy typically occurs before the segmenting of words into phonemes.

3. *Analytic writing* (analyzing and writing sounds heard in a word) typically occurs before *analytic reading*—that is, before sounding out words one sound (phoneme) at a time. In analytic writing, children begin typically to represent the first sound of the word with a letter, then the first and last sounds, and then other sounds, including vowels. The ability to analyze spoken words into sounds (phonemes) leads to the ability to read words by producing sounds for the letters and then blending them; this is "decoding" as phonics advocates usually conceive of it. However, such decoding is often a less effective as well as a less efficient process than sounding out words in chunks like onsets and rimes. In fact, children who have learned to sound out words in phonemes soon learn they need to sound out words in chunks again, especially as they encounter more and more multisyllabic words in texts.

4. Typically the *orthographic stage in reading* is reached slightly before the *orthographic stage in writing.* Children identify familiar words automatically and many new print words quickly in reading, using all they know about spelling patterns and the ways words are structured and spelled. Typically they read new print words by making analogies with chunks of familiar words, while also using prior knowledge and context. In writing, they

spell many familiar words conventionally and use what they know about spelling patterns to write parts of words they don't already know how to spell. They make effective use of strategies for reading, writing, and spelling independently.

> This is powerful evidence that children do not need to have phonemic awareness or phonics knowledge before learning to read. The evidence also suggests that the natural progression in learning to read is from wholes to parts.

Thus experimental and observational research both suggest that reading new print words by analogy with parts of already-known print words occurs easily, early, and before the ability to analyze words into sounds. This is powerful evidence that children do not need to have phonemic awareness or phonics knowledge before beginning to read words in familiar contexts, including texts. The evidence also suggests that the natural progression in learning to read is from wholes to parts.

RELATIONSHIPS BETWEEN PHONEMIC AWARENESS AND LEARNING TO READ

It is clear that there is a strong correlation between first graders' ability to identify separate phonemes and their scores on reading skills tests in first grade. That is, the two often go together. But which causes the other, or does the influence proceed in both directions? Reading researchers commonly express one of the following views regarding the relationship between phonemic awareness and learning to read:

- Phonemic awareness promotes learning to read.
- Learning to read promotes phonemic awareness.
- Learning to read and phonemic awareness are reciprocal: that is, each facilitates the other.

Phonemic Awareness Promotes Learning to Read

Various studies demonstrate that most children can be trained to hear phonemes and to segment words into phonemes (though some children need intensive tutoring to do so). Often, such studies have also been interpreted as evidence that teaching phonemic awareness causes, or at least facilitates, higher scores on standardized tests. These studies include, among others, Torgeson & Hecht, 1996; Vellutino et al., 1996; Ball & Blachman, 1991; Juel, Griffith, & Gough, 1986; Stanovich, Cuningham, & Freeman, 1985; Bradley & Bryant, 1985; Fox & Routh, 1976.

Defining phonemic awareness as "the ability to focus on and manipulate phonemes in spoken words," one subgroup of the National Reading Panel chose to "examine the scientific evidence relevant to the impact of phonemic awareness instruction on reading and spelling development" (2000b, p. 2-1). It is noteworthy that the group did not try to examine the opposite, namely the impact of learning to read on the development of phonemic awareness. There would not have been enough studies to compare in a statistical meta-analysis.

Doing a statistical meta-analysis of research studies, the panelists found that teaching phonemic awareness to young children produced, in comparison with control groups, a large "effect size" of 0.86 on posttests of phonemic awareness; a relatively small effect size of 0.34 on reading comprehension tests; and a moderate effect size of 0.53 when taking all the measures of word and reading skills together (NRP, 2000b, p. 2-3; Ehri, Nunes, et al., 2001, p. 261). It is important to note that "reading comprehension tests at the beginning levels consist of short sentences and conceptually simple ideas. The primary determiner of success is whether the words can be read" (Ehri, Nunes, et al., 2001, p. 277). It is also important to note that many of the analyzed studies involved teaching sounds along with letters, which is phonics and not merely phonemic awareness. When Krashen analyzed the data from studies where only phonemic awareness was taught, he did not find strong evidence that phonemic awareness alone had much effect on reading comprehension: "The six studies found of the impact of pure phonemic awareness training (without phonics) on reading comprehension gave a positive but modest overall effect size in favor of phonemic awareness training. Four studies had small samples, two showed no or very small effect sizes, and one [had] inconsistent results. Three involved languages other than English. Such results do not support the popular movement for universal phonemic awareness training" (Krashen, 2001a).

What Is an Effect Size?

In trying to generalize about the effects of systematic phonics instruction, the members of the National Reading Panel used a statistical concept called *effect size*. Effect size was calculated by subtracting the mean of the control group from the mean of the experimental group, with the difference expressed in standard deviation units: $d = 0.20$, for example. The panelists categorized effect sizes according to Cohen's rule of thumb (1988): an effect size between zero and 0.20 is considered small; an effect size of 0.50 is considered moderate; and an effect size of 0.80 is considered large. They also noted that "A treatment can be very effective but yield only a small effect size if instruction in the control group is also effective" and, conversely, that "if the control group's instruction is particularly ineffective . . . then the effect size is inflated" (2000b, p. 2-95).

Learning to Read Promotes Phonemic Awareness

Other researchers have documented the opposite: that learning to read promotes phonemic awareness. One example is Morais, Cary, Alegria, and Bertelson (1979), who assessed the phonemic segmentation ability of adult illiterates compared with a group who had learned to read beyond the usual age. They concluded that "Learning to read, whether in childhood or as an adult, evidently allows the ability [to segment words into phonemes] to manifest itself. Thus, it is not right to say that awareness of the phonetic structure of speech is a precondition for starting learning to read and write" (1979, p. 330). However, the authors do not describe how these older youth and adults learned to read, while they do say that "the ability to deal explicitly with the phonetic units of speech is not acquired spontaneously" (p. 330).

Other studies that have been interpreted as demonstrating that phonemic awareness is a consequence of learning to read are Mann (1986) and Wimmer, Landerl, et al. (1991). Krashen (2000a) also finds that phonemic awareness develops without special training, through learning to read and reading—though not necessarily for all children. Many children who begin with very low levels of phonemic awareness (PA), compared with their age-mates, eventually develop substantial levels of PA (e.g., Fox & Routh, 1983; Juel, 1988, as cited in Krashen, 2000a). Krashen observes: "The results presented here do not settle the issue of whether reading instruction or reading experience is the cause of PA, but they certainly cast doubt upon the strong view that direct PA training is necessary" (2000a).

Indeed, what all of these studies show most clearly is that phonemic awareness can be a result of learning to read, and that phonemic awareness does not have to precede the process of learning to read. Some interesting case studies show, in fact, that some effective adult readers may have low phonemic awareness (summarized in Krashen & McQuillan, 1998).

High Phonemic Awareness Not Necessary for Reading

In "Successful Dyslexics: A Constructivist Study of Passionate Interest Reading" (1995/1996),

Rosalie Fink reports on highly successful adults—including a Nobel laureate—who had been diagnosed as dyslexic in childhood. These twelve dyslexics' problems "included a history of difficulty with letter identification, word recognition, phonics, reading fluency, reading speed, spelling, laterality, writing, fine motor control, memory and learning a foreign language." Yet all had become highly successful in their chosen fields, and most have authored books and journal articles in their field. These highly successful adults still, however, have difficulties with basic phonological skills that severely limit their ability to sound out unfamiliar words.

How, then, did they become successful readers, most of them between the ages of 10 and 12? It was only when they developed and pursued a passionate interest through reading that they finally developed "basic word recognition and fluency." They learned to read by reading.

Learning to Read and Phonemic Awareness Facilitate Each Other

Some skills researchers have concluded from other research that phonemic awareness helps in learning to read, and that learning to read promotes phonemic awareness. For example, in a review of research on reading and phonological processing (which includes phonemic awareness), Tunmer and Nesdale (1985) point out that "Our review supports a causal role for phonological awareness in learning to read . . ." (p. 192). But they also point out that "Most researchers have neglected the probable causal role of learning to read in the development of phonological skills" (p. 192).

According to the abstract of a study that focused on possible relationships between phonemic awareness and reading words (not connected texts), "Findings are interpeted to show that phonemic segmentation skill may be a consequence of as much as a prerequisite to learning to read words" (Ehri & Wilce, 1980, p. 371). Perfetti, Beck, Bell, & Hughes (1987) hypothesize that "learning to read and phonemic awareness develop in tandem, in a reciprocal mutually supporting relationship"; they further state, "A corollary to this major premise is that phonemic awareness is not a unitary ability, but a constellation of abilities" (p. 284). Morais, Alegria, and Content (1987) came to the same conclusion about the reciprocal effects of phonemic awareness and learning to read. Wagner, Torgeson, and Rashotte (1994) provide evidence of bidirectional causality "from a latent variable longitudinal study" (p. 73). The abstract summarizes: "Causal relations between phonological processing abilities and reading-related knowledge [tests of isolated skills] are bi-directional" (p. 73). Wimmer, Landerl, Linortner, & Hummer (1991) titled their research article "The Relationship of Phonemic Awareness to Reading Acquisition: More Consequence Than Precondition but Still Important."

These groups of researchers have uncovered what may, in fact, be some complex interrelationships that commonly occur as an emergent reader becomes an independent reader. Some of these relationships were explored by Linda Ayres in her award-winning dissertation study (1993). Ayres investigated the efficacy of three training conditions upon the phonological awareness (including phonemic awareness) of kindergarten children, and the possible effects on reading achievement at the end of first grade. One hundred and five students completed the training study in the kindergarten year, while 92 remained in the study throughout first grade.

The children in the experimental groups received an experimental treatment for twenty minutes a day for ten weeks, in the fall of their kindergarten year. Each experimental group then received a different treatment in the winter. Ayres concluded that "The most important implication from this study is that training in phonological awareness is both possible and advantageous for children" (Ayres, 1993, p. 153). She observes that "The most effective means of instruction seems to begin with literature as a foundation for the direct instruction that will come later in the year," when it appears to be more effective (1993, p. 144).

It is also noteworthy, however, that children in the story mapping and retelling group showed a substantial gain in phonemic awareness during the first ten weeks, along with the children in groups that were specifically taught phonological awareness. Also, from the unexpected gains made by the control group, Ayres concluded that "students whose phonological awareness is less than completely developed are nevertheless capable of making progress in reading" (1993, p. 150). This data leads to the conjecture that phonological awareness and learning to read are linked in a mutually facilitative relationship (Ayres, 1993, p. 151).

Furthermore, Ayres (1993, p. 151) noted Ehri's (1979) caution that "if a skill is facilitative, as phonological awareness appears to be, the effect may last only temporarily." The controls will "catch up."

THE NATIONAL READING PANEL REPORT ON PHONICS

Chapter 11 discussed the controversy surrounding the National Reading Panel Report released in April 2000, noting in particular some of the careful and detailed critiques of that report as well as the limitations governing what research studies, and kinds of research studies, were included in the NRP's analyses. I also raised a concern about quality control with regard to the studies included, with particular reference to the study by Foorman, Francis, et al., (1997 and 1998).

Here, we shall focus on what the National Reading Panel report said about the teaching of phonics.

What Is "Reading," as Discussed in the National Reading Panel Report?

"Reading was defined to include several behaviors such as the following: reading real words in isolation or in context, reading pseudowords that can be pronounced but have no meaning, reading text aloud or silently, and comprehending text that is read silently or orally" (NRP, 2000c, p. 5)

Major Distortions in the Summary of the NRP Report

The official summary of the National Reading Panel Report includes inaccurate claims about the teaching of phonics, when compared with the detailed analysis of the subgroup on phonics. Within a stretch of two paragraphs, the writers of the summary on phonics in the widely distributed thirty-three-page booklet (NRP, 2000c) make several blanket statements that vastly overstate what the subgroup on phonics wrote in the detailed analysis. Let us take each of three misleading statements in turn and contrast them with statements from the detailed report.

Distortion

> From the summary booklet: "The meta-analysis revealed that systematic phonics instruction produces significant benefits for students in kindergarten through sixth grade and for children having difficulty learning to read" (NRP, 2000c, p. 9).

This implies that children in grades K–6 generally benefited from phonics instruction, but that is not true.

From the NRP detailed subgroup analysis:

■ Overall, the kindergartners and first graders showed higher reading scores (on various subtests within standardized tests) when phonics was taught systematically, compared with unsystematic or no teaching of phonics. However: (1) All of the "cases" (comparisons) of kindergartners in the studies involved children labeled "at risk," as did 9 of the 23 comparisons involving first graders, which would mean that 70% of the K–1 comparisons did not involve normally achieving readers (NRP, 2000b, p. 2-152). Of these groups, the greatest effect by far was found for the first graders deemed at risk: a difference (effect size) of 0.78, which is a large effect size. (2) The effects of phonics on the 14 comparisons involving normal but nonhomogenous groups of first graders were somewhat less—a difference of 0.48, which is a moderate effect size (p. 2-152). Among the at-risk kindergartners, the effect size favoring systematic phonics was only 0.58, which is also a moderate effect size.

■ Phonics instruction also correlated with higher test scores among "disabled" readers in grades 2–6 (p. 2-108), where disabled readers are defined as "older children of average or better intelligence who were not making normal progress in reading" (p. 2-82). However, panelist Linnea Ehri (2000) has noted that most of these readers were clustered in grade 2.

■ "Phonics instruction appears to contribute only weakly, if at all, in helping poor readers apply these [word reading] skills to read text and to spell words" (p. 2-108, referring to the grade 2–6 group).

■ "There were insufficient data to draw any conclusions about the effects of phonics instruction with normally developing readers above first grade" (p. 2-108).

■ "Phonics instruction failed to exert a significant impact on the reading performance of low-achieving readers in second through sixth grades" (p. 2-125; also p. 2-109), where low-achieving readers were defined as "older children who were progressing poorly in reading and who varied in intelligence with at least some of them achieving poorly in other academic areas" (p. 2-82).

■ Also, the researchers did not find significant gains in comprehension with the grade 2–6 group in general (p. 2-125).

■ Noting that phonics instruction produced less of an effect on oral reading than upon comprehension among kindergartners and first graders, the authors speculated as follows: "Why phonics skills facilitated reading comprehension more than oral reading is not clear. It may have to do with the nature of the tests. Standardized comprehension tests at this level generally use extremely short (usually one sentence) 'passages.' On these short passages, the effects of decoding should be strong" (p. 2-107). Certainly it seems fair to interpret this statement as indicating that the "comprehension" measures used with kindergartners and first graders say much more about word reading than about comprehension. It may also be noted that only 11 of the 75 comparisons, the 15% involving kindergartners and first graders, involved even such a limited measure of comprehension as a single sentence (Appendix E, p. 2-151).

■ Another passage from the report also casts doubt upon any claims about the effects of systematic phonics upon comprehension in the early grades. The authors are commenting upon an intensive, three-year tutoring program comparing the effects of synthetic versus embedded phonics instruction: "While reading comprehension depends upon other processes besides word reading, one would expect to see transfer, particularly in the primary grades where text reading is heavily influenced by word recognition skills" (p. 2-120). This further implies that in the studies involving younger children, measures of "comprehension" are not separable from measures of word recognition skills, as measured by standardized tests.

Phonics and Comprehension

"Systematic phonics instruction is focused on teaching children the alphabetic system and explicitly how to apply it to read and spell words. Phonics skills would be expected to show effects on text comprehension to the extent that phonics skills help children read words in texts. This is one reason why phonics instruction may have exerted less impact on text comprehension outcomes than on word reading outcomes, because the impact is indirect. In addition, although phonics programs do give children practice reading connected text, the purpose of this practice is centered on word recognition rather than on comprehending and thinking about the meaning of what is being read. This may be another reason why effect sizes on text comprehension were smaller than effect sizes on word reading" (NRP, 2000b, p. 2-115).

Furthermore, there are decades of evidence—from miscue research as well as other observational/ descriptive research—that focusing too much on word identification often keeps readers from focusing on meaning (e.g., J. Brown, Goodman, & Marek, 1996).

■ Still another statement from the same paragraph suggests that the authors of the subgroup report on phonics recognize that skilled word reading may not be as important in reading connected text as skills-emphasis researchers usually claim: "Another possibility is that compensatory processes are sufficiently strong to dilute the contribution that superior word recognition skill makes to text reading. That is, children read and comprehend text by utilizing their linguistic and background knowledge combined with their word reading skill" (p. 2-120). That, of course, is precisely what descriptive researchers such as Ken Goodman have documented for decades, through miscue studies especially. However, we wouldn't refer to these processes as "compensatory" processes, as if there were something unnatural about them. They simply reflect normal proficient reading and the fact that texts provide multiple and redundant cues to meaning. See, for example, my redundancy model of reading in Chapter 5.

Distortion

From the summary booklet: "The ability to read and spell words was enhanced in kindergartners who received systematic beginning phonics instruction. First graders who were taught phonics systematically were better able to decode and spell words and to read text orally, and they showed significant improvement in their ability to comprehend text" (NRP, 2000c, p. 9)

From the detailed report, some important qualifiers:

■ "Systematic phonics instruction was most effective in improving children's ability to decode regularly spelled words and pseudowords" (NRP, 2000b, p. 2-125; statistics omitted). "This was expected because the central focus of phonics programs is upon teaching children to apply the alphabetic system to read novel words" (p. 2-125).

■ "Phonics instruction with its emphasis on teaching letter-sound relations would be expected to improve beginning readers' ability to spell words by writing the sounds they hear. Studies with younger children commonly employed developmental spelling scoring systems that gave credit for phonetically plausible spellings, for example spelling *feet* as FET or *car* as KR (Tangel & Blachman, 1998; Morris & Perney, 1984). This may explain the sizeable effect observed on the spelling outcome" (p. 2-107). There is no independent evidence in the phonics analysis that the teaching of phonics improved conventional spelling, for students at any grade level.

Distortion

From the summary booklet: "Older children receiving phonics instruction were better able to decode and spell words and to read text orally, but their comprehension of text was not significantly improved" (NRP, 2000c, p. 9).

From the detailed report:

■ Again, note as above that systematic phonics instruction did not show a significantly greater effect upon normally achieving grade 2–6 students or the grade 2–6 students labeled "low-achieving," but only upon those considered "disabled" readers (NRP, 2000b, p. 2-125; also p. 2-109).

■ Regarding the older, grade 2-6 readers: "Phonics instruction appears to contribute only weakly, if at all, in helping poor readers apply these [word reading] skills to read text and to spell words" (p. 2-108).

■ "The evidence on older readers above first grade reviewed so far provides no information about the effects of phonics instruction on older students who began phonics instruction in kindergarten or first grade" (p. 2-109). (The panelists do, though, qualify this statement by reference to four comparisons that are "mainly suggestive," given the small number of cases; see p. 2-110.)

What About These Errors In the Influential Summary of the Report?

In a response to Elaine Garan's first published critique of the NRP report (2001a), Linnea Ehri and Steven Stahl had this to say:

> Garan expresses many concerns about the clarity and accuracy of the writing in the reports, particularly with regard to differences between the *Summary* and the *Reports of the Subgroups.* We admit that some of the writing is not as clear as it should be. And Garan rightly notes that conclusions resulting from the distillation process in the *Summary* sometimes lack the details, qualifiers, and cautions that appear in the more extensive *Reports of the Subgroups.* However, the number of mistakes is small and the robustness of the findings is overwhelming. (Ehri & Stahl, 2001, pp. 18–19)

Interpreting NRP Claims About Reading Growth

In the phonics section of the National Reading Panel report (2000b), the term *reading* usually refers to phonics and word identification skills and does not usually include comprehension. Only 11 of 75, or 15%, of the comparisons involving kindergartners and first graders and only 11 of 83, or 13%, of the comparisons involving grade 2–6 students involved comprehending "text" (2000b, p. 2-151). True, a different list on the same page indicates that 35 cases involved comprehending "text," but that amounted to 16% of the comparisons overall. Furthermore, "comprehending text" usually turned out to be reading and "comprehending" a single sentence, for the younger kindergarten and first-grade readers—the only age group for which systematic teaching of phonics showed a greater effect size overall than teaching phonics unsystematically or not at all.

Therefore, when the subgroup that analyzed phonics research mentions "growth in reading" or "reading growth," it is usually referring mostly or exclusively to growth on phonics-related skills, including word identification.

Negative or No Conclusions from the NRP Subgroup Report on Phonics

■ The researchers did not conclude that phonics is adequate as a way of teaching reading. In fact, they expressed their concern that phonics-only programs would not succeed in making every child a skilled reader (NRP, 2000b, p. 2-109).

■ The researchers did not find evidence that teaching more phonics is better than teaching less. Indeed, they noted that questions regarding how much phonics should be taught, and for how long, remain for future research to determine (NRP, 2000c, p. 10; 2000b, pp. 2–88 and 2–115).

■ The researchers did not conclude that one way of teaching phonics systematically was superior to any other way of teaching phonics systematically.

■ The researchers did not find any systematic phonics *program* to be superior to the others (p. 2-111). Specifically, the researchers did not find any direct instruction program to be superior to other kinds of programs for teaching phonics systematically. (Actually, they did not even investigate that question, because there were too few studies for consideration.)

■ The researchers did not find reason to recommend the teaching of phonics in isolation.

Nor is it true, as many people mistakenly assume, that systematic phonics instruction means a "direct instruction" *program*. There are specific direct instruction programs with a script that tells the teacher exactly what to say, but there are also many other ways of teaching phonics directly and systematically. The term *direct instruction* is something like the word *kleenex*, which is the brand name for a particular kind of facial tissue, but which has also become a generic term for any kind of facial tissue. That is, *direct instruction* originally referred to a specific scripted reading program, *DISTAR/Reading Mastery* but now is also used to describe any kind of direct teaching.

Summary of *Actual* NRP Findings

Here are key statements and data from the National Reading Panel report regarding phonemic awareness and phonics (2000b):

1. In comparison with "disabled" and normally progressing readers, at-risk students showed the largest effects from phonemic awareness training, especially with regard to "reading outcomes" (NRP, 2000b, p. 2-23).

2. Overall, teaching phonemic awareness to young children who were progressing normally as readers, to young children "at risk" of reading failure, and to older "disabled" readers (mostly in grades 2–6) produced, in comparison with control groups, a large "effect size" of 0.86 on posttests of phonemic awareness but only a relatively small effect size of 0.34 on reading comprehension tests (NRP, 2000b, p. 2-3; Ehri, Nunes, et al., 2001, p. 261). It is important to note that "reading comprehension tests at the beginning levels consist of short sentences and conceptually simple ideas. The primary determiner of success is whether the words can be read" (Ehri, Nunes, et al., 2001, p. 277).

3. When phonemic awareness is taught with letters—that is, when sounds are matched with letters—it is actually phonics instruction. "Teaching PA with letters helps students acquire PA more effectively than teaching PA without letters" (NRP, 2000b, p. 2-41). In fact, the difference is substantial. Thus phonemic awareness can be taught most effectively and most efficiently as part of phonics instruction in letter-sound relationships. (In the NRP report, none of the studies was included in both analyses.)

4. "Systematic phonics instruction was most effective in improving children's ability to decode regularly spelled words and pseudowords," with effect sizes of 0.67 and 0.60, respectively (p. 2-125). These are moderate to large effect sizes.

5. "Phonics instruction produced substantial reading growth among younger children at risk of developing future reading problems. Effect sizes were $d = 0.58$ for kindergartners at risk and $d = 0.74$ for first graders at risk" (p. 2-125).

6. "Phonics instruction also improved the reading performance of disabled readers (i.e., children with average IQs but poor reading) for whom the effect size was $d = .32$," a small effect size (p. 2-125).

7. "However, phonics instruction failed to exert a significant impact on the reading performance of low-achieving readers in second through sixth grades (i.e., children with reading difficulties and possibly other cognitive difficulties explaining their low achievement). The effect size was $d = 0.15$, which was not statistically greater than chance" (p. 2-125).

8. "Phonics instruction appears to contribute only weakly, if at all, in helping poor readers apply these [word reading] skills to read text and to spell words. There were insufficient data to draw any conclusions about the effects of phonics instruction with normally developing readers above first grade" (p. 2-108).

9. "The overall effect size of systematic phonics instruction in first grade was $d = 0.54$," a moderate effect size. The mean effect size for kindergarten was similar: $d = 0.56$. "The conclusion drawn is that systematic phonics instruction produces the biggest impact on growth in reading when it begins in kindergarten or first grade before children have learned to read independently" (p. 2-125).

10. Similarly, the effects of phonemic awareness training were by far the greatest for preschoolers and next greatest for kindergartners ($d = 0.95$), most of whom had probably not yet learned to read independently. The effect size for kindergartners was much greater than that for first graders ($d = 0.48$). It should be noted, however, that although preschoolers show the greatest effects when taught phonemic awareness, there is no evidence that phonemic awareness needs to be taught before kindergarten. It's simply that preschoolers are less aware of the separate phonemes in words and therefore learn more from phonemic awareness training.

With regard to these last two points, of course instruction in phonemic awareness and phonics will have the greatest effect upon children who cannot yet read independently.

We must remember, too, that when the National Reading Panel makes claims about children's growth in reading, the word *reading* refers mostly to word reading skills.

What, then, can reasonably be concluded with regard to the values of teaching phonics—letter-sound relationships and various skills—intensively and systematically to kindergartners and first graders?

■ Such teaching frequently promotes greater success at an early age on tests of phonemic awareness and skills related to reading words, plus a moderate temporary effect on tests of reading comprehension that use very short, simple passages that require little more than word identification.

■ Children considered at risk of reading failure in kindergarten and first grade seem to benefit the most from being taught phonics intensively and systematically, presumably because their skills are lowest at the outset.

■ Such teaching of phonics also benefits some "disabled" readers in grades 2–6: that is, children with at least average IQ who are not making normal progress in reading (NRP, 2000b, p. 2-82).

Considerations and Cautions

The National Reading Panel report itself includes various considerations and cautions with regard to the teaching of phonemic awareness and phonics. These are combined with other concerns, reminders, and cautions from earlier in this chapter:

1. Phonological skills, including phonemic awareness, do not need to be taught before a child begins to learn to read whole, interesting, and familiar texts—obviously with support. The same is true of phonics.

2. Whether taught apart from or during reading and writing, phonemic awareness develops best when sounds are taught in conjunction with letters—that is, when phonemic awareness is actually part of phonics instruction (NRP, 2000b, pp. 2–6, 2–33). This is important to remember as we read the following comments about teaching phonemic awareness.

3. "In addition to teaching PA [phonemic awareness] skills with letters, it is important for teachers to help children make the connection between the PA skills taught and their application to reading and writing tasks" (p. 2-33).

4. "One instructional activity that is maximally effective for teaching PA in a way that builds a bridge to reading and spelling is that of teaching children to invent phonemically more complete spellings of words.... The effect size [in a study by Ehri & Wilce, 1987] was large, $d = 0.97$. These findings indicate that teaching children to segment and spell helps them learn to read as well as spell words" (p. 2-39).

5. "In the NRP analysis, studies that spent between 5 and 18 hours teaching PA yielded very large effects on the acquisition of phonemic awareness. Studies that spent longer or less time than this also yielded significant effect sizes, but effects were moderate and only half as large" (p. 2-42).

6. "In the NRP data base, the average length of sessions [for teaching phonemic awareness] was 25 minutes." The National Reading Panel concluded "that sessions should probably not exceed 30 minutes in length" (p. 2-42).

7. The NRP analysis found that children learned phonemic awareness better when taught in small groups rather than in large groups or individually (p. 2-42). For teaching phonics in general, the panelists found that individual, small-group, and whole-class teaching all seemed to be effective (p. 2-124).

8. "In kindergarten, most children will be nonreaders and will have little phonemic awareness; so, PA instruction should benefit everyone. In first grade, some children will be reading and spelling already while others may know only a few letters and have no reading skill" (p. 2-42). In first and second grade, teachers should determine individual children's need for help in developing letter-sound knowledge, which includes phonemic awareness.

9. There are many ways that phonics can be taught intensively and systematically. These include synthetic and analytic phonics; analogy phonics, which involves teaching onsets and rimes and decoding new words by analogy; teaching the use of letter-sound knowledge along with context to identify unfamiliar words that readers encounter in texts ("phonics in context"); and teaching phonics through invented spelling ("phonics-through-spelling") (p. 2-81). (The NRP summary booklet describes phonics in context as "embedded phonics"; 2000c, p. 8.) The National Reading Panel clustered the various ways of teaching phonics into three categories: "(1) synthetic phonics programs which emphasized teaching students to convert letters (graphemes) into sounds (phonemes) and then to blend the sounds to form recognizable words; (2) larger-unit phonics programs which emphasized the analysis and blending of larger subparts of words (i.e., onsets, rimes, phonograms, spelling patterns) as well as phonemes; (3) miscellaneous phonics programs that taught phonics systematically but did this in other ways" (2000b, p. 2-85). These three ways of teaching phonics systematically did "not appear to differ significantly in their effectiveness," although there were slight differences in effect size (p. 2-85).

10. "It is important to note that acquiring phonemic awareness is a means rather than an end" (p. 2-33). More generally, "Phonics teaching is a means to an end" (p. 2-88).

And finally, the National Reading Panel cautions that "Phonics should not become the dominant component in a reading program, neither in the amount of time devoted to it nor in the significance attached" (p. 2-89).

In Chapter 14, then, we shall consider in more detail some of the most productive ways that phonics knowledge, phonemic awareness, and decoding skills can be fostered in a broadly based, comprehensive literacy program.

FOR FURTHER EXPLORATION

1. If you haven't already done so, read some of the critiques of the National Reading Panel report that were cited in Chapter 11, p. 260.

2. For research showing that the teaching of phonics can be just as effective in contemporary literacy programs as in a skills-based program, read McIntyre & Freppon, (1994).

3. For research on the many ways phonics is taught in contemporary literacy classrooms, read Dahl, Scharer, Lawson, & Grogan, (1999).

14 Teaching Comprehension Strategies and Phonics Skills

We believe that constructing meaning is the goal of comprehension. . . . True comprehension goes beyond literal understanding and involves the reader's interaction with text. If students are to become thoughtful, insightful readers, they must extend their thinking beyond a superficial understanding of the text

—Stephanie Harvey and Anne Goudvis

[In exemplary first-grade classrooms,] word-level, comprehension, vocabulary, spelling, and writing skills were typically taught in the context of actual reading and writing tasks.

—Center for English Learning and Achievement

Questions for Thought and Discussion

1. What are some reading "skills" that have traditionally been taught and tested? What are some differences between the traditional teaching of reading "skills" and the teaching of reading strategies?

2. What do you think are the most important strategies for readers to use in comprehending texts? In dealing with problem words?

3. How can teachers prepare themselves to teach reading strategies effectively?

4. How might we prepare to teach reading/thinking strategies through literature and short informational texts? Consider in detail, using specific texts as examples.

5. How do children commonly progress in their development of phonics-related skills and strategies?

6. How can we reflect that progression in a comprehensive literacy program?

7. How can we develop phonics-related skills and strategies during the shared reading experience, in particular?

8. Why and how is invented spelling so important in developing phonics knowledge? How can we promote children's development in inventing more sophisticated spellings, and how can we assess phonemic awareness as well as phonics knowledge through children's invented spellings?

9. Given this chapter's emphasis on teaching strategies and skills, what are some important points we should not lose sight of, as we plan a comprehensive literacy program for children?

Effective readers use a variety of reading strategies not only at what we might call the macro level, *with* texts and *among* texts, but at the micro level, for dealing with words not readily recognized in print.

This chapter provides a brief introduction to teaching comprehension strategies. These are cognitive strategies that we use not only for reading but for thinking, writing, doing mathematics and science, and making sense of our world. However, some students seriously need, and all can benefit from, instructional help in developing and using such strategies, especially in reading, and especially since reading instruction in the primary grades is increasingly being reduced to phonics and fluency. In truth, many adults who are not students could benefit from such help, too. Effective readers use such reading strategies not only at what we might call the macro level, *with* texts and *among* texts, but at the micro level, for dealing with words not readily recognized in print. Roughly the second half of the chapter focuses on teaching phonics (and phonemic awareness) within a comprehensive literacy program. This is important for emergent readers and for older readers who have never had adequate help in learning to use phonics knowledge and skills along with everything they know in reading texts appropriately, effectively, and efficiently. We should remember, though, that not all older struggling readers need this particular kind of help, and not all are able to benefit from additional help of this nature, even if they *seem* to need it—witness the highly successful adult readers and writers in Fink's study (1995/1996), discussed in Chapter 13.

Figure 14.1 shows the gradual release of responsibility model of instruction developed by Pearson and Gallagher (1983), and Figure 14.2 shows that model (inspired by Ritterskamp and Singleton [2001, p. 115]) applied to key aspects of a comprehensive literacy program as described in Chapter 12. This model indicates a progression from teacher modeling to shared reading and writing, to guided reading and writing in small groups, to sustained reading and writing. In other words, the model shows, from top to bottom, key literacy events that give increasing responsibility to learners. Typically this progression occurs again and again, cyclically, with many such teaching/learning opportunities occurring every day. Individual help is provided in

The gradual release of responsibility model of instruction

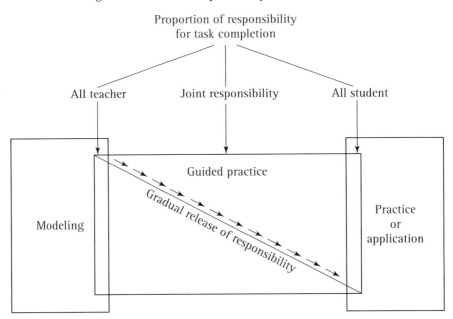

Figure 14.1   *Gradual release of responsibility model (Pearson & Gallagher 1983, after Campione, 1981).*

Reading and writing events in a first-grade comprehensive literacy classroom

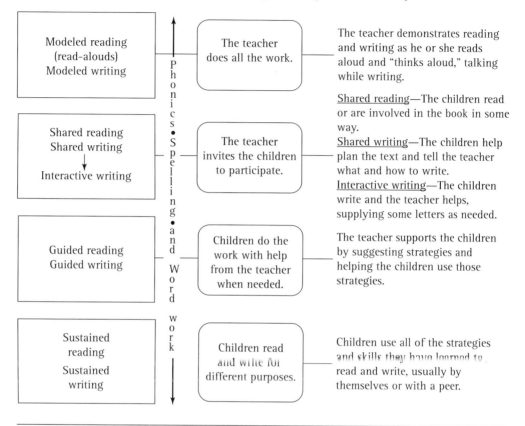

Figure 14.2   *Gradual release of responsibility model applied to daily literacy events (adapted from Ritterskamp & Singleton, 2001).*

teacher-student conferences if necessary. It's possible to hold brief conferences even at the secondary level, if the teacher establishes a reading workshop and/or a writing workshop in the classroom. Collaboration among peers also supports the learning process.

TEACHING READING STRATEGIES AT THE MACRO LEVEL

When my friends and I walked into Anne Ebner's first-grade classroom, we were astonished at the amount and quality of student-and-teacher-generated work that was displayed. Though it was only the seventh day of the school year, the walls were covered with children's writings and charts the teacher and children had composed together: caring and sharing rules, to which the children had signed on; a story of the month calendar with a piece of paper whereon the teacher had written, and a child had illustrated, what the class said about "what we did"; a list in response to the question "How do writers get their ideas?"; a list of spelling strategies; guidelines for "alone reading"; a list of books the children were recommending; the children's drawing and writing; and other evidence of their developing literacy.

One piece of chart paper that particularly caught my eye was a list of strategies good readers use. There were two strategies listed already, from the previous six days—strategies taught the previous year in kindergarten in that school:

Good readers use *background knowledge* to make sense of their reading.

Readers make *connections* about their reading.

That particular day, Anne was focusing on the strategy of making connections to one's own life. Here are my notes from that lesson, written as the sequence of activities unfolded:

1. Anne reads *The Relatives Came,* by Cynthia Rylant (1985). But before she begins reading, she tells the children that she will be focusing on background knowledge and especially making connections to their lives. She also tells the children that she has already put Post-its on pages she wants to come back to, after she's read the book aloud.

2. Anne demonstrates the strategy of making connections by sharing her own personal connections with the parts of the book where she has put the Post-its.

3. Before the time for alone reading, which follows, Anne asks the children to see if they can find something that generates personal connections with the book they have chosen to read. She gives each child a couple of Post-its to mark such spots. The books for alone reading are chosen from a number of bins of books arranged mostly by topic; some bins also have red, green, yellow, white, or other color dots indicating their difficulty.

4. While the children are doing alone reading, Anne sits down between two of them, reading a professional article herself but also helping the two readers with strategies as they need them. NOTE: She doesn't "give" them words; she "gives" them strategies by helping them use an appropriate strategy.

5. After read alone time, Anne begins the sharing by talking briefly about her professional article. It's an article from *Primary Voices,* she tells the children, and it's about starting writers' notebooks. She reads them a sentence about starting writers' notebooks in second grade. Anne tells the children her "connection" is she realizes that they, the children in her class, have been keeping writers' notebooks since kindergarten. Thus Anne demonstrates the kind of sharing she would like the children to do, at least eventually, with regard to the connections they make.

6. Several children share a connection and Anne responds by asking a question about the connection, or suggests a connection herself, based upon her knowledge of the student, if the child's sharing of something from the book hasn't actually included a connection. One child talks about "text-to-text" connections between two wordless picture books about the dog Carl; the child sees a pattern. Anne comments on the pattern and the background knowledge that the child drew upon in making the connection.

7. Anne brings this sequence of activities to a close by telling the children if they didn't have a chance to share their connection, they should keep the book with a sticky note right in the book.

We were amazed at the sophistication of the first grader's "text-to-text" connection, though later we learned that these strategies had been taught previously in kindergarten.

Anne's classroom is only one of several in the greater Denver area, and increasingly across the nation, that draws upon the work of Ellin Keene and Susan Zimmerman (1997), Stephanie Harvey (1998), Ann Goudvis (Harvey & Goudvis, 2000), and Chris Tovani (2000) to teach cognitive strategies that effective readers use. These educators and staff developers are affiliated with the Public Education and Business Coalition in Denver <*http://www.pebc.org*>.

The following strategies are emphasized by the PEBC staff developers, and most of these strategies are listed, with references from researchers, in Keene and Zimmerman (1997, p. 22–23):

- Using prior knowledge (schemas)
- Making connections (which requires prior knowledge/schemas)
- Drawing inferences (includes predicting, speculating, hypothesizing)
- Asking questions (of text and its connections to author, self, other texts, world)
- Determining importance in text (requires valuing, evaluating)
- Evoking images (visual and other sensory/mental images)
- Monitoring meaning and comprehension (for example, by paraphrasing)
- Employing fix-up strategies
- Synthesizing (requires analyzing and evaluating; may involve drawing analogies)
- Becoming metacognitively aware of the other strategies and determining when to use them

Each year in a school that has PEBC staff developers, each of the participating teachers focuses on three "new" strategies, while continuing to reinforce those previously emphasized.

"The cumulative effect of teaching comprehension strategies from kindergarten through high school is powerful" (Stephanie Harvey & Ann Goudvis, *Strategies That Work,* 2000, p. 26).

As you can readily see, this list of strategies includes three that have been emphasized in this book for getting words and meaning: predicting; monitoring comprehension; and employing fix-it strategies to correct, or try to correct, as needed. These three although and others are used at both the macro and micro levels, as defined previously. However, teaching all the listed strategies, again and again over time, enables readers to probe the meanings of texts much more deeply than typical instruction in "comprehension skills" does. This is partly because teaching reading strategies avoids the unnatural division into skills that the publishers of basal reading programs have made, if for no reason other than to show progression from grade to grade in the skills that are taught (e.g., Commission on Reading, 1988; see Rosenshine, 1980, on the inseparability of comprehension skills). Unlike the teaching of separate reading "skills," the teaching of reading strategies is supported by research (Pearson & Fielding, 1991; National Reading Panel, 2000b). Teaching reading strategies helps students—and even us, as teachers—to read more deeply, to probe a text more thoughtfully and thoroughly. Teaching reading strategies helps readers not only engage with and understand texts, but make connections with other texts, the world, and their own lives.

Outstanding Resources for Teachers

Harvey, S. (1998). *Nonfiction Matters: Reading, Writing, and Research in Grades 3–8.* York, ME: Stenhouse. An invaluable resource on these topics, Harvey's book includes several bibliographies of well-crafted materials to use with students, plus other print sources and models of different kinds of writing. My favorite bibliographies list picture books for science and social studies, many of which could be used in different ways with students of varying ages.

Harvey, S., & Goudvis, A. (2000). *Strategies That Work: Teaching Comprehension to Enhance Understanding.* York, ME: Stenhouse. This outstanding book discusses strategic thinking and reading, then focuses on five particular strategies, demonstrating how strategy instruction occurs in context. Several valuable appendices are included, among them "Great Books and Author Sets to Launch Strategy Instruction and Practice" and "Great Books for Teaching Content in History, Social Studies, Science, Music, Art and Literacy."

Keene, E. O., & Zimmerman, S. (1997). *Mosaic of Thought: Teaching Comprehension in a Reader's Workshop.* Portsmouth, NH: Heinemann. In this inspirational book, Keene and Zimmerman describe how they learned more about their own cognitive/reading strategies as they helped children develop such strategies—and in turn became better able to help children process and comprehend texts. Relevant to all levels, the book also suggests how we can help teachers understand these cognitive/reading strategies and then teach them.

Tovani, C. (2000). *I Read It, But I Don't Get It: Comprehension Strategies for Adolescent Readers.* York, ME: Stenhouse. From her experience as a high school teacher, Tovani shares how reading and English teachers at the junior high and secondary levels can teach reading strategies effectively. A highly valuable resource, her book extends the teaching practices of pioneers Keene and Harvey beyond the elementary and middle grades.

Wilhelm, J. (2001). *Improving Comprehension with Think-Aloud Strategies: Modeling What Good Readers Do.* New York: Scholastic. Think-alouds make audible the processes and strategies that a reader is using, and teacher modeling of the think-aloud strategy is important in "making strategic knowledge visible and available to students." This book is a valuable companion to the one described next.

Wilhelm, J., Baker, T. N., & Dube, J. (2001). *Strategic Reading: Guiding Students to Lifelong Literacy, 6–12.* Portsmouth, NH: Boynton/Cook. The teaching of reading strategies like visualization and questioning is only a small part of this book. Building on Wilhelm's *"You Gotta BE the Book"* (1995), the authors include chapters on such topics as a theory of teaching and a theory of teaching reading, authorial reading and democratic projects, teaching *before* reading, building on different strengths to make reading visible, and more.

Teaching Strategies in the Primary Grades

Especially in an election year, we routinely hear cries about how our nation's children can't even read at a basic level. Sometimes these critics of public education cite statistics from the latest National Assessment of Educational Progress. What most people don't realize, though, is that the "basic" level for fourth graders (the youngest group assessed) isn't described in terms of word identification or decoding skill, but in terms of reading strategies—namely, making connections and drawing simple inferences. The other two levels of fourth-grade achievement require even more sophisticated strategy use (NAEP, 1999, p. 19):

- "Fourth-grade students performing at the Basic level should demonstrate an understanding of the overall meaning of what they read. When reading text appropriate for fourth graders, they should be able to make relatively obvious connections between the text and their own experiences and extend the ideas in the text by making simple inferences."

- "Fourth-grade students performing at the Proficient level should be able to demonstrate an overall understanding of the text, providing inferential as well as literal information. When reading text appropriate to fourth grade, they should be able to extend the ideas in the text by making inferences, drawing conclusions, and making connections to their own experiences. The connection between the text and what the student infers should be clear."

- "Fourth-grade students performing at the Advanced level should be able to generalize about topics in the reading selection and demonstrate an awareness of how authors compose and use literary devices. When reading text appropriate to fourth grade, they should be able to judge text critically and, in general, give thorough answers that indicate careful thought."

It's true that the NAEP levels and level-setting procedures are fundamentally flawed and need to be revised (e.g., NAEP 1999, pp. 10–13), but it is also true that fourth graders should be able to meet at least the criteria for the basic level as described here—either in English or in their native language. But helping children learn to make connections and inferences is not just the job of the fourth-grade teacher; it's a responsibility shared with K–3 teachers as well.

Certain reading strategies can, and should, be taught and used in the primary grades, before teachers even help children learn words and phonics elements—though all of these may well be taught with the same text, if not during the same day. The most obvious strategy may be drawing inferences based upon prior knowledge and the pictures and words of a text, which is what we do when predicting what might happen next. Clearly, making connections is also a basic strategy, and asking questions is likely to come into play. When the teacher and children stop to discuss the appropriateness of their predictions, this is a form of monitoring comprehension. Furthermore, we can generate children's metacognitive awareness of these strategies and their usefulness by naming the strategies, demonstrating them, and involving children in applying the strategies themselves. Other reading strategies may also be demonstrated by the teacher and used by the children—even when the teacher simply reads a book aloud to the class for the first time.

One approach is to decide what strategy you want to teach and then to look for appropriate children's books, fiction as well as nonfiction. Another is to look through favorite children's books and see what strategies are most obviously required. Picture books—especially informational ones—can be good choices even for secondary students and adults, because the texts are relatively short. Most of the professional books I've recommended for teaching cognitive/reading strategies have bibliographies that can assist with either approach.

Captivated by the charm of the book *Owen,* by Kevin Henkes (1993), I have chosen it to illustrate selecting a book for young children and then deciding what strategies, if any, the book invites us to teach. *Owen* is the story of a little mouse named Owen who has a yellow blanket named Fuzzy. Fuzzy goes wherever Owen goes and participates in everything he does. A neighbor, Mrs. Tweezers, suggests to Owen's parents different strategies for getting Owen to give up his blanket, but Owen foils their attempts. Finally the situation becomes critical when Owen is about to start school. The pictures are delightful and the text is filled with gentle humor that adults, especially, will appreciate. For example, there are three incidents where Mrs. Tweezers "filled them in"—"them" being Owen's parents. The third is when it's time for school to start:

"Can't bring a blanket to school," said Mrs. Tweezers.
"Haven't you heard of saying no?"
Owen's parents hadn't.
Mrs. Tweezers filled them in.

In all three instances of Mrs. Tweezers' "helpfulness," the last two lines are repeated as a refrain. Sooner or later, many parents will laugh in sympathy with Owen's parents at the unsolicited advice from their neighbor. As for children, see what responses *you* receive in discussing these repeated incidents.

Upon a first reading of the book, it was immediately obvious that *Owen* would lend itself well to demonstrating and using certain cognitive/reading strategies: drawing upon prior knowledge and making connections, and drawing upon prior knowledge to make inferences—that is, predictions about what will happen next. Now that school has started, the problem of getting Owen to give up the blanket has to be solved, doesn't it? (Or does it?) But if so, how might it be solved? Clearly a kindergarten or first-grade class can be involved in hypothesizing how the problem might be solved—or not.

Other books by Kevin Henkes are especially appropriate for teaching young readers to use such reading strategies. Another of my favorites is *Chrysanthemum* (1991), about a mouse who loves her name until she starts school and other children tease her about the uncommon name. Like these two books, Henkes' picture books typically involve animal characters in situations that many young children can identify with—and adults, too, remembering their childhoods.

Remember Prior Knowledge!

While we're thinking about reading strategies, we need to keep in mind that many children may not have the background knowledge for simple picture books that we love and want to read to the class. Drawn by the illustrations and the simple text that reminded me of my childhood, I purchased one such book a year ago: *Spring Thaw*, by Steven Schnur, illustrated by Stacey Schuett (2000). But what would city children make of a sentence like "A wagon leaves the barn, its narrow wheels cutting deeply into the snow, turning it brown"? Would they realize that the snow was turning brown because it was melting and the horses' hooves cut through to the mud that was forming underneath? Before we can teach reading strategies, we often have to *provide* background knowledge for the text being read.

Teaching Strategies in the Intermediate and Middle Grades

In haste one day, I prepared a chart to share with a class of preservice teachers, showing reading strategies that one might teach from *A Boy Called Slow,* by Joseph Bruchac (1994). It's a Native American tale that describes the naming of a child who became a great leader of his people. I started reading the book to the class and immediately stumbled into a problem I hadn't anticipated: I needed to draw upon or to develop my students' prior knowledge to understand the very first sentence. Here is that opening sentence: "Many years ago, in the winter of 1831, a boy was born to the family of Returns Again of the Hunkpapa band of the Lakota Sioux." As soon as I read that sentence, I realized that just from listening to the sentence, my students probably didn't realize that Returns Again was the name of a person. I was right; most of them didn't. So we brainstormed for names that Native Americans had chosen, or might have chosen, to describe what a person did that was characteristic, such as Dances with Wolves. When I reread the opening sentence of the book more slowly, my students could then understand that Returns Again was someone's name. Figure 14.3 is the chart I prepared, with the addition of the strategy we needed to use in the very first sentence.

Before reading the final pages of the book, one could build upon students' prior experience in using reading strategies to have them predict what Slow will be renamed when he is considered an adult. This is a complex task that requires analyzing, synthesizing, inferring, and, of course, predicting. To break the task down into more manageable parts, I would photocopy four different sets of passages and give each set to one or two groups of students (see pages indicated in the chart). From each group's page(s), what would they predict Slow might be renamed? Predictions from the different groups would be listed, the text containing the photocopied pages would be reread, and the students would again be invited, as a class, to decide which predictions seem most likely. They would need to draw upon prior knowledge and information in the text, particularly from the photocopied pages. Ultimately, of course, I would read the ending of the book to the class. With this book, readers will almost certainly not make an accurate prediction regarding Slow's new name—unless they have read the subtitle of the book. However, they may decide that from the clues in the text, some of their names are more appropriate.

The individual reading strategies become quite complex and increasingly intertwined as students read more sophisticated texts and new genres. Here, for example, are some of Ellin Keene's reflections on inferring (Keene & Zimmerman, 1997):

■ "To infer as we read is to go beyond literal interpretation and to open a world of meaning deeply connected to our lives. We create an original meaning, a meaning born at the intersection of our background knowledge (schema), the words printed on a page, and our mind's capacity to merge that combination into something uniquely ours. We go beyond the literal and weave our own sense into the words we read. As we read further, that meaning is revised, enriched, sometimes abandoned, based on what we continue to read" (p. 149).

- "Inference is part rational, part mystical, part definable, and part beyond definition. Individuals' life experiences, logic, wisdom, creativity, and thoughtfulness, set against the text they are reading, form the crux of new meaning. Because each person's experiences are different, the art of inferring takes the reader beyond the text to a place only he or she can go" (pp. 147–148).

- "Inferring has many facets and great books provoke us to consider and use them all" (p. 153). Inference can be a prediction, a conclusion, a critical analysis of a text, an argument with an author, a recognition of propaganda, or "the play of imagination as we mentally expand text" (p. 153).

Keene asks us what the consequence is if children read for just the literal meaning or the facts of a text. In part, her answer is that children may be unable to recall important content because they have not made it their own. "Yet how often do we create the context for them to discuss, ponder, argue, restate, reflect, persuade, relate, write about, or otherwise work with the information we consider critical for them to recall? To push beyond the literal text, to make it personal and three-dimensional, to weave it into our own stories—*that* is to infer" (p. 152).

We must also not settle for mere summaries of what children read but instead help them learn to synthesize information and ideas.

Synthesis as Different from Summary

A summary is a listing of the parts and synthesis is somehow the creation of a whole. It requires real creative, critical thought. It should go on throughout the process of reading, not just at the end. (Keene, in Keene & Zimmerman, 1997, p. 173)

Synthesis is the process of ordering, recalling, retelling, and recreating into a coherent whole the information with which our minds are bombarded every day. . . . It is the process by which we forsake much of what we learn [or have been exposed to] in order to make sense of that which we determine is most pivotal for us. (p. 169)

Synthesis is about organizing the different pieces to create a mosaic, a meaning, a beauty, greater than the sum of each shiny piece. It is a complex process in which children, even the youngest, engage very naturally every day. (p. 169)

As these quotes from Ellin Keene make clear, reading strategies are not only complex but inseparably intertwined in actual use. For example, in reading the first fifty pages of *The Hours* (Cunningham, 1998) and trying to be metacognitively aware of my strategies, I noticed myself doing all of the following, recursively and not just in linear order: using prior knowledge to set purposes, make inferences, and determine the importance of and within small portions of text; using prior knowledge and information from the text to make predictions and construct hypotheses about larger patterns and possible future events in the text; synthesizing information to create larger patterns of understanding; questioning the text and the author's intentions and planned structure of the novel; and making metacognitive decisions about new purposes and strategies to use as I read further. As the staff developers at the PEBC have found, it's absolutely crucial for teachers to become aware of their own reading strategies—and perhaps to apply more of them, or to apply them more deliberately, as well. Consciously applying reading strategies, observing our own strategy use, and discussing with other teachers what we've done and learned is probably the best way for us to start thinking about how to foster students' use of reading strategies.

TEACHING READING STRATEGIES AT THE MICRO LEVEL

Of course there is no clear division between teaching reading strategies at the macro level, the level of texts, and teaching reading strategies at the micro level, the level of individual words and the strategies used to deal with them. Furthermore, teaching strategies at the macro level

Book information	Page(s) to draw upon This book has no page numbers. The pages begin with these words →	What strategies could be taught?	What will the strategy require? • Use prior knowledge • Use information in the text • Use information from other texts and sources	Questions or comments or notes
A Boy Called Slow, by Joseph Bruchac	"It was"	Predicting (a kind of inferring) and/or synthesizing	Information in the text; prior knowledge	What do you think they might name this boy? "If he were to take much longer eating," his uncle Four Horns said, "the food would bite him before he bites it!"
	"One summer"	Inferring, predicting	Information in the text	Questions: Do you think Slow will be given four names? Why or why not?
	"Slow longed"	Analyzing, synthesizing, inferring, predicting; determining relevance or importance	Information in the text; prior knowledge	If Slow is given four names, what do you think they might be?
	"Returns Again was" and the next page			
	"Slow was proud" and the next page			
	"Determined" and the next two pages			

Figure 14.3   *Strategies that could be taught with* A Boy Called Slow, *by Joseph Bruchac (1994).*

	Inferring word from context	Information in the text, prior knowledge	What do you think the word *travois* might mean, in the following passage? "Our Creator, Wakan-Tanka, loves the Lakota people," his uncle would tell him. "Wakan-Tanka saw that we had only our dogs to help us pull our travois and hunt buffalo. So Wakan-Tanka sent us a new animal as faithful as our dogs but able to pull our loads and carry us as quick as the whirlwind into the hunt, the *Shoong-Toñkah*, the 'Spirit Dog.'"
"Slow's uncle"			
"Determined"	Inferring word from context	Information in the text, prior knowledge	What do you think the word *coup* might mean, in the following passage? "The men began to make preparations. They put on their best clothing and brought out their paint to mark their faces and their horses. They uncovered their war shields and took out their coup sticks and their knives."

Figure 14-3 (Continued).

can help children use some of these same strategies in reading individual words, if this use is demonstrated and encouraged when students encounter difficult words in text.

> Teaching strategies at the macro level will help children use some of these same strategies in reading individual words . . . with teacher demonstrations and guidance.

In Chapter 9 I have already suggested some strategies for dealing with individual words, particularly during Retrospective Miscue Analysis sessions. Here, we will deal with three more topics: materials for a Reading Detective Club; considering micro-level reading strategies we ourselves use; plus using prompts and developing strategy charts and bookmarks with children.

A Reading Detective Club

What do detectives and good readers have in common? They look for clues (cues) to construct a meaningful scenario (text). That is, they try to solve the mystery by using the clues (cues) available to them, and their evolving hypotheses affect how they perceive and use—or miss—new clues (cues). Sometimes the new clues (cues) require them to abandon previous hypotheses (predictions) and formulate new ones. As they proceed in solving the mystery, the evolving scenario (text) teaches them more and more. Thus they increasingly use macro-level information to solve micro-level problems.

Debra Goodman has captured these and other parallels between good detectives and good readers in her book for teachers and students, *The Reading Detective Club: Solving the Mysteries of Reading* (1999). This text is not a workbook, even though it contains materials for students in the intermediate and middle grades to use. First, it offers teachers an excellent introduction to the reading process, explains the values of strategy lessons, and provides suggestions for establishing our own Reading Detective Club in the classroom. The heart of the book, however, is the detective cases for students to solve—often collaboratively. Discussion, not grading, is the means by which teachers can assess individual readers' continuing needs. The detective lessons, undertaken in a spirit of fun and sharing, help less proficient readers particularly to better understand what good readers do. As the less proficient and/or less confident readers begin to use language cues and reading strategies more effectively and efficiently, and to realize that their hypotheses and responses are valued, they typically begin also to develop better attitudes toward reading and to feel better about themselves as readers.

As an example, see Figure 14.4, which includes the first two pages of an extended case study, "The Case of the Messy Hands." After reading the case and supplying reasonable words for the smudges, see what you think is the "big idea" of this particular activity in the case.

There are other good resources for teaching reading strategies, especially Y. Goodman, D. Watson, and C. Burke, *Reading Strategies: Focus on Comprehension* (1996), which includes a wealth of strategy lessons, some for each of the language cueing systems that might need strengthening. However, I'll admit I especially like the playfulness of Debra Goodman's *The Reading Detective Club* (1999), because she plays up students' role of "linguistic detectives."

Quotable Quotes from *The Reading Detective Club*

"The Reading Detective Club helps young readers explore the wonders of the reading process and, at the same time, discover their own reading strengths and strategies. . . . My belief is that literacy learning in school can and should involve the same playfulness and delight as two-year-olds learning their mother tongue. . . .

Frank Smith (1988) talks about inviting our children to join "the literacy club." . . . I find that kids love being in a club, and they get really excited about solving their first case. That's partly because I really ham it up. As the "club sponsor" our job is to establish a playful and enjoyable atmosphere for language learning. I wrote these stories initially for my own students. I wanted them to know that language can be fun, interesting, and exciting. I wanted to show them that they are really smart kids who already know a lot about language" (Debra Goodman, 1999, p. ix).

The Case of the Messy Hands

Jacob was a famous detective. One day Michele stormed into Jacob's office shouting, "My stupid brother has done it again!"

Jacob asked, "What is it this time? Did he cross out some more words in your book?"

"No," said Michele, "This time he wanted to read my book. But he never washes his hands. Every time he touched my book with his grubby paws, he smudged up the words so I can't read them."

"Let me take a look," Jacob said. "I'll see what I can do." Michele handed Jacob the book.

Jacob said, "I think I can solve this case."

Psst: Work by yourself before you compare answers.

HINT!
If you can't think of a good guess for one of the smudges, keep reading. When you have read the whole story, go back and try again. Try to come up with a word that makes sense for each smudge.

THE THREE LITTLE PIGS

Once upon a 🖐 there were three little pigs.

One day the 🖐 pigs decided to go out into the

world to make their 🖐.

Each little pig 🖐 a house.

The first little pig built a house of 🖐.

The 🖐 little pig built a house of sticks.

The third little pig built a 🖐 of bricks.

One 🖐 a wolf saw the three little pigs.

"A little 🖐 will make a tasty meal for me,"

he 🖐.

Your solutions

1. _____

2. _____

3. _____

4. _____

5. _____

6. _____

7. _____

8. _____

9. _____

10. _____

Figure 14.4   *"The Case of the Messy Hands" (D. Goodman, 1999).*

DEBRIEFING:
The Case of the Messy Hands

*Readers Have Different Interpretations
When They Read*

*Congratulations on solving your second case! If you are working with
a group of friends, take a look at some of your friends' answers for each .
Use this chart to compare your answers.*

Number	My Answer	Friends' Answers	Clues We Used to Get Answers
1.	_____	_____	_____
2.	_____	_____	_____
3.	_____	_____	_____
4.	_____	_____	_____
5.	_____	_____	_____
6.	_____	_____	_____
7.	_____	_____	_____
8.	_____	_____	_____
9.	_____	_____	_____
10.	_____	_____	_____

Figure 14.4   *(Continued).*

Considering Strategies for Dealing with Words

One way to determine what strategies students might need to learn for dealing with problem words is to start by brainstorming the strategies we ourselves use. One group of preservice teachers came up with the following list:

- Skip it!
- Read on and see if that helps.
- Just go on—period.
- Come back to it if it seems important.
- Go back to the beginning of the sentence and reread.
- Sound it out.
- Ask my roommate.
- Look it up in the dictionary—but I don't really do that.

- Maybe try the glossary, if I'm reading a textbook and the word seems to be really important.
- Hope that the teacher will explain it in class!
- Don't worry about pronouncing it, but see if you can figure out what it means.
- Look at the word parts and see if they help with meaning.

We discussed in what order we usually use different reading strategies, to see if there were any patterns, and I later tried to draw generalizations from what we said (Figure 14.5). However, we all realized that this branching diagram was no more than one attempt to capture one pattern for dealing with problem words. Any given person, at any given time, might use different strategies or use strategies in a different order.

More recently, my students and I have concluded that "Try to make sense," or something of the sort, must be at the center of any diagram that attempts to capture the strategies that effective readers use. Our most recent attempts at a diagram begin with a circle in which we've written not only "THINK: What would make sense here?" but also "CHECK: Does that make sense here?" In

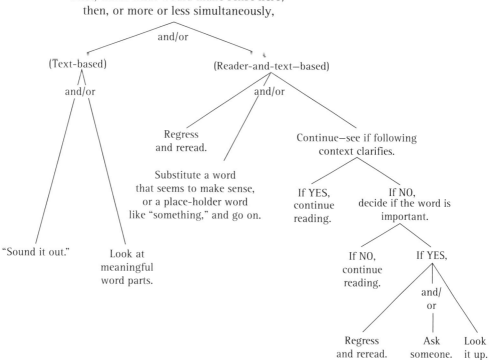

WHAT GOOD READERS DO MORE OR LESS AUTOMATICALLY BUT OTHER READERS MAY NEED HELP IN LEARNING TO DO

Figure 14.5   *Sample ordering of how good readers sometimes use strategies for dealing with problem words (Weaver, 1990, p. 15).*

other words, trying to make sense and monitoring for sense are crucial to effectively using other strategies for dealing with problem words (see diagram below). We invite you to elaborate upon the diagram, showing how more specific strategies intersect with these basic ones, or to develop your own list or visual of strategies for dealing with problem words.

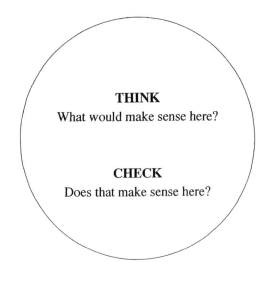

THINK

What would make sense here?

CHECK

Does that make sense here?

Using Prompts and Developing Strategy Charts and Bookmarks

As we demonstrate reading strategies with the whole class, we can discuss and use prompts that, over time, will help readers learn to use effective strategies for dealing with problem words. We can use prompts during shared, whole-class reading and within guided reading groups, then follow up with individual readers who need continued prompting.

Here, for example, are some prompts that Fountas and Pinnell (1996) suggest for supporting the reader's use of all sources of information (p. 161):

- "Check the picture."
- "Does that make sense?"
- "Does that look right?"
- "Does that sound right?"
- "You said (...). Can we say it that way?"
- "You said (...). Does that make sense?"
- "What's wrong with this?" (repeat what child said)
- "Try that again and think what would make sense."
- "Try that again and think what would sound right."
- "Do you know a word like that?" [if the child says a nonword close to the actual word]
- "Do you know a word that starts with those letters?"
- "Do you know a word that ends with those letters?"

- "What do you know that might help?"
- "What can you do to help yourself?"

Of course prompts often have to be used in sequence, in response to what the reader says and does. Here are some possibilities:

- "Check the picture. What is so-and-so doing? [for example] Try that word here. Does it fit? What else might fit?"
- "Look at the first letter(s). What word would fit here? Does that make sense?" and so forth.
- "Can you think of some words that would fit here? Try to sound out the word in chunks. Does that sound like a word? Does that word make sense here?" and so forth.
- "Does that sound like a word? Try again. Hmmm . . . that still doesn't sound like a word. Can you figure out what this *part* of the word [point to it] means? Okay, what do you think the word might mean?"
- "Does this word seem really important in the sentence? Why? What else could you do to get the word?" (focusing here on decision making and metacognitive awareness)
- "Does this word seem really important in the sentence? No? Okay, what do you want to do about it?" (helping readers understand that it's okay to decide that a word doesn't seem really important, and go on)

Of course whatever prompts we use must be not only tailored to the individual reader's strategies and needs but chosen according to what cues in the text would be particularly helpful. Sometimes, for instance, a quick glance at the sentence should tell us that the rest of the sentence isn't particularly helpful, so we wouldn't suggest that the reader back up and try the sentence again, or read on to see if the rest of the sentence helps. Also, we need to take into account the individual reader's personality, the particular text, and the reading situation. Though my general rule is "give a reader a strategy, not a word," we certainly don't want to make every problem word an opportunity for a strategy lesson, or to focus so much on getting the reader to use certain strategies that the reader gives up in frustration. With each reader and text, we need to develop a balance between teaching strategies and just helping the reader navigate the text successfully. We need also to consider whether the reader should be reading an easier text—or a more challenging one—the next time we work with the reader individually, to teach and guide the use of effective reading strategies.

Prompts are used, obviously, to promote reading strategies, and reminders of useful strategies can be displayed in the classroom. When teachers make charts or other classroom visuals of strategies good readers use, it is important to develop them together with the class. Notice, for example, that Anne, the first-grade teacher whose teaching of strategies I described earlier in the chapter, had started a list of strategies that good readers use. She would add to this over the school year as she demonstrated additional strategies and the children began to use them more consciously.

From such lists, the teacher can make bookmarks with increasingly complete and detailed strategies, over the school year and across the grades.

Figure 14.6 includes two examples that Lorraine Gillmeister-Krause, Grace Vento-Zogby, and I created together during one summer, not with students, but drawing upon our experiences in helping students develop such strategies. Generally speaking, the bookmark on the left is for independent readers in the primary grades (1996, T6.9a). The other is for independent readers in the intermediate grades and beyond. But I recommend using these only for ideas of what

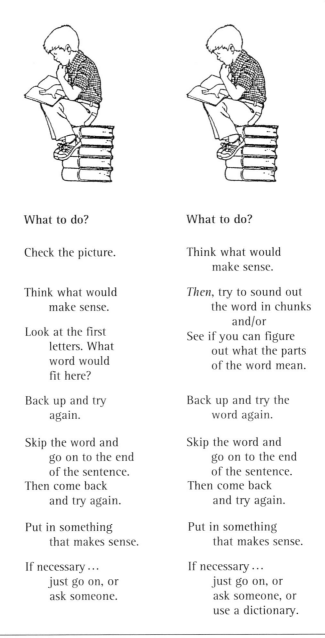

What to do?

What to do?

Check the picture.

Think what would
    make sense.

Think what would
    make sense.

Look at the first
    letters. What
    word would
    fit here?

Then, try to sound out
    the word in chunks
    and/or
See if you can figure
    out what the parts
    of the word mean.

Back up and try
    again.

Back up and try the
    word again.

Skip the word and
    go on to the end
    of the sentence.
Then come back
    and try again.

Skip the word and
    go on to the end
    of the sentence.
Then come back
    and try again.

Put in something
    that makes sense.

Put in something
    that makes sense.

If necessary...
    just go on, or
    ask someone.

If necessary...
    just go on, or
    ask someone, or
    use a dictionary.

Figure 14.6   *Sample bookmarks (Weaver, Gillmeister-Krause, & Vento-Zogby, 1996, p. T6.9a).*

strategies you want to help children develop, because students have more ownership over the bookmarks—and, we hope, the strategies—when the list of strategies is developed collaboratively.

In conclusion, if you'll look back at the strategies my students brainstormed (p. 338–339), you will notice that several of these strategies for dealing with words at the micro level of a text are the same or similar to those we use in dealing with whole texts, at the macro level (p. 329). The strategies explicit or implicit in both these lists include: try to make sense; use prior knowledge and the evolving sense to construct meaning(s), make predictions, monitor comprehension, and revise predictions if needed; and use fix-it strategies as needed. Of course either or both lists could be expanded, and other strategies could be added, too. But the aforementioned commonalities are basic, for they deal with constructing meaning from texts, and that is the basic purpose of reading.

TEACHING PHONICS AND PHONEMIC AWARENESS

How are phonics and phonemic awareness taught in comprehensive literacy classrooms? Phonics skills are not taught first. Figure 14.7 suggests the typical progression from whole texts to words and word parts, with phonics and phonemic awareness taught in the course of reading and writing interesting texts. During a shared reading experience, for example, phonics and phonemic awareness are taught when the teacher and children have read and reread a familiar predictable text, until the children have virtually memorized it.

First, however, the teacher will have guided the children in using and understanding such reading strategies as drawing inferences and predicting from the title and cover and from the pictures throughout the text. Thus, strategies are taught or reinforced before skills. If needed, the teacher will already have focused on certain concepts of print with that text, so the children will easily read from left to right and return down left. The teacher is also likely to have called the children's attention to particular words in the text—eventually, perhaps, by inviting individual children to use a pointer to show where a particular word is located in the text, or to frame the word with two fingers or two narrow sticky notes. Perhaps the predictable text rhymes, and after the first readings of the text, the teacher has covered up the second word of the rhyming pairs with sticky notes, inviting the children to predict the rhyme words. In short, the teacher and children will read and work with a text over several days, and—with emergent readers—might then attend to phonics

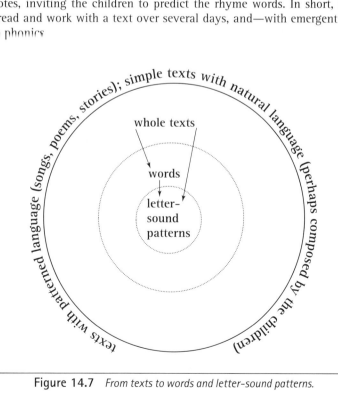

Figure 14.7 *From texts to words and letter-sound patterns.*

Why Teach Just Phonemic Awareness and Phonics, When We Can Teach All of the Following?

- Reading for meaning
- Strategies for understanding and reading texts
- Recognition of some interesting words and some high-utility words
- Phonics: letter-sound patterns, onsets and rimes
- Decoding new print words by using context and the parts of known words (such as onsets and rimes)
- Phonemic awareness

These aspects of reading can be taught even in preschool, as long as the children are not assessed for mastery. Each child will learn what he or she is ready to learn—as children and adults all do.

Chapters 11, 13, and 15 offer some of the research support for such a progression, and for integrating writing with reading. Focusing on reading strategies first keeps the children's attention on meaning, as they also discuss and enjoy the text together, relating it to their own lives and to other texts if relevant. Focusing on phonics a few days later postpones dealing with the more abstract elements of language, letters and sounds, but only for a very short time. It's not a matter of dealing with meaning in the fall and phonics in the winter and spring (though Ayres' [1993] research suggests that this, too, works better than focusing on phonics before attending to meaning in texts). Rather, comprehensive literacy classrooms teach and focus on everything cyclically, again and again, with each cycle taking a few days. During each cycle, teachers guide children in using strategies for constructing meaning from texts and for appreciating them; developing fluency through rereading texts; recognizing new print words and developing automaticity in recognizing them; developing skills for making connections between letter and sound relationships; and developing the ability to decode words, in context first. Writing strategies and skills are also employed and taught.

"Inventive" Spelling Promotes Phonics and Phonemic Awareness

In a detailed study of invented versus traditional spelling in first graders' writings, Linda Clarke (1988) examined the differing effects on learning to spell and read. At the end of the study, she found not only that the children who used invented spellings wrote much more (40.9 words on the average, compared to 13.2) and spelled substantially more words correctly (13.7 to 9.8), but that they read substantially more real words in an untimed situation and demonstrated better word attack skills on nonsense words from lists.

The National Reading Panel report (2000b) also reports positive effects for helping children invent spellings: "One instructional activity that is maximally effective for teaching PA [phonemic awareness] in a way that builds a bridge to reading and spelling is that of teaching children to invent phonemically more complex spellings of words. . . . The effect size [in a study by Ehri & Wilce, 1987] was large, $d = 0.97$. These findings indicate that teaching children to segment and spell [spoken words] helps them learn to read as well as to spell words" (p. 2-39).

It's important to keep in mind the typical developmental progression that we examined in Chapter 13 (pp. 312–314) and to teach various aspects of phonics accordingly. The following is a common developmental pattern for emerging readers, especially when their emergent writing is also encouraged and supported. Over time, children tend to

- read words mostly as wholes, especially in familiar contexts;
- begin to read words by analogy with chunks of familiar words—for example, to blend familiar onsets and rimes (see pp. 305–306 for a definition of these terms);
- begin to write the sounds they hear in words;
- begin to develop the ability to analyze written words into letters and their related sounds;
- begin to write more of the sounds they hear in words, then begin to represent sounds with patterns they've seen in words; and
- become independent readers and writers of predictable and simple, natural texts.

This sequence is reflected in Figure 14.8, which indicates (1) emergent reading and writing skills and strategies; (2) teaching and learning situations within which they are fostered and/or extended toward more sophisticated skills and strategies; and (3) some basic instructional procedures appropriate to each phase. These are phases we can expect to find among children in kindergarten and first grade, though such activities as those involved in the shared reading experience can be started with preschoolers and extended at least into second grade for some students, as needed.

When examining Figure 14.8, please keep in mind the following:

- This chart focuses on reading and writing activities that are especially important for promoting the development of reading. The development of writing is not addressed quite as thoroughly.
- The list of instructional suggestions certainly does not include every kind of reading and writing experience that could or should be included in comprehensive literacy classrooms at the earliest grades, nor does it include related oral language experiences or art.
- The suggested "teaching and learning environments" include only those that seem best for promoting the strategies and skills mentioned, not all of the environments that might conceivably be productive.
- The term *shared reading* stands for a sequence of activities, as explained most fully in Chapter 12. It does not just mean reading a text together.
- Phases of reading and writing are sometimes separated in the chart, to reflect typical developmental patterns more accurately. In each instance, the reading phase promotes the next phase of writing, or the writing phase promotes the next phase of reading. However, reading and writing should be taught together, not sequentially, as these phases might seem to imply.
- This chart does not include the many other opportunities in comprehensive literacy classrooms for children to make use of, or "practice," the strategies and skills they've been learning: during sustained reading and writing, including journal writing; and soon through literature circles and inquiry reading and writing, which at first must be led, guided, and scaffolded by the teacher.

Given these caveats, you may find the chart in Figure 14.8 useful in planning for strategy and skill instruction, particularly in kindergarten and first grade.

Of course we will continue to teach reading and writing strategies and skills to newly independent readers and writers. As we introduce children to many sophisticated and diverse texts, we must continue, across the years, to guide them in developing increasingly complex strategies and skills.

Developmental trends	Teaching and learning environments	Instructional suggestions and goals for emergent readers and writers
LOGOGRAPHIC READING PHASE AND SYMBOLIC WRITING PHASE May begin well before kindergarten.		
begin learning to attend to meaning first	guided reading (whole class, group, individual)	Help children read words in environmental contexts, such as signs, labels, brief directions, and eventually such texts as a morning message (composed by the teacher or by the teacher and children together). *Goals*: *Understand that print is meaningful and that context can help in reading words; begin to be functionally literate in the environment.
	read-aloud	Read to children a lot, and demonstrate how you predict and draw inferences from pictures and text. Encourage the children to do the same, as you read more and more books. *Goals*: *Enjoy the text, realize that we read to make meaning, and begin to develop reading strategies.
	shared reading	Help children develop strategies for predicting, drawing inferences, and making connections to text (and other strategies as relevant). *Goal*: *Learn to focus on making meaning from texts; develop strategies for doing so.
"write" with just pictures add "text" to pictures by using scribbles or other symbols that represent the child's meaning (individual words may not be separately represented)	write-aloud (demonstration); shared and guided writing; individual writing conferences	Help children write as best they can, whether it be a scribble, shapes, or other symbolic marks that at least begin to resemble letters (even if they are reversed or sideways). Begin to model strategies for writing, such as drawing a picture and then writing something with it. *Goal*: *Focus on conveying meaning, which thereby also reinforces the understanding that texts are supposed to mean something.

Figure 14.8

in reading, begin to attend not only to pictures but to interesting words	shared reading; guided reading; individual reading conferences	Engage children in repeatedly reading a familiar, predictable text. *New goals*: *Fluency, word recognition.

LOGOGRAPHIC WRITING PHASE

begin to use symbols that stand for words as they write	guided writing; individual writing conferences	Continue to encourage children to write the best they can. Point out when they have used symbols to stand for individual words and encourage this strategy. *Goal*: *Use symbols to represent words, not entire stretches of words.

LOGOGRAPHIC READING AND WRITING PHASES (more advanced)

read words mostly as wholes (on sight), especially in familiar contexts read words that they find personally meaningful before reading the little "glue" words like *a, an, the; and, but; in, on, to*; and pronouns, such as *this, that, these, those*	shared and guided reading; write-aloud and shared writing shared and guided reading; guided writing and individual writing conferences	Help children learn to identify and become familiar with new print words before focusing on parts of words, including phonics. *New goals*: *Developing automaticity in indentifying these new words. Start with words that are predictable from the context. Later (in the same reading/writing cycle or another cycle) focus on meaningful words that aren't so predictable. Finally—but still soon—start focusing on some of the glue words and pronouns within texts, since they occur so frequently in a text.
begin to use *letters* to represent words, though not necessarily to represent the sounds in words: a pre-phonemic phase of spelling	shared and guided reading and writing; individual reading and writing conferences; write-aloud	Continue to encourage children to write as best they can. Teach other strategies for writing, such as talking about what you want to write, both before and during writing, and getting feedback. *Writing goals*: * Begin to write some words as wholes, using remembered spellings. * Expand repertoire of writing strategies.

Figure 14.8   *(Continued).*

ANALOGIC READING PHASE		
begin to read new print words by	shared reading, guided reading,	In order to facilitate the emergence of this stage, teachers can have children predict rhyming
analogy with chunks of familiar words, often onset-rime chunks of one-syllable words	individual reading conferences	words in a text, then attend to the spellings of the rhymed part. With single-syllable words, this rhymed part of the word is also the rime part of the syllable. (Poems, songs, and predictable books with rhyme are excellent for this purpose.)
		Teachers can also focus on the onsets of words, starting with single-consonant onsets and later focusing on digraphs (two letters that make one sound) and initial consonant clusters. For a list of these, see appendix to this chapter. (Alphabet books are excellent for this purpose.)
		Begin to focus children's attention, during repeated shared readings and guided reading, on meaningful parts in words—particularly simple prefixes such as *un-* and simple affixes such as *-ing*.
		Reading and writing goals: * To read new print words by using familiar onset and rime patterns. * To begin to develop phonemic awareness and letter-sound correspondences. * To begin to grasp the "alphabetic principle," that there are correlations between letters and sounds. * To understand that words may have meaningful parts within them. * To use prefixes and suffixes in reading unfamiliar print words. * To internalize more and more of these chunks of words, which can then be used for writing as well as reading.
ANALOGIC TO ANALYTIC PHASE IN WRITING		
begin to write words using onsets, familiar rime patterns, and other patterns seen in print, such as prefixes and suffixes begin to use letters to represent some of the sounds in words: the beginnings of a phonemic phase of writing	write-aloud (modeling); shared and guided writing; individual writing conferences	Help children hear and write some of the sounds they hear in words, starting with initial consonants, and then other consonants, especially final consonant sounds—a sequence that follows developmental tendencies. *Goals*: * Increased phonemic awareness. * Ability to read new words more readily. * Ability to write well enough that their writing can be read by others.

Figure 14.8 *(Continued).*

write increasingly more of the sounds they hear in words, including vowel sounds	write-aloud (demonstration); shared and guided writing; individual writing conferences	Help children hear and write more of the sounds they hear in words, including vowel sounds. At this point you may also want to provide the conventional spelling, perhaps writing the child's text on the back of the page or, with the child's permission, lightly above the words as the child wrote them.
		Begin to teach simple strategies for checking and revising spelling, such as circling a word and asking for help later, or writing a word two or three times and choosing the one that looks best.
		Teach any other writing strategies or skills that at least some children might be ready to learn. For example, one such skill would be to put periods where the child stops to take a breath in reading his or her own work, then later adding a capital to the first word that comes after the period. One strategy might be to have a definite beginning, middle, and end to the writing.
		Writing and reading goals: * To increase their repertoire of writing strategies and skills, including spelling strategies. * To spell words they commonly write increasingly closer to the conventional spellings. * To increase phonemic awareness and letter-sound knowledge. * To identify individual letter sounds in reading unfamiliar print words, if or as needed.
ANALYTIC READING PHASE		
use knowledge of individual letter-sound correspondences in reading, if or as needed (using context, too, as needed)	shared reading, guided reading, and individual reading conferences	If trying to read unfamiliar print words in chunks isn't successful, even though the words are read in context, decide whether using some of the individual letter sounds would help. If so, guide readers in using them. *Goal*: Increase flexibility of strategies for reading words.

Figure 14.8   *(Continued)*.

INDEPENDENT READING PHASE

The newly independent reader can do all or most of the following:
* focus on meaning while reading;
* use three or more strategies to construct meaning from texts;
* use context and prior knowledge plus letter-sound knowledge to read words;
* read most unfamiliar print words (in suitable texts) by analogy with parts of known words;
* read a substantial number of words on sight, automatically;
* use context to understand many print words, as needed; and
* read simple informational texts as well as simple stories.

INDEPENDENT WRITING PHASE

The newly independent writer can do all or most of the following:
* convey meaning through writing;
* use some strategies for preparing to write, such as drawing and talking;
* use invented (constructed) spellings as needed, representing most consonant and vowel sounds accurately enough that the writing can be read by others;
* use strategies for checking and correcting spellings;
* spell many common words and some less common words conventionally; and
* employ some editing strategies, such as adding periods and capitals.

Figure 14.8 *(Continued).*

Shared Reading: Veteran and Novice Teacher Describe How They Do It

Fisher, B., & Fisher-Medvic, E. (2000). *Perspectives on Shared Reading: Planning and Practice.* Portsmouth, NH: Heinemann. An excellent resource.

Meanwhile, the most fundamental instructional framework for accomplishing many of the instructional goals in the chart is the shared reading experience, or rather the set and sequence of related experiences undertaken in conjunction with the reading of a shared text, usually a Big Book or other text that has been printed on paper (often by the teacher) large enough for all the children in a class or group to see. The next section of this chapter will illustrate with an extended example.

Shared Reading Most Important!

After discussing language experience reading, shared reading, assisted reading, and assisted reading with CD-ROM interactive stories, Moustafa concludes:

While teachers need to have all of these tools at their disposal, over time the single most important of these instructional strategies for the purpose of teaching reading, in my experience and the experience of knowledgeable colleagues, is shared reading with predictable stories. Shared reading of lots of predictable stories with knowledgeable teachers is a powerful and effective way to launch children into lifelong reading. Extensive, pleasant experiences with shared reading with predictable stories enables children to see themselves as readers and to become readers more quickly and more easily than any other single experience teachers can provide. (Margaret Moustafa, *Beyond Traditional Phonics: Research Discoveries and Reading Instruction*, 1997, p. 30)

The Shared Reading Experience—and More

Mr. Peters is a first-grade teacher. He also plays the guitar, which has helped him teach reading and writing through singing, though Mrs. Albers down the hall has been quite successful using just the audiocassettes and accompanying books in the Wee Sing® packages she bought at the local bookstore. Both of them also use Big Books and audiocassettes, and accompanying small books from Scholastic and other publishers.

Though the kindergarten teacher in Mr. Peters' school has used similar materials with the children, only a few of his first graders are almost independent readers and writers. Therefore, Mr. Peters uses the shared reading experience, with its many facets, as the mainstay of instruction in reading. He has been teaching his students the strategies of predicting and drawing inferences, and making connections to their own lives, along with phonics skills. He likes the shared reading approach to phonics because he can introduce and reinforce needed skills, teaching them intensively and systematically, starting with the developmentally easiest. Furthermore, this approach to phonics helps him avoid overdosing kids on phonics when they need very little if any basic instruction, while setting the stage for additional work with small groups and, in some instances, individual students. Indeed, he realizes, the beauty of the shared reading experience is that it provides a basic framework that allows for variety within it, to teach needed strategies and skills.

> "Shared reading is a time when the entire class gathers together to share a variety of literacy experiences by reading and discussing a variety of texts. Many of the texts are enlarged so that all the children can see the print and pictures and thus talk more easily about them. Shared reading is a noncompetitive time when children of different abilities and experiences learn from and with each other." (Bobbi Fisher, in *Perspectives on Shared Reading: Planning and Practice*, by Bobbi Fisher and Emily Fisher-Medvic, 2000, p. 3)

Early in November, Mr. Peters decided to launch another shared reading cycle with the old rhyme that some people know as "This Old Man" and others know as "Knick Knack Paddy Wack" (a copy is included in Weaver, Gillmeister-Krause, & Vento-Zogby, 1996). For the last three days, he's been singing the traditional rhyme to the accompaniment of the guitar, with the children chiming in. By now most of the children can easily sing the repetitive parts:

This old man, he played . . . ,
He played knick knack on my . . . .
With a knick knack, paddy wack
Give the dog a bone,
This old man came rolling home.

The children have also come up with their own ideas as to what "knick knack" and "paddy wack" might mean and have been tapping the eraser tips of their pencils on their elbows when they sing "knick knack" and slapping their knees when they sing "paddy wack." Of course they aren't all together rhythmically, and sometimes they drop their pencils, but they enjoy accompanying the song with this physical activity.

Mr. Peters decides it's time to connect their singing with print. But instead of copying the traditional version on chart paper for the children, Mr. Peters decides to copy a modified version he found in a professional book for teachers (Weaver, Gillmeister-Krause, & Vento-Zogby, 1996, p. T5.26). He chooses this version for two reasons: partly because it includes the six basic colors as rhyme words, but also because the rhymes are all spelled the same after the initial sound(s). At first, he writes only the initial verse on chart paper:

This old man, he played red,
He played knick knack on my bed,

> With a knick knack, paddy wack
> Give the dog a bone,
> This old man came rolling home.

Mr. Peters underlines the word *red* with a red marker and shows the children that the rhyming word is *bed*. Then he plays the guitar and sings this verse, with the children chiming in—though naturally some children are still singing the words to the first verse of the traditional rhyme. Mr. Peters reminds the children that the rhymed words are *red* and *bed,* and points to them again. They repeat these steps until most of the children are singing the rhyme with "red" and "bed." Then Mr. Peters puts down the guitar and uses a pointer to point to each word as he and the children sing the verse.

Most of the children still seem to be involved in the singing and able to attend to the written text, so after another round of the first verse, Mr. Peters asks who would like to come forward and frame the words *knick knack* with two fingers. Aliya volunteers first, pointing out *knick knack* in the first line. Trevor waves his hand, and Mr. Peters lets him frame the other instance of *knick knack,* in the third line. "I'll do *paddy wack,*" claims LaNorris, strutting to the front and framing the words with his fingers. Mr. Peters figures this is enough for one day, but Kevin quickly says "I'll do *red,*" and Carmen volunteers to do *bed.*

"Enough, enough," Mr. Peters cries in mock distress, after they have all sung the verse one last time—followed by an encore on demand. "I'll sing the whole song for you and tomorrow I'll have three more verses written out, okay?" He then sings the song with all six verses, which are as follows (without repeating the refrain here):

> This old man, he played red,
> He played knick knack on my bed.
>
> This old man, he played blue,
> He played knick knack with our glue.
>
> This old man, he played yellow,
> He played knick knack with a fellow.
>
> This old man, he played purple,
> He played knick knack with a burple.
>
> This old man, he played green,
> He played knick knack with the queen.
>
> This old man, he played orange,
> He played knick knack in Florange.

The children clap and yell, and Mr. Peters feels satisfied that he has successfully launched a new shared reading cycle.

Over the next few days, Mr. Peters and the children focus on predicting from prior knowledge and context, then on rimes and onsets. Here are some of the activities they engage in:

1. Mr. Peters cuts out squares of colored construction paper and invites the children to match the squares with the color words. This works fine except that John, who is colorblind in the blue-purple range, volunteers first. He chooses the purple square to match with the color word *blue,* so Mr. Peters intervenes gently. When a few children snicker, Mr. Peters asks the rest of the class to remind these children how to act and react when someone has made a mistake.

2. Mr. Peters covers all but the initial consonant(s) of the words that rhyme with the color words, and has the children predict these words as they read the song together. Again, Mr. Peters points at the words of the text, stopping when they have predicted a rhyming

word. He uncovers the rest of the word and the children check to see if the end of the word confirms their prediction. The children have previously focused on predicting rhymes in one-syllable words within other songs, poems, and stories, so this task of checking the letter patterns is a familiar one, but a little more demanding with some of the longer rhymes. Mr. Peters asks the children if *burple* is a real word, and some of the boys burp, but ultimately Mr. Peters says he couldn't find *burple* in the dictionary, so it must have been made up, to rhyme with *purple.*

3. The children and Mr. Peters add the rhyming words to their word wall. They have been categorizing the words by sound, so the children suggest that *red* and *bed* belong with words they already have on the wall that rhyme the same: *head, dead, said,* and *red* (which, they discover, is already on the word wall).

4. Mr. Peters wonders if it's time to subdivide their list into words that spell the /ed/ rhyme differently. The children agree, so they help him create three subcategories; add *bed* to the appropriate list; and then brainstorm for other words to add to the subcategories. No rhyming word they suggest spells the /ed/ rime as it's spelled in *said,* but they come up with words like *Fred, bread,* and /led/. Mr. Peters asks Kevin to use /led/ in a sentence, but he only mumbles something, so Mr. Peters suggests "Matt led us to victory." Students cheer, and Mr. Peters writes *led* in the list with *red* and *bed.* He considers whether to offer the spelling *lead* and point out the lead in their pencils, but he decides not to, because *lead* also spells the verb "to lead," which has a different pronunciation.

5. On another day, Mr. Peters and the children focus on the onsets of the rhyming words. Some of these onsets are already on their word wall, but the children decide to think of other words that start with *gl-, gr-,* and *fl-* and add these categories to the wall. They struggle with *gl-* words, offering such possibilities as *green, grow,* and *go,* so Mr. Peters suggests they leave this category until later. Meanwhile, though, they've suggested words with the *gr-* onset of *green,* so Mr. Peters helps them hear the *gr* in all the words, and writes these on the word wall. The onset *fl-* is easier, and the children suggest *fly, flip,* and *flop.* Some children again have difficulty hearing the difference between /l/ and /r/ in the consonant cluster, so they suggest *frog* and *fry.* Again Mr. Peters helps the children hear the difference and makes two lists, one of *fl-* words and one of *fr-* words. Mr. Peters makes a mental note to work with certain children on differentiating these onsets. Reiko and her brother will especially need help, he knows, since their native Japanese language does not have both of these sounds.

6. Mr. Peters guides the children in blending onsets and rimes to read simple words that some of the children do not know on sight. He illustrates such blending and the class does it together during shared reading, after which he gives certain children additional help during guided reading and individual conferences.

And so the days progress, and Mr. Peters thinks about introducing and working with another version of the same traditional song, one created by fourth graders for their buddies in a primary class to read; see Figure 14.9. Instead, however, he asks his children if they would like to write their own version of the song. Of course the children are excited about doing this, and they begin to brainstorm for possible rhyming pairs. It takes the class three sessions, over three days, to complete the process. They brainstorm for rhymes, select some and draft the new verses, and check to see if they are satisfied with their verses or need to make some changes. During this shared writing process, Mr. Peters helps the children compose the new rhyming lines if absolutely necessary; helps them decide if the lines have the right rhythm; and helps the children revise these lines when needed. As he writes what they compose, he also encourages the children to provide the spellings of some common words he thinks they already know how to spell, words that at least are in the "Common words" chart they've been compiling together. The children write a

This old man, was so nice,
He played knick knack with the mice.
With a knick knack paddy wack
Give the dog a bone,
This old man came rolling home.

Additional verses:
This old man, went to sleep,
He played knick knack counting sheep.

This old man, liked to run,
He played knick knack just for fun.

This old man, swam all day,
He played knick knack by the bay.

This old man, danced all night,
He played knick knack by the light.

This old man, jumped way up,
He played knick knack with his pup.

This old man, wasn't greedy,
He played knick knack with the needy.

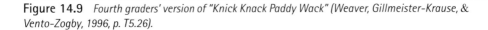

Figure 14.9 *Fourth graders' version of "Knick Knack Paddy Wack" (Weaver, Gillmeister-Krause, & Vento-Zogby, 1996, p. T5.26).*

needed word on another piece of chart paper at the front of the room, and then Mr. Peters and the class correct the spelling if necessary before he adds the word to the evolving draft. As he writes down certain other words in the verses they've composed, Mr. Peters helps the children hear the initial sounds and tell him what letters he should write. With words that end in a common rime and are already on their word wall, he sometimes invites the children to supply the rime—and he merely helps them find the word on the word wall if they offer another spelling for the end of this particular word. At the end of each line, Mr. Peters asks what punctuation mark is needed. At first he has to supply the commas, but the children quickly catch on, using the first verse as an example. They decide to put a comma at the end of the third line of each verse, too, though their original model didn't have a comma. After the song has been composed to the class' satisfaction, Mr. Peters demonstrates how he proofreads their text before publication.

The children decide they want to publish their song in two ways: by learning to sing it and then singing it for a kindergarten class next door, and by submitting their song for the next school newsletter, which includes one page from every class in the school. Mr. Peters points out that they should also learn to read their song, and they agree. As they work with the large copy, he uses this opportunity to help them blend onsets and rimes to read words that many of the children don't yet know in print. They also attend to single-sound onsets in some of the words, so as to promote phonemic awareness along with letter-sound knowledge.

On the weekend, Mr. Peters makes a one-page copy to submit to the monthly newsletter and for children to take home to their parents, plus small booklets, one verse per page, with room above the new verse for the children to draw a picture and with the refrain on the opposite page. He also makes some audiotapes for the listening center in the classroom, so that as many as three children at a time can listen to their song and read along during sustained reading and writing time the following week. During that week, some of the children listen repeatedly to the tape as they read, or at least turn the pages of, their book. Many of the children choose to illustrate their pages during sustained reading and writing time. A few simply read the booklet with the story they have composed together. Others ask for blank booklets they can draw and write in, preferring to create a new book rather than reread the song during that time. During shared reading time, Mr. Peters and the children continue to reread the song for a few days, and Mr. Peters gives additional help as needed in guided reading groups and individual conferences.

Meanwhile, on these same days, Mr. Peters is reading two or three books aloud to the children and giving them repeated opportunities to predict what will come next, along with opportunities to share how the characters or the stories relate to their own lives or other texts. During sustained reading and writing time, he conducts guided reading and writing groups and individual conferences while the rest of the children are rereading a familiar book or chart; listening to a book, poem, or song on tape (he and some of the parents have made most of these tapes themselves); "reading" the pictures in a book that they cannot read by themselves; reading with a buddy; drawing a picture and writing something with it; playing with magnetic letters to make words; writing in personal journals about events in their lives; writing something with a buddy; or reading or writing with a parent or older student who has come in to help. Every day Mr. Peters and the class sing the alphabet song together, while he plays the guitar.

By occupying most of the class in these literacy experiences and getting the children accustomed to asking each other for help when they're stuck with something, Mr. Peters has created time to help children with reading strategies and skills during guided reading in small groups, time to help with writing strategies and skills—especially spelling—during guided writing groups, and time to hold an individual reading and/or writing conference with each child about once a week. His teaching is based upon continuous assessment as the children engage in daily reading and writing. For example, when he sees that a child or a small group of children are writing more than one or two letters for the sounds in a word, he may assist their spelling development through interactive writing, perhaps offering the conventional way to spell certain sounds in a word or supplying silent letters. Continuous assessment enables him not only to plan for instruction but to decide which children need additional teaching and support from the learning support teacher, Mrs. Gaines, who fortunately supplements Mr. Peters' ways of teaching. Thank goodness for Mrs. Gaines!

Sometime after the holiday season, Mr. Peters plans to start literature study groups, too (Egawa, 1990), and for those children who seem ready, to guide them in reading and taking notes on informational texts. He also incorporates reading and writing into science and math, as well as social studies. It takes time to establish such routines, of course, but Mr. Peters has discovered that as a result of his whole-class, group, and individual teaching, almost all of his students leave his first-grade class having emerged as independent readers and writers of simple texts.

What reading and writing strategies and skills have been taught during these ten or so days?

1. Predicting, which requires drawing inferences and using prior knowledge; making connections to one's life (done mostly during the read-alouds)

2. Using context and letters to predict specific words; using the rest of the letters to confirm or show the need for correction

3. Onsets and rimes, and their use in chunking unfamiliar words—that is, reading them by analogy with the parts of known words. Also the use of onsets and rimes to help in spelling words.

4. Phonemic awareness (through the focus on onsets during reading experiences, and when Mr. Peters helped children in small groups and individual conferences hear some of the sounds in words they wanted to write, and to write letters for these sounds)

5. Phonics: letter-sound correspondences (see item 4), and blending onsets and rimes in decoding words

6. Spelling strategies, with particular emphasis on writing the sounds they hear in words. The more advanced spellers were taught strategies for identifying some (only two or three) possible misspellings and making the spellings more conventional.

7. Writing strategies. Those children who chose blank paper or booklets for writing were encouraged to draw a picture before they wrote, and/or to share their ideas with a classmate before and during writing.

In addition, what important attitudes were the children learning?

■ Reading is something "I can do," even though at first I need the support of my teacher and peers. I can write, too.

■ Reading and writing are fun.

■ When we work together and help each other, we learn better.

Intensive, Systematic Phonics

Though Mr. Peters doesn't teach phonics in isolation from reading, writing, and the texts children are enjoying, his teaching of phonics is nevertheless both intensive and systematic. It's intensive because Mr. Peters teaches phonics several ways each day, with attention to learning common rimes and onsets; using context and blending word parts to identify words (decoding); and developing letter-sound knowledge and phonemic awareness—the latter especially by helping children spell the sounds they hear in words. Not surprisingly, Mr. Peters teaches phonics and phonemic awareness through some of the means found successful in the National Reading Panel's meta-analysis—namely, learning common onsets and rime patterns and reading new print words by analogy with the parts of known print words ("analogy phonics"), and inventive spelling ("phonics-through-spelling"). Moreover, Mr. Peters' class exemplifies the kind of highly successful first-grade classroom described by researchers from the Center on English Learning and Achievement (1998; also Pressley, Allington, et al., 2001). Among the characteristics of such classrooms are a great deal of reading and writing, plus the teaching of skills in context. Each of these characteristics can be seen in the previous description of Mr. Peters' teaching. In addition, he reads good literature to the children, includes high-quality predictable books among the texts they use for shared reading, and employs interesting texts that allow him to focus on different phonic elements, particularly rime and onsets. He copies the texts of shorter books on chart paper for the children, so they can learn to read the texts together and attend to varying aspects of phonics. Less predictable Big Books are also used, and Mr. Peters helps children learn to figure out problem words by using context and blending together the familiar parts of the words. See Figure 14.10 for a list of books that are useful for teaching phonics, spelling, and words. Opitz's *Rhymes and Reasons* (2000) refers to many books you might want to use with young children.

In classrooms where phonics is taught as an integral part of daily reading and writing activities, children typically learn phonics as well as do children in classrooms where intensive, systematic phonics is taught in isolation (e.g., Freppon, 1991, which is also included in the National Reading Panel report, 2000b). They may even make better use of their phonics knowledge in reading (Freppon, 1991). They begin to develop effective reading strategies. They also learn to enjoy reading and writing and to feel good about their progress as readers and writers. Most important, though, children actually learn to read and write!

Recommended Books on Understanding and Teaching Phonics, Spelling, and Words

Primary Grades Especially

Dahl, K. L., Scharer, P. L., Lawson, L. L., & Grogan, P. R. (2001). *Rethinking Phonics: Making the Best Teaching Decisions.* Portsmouth, NH: Heinemann. Based upon research in reading and writing classrooms, this excellent book articulates and exemplifies six principles for effective phonics instruction. It includes a variety of strategies for developing phonics skills and discusses in detail ways of helping children who struggle with phonics.

Fountas, I. C., & Pinnell, G. S. (Eds.) (1999b). *Voices on Word Matters: Learning About Phonics and Spelling in the Literacy Classroom.* Portsmouth, NH: Heinemann. An excellent collection of articles, focusing on phonics and spelling in grades K–3.

Moustafa, M. (1997). *Beyond Traditional Phonics: Research Discoveries and Reading Instruction.* Portsmouth, NH: Heinemann. Focuses particularly on the research base for teaching phonics as described in this chapter, but also discusses the importance of shared reading and describes Moustafa's particular approach to teaching phonics in context, "whole-to-parts phonics." For more details on the latter, see especially Moustafa 1998 and 2000.

Opitz M. F. (2000). *Rhymes & Reasons: Literature and Language Play for Phonological Awareness.* Portsmouth, NH: Heinemann. Lists many wonderful books for use with young children and offers teaching suggestions to accompany them.

Strickland, D. S. (1998). *Teaching Phonics Today: A Primer for Educators.* Newark, DE: International Reading Association. Discusses issues with regard to the teaching of phonics; provides suggestions for helping children learn to use phonics as part of their overall reading development.

Wilde, S. (1997). *What's a Schwa Sound Anyway? A Holistic Guide to Phonetics, Phonics, and Spelling.* Portsmouth, NH: Heinemann. This book provides a wealth of background knowledge for teachers' understanding, including chapters on what children's invented spellings tell us about their development of phonics knowledge and what miscues tell us about children's use of phonics when they read.

Primary Grades and Beyond

Bear, D. R., Invernizzi, M., Templeton, S., & Johnston, F. (2000). *Words Their Way: Word Study for Phonics, Vocabulary and Spelling Instruction.* (2nd ed.). Upper Saddle River, NJ: Merrill/ Prentice Hall. This popular resource includes a wealth of teaching ideas. Grades 1–12.

Cunningham, P. M. (2000). *Phonics They Use: Words for Reading and Writing.* (3rd ed.). New York: Addison Wesley Longman. Excellent for teaching onsets and rimes (though often in isolation) plus understanding and reading longer words, including those that have meaningful parts within them.

Hughes, M., & Searle, D. (1997). *The Violent E and Other Tricky Sounds: Learning to Spell from Kindergarten Through Grade 6.* York, ME: Stenhouse. Describing children's spelling development throughout the elementary grades, this book enables teachers to recognize and monitor growth and to plan effective spelling programs for their students. The authors note that "The good spellers demonstrate that the basis for their success is their ability to understand the systematic nature of spelling, rather than the ability to learn a set of discrete spellings" (back cover).

Figure 14.10   *Resources for teaching phonics, spelling, and words.*

Laminack, L. L., & Wood, K. (1996). *Spelling in Use: Looking Closely at Spelling in Whole Language Classrooms.* Urbana, IL: National Council of Teachers of English. Includes a rich collection of student writing, which is analyzed in detail. Includes chapters to help teachers include parents in conversations about spelling and writing Grades K–8.

Pinnell, G. S., & Fountas, I. C. (Eds.) (1998). *Word Matters: Teaching Phonics and Spelling in the Reading/Writing Classroom.* Portsmouth, NH: Heinemann. The central goal of this extensive resource is to "teach children to become 'word solvers': readers who can take words apart while reading for meaning, and writers who can construct words while writing to communicate" (back cover).

Intermediate Grades Through High School

Allen, J. (1999). *Words, Words, Words: Teaching Vocabulary in Grades 4–12.* York, ME: Stenhouse. An invaluable resource for helping students understand and decipher the meanings of words, this book includes a chapter on alternatives to "Look it up in the dictionary!" and a chapter on reading as the heart of word-rich classrooms.

See some of the books in the "Primary Grades and Beyond" section.

Figure 14.10   *(Continued).*

A Perspective on Teaching Phonics

Politicians and policy makers, not to mention textbook publishers, increasingly promote "programs" to teach phonemic awareness and phonics. Teaching by program—more accurately, teaching a program rather than teaching the children—flies in the face of what knowledgeable teachers know and do. They know that exemplary phonics instruction will

- make provision for addressing the needs of children with varying backgrounds, native languages, and other instructional needs by using small-group, individual, and even extra tutorial help if needed;
- occur in a context where children are read to a lot—ideally, several times daily;
- occur only after such foundational experiences have developed the concept of reading for meaning, plus basic concepts about print (such as directionality and the concept of a written word);
- immerse childen in reading every day—shared, guided, and sustained reading in varying ways;
- include various kinds of assisted reading, in which children have the opportunity to match spoken with written words;
- include many writing experiences every day—such as guided writing, interactive writing, and sustained writing;
- encourage children to write and spell the best they can, and provide help in hearing and writing the sounds in words;
- require children to think, not passively complete worksheets or engage in oral drill;
- involve interaction and collaboration, between teacher and class and among children;

- derive partly from alphabet books, nursery rhymes, other poetry and stories with alliteration and/or rhyme and other sound effects; and

- relate to and derive from the reading and writing that the children are doing.

Only teacher-planned instruction can meet such criteria adequately, avoiding the "one-size-fits-all" approach that, in fact, leaves many children behind, making their reading of enjoyable and natural texts a dream deferred.

AND LET US KEEP IN MIND . . .

Were your reading experiences in school mostly positive, or negative? What kinds of experiences are we currently giving our own students during classroom reading time, and what are the effects? Do we need to make changes in what we're doing? To prompt your reflection, let me share an important reading memory that I drafted in a workshop conducted by the Public Education and Business Coalition in Denver:

> I already knew how to read when I entered school, just from my mother reading to me every day since I was little. Fortunately, I was allowed to read books of my own choosing in the elementary grades (once I had finished the Dick and Jane books independently in first grade). One reason independent reading was important is that nobody was looking over my shoulder to see if I got all the words right. Nobody previewed the book for me; I was allowed to discover its treasures myself. Nobody gave me vocabulary quizzes on words I encountered in the book. Nobody required me to do a book report or some other project on a book I had chosen (well, not on most of the books). Nobody even required me to journal about the book. Instead, the book was mine, all mine—to savor, to get lost in, and to identify with the adventures and values of the main character (usually male!). I was allowed just to be a reader instead of having to keep proving, again and again, that I could use certain strategies and skills, or even that I had actually read the book. What an exhilarating way for me to learn to read more and more challenging and interesting texts!
>
> My wish for every child would be to experience the same joy I did, and do, in reading.

So Let Us Not Forget . . .

Given this chapter's emphasis on teaching reading strategies and skills, let us not forget that there is *much* more to a good literacy program than direct teaching. Let us not forget, in particular, that sustained reading and writing are not merely the desired ends of instruction but the means of accomplishing our goal of helping students become adults who *choose* to read and write for many purposes—adults who are not only functionally literate, but joyfully literate.

And let us not forget that only teacher-planned instruction can come close to making this goal, this dream, a reality.

FOR FURTHER EXPLORATION

1. Develop your own visual representation of reading strategies, as preparation for teaching strategies and helping students develop a visual with you. You might develop a visual for macro-level strategies, one for micro-level strategies, and/or a visual for both. Feel free to draw upon your own strategies and the strategies other adults use, even if you would not plan to teach all of these strategies to the students in your class.

2. Use the following chart (Figure 14.11) to brainstorm for what cognitive/reading strategies you might teach, using a favorite book. The chart of *A Boy Called Slow* (Figure 14.3) may be useful as a model.

Book information	Page(s) to draw upon	What strategies could be taught?	What will the strategy require? • Use prior knowledge • Use information in the text • Use information from other texts and sources	Questions or comments or notes

Cognitive strategies for understanding include monitoring for meaning, inferring (includes predicting), making connections, creating mental images, synthesizing, analyzing, evaluating (includes determining importance), relating new to known, questioning, using fix-up strategies.

Figure 14.11   *Strategy chart.*

3. Following is a selection from the reading material given to an eleven-year-old boy in a special education classroom, with his miscues marked on the text (Figure 14.12). Examine the miscues to determine his apparent reading strengths and needs. Then discuss what kind of reading program you might design for this boy. Be specific and detailed.

light | *2 bake / 1 mim*
Gail and Ben can not get home. The ~~lake~~ is wide. "I can ~~make~~

You   Gail | *Gail*
a boat," said Ben. "~~Use~~ the ~~pail,~~" said Gail. "The ~~pail~~ is big,"

is | 1 Pete boat | 2 ... not | pail | Ben they said boat boat
~~said~~ Ben. "~~A nut~~ can make a ~~fine~~ boat." "~~Nail the sail to the pole,~~"

sailed   I   we
said Gail. Gail and Ben ~~set sail~~ in the boat. "~~It~~ is ~~wet~~ in the

is   to   is
boat," said Gail. "The boat ~~has~~ a hole in it." "Take the cap," ~~said~~

and eat   Gail   pail   said
Ben. "Use it to ~~bail.~~" Gail did ~~bail,~~ but the hole is big. "I ~~see~~

sail mad   pail   is
rain," said Gail. The ~~rain came.~~ "The ~~sail~~ is in the lake," ~~said~~

Tom   Pete
Gail. ~~Tim~~ is in the lake. ("Wait,") said ~~Ben.~~ "Save us," (said) Gail.

Tom   lake   Tim   Nut is
~~Tim~~ came up to the ~~boat.~~ "Tim can save us," said ~~Ben.~~ "~~Take his~~

Nut is   ride   Tim
tail," said Gail. "~~Get on~~ top," said Tim. Gail and Ben ~~rode~~ on ~~top~~

is   is
of Tim. "Tim ~~got~~ us home," ~~said~~ Gail. "Tim is a fine boat," said

Tim
~~Ben.~~

(The reader made some corrections, but most were prompted by the teacher. Since she did not indicate which were prompted and which were not, I have not marked any of the miscues as corrected.)

Figure 14.12 *Eleven-year-old's miscues.*

4. Susan Ohanian, author of *One Size Fits Few* (1999) and other books and articles, shares a significant teaching experience below (listserv message, 6/25/2001; used with permission). Reflect on her experience and what it suggests about learning and teaching, with particular regard to literacy.

> I confess that when I taught 3rd grade I didn't know a whole lot about reading, but when I discovered that my third graders, carefully segregated by the school as the worst readers in 3rd grade, didn't "hear" rhyme, this seemed significant to me. So I got all the library books I could find and read the kids rhyming books throughout the day. And I carefully salted their universe of "choice" books for the free reading period with lots of rhyming books.
>
> Each kid in the room discovered "rhyme." One by one. It was quite an earth-shattering occurrence—every time. And once that light bulb went off, they really did become energetic readers.
>
> I don't think I could have given them a shortcut. Actually I confess that before this pedagogical light bulb went off for me, I labored over showing them rhyming patterns in spelling words. To no avail. They just didn't "get" it. They "got" it after hearing me read a zillion books. And reading another zillion on their own. But their zillion was free choice. And a large variety of books brought different kids to that moment of awareness. My selection of their universe of texts was so varied that it was pretty close to "free" choice. I had an agenda but it wasn't oppressive to the kids. For a while it wasn't apparent either. Then suddenly a kid would look astonished and violate every principle of sustained silent reading by rushing up to me and announcing, "This book rhymes!!" It truly was an exciting moment.
>
> I don't know that anyone ever caught on that for the first six weeks of school ALL the books rhymed.

5. In "For Further Exploration" at the end of Chapter 12, you were invited to draw lines on a chart to indicate in which instructional settings reading strategies and skills might be taught. If you did that activity, see whether you have anything to add after reading the present chapter. If you didn't do that activity, you might do it now.

APPENDIX: ONSETS AND RIMES

ONSETS:
BEGINNING CONSONANT SOUNDS

Single Consonants

b	h	n	v
c	j	p	w
d	k	r	y
f	l	s	z
g	m	t	

Important Exceptions

qu = /kw/ blend as in *quick*
(the letter *q* is never used without *u*)
ph = /f/ sound as in *phone*
c = /s/ before *i, e,* or *y*, as in *city*
c = /k/ before *a, o,* or *u*, as in *cat*
g = /j/ before *i, e,* or *y*, as in *gem*
g = /g/ before *a, o,* or *u*, as in *good*

Rare Exceptions

ch = /k/ as in *character*
ch = /sh/ as in *chef*
s = /sh/ as in *sure*

Consonant Digraphs

ch as in *church*
sh as in *shoe*
th (voiceless) as in *thin*
th (voiced) as in *this*
wh (hw blend) as in *which*

Silent Consonants

gn = /n/ as in *gnat*
kn = /n/ as in *knife*
wr = /r/ as in *write*

Beginning Consonant Blends

(r family)	(l family)	(s letter)	(s family)	(no family)
br	bl	sc	scr	dw
cr	cl	sk	squ	tw
dr	fl	sm	str	thr
fr	gl	sn	spr	
gr	pl	sp	spl	
pr	sl	st	shr	
tr		sw	sch	
wr				

Onsets and rimes. From Fry, E. (1998). "The Most Common Phonograms." Reading Teacher 51: 620–622.

Most common phonograms in rank order based on frequency (number of uses in monosyllabic words)*

Frequency	Rime	Example words
26	-ay	jay say pay day play
26	-ill	hill Bill will fill spill
22	-ip	ship dip tip skip trip
19	-at	cat fat bat rat sat
19	-am	ham jam dam ram Sam
19	-ag	bag rag tag wag sag
19	-ack	back sack Jack black track
19	-ank	bank sank tank blank drank
19	-ick	sick Dick pick quick chick
19	-ell	bell sell fell tell yell
18	-ot	pot not hot dot got
18	-ing	ring sing king wing thing
18	-ap	cap map tap clap trap
18	-unk	sunk junk bunk flunk skunk
17	-ail	pail jail nail sail tail
17	-ain	rain pain main chain plain
17	-eed	feed seed weed need freed
17	-y	my by dry try fly
17	-out	pout trout scout shout spout
17	-ug	rug bug hug dug tug
16	-op	mop cop pop top hop
16	-in	pin tin win chin thin
16	-an	pan man ran tan Dan
16	-est	best nest pest rest test
16	-ink	pink sink rink link drink
16	-ow	low slow grow show snow
16	-ew	new few chew grew blew
16	-ore	more sore tore store score
15	-ed	bed red fed led Ted
15	-ab	cab dab jab lab crab
15	-ob	cob job rob Bob knob
15	-ock	sock rock lock dock block
15	-ake	cake lake make take brake
15	-ine	line nine pine fine shine
14	-ight	knight light right night fight
14	-im	swim him Kim rim brim
14	-uck	duck luck suck truck buck
14	-um	gum bum hum drum plum

* For a complete list of all example words see Fry (1998).

38 Phonograms in 600 Common Words*

	V-C/V-C-C	V-C-e/V-V-C	Diphthongs, r-controlled, others
a	at, am, ag, ack, ank, ap, an, ab	ay, ail, ain, ake	
e	ell, est, ed	eed	ew
i	ill, ip, ick, ing, in, ink, im	ine	ight
o	ot, op, ob, ock		out, ow, ore
u	unk, ug, uck, um		
y			y

Center for the Improvement of Early Reading Achievement (CIERA). (1998). Phonics and word recognition accuracy. No. 3 in the series Every child a reader, by E. H. Hiebert, P. D. Pearson, B. M. Taylor, V. Richardson, & S. G. Paris. Ann Arbor, MI: Michigan State University, CIERA. Based on Edward Fry's "The Most Common Phonograms." *Reading Teacher 51*: 520–622.

Foundations for Universal Literacy

Margaret Moustafa
California State University, Los Angeles

> Both experience and research suggest that children most readily become literate if reading and writing skills and strategies are taught and learned while the children are engaging in the kinds of real life experiences that engage all of us outside school—that is, reading and writing to enjoy, learn, inquire, persuade . . . . Under such circumstances, literacy is not just a future goal, a dream deferred perhaps forever, but a present and positive experience.
>
> —Constance Weaver

Questions for Thought and Discussion

1. What type(s) of literacy instruction and instructional materials benefit lower-achieving children the most? Why?

2. In addition to instruction, what factors affect children's literacy achievement?

3. How can educators and policy makers (government officials and members of boards of education) foster universal literacy?

Today the need for universal literacy is greater than it has ever been. In the Industrial Age those with low literacy skills could work in industrial, agricultural, and service-sector jobs that once required only minimal literacy skills. However, in today's Information Age, our individual and collective success depends on universal literacy.

How can we promote universal literacy? In this chapter I describe independent, peer-reviewed, replicated research on early readers, reading instruction, and access to age-appropriate books, especially as this research applies to lower-achieving students. Then I look at influences originating outside schools that affect instructional policy for lower-achieving students in elementary and secondary schools and suggest ways educators can influence policy to benefit all children.

EARLY READERS

In Chapter 11 we looked at a study done by Steven Kucer (1985) where a third-grade struggling reader read two stories, a "Pin for Dan" and "The Great Big Enormous Turnip." In "A Pin for Dan," the child shut down as a reader. At first she struggled with the text but then she gave up. In "The Great Big Enormous Turnip," the same child took giant steps toward becoming a proficient reader. At first she struggled with the text, but by the end of the text she was reading so fluently that she was maintaining the meaning of the text while changing the verb tense, a kind of behavior associated with proficient readers.

"A Pin for Dan" is a decodable text. Decodable texts are written with a limited set of letters, letter-sound correspondences, and/or words. Consequently, the syntax—or grammar, or flow of

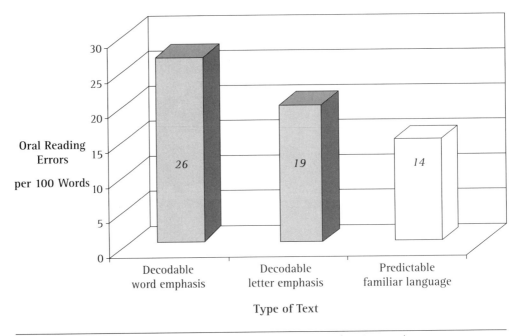

Figure 15.1 *Oral reading errors by type of text (Rhodes, 1979).*

the language—in decodable texts is unnatural. To the child in Kucer's study, the implicit message of "A Pin for Dan" was that reading is nonsense.

"The Great Big Enormous Turnip" is a predictable text. Predictable texts use language that is already familiar to children. To the child in Kucer's study, the implicit message of "The Great Big Enormous Turnip" was that reading makes sense.

How typical is the child in Kucer's study? Lynn Rhodes (1979) asked thirteen first-grade children to read a predictable story and two decodable stories. One of the decodable stories was written with a limited set of letter-sound correspondences and the other was written with a limited set of print words. She found three of the children read and retold the predictable and decodable stories equally well. But ten of the children, like the child in Kucer's study, responded differently to the different types of text. As shown in Figure 15.1, while the children averaged 26 miscues per hundred words on the story based on a limited set of print words and 19 miscues per hundred words on the story based on a limited set of letter-sound correspondences, they averaged only 14 oral reading miscues per hundred words on the story with familiar, natural-sounding language. More importantly, as shown in Figure 15.2, while they retold, on average, only 24% of the story based on a small number of print words and 52% of the story based on a small number of letter-sound correspondences, they retold 61% of the predictable story. These children, like the child in Kucer's study, had fewer oral reading miscues and better retellings on the predictable story than on the decodable stories.

Decodable texts belong to our traditional, parts-to-whole approach to reading instruction, where instruction begins with teaching letter-sound correspondences and/or individual words and then moves on to stories made up of the same letters and words. Predictable texts belong to the contemporary, whole-to-parts approach to reading instruction, where instruction begins with reading the story to the children until the children can read it themselves and then teaching

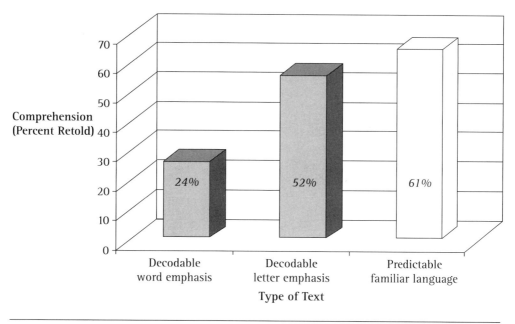

Figure 15.2 *Comprehension by type of text (Rhodes, 1979).*

the children the parts in the whole. What would account for the children's different responses to decodable and predictable text? *Language.* For example, read the following sentence.

If you haven't read Kuhn's book, you should read it.

The word *read* occurred twice in this sentence. Each time it was written exactly the same; yet each time you pronounced it differently. While you used your knowledge of letter-sound correspondences to pronounce these words, you also used your knowledge of English grammar. These two knowledge sources—your knowledge of letter-sound correspondences and your knowledge of English—function together as one coordinated system, much like when we run we use our feet, heart, lungs, and brain as a coordinated system, not as separable, sequential parts.

When children begin to read, they know much more about spoken language than they know about letter-sound correspondences. *Language is their strength.* Ken Goodman (1965), Tom Nicholson and his colleagues (1988), and Keith Stanovich (1991) studied how well children read single words in isolation versus words in stories. The *consistent* finding of this body of research is that children learning to read will read words in the context of a story better than outside the context of a story. For example, children learning to read may read *horse* as "house" in a list but read it correctly in a story about cowboys.

However, while language is children's strength, the language needs to be familiar language. Robert Ruddell (1965) and Susan Tatham (1970) studied children's responses to text with familiar language versus text with unfamiliar language. Like Kucer and Rhodes, they both found that children read text with familiar language better than text with unfamiliar language.

Because children use language they already know in order to read, the unnatural syntax of decodable stories makes it more difficult, not easier, for children to read. Hence, not surprisingly, in their review of research on decodable texts, Richard Allington and Haley Woodside-Jiron (1998a) found no well-constructed research that showed children become better readers through reading decodable texts. On the other hand, stories with familiar language, when combined with shared reading (described in Chapter 12) enable children to use what they know—language—to learn more.

Another problem with decodable texts is that they assume that children need to learn letter-phoneme correspondences in order to read. As D. J. Bruce (1964), Jerome Rosner (1974), Isabelle Liberman and her associates (1974), and many others (see Chapter 2 in Moustafa, 1997) have shown, children have difficulty analyzing spoken words into their constituent phonemes. For example, children have trouble analyzing the spoken word *smiles* into /s/, /m/, /i/, /l/, and /z/.

In fact, Robert Scholes (1998) showed that being able to analyze spoken words into phonemes is a limited consequence of becoming literate in an alphabetic script. Most of us use our knowledge of how words are spelled to determine how many phonemes are in a word. For example, when asked, most of us respond that there are three phonemes in the word *box*, rather than the four that there are.

How, then, do readers learn to independently figure out unfamiliar print words when learning to read an alphabetic script? For many children the process begins long before they go to school. Don Holdaway (1979) in New Zealand, Shirley Brice Heath (1982, 1983) in the United States, Gordon Wells (1985, 1986) in England, and Dina Feitelson and Zahava Goldstein (1986) in Israel studied children's preschool experiences with print and found that children who succeeded in traditional programs in school had been read to extensively in their preschool years. As Wells (1986) points out, being read to helps children understand the purposes and pleasures of print as well as learn the language we use in stories—language that we don't use in our daily conversations with children. For example, when we talk with children, we might say that someone is *mean*, but most versions of Cinderella say that Cinderella's stepmother was *cruel*.

Mary Ann Manning and her colleagues (1993), building on the work of Emilia Ferreiro and Ana Teberosky (1979/1982), found that preschool children go through several developmental stages in their understanding of a written sentence. Initially they think that only names of objects and people are written. Then, with more experience, they think that every word is written but they are not yet able to match spoken words to print words. Next they are able to match spoken words to print words and they can use word order to identify print words within a sentence. Finally, once children are able to use word order to identify print words within a sentence, they begin to use letter-sound correspondences in print words to figure out new print words.

Other researchers have shown that the sounds children use when they make letter-sound correspondences are not necessarily phonemes. Rebecca Treiman (1983) studied four-, five- and eight-year-old children and found that children learn to analyze spoken English into onsets and rimes before they learn to analyze them into phonemes. That is, they can analyze the spoken word *smiles* into /sm/ and /iles/ before they can analyze it into /s/, /m/, /i/, /l/, and /z/.

Finally, Usha Goswami (1986) found that children learning to read make analogies between familiar and unfamiliar print words to figure out how to pronounce unfamiliar print words, and they use letter-onset and letter-rime correspondences, not letter-phoneme correspondences, to do so. For example, children who have learned to recognize the print words *small* and *smile* can figure out that the letter string *sm-* is pronounced /sm/. Similarly, children who have learned to recognize the print words *cart* and *part* can figure out that the letter string *-art* is pronounced /art/. Then, when they encounter the print word *smart*, they can figure out how to pronounce it by themselves.

In my own work with first graders (Moustafa, 1995), I found that the children's knowledge of familiar print words accounted for their pronunciation of unfamiliar print words better than their knowledge of letter-phoneme correspondences did (see Chapters 5 and 13). I also found that the more print words children recognized, the better they figured out new print words.

William Tunmer and Andrew Nesdale (1985) studied six first-grade classes, three where instruction emphasized letter-phoneme correspondences and three where instruction ignored letter-phoneme correspondences. Their data show that at the end of the year the children who could pronounce more real print words could figure out more made-up print words, regardless of whether their instruction emphasized letter-phoneme correspondences or not.

In summary, as children have more and more experience with print, development proceeds, not from part to whole, but from whole to part: from being read to, to being able to read; from an understanding that print represents speech to being able to match spoken words to print words; from perceiving print words as whole units to being able to analyze print words into units that represent onsets and rimes. These research discoveries are but a part of the large body of independent research that has fostered new instructional strategies for beginning readers and writers such as daily read-alouds, shared reading, shared writing, phonics taught in context, reading/thinking strategies taught through meaningful texts, opportunities to self-select and read engaging books, and opportunities to write on self-selected topics, described in Chapters 10 and 12 in this book.

> In summary, as children have more and more experience with print, development proceeds, not from part to whole, but from whole to part: from being read to, to being able to read; from an understanding that print represents speech to being able to match spoken words to print words; from perceiving print words as whole units to being able to analyze print words into units that represent onsets and rimes.

EARLY READING INSTRUCTION

There is a large body of comparative research that has found that children with comprehensive literacy instruction such as shared reading, shared writing, phonics taught in context, and lots and lots of experiences of being read to and opportunities to read self-selected books and write on self-selected topics learn to make sense of print better than children with traditional, parts to-whole reading instruction.

For example, Ray Reutzel and Robert Cooter (1991) compared the end-of-year achievement of 53 children in two suburban first-grade classrooms with comprehensive reading instruction with 38 children in two suburban first-grade classrooms with traditional reading instruction. Using the *Gates-MacGinitie Reading Survey Test*, they found the children in the classrooms with comprehensive reading instruction achieved significantly better than the children in the classrooms with traditional reading instruction in total reading scores as well as on the vocabulary and comprehension subtest scores.

For another example, Penny Freppon (1991) compared 12 children in two first-grade classrooms with a comprehensive reading program that focused on meaning with 12 children in two first-grade classrooms with traditional reading programs in school districts that serve middle-income communities. She found the children in the two comprehensive classrooms not only had a better sense that reading was constructing meaning with print but also were almost twice as successful as the children in the traditional classrooms at sounding out words. (See Figure 15.3).

Many studies compare the achievement of lower-achieving children in classrooms with comprehensive reading instruction with their achievement in classrooms with traditional reading instruction. Colin Sacks and John Mergendoller (1997) studied 132 kindergartners in 11 classrooms. They found that the children who scored the lowest on entry into kindergarten improved the most in reading achievement in classrooms with comprehensive, meaning-emphasis reading instruction and improved the least in traditional phonics-oriented classrooms.

Jerry Milligan and Herbert Berg (1992) compared the end-of-year reading comprehension of 82 first-grade children with comprehensive reading instruction with 83 first-grade children with traditional parts-to-whole—word and letter-phoneme emphasis—reading instruction in a middle-income school district. While they found no significant difference between the two groups

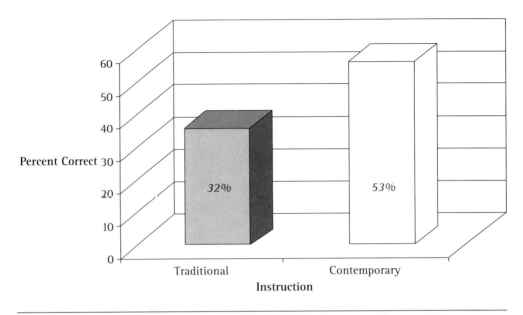

Figure 15.3   *Correctly sounding out words by type of instruction (Freppon, 1991).*

as a whole, they found the middle- and lower-achieving children with the comprehensive reading instruction were significantly better in reading comprehension than the middle- and lower-achieving children with traditional reading instruction. Of these two groups, the lower-achieving children benefited the most from comprehensive reading instruction. They also found that all the males—high-, middle-, and lower-achieving—with the comprehensive reading instruction comprehended text significantly better than the males with traditional reading instruction.

Lloyd Eldredge and his colleagues (1996) compared the effectiveness of shared reading with traditional round-robin reading (where children take turns reading a story orally) on 78 second-grade children's reading growth in a mixed-income community. They found that all the children—above-average, average, and below-average—had better comprehension with shared reading than with traditional round-robin reading as measured by the *Iowa Test of Basic Skills*. (See Figure 15.4.) However, the below-average children especially benefited from shared reading. The below-average children had almost half as many oral reading miscues in shared reading as they did in round-robin reading. (See Figure 15.5).

Richard Anderson and his colleagues (1991) studied 149 third-grade children in six classrooms from two schools, one in a middle-income neighborhood and one in a lower-income neighborhood. They asked the teachers to teach their students four lessons—two lessons with an emphasis on overall story meaning and two lessons with an emphasis on such things as letter-phoneme correspondences and accurate oral reading. They found that the lessons that emphasized overall story meaning led to better outcomes in relation to factors such as students' recall, oral reading, story interest, and lesson time. While all of the reading groups—high, average, and low—benefited from the emphasis on meaning, the average and low groups especially benefited from it.

Other studies compare the achievement of children in comprehensive and traditional classrooms in economically disadvantaged communities. Connie Juel and Cecilia Minden-Cupp (2000) looked at four first-grade classrooms in a school district serving economically disadvantaged children. Their data show that the children in the lowest reading groups gained the most in

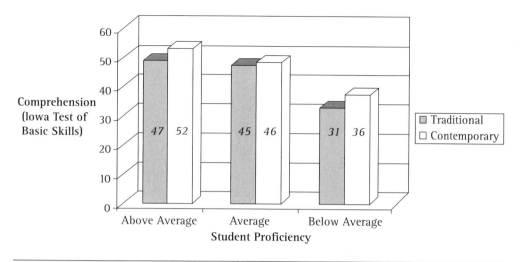

Figure 15.4 *Comprehension by type of instruction and student proficiency (Eldredge, Reutzel, and Hollingsworth, 1996).*

word reading in the two classrooms where they experienced the fewest phonics worksheets, used choral reading, and were taught letter-onset and letter-rime correspondences. The greatest gains among the children in the lowest reading groups occurred in the classroom where the teacher used no phonics worksheets with the low group and frequently asked the children to use their emerging knowledge of letter-sound correspondence and what makes sense in the text to figure out unfamiliar words in text.

Susan Cantrell (1999) studied children in eight multiage primary-grade classrooms in schools where at least 50% of the children were eligible for free or reduced-price lunch. She found that the

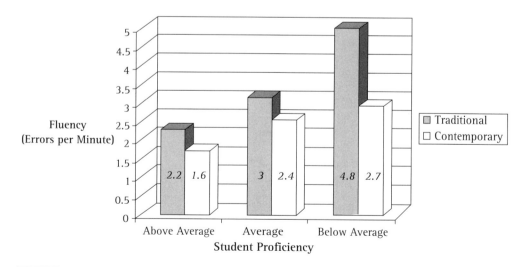

Figure 15.5 *Fluency (errors per minute) by type of instruction and student proficiency (Eldredge, Reutzel, and Hollingsworth, 1996).*

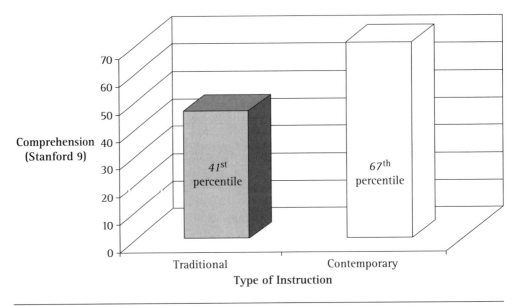

Figure 15.6 *Comprehension by type of instruction (Cantrell, 1999).*

22 focal children in the four classrooms where instruction focused on reading for meaning and skills taught in context achieved scores between the 50th and 76th percentile on the *Stanford 9* national norms in reading comprehension, spelling, and language, whereas the 19 focal children in the four classrooms where skills were taught out of context and meaning was not emphasized achieved scores that fell below the 50th percentile. (See Figure 15.6.)

Michael Knapp and his colleagues (1995) studied children in 140 classrooms, grades 1 through 6, in schools serving high-poverty communities. They found that both the lower-achieving and higher-achieving children in the classrooms with the most teaching for meaning, i.e., comprehensive reading and writing instruction, ended the year with significantly higher achievement than their counterparts in classrooms with traditional, skills-oriented reading and writing instruction.

Not surprisingly, then, when Karin Dahl and Penny Freppon (1995) studied kindergarten and first-grade inner-city children in classrooms with comprehensive and traditional reading and writing instruction, they found that in the classrooms with comprehensive reading instruction, all the children—both more proficient and less proficient readers and writers—either saw themselves as readers and writers or believed that they would be readers and writers. However, in the classrooms with traditional reading instruction, only the more proficient readers and writers saw themselves as readers and writers.

Most important, when looking at how we can achieve universal literacy, this body of research shows that low-achieving children achieve more with comprehensive, whole-to-parts reading instruction than children with traditional, parts-to-whole reading instruction.

Altogether, this body of research shows that all children—high-, middle-, and low-achieving children—achieve more with comprehensive, whole-to-parts reading and writing instruction than children with traditional, parts-to-whole reading and writing instruction. Most important, when looking at how we can achieve universal literacy, this body of research shows that low-achieving children achieve more with contemporary, whole-to-parts reading instruction than children with traditional, parts-to-whole reading instruction.

BEYOND DECODING

Reading is more than decoding (pronouncing) print. It is making sense of print. Schema researchers have shown that readers of all ages must first understand a topic to understand text on that topic. To illustrate, read the following passage written by John Bransford and Marcia Johnson (1972).

> A newspaper is better than a magazine, and on a seashore is a better place than a street. At first, it is better to run than walk. Also you may have to try several times. It takes some skill but it's easy to learn. Even young children can enjoy it. Once successful, complications are minimal. Birds seldom get too close. One needs lots of room. Rain soaks in very fast. Too many people doing the same thing can also cause problems. If there are no complications, it can be very peaceful. A rock will serve as an anchor. If things break loose from it, however, you will not get a second chance.

Most people who read this passage have difficulty making sense of it until they are told that the passage is about flying kites. If you didn't realize it was about flying kites when you read it, read it again and see if it makes more sense to you now that you know what it is about.

Researchers have shown that the more children know about a topic, the better they understand text on that topic. David Pearson, Jane Hansen, and Christine Gordon (1979) gave a passage about spiders to second-grade children who already knew a lot about spiders and to children who knew little about spiders. They found that the children who knew a lot about spiders before they read the passage were significantly better at answering questions on implicit information in the passage than the children who knew less about spiders before they read the passage.

Marjorie Lipson (1983) showed that children are better readers when they are reading on a familiar topic than when they are reading on an unfamiliar topic. She gave fourth-, fifth-, and sixth-grade children attending a Catholic school and fourth-, fifth-, and sixth-grade children attending a Hebrew school two reading passages, one entitled "First Communion" and the other entitled "Bar Mitzvah." She found the children attending the Catholic school read faster, recalled more, made fewer miscues, and made better inferences in the passage about the first communion than in the passage about the bar mitzvah. Similarly, the children attending the Hebrew school read faster, recalled more, made fewer miscues, and made better inferences in the passage about the bar mitzvah than in the passage about the first communion.

Barbara Taylor (1979) looked at the effect of background knowledge on the reading comprehension of below-average readers. She had third- and fifth-grade children read passages on a topic generally familiar to children—bird nest building—and on a topic generally unfamiliar to children—bee dancing. The third-grade children were average readers. The fifth-grade children were average and below-average readers. While all the children gave better retellings on the familiar topic than the unfamiliar topic, the below-average fifth-grade readers were most affected by the topic. As shown in Figure 15.7, when reading on an unfamiliar topic, their retellings were similar to those of average third-grade children. When reading on a familiar topic, their retellings approached those of the average fifth-grade readers.

Similarly, Donna Recht and Lauren Leslie (1988), building on the work of Spilich and his colleagues (1979) with adults, gave a passage about baseball to "low reading ability" and "high reading ability" seventh- and eighth-grade children, some of whom knew a lot about baseball and others who knew little about baseball. They found that the children who had more knowledge of baseball before they read the passage comprehended the passage on baseball significantly better than those with less knowledge of baseball before they read the passage, regardless of whether they had been classified as low-ability or high-ability readers. That is, the children with a "low

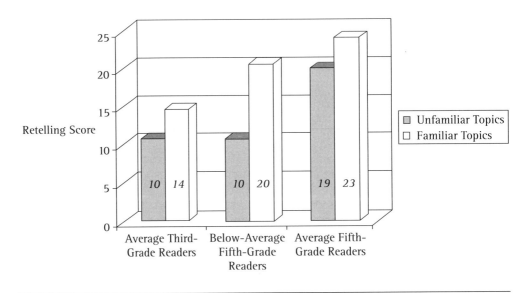

Figure 15.7 *Comprehension on familiar and unfamiliar topics (Taylor, 1979).*

reading ability" who had more prior knowledge of baseball comprehended the baseball passage significantly better than the children with a "high reading ability" who had less prior knowledge of baseball.

Finally, Kathleen Stevens (1982) showed that providing readers background knowledge on a topic before they read can improve reading comprehension of texts on that topic. She gave three classes of tenth graders a lesson on the Texan War and three classes a lesson on the U.S. Civil War. Then she asked the students to read a passage on the Alamo, a battle in the Texan War. She found that the students who were given background information about the Texan War before they read the passage on the Alamo understood the passage significantly better than the students who were not given relevant background information before they read the passage.

Altogether, this body of research shows that once children have acquired basic reading skills, whether they are "good readers" or "poor readers" is largely determined by the extent of their background knowledge on the topic of any given text.

> Altogether, this body of research shows that once children have acquired basic reading skills, whether they are "good readers" or "poor readers" is largely determined by the extent of their background knowledge on the topic of any given text.

BEYOND INSTRUCTION

While instructional materials and instruction are important, they are not sufficient. Children and their caretakers at home and at school need access to engaging, age-appropriate books. As mentioned earlier in this chapter, Dina Feitelson and Zahava Goldstein (1986), Don Holdaway (1979, 1982), Shirley Brice Heath (1982, 1983), and Gordon Wells (1985, 1986) have shown that children who are read to in their preschool years become better readers. Richard Anderson and his colleagues (1988) and Ina Mullis and his colleagues (1993) studied intermediate-grade elementary children and found that children who read more become better readers.

All this requires access to age-appropriate books. Jonathan Kozol (1991), Courtney Smith and her colleagues (1997), and Jeff McQuillan and his colleagues (1997) have shown that children

	Beverly Hills	Watts	Compton
Books in home	199	0.4	2.7
Books in class libraries	392	54	47
Books in school libraries	60,000	23,000	16,000
Books in public libraries	200,000	110,000	90,000
Bookstores	5	0	1

Figure 15.8 *Children's access to age-appropriate books by neighborhood (Smith, Constantino, & Krashen, 1997).*

in poor communities in the United States have less access to age-appropriate books at home, in school, and in public libraries. Smith and her colleagues have shown that while children in one affluent neighborhood, Beverly Hills, averaged 200 age-appropriate books per home, children in two nearby impoverished neighborhoods, Watts and Compton, lacked such resources. Children in Watts averaged 1 age-appropriate book for every two homes and children in Compton averaged 2.7 books per home. The children in the affluent neighborhood had more age-appropriate books in their homes than the children in the impoverished neighborhood had in their classrooms. (See Figure 15.8.)

Warwick Elley (1992), Stephen Krashen (1995), and Jeff McQuillan (1998) have each shown that access to age-appropriate books is a powerful predictor of reading achievement. Warwick Elley and Francis Mangubhai (1983) have shown that when children with limited access to books are provided with access to books, there is significant growth in literacy. (See Figure 15.9.) Just as highways are a necessary part of the infrastructure for commerce, access to age-appropriate books for children and their caretakers is a necessary part of the infrastructure for universal literacy.

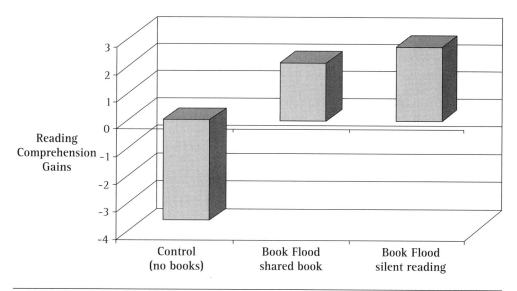

Figure 15.9 *Book flood program: long-term gains in reading comprehension, fourth grade (Elley & Mangubhai, 1983).*

Towards Universal Literacy

In this chapter I have touched on just some of the large body of independent, replicated, peer-reviewed research that has helped literacy educators move beyond traditional parts-to-whole reading instruction and into contemporary, meaning-based, whole-to-parts reading instruction. This body of research shows again and again that while all children benefit from contemporary reading instruction, lower-achieving children benefit the most. It also shows that language and background knowledge affect reading comprehension and that universal access to age-appropriate books is a prerequisite of universal literacy.

President George W. Bush has called reading a civil right. If we are to achieve the universal literacy he envisions, it is not enough for educators to be skilled in implementing comprehensive reading instruction. To flourish, teachers and children also need an infrastructure that supports universal literacy. Among other things, all teachers—but especially those serving low-achieving children—need appropriate instructional materials (e.g., predictable books for emergent readers), well-stocked classroom libraries, and the freedom to make professional decisions about the instructional needs of the children they serve. Among other things, all children—but especially low-achieving children—need easy access to engaging, age-appropriate books at school and at home and the time and freedom to self-select books to read that interest them.

The problem is, the body of knowledge described in this chapter and this book is not yet part of our general cultural knowledge. Those outside of education often see phonics as reading rather than phonics as a part of reading, or an aid to reading. Unaware of the role that language, background knowledge, and access to books play in reading and learning to read, they assume that if children don't do well on standardized tests, it must be because they don't know phonics.

Corporations with access to the media and to politicians have been successful in promoting the concept of "accountability" and consequently the use of norm-referenced tests, that is, tests constructed so that 50% of the examinees will score above the 50th percentile and 50% below the 50th percentile (see Falk, 2000), along with the dissemination of group test reports that include the scores of nonnative speakers of English still learning English averaged with the scores of native speakers of English (see, for example, Moustafa, 1999) to convince national, state, and local policy makers that there is a literacy crisis. Some corporations have then used the "crisis" to convince policy makers that their "research-based" programs (that is, products) will improve the literacy achievement of lower-achieving children (Taylor, 1998). They then provide test practice materials and multiple-choice tests where the questions are the same year after year (Linn, 2000), while politicians, and consequently administrators, pressure teachers to teach to the test. The resultant rising scores are then hailed as "proof" that their programs are "working."

Policy makers, often unaware of how the tests are being misused and of the large body of research that informs literacy educators, are overriding the expertise of reading/language arts specialists and implementing traditional educational policies that literacy educators learned a long time ago don't work. Among other things, policy makers in some states are mandating out-of-context training in phonemic awareness (see Chapter 13) and decodable texts for the primary grades (see Chapter 11). Additionally, for the first time in the history of reading education, we are now seeing decodable texts being sold to school districts for high school students.

To date, most of the schools that have shifted to an emphasis on out-of-context phonemic awareness instruction and decodable texts are schools serving children whose average reading scores on standardized tests are low. All indications are that these changes have been counterproductive—that they have produced results the opposite of their stated intent of improving literacy achievement. In 2001 the National Assessment of Educational Progress (NAEP), a federal program that has administered reading achievement tests to children in grades 4, 8, and 11 across the United States since 1972, reported that the reading scores of the fourth-grade children in the bottom 10% of the NAEP declined significantly from 1992 to 2000.

School is more than a place for corporations to make money. It is a place where individual and collective futures are made. As a society, we are remiss if we allow social policies to be made by the corporations that benefit from them. How can educators help move policy beyond where we are now to provide more effective literacy education for lower-achieving children?

More and more frequently we see articles in professional newspapers and journals urging educators to dialogue with politicians. As difficult as this is for many of us, it is necessary. There is too much at stake to not do so. However, it may not be sufficient. The voice of one education reporter who has never taken a class in education, much less been a classroom teacher, can easily outweigh the voice of thousands of experienced, overworked professional educators.

Ultimately the answer is education, education that provides the public with a basic understanding of the body of knowledge that informs successful literacy educators. Every college graduate must fulfill general education classes in math, science, and social science. Imagine if every college graduate were to have as one of his or her general education classes a class on how children learn to read and write. Then when college graduates go on to become reporters, politicians, and members of boards of education, they would know enough about how children become literate that policy makers and educators would share a common body of knowledge. It will take generations for us to get beyond the knowledge gap we now have between policy makers and educators. But if we begin now, we'll get there.

FOR FURTHER EXPLORATION

1. Respond again to the "Questions for Thought and Discussion" at the beginning of this chapter. Support your answers.

2. Find out what types of occupations the members of your local or state school board have. Find out what types of occupations the members of the education committee in your state legislature had before they were elected to their current positions. What are the possible implications?

3. Talk to a school board member or a legislator. Ask him or her the questions at the beginning of this chapter. Compare your notes with others who have also talked to legislators or school board members.

4. Plan a talk to your local school board. Outline a plan for helping lower-achieving children become better readers.

5. Write a letter to your state legislator. Ask him or her to support something that your community needs to do in order to improve the literacy achievement of lower-achieving children. Use a standard business-letter form.

Notes

CHAPTER 1

1. Function words are the "little words" that glue the content words together. The main types of function words are as follows: noun determiners (e.g., *the,* and *this* in the phrase *this boy*); verb auxiliaries (e.g., *will* in *will win*); prepositions (e.g., *by* in *by the lake*); and conjunctions (e.g., *because* and *and*). For a more thorough discussion of these and other parts of speech (grammatical categories), see Chapter 2. Also see Figure 8.4, p. 198.

2. In the TORP, there are eight to ten items designed to reveal each of three different teacher orientations:

   Phonics: 1, 2, 3, 6, 9, 10, 12, 20, 21, 22

   Skills: 4, 8, 11, 13, 14, 16, 19, 24, 25, 28

   Whole language: 5, 7, 15, 17, 18, 23, 26, 27

   That is, teachers who strongly agree with the phonics items have a strong phonics orientation, those who strongly agree with the skills items have a strong skills orientation, and those who strongly agree with the whole language items have a strong whole language orientation. It is possible to have more than one strong orientation. Since 1 is "strongly agree" and 5 is "strongly disagree" on the TORP, a low numerical score reflects strong agreement and a high score reflects strong disagreement.

   In research validating the TORP, the teachers were preidentified as having a phonics, skills, or whole language orientation before they took the TORP. For the 90 teachers in the study (30 in each group), the average (mean) scores were as follows:

	Phonics items	Skills items	Whole language items
Phonics group	19.47	24.37	30.37
Skills group	26.87	23.87	28.23
Whole language group	48.40	47.50	9.13

The greatest and perhaps most interesting difference is between the whole language groups and the other two (see DeFord, 1985).

CHAPTER 2

1. I am grateful to my colleague Jim Burns for introducing me to a similar activity and to the book from which these "lost words" are taken: Susan Kelz Sperling's *Poplollies and Bellibones: A Celebration of Lost Words* (1977). Given the brevity of Sperling's definitions, it is possible that some words may have been misused in my story. In any case, here are her definitions:

   Bellytimber—Food, provisions

   Blonke—A large, powerful horse

   Blore—To cry out or bleat and bray like an animal

Crinet —A hair

Drumly —Cloudy, sluggish

Fairney cloots —Small horny substances above the hoofs of horses, sheep, and goats

Flosh —A swamp or stagnant pool overgrown with weeds

Givel —To heap up

Icchen —To move, stir

Kexy —Dry, juiceless

Lennow —Flappy, limp

Maily —Speckled

Quetch —To moan and twitch in pain, shake

Samded —Half-dead

Shawk —Smell

Sparple —To scatter, spread about

Spiss —Thick, dense

Venenate —To poison

Wam —A scar, cicatrix

Wong —Meadowlands, commons

Yerd —To beat with a rod

Chapter 3

1. The omitted words are: (1) aren't, (2) Most, (3) three, (4) and, (5) 40, (6) of, (7) most, (8) is, (9) as, (10) Beavers, (11) dams, (12) They, (13) paws, (14) their, (15) tree, (16) pointed, (17) beaver, (18) tree, (19) about.

2. *Kalamazoo Gazette,* August 1, 1978, p. A-1. The article was a UPI tidbit originating in Chicago.

3. To see this for yourself, try a brief experiment with someone you know to be a reasonably proficient reader. First, locate a book that the person has not read, but that will not be especially difficult for him or her. Have the person begin reading a page aloud, and after a few lines stop the person's reading by suddenly turning out the light (if it is dark) or by putting your hand over the part being read. Then ask the person to tell you what words he or she saw beyond the word last focused upon. If you repeat this procedure several times, you will probably find that the person can report, on the average, about four additional words. Typically, the person will have picked up those words that complete a syntactic unit of some sort: thus, one person undertaking such an experiment reported the following, when the light was turned off five different times: *but rather because of; from the galactic rim; none completely satifactory; of the universe; but as the ship leaves.* The words perceived beyond the word focused upon consitute the person's *eye-voice span,* or *EVS:* the number of words the eye is ahead of the voice. In silent reading, of course, one has a similar *eye-memory span,* or *EMS:* the number of words the eye is ahead of the word being focused upon (Dechant, 1970, p. 18; see I. Anderson & Dearborn, 1952, pp. 127–136). The EVS and the EMS indicate the number of following words seen during one eye fixation, in addition to the

word being identified. These additional words may be used in identifying the word being focused upon.

4. I like the word *sneakers* best here, because its connotation seems to fit best with the description in the passage. Other good possibilities are *tennis shoes, gym shoes,* or the name brand of some kind of sports shoe. Check Bradbury to see which word he chose!

Chapter 4

1. When I tried to locate "Jimmy Hayes and Muriel" through a short story index, the entry under "Frogs, horned" referred me to an entry for horned *toads*. I have since discovered that so-called horned frogs do exist, though.

2. Here is the original passage:

> The crack of the rifle volley cut the suddenly still air. It appeared to go on, as a solid volley, for perhaps a full minute or a little longer.
>
> Some of the students dived to the ground, crawling on the grass in terror. Others stood shocked or half crouched, apparently believing the troops were firing into the air. Some of the rifle barrels were pointing upward.
>
> Near the top of the hill at the corner of Taylor Hall, a student crumpled over, spun sideways and fell to the ground, shot in the head.
>
> When the firing stopped, a slim girl, wearing a cowboy shirt and faded jeans, was lying face down on the road at the edge of the parking lot, blood pouring out onto the macadam, about 10 feet from this reporter.

3. My opinion supported the position of the family. The definitions in some of our major dictionaries suggested that the word *passenger* at least *could* be taken to include the operator of a vehicle. Ultimately, however, the Michigan Supreme Court ruled in support of the insurance company's interpretation, arguing that the "ordinary man" would not consider the operator of a vehicle to be one of its passengers (*Kinnavy v. Traill,* 1976).

4. One important point about such "grammatical" miscues is that they are not all grammatical in nature. Their origin may be phonological, as is the apparent omission of the past tense marker by speakers of African American Vernacular English. The past tense marker is absent from African American Vernacular English primarily when the base word is a regular verb ending in a consonant other than /t/ or /d/. In such cases, addition of the past tense ending results in a consonant cluster (the examples are mostly from Fasold & Wolfram, 1970, p. 45):

stopped /pt/	rubbed /bd/
looked /kt/	hugged /gd/
laughed /ft/	loved /vd/
unearthed /θt/	seethed /ðd/
missed /st/	raised /zd/
watched /čt/	judged /ǰd/
finished /št/	
	named /md/
	rained /nd/
	hanged /ŋd/
	called /ld/
	cured /rd/

In each case, the past tense ending is represented by /t/ or /d/. Word-final consonant clusters are especially likely to be simplified when they end in a /t/ or /d/, and virtually all speakers of English show some tendancy to omit the final /t/ or /d/ when it does not represent a tense marker. Such omission is particularly common when the word in quetion precedes a word that begins with a consonant, as in "She *just* left" or "I'll *find* the book." Speakers of so-called standard English occasionally omit a past tense /t/ or /d/ when the following word begins with a consonant, as in "I *missed* Mike" and "He *lived* near me." Speakers of African American Vernacular English simply carry this tendancy somewhat further, with the result that they are often perceived as consistently omitting past tense markers although in reality their usage varies, as it does for all of us. The same is true of other dialect features.

5. Note that in this approximation of African American Vernacular English, past time is not always indicated by the verb form itself, even for verbs that express the past by some means other than the mere addition of /t/ or /d/.

6. This nonsense word comes from an article by Robert Hillerich (1977, p. 301). Hillerich explains, "To arrive at the spelling, one could consider *n* as the most likely beginning letter, although the other reasonable possibilities are *kn* (*know*), *gn* (*gnaw*), *pn* (*pneumonia*), and *mn* (*mnemonic*). The /ē/ in medial position could be spelled *ae* (*aegis*), *e* (*between*), *ea* (*meat*), *ee* (*meet*), *ei* (*neither*), *ie* (*chief*), *eo* (*people*), *ey* (*keynote*), or *oe* (*amoeba*); /d/ is easy—it is *d* or *dd*; /ər/ could be *ar* (*liar*), *er* (*term*), *ir* (*first*), or (*worm*), *ur* (*turn*), *ear* (*learn*), *our* (*journey*), *eur* (*chauffeur*), or *yr* (*myrtle*); /l/ again is easy as either *l* or *ll*, but final /ē/ could be *ay* (*quay*), *i* (*ski*), *ee* (*see*), *ey* (*key*), *y* (*baby*), *e* (*be*), or *ois* (*chamois*). In fact, we have demonstrated that the nonsense word could be spelled in $5 \times 9 \times 2 \times 9 \times 2 \times 7$, or 11,340 different ways. Of course, if one were unfamiliar with the influence of position, seventeen different spellings of /ē/ would have to be considered for both occurrences, increasing the possibilities to 52,020!"

CHAPTER 5

1. In line 2, *basement* is misspelled as *bastement*. Line 2 ends with *the*, which is repeated at the beginning of line 3. In line 3, *boat* is misspelled as the word *boot*. In line 4 the word *through* is misspelled as the word *though*. At the end of line 4, *he* occurs, when the word should have been *she*. In line 5, the single word *apart* is written as two words, *a* and *part*. In the last line, *should've* is misspelled as *should of*.

2. It seems to me that "perception" more readily includes the possibility of error, and that "identification" and "recognition" imply *accurate* perception of the print on the page. Note, however, that all three indicate a decision on the part of the *brain*.

3. The words, in order of occurrence, are: *could, short, about, voice, trust, scarf, drank, ghost, which, stand.* For a similar list of mutilated words, see I. Anderson and Dearborn, 1952, p. 189; they reproduced the words by permission from a test constructed by L. L. Thurstone.

4. One interesting example of such experiments involved the reversal of two letters at the beginning or the middle or the end of a word, as with *vaiation, avitaion,* and *aviatino* for the word *aviation*. The words were hardest to identify when the reversal occurred at the beginning, and easiest to identify when the reversal occurred in the middle: thus, the experiment suggests that beginnings are most important in word perception and middles are least important (Bruner & O'Dowd, 1958).

5. The sentence reads, "This demonstrates that text becomes relatively illegible when a comparable proportion of randomly selected letters has been removed" (Adams, 1990, citing Miller & Friedman, 1957).

CHAPTER 12

1. This conclusion is not affected by the National Reading Panel's report that they could not find a substantial body of experimental research demonstrating the positive effects of sustained or "independent silent reading," as the panel called it. Indeed, they wrote that "Literally hundreds of correlational studies find that the best readers read the most and that poor readers read the least. These correlational studies suggest that the more that children read, the better their fluency, vocabulary, and comprehension" (National Reading Panel, 2000a, 12). However, the scarcity of experimental research does not demonstrate that silent reading *doesn't* promote reading comprehension, fluency, and vocabulary. Indeed, the panelists themselves emphasize this point (p. 13).

References

Adams, M. J. (1990). *Beginning to Read: Thinking and Learning About Print.* Cambridge: MIT Press.

Adams, M. J. (1999). Report to the Arizona State Task Force. September 9.

Adams, M. J., & Bruck, M. (1995). "Resolving the 'Great Debate.'" *American Educator* 19(7): 10–20.

Adams, M. J., & Collins, A. (1979). "A Schema-Theoretic View of Reading." *New Directions in Discourse Processing,* ed. R. O. Freedle, 1–22. Norwood, NJ: Ablex.

Adams, M. J., Treiman, R., et al. (1998). "Reading, Writing, and Literacy." *Handbook of Child Psychology, 5th ed. Volume 4: Child Psychology in Practice.* pp. 275–355. New York: Wiley.

Allen, J. (1995). *It's Never Too Late: Leading Adolescents to Lifelong Literacy.* Portsmouth, NH: Heinemann.

Allen, J. (1999). *Words, Words, Words: Teaching Vocabulary in Grades 4–12.* York, ME: Stenhouse.

Allen, J., & Gonzalez, K. (1998). *There's Room for Me Here: Literacy Workshop in the Middle School.* York, ME: Stenhouse.

Allington, R. L. (1983). "The Reading Instruction Provided Readers of Differing Abilities." *Elementary School Journal* 83: 548–559.

Allington, R. L. (1998). "More on the Schools We Have Versus the Schools We Need." *Practicing What We Know: Informed Reading Instruction,* ed. C. Weaver, 554–565. Urbana, IL: National Council of Teachers of English.

Allington, R. L. (2001). *What Really Matters for Struggling Readers: Designing Research-Based Programs.* New York: Addison Wesley Longman.

Allington, R. L. (2002). *Inadequate Evidence.* Portsmouth, NH: Heinemann.

Allington, R. L., & Woodside-Jiron, H. (1998a). "Decodable Text in Beginning Reading: Are Mandates and Policy Based on Research?" *ERS Spectrum: Journal of Research and Information* 16(3): 3–11.

Allington, R. L., & Woodside-Jiron, H. (1998b). "Thirty Years of Research in Reading: When Is a Research Summary Not a Research Summary?" *In Defense of Good Teaching: What Teachers Need to Know About the "Reading Wars,"* ed. K. S. Goodman, 143–153. York, ME: Stenhouse.

Allington, R. L., & Woodside-Jiron, H. (1999). "The Politics of Literacy Teaching: How 'Research' Shaped Educational Policy." *Educational Researcher* 28(8): 4–13.

Allsburg, C. V. (1987). *The Z Was Zapped: A Play in Twenty-Six Acts.* Boston: Houghton Mifflin.

Altwerger, B., & Strauss, S. L. (2002). "The Business Behind Testing." *Language Arts* 79(3): 256–262.

Ames, W. S. (1966). "The Development of a Classification Scheme of Contextual Aids." *Reading Research Quarterly* 2: 57–82.

Anderson, I. H., & Dearborn, W. F. (1952). *The Psychology of Teaching Reading.* New York: Ronald.

Anderson, R. B., St. Pierre, R. G., Proper, E. C., & Stebbins, L. B. (1978). "Pardon Us, but What Was the Question Again? A Response to the Critique of the Follow Through Evaluation." *Harvard Educational Review* 48: 161–170.

Anderson, R. C. (1994). "Role of the Reader's Schema in Comprehension, Learning, and Memory." *Theoretical Models and Processes of Reading,* ed. R. B. Ruddell, M. R. Ruddell, & H. Singer, 469–482. Newark, DE: International Reading Association.

Anderson, R. C., & Freebody, P. (1983). "Reading Comprehension and the Assessment and Acquisition of Word Knowledge." *Advances in Reading/Language Research,* ed. B. Hutson, 231–256. Greenwich, CT: JAI.

Anderson, R. C., Hiebert, E. H., Scott, J. A., & Wilkinson, I. A. G. (1985). *Becoming a Nation of Readers: The Report of the Commission on Reading.* Washington, D.C.: U.S. Department of Education, National Institute of Education.

Anderson, R. C., Spiro, R. J., & Anderson, M. C. (1977). "Schemata as Scaffolding for the Representation of Meaning in Connected Discourse." (Tech. Rep. no. 24.) ERIC: ED 136236. Urbana, IL: Center for the Study of Reading.

Anderson, R. C., Wilkinson, I. A. G., & Mason, J. M. (1991). "A Microanalysis of the Small-Group Guided Reading Lesson: Effects of an Emphasis on Global Story Meaning." *Reading Research Quarterly* 36: 417–441.

Anderson, R. C., Wilson, P. T., & Fielding, L. G. (1988). "Growth in Reading and How Children Spend Their Time Outside of School." *Reading Research Quarterly* 23: 285–303.

The Ann Arbor Decision: Memorandum Opinion and Order and the Educational Plan. (1979). Arlington, VA: Center for Applied Linguistics.

Applebee, A. N., Langer, J. A., et al. (1988). *Who Reads Best? Factors Related to Reading Achievement in Grades 3, 7, and 11.* Princeton, NJ: National Assessment of Educational Progress, Educational Testing Service.

Artley, A. S. (1943). "Teaching Word-Meaning Through Context." *Elementary English Review* 20(2): 68–74.

Atwell, N. (1998). *In the Middle: New Understandings About Writing, Reading, and Learning.* Portsmouth, NH: Heinemann.

Avery, C. (1993). . . . *And with a Light Touch: Learning About Reading, Writing, and Teaching with First Graders.* Portsmouth, NH: Heinemann.

Ayres, L. R. (1993). *The Efficacy of Three Training Conditions on Phonological Awareness of Kindergarten Children and the Longitudinal Effect of Each on Later Reading Acquisition.* Oakland, MI: Oakland University. Unpublished doctoral dissertation.

Ayres, L. R. (1998). "Literacy Learning in a Whole Language Classroom: Reading Concepts and Reading Strategies First Graders Know and Use." *Reconsidering a Balanced Approach to Reading,* ed. C. Weaver, 209–255. Urbana, IL: National Council of Teachers of English.

Baker, L., & Brown, A. L. (1984). "Cognitive Monitoring in Reading." *Understanding Reading Comprehension,* ed. J. Flood, 21–44. Newark, DE: International Reading Association.

Baldwin, R. S., & Schatz, E. K. (1985). "Context Clues Are Ineffective with Low Frequency Words in Naturally Occurring Prose." *Issues in Literacy: A Research Perspective (Thirty-Fourth Yearbook of the National Reading Conference),* ed. J. A. Niles & R. V. Lalik, 132–135. Rochester, NY: National Reading Conference.

Ball, Z. (1962). *Bristle Face.* New York: Holiday House.

Balota, D. A., Pollatsek, A., et al. (1985). "The Interaction of Contextual Constraints and Parafoveal Visual Information in Reading." *Cognitive Psychology* 17: 364–390.

Banks, W. P., Oka, E., & Shugarman, S. (1981). "Internal Speech: Does Recoding Come Before Lexical Access?" *Perception of Print: Reading Research in Experimental Psychology,* ed. O. J. L. Tzeng & H. Singer, 137–170. Englewood Cliffs, NJ: Prentice-Hall.

Baratz, J., & Stewart, W. (1970). *Friends.* Washington, D.C.: Education Study Center.

Barr, J. (1949). *Little Circus Dog.* Chicago: Albert Whitman.

Barrera, R. B., Thompson, V. D., Dressman, M., & Multicultural Booklist Committee editors. (1997). *Kaleidoscope: A Multicultural Booklist for Grades K–8.* Urbana, IL: National Council of Teachers of English.

Bartoli, J., & Botel, M. (1988). *Reading/Learning Disability: An Ecological Approach.* New York: Teachers College Press.

Bateman, B. D. (1974). "Educational Implications of Minimal Brain Dysfunction." *The Reading Teacher* **27**: 662–668.

Baumann, J. F., Hoffman, J. V., Moon, J., & Duffy-Hester, A. M. (1998). "Where Are Teachers' Voices in the Phonics/Whole Language Debate? Results from a Survey of U.S. Elementary Classroom Teachers." *Reading Teacher* **51**: 636–650.

Bear, D. R., Invernizzi, M., Templeton, S., & Johnson, F. (2000). *Words Their Way: Word Study for Phonics, Vocabulary, and Spelling Instruction.* Upper Saddle River, NJ: Merrill.

Beck, I. L., McKeown, M. G., & McCaslin, E. S. (1983). "Vocabulary Development: All Contexts Are Not Created Equal." *Elementary School Journal* **83**(3): 177–181.

Beck, W. S. (1957). *Modern Science and the Nature of Life.* New York: Harcourt, Brace.

Bennett, J. (1987). *Noisy Poems.* New York: Oxford University Press.

Berdiansky, B., Cronnell, B., et al. (1969). *Spelling-Sound Relations and Primary Form-Class Descriptions for Speech-Comprehension Vocabularies of 6–9-Year-Olds.* Inglewood, CA: Southwest Regional Laboratory for Educational Research and Development.

Berenstain, S., & Berenstain, J. (1971). *Bears in the Night.* New York: Random House.

Bertrand, J. E., & Stice, C. F. (Eds.). (1995). *Empowering Children at Risk of School Failure: A Better Way.* Norwood, MA: Christopher-Gordon.

Biemiller, A. (1970). "The Development of the Use of Graphic and Contextual Information as Children Learn to Read." *Reading Research Quarterly* **1**: 77–96.

Bishop, J. E. (1993, Oct. 12). "Stroke Patients Yield Clues to Brain's Ability to Create Language." *Wall Street Journal* **74**(253): 1, 6.

Blachman, B. A. (2000). "Phonological Awareness." *Handbook of Reading Research, Vol. 3,* ed. M. L. Kamil, P. B. Mosenthal, P. D. Pearson, & R. Barr, Vol. 3. Mahwah, NJ: Erlbaum.

Bloome, D. (1985). "Reading as a Social Process." *Language Arts* **62**: 134–142.

Bloome, D., & Green, J. (1985). "Looking at Reading Instruction: Sociolinguistic and Ethnographic Approaches." *Contexts of Reading,* ed. C. N. Hedley & A. N. Baratta, 167–184. Norwood, NJ: Ablex.

Bloomfield, L. (1942). "Linguistics and Reading." *The Elementary English Review* **19**: 125–130, 183–186.

Board, P. (1976). Retelling Form. Toronto: University of Toronto. Unpublished.

Boatner, M. T., Gates, J. E., & Makkai, A. (1987). *A Dictionary of American Idioms,* 2nd ed. New York: Barrons.

Bomer, R. (1995). *Time for Meaning: Crafting Literate Lives in Middle & High School.* Portsmouth, NH: Heinemann.

Booth, D. (Ed.). (1996). *Literacy Techniques For Building Successful Readers and Writers.* York, ME: Stenhouse.

Booth, D. (1998). *Guiding the Reading Process: Techniques and Strategies for Successful Instruction in K–8 Classrooms.* York, ME: Stenhouse.

Bormuth, J. R. (1975). "Literacy in the Classroom." *Help for the Reading Teacher: New Directions in Research,* ed. W. D. Page, 60–89. Urbana, IL: National Council of Teachers of English.

Bradbury, R. (1957). *Dandelion Wine.* Garden City, NY: Doubleday.

Bradley, L., & Bryant, P. E. (1983). "Categorizing Sounds and Learning to Read—A Causal Connection." *Nature* **301**: 419–421.

Bradley, L., & Bryant, P. E. (1985). *Rhyme and Reason in Reading and Spelling. I. A. R. L. D. Monographs, No. 1.* Ann Arbor: University of Michigan Press.

Brandt, R. (1998). *Powerful Learning.* Alexandria, VA: Association for Supervision and Curriculum Development.

Bransford, J. D., & Johnson, M. K. (1972). "Contextual Prerequisites for Understanding: Some Investigations of Comprehension and Recall." *Journal of Verbal Learning and Verbal Behavior* 11: 717–726.

Bransford, J. D., & McCarrell, N. S. (1974). "A Sketch of a Cognitive Approach to Comprehension: Some Thoughts About Understanding What It Means to Comprehend." *Cognition and the Symbolic Processes,* ed. W. B. Wiemer & D. S. Palermo, 189–229. Hillsdale, NJ: Erlbaum.

Braunger, J., & Lewis, J. P. (1997). *Building a Knowledge Base in Reading.* Portland, OR, Urbana, IL, Newark, DE: Northwest Regional Educational Laboratory, National Council of Teachers of English, International Reading Association.

Bridges, L. (1997). *Writing As a Way of Knowing.* York, ME: Stenhouse.

Bridwell, N. (1966). *Clifford Takes a Trip.* New York: Scholastic.

Brinkley, E. H. (1998). "What's Religion Got to Do with Attacks on Whole Language?" *In Defense of Good Teaching: What Teachers Need to Know About the "Reading Wars,"* ed. K. S. Goodman, 57–69. York, ME: Stenhouse.

Brooks, E. (1996). *Just-Right Books for Beginning Readers: Leveled Booklists and Reading Strategies.* New York: Scholastic.

Brown, C. (1965). *Manchild in the Promised Land.* New York: Macmillan.

Brown, H., & Cambourn, B. (1990). *Read and Retell: A Strategy for the Whole Language/Natural Learning Classroom.* Portsmouth, NH: Heinemann.

Brown, J. (1997). *An Integrated View of Context: Implications of Miscue Analysis.* Tucson: University of Arizona. Program in Language and Literacy. Unpublished doctoral dissertation.

Brown, J., Goodman, K. S., & Marek, A. M. (1996). *Studies in Miscue Analysis: An Annotated Bibliography.* Newark, DE: International Reading Association.

Brown, M. (1998). *Arthur's Birthday.* New York: Little, Brown.

Brown, R. (1970). "Psychology and Reading: Commentary on Chapters 5 to 10." *Basic Studies on Reading,* ed. H. Levin & J. P. Williams, 164–187. New York: Basic Books.

Bruce, D. J. (1964). "The Analysis of Word Sounds." *British Journal of Educational Psychology* 34: 158–170.

Bruchac, J. (1994). *A Boy Called Slow.* Illus. Rocco Baviera. New York: Putnam & Grosset.

Bruner, J. S. (1983a). *Child's Talk: Learning to Use Language.* Oxford: Oxford University Press.

Bruner, J. S. (1983b). Development of a Transactional Self. *New Directions in Studying Children: Speeches from the Conference of the Erickson Institute, April 29–30.* Chicago.

Bruner, J. S. (1986). *Actual Minds, Possible Worlds.* Cambridge: Harvard University Press.

Bruner, J. S., & O'Dowd, D. (1958). "A Note on the Informativeness of Parts of Words." *Language and Speech,* 1: 98–101.

Burgess, A. (1963). *A Clockwork Orange.* New York: Norton.

Burke, J. (2001). *Illuminating Texts: How to Teach Students to Read the World.* Portsmouth, NH: Heinemann.

Burling, R. (1973). *English in Black and White.* New York: Holt, Rinehart.

Bush, G. W. (2001). "No Child Left Behind." Washington, D.C.: United States Department of Education.

Calkins, L., Montgomery, K., Santman, D., Falk, B., & Teachers College (Columbia Univ.) Reading and Writing Project Members. (1998). *A Teacher's Guide to Standardized Reading Tests: Knowledge Is Power.* Portsmouth, NH: Heinemann.

Campbell, R., & Butterworth, B. (1985). "Phonological Dyslexia and Dysgraphia in a Highly Literate Subject: A Developmental Case with Associated Deficits and Phonemic Processing and Awareness." *The Quarterly Journal of Experimental Psychology* 37A: 437–475.

Campione, J. (1981). Learning, Academic Achievement, and Instruction. Paper presented at the second annual conference on Reading Research of the Center for the Study of Reading, New Orleans, April.

Cantrell, S. C. (1999). "Effective Teaching and Literacy Learning: A Look Inside Primary Classrooms." *The Reading Teacher* 52(4): 370–378.

Carbo, M. (1978). "Teaching Reading with Talking Books." *The Reading Teacher* 32: 267–273.

Carbo, M. (1988). "Debunking the Great Phonics Myth." *Phi Delta Kappan* 70: 226–240.

Carey, R. F., Harste, J. C., et al. (1981). "Contextual Constraints and Discourse Processes: A Replication Study." *Reading Research Quarterly* 16: 201–212.

Carpenter, P. A., & Just, M. A. (1983). "What Your Eyes Do While Your Mind Is Reading." *Eye Movements in Reading: Perceptual and Language Processes,* ed. K. Rayner, 275–307. New York: Academic Press.

Cattell, J. M. (1947). *Man of Science, 1860–1944.* Lancaster, PA: Science Press.

Center on English Learning and Achievement. (1998). "Characteristics of Effective Literacy Teachers." *English Update: A Newsletter from the Center on English Learning and Achievement* (Spring): 1, 8.

Chambers, A. (1996). *The Reading Environment: How Adults Help Children Enjoy Books.* York, ME: Stenhouse.

Chappell-Carr, J. (1999). *A Child Went Forth: Reflective Teaching with Young Readers and Writers.* Portsmouth, NH: Heinemann.

Charlesworth, R., Hart, C. H., Burts, D. C., & DeWolf, M. (1993). "The LSU Studies: Building a Research Base for Developmentally Appropriate Practice." *Advances in Early Education and Day Care: Perspectives on Developmentally Appropriate Practice,* ed. S. Reifel, Vol. 5. Greenwich: JAI.

Chomsky, C. (1972). "Stages in Language Development and Reading Exposure." *Harvard Educational Review* 42: 1–33.

Chomsky, C. (1976). "After Decoding: What?" *Language Arts* 53: 228–296, 314.

Chomsky, N. (1965). *Aspects of the Theory of Syntax.* Cambridge: MIT Press.

Chomsky Higgins, P. (1998). "Teaching Strategies and Skills During Readers' Workshop: Setting the Stage for Successful Readers and Writers." *Practicing What We Know: Informed Reading Instruction,* ed. C. Weaver, 140–153. Urbana, IL: National Council of Teachers of English.

Christian, P. (1995). *The Bookstore Mouse.* San Diego: Harcourt Brace.

Clarke, L. K. (1988). "Invented Versus Traditional Spelling in First Graders' Writings: Effects on Learning to Spell and Read." *Research in the Teaching of English* 22(3): 281–309.

Clay, M. (1979). *Stones: The Concepts About Print Test.* Portsmouth, NH: Heinemann.

Clay, M. (1985). *The Early Detection of Reading Difficulties.* Portsmouth, NH: Heinemann.

Clay, M. M. (1991). *Becoming Literate: The Construction of Inner Control.* Portsmouth, NH: Heinemann.

Clay, M. M. (1993a). *An Observation Survey of Early Literacy Achievement.* Portsmouth, NH: Heinemann.

Clay, M. M. (1993b). *Sand (A "Concepts About Print" Test).* Portsmouth, NH: Heinemann.

Clay, M. M. (1993c). *Stones (A "Concepts About Print" Test).* Portsmouth, NH: Heinemann.

Clowes, G. A. (1999). Reading Is Anything but Natural: An Interview with G. Reid Lyon. <*www.heartland .org/education/jul99/lyon/htm*>.

Clymer, T. L. (1963). "The Utility of Phonic Generalizations in the Primary Grades." *The Reading Teacher* 16: 252–258.

Cohen, J. (1988). *Statistical Power Analysis for the Behavior Sciences,* 2nd ed. Hillsdale, NJ: Erlbaum.

Cole, W. (1981). *Poem Stew.* New York: Lippincott.

Coles, G. (1998). *Reading Lessons: The Debate over Literacy.* New York: Hill & Wang.

Coles, G. (2000). *Misreading Reading: The Bad Science That Hurts Children.* Portsmouth, NH: Heinemann.

Coles, G. (2001). "Teaching Reading: Using the 'Scientific' Hickory Stick." *Phi Delta Kappan* 83(3).

Coles, G. (Forthcoming, 2003). *Reading Unmentionables: Damaging Reading Education While Seeming to Fix It*. Portsmouth, NH: Heinemann.

Commission on Reading. (1988). Report on Basal Readers (position statement). Urbana, IL: National Council of Teachers of English.

Comte, A. (1830/1988). *Introduction to Positive Philosophy*. Indianapolis, IN: Hacket.

Cooper, H. (1998). *Synthesizing Research: A Guide for Literature Reviews*. Thousand Oaks, CA: Sage.

Cowley, J. (1984). *I'm the King of the Mountain*. Katonah, NY: Richard C. Owen.

Cronnell, B. A. (1970). *Spelling-to-Sound Correspondences for Reading vs. Sound-to-Spelling Correspondences*. Technical Note TN2-70-15. Los Alamitos, CA: Southwest Regional Laboratory.

Cunningham, J. W. (2001). "The National Reading Panel Report." *Reading Research Quarterly* 36(3): 326–335.

Cunningham, M. (1998). *The Hours*. New York: Picador USA.

Cunningham, P. M. (1977). "Teachers' Correction Responses to Black Dialect Miscues Which Are Non-Meaning Changing." *Reading Research Quarterly* 12: 637–653.

Cunningham, P. M. (2000). *Phonics They Use: Words for Reading and Writing*. New York: Longman.

Dahl, K. L., & Freppon, P. A. (1991). "Literacy Learning in Whole Language Classrooms: An Analysis of Low Socioeconomic Urban Children Learning to Read and Write in Kindergarten." *Learner Factors/Teacher Factors: Issues in Literacy Research and Instruction*, ed. J. Zutell & S. McCormick, 149–158. Chicago: National Reading Conference.

Dahl, K. L., & Freppon, P. A. (1992). Learning to Read and Write in Inner-City Schools: A Comparison of Children's Sense-Making in Skills-Based and Whole Language Classrooms. Washington, D.C.: U.S. Department of Education.

Dahl, K. L., & Freppon, P. A. (1995). "A Comparison of Innercity Children's Interpretations of Reading and Writing Instruction in the Early Grades in Skills-Based and Whole Language Classrooms." *Reading Research Quarterly* 30(1): 50–74.

Dahl, K. L., Purcell-Gates, V., & Freppon, P. A. (1989). Ways That Inner-City Children Make Sense of Traditional Reading and Writing Instruction in the Early Grades. Final report to the Office of Educational Research and Improvement. Washington, D.C.: U.S. Department of Education. (Grant No. R117E00134).

Dahl, K. L., Scharer, P. L., Lawson, L. L., & Grogan, P. R. (1999). "Phonics Instruction and Student Achievement in Whole Language First-Grade Classrooms." *Reading Research Quarterly* 34(3): 312–341.

Dahl, K. L., Scharer, P. L., Lawson, L. L., & Grogan, P. R. (2001). *Rethinking Phonics: Making the Best Teaching Decisions*. Portsmouth, NH: Heinemann.

Dahl, R. (1950). "Poison." *Someone Like You*. New York: Knopf.

Daniels, H. (1994). *Literature Circles: Voice and Choice in the Student-Centered Classroom*. York, ME: Stenhouse.

Daniels, H. (2002). *Literature Circles: Voice and Choice in Book Clubs and Reading Groups*. York, ME: Stenhouse.

Daniels, H., Zemelman, S., & Bizar, M. "Whole Language Works: Sixty Years of Research." *Educational Leadership* 57(2): 32–37.

Davenport, R. (2002). *Miscues Not Mistakes: Miscue Analysis in the Classroom*. Portsmouth, NH: Heinemann.

Davey, B. (1983). "Think-Aloud—Modeling the Cognitive Processes of Reading Comprehension." *Journal of Reading* 27: 44–47.

Davies-Samway, K., & Whang, G. (1995). *Literature Study Circles in a Multicultural Classroom*. York, ME: Stenhouse.

Davison, A., & Green, G. (Eds.). (1988). *Linguistic Complexity and Text Comprehension: Readability Issues Reconsidered*. Mahweh, NJ: Lawrence Erlbaum.

Dechant, E. V. (1970). *Improving the Teaching of Reading*. Englewood Cliffs, NJ: Prentice Hall.

DeFord, D. E. (1985). "Validating the Construct of Theoretical Orientation in Reading Instruction." *Reading Research Quarterly* 20: 351–367.

DeFord, D. E., Lyons, C. A., & Pinnell, G. S. (Eds.). (1991). *Bridges to Literacy: Learning from Reading Recovery*. Portsmouth, NH: Heinemann.

Desberg, P., Elliott, D. E., et al. (1980). "American Black English and Spelling." *Cognitive Processes in Spelling,* ed. V. Frith, 69–84. New York: Academic.

Dewey, J., & Bentley, A. F. (1949). *Knowing and the Known*. Boston: Beacon.

Dodge, R. (1900). "Visual Perceptions During Eye Movement." *Psychological Review* VII: 454–465.

Dombey, H., Moustafa, M., & the Centre for Language in Primary Education. (1998). *Whole-to-Part Phonics: How Children Learn to Read and Spell*. Portsmouth, NH: Heinemann.

Donahue, P. L., Voelkl, K. E., Campbell, J. R., & Mazzeo, J. (1999). *NAEP 1998 Reading Report Card for the Nation*. Washington, D.C.: U.S. Department of Education, Office of Educational Research and Improvement, National Center for Education Statistics.

Duckett, P. (2001). First-Grade Beginning Readers' Use of Pictures and Print as They Read. Tucson: University of Arizona. Department of Language, Reading and Culture. Unpublished doctoral dissertation.

Duke, N. K. (2000). "Print Environments and Experiences Offered to First-Grade Students in Very Low- and Very High-SES School Districts." *Reading Research Quarterly* 35(4): 456–457.

Dulin, K. L. M. (1969). "New Research on Context Clues." *Journal of Reading* 13: 33–38, 53.

Dunrea, O. (1988). *Deep Down Underground*. New York: Macmillan.

Durkin, D. (1966). *Children Who Read Early: Two Longitudinal Studies*. New York: Teachers College Press.

Egawa, K. (1990). "Harnessing the Power of Language: First Graders' Literature Engagement with *Owl Moon*." *Language Arts* 67: 582–588.

Ehri, L. C. (1979). "Linguistic Insight: Threshold of Reading Acquisition." *Reading Research: Advances in Theory and Practice,* ed. T. Waller & G. E. MacKinnon, 63–114. New York: Academic.

Ehri, L. C. (1991). "Development of the Ability to Read Words." *Handbook of Reading Research, Vol. 2,* ed. R. Barr, M. Kamil, P. Mosenthal, & P. D. Pearson, 383–417. New York: Longman.

Ehri, L. C. (1994). "Development of the Ability to Read Words: Update." *Theoretical Models and Processes of Reading,* ed. H. Singer & R. B. Ruddell, 323–359. Newark, DE: International Reading Association.

Ehri, L. C. (1995). "Phases of Development in Reading Words." *Journal of Research in Reading* 18: 116–125.

Ehri, L. C. (1998). "Grapheme-Phoneme Knowledge Is Essential for Learning to Read Words in English." *Word Recognition in Beginning Literacy,* ed. J. Metsala & L. Ehri. Mahwah, NJ: Erlbaum.

Ehri, L. C. (2000). *The Report of the National Reading Panel*. Presented at the International Reading Association Convention, Indianapolis, May 2.

Ehri, L. C., Nunes, S. R., Willows, D. M., Schuster, B. V., Yaghoub-Zadeh, Z., & Shanahan, T. (2001). "Phonemic Awareness Instruction Helps Children Learn to Read: Evidence from the National Reading Panel's Meta-Analysis." *Reading Research Quarterly* 36(3): 250–287.

Ehri, L. C., & Stahl, S. A. (2001). "Beyond the Smoke and Mirrors: Putting Out the Fire." *Phi Delta Kappan* 82(1): 17–20.

Ehri, L. C., & Wilce, L. S. (1980). "The Influence of Orthography on Readers' Conceptulization of the Phonemic Structure of Words." *Applied Psycholinguistics* 1: 371–385.

Ehri, L. C., & Wilce, L. S. (1987). "Does Learning to Spell Help Beginners Learn to Read Words?" *Reading Research Quarterly* 22: 48–65.

Ehrlich, S. F., & Rayner, K. (1981). "Contextual Effects on Word Perception and Eye Movements During Reading." *Journal of Verbal Learning and Verbal Behavior* 20: 641–655.

Eldredge, J. L. (1991). "An Experiment with a Modified Whole Language Approach in First-Grade Classrooms." *Reading Research and Instruction* 30: 21–38.

Eldredge, J. L., & Butterfield, D. (1986). "Alternatives to Traditional Reading Instruction." *Reading Teacher* 40: 32–37.

Eldredge, J. L., Reutzel, D. J., & Hollingsworth, P. M. (1996). "Comparing the Effectiveness of Two Oral Reading Practices: Round-Robin Reading and the Shared Book Experience." *Journal of Literacy Research* 28(2): 201–225.

Elley, W. (1989). "Vocabulary Acquisition from Listening to Stories Read Aloud." *Reading Research Quarterly* 24: 174–187.

Elley, W. (1991). "Acquiring Literacy in a Second Language: The Effect of Book-Based Programs." *Language Learning* 41(3): 375–411.

Elley, W. (1992). *How in the World Do Students Read? The IEA Study of Reading Literacy.* The Hague, Netherlands: International Association for the Evaluation of Education Achievement.

Elley, W. (1998). *Raising Literacy Levels in Third World Countries: A Method That Works.* Culver City, CA: Language Education Associates.

Elley, W., & Mangubhai, F. (1983). "The Impact of Reading on Second Language Learning." *Reading Research Quarterly* 19: 53–67.

Engelmann, S. (1975). *DISTAR Reading: An Instructional System.* Chicago: Science Research Associates.

Engelmann, S. (1980). *Direct Instruction.* Englewood Cliffs, NJ: Educational Technology.

Engelmann, S., Johnson, G., Carnine, L., Meyer, L., Becker, W., & Eisel, J. (1988). *Corrective Reading.* Chicago: Science Research Associates.

Erdmann, B., & Dodge, R. (1898). *Psychologische Untersuchungen uber das Lesen, auf Experimenteller Grundlage.* Halle. As cited in E. B. Huey, *The Psychology and Pedagogy of Reading,* 1908/1968, Cambridge: MIT Press.

Evans, M., & Carr, T. (1985). "Cognitive Abilities, Conditions of Learning, and the Early Development of Reading Skill." *Reading Research Quarterly* 20: 327–350.

Falk, B. (2000). *The Heart of the Matter: Using Standards and Assessment to Learn.* Portsmouth, NH: Heinemann.

Fasold, R. W., & Wolfram, W. (1970). "Some Linguistic Features of Negro Dialect." *Teaching Standard English in the Inner City,* ed. R. W. Fasold & R. W. Shuy, 41–86. Arlington, VA: Center for Applied Linguistics.

Feitelson, D., & Goldstein, Z. (1986). "Patterns of Book Ownership and Reading to Young Children in Israel School-Oriented and Nonschool-Oriented Families." *The Reading Teacher* 39: 924–930.

Ferreiro, E., & Teberosky, A. (1979/1982). *Literacy Before Schooling.* Portsmouth, NH: Heinemann.

Fielding, L. G., & Pearson, P. D. (1994). "Reading Comprehension: What Works." *Educational Leadership* (February): 62–68.

Fiesta (1971). From the Houghton Mifflin Reading Program. Boston: Houghton Mifflin.

Fink, R. P. (1995/1996). "Successful Dyslexics: A Constructivist Study of Passionate Interest Reading." *Journal of Adolescent and Adult Literacy* 39(4): 268–280.

Fisher, B. (1995). *Thinking and Learning Together: Curriculum and Community in a Primary Classroom.* Portsmouth, NH: Heinemann.

Fisher, B., & Fisher-Medvic, E. (2000). *Perspectives on Shared Reading: Planning and Practice.* Portsmouth, NH: Heinemann.

Fisher, D. F., & Shebilske, W. L. (1985). "There Is More That Meets the Eye Than the Eyemind Assumption." *Eye Movements and Human Information Processing,* ed. R. Groner, G. W. McConkie, & C. Menz, 149–157. Amsterdam: Elsevier.

Fitzgerald, S. (1986). "Beginning Reading and Writing Through Singing: A Natural Approach." *Highway One* 7(2): 6–12.

Five, C. L., & Egawa, K. (1998a). "Literacy Workshop Across the Day." *School Talk* 3(4): 8.

Five, C. L., & Egawa, K. (1998b). "Reading and Writing Workshop: What Is It, and What Does It Look Like?" *School Talk* 3(4): 1–3.

Five, C. L., & Egawa, K., eds. (1998c). "Reading and Writing Workshop." *School Talk* 3(4).

Fleischman, P. (1988). *Joyful Noise: Poems for Two Voices.* New York: Harper & Row.

Flesch, R. (1955). *Why Johnny Can't Read.* New York: Harper & Row.

Fletcher, J. M., & Lyon, G. R. (1998). "Reading: A Research-Based Approach." *What's Gone Wrong in America's Classrooms?,* ed. W. M. Evers, 49–90. Stanford, CA: Hoover Institution Press.

Fletcher, R., & Portalupi, J. (1998). *Craft Lessons: Teaching Writing K–8.* York, ME: Stenhouse.

Fletcher, R., & Portalupi, J. (2001). *Writing Workshop: The Essential Guide.* Portsmouth, NH: Heinemann.

Flippo, R. F. (1998). "Points of Agreement: A Display of Professional Unity in Our Field." *The Reading Teacher* 52(1): 30–40.

Flippo, R. F. (1999). *What Do the Experts Say?* Portsmouth, NH: Heinemann.

Flurkey, A. D. (1997). *Reading as Flow: A Linguistic Alternative to Fluency.* Tucson: University of Arizona. Unpublished doctoral dissertation.

Flurkey, A. D. (1998). *Reading as Flow: A Linguistic Alternative to Fluency.* Tucson: University of Arizona Program in Language and Literacy.

Foorman, B., et al. (1999). "The Dimensionality of Phonological Awareness: An Application of the Item Response Theory." *Journal of Educational Psychology* 91(September): 439–449.

Foorman, B., Francis, D., Fletcher, J., Schatschneider, C., & Mehta, P. (1998). "The Role of Instruction in Learning to Read: Preventing Reading Failure in At-Risk Children." *Journal of Educational Psychology* 90: 37–55.

Foorman, B., Francis, D., Winikates, D., Mehta, P., Schatschneider, C., & Fletcher, J. M. (1997). "Early Interventions for Children with Reading Disabilities: Study Designs and Preliminary Findings." *Scientific Studies in Reading* 1: 255–276.

Foorman, B. R., Francis, D. J., Beeler, T., Winikates, D., & Fletcher, J. M. (1997). "Early Interventions for Children with Reading Problems: Study Designs and Preliminary Findings." *Learning Disabilities: A Multidisciplinary Journal* 8(1): 63–71.

Fountas, I. C., & Pinnell, G. S. (1996). *Guided Reading: Good First Teaching for All Children.* Portsmouth, NH: Heinemann.

Fountas, I. C., & Pinnell, G. S. (1999a). *Matching Books to Readers: Using Leveled Books in Guided Reading, K–3.* Portsmouth, NH: Heinemann.

Fountas, I. C., & Pinnell, G. S. (Eds.). (1999b). *Voices on Word Matters: Learning About Phonics and Spelling in the Literacy Classroom.* Portsmouth, NH: Heinemann.

Fountas, I. C., & Pinnell, G. S. (2000). *Guiding Readers and Writers: Grades 3–6.* Portsmouth, NH: Heinemann.

Fox, B., & Routh, D. (1983). "Reading Disability, Phonemic Analysis, and Dysphonetic Spelling: A Follow-up Study." *Journal of Clinical Child Psychology* 12(1): 28–32.

Frank, R. (1980). "Context and Reading Acquisition." *Journal of Reading* 24: 11–15.

Fraser, J., & Skolnick, D. (1994). *On Their Way: Celebrating Second Graders as They Read and Write.* Portsmouth, NH: Heinemann.

Freire, P. (1970). *Pedagogy of the Oppressed.* New York: Herder and Herder.

Freppon, P. (1991). "Children's Concepts of the Nature and Purpose of Reading in Different Instructional Settings." *Journal of Reading Behavior* 23(2): 139–163.

Freppon, P. (1993). Making Sense of Reading and Writing in Urban Classrooms: Understanding At-Risk Children's Knowledge Construction in Different Curricula. Final Report to the Office of Educational Research and Improvement. Washington, D.C.: U.S. Department of Education. (Grant Award No. R117E102361-91).

Freppon, P. (1995). "Low-Income Children's Literacy Interpretations in a Skills-Based and a Whole-Language Classroom." *Journal of Reading Behavior* 27: 505–533.

Freppon, P. A., & Dahl, K. L. (1991). "Learning About Phonics in a Whole Language Classroom." *Language Arts* 68: 190–197.

Freppon, P. A., & Headings, L. (1996). "Keeping It Whole in Whole Language: A First Grade Teacher's Instruction in an Urban Whole Language Classroom." *Balanced Instruction: Strategies and Skills in Whole Language,* ed. E. McIntyre & M. Pressley, 65–82. Norwood, MA: Christopher-Gordon.

Freppon, P., & McIntyre, E. (1999). "A Comparison of Young Children Learning to Read in Different Instructional Settings." *Journal of Educational Research* 92(4): 206–217.

Fries, C., Fries, A., Wilson, R., & Rudolph, M. (1966). *Merrill Linguistic Readers,* Vol. 2. Charles E. Merrill Books, Inc.

Frith, U. (1985). "Beneath the Surface of Developmental Dyslexia." *Surface Dyslexia: Neuropsychological and Cognitive Analyses of Phonological Reading,* ed. K. E. Patterson, J. C. Marshall, & M. Colthart, 301–330. Mahwah, NJ: Erlbaum.

Fry, E. (1998). "The Most Common Phonograms." *Reading Teacher* 51: 620–622.

Gambrell, L. (1996). "Creating Classroom Cultures That Foster Reading Motivation." *Reading Teacher* 50: 14–25.

Garan, E. M. (2001a). "Beyond the Smoke and Mirrors: A Critique of the National Reading Panel Report on Phonics." *Phi Delta Kappan* 82(7): 500–506.

Garan, E. M. (2001b). "More Smoking Guns: A Response to Linnea Ehri and Steven Stahl." *Phi Delta Kappan,* 83(1): 21–27.

Garan, E. M. (2001c). "What Does the Report of the National Reading Panel *Really* Tell Us About Teaching Phonics?" *Language Arts* 77(5): 59–68.

Garan, E. M. (2002). *Resisting Reading Mandates: How to Triumph with the Truth.* Portsmouth, NH: Heinemann.

Gates, D. D. (1979). *The Use of Contextual Information for Word Identification by Elementary School Children.* Berkeley: University of California.

Geisel, T. S. (1972). *In a People House.* New York: Random House.

Gersten, R., & Keating, T. (1987). "Long-Term Benefits from Direct Instruction." *Educational Leadership* 44(6): 28–31.

Gibson, E. J. (1972). "Reading for Some Purpose." *Language by Ear and by Eye,* ed. J. F. Kavanagh & I. G. Mattingly, 3–19. Cambridge: MIT Press.

Gibson, E. J., & Levin, H. (1975). *The Psychology of Reading.* Cambridge: MIT Press.

Gibson, E. J., Shurcliff, A., et al. (1970). "Utilization of Spelling Patterns by Deaf and Hearing Subjects." *Basic Studies on Reading,* ed. H. Levin & J. P. Williams, 57–73. New York: Basic Books.

Glushko, R. J. (1979). "The Organization and Activation of Orthographic Knowledge in Reading Aloud." *Journal of Experimental Psychology: Human Perception and Performance* 5: 674–691.

Goetz, L. G. (1966). *A Camel in the Sea.* New York: McGraw-Hill.

Gollasch, F. V. (1980). Reader's Perception in Detecting and Processing Embedded Errors in Meaningful Text. UMI# AAC 81-07445. Tucson: University of Arizona.

Goodling, W. F. (1997, October). Reading Excellence Act. (Staff discussion draft). Washington, D.C.: U.S. House of Representatives, Committee on Education and the Workforce. [Draft obtained via the International Reading Association].

Goodman, D. (1999). *The Reading Detective Club: Solving the Mysteries of Reading, a Teacher's Guide.* Portsmouth, NH: Heinemann.

Goodman, K. S. (1965). "A Linguistic Study of Cues and Miscues in Reading." *Elementary English* **42**: 639–643.

Goodman, K. S. (1967). "Reading: A Psycholinguistic Guessing Game." *Journal of the Reading Specialist* **6**: 126–135.

Goodman, K. S. (1973). "Miscues: Windows on the Reading Process." *Miscue Analysis: Applications to Reading Instruction,* 3–14. Urbana, IL: ERIC and the National Council of Teachers of English.

Goodman, K. S. (1976). "What We Know About Reading." *Findings of Research in Miscue Analysis,* ed. P. D. Allen & D. J. Watson, 57–70. Urbana, IL: ERIC and the National Council of Teachers of English.

Goodman, K. S. (1978). "The Reading Process." *Reading of American Children Whose Language Is a Stable Rural Dialect of English or a Language Other Than English.* Final report, Project NIE-C-00-3-0087. Washington, DC: U.S. Department of Health, Education, and Welfare.

Goodman, K. S. (1982a). *Language and Literacy: The Selected Writings of Kenneth S. Goodman.* Boston: Routledge and Kegan Paul.

Goodman, K. S. (1982b). "Miscue Analysis: Theory and Reality in Reading." *Language and Literacy: The Selected Writings of Kenneth S. Goodman,* ed. F. Gollasch, 2: 103–113. Boston: Routledge and Kegan Paul.

Goodman, K. S. (1986a). "Revaluing Readers and Reading." *Revaluing Troubled Readers: Two Papers.* Tucson: University of Education, Program in Language and Literacy. **Occasional Papers # 15**: 1–11.

Goodman, K. S. (1986b). *What's Whole in Whole Language?* Portsmouth, NH: Heinemann.

Goodman, K. S. (1994). "Reading, Writing, and Written Texts: A Transactional Sociopsycholinguistic View." *Theoretical Models and Processes of Reading,* ed. R. B. Ruddell, M. R. Ruddell, & H. Singer, 1093–1130. Newark, DE: International Reading Association.

Goodman, K. S. (1996). *On Reading.* Portsmouth, NH: Heinemann.

Goodman, K. S. (1998). *In Defense of Good Teaching: What Teachers Need to Know About the "Reading Wars."* York, ME: Stenhouse.

Goodman, K. S., & Buck, C. (1973). "Dialect Barriers to Reading Comprehension Revisited." *The Reading Teacher* **27**: 6–12.

Goodman, K. S., & Burke, C. L. (1973). *Theoretically Based Studies of Patterns of Miscues in Oral Reading Performance.* Detroit: Wayne State University. ERIC:ED 079 708.

Goodman, K. S., & Gollasch, F. V. (1980). "Word Omissions: Deliberate and Non-Deliberate." *Reading Research Quarterly* **16**(1): 6–31.

Goodman, K. S., & Goodman, Y. M. (1978). *Reading of American Children Whose Language Is a Stable Rural Dialect of English or a Language Other Than English.* Final report, Project NIE-C-00-3-0087. Washington, D.C.: U.S. Department of Health, Education, and Welfare.

Goodman, K. S., & Goodman, Y. M. (1979). "Learning to Read Is Natural." *Theory and Practice of Early Reading,* Vol. 1, ed. L. B. Resnick & P. W. Weaver, 137–154. Hillsdale, NJ: Erlbaum.

Goodman, Y. M. (1976). "Strategies for Comprehension." *Findings of Research in Miscue Analysis: Classroom Implications,* ed. P. D. Allen & D. Watson, 94–102. Urbana, IL: ERIC Clearinghouse on Reading and Communication Skills and the National Council of Teachers of English.

Goodman, Y. M. (1978). "Kid Watching: An Alternative to Testing." *National Elementary Principal* 57(June): 41–45.

Goodman, Y. M. (1985). "Kidwatching: Observing Children in the Classroom." *Observing the Language Learner,* ed. A. Jaggar & M. T. Smith-Burke, 9–18. Newark, DE: International Reading Association.

Goodman, Y. M. (1996a). *Notes from a Kidwatcher: Selected Writings of Yetta M. Goodman.* Portsmouth, NH: Heinemann.

Goodman, Y. M. (1996b). "Revaluing Readers While Readers Revalue Themselves: Retrospective Miscue Analysis." *The Reading Teacher* 49(8): 600–609.

Goodman, Y. M., & Goodman, K. S. (1994). "To Err Is Human: Learning About Language Processes by Analyzing Miscues." *Theoretical Models and Processes of Reading,* 4th ed., R. B. Ruddell, M. R. Ruddell, & H. Singer, 104–123. Newark, DE: International Reading Association.

Goodman, Y. M., & Marek, A. (1989). "Retrospective Miscue Analysis: Two Papers." Tucson: University of Arizona. Program in Language and Literacy.

Goodman, Y. M., & Marek, A. M. (1996). *Retrospective Miscue Analysis: Revaluing Readers and Reading.* Katonah, NY: Richard C. Owen.

Goodman, Y. M., Watson, D. J., & Burke, C. L. (1987). *Reading Miscue Inventory: Alternative Procedures.* Katohan, NY: Richard C. Owen.

Goodman, Y. M., Watson, D. J., & Burke, C. L. (1996). *Reading Strategies: Focus on Comprehension,* 2nd ed. Katonah, NY: Richard C. Owen.

Goswami, U. (1986). "Children's Use of Analogy in Learning to Read: A Developmental Study." *Journal of Experimental Psychology* 42: 73–83.

Goswami, U. (1988). "Orthographic Analogies and Reading Development." *Quarterly Journal of Experimental Psychology* 40A(2): 239–268.

Goswami, U. (1993). "Toward an Interactive Analogy Model of Reading Development: Decoding Vowel Graphemes in Beginning Reading." *Journal of Experimental Child Psychology* 56: 443–475.

Goswami, U., & Bryant, P. (1990). *Phonological Skills and Learning to Read.* Hove, East Sussex: Lawrence Erlbaum.

Goswami, U., & Mead, F. (1992). "Onset and Rime Awareness and Analogies in Reading." *Reading Research Quarterly* 27: 150–162.

Gough, P. (1972). "One Second of Reading." *Language by Ear and by Eye,* ed. J. F. Kavanagh & I. G. Mattingly, 331–358. Cambridge: MIT Press.

Gough, P. B., & Hillinger, M. L. (1980). "Learning to Read: An Unnatural Act." *Bulletin of the Orton Society* 30: 180–196.

Graves, D. (1989–92). The Reading/Writing Teacher's Companion Series. Portsmouth. NH: Heinemann.

Graves, D. (1989a). *Experiment with Fiction.* Portsmouth, NH: Heinemann.

Graves, D. (1989b). *Investigate Nonfiction.* Portsmouth, NH: Heinemann.

Graves, D. (1990a). *Discover Your Own Literacy.* Portsmouth, NH: Heinemann.

Graves, D. (1990b). *A Fresh Look at Writing.* Portsmouth, NH: Heinemann.

Graves, D. (1991). *Build a Literate Classroom.* Portsmouth, NH: Heinemann.

Graves, D. (1992). *Explore Poetry.* Portsmouth. NH: Heinemann.

Greene, G. (1940). *The Power and the Glory.* New York: Viking.

Griffith, P., Klesius, J., & Kromey, J. (1992). "The Effect of Phonemic Awareness on the Literacy Development of First Grade Children in a Traditional or a Whole Language Classroom." *Journal of Research in Childhood Education* 6(2): 85–92.

Grossen, B. (1997). A Synthesis of Research on Reading from the National Institute of Child Health and Human Development. *<www.nrrf.org/synthesis.research.htm>*

Gunning, R. G. (1988). Decoding Behavior of Good and Poor Second Grade Students. Paper presented at the annual meeting of the International Reading Association, Toronto.

Gunning, R. G. (1995). "Word Building: A Strategic Approach to the Teaching of Phonics." *The Reading Teacher* 48: 484–488.

Gwynne, F. (1987). *The Sixteen Hand Horse*. New York: Simon & Schuster.

Gwynne, F. (1988a). *A Chocolate Moose for Dinner*. New York: Simon & Schuster.

Gwynne, F. (1988b). *The King Who Rained*. New York: Simon & Schuster.

Gwynne, F. (1990). *Little Pigeon Toad*. New York: Simon & Schuster.

Hagerty, P., Hiebert, E. H., & Owens, M. (1989). "Students' Comprehension, Writing, and Perceptions in Two Approaces to Literacy Instruction." *Cognitive and Social Perspectives in Literacy Research and Instruction: Thirty-Eighth Yearbook of the National Reading Conference*, ed. S. McCormick & J. Zutell, 453–459. Chicago: National Reading Conference.

Halliday, M. A. K. (1975). *Learning How to Mean: Explorations in the Development of Language*. London: Elsevier.

Halliday, M. A. K. (1980). "Text and Context: Aspects of Language in Socio-Semiotic Perspective." *Sophia Linguistica VI*. Tokyo: Sophia University Press.

Hammill, D. D. (1977). "The Effects of Spelling Instruction: A Preliminary Study." *Elementary School Journal* 78: 67–72.

Hanna, R. R., et al. (1966). Phoneme Grapheme Correspondences as Cues to Spelling Improvement. Washington D.C.: Government Printing Office. USOE Publication No. 32008.

Hansen, J., & Graves, D. (1988). *The Writing and Reading Process*. Portsmouth, NH: Heinemann.

Harper, R. J., & Kilarr G. (1977). "The Law and Reading Instruction." *Language Arts* 54: 913–919.

Harris, A. J., & Clark, M. K. (1965). *Opening Doors*. New York: Macmillan.

Harste, J. C. (1978). "Understanding the Hypothesis, It's the Teacher That Makes the Difference: Part II." *Reading Horizons* 18: 89–98.

Hart-Hewins, L., & Wells, J. (1999). *Better Books! Better Readers! How to Choose, Use, and Level Books for Children in the Primary Grades*. York, ME: Stenhouse.

Harvey, S. (1998). *Nonfiction Matters: Reading, Writing, and Research in Grades 3–8*. York, ME: Stenhouse.

Harvey, S., & Goudvis, A. (2000). *Strategies That Work: Teaching Comprehension to Enhance Understanding*. York, ME: Stenhouse.

Harwayne, S. (1992). *Lasting Impressions: Weaving Literature into the Writing Workshop*. Portsmouth, NH: Heinemann.

Harwayne, S. (2001). *Writing Across Childhood*. Portsmouth, NH: Heinemann.

Haskell, D. W., et al. (1992). "Effects of Three Orthographic/Phonological Units on First-Grade Reading." *Remedial and Special Education* 13: 40–49.

Heald-Taylor, G. (1989). *The Administrator's Guide to Whole Language*. Katonah, NY: Richard C. Owen.

Heath, S. B. (1982). "What No Bedtime Story Means: Narrative Skills at Home and School." *Language in Society* 2: 49–76.

Heath, S. B. (1983). *Ways with Words: Language, Life, and Work in Communities and Classrooms.* New York: Cambridge University Press.

Hendrick-Keefe, C. (1996). *Label-Free Learning.* York, ME: Stenhouse.

Henkes, K. (1991). *Chrysanthemum.* New York: Mulberry (William Morrow & Co.).

Henkes, K. (1993). *Owen.* New York: Greenwillow.

Hill, B. C., Johnson, N. J., & Noe, K. L. S. (Eds.). (1995). *Literature Circles and Response.* Norwood, MA: Christopher-Gordon.

Hill, S. (2000). *Phonics.* York, ME: Stenhouse.

Hillerich, R. L. (1977). "Let's Teach Spelling—Not Phonetic Misspelling." *Language Arts* 54: 301–307.

Hindley, J. (1996). *In the Company of Children.* York, ME: Stenhouse.

Hindley, J. (1990). *Inside Reading and Writing Workshop: A Visit to Room 305.* Four inservice videotapes. York, ME: Stenhouse.

Hoban, R. (1964). *Bread and Jam for Frances.* New York: Harper & Row.

Hochberg, J. (1970). "Components of Literacy: Speculations and Exploratory Research." *Basic Studies on Reading,* ed. H. Levin & J. P. Williams, 74–89. New York: Basic Books.

Hoffmann, P. R., & Norris, J. A. (1994). "Whole Language and Collaboration Work: Evidence from At-Risk Kindergarteners." *Journal of Childhood Communication Disorders* 16(1): 41–48.

Hogaboam, T. (1983). "Reading Patterns in Eye Movement Data." *Eye Movements in Reading,* ed. K. Rayner, 309–332. New York: Academic.

Holdaway, D. (1979). *The Foundations of Literacy.* Portsmouth, NH: Heinemann.

Holdaway, D. (1982). "Shared Book Experience: Teaching Reading Using Favorite Books." *Theory into Practice* 21(4): 293–300.

Horn Book Guide, Interactive, The. (1998). Portsmouth, NH: Heinemann.

House, E. R., Glass, G. V., McLean, L. D., & Walker, D. F. (1978). "No Simple Answer: Critique of the Follow Through Evaluation." *Harvard Educational Review* 48: 128–60.

Hoyt, L. (2000). *Snapshots: Literacy Minilessons up Close.* Portsmouth, NH: Heinemann.

Hudelson-Lopez, S. (1977). "Children's Use of Contextual Clues in Reading Spanish." *The Reading Teacher* 30: 735–740.

Huey, E. B. (1908/1968). *The Psychology and Pedagogy of Reading.* Cambridge: MIT Press.

Hughes, M., & Searle, D. (1997). *The Violent E and Other Tricky Sounds: Learning to Spell from Kindergarten Through Grade 6.* York, ME: Stenhouse.

Hughes, M. A. (1977). *Word Identification and Comprehension in Learning to Read.* Ontario, Canada: University of Toronto.

Hunt, B. C. (1974–1975). "Black Dialect and Third and Fourth Graders' Performance on the Gray Oral Reading Test." *Reading Research Quarterly* 10(1): 103–123.

Internal Revenue Service. (1985). *1040 Federal Income Tax Forms and Instructions.* Washington, D.C.: Internal Revenue Service.

International Reading Association. (1999). *Using Multiple Methods of Beginning Reading Instruction: A Position Statement of the International Reading Association.* Newark, DE: International Reading Association.

Iran-Nejad, A. (1980). *The Schema: A Structural or a Functional Pattern.* Technical Report No. 159. Urbana, IL: University of Illinois, Center for the Study of Reading.

Iran-Nejad, A., & Ortony, A. (1984). "A Biofunctional Model of Distributed Mental Content, Mental Structures, Awareness, and Attention." *The Journal of Mind and Behavior* 5: 171–210.

Jobe, R., & Dayton-Sakari, M. (1999). *Reluctant Readers: Connecting Students and Books for Successful Reading Experiences.* York, ME: Stenhouse.

Johns, J. L. (1986). "Students' Perceptions of Reading: Thirty Years of Inquiry." *Metalinguistic Awareness and Beginning Literacy,* ed. J. D. B. Yaden & S. Templeton, 31–40. Portsmouth, NH: Heinemann.

Johnston, P. H. (1997). *Knowing Literacy: Constructive Literacy Assessment.* York, ME: Stenhouse.

Johnston, P. H. (2000). *Running Records: A Self-Tutoring Guide.* York, ME: Stenhouse.

Juel, C. (1988). "Learning to Read and Write: A Longitudinal Study of 54 Children from First Through Fourth Grades." *Journal of Educational Psychology* 80(4): 437–447.

Juel, C., Griffith, P. L., & Gough, P. B. (1986). "Acquisition of Literacy: A Longitudinal Study of Children in First and Second Grade." *Journal of Educational Psychology* 78(4): 243–255.

Juel, C., & Minden-Cupp, C. (2000). "Learning to Read Words: Linguistic Units and Instructional Strategies." *Reading Research Quarterly* 35(4): 458–492.

Juel, C., & Roper/Schneider, D. (1985). "The Influence of Basal Readers on First Grade Reading." *Reading Research Quarterly* 20(2): 134–152.

Just, M., & Carpenter, P. (1980). "A Theory of Reading: From Eye Fixations to Comprehension." *Psychological Review* 87: 329–354.

Just, M., & Carpenter, P. (1987). *The Psychology of Reading and Language Comprehension.* Newton, MA: Allyn & Bacon.

Kameenui, E. J., Simmons, D.C., Chard, O., & Dickson, S. (1997). "Direct Instruction Reading." *Instructional Models in Reading,* ed. S. A. Stahl & D. A. Hayes, 59–84. Mahwah, NJ: Erlbaum.

Karnes, M. B., Shwedel, A. M., & Williams, M. B. (1983). "A Comparison of Five Approaches for Educating Young Children from Low-Income Homes." *As the Twig Is Bent . . . : Lasting Effects of Preschool Programs,* Consortium for Longitudinal Studies, 133–169. Hillsdale, NJ: Erlbaum.

Keefe, C. H. (1996). *Label Free Learning: Supporting Learners with Disabilities.* York, ME: Stenhouse.

Keene, E. O., & Zimmermann, S. (1997). *Mosaic of Thought: Teaching Comprehension in a Reader's Workshop.* Portsmouth, NH: Heinemann.

Killgallon, D. (1997). *Sentence Composition for Middle School: A Worktext on Sentence Variety and Maturity.* Portsmouth, NH: Heinimann.

King, D. R., & Watson, D. J. (1983). "Reading as Meaning Construction." *Integrating the Language Arts in the Elementary School,* ed. B. A. Busching & J. I. Schwartz, 70–77. Urbana, IL: National Council of Teachers of English.

Kirtley, C., Bryant, P., et al. (1989). "Rhyme, Rime and the Onset of Reading." *Journal of Experimental Psychology* 48: 224–245.

Kitagawa, M. (2000). *Enter Teaching! The Essential Guide for Teachers New to Grades 3–6.* Portsmouth, NH: Heinemann.

Klesius, J. P., Griffith, P. L., & Zielonka, P. (1991). "A Whole Language and Traditional Instruction Comparison: Overall Effectiveness and Development of the Alphabetic Principle." *Reading Research and Instruction* 30: 47–61.

Knapp, M., Adelman, N., Marder, C., McCollum, H., Needels, M., Padilla, C., Shields, P., Turnbull, B., & Zucker, A. (1995). *Teaching for Meaning in High-Poverty Classrooms.* New York: Teachers College Press.

Kobrin, B. (1988). *Eyeopeners! How to Choose and Use Children's Books About Real People, Places, and Things.* New York: Viking Penguin.

Koestler, A. (1969). "Beyond Atomism and Holism—The Concept of the Holon." *Beyond Reductionism,* ed. A. Koestler & J. R. Smythies, 192–227. New York: Macmillan.

Kohler, I. (1962). "Experiments with Goggles." *Scientific American* 206: 62–72.

Kohn, A. (1999). *The Schools Our Children Deserve: Moving Beyond Traditional Classrooms and "Tougher Standards."* Boston: Houghton Mifflin.

Kolers, P. A. (1969). "Reading Is Only Incidentally Visual." *Psycholinguistics and the Teaching of Reading,* ed. K. S. Goodman & J. T. Fleming, 8–16. Newark, DE: International Reading Association.

Kooy, M., & Wells, J. (1996). *Reading Response Logs: Inviting Students to Explore Novels, Short Stories, Plays, Poetry, and More.* Portsmouth, NH: Heinemann.

Kozol, J. (1991). *Savage Inequalities: Children in America's Schools.* New York: Crown.

Krashen, S. D. (1993). *The Power of Reading: Insights from the Research.* Englewood, CO: Libraries Unlimited.

Krashen, S. D. (1995). "School Libraries, Public Libraries, and the NAEP Reading Scores." *School Library Media Quarterly* 235–237.

Krashen, S. D. (1999). *Three Arguments Against Whole Language and Why They Are Wrong.* Portsmouth, NH: Heinemann.

Krashen, S. D. (2000a). "Does Phonemic Awareness Develop Without Special Training?" <*www.languagebooks.com*>.

Krashen, S. D. (2000b). "Low PA Can Read OK." <*www.languagebooks.com*>.

Krashen, S. D. (2000c). "The National Reading Panel: Errors and Omissions." *Education Week,* May 20. Bethesda, MD, Language Education Associates.

Krashen, S. D. (2000d). "The National Reading Panel Report on Phonics: Consistent with and Supportive of the Comprehension Hypothesis (We Learn to Read by Reading)." <*www.languagebooks.com*>.

Krashen, S. D. (2001a). "Does 'Pure' Phonemic Awareness Training Affect Reading Comprehension?" *Perceptual and Motor Skills* 93: 356–358.

Krashen, S. D. (2001b). "More Smoke and Mirrors: A Critique of the National Reading Panel Report on 'Fluency.'" *Phi Delta Kappan* 83(2): 118–121.

Krashen, S. D. (In press). "Recreational Reading." *Literacy in America: An Encyclopedia,* ed. B. Guzzetti. Santa Barbara, CA: ABC Publishers.

Krashen, S. D., & McQuillan, J. (1998). "The Case for Late Intervention: Once a Good Reader, Always a Good Reader." *Reconsidering a Balanced Approach to Reading,* ed. C. Weaver, 409–422. Urbana, IL: National Council of Teachers of English.

Kucer, S. B. (1985). "Predictability and Readability: The Same Rose with Different Names?" *Claremont Reading Conference Forty-Ninth Yearbook,* ed. M. Douglass, 229–246. Claremont, CA: Claremont Graduate School.

Kucer, S. B. (1992). "Six Bilingual Mexican-American Students' and Their Teachers' Interpretations of Cloze Literacy Lessons." *The Elementary School Journal* 92: 555–570.

Lakoff, G. (1968). "Instrumental Adverbs and the Concept of Deep Structure." *Foundations of Language* 4: 4–29.

Laminack, L. L., & Wood, K. (1996). *Spelling in Use: Looking Closely at Spelling in Whole Language Classrooms.* Urbana, IL: National Council of Teachers of English.

Lefton, L. A., & Spragins, A. B. (1974). "Orthographic Structure and Reading Experience Affect the Transfer from Iconic to Short-Term Memory." *Journal of Experimental Psychology* 103: 775–781.

Lenel, J. C., & Cantor, J. H. (1981). "Rhyme Recognition and Phonemic Perception in Young Children." *Journal of Psycholinguistic Research* 10: 57–68.

Leslie, L., & Caldwell, J. (2001). *Qualitative Reading Inventory–3.* New York: Longman.

Levande, D. I. (1989). "Theoretical Orientation to Reading and Classroom Practice." *Reading Improvement* 26: 274–280.

Levy, S. (1996). *Starting from Scratch: One Classroom Builds Its Own Curriculum.* Portsmouth, NH: Heinemann.

Liberman, I., & Liberman, A. (1992). "Whole Language Versus Code Emphasis: Underlying Assumptions and Their Implications for Reading Instruction." *Reading Acquisition,* ed. P. B. Gough, L. C. Ehri, & R. Treiman, 343–366. Hillsdale, NJ: Erlbaum.

Liberman, I., Shankweiler, D., Fricker, F. W., & Carter, B. (1974). "Explicit Syllable and Phoneme Segmentation in the Young Child." *Journal of Experimental Child Psychology* 18: 201–212.

Lindamood, C. H., & Lindamood, P. C. (1994). *Auditory Discrimination in Depth.* Austin, TX: PRO-ED.

Linn, R. L. (2000). "Assessments and Accountability." *Educational Researcher* 29(2): 4–16.

Lipson, M. Y. (1983). "The Influence of Religious Affiliation on Children's Memory for Text Information." *Reading Research Quarterly* 18: 448–457.

Lovett, M. W., Borden, S. L., DeLuca, T., Lacerenza, L., Benenson, N. J., & Brackstone, D. (1994). "Treating the Core Deficits of Developmental Dyslexia: Evidence of Transfer of Learning After Phonologically- and Strategy-Based Reading Training Programs." *Developmental Psychology* 30: 805–822.

Lundberg, I., Frost, J., & Peterson, O. P. (1988). "Effects of an Extensive Program for Stimulating Phonological Awareness in Preschool Children." *Reading Research Quarterly* 23: 263–284.

Lyon, G. R. (1995). "Toward a Definition of Dyslexia." *Annals of Dyslexia,* 65.

Lyon, G. R. (1997). Statement of G. R. Lyon, Ph.D., before the Committee on Education and the Workforce, U.S. House of Representatives. Washington, D.C. July 10. Available: <*www.edworkforce.house.gov*>.

Lyon, G. R. (1998). "Why Reading Is Not a Natural Process." *Educational Leadership* (March): 14–18.

Lyon, G. R. (2001a). Statement of Dr. G. Reid Lyon, before the Subcommittee on Education Reform, Committee on Education and the Workforce, U.S. House of Representatives. Washington, D.C. March 8. Available: <*www.edworkforce.house.gov*>.

Lyon, G. R. (2001b). "What Does Quality Reading Instruction Look Like?" Speech, "What's Working in Reading?" Conference, spons. Charlotte Chamber of Commerce, January 19, Charlotte, NC. <*www charlottechamber com/files/eduhatstranscript pdf*>

Lyon, G. R., & Moats, L. C. (1997). "Critical Conceptual and Methodological Considerations in Reading Intervention Research." *Journal of Learning Disabilities* 30: 578–588.

MacKenzie, T. (Ed.). (1992). *Readers' Workshop: Bridging Literature and Literacy.* Toronto, Ontario, Canada: Irwin.

Maniates, H., Doerr, B., & Golden, M. (2001). *Teach Our Children Well: Essential Strategies for the Urban Classroom.* Portsmouth, NH: Heinemann.

Mann, V. A. (1986). "Phonological Awareness: The Role of Reading Experience." *Cognition* 24: 65–92.

Manning, M., Manning, G., & Long, R. (1994). *Theme Immersion: Inquiry-Based Curriculum in Elementary and Middle Schools.* Portsmouth, NH: Heinemann.

Manning, M., Manning, G., Long, R., & Kamii, C. (1993). "Preschoolers' Conjectures About Segments of a Written Sentence." *Journal of Research in Childhood Education* 8(1): 5–11.

Manzo, K. K. (2000). "Reading Panel Urges Phonics for All in K–6." *Education Week,* April 19.

Marcel, A. J., & Patterson, K. E. (1978). "Word Recognition and Production: Reciprocity in Clinical and Normal Studies." *Attention and Performance VII,* ed. J. Peguin. 209–226. Hillsdale, NJ: Erlbaum.

Marcon, R. A. (1995). "Doing the Right Thing for Children: Linking Research and Policy Reform in the District of Columbia Public Schools." *Young Children* (November): 8–20.

Marek, A. M. (1989). "Using Evaluation as an Instructional Strategy for Adult Readers." *The Whole Language Evaluation Book,* ed. K. S. Goodman, Y. M. Goodman, & W. J. Hood. 157–164. Portsmouth, NH: Heinemann.

Marek, A. M. (1992). Retrospective Miscue Analysis Lesson Plan. Distributed at a session on miscue analysis at the International Reading Association annual convention, Orlando, May.

Marks, L. E., & Miller, G. A. (1964). "The Role of Semantic and Syntactic Constraints in the Memorization of English Sentences." *Journal of Verbal Learning and Verbal Behavior* **3**: 1–5.

Marshall, E. (1981). *Three by the Sea.* New York: Dial.

Marshall, J. (1972). *What's the Matter with Carruthers?* Boston: Houghton Mifflin.

Marsonet, M. (1995). *Science, Reality, and Language.* Albany, NY: State University of New York Press.

Martens, P. (1997). "What Miscue Analysis Reveals About Word Recognition and Repeated Reading: A View Through the Miscue Window." *Language Arts* **74**(8): 600–609.

Martens, P. M., Goodman, K. S., & Goodman, Y. M. (1993). The Making of a Proficient Reader: Repeated Reading? Or, Continued Wide Reading? National Reading Conference, Charleston, SC, December 1–4.

McCarrier, A., Pinnell, G. S., & Fountas, I. C. (2000). *Interactive Writing: How Language & Literacy Come Together, K–2.* Portsmouth, NH: Heinemann.

McCaughey, M. W., Juola, J. F., et al. (1980). "Whole-Word Units Are Used Before Orthographic Knowledge In Perceptual Development." *Journal of Experimental Child Psychology* **30**: 411–421.

McCawley, J. D. (1968). "The Role of Semantics in Grammar." *Universals in Linguistic Theory,* ed. E. Bach & R. T. Harms, 124–169. New York: Holt, Rinehart.

McClelland, J. L., & O'Regan, J. K. (1981). "Expectations Increase the Benefit Derived from Parafoveal Visual Information in Reading Words Aloud." *Journal of Experimental Psychology: Human Perception and Performance* **7**(3): 634–644.

McConkie, G. W., & Zola, D. (1981). "Language Constraints and the Functional Stimulus in Reading." *Interactive Processes in Reading,* ed. A. M. Lesgold & C. A. Perfetti, 155–175. Hillsdale, NJ: Erlbaum.

McCormick-Calkins, L. (1983). *Lessons from a Child.* Portsmouth, NH: Heinemann.

McCormick-Calkins, L. (1987). *The Writing Workshop Video: A World of Difference.* Portsmouth, NH: Heinemann.

McCormick-Calkins, L. (1994). *The Art of Teaching Writing.* Portsmouth, NH: Heinemann.

McCormick-Calkins, L., & Harwayne, S. (1990). *Living Between the Lines.* Portsmouth, NH: Heinemann.

McCullough, C. M. (1943). "Learning to Use Context Clues." *Elementary English Review* **20**(4): 140–143.

McGovern, A. (1968). *Stone Soup.* Illus. Winslow Pinney Pels. New York: Scholastic.

McIntyre, E., & Freppon, P. (1994). "A Comparison of Children's Development of Alphabetic Knowledge in a Skills-Based and a Whole Language Classroom." *Research in the Teaching of English* **28**(4): 391–417.

McKean, K. (1981). "Beaming New Light on the Brain." *Discover* **2**: 30–33.

McKean, K. (1985). "In Search of the Unconscious Mind." *Discover* **6**: 12–14, 16, 18.

McKenna, M. C., Stratton, B. D., Grindler, M. C., & Jenkins, S. J. (1995). "Differential Effects of Whole Language and Traditional Instruction on Reading Attitudes." *Journal of Reading Behavior* **27**: 19–44.

McMahon, S. I., & Raphael, T. E. (Eds.). (1997). *The Book Club Connection: Literacy Learning and Classroom Talk.* New York: Teachers College Press, International Reading Association.

McMillan, B. (1990). *One Sun: A Book of Terse Verse.* New York: Holiday House.

McPike, E. (1998). "Introduction to Adams, M. J., B. R. Foorman, I. Lundberg, and T. Beeler, 'The Elusive Phoneme.'" *American Educator* **22**(Spring/Summer): 18–19.

McQuillan, J. (1997). "The Effects of Incentives on Reading." *Reading Research and Instruction* **36**: 111–125.

McQuillan, J. (1998). *The Literary Crisis: False Claims, Real Solutions.* Portsmouth, NH: Heinemann.

McQuillan, J., LeMoine, N., Brandlin, E., & O'Brien, B. (1997). "The (Print-) Rich Get Richer: Library Access in Low- and High-Achieving Elementary Schools." *California Reader* **30**(2): 23–25.

Meek, M. (1983). *Achieving Literacy.* London: Routledge & Kegan Paul.

Meek, M. (1988). *How Texts Teach What Readers Learn.* Exeter: Thimble.

Meier, D. (1981). "Why Reading Tests Don't Test Reading." *Dissent* (Fall): 457–466.

Menosky, D. (1971). *A Psycholinguistic Description of Oral Reading Miscues Generated During the Reading of Varying Portions of Text by Selected Readers from Grades Two, Four, Six, and Eight.* Detroit: Wayne State University. Unpublished doctoral dissertation.

Mercer-Krogness, M. (1995). *Just Teach Me, Mrs. K.: Talking, Reading, and Writing with Resistant Adolescent Learners.* Portsmouth, NH: Heinemann.

Metcalf, S. (2002). "Reading Between the Lines." *The Nation,* Jan. 28, 18–22.

Mewhort, D. J. K., & Campbell, A. J. (1981). "Toward a Model of Skilled Reading: An Analysis of Performance in Tachistoscopic Tasks." *Reading Research: Advances in Theory and Practice,* G. E. MacKinnon & T. G. Waller, Vol. 3: 39–118. New York: Academic.

Miller, G. A. (1956). "The Magical Number Seven, Plus or Minus Two: Some Limits on Our Capacity for Processing Information." *Psychological Review* 63: 81–92.

Miller, G. A., Bruner, J. S., & Postman, L. (1954). "Familiarity of Letter Sequences and Tachistoscopic Identification." *Journal of Genetic Psychology* 84: 129–139.

Miller, G. A., & Friedman, E. A. (1957). "The Reconstruction of Mutilated English Texts." *Information and Control* 1: 38–55.

Miller, G. A., & Gildea, P. M. (1987). "How Children Learn Words." *Scientific American* 257(3): 94–99.

Milligan, J. L., & Berg, H. (1992). "The Effect of Whole Language on the Comprehending Ability of First Grade Children." *Reading Improvement* 29(3): 146–154.

Mills, C. W. (1959). *The Sociological Imagination.* New York: Oxford University Press.

Miramontes, O. B. (1990). "A Comparative Study of English Oral Reading Skills in Differently Schooled Groups of Hispanic Students." *Journal of Reading Behavior* 22: 373–394.

Moats, L. C. (1999). *Teaching Reading Is Rocket Science.* Washington, D.C.: American Federation of Teachers.

Morais, J., Alegria, J., & Content, A. (1987). "The Relationships Between Segmental Analysis and Alphabetic Literacy: An Interactive View." *European Bulletin of Cognitive Psychology* 7(5): 415–438.

Morais, J., Cary, L., Alegria, J., & Bertelson, P. (1979). "Does Awareness of Speech as a Sequence of Phones Arise Spontaneously?" *Cognition* 7: 323–331.

Morris, D. (1999). *The Howard Street Tutoring Manual.* New York: Guilford.

Morris, D., & Perney, J. (1984). "Developmental Spelling as a Predictor of First Grade Reading Achievement." *Elementary School Journal* 84: 441–457.

Morrow, L. M. (1992). "The Impact of a Literature-Based Program on Literacy Achievement, Use of Literature, and Attitudes of Children from Minority Backgrounds." *Reading Research Quarterly* 27: 251–275.

Morrow, L. M., O'Connor, E. M., & Smith, J. K. (1990). "Effects of a Story Reading Program on the Literacy Development of *At-Risk* Kindergarten Children." *Journal of Reading Behavior* 22: 255–275.

Moustafa, M. (1990). *An Interactive/Cognitive Model of the Acquisition of a Graphophonemic System by Young Children.* Los Angeles: University of Southern California. Unpublished doctoral dissertation.

Moustafa, M. (1995). "Children's Productive Phonological Recoding." *Reading Research Quarterly* 30(3): 464–476.

Moustafa, M. (1997). *Beyond Traditional Phonics: Research Discoveries and Reading Instruction.* Portsmouth, NH: Heinemann.

Moustafa, M. (1998). "Reconceptualizing Phonics Instruction." *Reconsidering a Balanced Approach to Reading,* ed. C. Weaver, 135–157. Urbana, IL: National Council of Teachers of English.

Moustafa, M. (1999). "Report Card on California's Standardized Testing and Reporting (STAR) Program: When Is Public Information Misinformation?" *The California Reader* (Spring).

Moustafa, M. (2000). "Phonics Instruction." *Beginning Reading and Writing,* ed. D. Strickland & L. M. Morrow, 121–133. New York, Newark, DE: Teachers College Press, International Reading Association.

Moustafa, M., & Land, R. E. (2002). "The Reading Achievement of Economically Disadvantaged Children in Urban Schools Using Open Court vs. Comparably Disadvantaged Children in Urban Schools Using Non-scripted Reading Programs." *Urban Learning, Teaching, and Research Yearbook,* ed. F. Uy, in press.

Moustafa, M., & Maldonado-Colon, E. (1999). "Whole-to-Parts Phonics Instruction: Building on What Children Know to Help Them Know More." *The Reading Teacher* 52(5): 448–458.

Mullis, I. V. S., Campbell, J., & Farstrup, A. E. (1993). *NAEP 1992 Reading Report Card for the Nation and the States.* Washington, D.C.: National Center for Educational Statistics.

Murphy, S. (1986). "Children's Comprehension of Deictic Categories in Oral and Written Language." *Reading Research Quarterly* 21: 118–131.

Murray, D. M. (1990). *Crafting a Life in Essay, Story, Poem.* Portsmouth, NH: Heinemann.

Nagy, N., Campenni, E., & Shaw, J. (2000). A Survey of Sustained Silent Reading Practices in Seventh-Grade Classrooms. International Reading Association.

Nagy, W. E. (1995). On the Role of Context in First- and Second-Language Vocabulary Learning. ERIC 391152, technical report #627. Urbana, IL: Center for the Study of Reading.

Nagy, W. E., & Anderson, R. C. (1984). "How Many Words Are There in Printed School English?" *Reading Research Quarterly* 19: 304–330.

Nagy, W. E., Anderson, R. C., & Herman, P. A. (1987). "Learning Word Meanings from Context During Normal Reading." *American Educational Research Journal* 24: 237–270.

Nagy, W. E., Herman, P. A., et al. (1985). "Learning Words from Context." *Reading Research Quarterly* 20: 233–253.

Nagy, W. E., & Herman, P. A. (1987). "Breadth and Depth of Vocabulary Knowledge: Implications for Acquisition and Instruction." *The Nature of Vocabulary Acquisition,* ed. M. McKeown & M. Curtis, 19–35. Hillsdale, NJ: Erlbaum.

National Assessment of Educational Progress (1999). *NAEP 1998 Reading Report Card for the Nation and the States.* Washington, D.C.: National Center for Education Statistics, U.S. Department of Education. March. NCES 1999-500.

National Assessment of Educational Progress (2001). *The Nation's Report Card: Fourth Grade Reading.* Washington, D.C.: National Center for Education Statistics, U.S. Department of Education. NCES 2001-499.

National Education Association, Task Force on Reading. (2000). *A Complete Reading Program.* Washington, DC: National Education Association.

National Institute of Child Health and Human Development. (2000). National Reading Panel Reports Combination of Teaching Phonics, Word Sounds, Giving Feedback on Oral Reading Most Effective Way to Teach Reading. April 13. <*www.nichd.nih.gov/new/releases/nrp.cfm*>.

National Reading Panel (2000a). "Minority View." By Joanne Yatvin. Washington, D.C.: Included within book that presents the subgroup reports (NRP, 2000b). <*http://nichd.nih.gov/publications/nrp/minority View.pdf*>.

National Reading Panel (2000b). *Report of the National Reading Panel: An Evidence-Based Assessment of the Scientific Research Literature on Reading and Its Implications for Reading Instruction, Reports of the Subgroups* [book]. Washington, DC: National Institute of Child Health and Human Development. <*http://www.nichd.nih.gov/publications/nrp/report.htm*>.

National Reading Panel (2000c). *Report of the National Reading Panel: Teaching Children to Read—An Evidence-Based Assessment of the Scientific Research Literature on Reading and Its Implications for Reading Instruction.* [Summary.]. Washington, D.C.: National Institute of Child Health and Human Development. 33 pp. *<http://www.nichd.nih.gov/publications/nrp/smallbook/pdf>*. The alleged findings can be accessed at *<http://www.nihd.nih.gov/publications/nrp/findings.htm>*.

New Zealand National Film Unit. (1990). *I Can Read.* Portsmouth, NH: Heinemann.

Nicholson, T. (1991). "Do Children Read Words Better in Context or in Lists? A Classic Study Revisited." *Journal of Educational Psychology* **83**: 444–450.

Nicholson, T. (1997). "Closing the Gap on Reading Failure: Social Background, Phonemic Awareness, and Learning to Read." *Foundation of Reading Acquisition and Dyslexia,* ed. B. A. Blachman, 381–408. Mahwah, NJ: Erlbaum.

Nicholson, T., Lillas, C., & Rzuska, M. A. (1988). "Have We Been Misled by Miscues?" *The Reading Teacher* **42**: 6–10.

Ninio, A., & Bruner, J. S. (1978). "The Achievement and Antecedents of Labeling." *Journal of Child Language* **5**: 1–15.

Nix, D., & Schwarz, M. (1979). "Toward a Phenomenology of Reading Comprehension." *New Directions in Discourse Processing,* ed. R. Freedle, 183–196. Norwood, NJ: Ablex.

"No Child Left Behind." (2002). Public Law 107, Jan. 8, 2002, a reauthorization of the Elementary and Secondary Education Act. Washington, DC.

Noble, T. H. (1980). *The Day Jimmy's Boa Ate the Wash.* Illus. S. Kellogg. New York: Puffin.

Norris, J. A. (1988). "Using Communication Strategies to Enhance Reading Acquisition." *The Reading Teacher* **47**: 668–673.

Norris, J. A. (1991). "From Frog to Prince: Using Written Language as a Context for Language Learning." *Topics in Language Disorders* **12**(1): 66–81.

Norris, J. A. (1998). "I Could Read If I Just Had a Little Help." *Practicing What We Know: Informed Reading Instruction,* ed. C. Weaver, 513–565. Urbana, IL: National Council of Teachers of English.

Norris, J. A., & Hoffman, P. R. (No date). *Improving Oral and Written Language Abilities in Mild-Moderately Handicapped Children.* Department of Communication Sciences and Disorders. Baton Rouge, LA: Louisiana State University.

North Central Regional Educational Laboratory. (1996). *Collaboration in Education.* Portsmouth, NH: Heinemann.

Obligado, L. (1983). *Faint Frogs Feeling Feverish, and Other Terrifically Tantalizing Tongue Twisters.* New York: Puffin.

Ohanian, S. (1999). *One Size Fits Few.* Portsmouth, NH: Heinemann.

Olofsson, A., & Lundberg, I. (1985). "Evaluation of Long Term Effects of Phonemic Awareness Training in Kindergarten: Illustrations of Some Methodological Problems in Evaluation Research." *Scandanavian Journal of Psychology* **26**: 21–34.

Open Court. (1995). *Open Court Reading Collections for Young Scholars.* Chicago: SRA/McGraw-Hill.

Opening Doors, in The Macmillan Reading Program, A. J. Harris & M. K. Clark, Senior Authors. (1965). New York: Macmillan.

Opitz, M., & Ford, M. (2001). *Reaching Readers: Flexible & Innovative Strategies for Guided Reading.* Portsmouth, NH: Heinemann.

Opitz, M. F. (2000). *Rhymes & Reasons: Literature and Language Play for Phonological Awareness.* Portsmouth, NH: Heinemann.

Opitz, M. F., & Rasinski, T. V. (1998). *Good-Bye Round Robin: 25 Effective Oral Reading Strategies.* Portsmouth, NH: Heinemann.

Oppenheim, J., Brenner, B., & Boegehold, B. D. (1986). *Choosing Books for Kids.* New York and Toronto: Ballantine.

O'Regan, J. K. (1979). "Moment to Moment Control of Eye Saccades as a Function of Textual Parameters in Reading." *Processing of Visible Language (Vol. 1),* ed. P. A. Kolers, M. E. Wrolstad, &H. Bouma, 49–60. New York: Plenum.

Orton Dyslexia Society Research Committee. (1994). "Operational Definition of Dyslexia." *Perspectives* 20(5): 4.

Palermo, D. S. (1978). *Psychology of Language.* Glenview, IL: Scott, Foresman.

Paterson, F. (1998). "Mandating Methodology: Promoting the Use of Phonics Through State Statute." *In Defense of Good Teaching: What Teachers Need to Know About the "Reading Wars,"* ed. K. S. Goodman, 107–125. York, ME: Stenhouse.

Paterson, F. (2000). "The Politics of Phonics." *Journal of Curriculum and Supervision* 15(3): 179–211.

Paulson, E. J. (1999). *Reading as a Perceptual, Psychological Process: An Eye Movements and Miscue Analysis Study.* Las Vegas: International Academy of Linguistics, Behavioral and Social Sciences.

Paulson, E. J. (2000). *Adult Readers' Eye Movements During the Production of Oral Miscues.* Tucson: University of Arizona. Program in Language and Literacy. Unpublished doctoral dissertation.

Paulson, E. J. (In press). "Are Oral Reading Word Omissions and Substitutions Caused by Careless Eye Movements?" *Journal of Reading Psychology.*

Paulson, E. J., & Goodman, K. S. (1998). "Influential Studies in Eye-Movement Research." *Reading Online.* *<www.readingonline.org/research/eyemove.html>.*

Pearson, P. D. (1978). "On Bridging Gaps and Spanning Chasms." *Curriculum Inquiry* 8: 353–362.

Pearson, P. D., & Fielding, L. (1991). "Comprehension Instruction." *Handbook of Reading Research: Volume II,* ed. R. Barr, M. L. Kamil, P. Mosenthal, & P. D. Pearson, 815–860. White Plains, NY: Longman.

Pearson, P. D., & Gallagher, M. C. (1983). "The Instruction of Reading Comprehension." *Contemporary Educational Psychology* 8(3): 317–344.

Pearson, P. D., Hansen, J., & Gordon, C. (1979). "The Effect of Background Knowledge on Young Children's Comprehension of Explicit and Implicit Information." *Journal of Reading Behavior* 11(3): 201–209.

Pearson, P. D., & Johnson, D. D. (1978). *Teaching Reading Comprehension.* New York: Holt, Rinehart.

Pearson, P. D., Roehler, L. R., Dole, J. A., & Duffy, G. G. (1992). "Developing Expertise in Reading Comprehension." *What Research Has to Say About Reading Instruction,* ed. S. J. Samuels & A. E. Farstrup, 145–199. Newark, DE: International Reading Association.

Pearson, P. D., & Stephens, D. (1994). "Learning About Literacy: A 30-Year Journey." *Elementary Reading Instruction: Process and Practice,* ed. C. Gordon, G. D. Labercane, & W. R. McEachern, 22–42. Glenview, IL: Ginn Press.

Peirce, C. S. (1955). "The Fixation of Belief." *Philosophical Writings of Peirce,* ed. J. Buchler, 5–22. New York: Dover.

Perfetti, C. A. (1985). *Reading Ability.* New York: Oxford University Press.

Perfetti, C. A., Beck, I., Bell, L., & Hughes, C. (1987). "Phonemic Knowledge and Learning to Read Are Reciprocal: A Longitudinal Study of First Grade Children." *Merrill-Palmer Quarterly* 33: 283–319.

Perfetti, C. A., Bell, L. C., et al. (1988). "Automatic (Prelexical) Phonetic Activation in Silent Word Reading: Evidence from Backward Masking." *Journal of Memory and Language* 27: 59–70.

Perkins, A. (1969). *Hand, Hand, Fingers, Thumb.* New York: Random House.

Peterson, M. E., & Haines, L. P. (1992). "Orthographic Analogy Training with Kindergarten Children: Effects on Analogy Use, Phonemic Segmentation, and Letter-Sound Knowledge." *Journal of Reading Behavior* 24(1): 109–127.

Peterson, R. (1992). *Life in a Crowded Place: Making a Learning Community*. Portsmouth, NH: Heinemann.

Peterson, R., & Eeds, M. (1990). *Grand Conversations: Literature Groups in Action*. New York: Scholastic.

Phelan, P. (Ed.). (1996). *High Interest—Easy Reading: An Annotated Booklist for Middle School and Senior High School*. Urbana, IL: National Council of Teachers of English.

Pilgreen, J. L. (2000). *The SSR Handbook: How to Organize and Manage a Sustained Silent Reading Program*. Portsmouth, NH: Heinemann.

Pinnell, G. S., & Fountas, I. C. (Eds.). (1998). *Word Matters: Teaching Phonics and Spelling in the Reading/ Writing Classroom*. Portsmouth, NH: Heinemann.

P. L. 107. (2002). "No Child Left Behind." Reauthorization of the Elementary and Secondary Education Act, Jan 8, 2002. Washington, D.C.

Pollatsek, A., Lesch, M., et al. (1992). "Phonological Codes Are Used in Integrating Information Across Saccades in Word Identification and Reading." *Journal of Experimental Psychology: Human Perception and Performance* 18(1): 148–162.

Porter, W. S. (1936). "Jimmy Hayes and Muriel." *The Complete Works of O. Henry*. Garden City, NY: Doubleday, Doran.

Pressley, M., Allington, R. L., Wharton-McDonald, R., Block, C. C., & Morrow, L. M. (2001). *Learning to Read: Lessons from Exemplary First-Grade Classrooms*. New York: Guilford.

Purcell-Gates, V. (1988). "Lexical and Syntactic Knowledge of Written Narrative Held by Well-Read-to Kindergarteners and Second Graders." *Research in the Teaching of English* 22: 128–160.

Purcell-Gates, V., McIntyre, E., & Freppon, P. (1995). "Learning Written Storybook Language in School: A Comparison of Low SES Children in Skills-Based and Whole Language Classrooms." *American Educational Research Journal* 32: 659–685.

Raphael, T. E., & McMahon, S. I. (1994). "Book Club: An Alternative Framework for Reading Instruction." *The Reading Teacher* 42(2): 102–116.

Rasinski, T. V., & DeFord, D. E. (1988). "First Graders' Conceptions of Literacy: A Matter of Schooling." *Theory into Practice* 27(1): 53–61.

Rayner, K. (1981). "Eye Movements and the Perceptual Span in Reading." *Neuropsychological and Cognitive Processes in Reading,* ed. F. Pirozzolo & M. Wittrock, 145–65. New York: Academic.

Rayner, K. (1997). "Understanding Eye Movements in Reading." *Scientific Studies in Reading* 1(4): 317–339.

Rayner, K., & Morris, R. (1992). "Eye Movement Control in Reading: Evidence Against Semantic Preprocessing." *Journal of Experimental Psychology: Human Perception and Performance* 18: 163–172.

Rayner, K., & Pollatsek, A. (1989). *The Psychology of Reading*. Englewood Cliffs, NJ: Prentice Hall.

Rayner, K., & Sereno, S. C. (1994). "Eye Movements in Reading: Psycholinguistic Studies." *Handbook of Psycholinguistics,* ed. M. A. Gernsbacher, 57–81. San Diego, CA: Academic.

Rayner, K., & Well, A. D. (1996). "Effects of Contextual Constraint on Eye Movements in Reading: A Further Examination." *Psychonomic Bulletin & Review* 3(4): 504–509.

Reading Deficit Elimination Act. (2000). HR 4307, introduced by Rep. W. F. Gooding, April 13, 2000; S 2452, introduced by Sen. P. Coverdale. U.S. Congress, Washington, D.C.

Reading Excellence Act. (1998). HB 2614, introduced by Rep. W. F. Gooding, Oct. 21, 1998; S 1596, introduced by Sen. P. Coverdale. U.S. Congress, Washington, D.C.

Reading House Series: Comprehension and Vocabulary. (1980). New York: Random House.

Recht, D. R., & Leslie, L. (1988). "Effect of Prior Knowledge on Good and Poor Readers' Memory of Text." *Journal of Educational Psychology* 80: 16–20.

Reichle, E. D., Pollatsek, A., Fisher, D. L., & Rayner, K. (1998). "Toward a Model of Eye Movement Control in Reading." *Psychological Review* 105(1): 125–157.

Reid, J. F. (1958). "An Investigation of Thirteen Beginners in Reading." *Acta Psychologica* **14**(4): 295–313.

Reutzel, D. R., & Cooter, R. B. (1991). "Whole Language: Comparative Effects on First-Grade Reading Achievement." *Journal of Educational Research* **83**(5): 252–257.

Reynolds, R. E., Taylor, M. A., et al. (1982). "Cultural Schemata and Reading Comprehension." *Reading Research Quarterly* **17**: 353–366.

Rhodes, L. K. (1979). "Comprehension and Predictability: An Analysis of Beginning Reading Materials." *New Perspectives on Comprehension,* ed. J. C. Harste & R. Carey, 100–130. Bloomington, IN: School of Education, Indiana University.

Rhodes, L. K., & Dudley-Marling, C. (1996). *Readers and Writers with a Difference: A Holistic Approach to Teaching Struggling Readers and Writers.* Portsmouth, NH: Heinemann.

Richgels, D. J., Poremba, K. J., & McGee, L. M. (1996). "Kindergartners Talk About Print: Phonemic Awareness in Meaningful Contexts." *The Reading Teacher* **49**(8): 632–642.

Rief, L. (1992). *Seeking Diversity: Language Arts with Adolescents.* Portsmouth, NH: Heinemann.

Rief, L. (1998). *Vision & Voice: Extending the Literacy Spectrum.* Portsmouth, NH: Heinemann.

Rigg, P. (1978). "Dialect and /in/ for Reading." *Language Arts* **55**: 285–290.

Ritterskamp, P., & Singleton, J. (2001). "Interactive Calendar." *The Reading Teacher* **55**(2): 114–129.

Rogovin, P. (2001). *The Research Workshop: Bringing the World into Your Classroom.* Portsmouth, NH: Heinemann.

Romano, T. (1995). *Writing with Passion: Life Stories, Multiple Genres.* Portsmouth, NH: Heinemann.

Rosenblatt, L. (1964). "The Poem as Event." *College English* **26**: 123–128.

Rosenblatt, L. (1978/1996). *The Reader, the Text, the Poem: The Transactional Theory of the Literary Work.* Carbondale, IL: Southern Illinois University Press.

Rosenblatt, L. (1983). *Literature as Exploration.* New York: Modern Language Association.

Rosenshine, B. (1980). "Skill Hierarchies in Reading Comprehension." *Theoretical Issues in Reading Comprehension,* ed. R. J. Spiro, B. C. Bruce, & W. F. Brewer, 535–554. Hillsdale, NJ: Lawrence Erlbaum.

Rosner, J. (1974). "Auditory Analysis Training with Prereaders." *The Reading Teacher* **27**: 379–384.

Ross, J. R. (1967). Constraints on Variables in Syntax. Cambridge: MIT. Unpublished doctoral dissertation.

Ross, J. R. (1974). "Three Batons for Cognitive Psychology." *Cognition and the Symbolic Processes,* ed. W. B. Werner & D. S. Palermo, 63–124. Hillsdale, NJ: Erlbaum.

Ross-Lipson, E. (1991). *The New York Times Parent's Guide to the Best Books for Children.* New York: Times Books (Random House).

Routman, R. (1994a). *The Blue Pages: Resources for Teachers* from *Invitations: Changing as Teachers and Learners K–12.* Portsmouth, NH: Heinemann.

Routman, R. (1994b). *Invitations: Changing as Teachers and Learners K–12.* Portsmouth, NH: Heinemann.

Routman, R. (1999). *Conversations: Strategies for Teaching, Learning, and Evaluating.* Portsmouth, NH: Heinemann.

Ruddell, R. B. (1965). "The Effect of Oral and Written Patterns of Language Structure on Reading Comprehension." *The Reading Teacher* **18**: 270–275.

Ruddell, R. B., Ruddell, M. R., & Singer, H. (1994). *Theoretical Models and Processes of Reading.* Newark, DE: International Reading Association.

Rumelhart, D. E. (1980). "Schemata: The Building Blocks of Cognition." *Theoretical Issues in Reading Comprehension,* ed. R. J. Spiro, B. C. Bruce, & W. F. Brewer, 33–58. Hillsdale, NJ: Erlbaum.

Rumelhart, D. E., & McClelland, J. L. (1986). *Parallel Distributed Processing: Explorations in the Microstructure of Cognition.* Cambridge: MIT Press.

Rylant, C. (1985). *The Relatives Came.* Ill. S. Gammell. New York: Aladdin.

Sachs, J. D. (1967). "Recognition Memory for Syntactic and Semantic Aspects of Connected Discourse." *Perception and Psychophysics* 2: 437–442.

Sacks, C. H., & Mergendoller, J. R. (1997). "The Relationship Between Teachers' Theoretical Orientation Toward Reading and Student Outcomes in Kindergarten Children with Different Initial Reading Abilities." *American Educational Research Journal* 34(4): 721–739.

Samuels, B. G., & Beers, G. K. (Eds.). (1996). *Your Reading: An Annotated Booklist for Middle School and Junior High.* Urbana, IL: National Council of Teachers of English.

Santa, C. (1976–77). "Spelling Patterns and the Development of Flexible Word Recognition Strategies." *Reading Research Quarterly* 12: 125–144.

Santa, C. (1998). *Early Steps: Learning from a Reader.* Kalispell, MT: Scott.

Santa, C., & Hoien, T. (1999). "An Assessment of Early Steps: A Program for Early Intervention of Reading Problems." *Reading Research Quarterly* 34: 54–79.

Santa, C. M. (1981). "Children's Reading Comprehension: A Final Word." *Children's Prose Comprehension: Research and Practice,* ed. C. M. Santa & B. L. Hayes, 157–170. Newark, DE: International Reading Association.

Schatschneider, C., Francis, D., Foorman, B., Fletcher, J., & Mehta, P. (1999). "The Dimensionality of Phonological Awareness: An Application of Item Response Theory." *Journal of Experimental Child Psychology* 91: 439–449.

Schatz, E. K., & Baldwin, R. S. (1986). "Context Clues Are Unreliable Predictors of Word Meanings." *Reading Research Quarterly* 21: 439–453.

Schnur, S. (2000). *Spring Thaw.* Illus. Stacey Schuett. New York: Penguin.

Scholes, R. J. (1998). "The Case Against Phonemic Awareness." *Journal of Research in Reading* 21(3): 177–180.

Schwantes, F. M., Boesl, S. L., et al. (1980). "Children's Use of Context in Word Recognition: A Psycholinguistic Guessing Game." *Child Development* 51: 730–736.

Schweinhart, L. J., & Weikart, D. P. (1997). "The High/Scope Preschool Curriculum Comparison Study Through Age 23." *Early Childhood Research Quarterly* 12: 117–143.

Schweinhart, L. J., Weikart, D. P., & Larner, M. B. (1986). "Consequences of Three Preschool Curriculum Models Through Age 15." *Early Childhood Research Quarterly* 1: 15–45.

Science Research Associates (1988). *Reading Mastery.* New York: SRA, Macmillan/McGraw-Hill.

Science Research Associates (1995). *Open Court.* Chicago: SRA/McGraw-Hill.

Science Research Associates (1999). *SRA/Open Court Phonics.* New York: SRA/McGraw-Hill.

Science Research Associates/McGraw-Hill (1999). *Research Related to Open Court Collections for Young Scholars.* Mahwah, NJ: SRA/McGraw-Hill.

Seidenberg, M. S., & McClelland, J. L. (1989). "A Distributed, Developmental Model of Word Recognition and Naming." *Psychological Review* 96: 523–568.

Selinker, L. (1972). "Interlanguage." *International Review of Applied Linguistics in Language* 3: 209–231.

Serafini, F. (2001). *The Reading Workshop: Creating Space for Readers.* Portsmouth, NH: Heinemann.

Seton, A. (1954). *Katherine.* Boston: Houghton Mifflin.

Shannon, C. E. (1948). "A Mathematical Theory of Information." *Bell System Technical Journal* 27: 379–423, 623–656.

Shapiro, J. (1990). "Research Perspectives on Whole-Language." *Whole-Language: Practice and Theory,* ed. V. Froese, 269–305. Boston: Allyn & Bacon.

Share, D. L., & Stanovich, K. E. (1995). "Cognitive Processes in Early Reading Development: Accommodating Individual Differences in a Model of Acquisition." *Issues in Education* 1(1): 1–57.

Short, K. G. (1997). *Literature As a Way of Knowing.* York, ME: Stenhouse.

Short, K. G., Harste, J. C., & Burke, C. (1996). *Creating Classrooms for Authors and Inquirers.* Portsmouth, NH: Heinemann.

Short, K. G., & Pierce, K. M. (Eds.). (1998). *Talking About Books: Literature Discussion Groups in K–8 Classrooms.* Portsmouth, NH: Heinemann.

Short, K. G., Schroeder, J., Laird, J., Kauffman, G., Ferguson, M. J., & Crawford, K. M. (1996). *Learning Together Through Inquiry: From Columbus to Integrated Curriculum.* York, ME: Stenhouse.

Simon, D. P., & Simon, H. A. (1973). "Alternative Uses of Phonemic Information in Spelling." *Review of Educational Research* **43**: 115–137.

Simons, H. D., & Amon, P. (1989). "Child Knowledge and Primerese Text: Mismatches and Miscues." *Research in the Teaching of English* **23**: 380–398.

Slavin, R. *Success for All* (a comprehensive school restructuring program). Baltimore, MD: Success for All Foundation. *<www.successforall.net/curriculum/sfa.htm>*

Slavin, R. E., et al. (1996). *Every Child, Every School: Success for All.* Newberry Park, CA: Corwin.

Smith, C., Constantino, R., & Krashen, S. (1997). "Differences in Print Environments for Children in Beverly Hills, Compton, and Watts." *The Emergency Librarian* **24**(4): 8–9.

Smith, E. B., Goodman, K. S., et al. (1970). *Language and Thinking in the Elementary School.* New York: Holt, Rinehart.

Smith, F. (Ed.). (1973). *Psycholinguistics and Reading.* New York: Holt, Rinehart and Winston.

Smith, F. (1975). *Comprehension and Learning: A Conceptual Framework for Teachers.* Katonah, NY: Richard C. Owen.

Smith, F. (1979/1996). *Reading Without Nonsense.* New York: Teachers College Press.

Smith, F. (1988). *Joining the Literacy Club: Further Essays into Education.* Portsmouth, NH: Heinemann.

Smith, F. (1971/1994). *Understanding Reading: A Psycholinguistic Analysis of Reading and Learning to Read.* (5th ed.). Hillsdale, NJ: Erlbaum.

Smith, J. W. A., & Elley, W. B. (1995). *Learning to Read in New Zealand.* Katanah, NY: Richard C. Owen.

Smith, K. (1995). "Bringing Children and Literature Together in the Elementary Classroom." *Primary Voices, K–6* 3(2): 22–32.

Snow, C. E., Burns, M. S., & Griffin, P. (1998). *Preventing Reading Difficulties in Young Children.* Washington, D.C.: National Academy Press.

Spache, G. (1978). *Good Reading for Poor Readers* (rev. 10th ed.). Champaign, IL: Garrard.

Sperling, S. K. (1977). *Poplollies and Bellibones: A Celebration of Lost Words.* New York: Clarkson N. Potter.

Spilich, G. J., Vesonder, G. T., Chiesi, H. L., & Voss, J. F. (1979). "Test Processing in Domain-Related Information for Individuals with High and Low Domain Knowledge." *Journal of Verbal Learning and Verbal Behavior* **18**: 275–290.

Spoehr, K. T. (1981). "Word Recognition in Speech and Reading: Toward a Theory of Language Processing." *Perspectives on the Study of Speech,* ed. P. D. Eimas & J. L. Miller, 239–282. Hillsdale, NJ: Erlbaum.

Stahl, S. A. (1999). "Why Innovations Come and Go (and Mostly Go): The Case of Whole Language." *Educational Researcher* **28**: 13–23.

Stahl, S. A., McKenna, M. C., & Pagnucco, J. R. (1994). "The Effects of Whole Language Instruction: An Update and a Reappraisal." *Educational Psychologist* **29**: 175–185.

Stahl, S. A., & Shield, T. G. (1992). "Teaching Meaning Vocabulary: Productive Approaches for Poor Readers." *Reading and Writing Quarterly: Overcoming Learning Disabilities* **8**: 223–241.

Stanovich, K. E. (1980). "Toward an Interactive-Compensatory Model of Individual Differences in the Development of Reading Fluency." *Reading Research Quarterly* 16: 32–71.

Stanovich, K. E. (1984). "The Interactive-Compensatory Model of Reading: A Confluence of Developmental, Experimental, and Educational Psychology." *Remedial and Special Education* 5: 11–19.

Stanovich, K. E. (1986). "Matthew Effects in Reading: Some Consequences of Individual Differences in the Acquisition of Literacy." *Reading Research Quarterly* 21: 360–406.

Stanovich, K. E. (1991). "Word Recognition: Changing Perspectives." *Handbook of Reading Research* Vol. 2, ed. R. Barr, M. L. Kamil, P. B. Mosenthal, & P. D. Pearson, 418–452. New York: Longman.

Stanovich, K. E. (1992). "The Psychology of Reading: Evolutionary and Revolutionary Developments." *Annual Review of Applied Linguistics* 12: 3–30.

Stanovich, K. E. (1993/1994). "Romance and Reality." *Reading Teacher* 47(December/January): 289–291.

Stephens, D. (1991). *Research on Whole Language: Support for a New Curriculum.* Katonah, NY: Richard C. Owen.

Stephens, D. (1998). "Foreword: Research as Inquiry." *Reconsidering a Balanced Approach to Reading,* ed. C. Weaver, ix–xiii. Urbana, IL: National Council of Teachers of English.

Stevens, K. C. (1982). "Can We Improve Reading by Teaching Background Information?" *Journal of Reading* 25: 326–329.

"Sticking to the Script." (2000). *Time Magazine: Time Classroom.* Teacher's Guide, March 6.

Stipek, D. J., Feiler, R., Daniels, D., & Milburn, S. (1995). "Effects of Different Instructional Approaches on Young Children's Achievement and Motivation." *Child Development* 66: 209–223.

Strauss, S. L. (2001). "An Open Letter to Reid Lyon." *Educational Researcher* (June/July): 26–33.

Strickland, D. S. (1998). *Teaching Phonics Today: A Primer for Educators.* Newark, DE: International Reading Association.

Strickland, K. (1995). *Literacy Not Labels: Celebrating Students' Strengths Through Whole Language.* Portsmouth, NH: Heinemann.

Strickland, K., & Strickland, J. (1999). *Making Assessment Elementary.* Portsmouth, NH: Heinemann.

Stuart, M. (1999). "Getting Ready for Reading: Early Phoneme Awareness and Phonics Teaching Improves Reading and Spelling in Inner-City Second Language Learners." *British Journal of Educational Psychology* 69: 587–605.

Stuart-Hamilton, I. (1986). "The Role of Phonemic Awareness in the Reading Style of Beginning Readers." *British Journal of Educational Psychology* 56: 271–285.

Sulzby, E. (1985). "Children's Emergent Reading of Favorite Storybooks: A Developmental Study." *Reading Research Quarterly* 20: 458–481.

Sutton, W. K. (Ed.). (1997). *Adventuring with Books: A Booklist for Pre–K–Grade 6.* Urbana, IL: National Council of Teachers of English.

Swartz, S. L., & Klein, F. A. (Eds.). (1997). *Research in Reading Recovery.* Portsmouth, NH: Heinemann.

Taberski, S. (1996). *A Close-up Look at Teaching Reading: Focusing on Children and Our Goals.* (Video.) Portsmouth, NH: Heinemann.

Taberski, S. (2000). *On Solid Ground: Strategies for Teaching Reading K–3.* Portsmouth, NH: Heinemann.

Tanenhaus, M. K., Flanigan, H., et al. (1980). "Orthographic and Phonological Activation in Auditory and Visual Word Recognition." *Memory and Cognition* 8: 513–520.

Tangel, D., & Blachman, B. (1995). "Effect of Phoneme Awareness Instruction on the Invented Spelling of First-Grade Children: A One-Year Follow-Up." *Journal of Reading Behavior* 27: 153–185.

Tatham, S. (1970). "Reading Comprehension of Materials Written with Select Oral Language Patterns: A Study at Grades Two and Four." *Reading Research Quarterly* 5: 402–426.

Taylor, B. (1979). "Good and Poor Readers' Recall of Familiar and Unfamiliar Text." *Journal of Reading Behavior* 11: 375–388.

Taylor, D. (1998). *Beginning to Read and the Spin Doctors of Science: The Political Campaign to Change America's Mind About How Children Learn to Read.* Urbana, IL: National Council of Teachers of English.

Taylor, M. D. (1976). *Roll of Thunder, Hear My Cry.* New York: Bantam.

Taylor, W. L. (1953). "Cloze Procedure: A New Tool for Measuring Readability." *Journalism Quarterly* 30: 415–433.

Tierney, R. J., & Readence, J. E. (1999). *Reading Strategies and Practices: A Compendium.* Boston: Allyn and Bacon.

Tinker, M. A. (1936). "Reliability and Validity of Eye-Movement Measures of Reading." *Journal of Experimental Psychology* 19: 732–746.

Tolstoy, A. (1971). "The Great Big Enormous Turnip." In *Scott Foresman Reading Systems.* Glenview, IL: Scott Foresman.

Tomlinson, C. M. (Ed.). (1998). *Children's Books from Other Countries.* Lanham, MD: Scarecrow Press.

Torgeson, J. K., & Hecht, S. A. (1996). "Preventing and Remediating Disabilities: Instructional Variables That Make a Difference for Special Students." *The First R: Every Child's Right to Read,* ed. M. F. Graves, P. Van Den Brock, & B. M. Taylor, 133–159. New York: Teachers College Press.

Torgeson, J. K., Wagner, R. K., Rashotte, C. A., Alexander, A. W., & Conway, T. (1997). "Preventative and Remedial Interventions for Children with Severe Reading Disabilities." *Learning Disabilities: A Multidisciplinary Journal* 8: 51–62.

Torgeson, J. K., Wagner, R. K., & Rashotte, C. A. (1997). "Prevention and Remediation of Severe Reading Disabilities: Keeping the End in Mind." *Scientific Studies in Reading* 1: 217–234.

Torgeson, J. K., Wagner, R. K., Rashotte, C. A., Rose, E., Lindamood, P., Conway, T., & Garvan, C. (1999). "Preventing Reading Failure in Young Children with Phonological Processing Disabilities: Group and Individual Responses to Instruction." *Journal of Educational Psychology* 91: 579–593.

Tovani, C. (2000). *I Read It, but I Don't Get It: Comprehension Strategies for Adolescent Readers.* York, ME: Stenhouse.

Tovey, D. R. (1979). "Teachers' Perceptions of Children's Reading Miscues." *Reading Horizons* 19: 302–307.

Tovey, D. R. (1980). "Children's Grasp of Phonics Terms vs. Sound-Symbol Relationships." *The Reading Teacher* 33: 431–437.

Traw, R. (1996). "Large-Scale Assessment of Skills in a Whole Language Curriculum: Two Districts' Experiences." *Journal of Educational Research* 89: 323–339.

Traweek, K., & Berninger, V. (1997). "Comparisons of Beginning Literacy Programs: Alternative Paths to the Same Learning Outcomes." *Learning Disability Quarterly* 20: 160–168.

Treiman, R. (1983). "The Structure of Spoken Syllables: Evidence from Novel Word Games." *Cognition* 15: 49–74.

Treiman, R. (1985). "Onsets and Rimes as Units of Spoken Syllables: Evidence from Children." *Journal of Experimental Child Psychology* 39: 161–181.

Treiman, R. & Baron, J. (1981). "Segmental Analysis Ability: Development and Relation to Reading Ability." *Reading Research: Advances in Theory and Practice,* Vol. 3, ed. G. E. MacKinnon & T. G. Waller, 159–198. New York: Academic.

Treiman, R., & Chafetz, J. (1987). "Are There Onset- and Rime-Like Units in Printed Words?" *Attention and Performance XII: The Psychology of Reading,* ed. M. Coltheart, 281–298. Hillsdale, NJ: Erlbaum.

Trelease, J. (1995). *The Read-Aloud Handbook.* New York: Penguin.

Troia, G. A. (1999). "Phonological Intervention Research: A Critical Review of the Experimental Methodology." *Reading Research Quarterly* 34(1): 28–52.

Tunmer, W., & Chapman, J. (1998). "Language Prediction Skill, Phonological Recoding Ability, and Beginning Reading." *Reading and Spelling: Development and Disorders,* ed. C. Hulme & R. Joshi, 33–67. Mahwah, NJ: Erlbaum.

Tunmer, W., & Hoover, W. (1993). "Phonological Recoding Skill and Beginning Reading." *Reading and Writing: An Interdisciplinary Journal* 5: 161–179.

Tunmer, W. E., & Nesdale, A. R. (1985). "Phonemic Segmentation Skill and Beginning Reading." *Journal of Educational Psychology* 77(4): 417–427.

Tunnell, M. O., & Jacobs, J. S. (1989). "Using 'Real' Books: Research Findings on Literature Based Reading Instruction." *The Reading Teacher* 42: 470–477.

Turner, R. L. (1989). "The 'Great' Debate: Can Both Carbo and Chall Be Right?" *Phi Delta Kappan* 71: 276–283.

Underwood, G., Clews, S., et al. (1990). "How Do Readers Know Where to Look Next? Local Information Distributions Influence Eye Fixations." *Quarterly Journal of Experimental Psychology* 42A(1): 39–65.

Van Allen, R. (1976). *Language Experiences in Education.* Boston: Houghton Mifflin.

Vellutino, F. R. (1991a). "Cognitive and Neuropsychological Foundations of Word Identification in Poor and Normally Developing Readers." *Handbook of Reading Research,* ed. R. Barr, M. L. Kamil, P. B. Mosenthal, & P. D. Pearson, Vol. 2: 571–608. New York: Longman.

Vellutino, F. R. (1991b). "Introduction to Three Studies on Reading Acquisition: Convergent Findings on Theoretical Foundations of Code-Oriented Versus Whole-Language Approaches to Reading Instruction." *Journal of Educational Psychology* 83: 437–443.

Vellutino, F. R., et al. (1996). "Cognitive Profiles of Difficult-to-Remediate and Readily Remediated Poor Readers: Early Intervention as a Vehicle for Distinguishing Between Cognitive and Experiential Deficits as Basic Causes of Specific Reading Disability." *Journal of Educational Psychology* 88: 601–638.

Vellutino, F. R., & Scanlon, D. M. (1987). "Phonological Coding, Phonological Awareness, and Reading Ability. Evidence from a Longitudinal and Experimental Study." *Merrill Palmer Quarterly* 33: 321–363.

Venezky, R. L. (1967). "English Orthography: Its Graphical Structure and Its Relation to Sound." *Reading Research Quarterly* 2: 75–106.

Venezky, R. L. (1970a). "Regularity in Reading and Spelling." *Basic Studies on Reading,* ed. H. Levin & J. P. Williams, 30–42. New York: Basic Books.

Venezky, R. L. (1970b). *The Structure of English Orthography.* The Hague: Mouton.

Wagner, R. K., & Torgeson, J. K. (1987). "The Nature of Phonological Processing and Its Causal Role in the Acquisition of Reading Skills." *Psychological Bulletin* 101: 192–212.

Wagner, R. K., Torgesen, J. K., & Rashotte, C. A. (1994). "Development of Reading-Related Phonological Processing Abilities: New Evidence of Bidirectional Causality from a Latent Variable Longitudinal Study." *Developmental Psychology* 30(1): 73–87.

Wagstaff, J. (No date). *Phonics That Work! New Strategies for the Reading/Writing Classroom.* New York: Scholastic.

Walcutt, C. C., & McCracken, G. (1975). *Lippincott Basic Reading.* New York: Macmillan.

Watson, D. J. (1996). *Making a Difference: Selected Writings of Dorothy Watson.* Portsmouth, NH: Heinemann.

Watson, D. J., & Hoge, S. (1987). "Reader-Selected Miscues." *Retrospective Miscue Analysis: Revaluing Readers and Reading,* ed. Y. M. Goodman & A. M. Marek, 157–164. Katonah, NY: Richard C. Owen.

Wayman, J. (1980). *The Other Side of Reading.* Carthage, IL: Good Apple.

Weaver, C. (1985). "Parallels Between New Paradigms in Science and in Reading and Literary Theories: An Essay Review." *Research in the Teaching of English* 19: 298–316.

Weaver, C. (1990). *Understanding Whole Language: From Principles to Practice.* Portsmouth, NH: Heinemann.

Weaver, C. (1994a). *Reading Process and Practice: From Socio-Psycholinguistics to Whole Language.* Portsmouth, NH: Heinemann.

Weaver, C. (1994b). "Reconceptualizing Reading and Dyslexia." *Journal of Childhood Communication Disorders* **16**(1): 23–25.

Weaver, C. (Ed.). (1994c). *Success at Last!: Helping Students with AD(H)D Achieve Their Potential.* Portsmouth, NH: Heinemann.

Weaver, C. (1998a). "Experimental Research: On Phonemic Awareness and on Whole Language." *Reconsidering a Balanced Approach to Reading,* ed. C. Weaver, 321–371. Urbana, IL: National Council of Teachers of English.

Weaver, C. (1998b). *Practicing What We Know: Informed Reading Instruction.* Urbana, IL: National Council of Teachers of English.

Weaver, C. (Ed.). (1998c). *Reconsidering a Balanced Approach to Reading.* Urbana, IL: National Council of Teachers of English.

Weaver, C., & Brinkley, E. H. (1998). "Phonics, Whole Language, and the Religious and Political Right." *In Defense of Good Teaching: What Teachers Need to Know About the "Reading Wars,"* ed. K. S. Goodman, 127–141. York, ME: Stenhouse.

Weaver, C., Gillmeister-Krause, L., & Vento-Zogby, G. (1996). *Creating Support for Effective Literacy Education.* Portsmouth, NH: Heinemann.

Weaver, C., with Stone, S. (1998). "From Reading Strategies to Strategies for Teaching in Tutorial and Small Group Situations." *Practicing What We Know: Informed Reading Instruction,* ed. C. Weaver, 490–512. Urbana, IL: National Council of Teachers of English.

Weber, R. (1970). "First-Graders' Use of Grammatical Context in Reading." *Basic Studies on Reading,* ed. H. Levin & J. P. Williams, 147–163. New York: Basic Books.

Weinberg, S. (1992). *Dreams of a Final Theory.* New York: Pantheon.

Wells, G. (1985). "Preschool Literacy-Related Activities and Success in School." *Literacy, Language, and Learning,* ed. D. R. Olson, N. Torrance, & A. Hildyard, 229–255. New York: Cambridge University Press.

Wells, G. (1986). *The Meaning Makers: Children Learning Language and Using Language to Learn.* Portsmouth, NH: Heinemann.

Whitmore, K. F., & Crowell, C. G. (1994). *Inventing a Classroom: Life in a Bilingual, Whole Language Learning Community.* York, ME: Stenhouse.

Wilde, S. (1997). *What's a Schwa Sound Anyway? A Holistic Guide to Phonetics, Phonics, and Spelling.* Portsmouth, NH: Heinemann.

Wilde, S. (2000). *Miscue Analysis Made Easy: Building on Student Strengths.* Portsmouth, NH: Heinemann.

Wilhelm, J. D. (1995). "*You Gotta BE the Book.*" New York: Teachers College; Urbana, IL: National Council of Teachers of English.

Wilhelm, J. (2001). *Improving Comprehension with Think-Aloud Strategies: Modeling What Good Readers Do.* New York: Scholastic.

Wilhelm, J., Baker, T. N., & Dube, J. (2001). *Strategic Reading: Guiding Students to Lifelong Literacy, 6–12.* Portsmouth, NH: Boynton/Cook.

Williamson, J. (1961). *The Glorious Conspiracy.* New York: Knopf.

Wilson, K., & Norman, C. (1998). "Differences in Word Recognition Based on Approach to Reading Instruction." *Alberta Journal of Educational Research* **44**: 221–230.

Wilson, P. (2000). The Effects of Comprehension on Reading Development. Paper presented at the Michigan Reading Association Conference, March.

Wimmer, H., Landerl, K., Linortner, R., & Hummer, P. (1991). "The Relationship of Phonemic Awareness to Reading Acquisition: More Consequence than Precondition but Still Important." *Cognition* **40**: 219–249.

Wise, B. W., Olson, R. K., et al. (1990). "Subsyllabic Units as Aids in Beginning Readers' Word Learning: Onset-Rime Versus Post-Vowel Segmentation." *Journal of Experimental Child Psychology* **49**: 1–19.

Wiseman, B. (1978). *Morris Has a Cold.* New York: Dodd, Mead.

Wolverton, G. S., & Zola, D. (1983). "The Temporal Characteristics of Visual Information Extraction During Reading." *Eye Movements in Reading: Perceptual and Language Processes,* ed. K. Rayner, 41–51. New York: Academic.

Wood, M. N. (1976). *A Multivariate Analysis of Beginning Readers' Recognition of Taught Words in Four Contextual Settings.* Denton, TX: Texas Women's University.

Worsnop, C. (1996). "The Beginnings of Retrospective Miscue Analysis." *Retrospective Miscue Analysis: Revaluing Readers and Reading,* ed. Y. M. Goodman & A. M. Marek, 151–156. Katonah, NY: Richard C. Owen.

Wylie, R. E., & Durrell, D. D. (1970). "Teaching Vowels Through Phonograms." *Elementary English* **47**: 787–791.

Yatvin, J. (2000). *Report of the National Reading Panel: Minority View.* Presentation at the International Reading Association. Indianapolis, IN, May 2.

Yatvin, J. (2001). "Hasty and Unconsidered." *Phi Delta Kappan* **82**(10): 801.

Yatvin, J. (2002). "Babes in the Woods: The Wanderings of the National Reading Panel." *Phi Delta Kappan* **83**(5): 364–369.

Yopp, H. K. (1995). "A Test for Assessing Phonemic Awareness in Young Children." *The Reading Teacher* **49**: 20–29.

Zemelman, S., Daniels, H., & Bizar, M. (1999). *Rethinking High School: Best Practice in Action.* Portsmouth, NH: Heinemann.

Index